RAC
Road Atlas
Britain & Ireland

CONTENTS

Key to map pages — ii

Mileage chart — iii

Key to map symbols — iv-v

Route planning map
(40 miles to 1 inch) — vi-vii

Road map section
Britain (4.16 miles to 1 inch) — 2-109

Ireland road maps
(15.8 miles to 1 inch) — 110-113

M25 London orbital motorway map — 114-115

London urban map
(1.1 miles to 1 inch) — 116-117

London central map
(5.1 inches to 1 mile) — 118-119

Urban area maps — 120-133
(1.25 miles to 1 inch with town plans)
Southampton and Portsmouth — 120-121
Cardiff and Newport — 122
Bristol — 123
West Midlands — 124-125
Merseyside — 126-127
Greater Manchester — 128-129
Newcastle upon Tyne — 130
Edinburgh — 131
Glasgow — 132-133

Index to place names in Britain & Ireland — 134-162

Specially prepared by Bartholomew Mapping Solutions
© Bartholomew Ltd 2001, a subsidiary of HarperCollins*Publishers* Ltd.
77-85 Fulham Palace Road, Hammersmith, London W6 8JB.

HarperCollins*Publishers* website: www.fireandwater.com

Mapping generated from Bartholomew digital databases.

Bartholomew website: www.bartholomewmaps.com

The contents of this publication are believed correct at the time of printing. Nevertheless, the publisher can accept no responsibility for errors or omissions, changes in the detail given, or for any expense or loss thereby caused.

The representation of a road, track or footpath is no evidence of a right of way.

Printed in Italy

ISBN 0 00 763716 0 Spiral   OG11067 BDC

Imp 001

e-mail: roadcheck@harpercollins.co.uk

KEY TO MAP PAGES

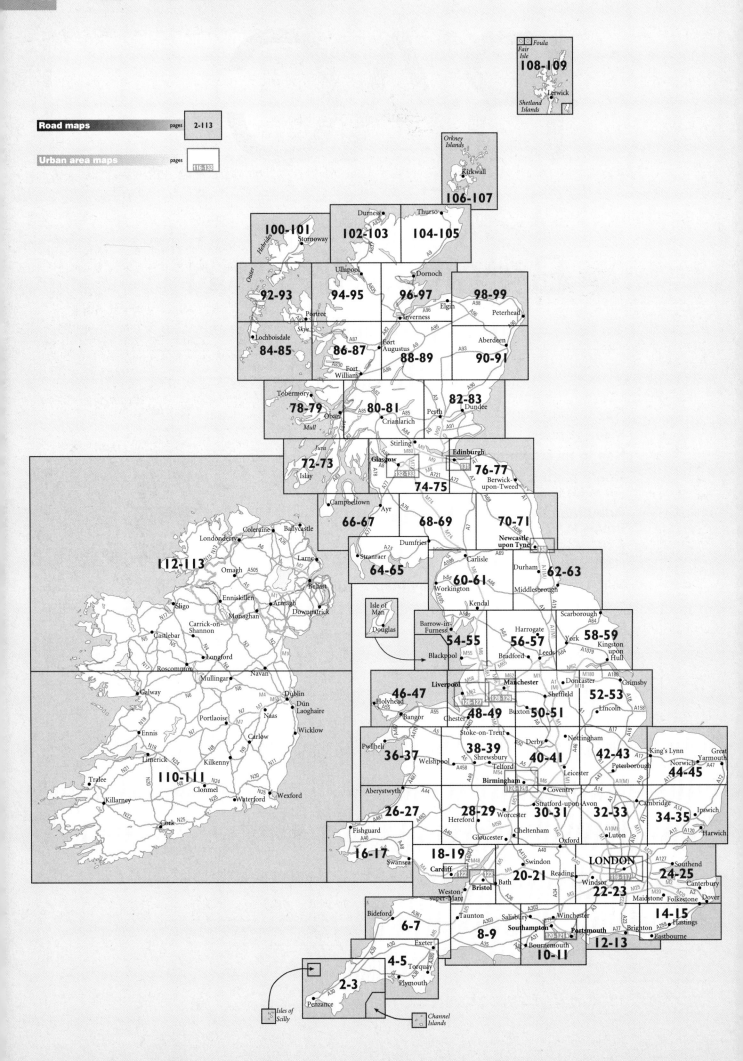

Road maps pages **2-113**

Urban area maps pages **116-133**

GREAT BRITAIN DISTANCE CHART

DISTANCE IN KILOMETRES

This is a triangular distance chart for Great Britain. Cities run diagonally through the chart. The upper-right triangle gives distances in kilometres, and the lower-left triangle gives distances in miles. The cities, in order along the diagonal, are: ABERDEEN, ABERYSTWYTH, AYR, BIRMINGHAM, BRADFORD, BRISTOL, CAMBRIDGE, CARDIFF, CARLISLE, COVENTRY, DERBY, DONCASTER, DOVER, EDINBURGH, EXETER, FISHGUARD, FORT WILLIAM, GLASGOW, GLOUCESTER, HARWICH, HOLYHEAD, HULL, INVERNESS, KENDAL, LEEDS, LEICESTER, LINCOLN, LIVERPOOL, MANCHESTER, NEWCASTLE UPON TYNE, NORWICH, NOTTINGHAM, OXFORD, PENZANCE, PERTH, PLYMOUTH, PORTSMOUTH, SALISBURY, SHEFFIELD, SHREWSBURY, SOUTHAMPTON, SOUTHEND-ON-SEA, STOKE-ON-TRENT, STRANRAER, THURSO, WORCESTER, YORK, LONDON.

DISTANCE IN KILOMETRES (upper-right triangle, read row by row)

	km values (left to right)
ABERDEEN	689 288 652 525 779 772 787 348 678 631 554 943 208 896 776 253 235 723 869 679 566 169 420 531 660 624 531 533 377 789 628 779 1069 135 977 904 866 584 628 872 858 592 370 365 689 509 816
ABERYSTWYTH	492 179 285 217 319 187 341 211 224 278 476 489 335 87 681 494 164 444 175 366 761 269 293 235 306 158 228 447 417 248 238 507 554 407 340 251 121 307 396 174 507 958 153 335 340
AYR	455 328 583 571 591 151 481 435 385 734 127 700 579 227 53 526 682 483 402 333 224 335 470 449 335 336 238 613 436 554 872 153 772 681 634 388 423 668 666 388 82 529 484 340 621
BIRMINGHAM	182 138 161 161 304 32 66 153 285 452 256 267 64 457 82 265 232 209 787 232 175 68 142 142 125 331 249 84 98 428 517 328 225 179 122 69 201 232 68 470 903 45 206 171
BRADFORD	309 249 333 177 190 117 55 426 323 439 372 517 330 253 354 254 106 578 100 15 162 119 100 56 156 283 122 270 599 389 499 397 352 61 164 377 351 114 343 774 217 51 312
BRISTOL	235 72 431 148 204 288 338 579 117 248 771 584 56 311 368 348 832 359 314 185 264 261 253 470 328 222 108 290 644 190 146 82 261 167 117 259 195 597 1028 100 346 196
CAMBRIDGE	286 425 129 146 179 185 549 340 404 752 565 193 105 383 201 826 348 228 101 134 270 240 381 93 127 127 497 637 425 200 225 179 232 211 101 191 591 1022 116 256 85
CARDIFF	439 185 227 314 351 587 190 175 779 592 93 364 343 370 840 367 336 222 301 261 275 491 380 245 161 362 652 262 217 150 286 167 185 299 220 605 1036 116 367 237
CARLISLE	330 283 233 582 148 549 428 340 153 375 531 331 251 401 72 183 319 298 183 185 90 460 285 402 721 212 621 529 483 237 517 515 237 166 597 333 187 470
COVENTRY	72 151 253 497 265 304 669 483 92 233 262 183 731 257 187 37 116 151 330 219 77 76 438 542 338 203 162 134 100 179 200 93 496 927 66 204 138
DERBY	87 309 431 322 311 623 436 150 251 248 146 684 211 109 45 82 129 90 264 217 24 148 494 496 394 272 235 56 103 251 240 56 449 880 116 140 187
DONCASTER	364 346 417 365 573 286 237 303 267 74 607 161 50 106 64 130 80 179 228 72 217 578 418 478 344 314 27 158 320 280 105 399 803 203 53 262
DOVER	718 396 581 932 745 312 188 533 386 996 517 420 264 319 426 404 566 262 306 209 554 808 460 201 256 365 352 220 116 346 748 1192 296 441 114
EDINBURGH	697 576 225 69 523 661 480 397 261 220 330 476 415 331 333 181 418 570 869 72 769 697 658 383 420 665 650 385 200 457 481 301 608
EXETER	365 888 702 174 399 486 449 949 476 431 303 381 378 370 587 430 340 212 158 761 69 203 140 378 285 171 344 312 715 1146 217 463 282
FISHGUARD	768 581 269 537 262 423 829 356 383 322 393 254 315 534 504 335 335 537 640 438 394 330 338 208 365 475 261 594 1025 238 422 430
FORT WILLIAM	187 715 871 671 591 108 412 523 658 637 523 525 415 801 624 742 1061 171 961 869 822 576 612 856 855 576 309 285 673 526 810
GLASGOW	528 684 484 404 280 225 336 471 451 336 338 228 615 438 555 874 100 774 882 636 389 425 669 668 389 135 476 486 340 623
GLOUCESTER	277 282 275 776 303 257 129 208 212 196 414 286 171 74 346 587 246 171 106 211 119 143 232 138 541 972 43 290 175
HARWICH	497 306 922 462 352 206 238 368 341 486 129 232 203 557 734 468 253 259 293 333 264 97 288 697 1118 290 361 117
HOLYHEAD	346 732 259 262 274 299 148 198 397 465 272 325 658 544 528 457 389 191 162 425 463 191 497 929 238 306 402
HULL	620 200 88 146 68 198 148 190 232 132 257 637 431 537 385 346 105 216 360 303 162 417 816 277 64 278
INVERNESS	473 584 713 677 584 586 430 842 681 832 1122 188 1030 958 919 637 681 925 911 645 415 196 742 562 869
KENDAL	111 246 225 111 121 138 383 220 330 649 285 549 457 410 161 200 444 451 164 238 669 261 142 406
LEEDS	154 114 114 64 154 278 114 265 603 396 504 393 354 53 172 360 343 116 349 780 212 37 304
LEICESTER	79 162 135 291 182 40 111 475 375 238 200 101 114 214 195 82 484 909 103 159 150
LINCOLN	195 151 248 164 58 190 554 489 454 317 278 74 185 303 235 134 463 874 174 122 211
LIVERPOOL	50 249 346 148 249 550 396 451 383 320 110 93 341 337 80 349 780 171 150 325
MANCHESTER	219 307 100 227 542 397 443 351 311 61 108 331 330 58 351 782 161 108 303
NEWCASTLE UPON TYNE	412 251 402 760 241 660 529 491 208 307 505 483 270 256 626 380 125 441
NORWICH	193 220 587 653 515 296 319 235 296 304 164 274 626 1038 259 286 171
NOTTINGHAM	157 512 492 417 278 240 61 127 254 228 80 451 877 122 125 192
OXFORD	397 644 298 127 97 209 162 103 156 169 568 1028 87 277 95
PENZANCE	933 125 360 298 576 443 328 502 484 887 1318 375 636 439
PERTH	842 769 731 449 492 737 723 457 235 385 554 373 681
PLYMOUTH	272 209 451 354 240 414 385 787 1226 286 536 351
PORTSMOUTH	64 336 290 32 191 293 695 1154 214 397 124
SALISBURY	306 225 35 204 246 649 1115 150 373 142
SHEFFIELD	130 307 290 77 402 834 171 84 253
SHREWSBURY	262 301 53 438 877 76 214 240
SOUTHAMPTON	200 280 682 1122 171 380 130
SOUTHEND-ON-SEA	274 681 1107 220 357 63
STOKE-ON-TRENT	402 842 97 161 245
STRANRAER	612 499 352 636
THURSO	938 758 107
WORCESTER	256 171
YORK	315

DISTANCE IN MILES (lower-left triangle, read row by row)

City	mile values (left to right)
ABERDEEN	428
ABERYSTWYTH	179 306
AYR	405 111 283
BIRMINGHAM	326 177 204 113
BRADFORD	484 135 362 86 192
BRISTOL	480 198 355 100 155 146
CAMBRIDGE	489 116 367 100 207 45 178
CARDIFF	216 212 94 189 110 268 264 273
CARLISLE	421 131 299 20 118 92 80 115 205
COVENTRY	392 139 270 41 73 127 91 141 176 45
DERBY	344 173 239 95 34 179 111 195 145 94 54
DONCASTER	586 296 456 177 265 210 115 218 362 157 192 226
DOVER	129 304 79 281 201 360 341 365 92 309 268 215 446
EDINBURGH	557 208 435 159 273 73 211 118 341 165 200 259 246 433
EXETER	482 54 360 166 231 154 251 109 266 189 193 227 361 358 227
FISHGUARD	157 423 141 400 321 479 467 484 211 416 387 356 579 140 552 477
FORT WILLIAM	146 307 33 284 205 363 351 368 95 300 271 240 463 43 436 361 116
GLASGOW	449 102 327 51 157 35 120 58 233 57 93 147 194 325 108 167 444 328
GLOUCESTER	540 276 424 165 220 193 65 226 330 145 156 188 117 411 248 334 541 425 172
HARWICH	422 109 300 144 158 229 238 213 206 163 154 166 331 298 302 163 417 301 175 309
HOLYHEAD	352 209 250 130 66 216 125 230 156 114 91 46 240 222 279 263 367 251 171 190 215
HULL	105 473 207 439 359 517 513 522 249 454 425 377 619 162 590 515 67 174 482 573 455 385
INVERNESS	261 167 139 144 92 223 216 228 45 160 131 100 321 137 296 221 256 140 188 287 161 124 294
KENDAL	330 182 208 109 9 195 142 209 114 116 68 31 261 205 268 238 325 209 160 219 163 55 363 69
LEEDS	410 146 292 42 101 115 63 138 198 23 28 66 164 296 188 200 409 293 96 137 91 443 153 96
LEICESTER	388 190 279 88 74 164 83 187 185 72 51 40 198 258 237 244 396 280 129 148 186 42 421 140 71 49
LINCOLN	330 98 208 88 62 162 168 162 114 108 80 81 265 206 235 158 325 280 132 123 363 69 71 101 121
LIVERPOOL	331 142 209 78 35 157 149 171 115 94 56 50 251 207 230 196 326 210 112 212 123 92 364 75 40 84 94 31
MANCHESTER	234 278 148 206 97 292 237 305 56 205 164 111 352 104 365 332 258 142 257 302 247 118 267 86 96 181 154 155 136
NEWCASTLE UPON TYNE	490 259 381 155 176 204 58 236 286 136 135 142 163 360 267 313 498 382 178 80 289 144 523 238 173 113 102 215 191 256
NORWICH	390 154 271 52 76 138 79 152 177 48 15 45 190 260 211 208 388 272 106 144 169 82 423 137 71 25 36 92 62 156 126
NOTTINGHAM	484 148 344 61 168 67 79 100 250 47 92 135 130 354 132 208 461 345 46 126 202 160 517 205 165 69 118 155 141 250 137 94
OXFORD	664 315 542 266 372 180 309 225 448 272 307 359 344 540 98 334 659 543 215 346 409 396 697 403 375 295 344 342 337 472 365 318 247
PENZANCE	84 344 95 321 242 400 396 405 132 337 308 260 502 45 473 398 106 62 365 456 338 268 117 177 246 326 304 246 247 150 406 306 400 580
PERTH	607 253 480 204 310 118 264 163 386 210 245 297 286 478 43 272 597 481 153 291 328 334 640 341 313 233 282 280 275 410 320 259 185 78 523
PLYMOUTH	562 211 423 140 247 91 124 135 329 126 169 214 125 433 126 245 540 424 106 157 284 239 595 284 244 148 197 238 218 329 184 173 79 224 478 169
PORTSMOUTH	538 170 394 111 219 51 140 92 300 101 146 195 159 409 87 205 511 395 66 161 242 215 571 255 220 124 173 199 193 305 198 149 66 185 454 130 40
SALISBURY	363 156 241 76 38 162 111 178 147 83 35 17 227 238 235 210 358 242 131 182 149 65 396 100 33 63 46 69 38 130 358 279 280 209 190
SHEFFIELD	390 75 263 43 102 104 144 104 169 62 64 98 219 261 177 129 380 264 74 101 134 423 124 107 71 115 58 67 203 184 79 101 275 306 220 180 140 81
SHREWSBURY	542 191 415 125 234 73 131 115 321 111 156 199 137 413 106 227 532 416 78 184 264 224 575 276 224 138 189 212 206 314 189 158 94 204 458 149 20 22 191 163
SOUTHAMPTON	533 246 414 144 218 161 63 186 320 124 149 174 72 404 214 295 531 415 144 222 205 300 102 212 51 83 50 36 168 170 50 105 301 284 239 182 153 48 33 174 170
SOUTHEND-ON-SEA	368 108 241 42 71 121 119 137 147 35 65 215 239 194 162 358 242 86 179 119 101 401 102 72 51 83 50 36 168 170 50 105 301 284 239 182 153 48 33 174 170
STOKE-ON-TRENT	230 315 51 292 213 371 367 376 103 326 248 465 124 444 369 192 84 336 433 309 259 258 148 211 288 217 218 159 389 280 353 551 146 489 432 403 250 272 424 423 250
STRANRAER	227 595 329 561 481 639 635 644 371 576 547 499 741 284 712 637 177 296 604 695 577 507 122 416 485 565 543 485 486 389 645 545 639 819 239 762 717 693 518 545 697 688 523 380
THURSO	428 95 301 28 135 62 103 72 207 41 72 126 184 299 135 148 418 302 27 180 148 172 461 162 132 64 108 106 100 233 344 178 133 93 106 47 106 137 60 310 583
WORCESTER	316 208 211 128 32 215 159 228 116 127 87 33 274 187 288 262 327 180 224 190 40 349 88 23 99 76 54 178 78 178 78 395 232 333 247 232 52 13 236 222 100 219 471 159
YORK	507 211 386 106 194 122 53 147 292 86 116 163 71 378 175 267 503 387 109 73 250 173 540 252 189 93 131 202 188 274 106 119 59 273 423 218 77 88 157 149 81 39 152 395 662 106 196

DISTANCE IN MILES

KEY TO MAP SYMBOLS

Road maps (pages 2-109)

ROAD INFORMATION

M4	Motorway
30 — 29	Motorway junction with full / limited access
Maidstone / Birch / Sarn	Motorway service area with off road / full / limited access
A48	Primary dual / single carriageway
	With passing places
A30	'A' road dual / single carriageway
	With passing places
B1403	'B' road dual / single carriageway
	With passing places
	Minor road
	Restricted access due to road condition or private ownership
▬▬▬▬ ═══ ▬ ▬ ▬ ═ ═ ═	Road projected or under construction
⊗	Multi-level junction (occasionally with junction number)
○■○ ═○═ ○	Roundabout
10	Road distance in miles
⟩▪▪▪▪⟨	Road tunnel
→ →	Steep hill (arrows point downhill)
× Toll	Level crossing / Toll

OTHER TRANSPORT INFORMATION

Poole 2½ hrs (3 hrs)	Car ferry route with journey times; daytime and (night-time)
○ →	Railway line / Station / Tunnel
✈	Airport with scheduled services
Ⓗ	Heliport
Ⓟ	Park and Ride site

CITIES , TOWNS & VILLAGES

	Built up area
□ ▫ ▫	Town / Village / Other settlement
Peterhead	Primary route destination
St Ives	Seaside destination

OTHER FEATURES

▬·▬·▬·▬·	National boundary
▬·▬·▬·▬·	County / Unitary Authority boundary
	National / Regional park
	Forest park boundary
Danger Zone	Military range
	Woodland
•468	Spot height in metres
▲941	Summit height in metres
	Lake / Dam / River / Waterfall
	Canal / Dry canal / Canal tunnel
	Beach
14	Adjoining page indicator

TOURIST INFORMATION

A selection of tourist detail is shown on the mapping. It is advisable to check with the local tourist information office regarding opening times and facilities available.

𝒊 𝒊	Tourist information office (all year / seasonal)
🚂 ┄•┄•┄	Preserved railway
⚔ 1738	Battlefield
�	Ancient monument
✚	Ecclesiastical building
⌂	Castle
⌂	Historic house (with or without garden)
❀	Garden
🏛	Museum / Art gallery
£	Factory shop village
⊞	Theme park
⚐	Major sports venue
⊠	Motor racing circuit
⚘	Racecourse
⊠	Country park
➹	Nature reserve
🐘	Wildlife park or Zoo
★	Other interesting feature
⚑	Golf course
(NT) (NTS)	National Trust property / National Trust for Scotland
(MNT)	Manx National Trust (Isle of Man)

London central map (pages 118-119)

Dual A4	Primary route	Main / Other railway station	Tourist information centre
Dual A302	'A' road	LRT / Bus or coach station	Cinema / Theatre
B240	'B' road	Leisure and tourism	Major hotel
	Other road	Shopping	Embassy
	Street market / Pedestrian street	Administration and law	Church
	Track / Path	Health and welfare	Mosque
	One way street / Access restriction	Education	Synagogue
	Ferry	Industry and commerce	Mormon — Other place of worship
	Borough boundary	Public open space	Car park / Public toilet
	Postal district boundary	Park / Garden / Sports ground	POL — Fire Sta — PO — Police station / Fire station / Post office

Urban area maps (pages 120-133)

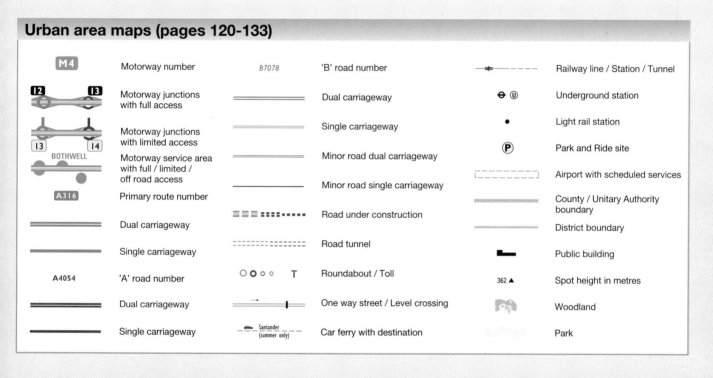

M4	Motorway number	B7078	'B' road number	Railway line / Station / Tunnel
12 13	Motorway junctions with full access		Dual carriageway	Underground station
13 14	Motorway junctions with limited access		Single carriageway	Light rail station
BOTHWELL	Motorway service area with full / limited / off road access		Minor road dual carriageway	Park and Ride site
A316	Primary route number		Minor road single carriageway	Airport with scheduled services
	Dual carriageway		Road under construction	County / Unitary Authority boundary
	Single carriageway		Road tunnel	District boundary
A4054	'A' road number	O O o o T	Roundabout / Toll	Public building
	Dual carriageway		One way street / Level crossing	362 ▲ Spot height in metres
	Single carriageway	Santander (summer only)	Car ferry with destination	Woodland
				Park

City and town centre plans (pages 120-133)

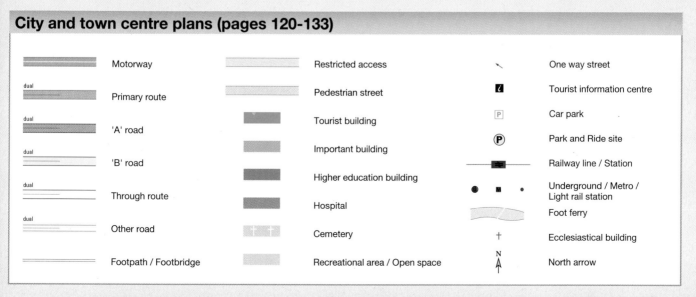

	Motorway		Restricted access	One way street
dual	Primary route		Pedestrian street	Tourist information centre
dual	'A' road		Tourist building	Car park
dual	'B' road		Important building	Park and Ride site
dual	Through route		Higher education building	Railway line / Station
dual	Other road		Hospital	Underground / Metro / Light rail station
			Cemetery	Foot ferry
	Footpath / Footbridge		Recreational area / Open space	Ecclesiastical building
				N Ⓐ North arrow

ROUTE PLANNING MAP OF GREAT BRITAIN AND IRELAND

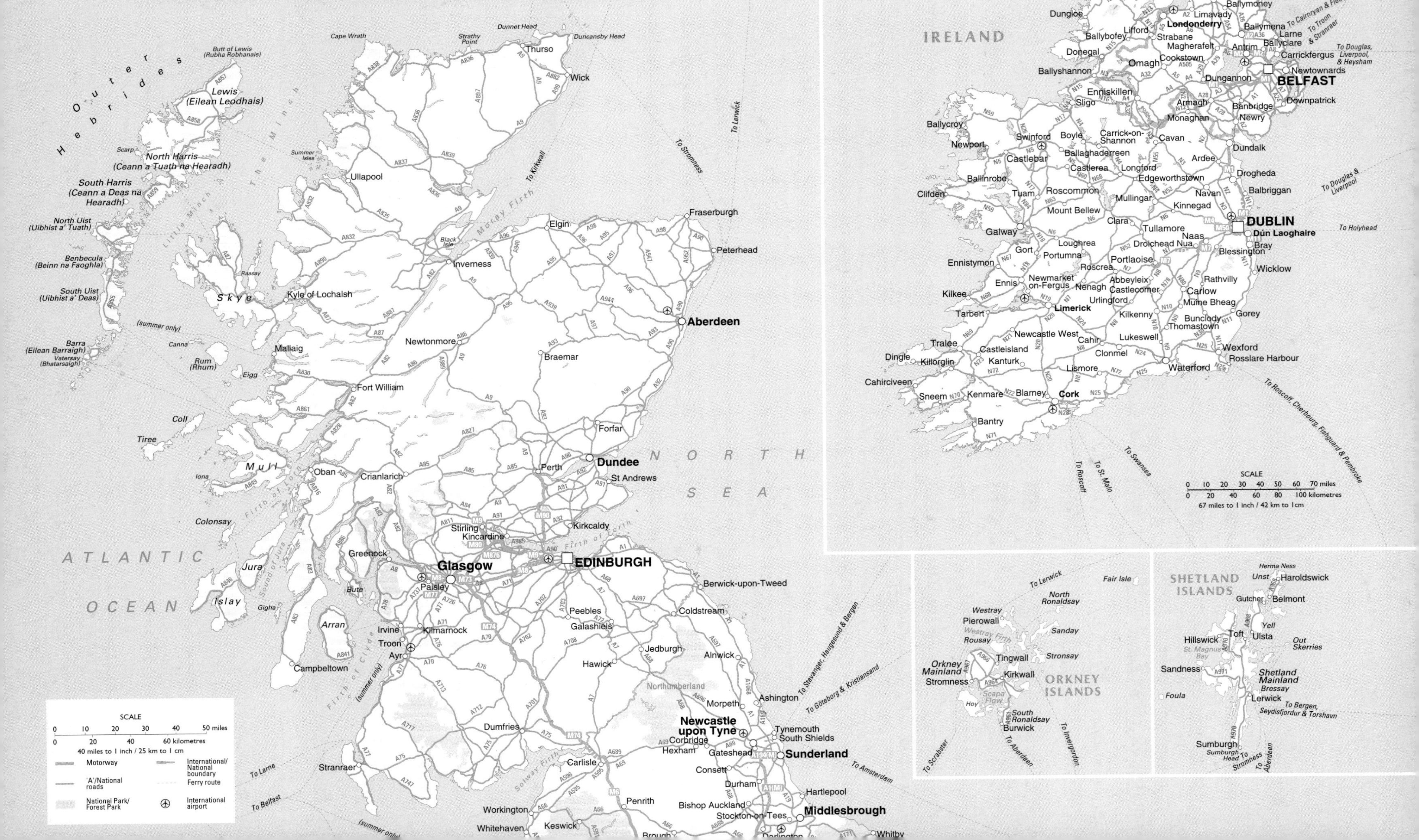

IRELAND

To Douglas, Liverpool, Fleetwood
To Cairnryan & Troon
To Douglas & Liverpool
To Heysham
To Stranraer
To Holyhead

BELFAST
Newtownards
Larne
Ballyclare
Carrickfergus
Bangor
Downpatrick
Newtownards
Ballycastle
Ballymoney
Antrim
Ballymena
Coleraine
Limavady
Londonderry
Magherafelt
Strabane
Cookstown
Omagh
Lifford
Dungannon
Armagh
Monaghan
Dungloe
Ballybofey
Donegal
Enniskillen
Cavan
Carrick-on-Shannon
Sligo
Ballyshannon
Swinford
Boyle
Ballaghaderreen
Longford
Castlerea
Roscommon
Mount Bellew
Ballymote
Castlebar
Newport
Ballycroy
Ballinrobe
Tuam
Clifden
Galway
Gort
Portumna
Ennistymon
Ennis
Newmarket-on-Fergus
Nenagh
Loughrea
Kilkee
Tarbert
Killorglin
Tralee
Listowel
Newcastle West
Kanturk
Castleisland
Dingle
Cahirciveen
Sneem
Kenmare
Blarney
Bantry
Cork

Banbridge
Newry
Dundalk
Ardee
Drogheda
Balbriggan
Navan
Kinnegad
Edgeworthstown
Mullingar
Clara
Tullamore
Droichead Nua
Portlaoise
Abbeyleix
Roscrea
Castlecomer
Urlingford
Kilkenny
Thomastown
Cahir
Lismore
Clonmel

DUBLIN
Dún Laoghaire
Bray
Wicklow
Blessington
Rathvilly
Carlow
Muine Bheag
Bunclody
Gorey
Wexford
Rosslare Harbour
Waterford

To Roscoff, Cherbourg, Fishguard & Pembroke
To Swansea
To St Malo
To Roscoff

SCALE
0 10 20 30 40 50 60 70 miles
0 20 40 60 80 100 kilometres
67 miles to 1 inch / 42 km to 1 cm

SHETLAND ISLANDS
Herma Ness
Haroldswick
Unst
Belmont
Gutcher
Yell
Out Skerries
Toft
Ulsta
Shetland Mainland
Bressay
Lerwick
Sandness
Hillswick
St Magnus Bay
Sumburgh
Sumburgh Head
Foula
To Bergen, Seydisfjordur & Torshavn
To Aberdeen

ORKNEY ISLANDS
Fair Isle
North Ronaldsay
Westray
Sanday
Stronsay
Pierowall
Rousay
Kirkwall
Tingwall
Stromness
Orkney Mainland
Scapa Flow
South Ronaldsay
Burwick
To Lerwick
To Invergordon
To Aberdeen
To Scrabster

To Stavanger, Haugesund & Bergen
To Amsterdam
To Göteborg, Kristiansand & Bergen

Tynemouth
South Shields
Sunderland
Hartlepool
Middlesbrough
Whitby
Ashington
Morpeth
Newcastle upon Tyne
Gateshead
Consett
Durham
Bishop Auckland
Stockton-on-Tees
Hexham
Corbridge
Berwick-upon-Tweed
Coldstream
Alnwick
Penrith
Brough

N O R T H   S E A

To Leith
To Stromness

Peterhead
Fraserburgh
Aberdeen
Elgin
Forfar
Dundee
St Andrews
Braemar
Perth
Kirkcaldy
EDINBURGH
Firth of Forth
GLASGOW
Paisley
Stirling
Kincardine
Inverness
Newtonmore
Fort William
Crianlarich
Oban
Kilmarnock
Irvine
Troon
Ayr
Campbeltown
Stranraer
Dumfries
Peebles
Galashiels
Hawick
Jedburgh
Carlisle
Keswick
Workington
Whitehaven
Wick
Thurso
Dunnet Head
Duncansby Head
Strathy Point
Cape Wrath
Ullapool
Kyle of Lochalsh
Mallaig

Butt of Lewis (Rubha Robhanais)
Lewis (Eilean Leòdhais)
North Harris (Ceann a Tuath na Hearadh)
South Harris (Ceann a Deas na Hearadh)
North Uist (Uibhist a Tuath)
Benbecula (Beinn na Faoghla)
South Uist (Uibhist a Deas)
Barra (Eilean Bharraigh)
Vatersay (Bhatarsaigh)

The Minch
Little Minch
Skye
Rum (Rhum)
Eigg
Canna
Coll
Tiree
Iona
Mull
Colonsay
Jura
Islay
Gigha
Arran
Bute
Sound of Jura
Firth of Clyde

Moray Firth
Black Isle
Solway Firth

To Kirkwall
To Lerwick
To Larne
To Belfast

ATLANTIC OCEAN

SCALE
0 10 20 30 40 50 miles
0 20 40 60 kilometres
40 miles to 1 inch / 25 km to 1 cm

Motorway
'A'/National roads
National Park/ Forest Park
International/ National boundary
Ferry route
International airport

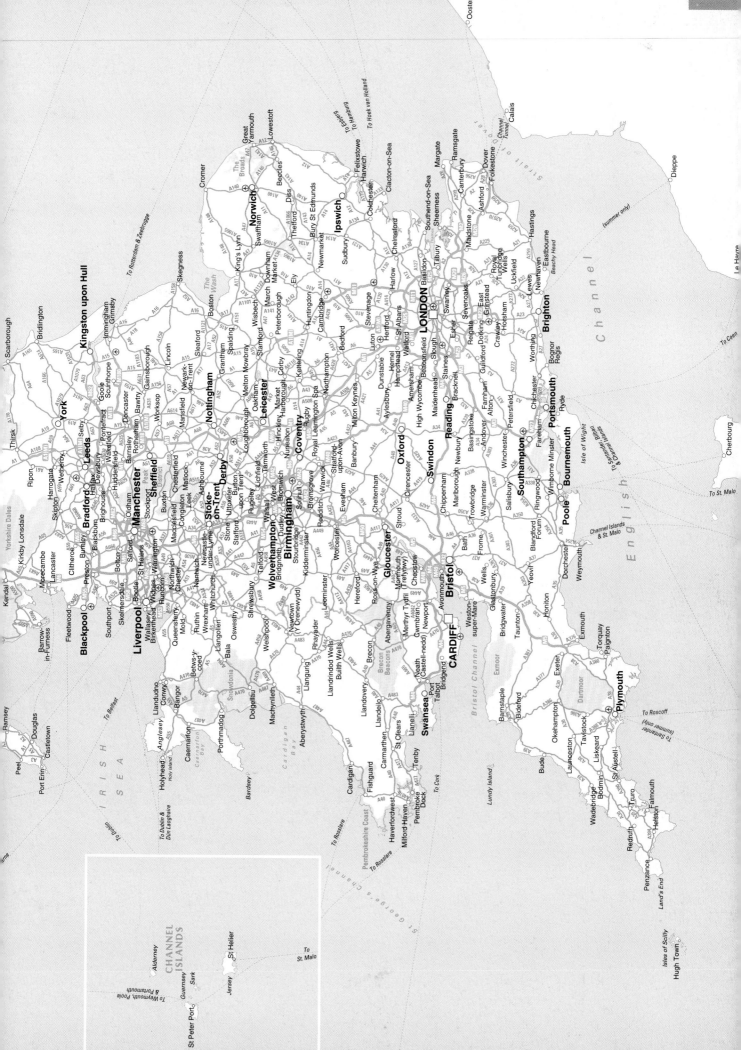

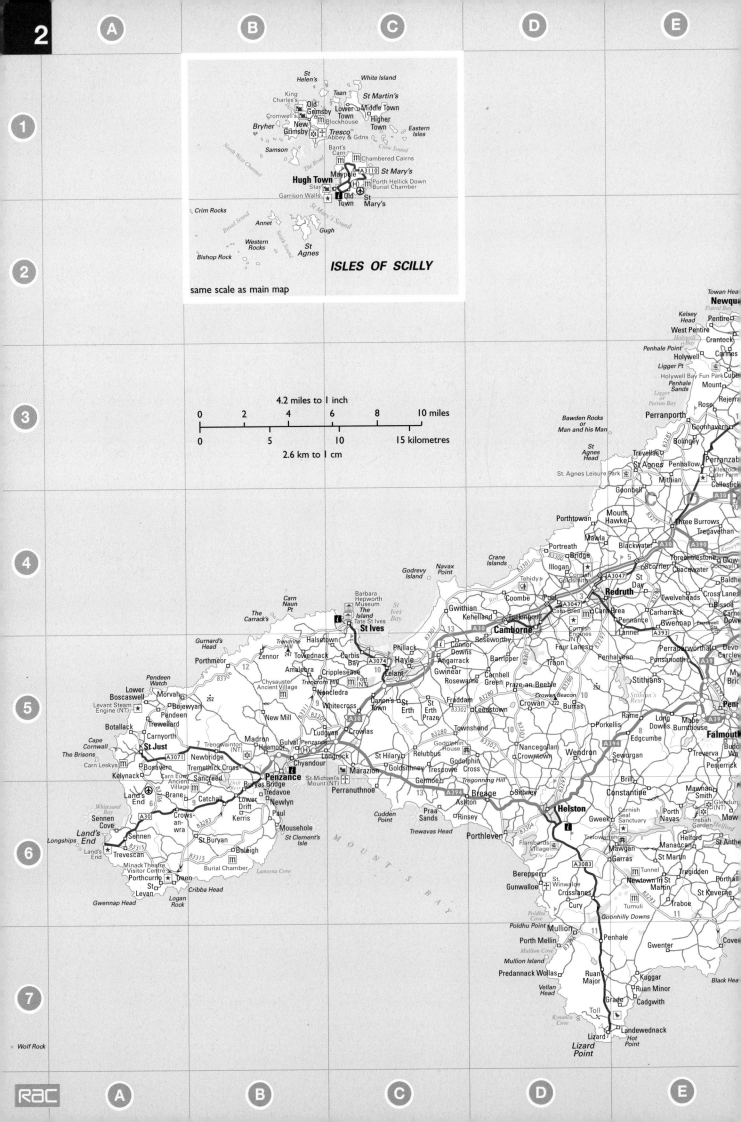

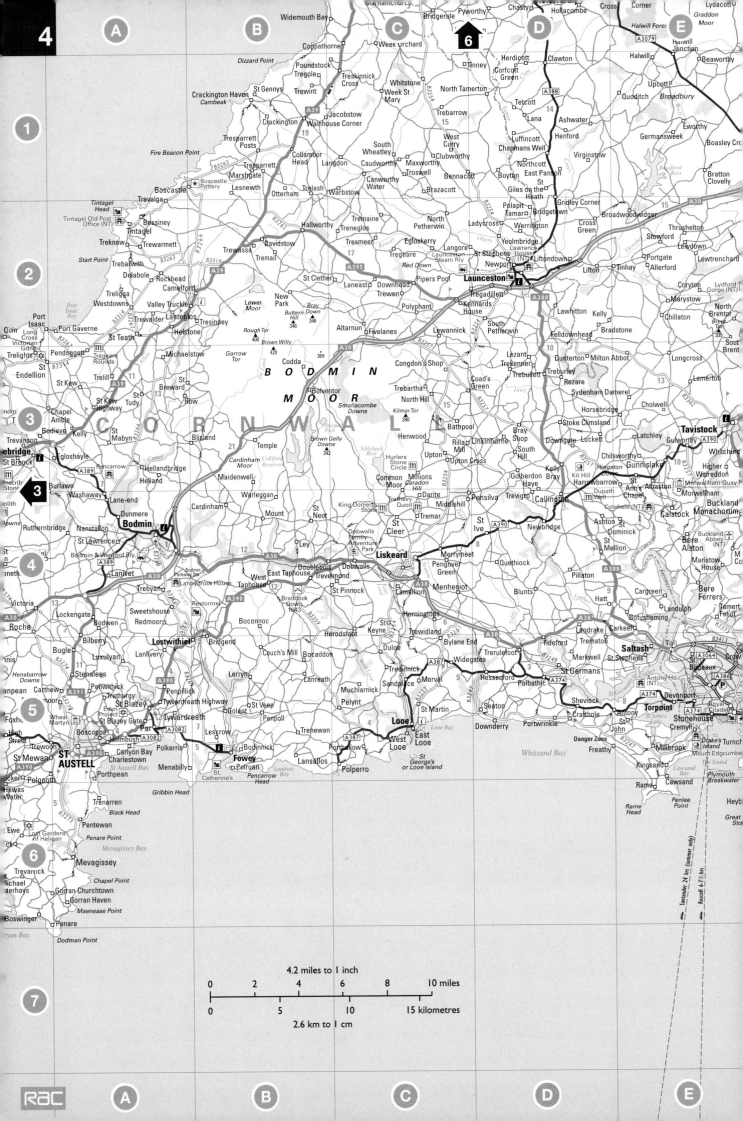

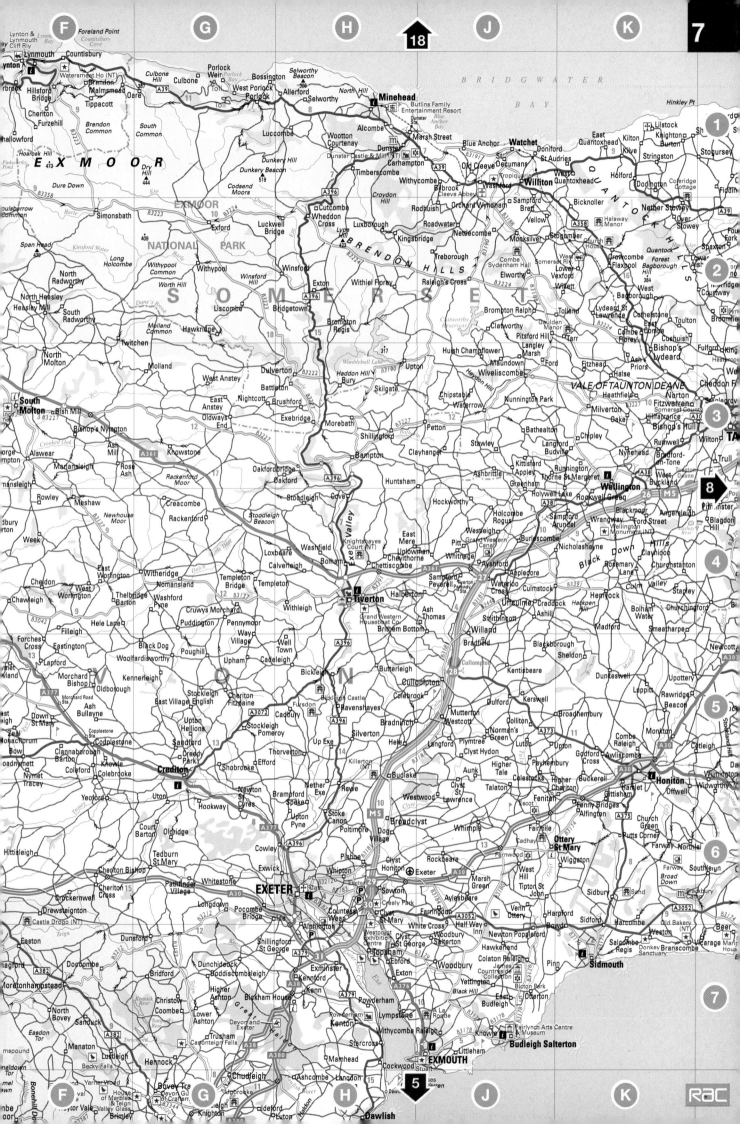

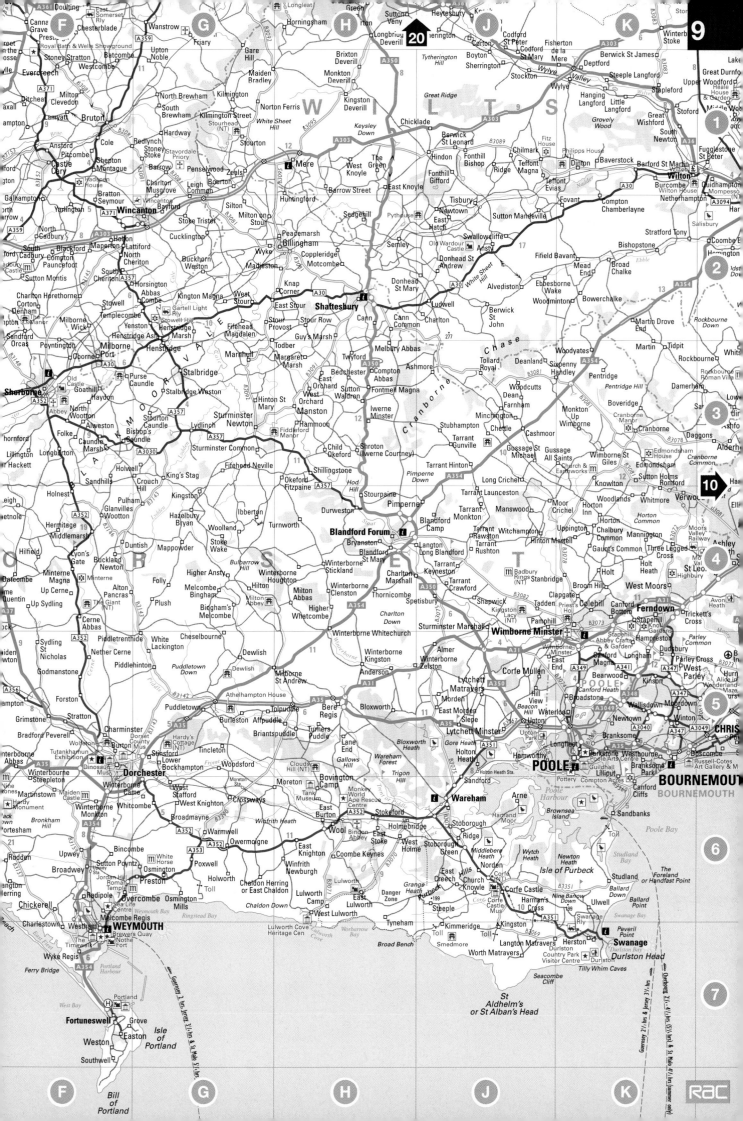

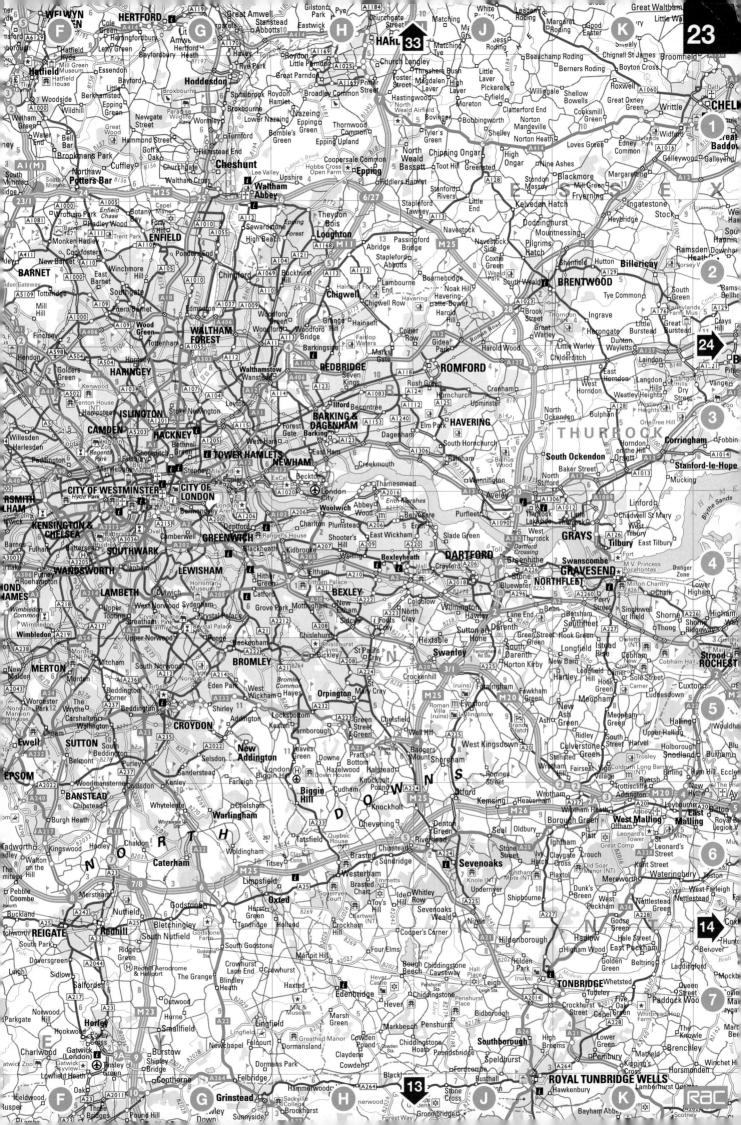

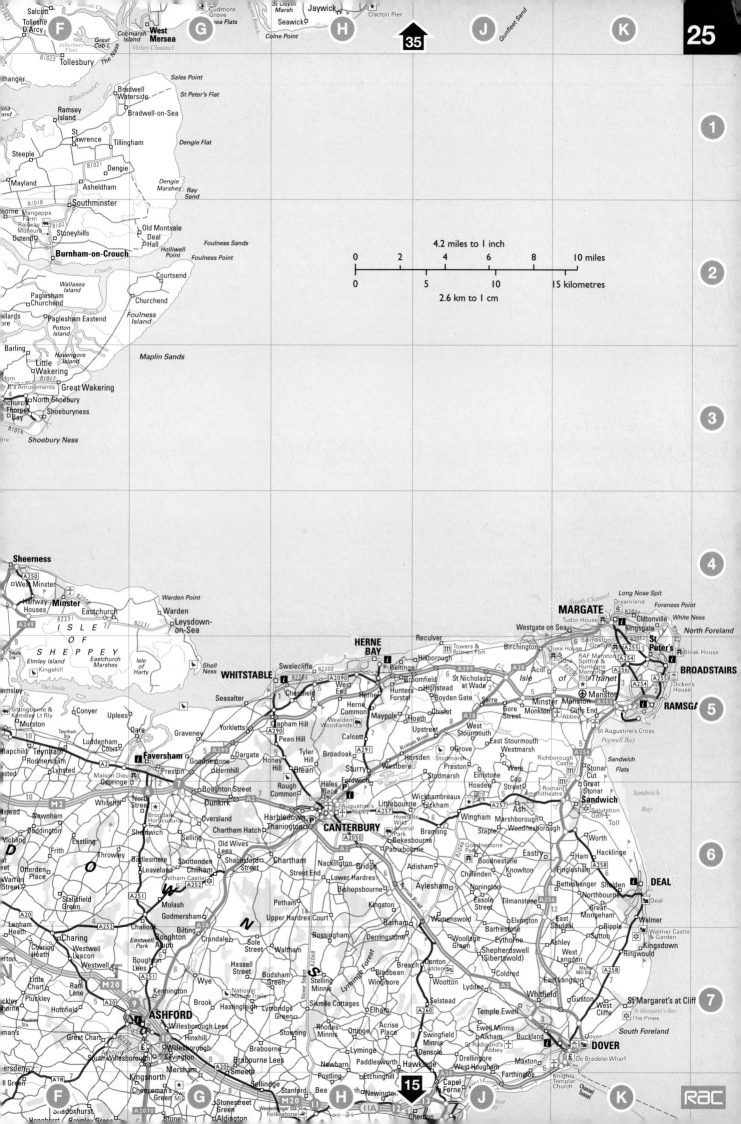

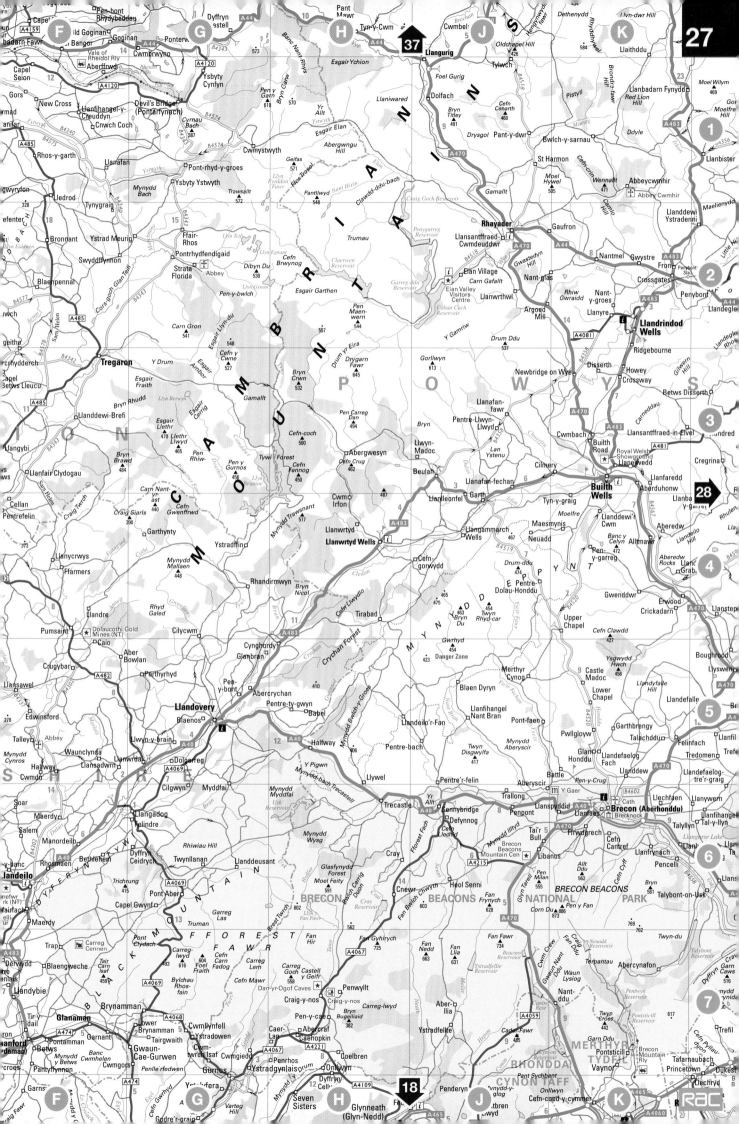

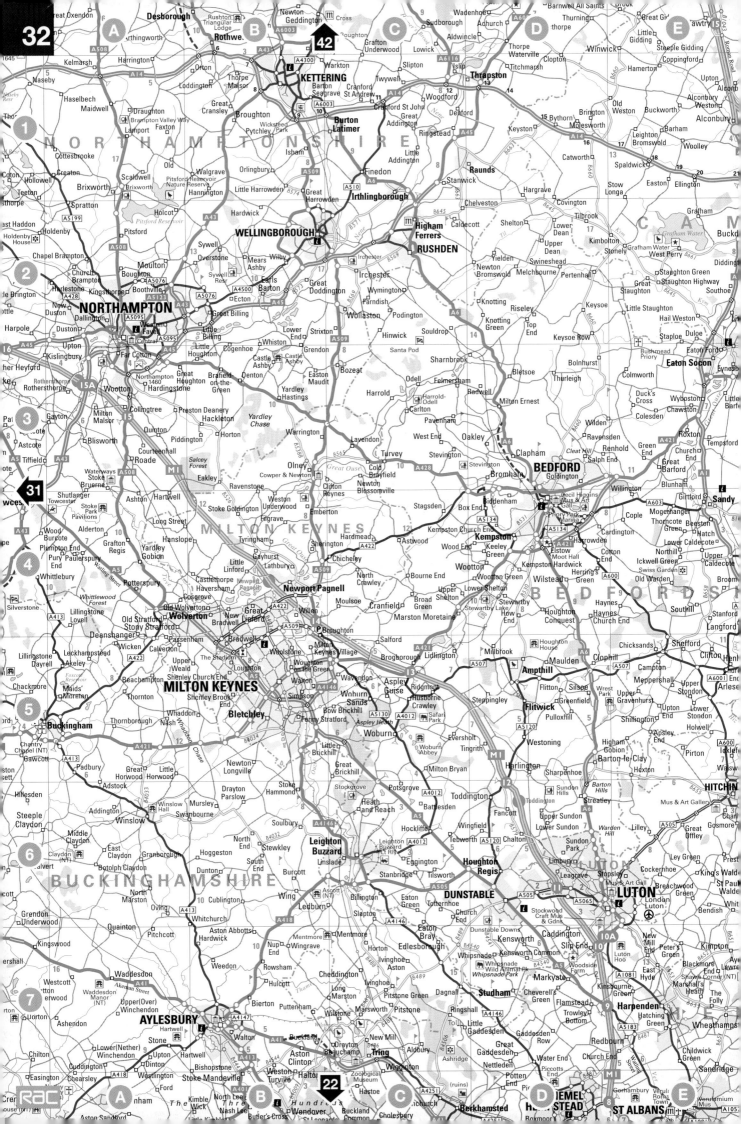

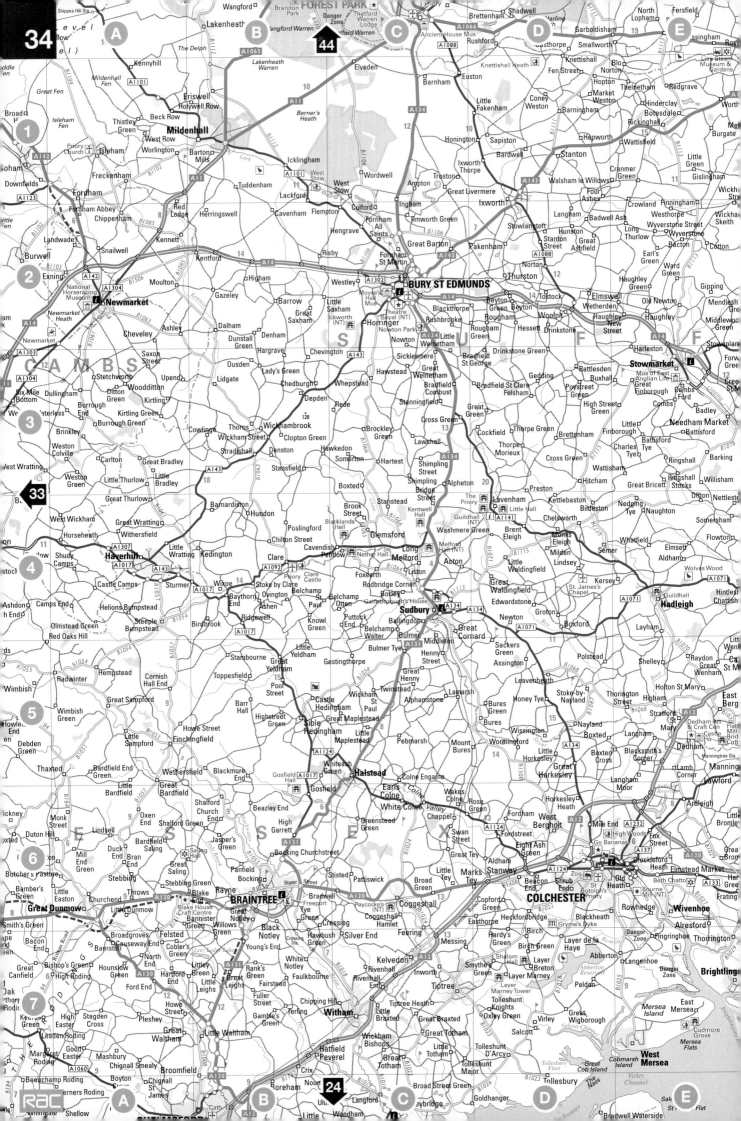

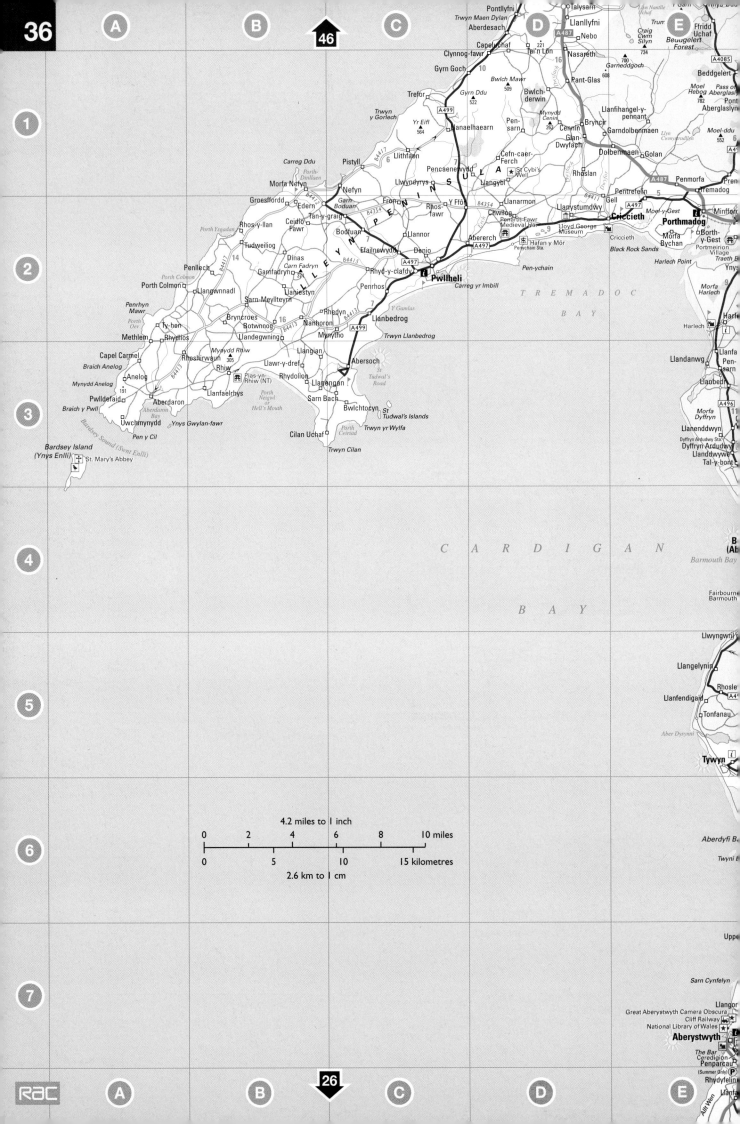

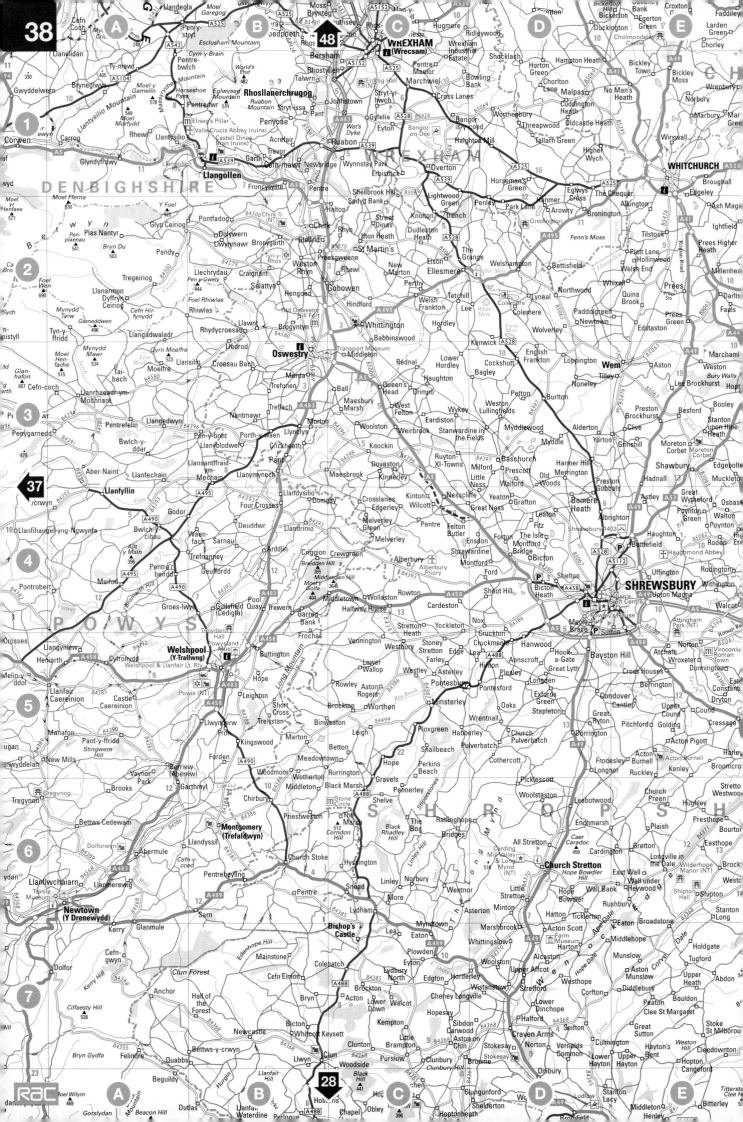

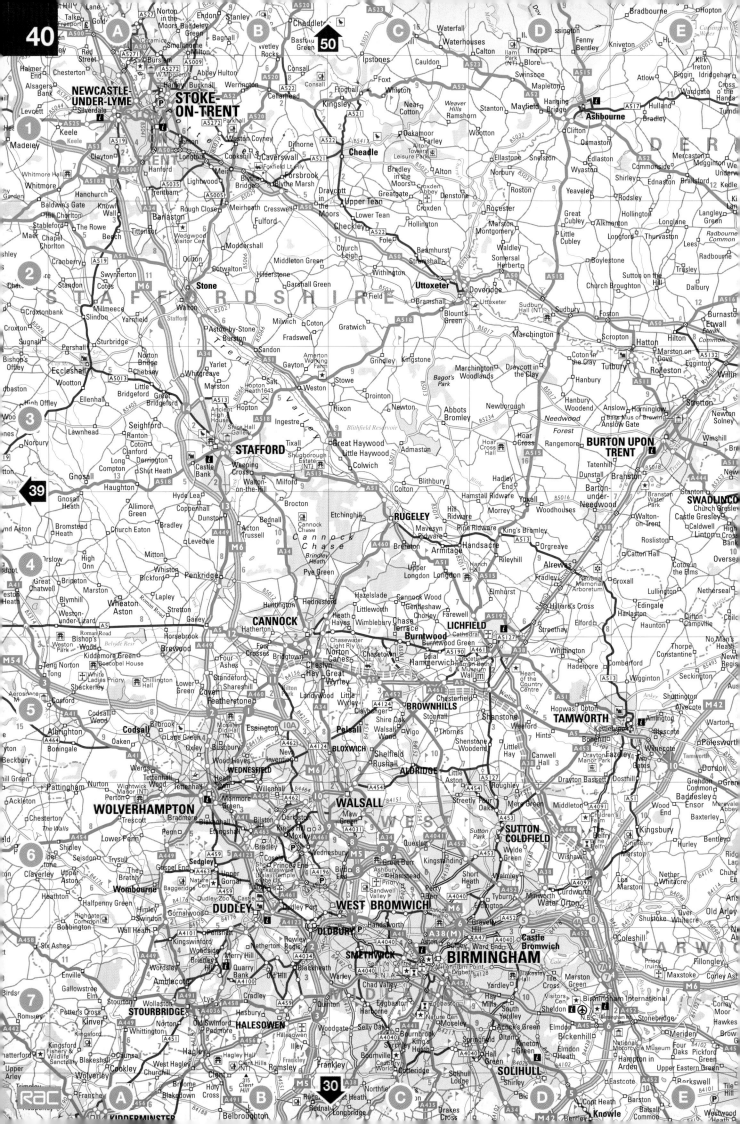

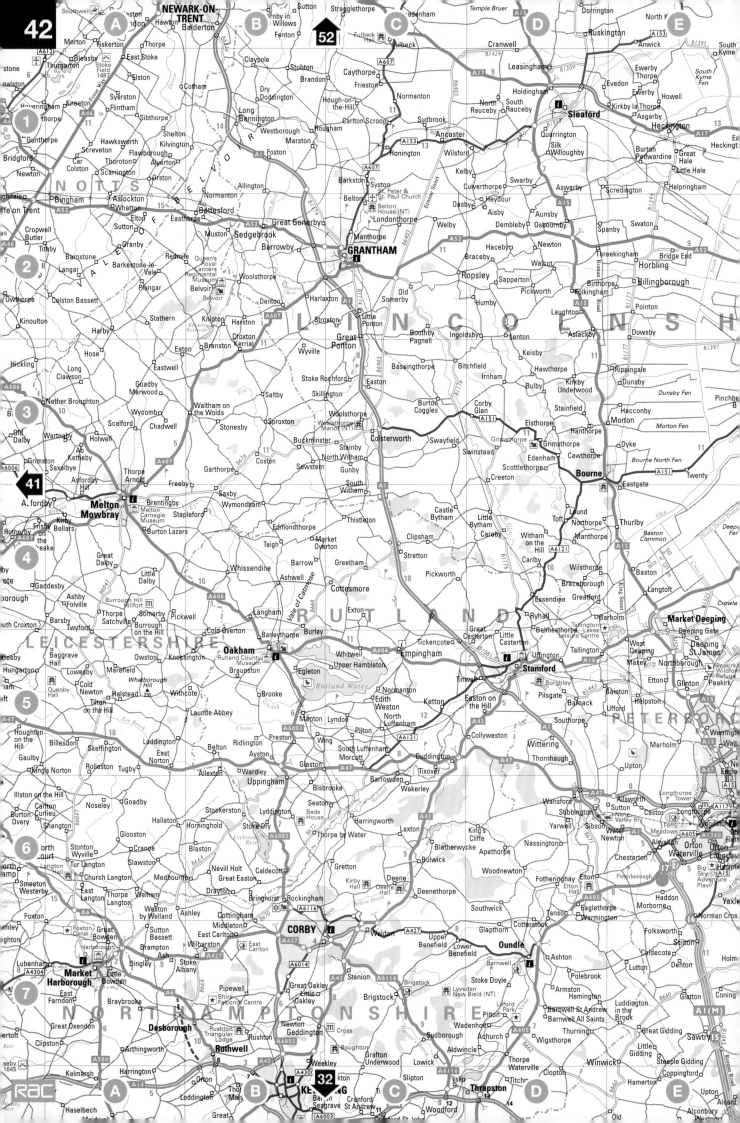

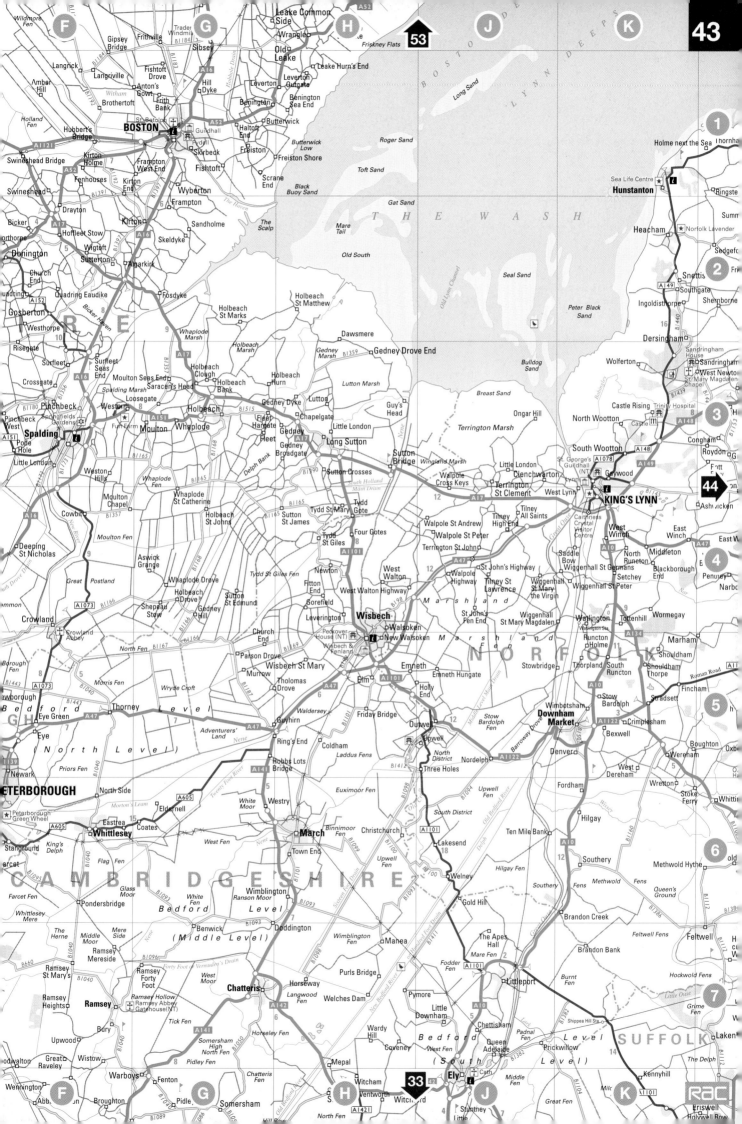

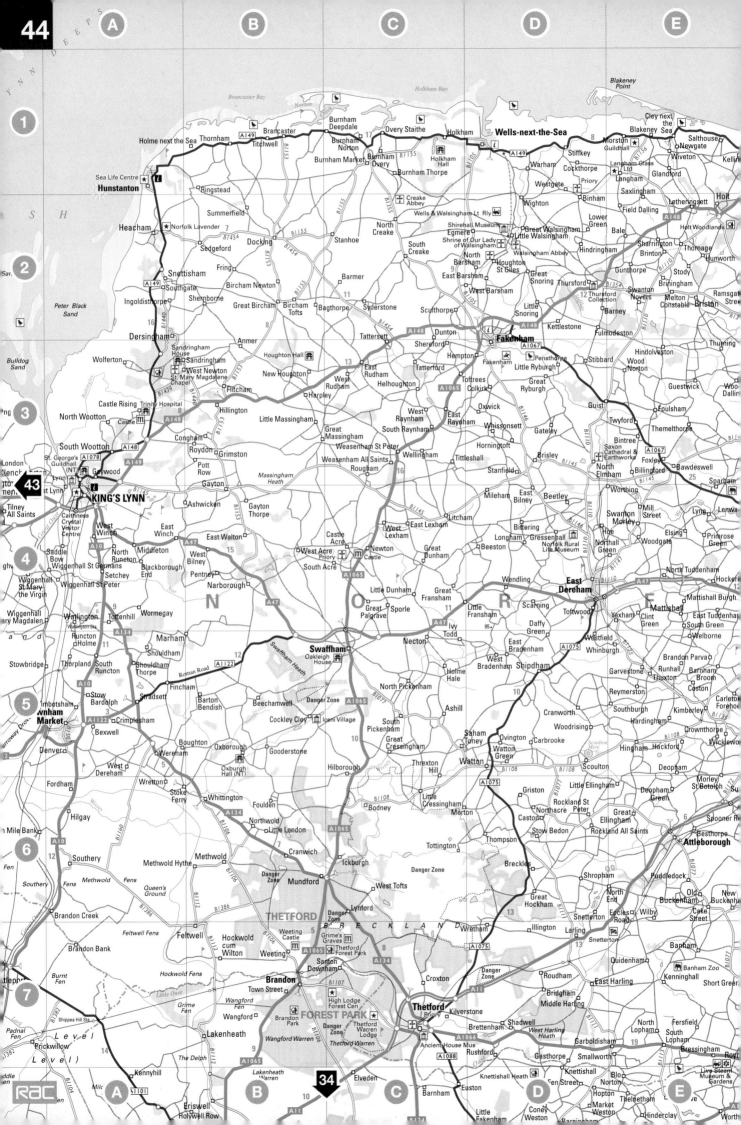

A1033

Holmpton

trington
59
Haven Side
Welwick
Weeton
7
Out Newton
Skeffling
Easington
6
B1445
G

Cherry Cobb Sands
Foulholme Sands

Immingham Dock

MOUTH OF THE HUMBER

Sunk Island
Old Hall

EAST RIDING OF YORKSHIRE

Kilnsea

Sunk Island Sands
Skeffling Clays
Kilnsea Clays

Spurn Head

NORTH

A180
Healing
A1136
West Marsh
Wellholme Galleries
A180
GRIMSBY
National Fishing Heritage Centre
CLEETHORPES
Cleethorpes Coast Light Rly
Cleethorpes Discovery Centre
Pleasure Island
Humberston

Great Coates
EAST

A46
Scartho
A1098

Aylesby
A46
Laceby
A16
6
Bradley

LINCOLNSHIRE
B1219
New Waltham
18

Barnoldby le Beck
Brigsley
Ashby cum Fenby
B1203
Waltham
Holton le Clay
A1031
Tetney Lock

Beelsby
Hatcliffe
Grainsby
Tetney
North Cotes

anby
Wold Newton
16
A18
A16
North Thoresby
B1201
Marsh Chapel
Eskham
Wragholme
Meals

Swinhope
East Ravendale
17
Churchthorpe
Fulstow
Grainthorpe
Donna Nook
North Somercotes

brook
Ludborough
Covenham St Bartholomew
Covenham Resr
Ludney
Conisholme
Church End
A1031

North Ormsby
Utterby
Covenham St Mary
Yarburgh
South Somercotes
Saltfleet

Kelstern
Fotherby
Little Grimsby
Alvingham
Skidbrooke

North Elkington
North Cockerington
Saltfleetby St Clements

ford agna
A631
Welton le Wold
South Elkington
Keddington
South Cockerington
Saltfleetby All Saints
11
Theddlethorpe St Helen

Burgh on Bain
A157
Louth
Grimoldby
Manby
B1200
A1031
Theddlethorpe All Saints

15
Gayton le Wold
Hallington
1
A16
Stewton
Little Carlton

Donington on Bain
Raithby
Tathwell
Legbourne
North Reston
South Reston
Great Carlton
Gayton le Marsh
15
Mablethorpe
Trusthorpe
A1104

Benniworth
Little Cawthorpe
Withern
Strubby
8
Thorpe
A52

Market Stainton
Stenigot
150
Cadwell Park
Cawkwell
Haugham
Muckton
Authorpe
Tothill
Maltby le Marsh
Beesby
Sutton on Sea
Sandilands

Asterby
A153
13
Scamblesby
Farforth
Ruckland
Burwell
Belleau
Claythorpe
Aby
Markby
Saleby
Sutton le Marsh
Hannah
16

Goulceby
Ranby
Oxcombe
Farforth
White Pit
Swaby
South Thoresby
A1111
9

S
B1225
Hemingby
Belchford
Little London
South Ormsby
Driby
Rigsby
Bilsby B1449
Huttoft
13

Vispington
Edlington
West Ashby
Fulletby
Tetford
Salmonby
Brinkhill
Somersby
Well
A1104
Farlesthorpe
Anderby
Mumby
Authorpe Row

Thimbleby
Low Toynton
Ashby Puerorum
Harrington
Harrington Hall
Ulceby Cross
Ulceby
Alford
Cumberworth
A52

Langton
B1190
Greetham
Langton
Aswardby
4
Skendleby
Willoughby
Hogsthorpe
Chapel St Leonards

Horncastle
High Toynton
Winceby 1643
Hagworthingham
Sausthorpe
A158
Welton le Marsh
A1028
Claxby
Sloothby

Thornton
Mareham on the Hill
Lusby
Raithby
Partney
Scremby
Orby
Addlethorpe
Fantasy Island
Ingoldmells Point
Ingoldmells

Dalderby
A153
Hameringham
Asgarby
Hundleby
Ashby by Partney
12
Candlesby
Orby Marsh
Butlins Family Entertainment Resort, Skegness

Roughton
8
Wood Enderby
Claxby Pluckacre
Mavis Enderby
Spilsby
Great Steeping
Bratoft
Burgh le Marsh
Burgh Marsh
Winthorpe

Kirkby on Bain
Moorby
Miningsby
Old Bolingbroke
Halton Holegate
Toynton All Saints
Irby in the Marsh
A158

Haltham
West Keal
East Keal
Toynton St Peter
Little Steeping
Firsby
Church Farm Museum
Skegness
Skegness Natureland Seal Sanctuary

Mareham le Fen
A155
East Kirkby
Hagnaby
A16
Toynton Fen Side
Thorpe St Peter
Croft

Tumby
Revesby
Keal Cotes
Stickford
Fendike Corner
Thorpe Culvert
5
A52
Seacroft
Croft Marsh

Tattershall
Moor Side
Tumby Woodside
New Bolingbroke
Wainfleet Bank
Keys Toft
Havenhouse Sta
Gibraltar Point

Coningsby
Tattershall (NT)
Midville
New Leake
Eastville
Friskney Eaudyke
Friskney
Wainfleet All Saints
Gibraltar

Hawthorn Hill
New York
Scrub Hill
Stickney
Carrington
East Fen
Lade Bank
Wainfleet Sand
Gibraltar Pt

Chapel Hill
West Fen
B1192
Northlands
A16
Trader Windmill
B1184
Wrangle Lowgate
Friskney Flats

Wildmore Fen
Gipsey Bridge
Frithville
Sibsey
B1184
Wrangle
A52
BOSTON DEEPS

THE WASH

LYNN DEEPS

43

Langriville
Anton's Gowt
Fishtoft Drove
Old Leake
Leake Hurn's End
Leverton
Leverton Outgate

4.2 miles to 1 inch
0   2   4   6   8   10 miles
0   5   10   15 kilometres
2.6 km to 1 cm

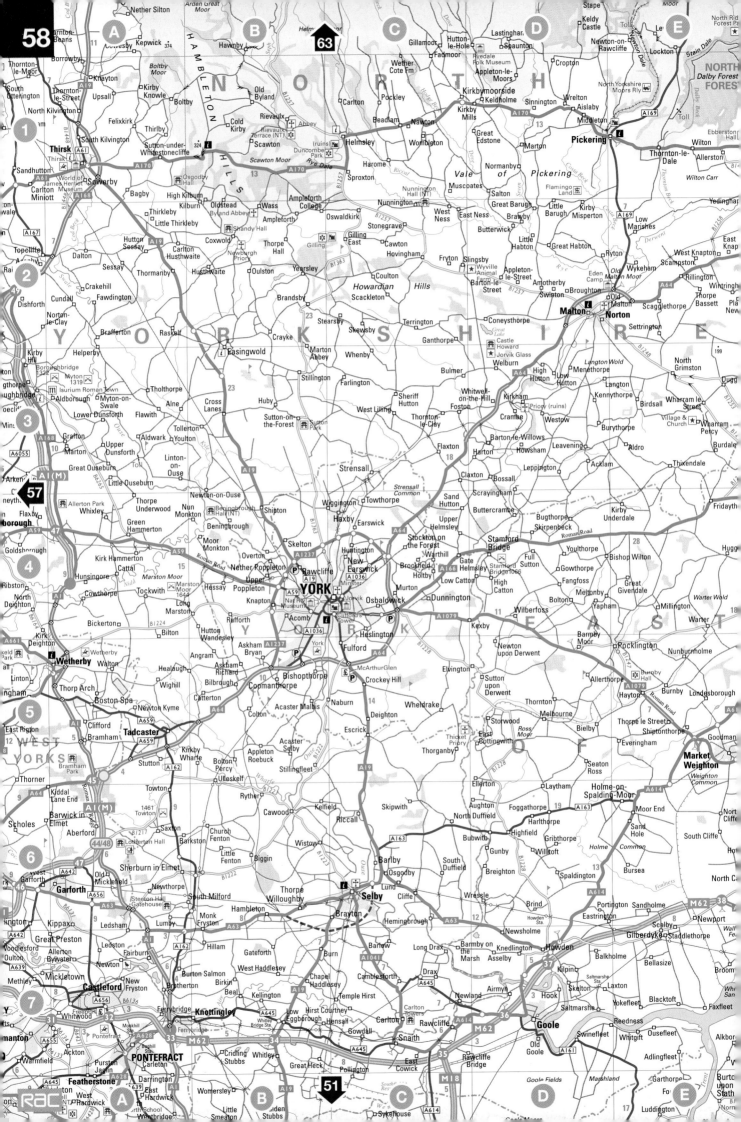

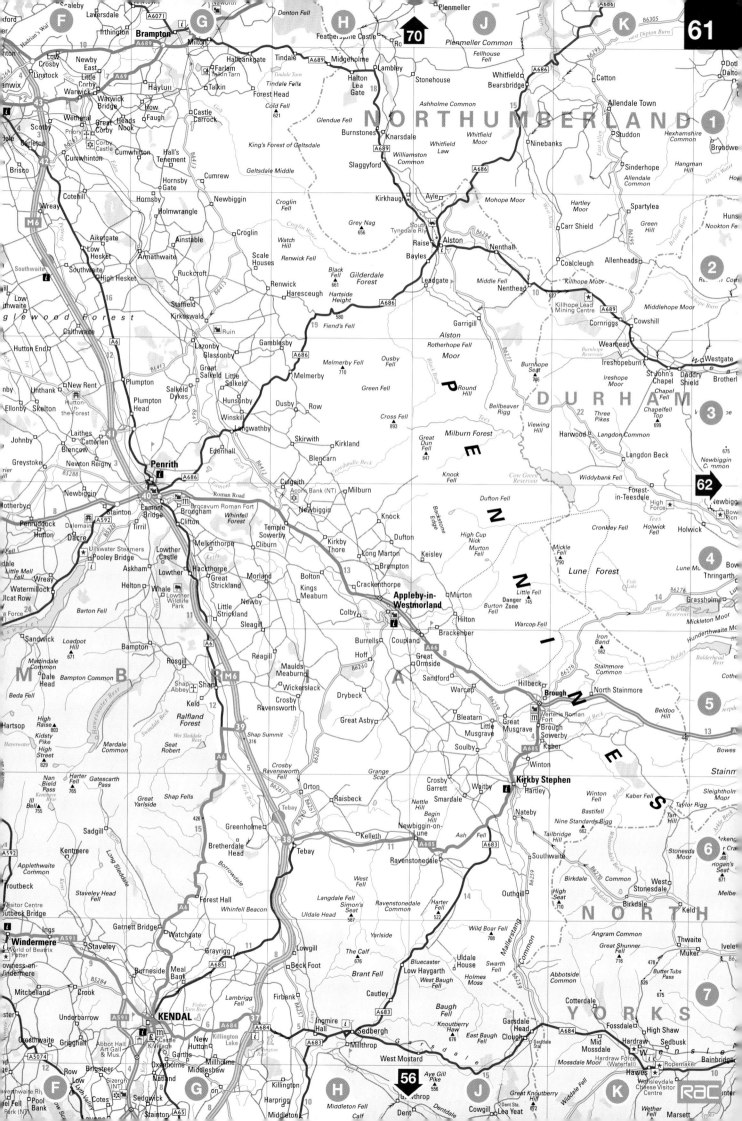

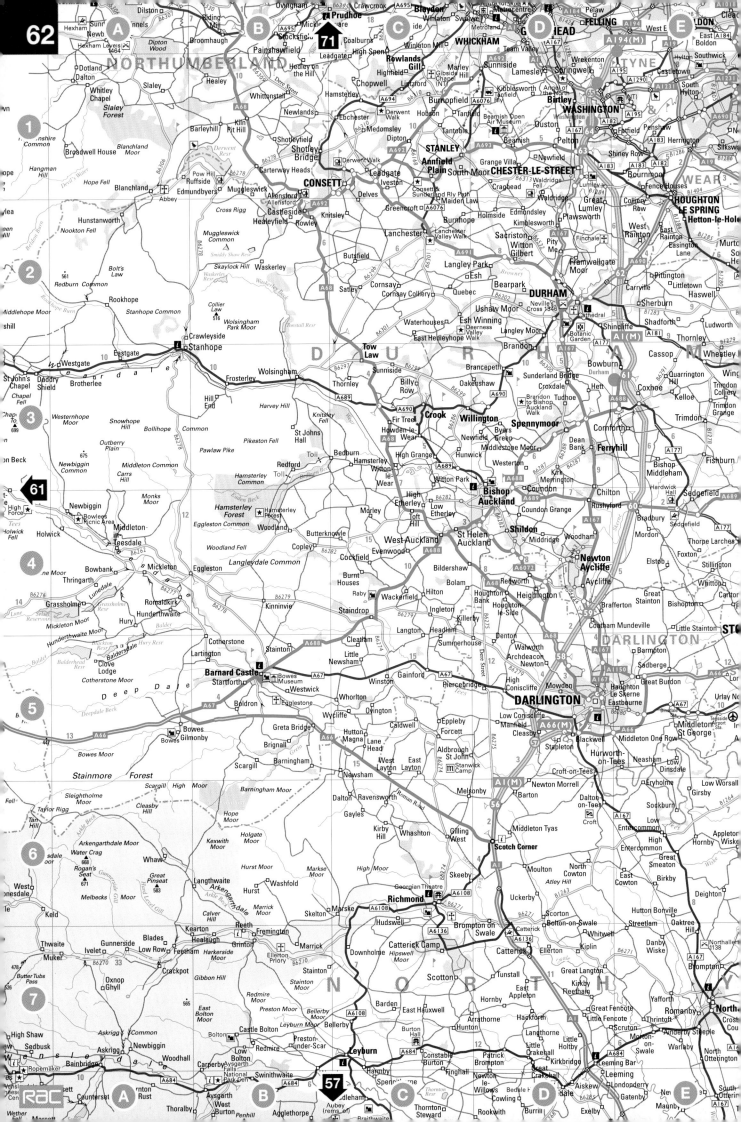

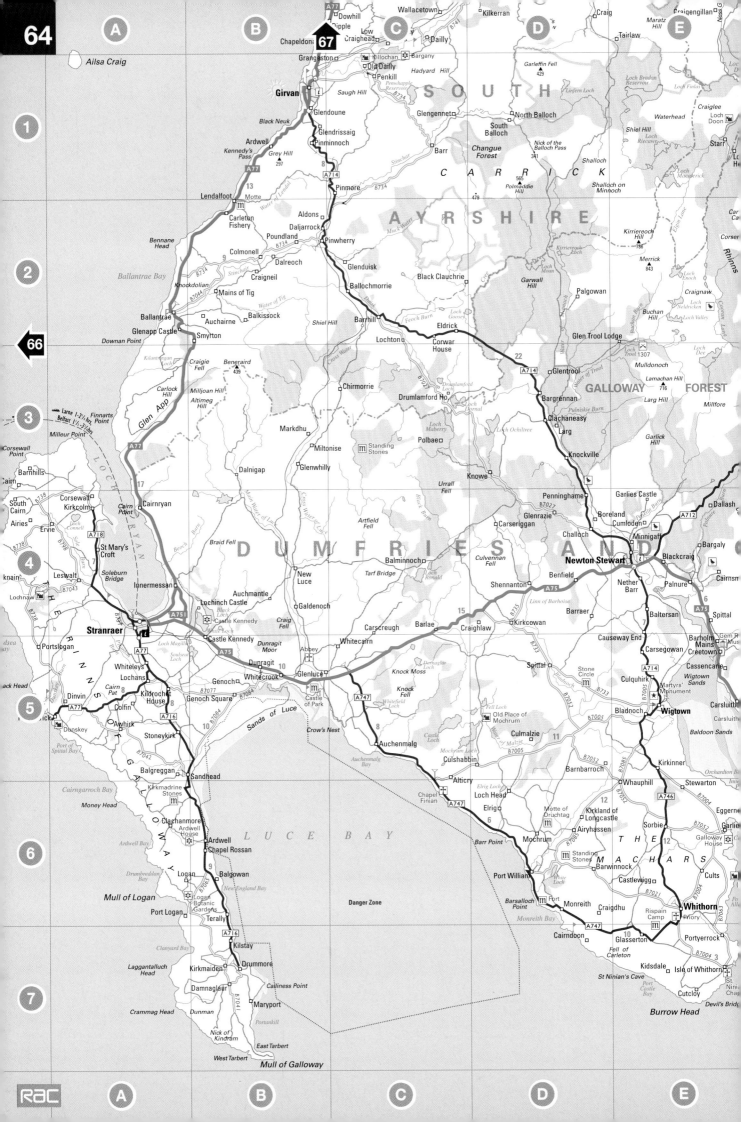

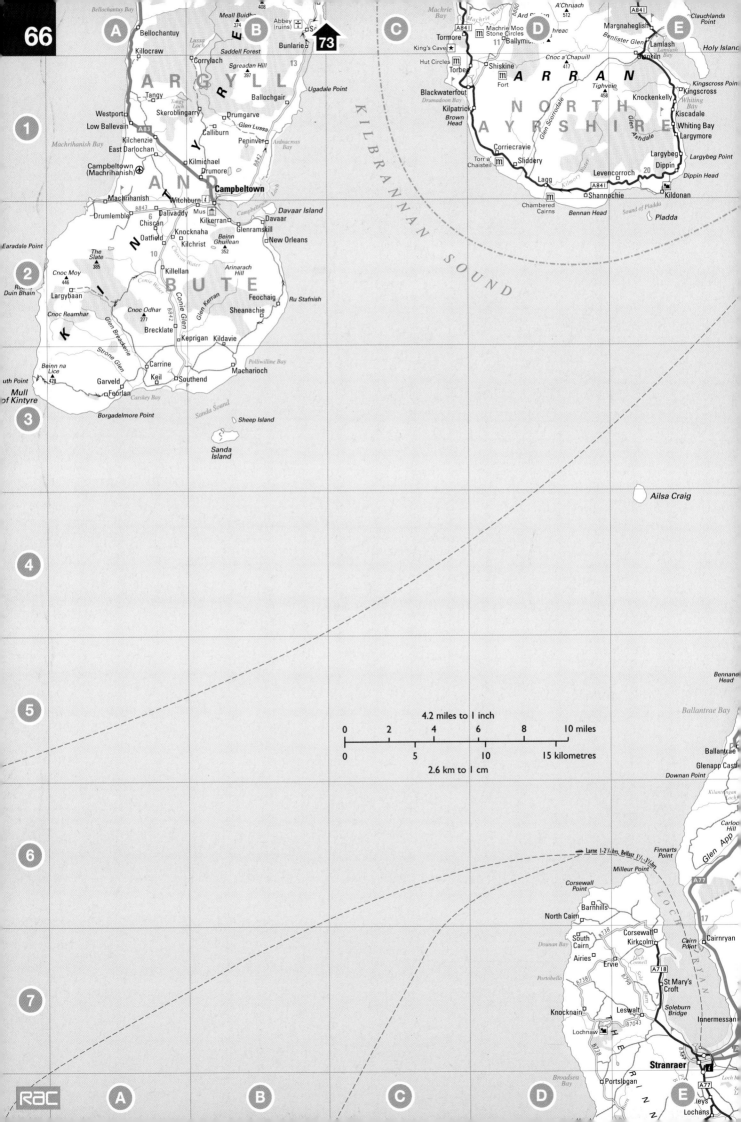

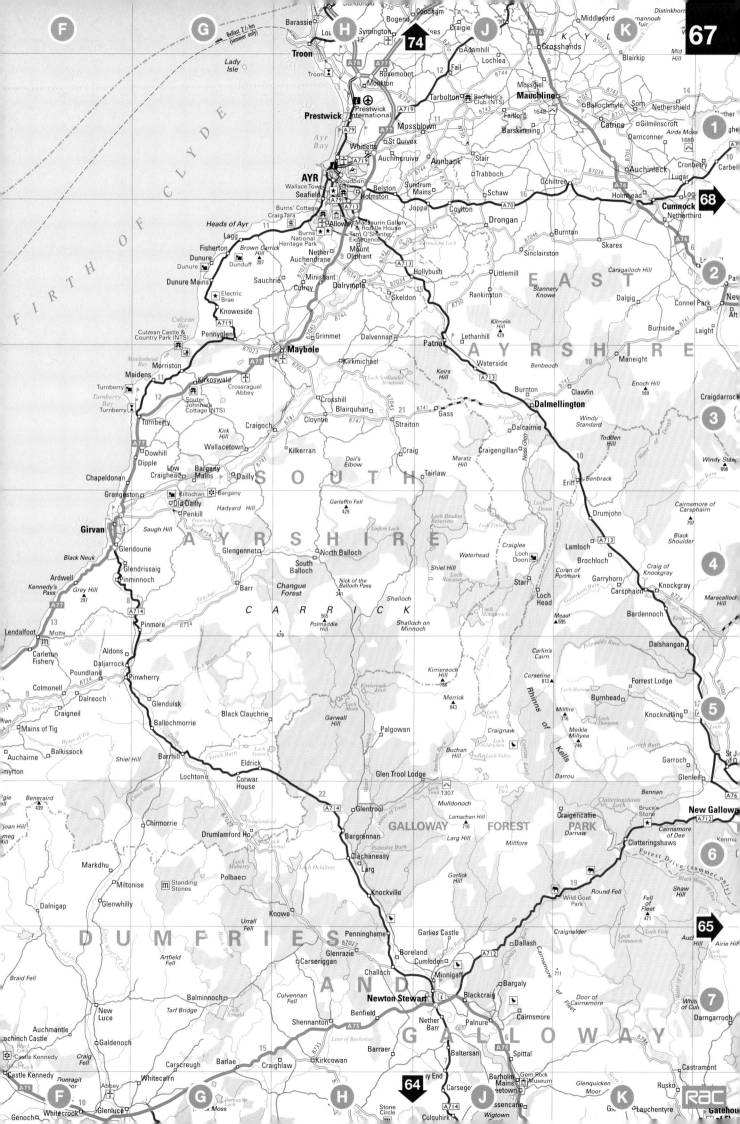

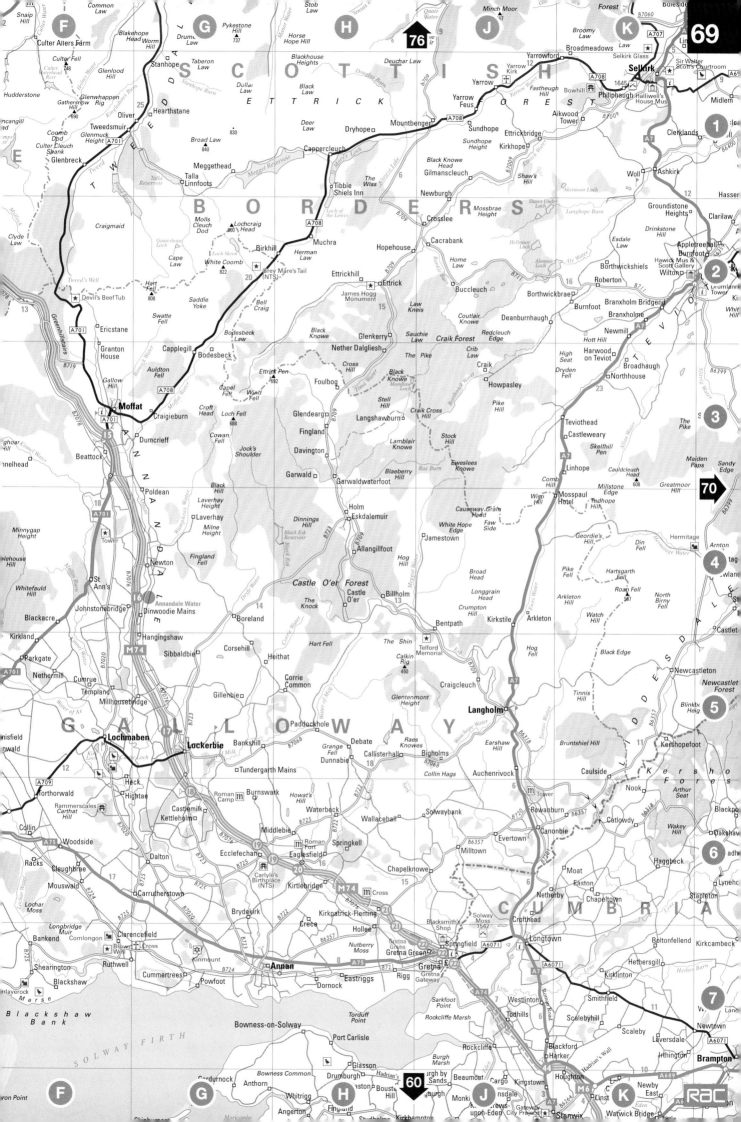

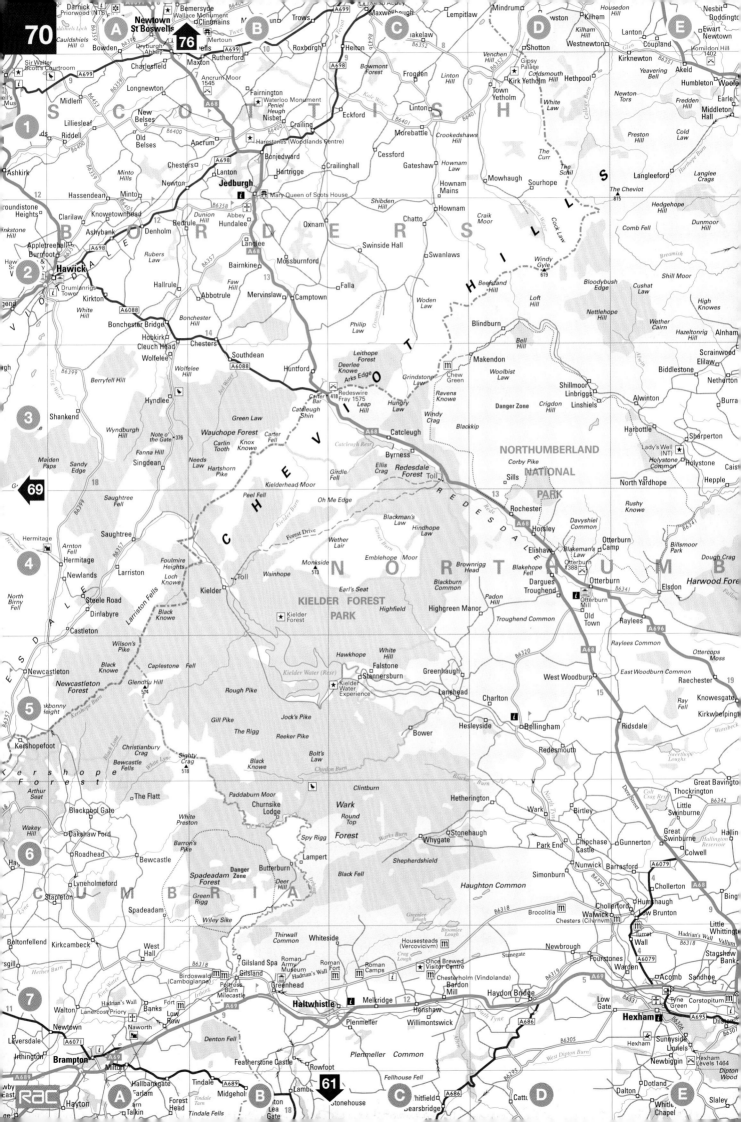

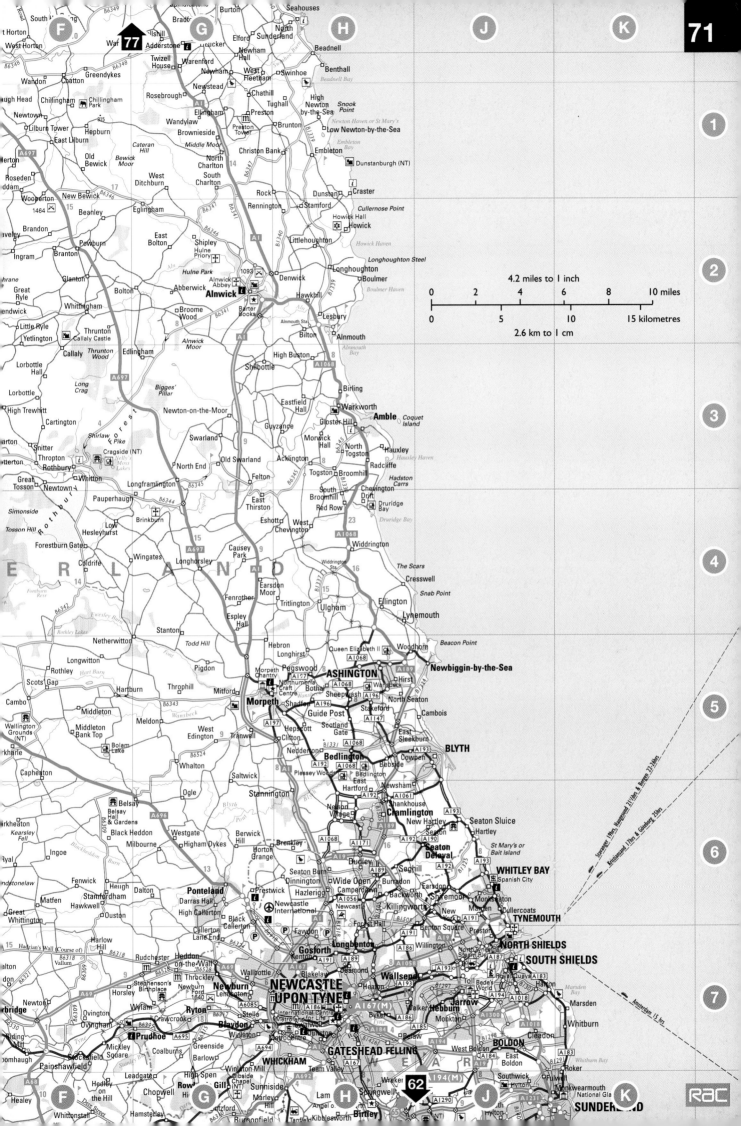

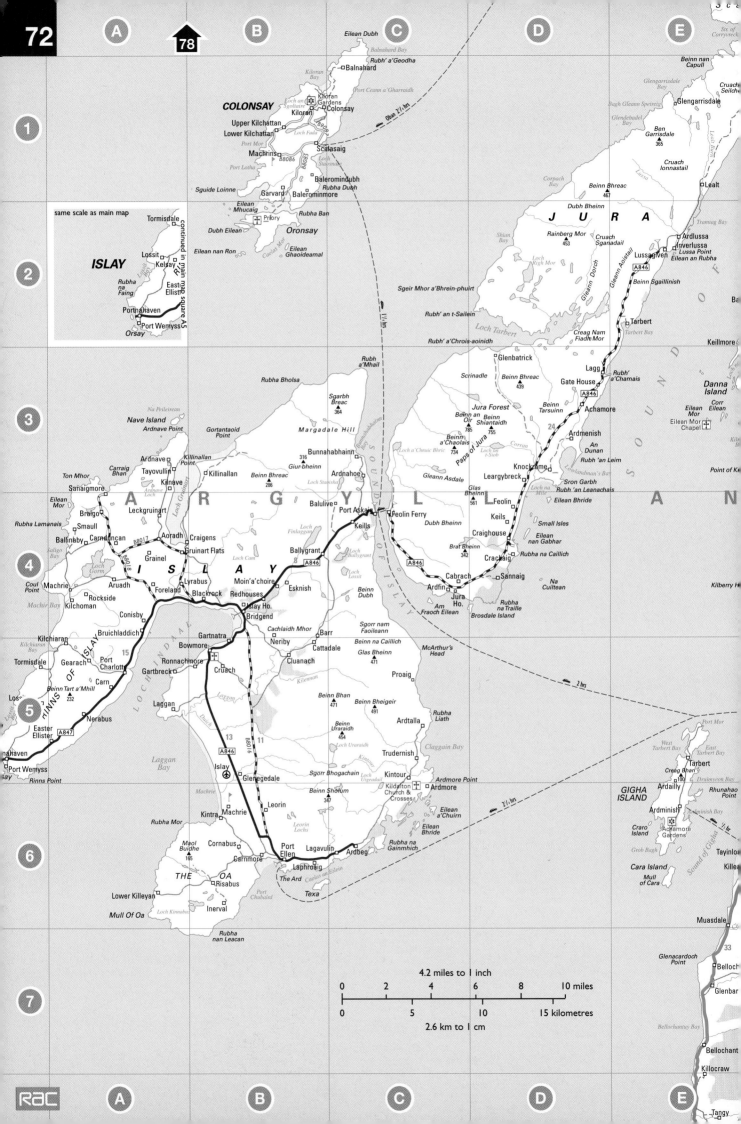

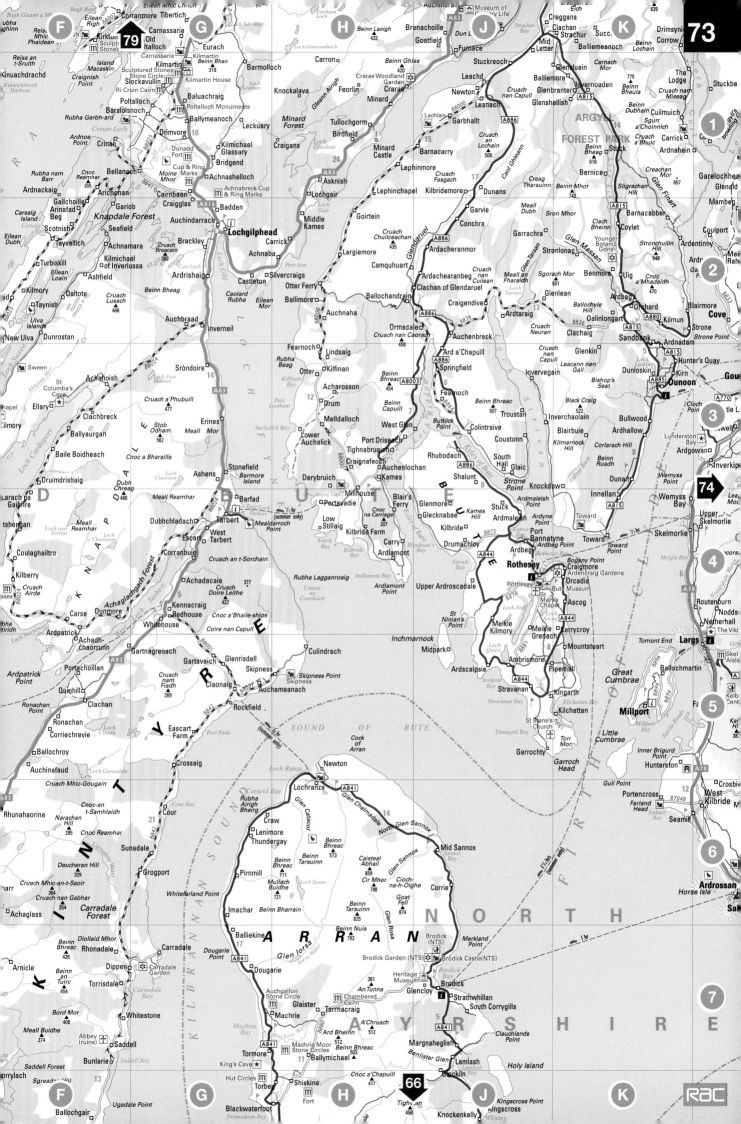

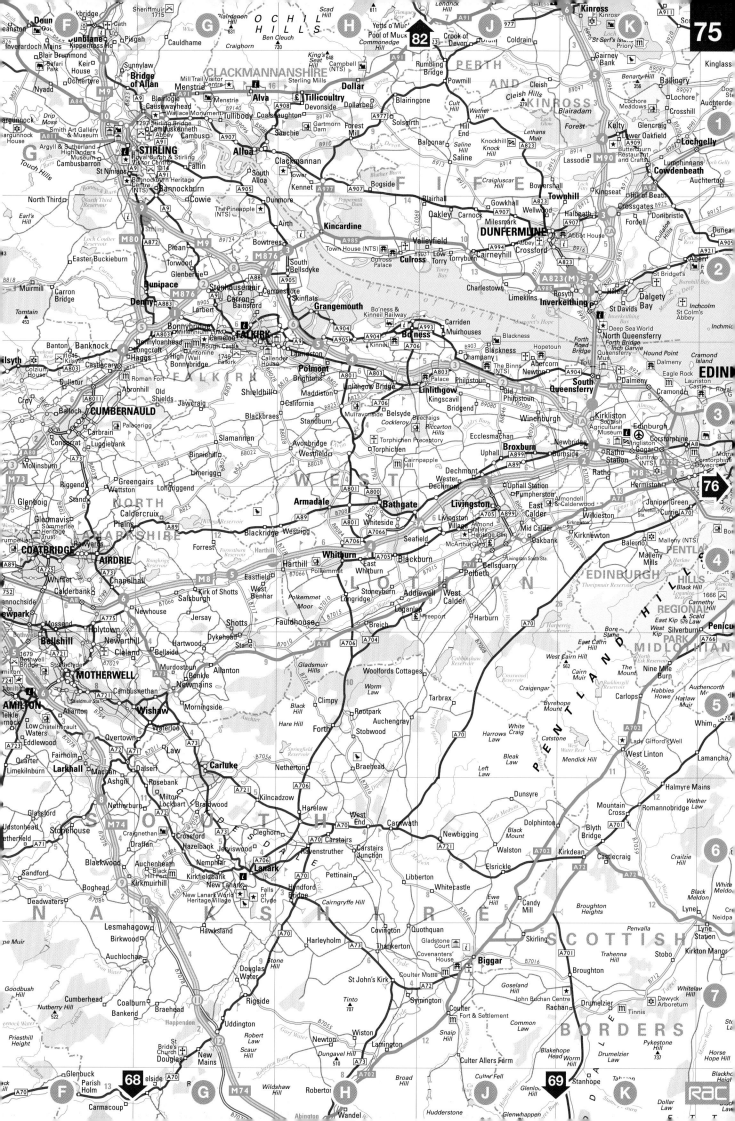

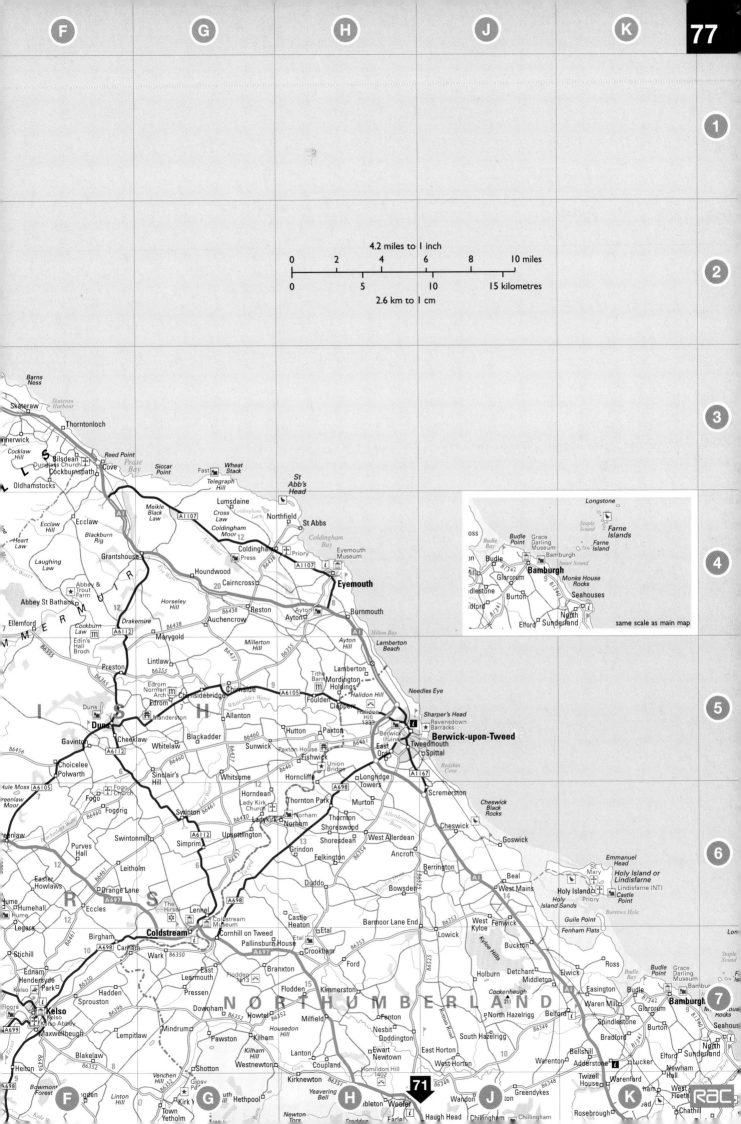

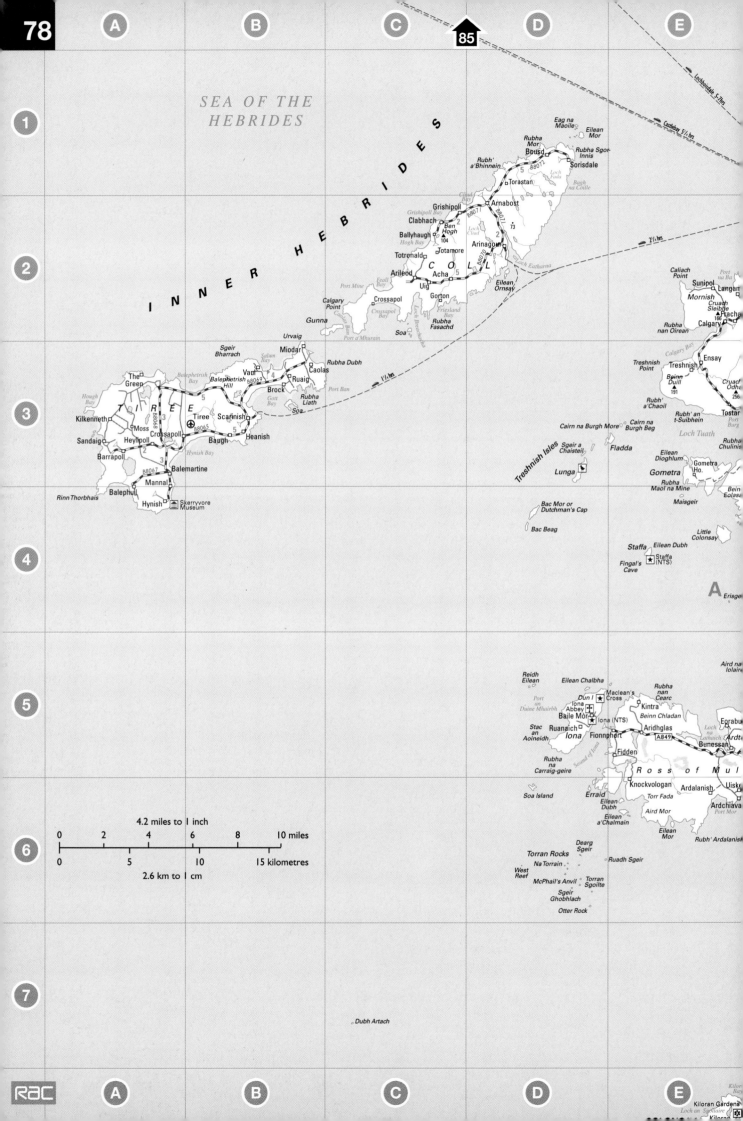

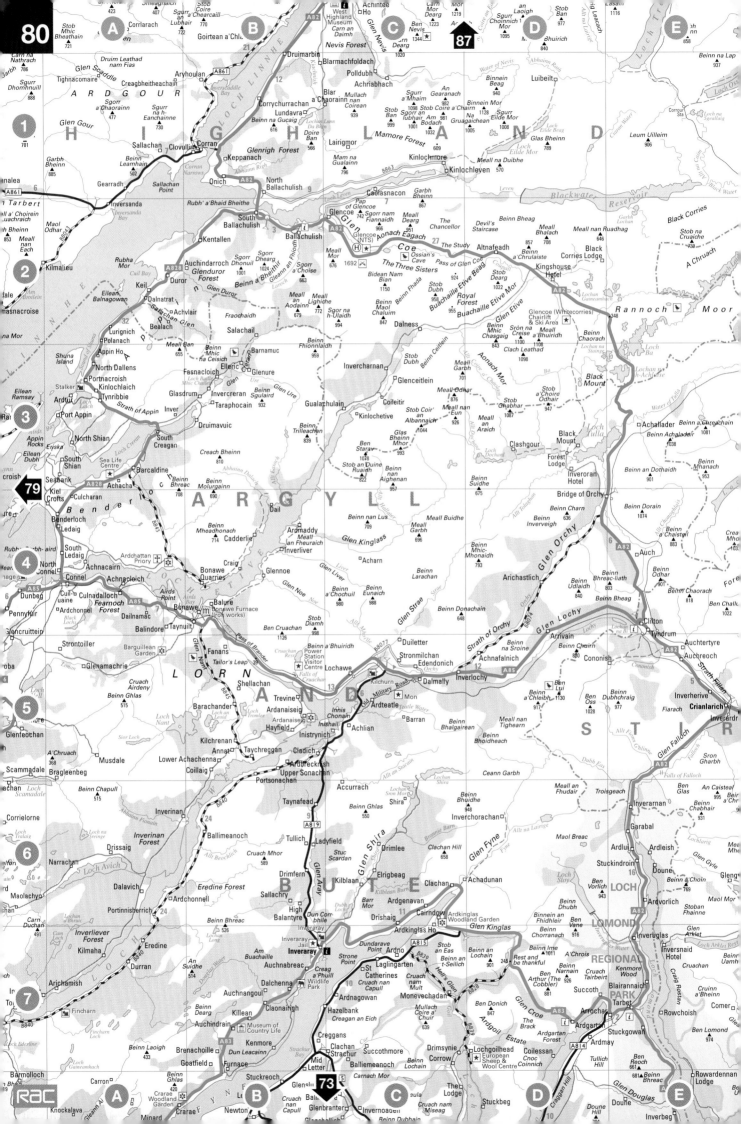

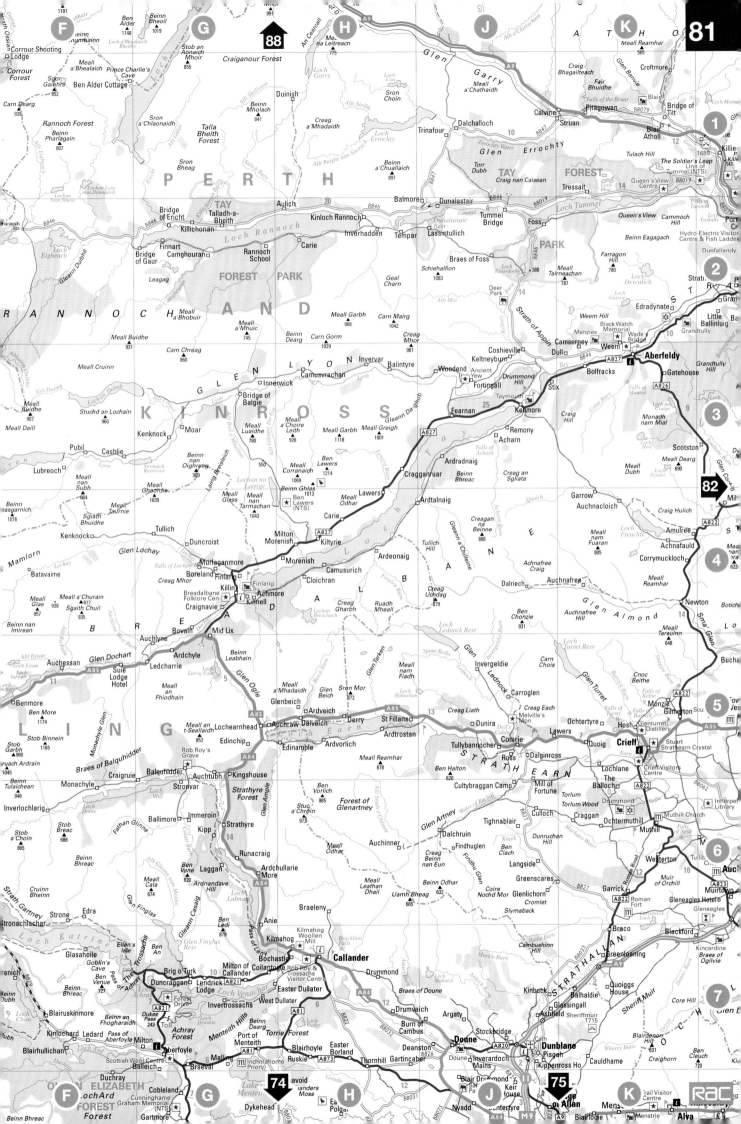

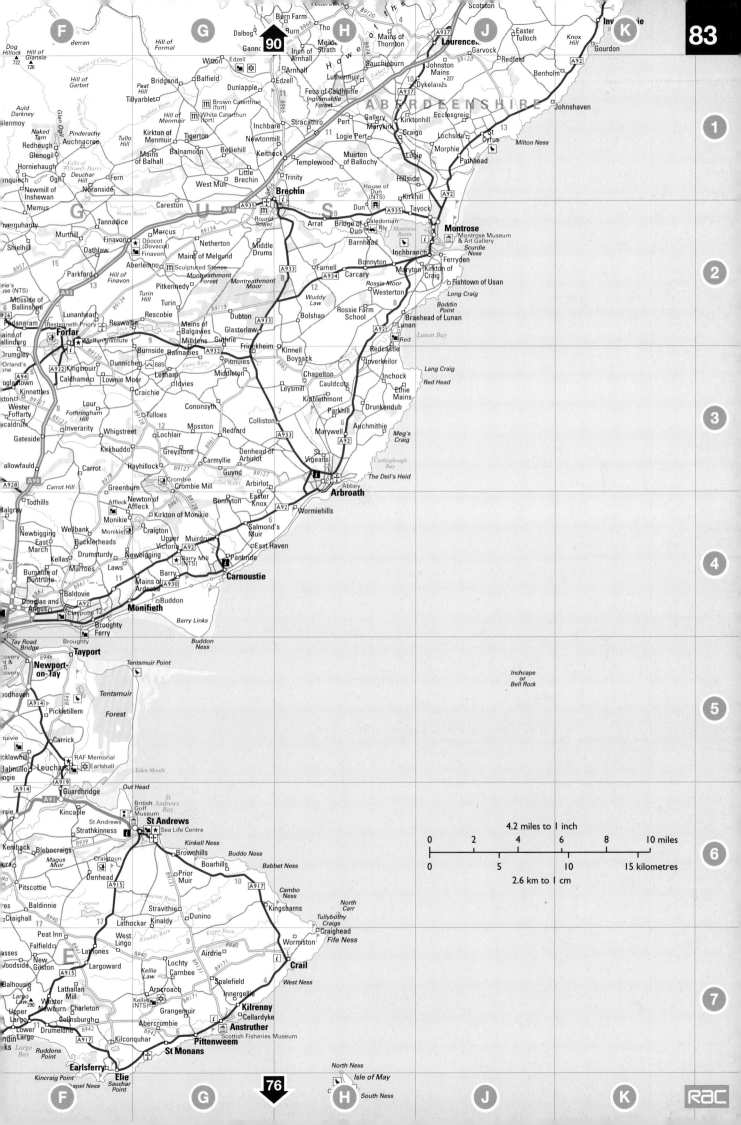

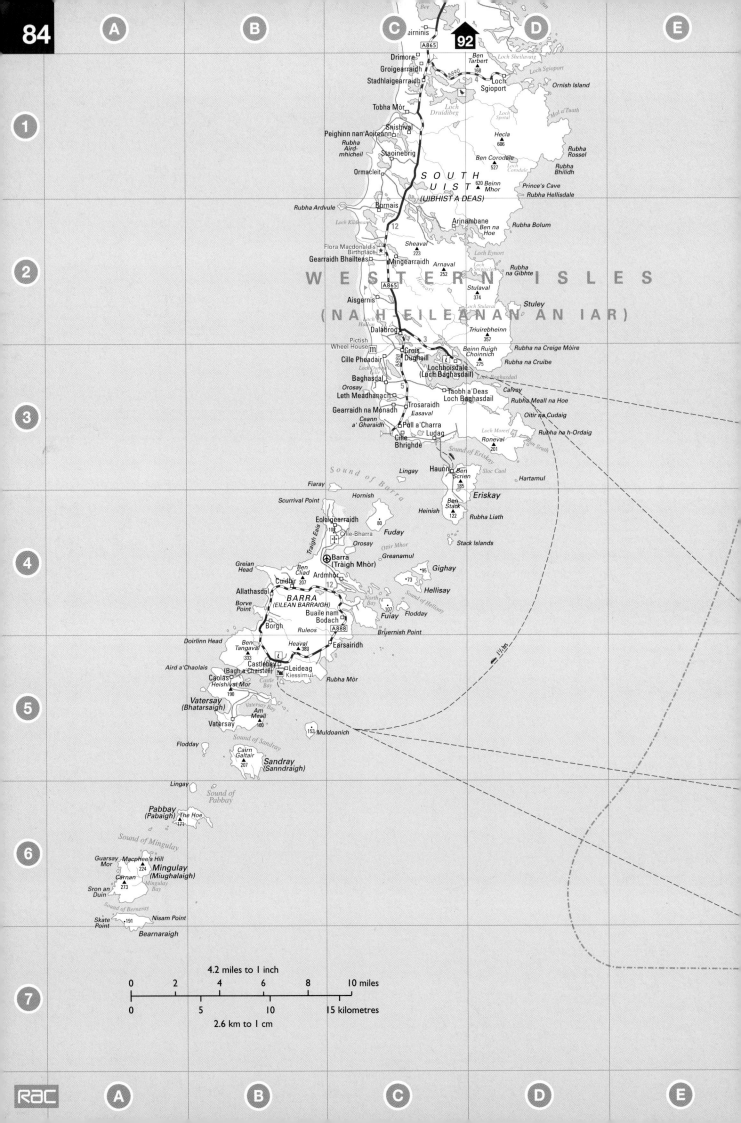

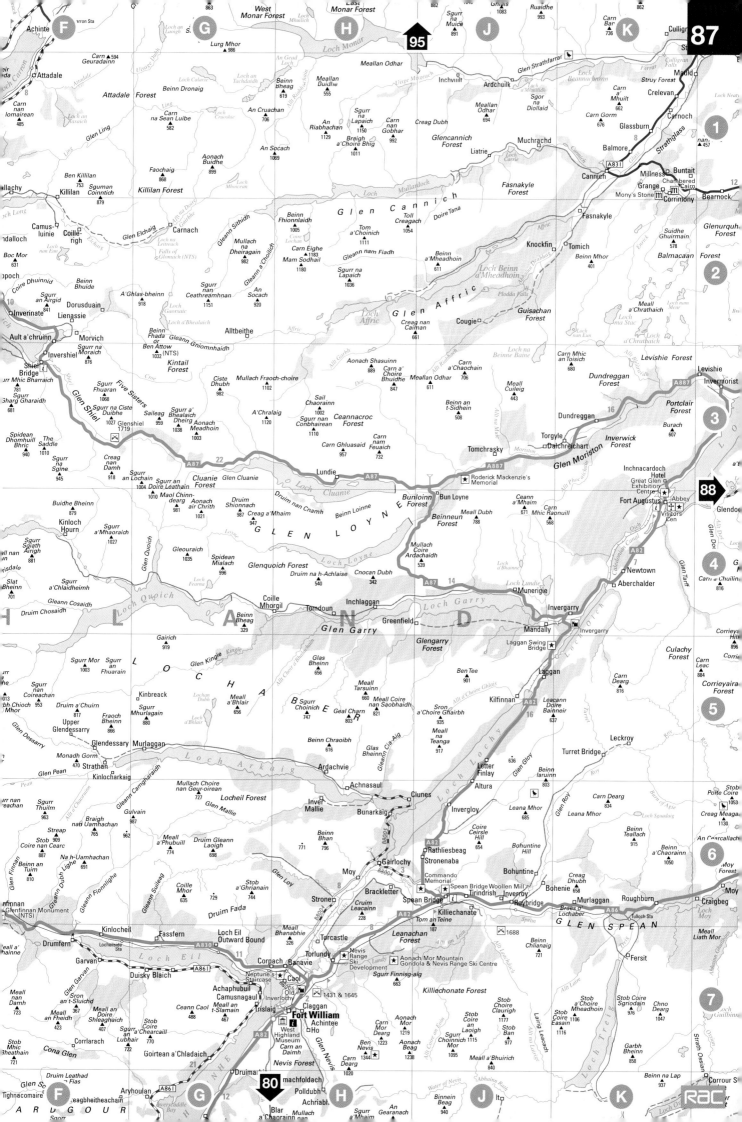

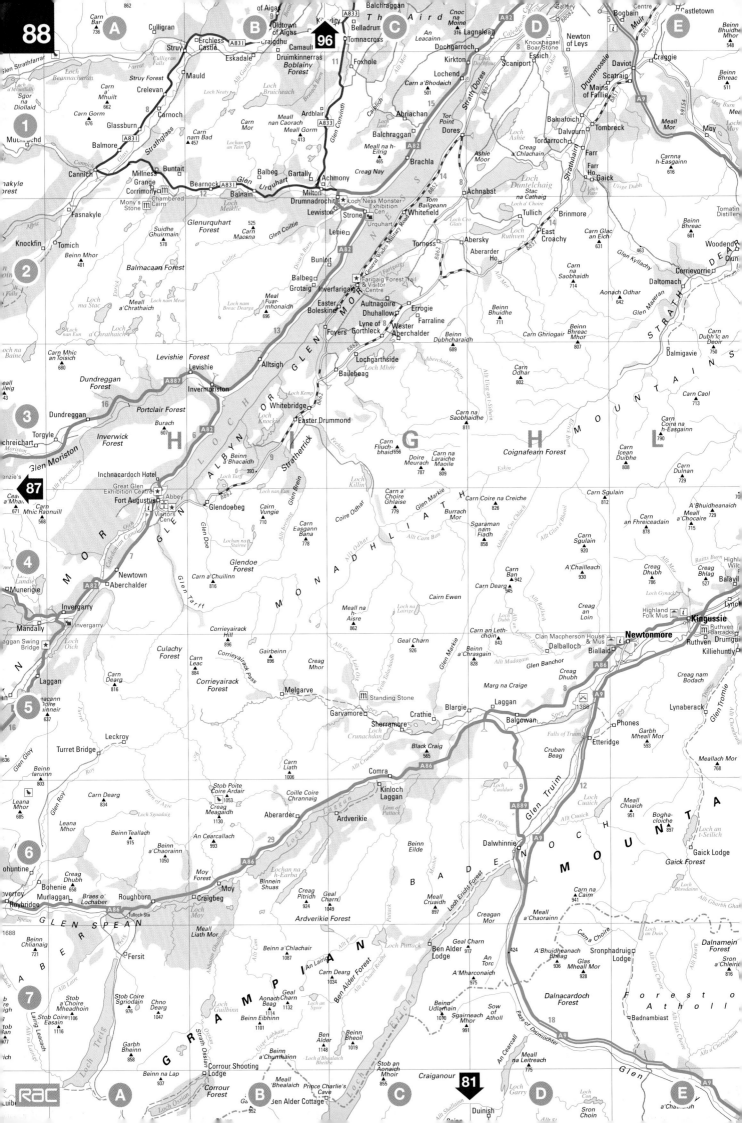

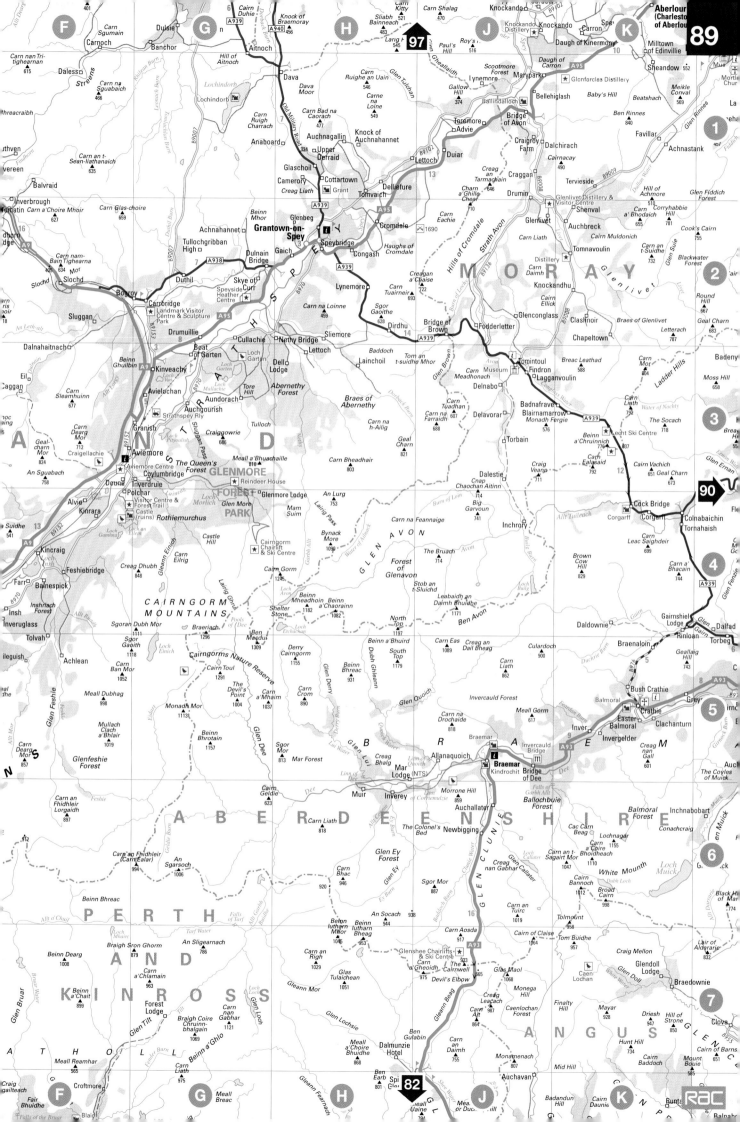

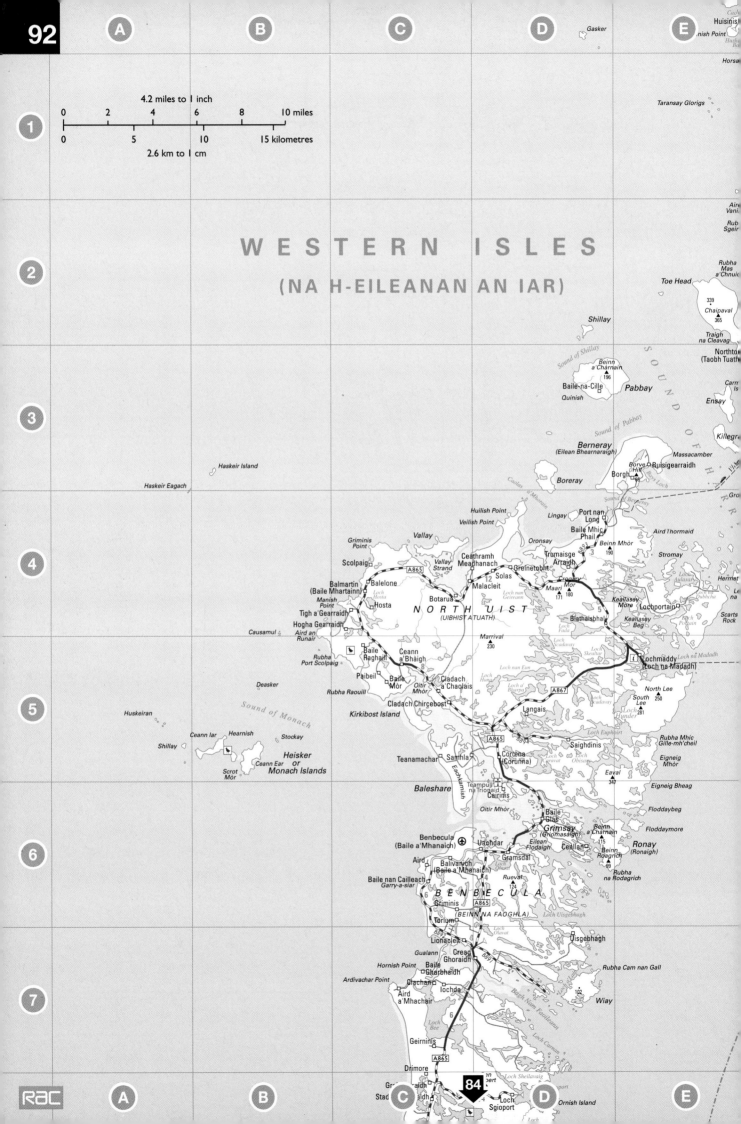

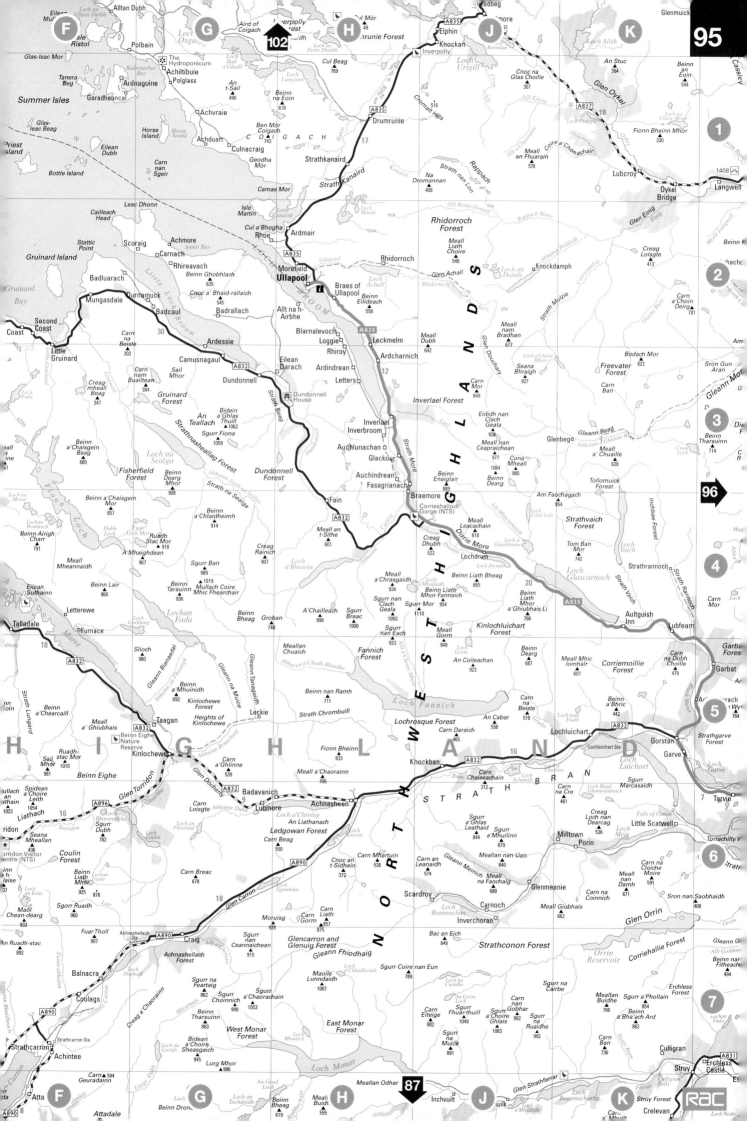

Portgower
Culgower
Colbhe 538 104 Creag a'Chrionaich Lothbeg Kilmote
Gordonbush 394 Lothbeg Lo more
Kilbraur Hill Lothbeg Point
Carrol Rock 323 Kintradwell
Killin Achrimsdale
West Clyne Greenhill
Cagar Feosaig Clynelish Dalchalm
Killin Rock
East Brora
Backies Brora
Beinn 'Bhragaidh Dol
Dunrobin Castle Sta
Dunrobin Castle
Golspie

ittleferry
arpenny
Embo
bo Street

ornoch
FIRTH
Dornoch Point
Whiteness Sands Innis Mhor Port Mor Tarbat Ness Wilkhaven
Balcherry Innis Bheag Portmahomack Hilton Bindal
Inver Rockfield
Balnagall Lochslin Tarrel
Rhynie Balaldie Geanies Ho.
ndhu Hill of Cadboll
Fearn Tullich Hilton of Cadboll
Fearn Abbey
Clay of Allan Shandwick Balintore
kerville
Chapelhill
Nigg Hill of Nigg

Castlecraig North Sutor
Sutor Stacks utors of Cromarty e Head

MORAY FIRTH

Kirkwall, Orkney 16.9hrs

98

Halliman Skerries Lossiemouth Fisheries and Communities Mus
Covesea Skerries
Clashach Point Stotfield
Covesea Branderburgh Lossiemouth
Hopeman Gordonstoun Oakenhead
Burghead Well Duffus St Peter's Church Salterhill Lossie Forest
Burghead Cummingstown Roseisle Innes Boar's Head Rock
Duffus Links Innes Canal
Roseisle Forest Findrassie A941 Palace of Spynie Lochh
Findhorn Buthill Quarrywood Old Mills Bishopmill Cath (ruins) Urquhart
Burghead Bay Hempriggs Coltfield Ardgye Mus Elgin Muir of Lochs
Muirhead Miltonhill New Johnstons Cashmere New Bax
Culbin Forest Findhorn Bay Alves Cloves Pittendreich Elgin Visitor Centre Moss of Barmuckity Vis Ce
Wellhill Kinloss Motor Museum Palmerscross Lhanbryde A96
Kintessack Invererne Grange Hall Toreduff Miltonduff Mosstodloch
Moy House Springfield Hillside Miltonhill Longmorn Orbliston Focha
Brodie Dyke Hillside Paddockhaugh Birnie Church Fogwatt Altonside
Nairn (NTS) Forres Mains of Burgie Cloddach Blackhills Inchber
Kingsteps Macbeth's Sueno's Stone Monaughty Forest Heldon Hill Thomshill Whitewreath
Tradespark Hillock Falconer Museum Califer Pluscarden 234 Auchtertyre
Household Boath Newton Blervie Priory Barnhill Crofts of Findlay's Teindland Forest
Auldearn Dovecot of Dalvey Castle Heldon Hill Buinach Seat Wood of Dundurcas
Delnies (NTS) Rafford Dallas Kellas Leanoch 262
Hilton of Auldearn Altyre Tulloch Forest Glenlatterach Boat o' Brig
Piperhill 1645 Boghole Whitemire Woods Briach Hill of the Wangie Bardon Brylach Kirkhill
kackle Tradespark Fm Conicavel 319 Craigend Hill Aberlour Knock More
Moss-side Laiken Milton Darnaway Mains of Sluie Edinvale Dallas 325 Aberlour
Torrich Forest Darnaway Forest Phorp Romach Hill Mill Buie Cairn Pikey Hill The Aochinroath
Regoul Presley 313 355 Uish 355 Kettles A9015
Culcharry Fornighty Drumine Ardoch 365 Rothes
Cawdor Forest Tomnamoon Meikle Hill Craigroy Glen Grant &
allaschyle Littlemill Lethen Bar Hill of Tomechole Caperdonich Knock More
Achindown Randolph's 344 MORAY Cairn na Distillery Ben Aigan
Clunas Leap Carn Cailliche Hill of Dandaleith 471
Bruachmay Redburn Relugas Carnachie 404 Stob Hunt Whiteacen ggie
Balmore Ardclach 359 Cairn Cattoch Hill Telford
Cairn Bell Tower Mount 369 Bridge Craigell
a'Chrasgie Ferness Daltra Carn Elchies Forest Ringorm Aberlour
401 Ghiubhais Robertstown Archiestown (Charlestown of
Easter 430 Upper Cardow Aberlour)
Galcantray Dulsie Cairn Knockando A95
sich Duhie Tomdow Carn Speyview Dufftown
est Miltown Kitty Carron Daugh of
Carn Banchor Carn Shalag 470 Knockando Kinermony Milltown of
Sgumain Hill of Aitnoch Sliabh Knockando Edinvillie Balvenie
Carnoch Bainneach Larig Hill Distillery Daugh of Carron Sheandow
456 483 545 Paul's Hill Carron Dufftown
Carn nan Tri- Knock of Glenfarclas B9138 553
tighearnan Braemoray Roy's Hill Distillery
615 Carn 516 Baby's Hill
466 ighe an Carne Gallow Meikl
Carn na Jain 89 Hill otmore Maryp Beatshach Conval
546 374 Forest Bellehiglash Hill

F G H J K RAC

A9 A940 A939 A96 A95 A941 A98

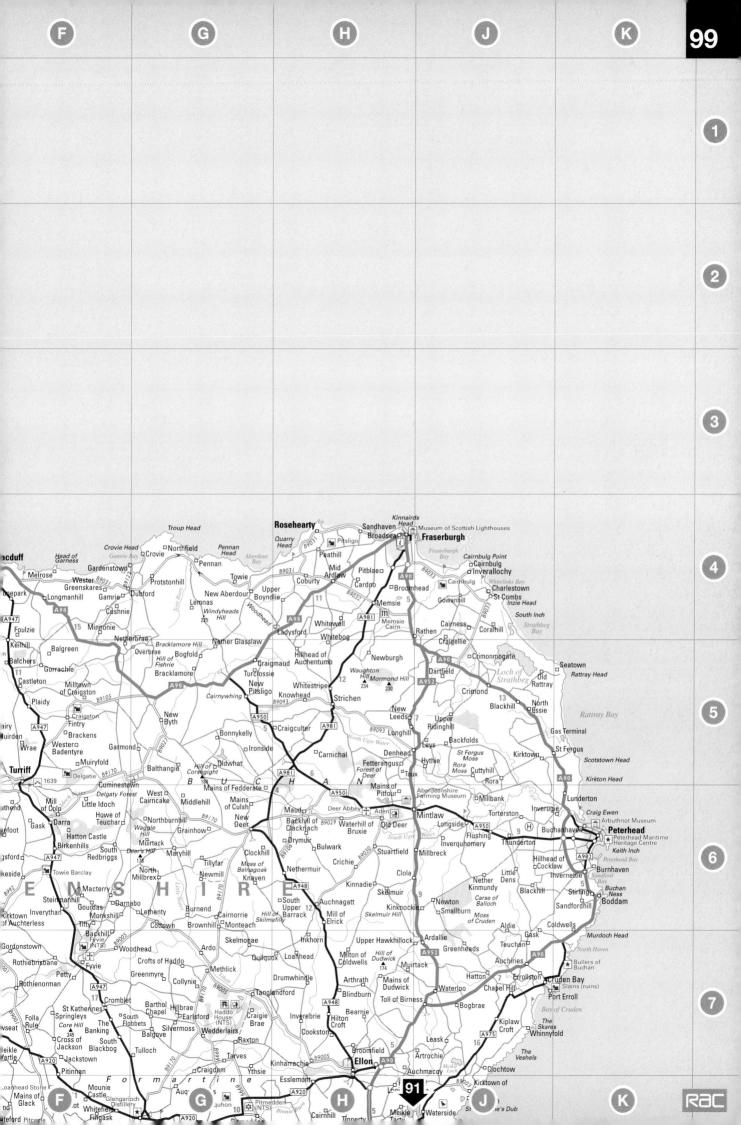

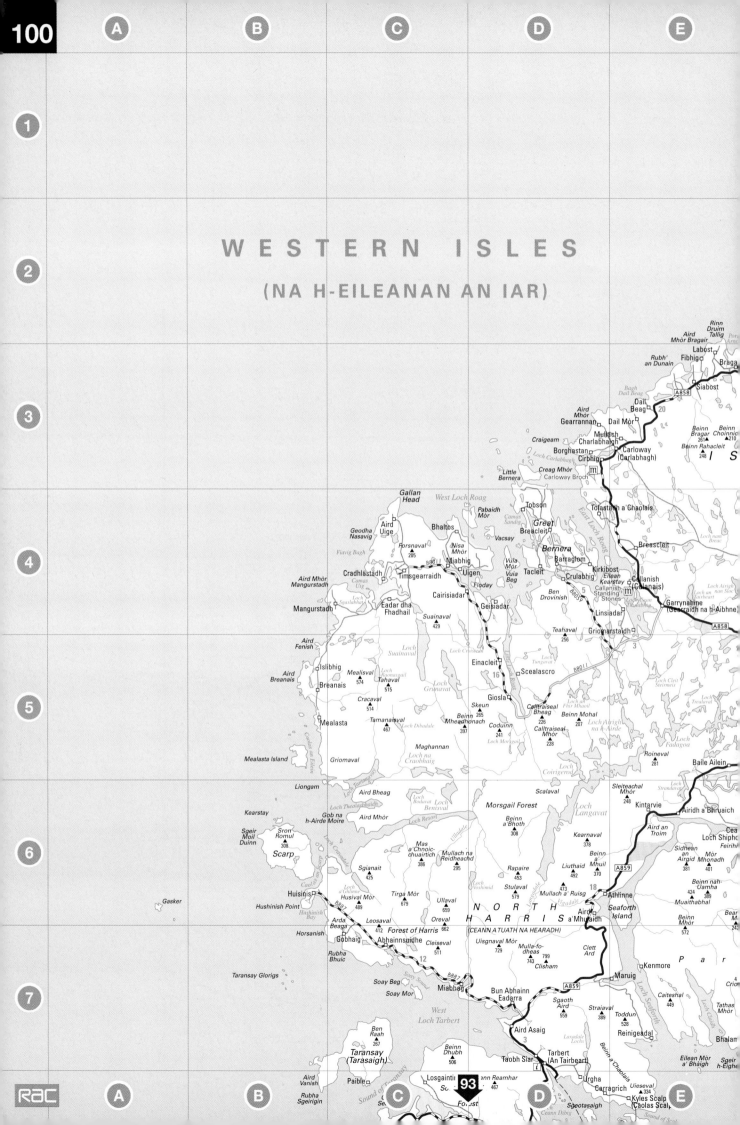

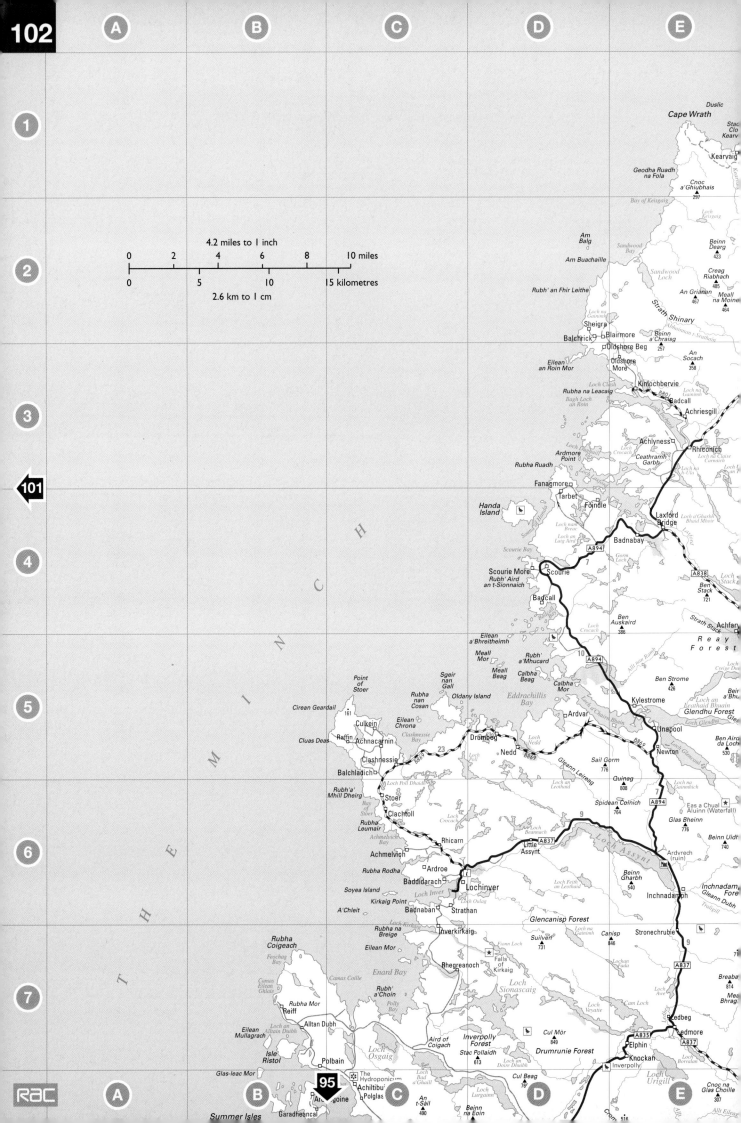

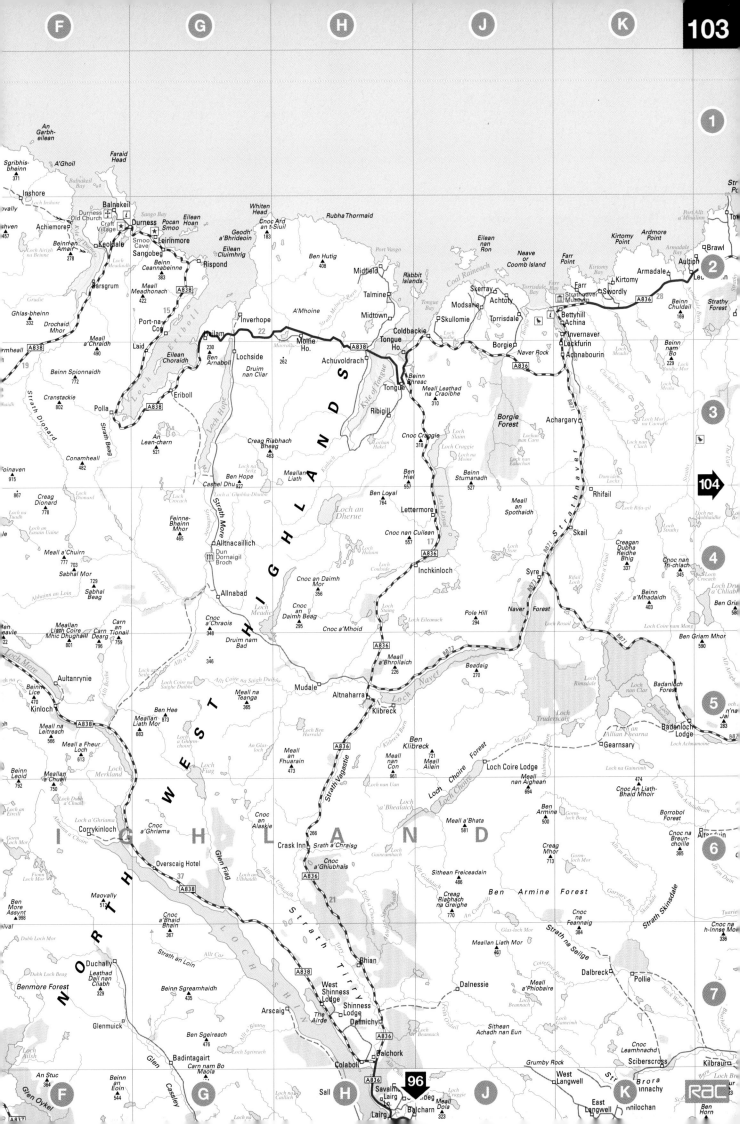

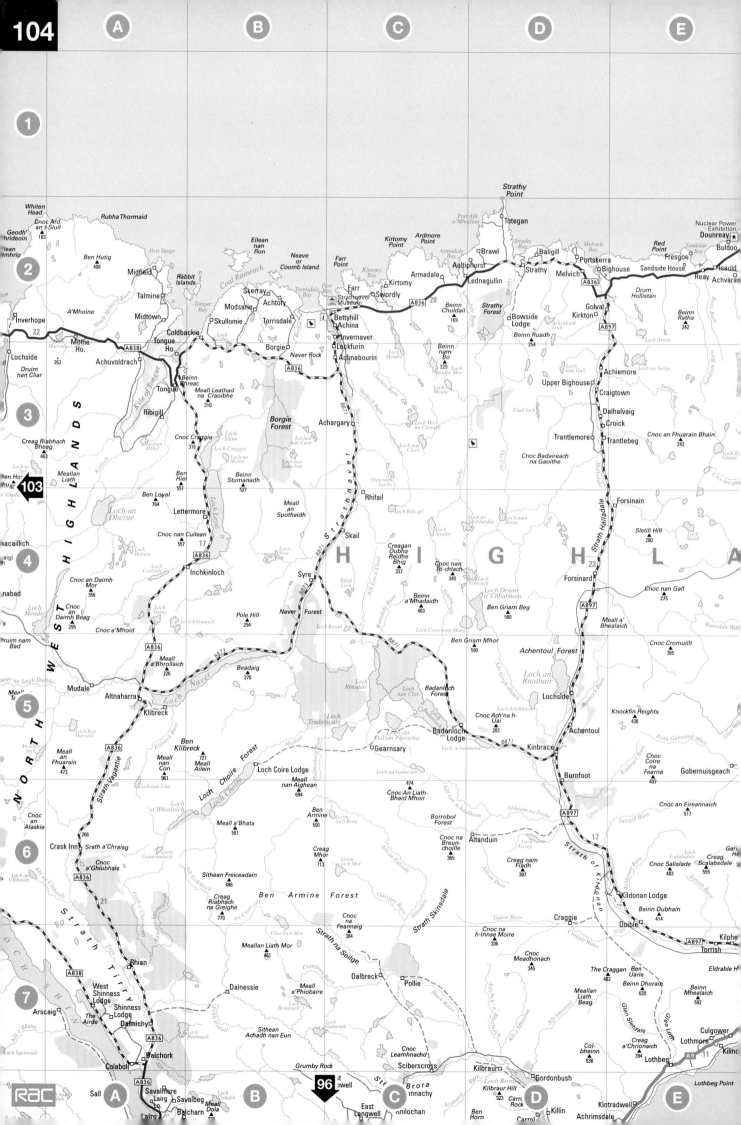

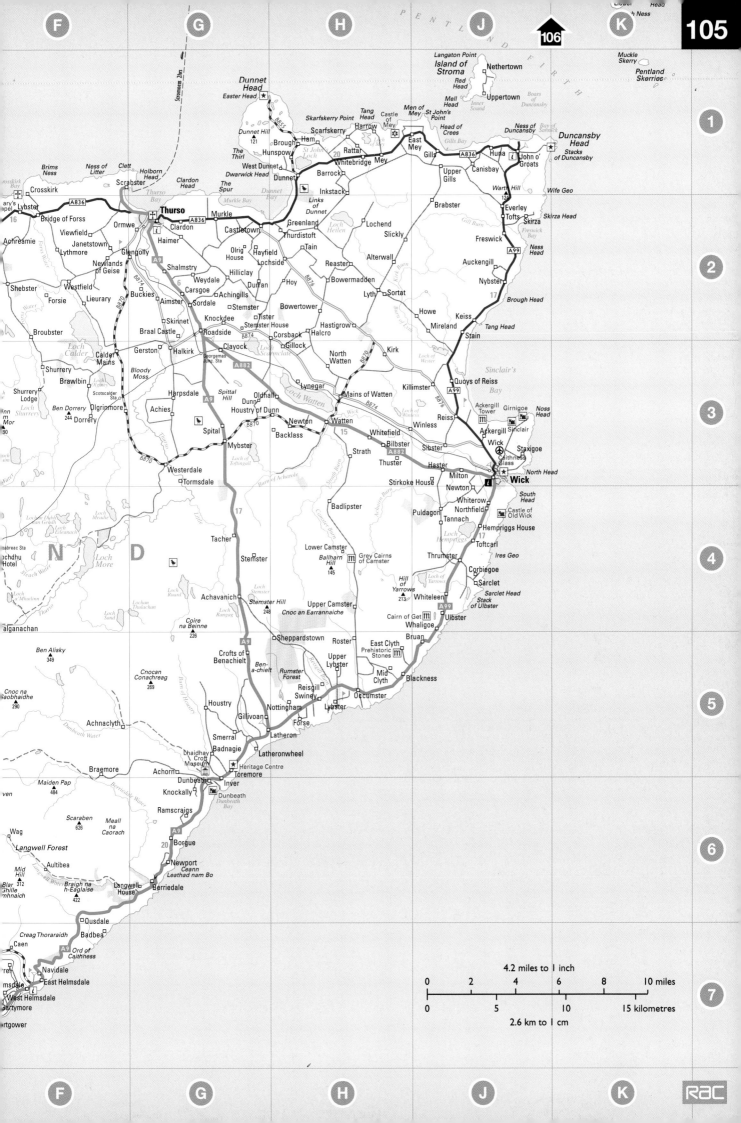

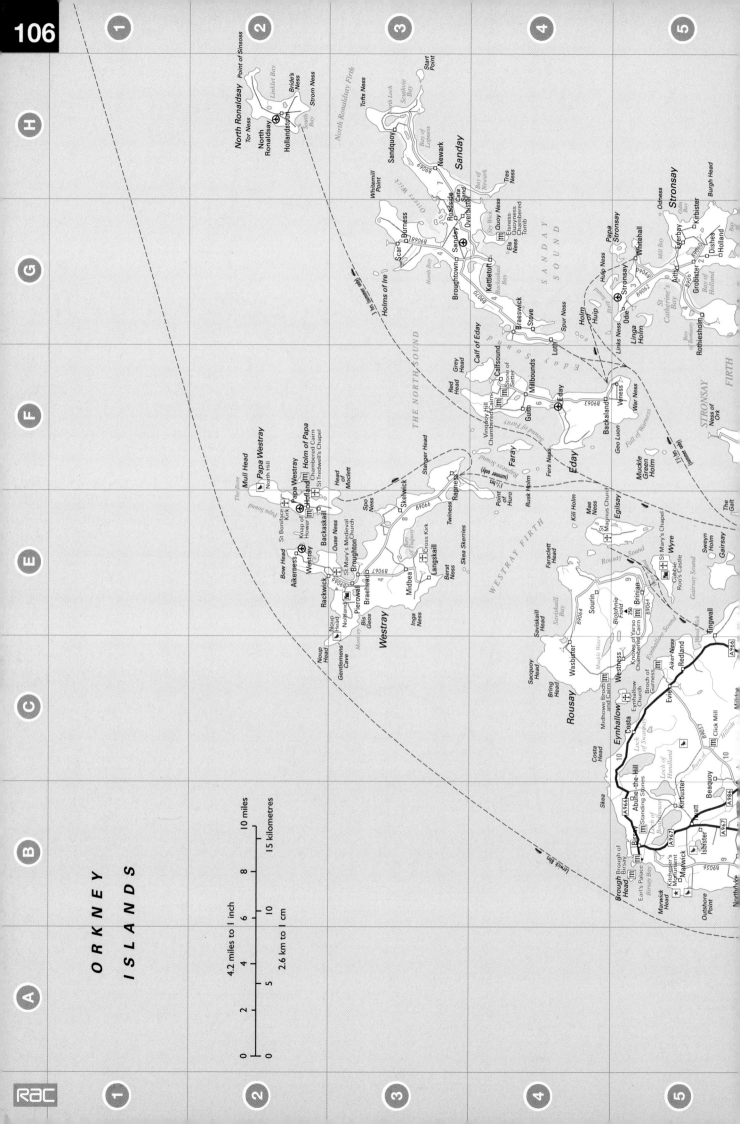

ORKNEY ISLANDS

4.2 miles to 1 inch

2.6 km to 1 cm

10 miles

15 kilometres

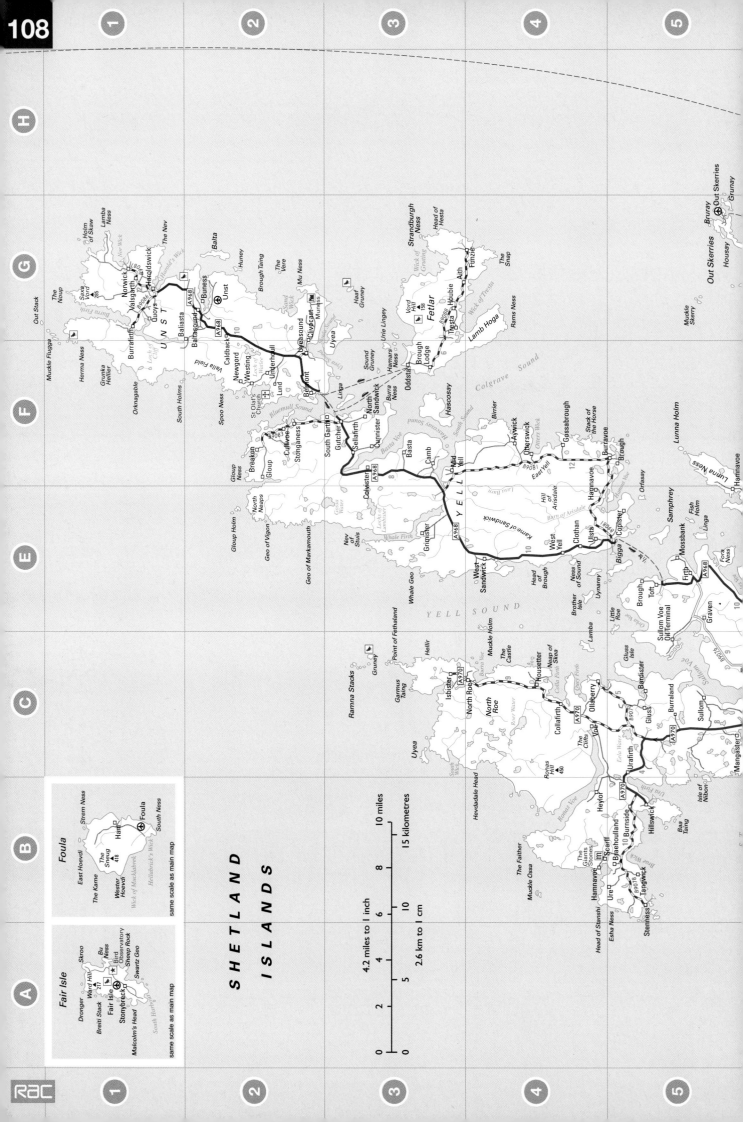

SHETLAND ISLANDS

Fair Isle

Dronger
Skroo
Bu Ness
Ward Hill 217
Breiti Stack
Bird Observatory
Sheep Geo
Fair Isle
Stonybreck
Swartz Geo
Malcolm's Head
South Harbour

same scale as main map

Foula

Strem Ness
East Hoevdi
The Kame
The Sneug 418
Wester Hoevdi
Ham
Foula
South Ness
Wick of Mucklabreck
Hellabrick's Wick

same scale as main map

4.2 miles to 1 inch
2.6 km to 1 cm

0 2 4 5 6 8 10
10 miles
15 kilometres

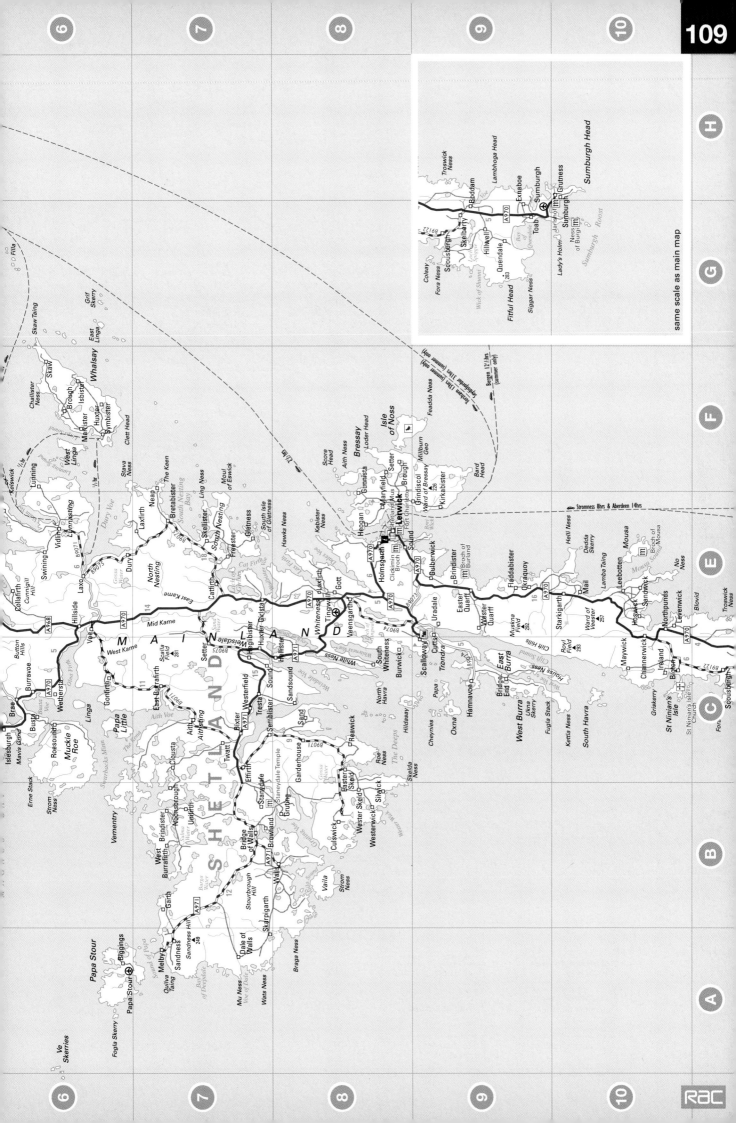

RAC

KEY TO MAP SYMBOLS

Motorway — under constr. — M1

Junction number — restricted access ①②

'A'/National primary — dual carriageway — N8

'A'/National secondary — dual carriageway — under constr. — N71

'B'/Regional road — dual carriageway — under constr. — B45

Road distances (in miles) — 13

Railway

Car ferry

Airport ✈

International boundary

National park

Regional/Forest park

Urban area

Beach

Canal

RAC

BELFAST

N
0 ——— 200 yds
0 ——— 200 m

Stranraer (Sea Cat) and
Isle of Man Ferry Terminals
Odyssey Complex

University of Ulster

P.O.

PETER'S HILL

Smithfield Market
Smithfield Sq. North

Millfield Technical College

Old Museum Arts Centre

Technical College

Royal Belfast Academical Institution

City Hall

Linen Hall Library

Victoria Sq.
Victoria Centre

Court House

Royal Courts of Justice

Waterfront Hall

Central Station

Grand Opera House

Crown Liquor Saloon

Group Theatre

Ulster Hall

BBC

Bus Station

Gt. Victoria Street Station

Gt. Northern Mall

Cinema

Ormeau Baths Gallery

St. Anne's Cathedral

Clock Tower

Custom House

Queen Elizabeth Bridge

Queen's Bridge

Bridge End

Lookout

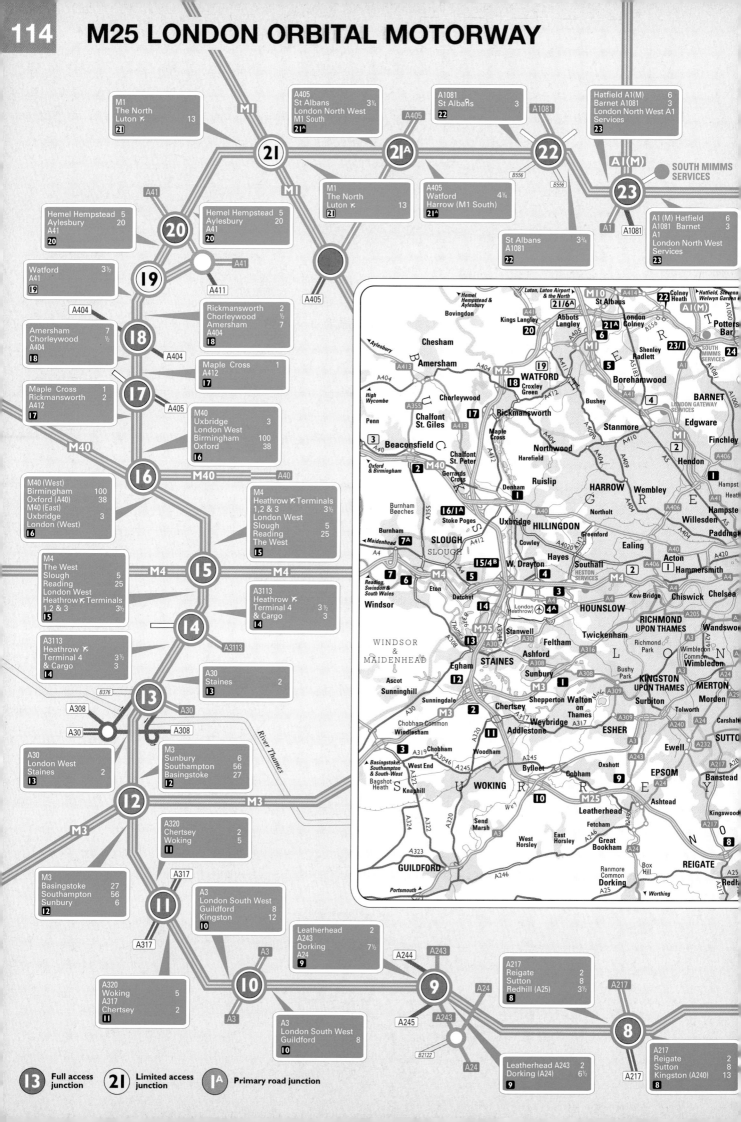

M1
The North
Luton ✈   13
21

A405
St Albans   3¼
London North West
M1 South
21ᴬ

A1081
St Albans   3
22

Hatfield A1(M)   6
Barnet A1081   3
London North West A1
Services
23

21   **21**ᴬ   **22**

A1(M)   SOUTH MIMMS SERVICES

23

M1
The North
Luton ✈   13
21

A405
Watford   4¼
Harrow (M1 South)
21ᴬ

St Albans   3¾
A1081
22

A1 (M) Hatfield   6
A1081 Barnet   3
A1
London North West
Services
23

Hemel Hempstead   5
Aylesbury   20
A41
20

Hemel Hempstead   5
Aylesbury   20
A41
20

20

Watford   3½
A41
19

19

Rickmansworth   2
Chorleywood   ½
Amersham   7
A404
18

Amersham   7
Chorleywood   ½
A404
18

18

Maple Cross   1
A412
17

Maple Cross   1
Rickmansworth   2
A412
17

17

M40
Uxbridge   3
London West
Birmingham   100
Oxford   38
16

M40 (West)
Birmingham   100
Oxford (A40)   38
M40 (East)
Uxbridge   3
London (West)
16

16

M4
Heathrow ✈ Terminals
1, 2 & 3   3½
London West
Slough   5
Reading   25
The West
15

M4
The West
Slough   5
Reading   25
London West
Heathrow ✈ Terminals
1, 2 & 3   3½
15

15

A3113
Heathrow ✈
Terminal 4   3½
& Cargo   3
14

A3113
Heathrow ✈
Terminal 4   3½
& Cargo   3
14

14

A30
Staines   2
13

13

A30
London West
Staines   2
13

M3
Sunbury   6
Southampton   56
Basingstoke   27
12

12

A320
Chertsey   2
Woking   5

M3
Basingstoke   27
Southampton   56
Sunbury   6
12

11

A3
London South West
Guildford   8
Kingston   12
10

A320
Woking   5
A317
Chertsey   2
11

Leatherhead   2
A243
Dorking   7½
A24
9

10

A3
London South West
Guildford   8
10

9

A217
Reigate   2
Sutton   8
Redhill (A25)   3½
8

Leatherhead A243   2
Dorking (A24)   6½
9

8

A217
Reigate   2
Sutton   8
Kingston (A240)   13
8

13 Full access junction   **21** Limited access junction   **1**ᴬ Primary road junction

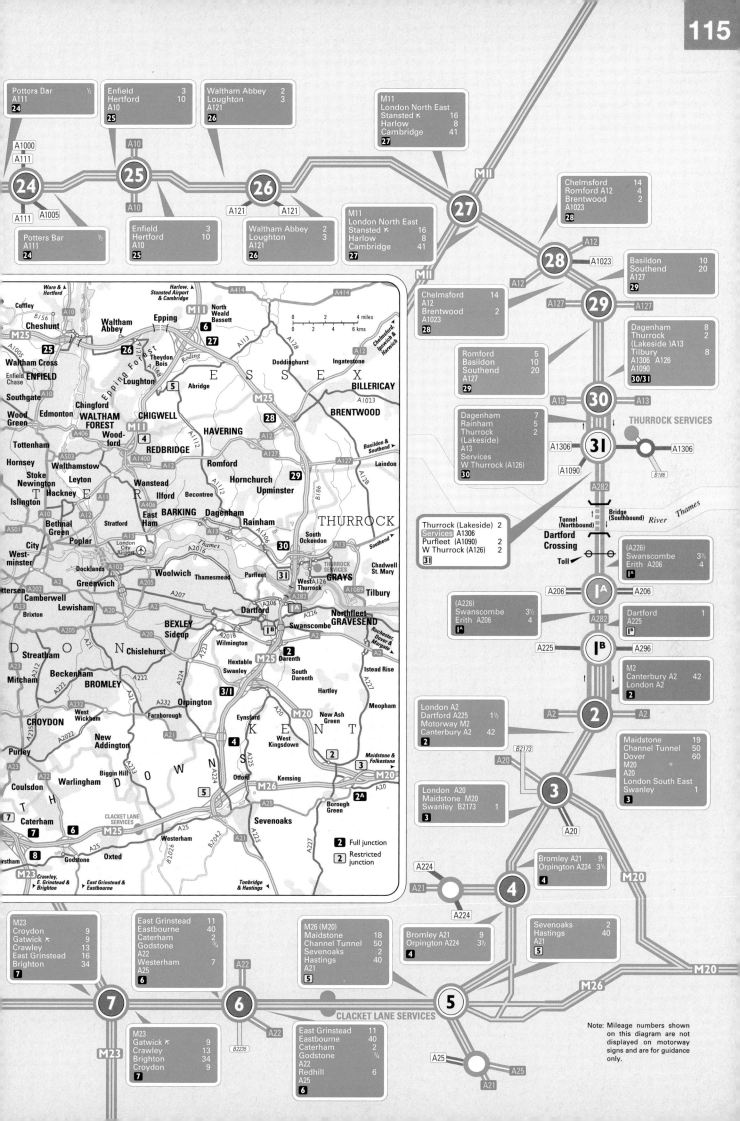

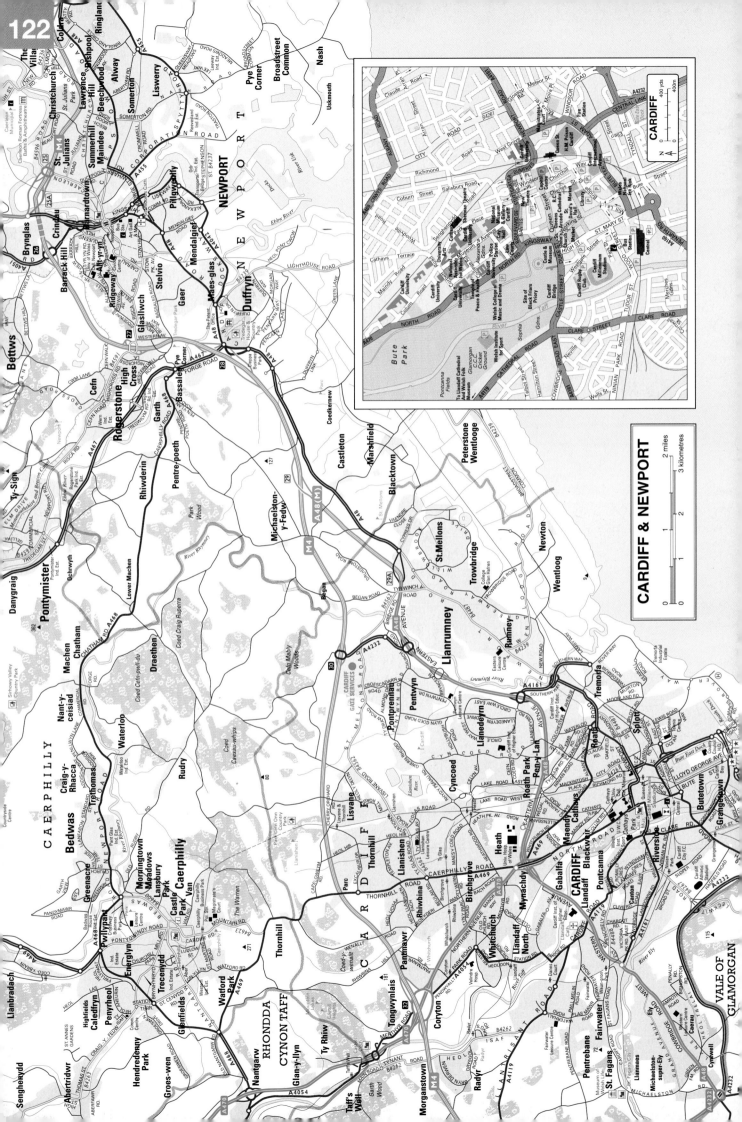

CARDIFF

CARDIFF & NEWPORT

GREATER MANCHESTER

Rainford
Billinge
Chadwick
Garswood
Ashton in Makerfield
WIGAN DISTRICT
Golborne
Lowton
Town of Lowton

Moss Bank
Haydock Park Race Course
Haydock Park

EAST LANCASHIRE ROAD

Denton's Green
Newtown
Eccleston
West Park
ST. HELENS
Blackbrook
Haydock
ST. HELENS DISTRICT

Toll Bar
Grange Park
Portico
Ravenhead
Parr
Broad Oak
Derbyshire Hill
Newton-le-Willows
Wargrave
Vulcan Village

Prescot
Eccleston Park
Thatto Heath
Peasley Cross
Sutton Park
Sutton Oak
Collins Green
Winwick

Holt
Nutgrove
Sutton Heath
Marshall's Cross
Sutton Leach
Burtonwood

Whiston Cross
Whiston
Rainhill
Clock Face
Burtonwood Services
Hulme
Cinnamon Brow
Longford

Windy Arbor
Rainhill Stoops
Sutton Manor
Bold Heath
Callands
Dallam
Bewsey
Orford

Town End
Cronton
Lunts Heath
Lingley Green
Old Hall
WARRINGTON

Tarbock Green
Cronton
Lunts Heath
Farnworth
Penketh
Great Sankey
Sankey Bridges
Howley
WARRINGTON

Hough Green
Appleton
Halton
Crow Wood
Cuerdley Cross
Latchford

Ditton
Ball o' Ditton
Halton Kingsway
Moss Bank
Lower Walton
Stockton Heath
Cobbs

Woodend
WIDNES
Higher Walton
Hillcliffe

West Bank
Hale Bank
HALTON
Astmoor
Castlefields
Higher Whitley

Hale
RUNCORN
Halton Brook
Grange

Weston Point
Beechwood
Weston
Stretton

VALE ROYAL BOROUGH
Frodsham Marshes
Frodsham

Ince Marshes
Helsby
Woodhouses
Acton Bridge

LIVERPOOL

Police Station
Liverpool John Moores University (JMU)
Walker Art Gallery
Liverpool Museum
Coach Sta.
William Brown St.
St. John's Garden
Empire Theatre
St. George's Hall
Mersey Tunnels Entrance
Old Haymarket
Royal Court Theatre
St. John's P.O. Precinct
The Beacon
Cotton Exchange
Moorfields (Underground)
Municipal Offices
Western Approaches Museum
Conservation Centre
Clayton Sq. Shopping Centre
Town Hall
Bus Station
Cavern Club
James St. (JMU)
Mersey Tunnel Exit
Royal Liver Building
Passport Office
Cunard Building
Derby Sq.
Queen Elizabeth II Crown Court
Bluecoat Arts Centre
P.O. (Underground)
Port of Liverpool Building
Chavasse Park
Mersey Ferry Terminal
Graving Docks
Fire Station
Canning Police H.Q.
Museum of Liverpool Life
Half Tide Dock
Maritime Museum & H.M. Customs Museum
Tate Liverpool
Albert Dock
Albert Dock Village

N
0   200 yds
0   200m

GREATER MANCHESTER

0   1   2 miles
0   1   2   3 kilometres

MANCHESTER

N

0   400 yds
0   400m

Use of the Index

The letters and numbers around the page edges of the main map section form the referencing system used in this atlas.
To find a place name first turn to the map page shown in bold type in the index, then locate the grid square indicated by the following letter and number.
The following list of abbreviations shows the counties for England and Wales and the councils for Scotland which appear in this atlas.
Where more than one place has the same name, each can be distinguished by the abbreviated county or council name shown after the place name.

Abbreviations

Aber.	Aberdeenshire
Arg. & B.	Argyll & Bute
B'burn.	Blackburn with Darwen
B. & H.	Brighton & Hove
B. & N.E.Som.	Bath & North East Somerset
B.Gwent	Blaenau Gwent
Beds.	Bedfordshire
Bourne.	Bournemouth
Brack.F.	Bracknell Forest
Bucks.	Buckinghamshire
Caerp.	Caerphilly
Cambs.	Cambridgeshire
Carmar.	Carmarthenshire
Cere.	Ceredigion
Chan.I.	Channel Islands
Ches.	Cheshire
Cornw.	Cornwall
Cumb.	Cumbria
D. & G.	Dumfries & Galloway
Darl.	Darlington
Denb.	Denbighshire
Derbys.	Derbyshire
Dur.	Durham
E.Ayr.	East Ayrshire
E.Dun.	East Dunbartonshire
E.Loth.	East Lothian
E.Renf.	East Renfrewshire
E.Riding	East Riding of Yorkshire
E.Suss.	East Sussex
Edin.	Edinburgh
Falk.	Falkirk
Flints.	Flintshire
Glas.	Glasgow
Glos.	Gloucestershire
Gt.Lon.	Greater London
Gt.Man.	Greater Manchester
Gwyn.	Gwynedd
Hants.	Hampshire
Hart.	Hartlepool
Here.	Herefordshire
Herts.	Hertfordshire
High.	Highland
I.o.A.	Isle of Anglesey
I.o.M.	Isle of Man
I.o.S.	Isles of Scilly
I.o.W.	Isle of Wight
Inclyde	Inverclyde
Lancs.	Lancashire
Leic.	Leicester
Leics.	Leicestershire
Lincs.	Lincolnshire
M.K.	Milton Keynes
M.Tyd.	Merthyr Tydfil
Med.	Medway
Mersey.	Merseyside
Middbro.	Middlesbrough
Midloth.	Midlothian
Mon.	Monmouthshire
N.Ayr.	North Ayrshire
N.E.Lincs.	North East Lincolnshire
N.Lan.	North Lanarkshire
N.Lincs.	North Lincolnshire
N.P.T.	Neath Port Talbot
N.Som.	North Somerset
N.Yorks.	North Yorkshire
Norf.	Norfolk
Northants.	Northamptonshire
Northumb.	Northumberland
Nott.	Nottingham
Notts.	Nottinghamshire
Ork.	Orkney
Oxon.	Oxfordshire
P. & K.	Perth & Kinross
Pembs.	Pembrokeshire
Peter.	Peterborough
Plym.	Plymouth
Ports.	Portsmouth
R. & C.	Redcar & Cleveland
R.C.T.	Rhondda Cynon Taff
Read.	Reading
Renf.	Renfrewshire
Rut.	Rutland
S'end	Southend
S'ham.	Southampton
S.Ayr.	South Ayrshire
S.Glos.	South Gloucestershire
S.Lan.	South Lanarkshire
S.Yorks.	South Yorkshire
Sc.Bord.	Scottish Borders
Shet.	Shetland
Shrop.	Shropshire
Slo.	Slough
Som.	Somerset
Staffs.	Staffordshire
Stir.	Stirling
Stock.	Stockton-on-Tees
Stoke	Stoke-on-Trent
Suff.	Suffolk
Surr.	Surrey
Swan.	Swansea
Swin.	Swindon
T. & W.	Tyne & Wear
Tel. & W.	Telford & Wrekin
Thur.	Thurrock
V. of Glam.	Vale of Glamorgan
W'ham	Wokingham
W. & M.	Windsor & Maidenhead
W.Berks.	West Berkshire
W.Dun.	West Dunbartonshire
W.Isles	Western Isles (Na h-Eileanan an Iar)
W.Loth.	West Lothian
W.Mid.	West Midlands
W.Suss.	West Sussex
W.Yorks.	West Yorkshire
Warks.	Warwickshire
Warr.	Warrington
Wilts.	Wiltshire
Worcs.	Worcestershire
Wrex.	Wrexham

A

A'Chill **85** H4
Ab Kettleby **42** A3
Abbas Combe **9** G2
Abberley **29** G2
Abberton *Essex* **34** E7
Abberton *Worcs.* **29** J3
Abberwick **71** G2
Abbess Roding **33** J7
Abbey Dore **28** C5
Abbey Hulton **40** B1
Abbey St. Bathans **77** F4
Abbey Village **56** B7
Abbey Wood **23** H4
Abbeycwmhir **27** K1
Abbeystead **55** J4
Abbeytown **60** C1
Abbotrule **70** B2
Abbots Bickington **6** B4
Abbots Bromley **40** C3
Abbots Langley **22** E1
Abbots Leigh **19** J4
Abbots Morton **30** B3
Abbots Ripton **33** F1
Abbot's Salford **30** B3
Abbotsbury **8** E6
Abbotsham **6** C3
Abbotskerswell **5** J4
Abbotsley **33** F3
Abbotts Ann **21** G7
Abbottswood **10** E2
Abdon **38** E7
Aber **26** D4
Aber-banc **26** C4
Aber Bargoed **18** E1
Aber Bowlan **17** K1
Aber-Cywarch **37** H4
Aber-Ilia **27** J7
Aber-Naint **38** A3
Aber-nant **18** D1
Aberaeron **26** D2
Aberaman **18** D1
Aberangell **37** H5
Aberarad **17** G1
Aberarder **88** B6
Aberarder House **88** D2
Aberargie **82** C6
Aberarth **26** D2
Aberavon **18** A3
Aberbeeg **19** F1
Abercanaid **18** D1
Abercarn **19** F2
Abercastle **16** B1
Abercegir **37** H5
Aberchalder **87** K4
Aberchirder **98** E5
Abercorn **75** J3
Abercraf **27** H7
Abercrombie **83** G7
Abercrychan **27** G5
Abercwmboi **18** D1
Abercych **26** B4
Abercynafon **27** K7
Abercynon **18** D2
Aberdalgie **82** B5
Aberdare **18** C1
Aberdaron **36** A3
Aberdaugleddau (Milford Haven) **16** C4
Aberdeen **91** H4
Aberdeen Airport **91** G3
Aberdesach **46** C7
Aberdour **75** K2
Aberdovey (Aberdyfi) **37** F6
Aberduhonw **27** K3
Aberdulais **18** A2
Aberdyfi (Aberdovey) **37** F6
Aberedw **27** K4
Abereiddy **16** B1
Abererch **36** D2
Aberfan **18** D1
Aberfeldy **81** K3
Aberffraw **46** B6
Aberffrwd **27** F1
Aberford **57** K6
Aberfoyle **81** G7
Abergarw **18** C3
Abergavenny (Y Fenni) **28** C7
Abergele **47** H5
Abergiar **26** E4
Abergorlech **17** J1
Abergwaun (Fishguard) **16** C1
Abergwesyn **27** H3
Abergwili **17** H2
Abergwydol **37** G5
Abergwynant **37** F4
Abergwynfi **18** B2
Abergwyngregyn **46** E5
Abergynolwyn **37** F5
Aberhafesp **37** K6
Aberhonddu (Brecon) **27** K6
Aberhosan **37** H6
Aberkenfig **18** B3
Aberlady **76** C2
Aberlemno **83** G2
Aberllefenni **37** G5
Aberlour (Charlestown of Aberlour) **97** K7
Abermad **26** E1
Abermaw (Barmouth) **37** F4
Abermeurig **26** E3
Abermule **38** A6
Abernant **17** G2
Abernethy **82** C6
Abernyte **82** D4
Aberpergwm **18** B1
Aberporth **26** B3
Aberriw (Berriew) **38** A5
Aberscross **96** E1
Abersky **88** C2
Abersoch **36** C3
Abersychan **19** F1
Abertawe (Swansea) **17** K5
Aberteifi (Cardigan) **26** A4
Aberthin **18** D4
Abertillery **19** F1
Abertridwr *Caerp.* **18** E3
Abertridwr *Powys* **37** K4
Abertysswg **18** E1
Aberuthven **82** A6
Aberyscir **27** J6
Aberystwyth **36** E7
Abhainnsuidhe **100** C7
Abingdon **21** H2
Abinger Common **22** E7
Abinger Hammer **22** D7
Abington **68** E1
Abington Pigotts **33** G4
Abingworth **12** E5
Ablington **20** E1
Abney **50** E5
Aboyne **90** D5
Abram **49** F2
Abriachan **88** C1
Abridge **23** H2
Abronhill **75** F3
Abson **19** K4
Abthorpe **31** H4
Abune-the-Hill **106** B5
Aby **53** H5
Acaster Malbis **58** B5
Acaster Selby **58** B5
Accrington **56** C7
Accurrach **80** C6
Acha **78** C2
Achacha **80** A3
Achadacaie **73** G4
Achadh-chaorrunn **73** F5
Achadh Mòr **101** F5
Achadunan **80** C6
Achagavel **79** J2
Achaglass **73** F6
Achahoish **73** F3
Achalader **82** C3
Achallader **80** E3
Achamore **72** D3
Achandunie **96** D4
Achany **96** C1
Achaphubuil **87** G7
Acharacle **79** H1
Achargary **104** C3
Acharn *Arg. & B.* **80** C4
Acharn *P. & K.* **81** J3
Acharonich **79** F4
Acharosson **73** H3
Achateny **79** G1
Achath **91** F3
Achavanich **105** G4
Achduart **95** G1
Achentoul **104** D5
Achfary **102** E4
Achgarve **94** E2
Achiemore *High.* **103** F2
Achiemore *High.* **104** D3
Achies **105** G3
Achiltibuie **95** G1
Achina **104** C2
Achindown **97** F7
Achinduich **96** C1
Achingills **105** G2
Achintee **95** F7
Achintee House **87** H7
Achintraid **86** E1
Achlean **89** F5
Achleanan **79** G2
Achleek **79** J2
Achlian **80** C5
Achlyness **102** E3
Achmelvich **102** C6
Achmony **88** B1
Achmore *High.* **86** E1
Achmore *High.* **95** G2
Achmore *Stir.* **81** G4
Achnaba **73** H2
Achnabat **88** C1
Achnabourin **104** C3
Achnacairn **80** A4
Achnacarnin **102** C5
Achnaclerach **96** B5
Achnacloich *Arg. & B.* **80** A4
Achnacloich *High.* **86** B4
Achnaclyth **105** F5
Achnacraig **79** F3
Achnacroish **79** K3
Achnadrish **79** F2
Achnafalnich **80** D5
Achnafauld **81** K4
Achnagairn **96** C7
Achnagarron **96** D4
Achnaha *High.* **79** H3
Achnaha *High.* **79** F1
Achnahanat **96** C2
Achnahannet **89** G2
Achnalea **79** K1
Achnamara **73** F2
Achnanellan **79** J1
Achnasaul **87** H6
Achnasheen **95** H6
Achnashelloch **73** G1
Achnastank **89** K1
Achorn **105** G5
Achosnich *High.* **96** E2
Achosnich *High.* **79** F1
Achreamie **105** F2
Achriabhach **80** C1
Achriesgill **102** E3
Achrimsdale **97** G1
Achtoty **103** J2
Achurch **42** D7
Achuvoldrach **103** H3
Achvaich **96** E2
Achvarasdal **104** E2
Achvlair **80** A2
Achvraie **95** G1
Ackergill **105** J3
Acklam *Middbro.* **63** F5
Acklam *N.Yorks.* **58** D3
Ackleton **39** G6
Acklington **71** H3
Ackton **57** K7
Ackworth Moor Top **51** G1
Acle **45** J4
Acock's Green **40** D7
Acol **25** J5
Acomb *Northumb.* **70** E7
Acomb *York* **58** B4
Aconbury **28** E5
Acre **56** C7
Acrefair **38** B1
Acrise Place **15** G3
Acton *Ches.* **49** F7
Acton *Gt.Lon.* **22** E4
Acton *Shrop.* **38** C7
Acton *Suff.* **34** C4
Acton *Worcs.* **29** H2
Acton Beauchamp **29** F3
Acton Bridge **48** E5
Acton Burnell **38** E5
Acton Green **29** F3
Acton Pigott **38** E5
Acton Round **39** F6
Acton Scott **38** D7
Acton Trussell **40** B4
Acton Turville **20** B3
Adamhill **74** C7
Adbaston **39** G3
Adber **8** E2
Adderbury **31** F5
Adderley **39** F2
Adderstone **77** K7
Addiewell **75** H4
Addingham **57** F5
Addington *Bucks.* **31** J6
Addington *Gt.Lon.* **23** G5
Addington *Kent* **23** K6
Addlestone **22** D5
Addlethorpe **53** J6
Adel **57** H6
Adeney **39** G4
Adfa **37** K5
Adforton **28** C1
Adisham **15** H2
Adlestrop **30** D6
Adlingfleet **58** E7
Adlington *Ches.* **49** J4
Adlington *Lancs.* **49** F1
Admaston *Staffs.* **40** C3
Admaston *Tel. & W.* **39** F4
Admington **30** C4
Adsborough **8** B2
Adstock **31** J5
Adstone **31** G3
Adversane **12** D4
Advie **89** J1
Adwalton **57** H7
Adwell **21** K2
Adwick le Street **51** H2
Adwick upon Dearne **51** G2
Ae Village **68** E5
Affleck **91** G2
Affpuddle **9** H5
Afon-wen **47** K5
Afton Bridgend **68** B2
Agglethorpe **57** F1
Aigburth **48** C4
Aignis **101** G4
Aike **59** G5
Aikerness **106** D2
Aikers **107** D8
Aiketgate **61** F2
Aikshaw **60** C2
Aikton **60** D1
Aikwood Tower **69** K1
Ailey **28** C4
Ailsworth **42** E6
Aimster **105** G2
Ainderby Quernhow **57** J1
Ainderby Steeple **62** E7
Aingers Green **35** F7
Ainsdale **48** C1
Ainstable **61** G2
Ainsworth **49** G1
Ainthorpe **63** J6
Aintree **48** C3
Aird **92** C6
Aird a' Mhachair **92** C7
Aird a' Mhulaidh **100** D6
Aird Asaig **100** D7
Aird Dhail **101** G1
Aird Leimhe **93** G3
Aird Mhige **93** G2
Aird Mhighe **93** F3
Aird of Sleat **86** B4
Aird Thunga **101** G4
Aird Uige **100** C4
Airdrie *Fife* **83** G7
Airdrie *N.Lan.* **75** F4
Airidh a' Bhruaich **100** E6
Airieland **65** H5
Airies **66** D7
Airigh-drishaig **86** D1
Airmyn **58** D7
Airntully **82** B4
Airor **86** D4
Airth **75** G2
Airton **56** E4
Airyhassen **64** D6
Aisby *Lincs.* **52** B3
Aisby *Lincs.* **42** D2
Aisgernis **84** C2
Aiskew **57** H1
Aislaby *N.Yorks.* **63** K6
Aislaby *N.Yorks.* **58** D1
Aislaby *Stock.* **63** F5
Aisthorpe **52** C4
Aith *Ork.* **107** B6
Aith *Ork.* **106** F5
Aith *Shet.* **109** C7
Aith *Shet.* **108** F3
Aitnoch **89** G1
Akeld **70** E1
Akeley **31** J5
Akenham **35** F4
Albaston **4** E3
Alberbury **38** C4
Albourne **13** F5
Albrighton *Shrop.* **40** A5
Albrighton *Shrop.* **38** D4
Alburgh **45** G7
Albury *Herts.* **33** H6
Albury *Surr.* **22** D7
Albury Heath **22** D7
Alby Hill **45** F2
Alcaig **96** C6
Alcaston **38** D7
Alcester **30** B3
Alciston **13** J6
Alcombe **7** H1
Alconbury **32** E1
Alconbury Hill **32** E1
Alconbury Weston **32** E1
Aldborough *N.Yorks.* **57** K3
Aldborough *Norf.* **45** F2
Aldbourne **21** F4
Aldbrough **59** J6
Aldbrough St. John **62** C5
Aldburgh **57** H2
Aldbury **32** C7
Aldclune **82** A1
Aldeburgh **35** J3
Aldeby **45** J6
Aldenham **22** E2
Alderbury **10** C2
Alderford **45** F4
Alderholt **10** C3
Alderley **20** A2
Alderley Edge **49** H5
Alderman's Green **41** F7
Aldermaston **21** J5
Aldermaston Soke **21** K5
Aldermaston Wharf **21** K5
Alderminster **30** D4
Alderney Airport **3** J4
Aldersey Green **48** D7
Aldershot **22** B6
Alderton *Glos.* **29** J5
Alderton *Northants.* **31** J4
Alderton *Shrop.* **38** D3
Alderton *Suff.* **35** H4
Alderton *Wilts.* **20** B3
Alderwasley **51** F7
Aldfield **57** H3
Aldford **48** D7
Aldham *Essex* **34** D6
Aldham *Suff.* **34** E4
Aldie *Aber.* **91** J1
Aldie *High.* **96** E3
Aldingbourne **12** C6
Aldingham **55** F2
Aldington *Kent* **15** F4
Aldington *Worcs.* **30** B4
Aldivalloch **90** B2
Aldochlay **74** B1
Aldons **67** F5
Aldreth **33** H1
Aldridge **40** C5
Aldringham **35** J2
Aldro **58** E3
Aldsworth **30** C7
Aldunie **90** B2
Aldville **82** A4
Aldwark *Derbys.* **50** E7
Aldwark *N.Yorks.* **57** K3
Aldwick **12** C7
Aldwincle **42** D7
Aldworth **21** J4
Alexandria **74** B3
Alfardisworthy **6** A4
Alfington **7** K6
Alfold **12** D3
Alfold Crossways **12** D3
Alford *Aber.* **90** D3
Alford *Lincs.* **53** H5
Alford *Som.* **9** F1
Alfreton **51** G7
Alfrick **29** G3
Alfriston **13** J6
Algarkirk **43** F2
Alhampton **9** F1
Alkborough **58** E7
Alkerton **30** E4
Alkham **15** H3
Alkington **38** E2
Alkmonton **40** D2
All Cannings **20** D5
All Saints South Elmham **45** H7
All Stretton **38** D6
Allaleigh **5** J5
Allanaquoich **89** J5
Allancreich **90** D5
Allangillfoot **69** H4
Allanton *D. & G.* **68** E5
Allanton *N.Lan.* **75** G5
Allanton *S.Lan.* **75** F5
Allanton *Sc.Bord.* **77** G5
Allardice **91** G7
Allathasdal **84** B4
Allendale Town **61** K1
Allenheads **61** K2
Allen's Green **33** H7
Allensford **62** B1
Allensmore **28** D5
Aller **8** C2
Allerby **60** B3
Allerford *Devon* **6** C7
Allerford *Som.* **7** H1
Allerston **58** E1
Allerthorpe **58** D5
Allerton *Mersey.* **48** D4
Allerton *W.Yorks.* **57** G6
Allerton Bywater **57** K7
Allesley **40** E7
Allestree **41** F2
Allexton **42** B5
Allgreave **49** J6
Allhallows **24** E4
Allhallows-on-Sea **24** E4
Alligin Shuas **94** E6
Allimore Green **40** A4
Allington *Lincs.* **42** B1
Allington *Wilts.* **10** D1
Allington *Wilts.* **20** D5
Allithwaite **55** G2
Allnabad **103** G4
Alloa **75** G1
Allonby **60** B2
Alloway **67** H2
Allscot **39** G6
Allt na h-Airbhe **95** H2
Allt-na-subh **87** F2
Alltachonaich **79** J2
Alltan Dubh **102** B7
Alltbeithe **87** G2
Alltforgan **37** J3
Alltmawr **27** K4
Alltnacaillich **103** G4
Alltsigh **88** B3
Alltwalis **17** H1
Alltwen **18** A1
Alltyblaca **26** E4
Almeley **28** C3
Almer **9** J5
Almington **39** F2
Almiston Cross **6** B3
Almondbank **82** B5
Almondbury **50** D1
Almondsbury **19** J3
Alne **57** K3
Alness **96** D5
Alnham **70** E2
Alnmouth **71** H2
Alnwick **71** G2
Alphamstone **34** C5
Alpheton **34** C3
Alphington **7** H6
Alpington **45** G5
Alport **50** E6
Alpraham **48** E7
Alresford **34** E6
Alrewas **40** D4
Alrick **82** C1
Alsager **49** G7
Alsagers Bank **40** A1
Alsop en le Dale **50** D7
Alston *Cumb.* **61** J2
Alston *Devon* **8** C4
Alstone **29** J5
Alstonefield **50** D7
Alswear **7** F3
Altanduin **104** D6
Altarnun **4** C2
Altass **96** C1
Altens **91** H4
Alterwall **105** H2
Altham **56** C6
Althorne **25** F2
Althorpe **52** B2
Alticry **64** C5
Altnafeadh **80** D2
Altnaharra **103** H5
Altofts **57** J7
Alton *Derbys.* **51** F6
Alton *Hants.* **11** J1
Alton *Staffs.* **40** C1
Alton Barnes **20** E5
Alton Pancras **9** F4
Alton Priors **20** E5
Altonside **97** K6
Altrincham **49** G4
Altura **87** J6
Alva **75** G1
Alvanley **48** D5
Alvaston **41** F2
Alvechurch **30** B1
Alvecote **40** E5
Alvediston **9** J2
Alveley **39** G7
Alverdiscott **6** D3
Alverstoke **11** H5
Alverstone **11** G6
Alverton **42** A1
Alves **97** J5
Alvescot **21** F1
Alveston *S.Glos.* **19** K3
Alveston *Warks.* **30** D3
Alvie **89** F4
Alvingham **53** G3
Alvington **19** K1
Alwalton **42** E6
Alweston **9** F3
Alwinton **70** E3
Alwoodley Gates **57** J5
Alyth **82** D3
Amalebra **2** B5
Amber Hill **43** F1
Ambergate **51** F7
Amberley *Glos.* **20** B1
Amberley *W.Suss.* **12** D5
Amble **71** H3
Amblecote **40** A7
Ambleside **60** E6
Ambleston **16** D2
Ambrismore **73** J5
Ambrosden **31** H7
Amcotts **52** B1
Amersham **22** C2
Amesbury **20** E7
Amington **40** E5
Amisfield **69** F5
Amlwch **46** C3
Amlwch Port **46** C3
Ammanford (Rhydaman) **17** K3
Amotherby **58** D2
Ampfield **10** E2
Ampleforth **58** B2
Ampleforth College **58** B2
Ampney Crucis **20** D1
Ampney St. Mary **20** D1
Ampney St. Peter **20** D1
Amport **21** G7
Ampthill **32** D5
Ampton **34** C1
Amroth **16** E4
Amulree **81** K4
An Tòb (Leverburgh) **93** F3
An Tairbeart (Tarbert) **100** D7
Anaboard **89** H1
Anaheilt **79** K1
Ancaster **42** C1
Anchor **38** A7
Ancroft **77** H6
Ancrum **70** B1
Ancton **12** C6
Anderby **53** J5
Anderson **9** H5
Anderton **49** F5
Andover **21** G7
Andover Down **21** G7
Andoversford **30** B6
Andreas **54** D4
Anelog **36** A3
Angarrack **2** C5
Angersleigh **7** K4
Angerton **60** D1
Angle **16** B4
Angler's Retreat **37** G6
Angmering **12** D6
Angram **58** B5
Anie **81** G6
Ankerville **97** F4
Anlaby **59** G7
Anmer **44** B3
Anna Valley **21** G7
Annan **69** G7
Annaside **54** D1
Annat *Arg. & B.* **80** B5
Annat *High.* **94** E6
Annbank **67** J1
Annesley **51** H7
Annesley Woodhouse **51** H7
Annfield Plain **62** C1
Annscroft **38** D5
Ansdell **55** G7
Ansford **9** F1
Ansley **40** E6
Anslow **40** E3
Anslow Gate **40** D3
Anstey *Herts.* **33** H5
Anstey *Leics.* **41** H5
Anstruther **83** G7
Ansty *W.Suss.* **13** F4
Ansty *Warks.* **41** F7
Ansty *Wilts.* **9** J2
Anthill Common **11** H3
Anthorn **60** C1
Antingham **45** G2
Anton's Gowt **43** F1
Antony **4** D5
Antrobus **49** F5
Anvil Corner **6** B5
Anwick **52** E7
Anwoth **65** F5
Aoradh **72** A4
Apethorpe **42** D6
Apley **52** E5
Apperknowle **51** F5
Apperley **29** H6
Appin House **80** A3
Appleby **52** C1
Appleby-in-Westmorland **61** H4
Appleby Magna **41** F4
Appleby Parva **41** F5
Applecross **94** D7
Appledore *Devon* **6** C2
Appledore *Devon* **7** J4
Appledore *Kent* **14** E5
Appledore Heath **14** E4
Appleford **21** J2
Appleshaw **21** G7
Applethwaite **60** D4
Appleton **21** H1
Appleton-le-Moors **58** D1
Appleton-le-Street **58** D2
Appleton Roebuck **58** B5
Appleton Thorn **49** F4
Appleton Wiske **62** E6
Appletreehall **70** A2
Appletreewick **57** F3
Appley **7** J3
Appley Bridge **48** E1
Apse Heath **11** G6
Apsley **22** D1
Apsley End **32** E5
Apuldram **12** B6
Arberth (Narberth) **16** E3
Arbirlot **83** G3
Arborfield **22** A5
Arborfield Cross **22** A5
Arborfield Garrison **22** A5

Arbroath 83 H3
Arbuthnott 91 G7
Archdeacon Newton 62 D5
Archiestown 97 K7
Arclid 49 G6
Ard a' Chapuill 73 J3
Ardachearanbeg 73 J2
Ardacheranmor 73 J2
Ardachoil 79 J4
Ardachu 96 D1
Ardachvie 87 H5
Ardailly 72 E5
Ardalanish 78 E6
Ardallie 91 J1
Ardanaiseig 80 B5
Ardaneaskan 86 E1
Ardanstur 79 K6
Ardantiobairt 79 H2
Ardantrive 79 K5
Ardarroch 86 E1
Ardbeg Arg. & B. 73 J4
Ardbeg Arg. & B. 72 C6
Ardbeg Arg. & B. 73 K2
Ardblair 88 B1
Ardbrecknish 80 B5
Ardcharnich 95 H3
Ardchiavaig 78 E6
Ardchonnel 80 A4
Ardchonnell 80 A6
Ardchrishnish 79 F5
Ardchronie 96 D3
Ardchuilk 87 J1
Ardchullarie More 81 G6
Ardchyle 81 G5
Arddlin 38 B4
Ardeley 33 G6
Ardelve 86 E2
Arden 74 B2
Ardencaple House 79 J6
Ardens Grafton 30 C3
Ardentallan 79 K5
Ardentinny 73 K2
Ardeonaig 81 H4
Ardersier 96 E6
Ardery 79 J1
Ardessie 95 G3
Ardfad 79 J6
Ardfern 79 K7
Ardfin 72 C4
Ardgartan 80 D7
Ardgay 96 C2
Ardgenavan 80 C6
Ardgowan 74 A3
Ardgowse 90 E3
Ardgye 97 J5
Ardhallow 73 K3
Ardheslaig 94 D6
Ardiecow 98 D4
Ardinamar 79 J6
Ardindrean 95 H3
Ardingly 13 G4
Ardington 21 H3
Ardintoul 86 E2
Ardkinglas House 80 C6
Ardlair 90 D2
Ardlamont 73 H4
Ardleigh 34 E6
Ardleish 80 E6
Ardler 82 D3
Ardley 31 G6
Ardlui 80 E6
Ardlussa 72 E2
Ardmaddy 80 B4
Ardmair 95 H2
Ardmaleish 73 J4
Ardmay 80 D7
Ardmenish 72 D3
Ardmhór 84 C4
Ardminish 72 E6
Ardmolich 86 D7
Ardmore Arg. & B. 72 C6
Ardmore Arg. & B. 79 J5
Ardmore Arg. & B. 74 B3
Ardmore High. 96 E3
Ardnackaig 73 F1
Ardnacross 79 G3
Ardnadam 73 K3
Ardnadrochit 79 J4
Ardnagoine 95 F1
Ardnagowan 80 C7
Ardnagrask 96 C7
Ardnahein 74 A1
Ardnahoe 72 C3
Ardnarff 86 E1
Ardnastang 79 K1
Ardnave 72 A3
Ardno 80 C7
Ardo 91 G1
Ardoch D. & G. 68 D3
Ardoch Moray 97 J6
Ardoch P. & K. 82 B4
Ardochrig 74 E6
Ardoyne 90 E2
Ardpatrick 73 F4
Ardpeaton 74 A2
Ardradnaig 81 J3
Ardrishaig 73 G2
Ardroe 102 C6
Ardrossan 74 A6
Ardscalpsie 73 J5
Ardshave 96 E2
Ardshealach 79 H1
Ardshellach 79 J6
Ardsley 51 F2
Ardslignish 79 G1
Ardtalla 72 C5
Ardtalnaig 81 H4
Ardtaraig 73 J2
Ardteatle 80 C5
Ardtoe 86 C7
Ardtornish 79 J3
Ardtrostan 81 H5
Ardtur 80 A3
Arduaine 79 K7
Ardullie 96 C5
Ardura 79 H4
Ardvar 102 D5
Ardvasar 86 C4
Ardveich 81 H5
Ardverikie 88 C6
Ardvorlich Arg. & B. 80 E6
Ardvorlich P. & K. 81 H5
Ardwall 65 F5
Ardwell D. & G. 64 B6
Ardwell Moray 90 B1
Ardwell S.Ayr. 67 F4
Areley Kings 29 G1
Arford 12 B3
Argaty 81 J7
Argoed 18 E2
Argoed Mill 27 J2
Argrennan 65 H5
Arichamish 80 A7
Arichastlich 80 D4
Arichonan 73 F1
Aridhglas 78 E5
Arienskill 86 D6
Arileod 78 C2
Arinacrinachd 94 D6
Arinafad Beg 73 F2
Arinagour 78 D2
Arinambane 84 C2
Arisaig 86 C6
Arivegaig 79 H1
Arkendale 57 J3
Arkesden 33 H5
Arkholme 55 J2
Arkleby 60 C3
Arkleside 57 F1
Arkleton 69 J4
Arkley 23 F2
Arksey 51 H2
Arkwright 51 G5
Arlary 82 C7
Arlecdon 60 B5
Arlesey 32 E5
Arleston 39 F4
Arley 49 F4
Arlingham 29 G7
Arlington Devon 6 E1
Arlington E.Suss. 13 J6
Arlington Glos. 20 E1
Arlington Beccott 6 E1
Armadale High. 104 C2
Armadale High. 86 C4
Armadale W.Loth. 75 H4
Armathwaite 61 G2
Arminghall 45 G5
Armitage 40 C4
Armscote 30 D4
Armston 42 D7
Armthorpe 51 J2
Arnabost 78 D2
Arncliffe 56 E2
Arncliffe Cote 56 E2
Arncroach 83 G7
Arne 9 J6
Arnesby 41 J6
Arngask 82 C6
Arngibbon 74 E1
Arngomery 74 E1
Arnhall 83 H1
Arnicle 73 F7
Arnipol 86 D6
Arnisdale 86 E3
Arnish 94 C7
Arniston Engine 76 B4
Arnol 101 F3
Arnold 41 H1
Arnprior 74 E1
Arnside 55 H2
Arowry 38 D2
Arrad Foot 55 G1
Arradoul 98 C4
Arram 59 G5
Arrat 83 H2
Arrathorne 62 C7
Arreton 11 G6
Arrington 33 G3
Arrivain 80 D4
Arrochar 80 E7
Arrow 30 B3
Arscaig 103 H7
Arthington 57 H5
Arthingworth 42 A7
Arthog 37 F4
Arthrath 91 H1
Arthurstone 82 D3
Artrochie 91 J1
Aruadh 72 A4
Arundel 12 D6
Aryhoulan 80 B1
Asby 60 B4
Ascog 73 K4
Ascot 22 C5
Ascott 30 E5
Ascott-under-Wychwood 30 D7
Ascreavie 82 E2
Asenby 57 J2
Asfordby 42 A4
Asfordby Hill 42 A4
Asgarby Lincs. 53 G6
Asgarby Lincs. 42 E1
Ash Kent 15 H2
Ash Kent 24 C5
Ash Som. 8 D2
Ash Surr. 22 B6
Ash Barton 6 D5
Ash Bullayne 7 F5
Ash Magna 38 E2
Ash Mill 7 F3
Ash Priors 7 K3
Ash Thomas 7 J4
Ash Vale 22 B6
Ashampstead 21 J4
Ashbocking 35 F3
Ashbourne 40 D1
Ashbrittle 7 J3
Ashburnham Place 13 K5
Ashburton 5 H4
Ashbury Devon 6 D6
Ashbury Oxon. 21 F3
Ashby 52 C2
Ashby by Partney 53 H6
Ashby cum Fenby 53 F2
Ashby de la Launde 52 D7
Ashby de la Zouch 41 F4
Ashby Folville 42 A4
Ashby Magna 41 H6
Ashby Parva 41 H7
Ashby Puerorum 53 G5
Ashby St. Ledgers 31 G2
Ashby St. Mary 45 H5
Ashchurch 29 J5
Ashcombe 5 K3
Ashcott 8 D1
Ashdon 33 J4
Ashe 21 J7
Asheldham 25 F1
Ashen 34 B4
Ashenden 14 D4
Ashendon 31 J7
Ashens 73 G3
Ashfield Arg. & B. 73 F2
Ashfield Stir. 81 J7
Ashfield Suff. 35 G2
Ashfield Green 35 G1
Ashfold Crossways 13 F4
Ashford Devon 5 G6
Ashford Devon 6 D2
Ashford Hants. 10 C3
Ashford Kent 15 F3
Ashford Surr. 22 D4
Ashford Bowdler 28 E1
Ashford Carbonel 28 E1
Ashford Hill 21 J5
Ashford in the Water 50 E6
Ashgill 75 F5
Ashiestiel 76 C7
Ashill Devon 7 J4
Ashill Norf. 44 C5
Ashill Som. 8 C3
Ashingdon 24 E2
Ashington Northumb. 71 H5
Ashington Som. 8 E2
Ashington W.Suss. 12 E5
Ashkirk 69 K1
Ashleworth 29 H6
Ashley Cambs. 33 K2
Ashley Ches. 49 G4
Ashley Devon 6 E4
Ashley Glos. 20 C2
Ashley Hants. 10 E1
Ashley Hants. 10 D5
Ashley Kent 15 H3
Ashley Northants. 42 A6
Ashley Staffs. 39 G2
Ashley Wilts. 20 B5
Ashley Green 22 C1
Ashley Heath 10 C4
Ashmanhaugh 45 H3
Ashmansworth 21 H6
Ashmansworthy 6 B4
Ashmore Dorset 9 J3
Ashmore P. & K. 82 C2
Ashorne 30 E3
Ashover 51 F6
Ashow 30 E1
Ashperton 29 F4
Ashprington 5 J5
Ashreigney 6 E4
Ashtead 22 E6
Ashton Ches. 48 E6
Ashton Cornw. 2 C6
Ashton Cornw. 4 D4
Ashton Here. 28 E2
Ashton Northants. 42 D7
Ashton Northants. 31 J4
Ashton Common 20 B6
Ashton-in-Makerfield 48 E3
Ashton Keynes 20 D2
Ashton under Hill 29 J5
Ashton-under-Lyne 49 J3
Ashton upon Mersey 49 G3
Ashurst Hants. 10 E3
Ashurst Kent 13 J3
Ashurst W.Suss. 12 E5
Ashurstwood 13 H3
Ashwater 6 B6
Ashwell Herts. 33 F5
Ashwell Rut. 42 B4
Ashwellthorpe 45 F6
Ashwick 19 K7
Ashwicken 44 B4
Ashybank 70 A2
Askam in Furness 55 F2
Askern 51 H1
Askerswell 8 E5
Askett 22 B1
Askham Cumb. 61 G4
Askham Notts. 51 K5
Askham Bryan 58 B5
Askham Richard 58 B5
Asknish 73 H1
Askrigg 62 A7
Askwith 57 G5
Aslackby 42 D2
Aslacton 45 F6
Aslockton 42 A1
Asloun 90 D3
Aspall 35 F2
Aspatria 60 C2
Aspenden 33 G6
Aspley Guise 32 C5
Aspull 49 F2
Asselby 58 D7
Assington 34 D5
Astbury 49 H6
Astcote 31 H3
Asterby 53 F5
Asterley 38 C5
Asterton 38 C6
Asthall 30 D7
Asthall Leigh 30 E7
Astley Shrop. 38 E4
Astley Warks. 41 F7
Astley Worcs. 29 G2
Astley Abbotts 39 G6
Astley Bridge 49 G1
Astley Cross 29 G2
Astley Green 49 G3
Aston Ches. 39 F1
Aston Ches. 48 E5
Aston Derbys. 50 D4
Aston Flints. 48 C6
Aston Here. 28 D1
Aston Herts. 33 F6
Aston Oxon. 21 G1
Aston S.Yorks. 51 G4
Aston Shrop. 38 E3
Aston Staffs. 39 G1
Aston Tel. & W. 39 F5
Aston W'ham 22 A3
Aston W.Mid. 40 C7
Aston Abbotts 32 B7
Aston Botterell 39 F7
Aston-by-Stone 40 B2
Aston Cantlow 30 C3
Aston Clinton 32 B7
Aston Crews 29 F6
Aston Cross 29 J5
Aston End 33 F6
Aston Eyre 39 F6
Aston Fields 29 J1
Aston Flamville 41 G6
Aston Ingham 29 F6
Aston juxta Mondrum 49 F7
Aston le Walls 31 F3
Aston Magna 30 C5
Aston Munslow 38 E7
Aston on Clun 38 C7
Aston on Trent 41 G3
Aston Rogers 38 C5
Aston Rowant 22 A2
Aston Sandford 22 A1
Aston Somerville 30 B5
Aston Subedge 30 C4
Aston Tirrold 21 J3
Aston Upthorpe 21 J3
Astwick 33 F5
Astwood 32 C4
Astwood Bank 30 B2
Aswarby 42 D1
Aswardby 53 G5
Aswick Grange 43 G4
Atch Lench 30 B3
Atcham 38 E5
Athelington 35 G1
Athelney 8 C2
Athelstaneford 76 D3
Atherington 6 D3
Atherstone 41 F6
Atherstone on Stour 30 D3
Atherton 49 F2
Athlinne 100 D6
Atlow 40 E1
Attadale 87 F1
Attenborough 41 H2
Atterby 52 C3
Attleborough Norf. 44 E6
Attleborough Warks. 41 F6
Attlebridge 45 F4
Atwick 59 H4
Atworth 20 B5
Aubourn 52 C6
Auch 80 E4
Auchairne 67 F5
Auchallater 89 J6
Auchameanach 73 G5
Aucharnie 98 E6
Aucharrigill 96 B1
Auchattie 90 E5
Auchavan 82 C1
Auchbraad 73 G2
Auchbreck 89 K2
Auchenblae 91 F7
Auchenbothie 74 B3
Auchenbrack 68 C4
Auchenbreck 73 J2
Auchencairn 65 J5
Auchencrow 77 G4
Auchendinny 76 A4
Auchendolly 65 H4
Auchenfoyle 74 B3
Auchengray 75 H5
Auchenhalrig 98 B4
Auchenheath 75 G6
Auchenhessnane 68 D4
Auchenlochan 73 H3
Auchenmalg 64 C5
Auchenrivock 69 J5
Auchentiber 74 B6
Auchenvennal 74 A2
Auchessan 81 F5
Auchgourish 89 G3
Auchinafaud 73 F5
Auchincruive 67 H1
Auchindarrach 73 G2
Auchindarroch 80 B2
Auchindrain 80 B7
Auchindrean 95 H3
Auchininna 98 E6
Auchinleck 67 K1
Auchinloch 74 E3
Auchinner 81 H6
Auchinroath 97 K6
Auchintoul Aber. 90 D3
Auchintoul Aber. 98 E5
Auchintoul High. 96 C1
Auchiries 91 J1
Auchleven 90 E2
Auchlochan 75 G7
Auchlunachan 95 H3
Auchlunies 91 G5
Auchlunkart 98 B6
Auchlyne 81 G5
Auchmacoy 91 H1
Auchmair 90 B2
Auchmantle 64 B4
Auchmithie 83 H3
Auchmuirbridge 82 D7
Auchmull 90 D7
Auchnabony 65 H6
Auchnabreac 80 B7
Auchnacloich 81 K4
Auchnacraig 79 J5
Auchnacree 83 F1
Auchnafree 81 K4
Auchnagallin 89 H1
Auchnagatt 99 H6
Auchnaha 73 H2
Auchnangoul 80 B7
Aucholzie 90 B5
Auchorrie 90 E4
Auchraw 81 G5
Auchreoch 80 E5
Auchronie 90 C6
Auchterarder 82 A6
Auchtercairn 94 E4
Auchterderran 76 A1
Auchterhouse 82 E4
Auchtermuchty 82 D6
Auchterneed 96 B5
Auchtertool 76 A1
Auchtertyre Angus 82 D3
Auchtertyre Moray 97 J6
Auchtertyre Stir. 80 E5
Auchtubh 81 G5
Auckengill 105 J2
Auckley 51 J2
Audenshaw 49 J3
Audlem 39 F1
Audley 49 G7
Audley End 33 J5
Auds 98 E4
Aughton E.Riding 58 D6
Aughton Lancs. 48 C2
Aughton Lancs. 55 J3
Aughton S.Yorks. 51 G4
Aughton Park 48 D2
Auldearn 97 G6
Aulden 28 D3
Auldhame 76 D2
Auldhouse 74 E5
Aulich 81 H2
Ault a' chruinn 87 F2
Ault Hucknall 51 G6
Aultanrynie 103 F5
Aultbea 94 E3
Aultgrishan 94 D3
Aultguish Inn 95 K4
Aultibea 105 F6
Aultiphurst 104 D2
Aultmore 98 C5
Aultnagoire 88 C2
Aultnamain Inn 96 D3
Aultnapaddock 98 B6
Aulton 90 E2
Aultvoulin 86 D4
Aundorach 89 G3
Aunk 7 J5
Aunsby 42 D2
Auquhorthies 91 G2
Aust 19 J3
Austerfield 51 J3
Austonley 50 D2
Austrey 40 E5
Austwick 56 C3
Authorpe 53 H4
Authorpe Row 53 J5
Avebury 20 D4
Aveley 23 J3
Avening 20 B2
Averham 51 K7
Aveton Gifford 5 G6
Avielochan 89 G3
Aviemore 89 F3
Avington Hants. 11 G1
Avington W.Berks. 21 G5
Avoch 96 D6
Avon 10 C5
Avon Dassett 31 F3
Avonbridge 75 H3
Avonmouth 19 J4
Avonwick 5 H5
Awbridge 10 E2
Awhirk 64 A5
Awkley 19 J3
Awliscombe 7 K5
Awre 20 A1
Awsworth 41 G1
Axbridge 19 H6
Axford Hants. 21 K7
Axford Wilts. 21 F4
Axminster 8 B5
Axmouth 8 B5
Aycliffe 62 D4
Aydon 71 F7
Aylburton 19 K1
Ayle 61 J2
Aylesbeare 7 J6
Aylesbury 32 B7
Aylesby 53 F2
Aylesford 14 C2
Aylesham 15 H2
Aylestone 41 H5
Aylmerton 45 F2
Aylsham 45 F3
Aylton 29 F5
Aymestrey 28 D2
Aynho 31 G5
Ayot St. Lawrence 32 E7
Ayot St. Peter 33 F7
Ayr 67 H1
Aysgarth 57 F1
Ayshford 7 J4
Ayside 55 G1
Ayston 42 B5
Aythorpe Roding 33 J7
Ayton P. & K. 82 C6
Ayton Sc.Bord. 77 H4
Aywick 108 E4
Azerley 57 H2

B

Babbacombe 5 K4
Babbinswood 38 C2
Babcary 8 E2
Babel 27 H5
Babell 47 K5
Babeny 5 G3
Babraham 33 J4
Babworth 51 J4
Bac 101 G3
Back of Keppoch 86 C6
Backaland 106 E4
Backaskaill 106 D2
Backbarrow 55 G1
Backburn 90 D1
Backfolds 99 J5
Backford 48 C5
Backhill 91 F1
Backhill of Clackriach 99 H6
Backhill of Trustach 90 E5
Backies High. 97 F1
Backies Moray 98 C5
Backlass 105 H3
Backside 90 C1
Backwell 19 H5
Backworth 71 H6
Bacon End 33 J7
Baconsthorpe 45 F2
Bacton Here. 28 C5
Bacton Norf. 45 H2
Bacton Suff. 34 E2
Bacup 56 D7
Badachro 94 D4
Badanloch Lodge 104 C5
Badavanich 95 H6
Badbea 105 F7
Badbury 20 E3
Badby 31 G3
Badcall High. 102 D4
Badcall High. 102 E3
Badcaul 95 G2
Baddeley Green 49 J7
Badden 73 G2
Baddesley Ensor 40 E6
Baddidarach 102 C6
Badenscoth 90 E1
Badenyon 90 B3
Badger 39 G6
Badgerbank 49 H5
Badgers Mount 23 H5
Badgeworth 29 J7
Badgworth 19 G6
Badicaul 86 D2
Badingham 35 H2
Badintagairt 103 G7
Badlesmere 15 F2
Badley 34 E3
Badlipster 105 H4
Badluarach 95 F2
Badminton 20 B3
Badnaban 102 C6
Badnabay 102 E4
Badnafrave 89 K3
Badnagie 105 G5
Badnambiast 88 E7
Badninish 96 E2
Badrallach 95 G2
Badsey 30 B4
Badshot Lea 22 B7
Badsworth 51 G1
Badwell Ash 34 D2
Badyo 82 A1
Bae Cinmel (Kinmel Bay) 47 H4
Bae Colwyn (Colwyn Bay) 47 G5
Bae Penrhyn (Penrhyn Bay) 47 G4
Bag Enderby 53 G5
Bagby 57 K1
Bagendon 20 D1
Baggrave Hall 42 A5
Baggrow 60 C2
Bagh a' Chaisteil (Castlebay) 84 B5
Baghasdal 84 C3
Bagillt 48 B5
Baginton 30 E1
Baglan 18 A2
Bagley 38 D3
Bagnall 49 J7
Bagnor 21 H5
Bagshot Surr. 22 C5
Bagshot Wilts. 21 G5
Bagstone 19 K3
Bagthorpe Norf. 44 B2
Bagthorpe Notts. 51 G7
Baguley 49 H4
Bagworth 41 G5
Bagwyllydiart 28 D6
Baildon 57 G6
Baile a' Mhanaich (Balivanich) 92 C6
Baile Ailein 100 E5
Baile an Truiseil 101 F2
Baile Boidheach 73 F3
Baile Gharbhaidh 92 C7
Baile Glas 92 D6
Baile Mhartainn (Balmartin) 92 C4
Baile Mhic Phail 92 D4
Baile Mòr Arg. & B. 78 D5
Baile Mòr W.Isles 92 C5
Baile-na-Cille 92 D3
Baile nan Cailleach 92 C6
Baile Raghaill 92 C5
Bailebeag 88 C3
Baileguish 89 F5
Bailetonach 86 C7
Bailiesward 90 C1
Bainbridge 62 A7
Bainsford 75 G2
Bainshole 90 E1
Bainton E.Riding 59 F4
Bainton Peter. 42 D5
Bairnkine 70 B2
Bakebare 90 B1
Baker Street 24 C3
Baker's End 33 G7
Bakewell 50 E6
Bala 37 J2
Balachuirn 94 B7
Balafark 74 E1
Balaldie 97 F4
Balavil 88 E4
Balbeg High. 88 B1
Balbeg High. 88 B2
Balbeggie 82 C5
Balbirnie 82 D7
Balbithan 91 F3
Balblair High. 96 E5
Balblair High. 96 C2
Balcharn 96 C1
Balcherry 97 F3
Balchers 99 F5
Balchladich 102 C5
Balchraggan High. 96 C7
Balchraggan High. 88 C1
Balchrick 102 D2
Balcombe 13 G3
Balcurvie 82 E7
Baldernock 74 D3
Baldersby 57 J2
Balderstone 56 B6
Balderton 52 B7
Baldhu 2 E4
Baldinnie 83 F6
Baldock 33 F5
Baldovie Angus 82 E2
Baldovie Dundee 83 F4
Baldrine 54 D5
Baldslow 14 C6
Baldwin 54 C5
Baldwinholme 60 E1
Baldwin's Gate 39 G1
Bale 44 E2
Balelone 92 C4
Balemartine 78 A3
Balendoch 82 D3
Balephuil 78 A3
Balerno 75 K4
Balernock 74 A2
Baleromindubh 72 B1
Balerominmore 72 B1
Balevulin 79 F5
Balfield 83 G1
Balfour Aber. 90 D5
Balfour Ork. 107 D6
Balfron 74 D2
Balfron Station 74 D2
Balgedie 82 C7
Balgonar 75 J1
Balgove 91 G1
Balgowan D. & G. 64 B6
Balgowan High. 88 D5
Balgown 93 J5
Balgray 83 F4
Balgreen 99 F5
Balgreggan 64 A5
Balgy 94 E6
Balhaldie 81 K7
Balhalgardy 91 F2
Balhary 82 D3
Balhelvie 82 E5
Balhousie 83 F7
Baliasta 108 F2
Baligill 104 D2
Baligrundle 79 K4
Balindore 80 A4
Balintore 97 F4
Balintraid 96 E4
Balintyre 81 H3
Balivanich (Baile a' Mhanaich) 92 C6
Balkeerie 82 E3
Balkholme 58 D7
Balkissock 67 F5
Ball 38 C3
Ball Haye Green 49 J7
Ball Hill 21 H5
Ballabeg 54 B6
Ballacannell 54 D5
Ballacarnane Beg 54 C5
Ballachulish 80 B2
Balladoole 54 B7
Ballafesson 54 B6
Ballagyr 54 B5
Ballajora 54 D4
Ballakilpheric 54 B6
Ballamodha 54 B6
Ballantrae 66 E5
Ballards Gore 25 F2
Ballasalla I.o.M. 54 B6
Ballasalla I.o.M. 54 C4
Ballater 90 B5
Ballaterach 90 C5
Ballaugh 54 C4
Ballaveare 54 C6
Ballechin 82 A2
Balleich 81 G7
Ballencrieff 76 C3
Ballidon 50 E7
Balliekine 73 G7
Balliemeanoch 80 C7
Balliemore Arg. & B. 73 K1
Balliemore Arg. & B. 79 K5
Ballig 54 B5
Ballimeanoch 80 B6
Ballimore Arg. & B. 73 H2
Ballimore Stir. 81 G6
Ballinaby 72 A4
Ballindean 82 D5
Ballingdon 34 C4
Ballinger Common 22 C1
Ballingham 28 E5
Ballingry 75 K1
Ballinlick 82 A3
Ballinluig P. & K. 82 A2
Ballinluig P. & K. 82 B2
Ballintuim 82 C2
Balloch Angus 82 E2
Balloch High. 96 E7
Balloch N.Lan. 75 F3
Balloch W.Dun. 74 B2
Ballochan 90 D5
Ballochandrain 73 H2
Ballochford 90 B1
Ballochgair 66 B1
Ballochmartin 73 K5
Ballochmorrie 67 G5
Ballochmyle 67 K1
Ballochroy 73 F5
Ballogie 90 D5
Balls Cross 12 C4
Ballyaurgan 73 F3
Ballygown 79 F3
Ballygrant 72 B4
Ballyhaugh 78 C2
Ballymeanoch 73 G1
Ballymichael 73 H7
Balmacara 86 E2
Balmaclellan 65 G3
Balmacneil 82 A2
Balmadies 83 G3
Balmae 65 G6
Balmaha 74 C1
Balmalcolm 82 E7
Balmartin (Baile Mhartainn) 92 C4
Balmeanach Arg. & B. 79 H3
Balmeanach Arg. & B. 79 F4
Balmedie 91 H3
Balmerino 82 E5
Balmerlawn 10 E4
Balminnoch 64 C4
Balmore E.Dun. 74 E3
Balmore High. 97 F7
Balmore High. 87 K1
Balmore High. 93 H7
Balmore P. & K. 81 J2
Balmullo 83 F5
Balmungie 96 E6
Balmyle 82 B2
Balnaboth 82 E1
Balnabruaich 96 E4
Balnacra 95 F7
Balnafoich 88 D1
Balnagall 97 F3
Balnagown Castle 96 E4
Balnaguard 82 A2
Balnaguisich 96 D4
Balnahard Arg. & B. 72 C1
Balnahard Arg. & B. 79 F4
Balnain 88 B1
Balnakeil 103 F2
Balnaknock 93 K5
Balnamoon 83 G1
Balnapaling 96 E5
Balnespick 89 F4
Balquhidder 81 G5
Balsall 30 D1
Balsall Common 30 D1
Balscote 30 E4
Balsham 33 J3
Baltasound 108 F2
Balterley 49 G7
Baltersan 64 E4
Balthangie 99 G5
Balthayock 82 C5
Baltonsborough 8 E1
Baluachraig 73 G1
Balulive 72 C4
Balure Arg. & B. 80 B4
Balure Arg. & B. 79 K4
Balvaird 96 C6
Balvarran 82 B1
Balvicar 79 J6
Balvraid High. 86 E3
Balvraid High. 89 F1
Bamber Bridge 55 J7
Bamber's Green 33 J6
Bamburgh 77 K7
Bamff 82 D2
Bamford 50 E4
Bampton Cumb. 61 G5
Bampton Devon 7 H3
Bampton Oxon. 21 G1
Banavie 87 H7
Banbury 31 F4
Banc-y-ffordd 17 H1
Bancffosfelen 17 H3
Banchor 97 G7
Banchory 91 F5
Banchory-Devenick 91 H4
Bancyfelin 17 G3
Bandon 82 D7
Banff 98 E4
Bangor 46 D5
Bangor-is-y-coed 38 C1
Bangor Teifi 26 C4
Banham 44 E7
Bank 10 D4
Bank End 55 F1
Bank Newton 56 E4
Bank Street 29 F2
Bankend D. & G. 69 F7
Bankend S.Lan. 75 G7
Bankfoot 82 B4
Bankhead Aber. 90 E3
Bankhead Aber. 90 E4
Bankhead Aberdeen 91 G4
Bankhead D. & G. 65 H6
Banknock 75 F3
Banks Cumb. 70 A7
Banks Lancs. 55 G7
Bankshill 69 G5
Banningham 45 G3
Bannister Green 33 K6
Bannockburn 75 G1
Banstead 23 F6
Bantham 5 G6
Banton 75 F3
Banwell 19 G6
Bapchild 25 F5
Baptiston 74 D2
Bar Hill 33 G2
Barabhas (Barvas) 101 F2
Barachander 80 B5
Barassie 74 B7
Barbaraville 96 E4
Barber Booth 50 D4
Barbon 56 B1
Barbrook 7 F1
Barby 31 G1

Barcaldine 80 A3
Barcaple 65 G5
Barcheston 30 D4
Barcombe 13 H5
Barcombe Cross 13 H5
Barden 62 C7
Bardennoch 67 K4
Bardfield End Green 33 K5
Bardfield Saling 33 K6
Bardister 108 C5
Bardney 52 E6
Bardon *Leics.* 41 G4
Bardon *Moray* 97 K6
Bardon Mill 70 C7
Bardsea 55 G2
Bardsey 57 J5
Bardsley 49 J2
Bardwell 34 D1
Barewood 28 C3
Barfad 73 G4
Barford *Norf.* 45 F5
Barford *Warks.* 30 D2
Barford St. John 31 F5
Barford St. Martin 10 B1
Barford St. Michael 31 F5
Barfrestone 15 H2
Bargaly 64 E4
Bargany Mains 67 G3
Bargoed 18 E2
Bargrennan 64 D3
Barham *Cambs.* 32 E1
Barham *Kent* 15 G2
Barham *Suff.* 35 F3
Barharrow 65 G5
Barholm 42 D4
Barholm Mains 64 E5
Barkby 41 J5
Barkby Thorpe 41 J5
Barkestone-le-Vale 42 A2
Barkham 22 A5
Barking *Gt.Lon.* 23 H3
Barking *Suff.* 34 E3
Barking & Dagenham 23 H3
Barkingside 23 H3
Barkisland 50 C1
Barkston *Lincs.* 42 C1
Barkston *N.Yorks.* 57 K6
Barkway 33 G5
Barlae 64 C4
Barlaston 40 A2
Barlavington 12 C5
Barlborough 51 G5
Barlby 58 C6
Barlestone 41 G5
Barley *Herts.* 33 G5
Barley *Lancs.* 56 D5
Barleycroft End 33 H6
Barleyhill 62 B1
Barleythorpe 42 B5
Barling 25 F3
Barlings 52 D5
Barlow *Derbys.* 51 F5
Barlow *N.Yorks.* 58 C7
Barlow *T. & W.* 71 G7
Barmby Moor 58 D5
Barmby on the Marsh 58 C7
Barmer 44 C2
Barmolloch 73 G1
Barmoor Lane End 77 J6
Barmouth (Abermaw) 37 F4
Barmpton 62 E5
Barmston 59 H4
Barnacabber 73 K2
Barnacarry 73 J1
Barnack 42 D5
Barnacle 41 F7
Barnamuc 80 B3
Barnard Castle 62 B5
Barnard Gate 31 F7
Barnardiston 34 B4
Barnard's Green 29 G4
Barnbarroch *D. & G.* 64 D5
Barnbarroch *D. & G.* 65 J5
Barnburgh 51 G2
Barnby 45 J6
Barnby Dun 51 J2
Barnby in the Willows 52 B7
Barnby Moor 51 J4
Barndennoch 68 D5
Barnes 23 F4
Barnet 23 F2
Barnetby le Wold 52 D2
Barney 44 D2
Barnham *Suff.* 34 C1
Barnham *W.Suss.* 12 C6
Barnham Broom 44 E5
Barnhead 83 H2
Barnhill 97 J6
Barnhills 66 D6
Barningham *Dur.* 62 B5
Barningham *Suff.* 34 D1
Barnoldby le Beck 53 F2
Barnoldswick 56 D5
Barns Green 12 E4
Barnsdale Bar 51 H1
Barnsley *Glos.* 20 D1
Barnsley *S.Yorks.* 51 F2
Barnstaple 6 D2
Barnston *Essex* 33 K7
Barnston *Mersey.* 48 B4
Barnstone 42 A2
Barnt Green 30 B1
Barnton 49 F5
Barnwell All Saints 42 D7
Barnwell St. Andrew 42 D7
Barnwood 29 H7
Barr *Arg. & B.* 72 B4
Barr *High.* 79 H2
Barr *S.Ayr.* 67 G4
Barr Hall 34 B5
Barra (Tràigh Mhòr) Airport 84 C4
Barrackan 79 J7
Barraer 64 D4
Barraglom 100 D4
Barrahormid 73 F2
Barran 80 C5
Barrapoll 78 A3
Barrasford 70 E6
Barravullin 79 K7
Barregarrow 54 C5
Barrhead 74 D5
Barrhill 67 G5
Barrington *Cambs.* 33 G4
Barrington *Som.* 8 C3
Barripper 2 D5
Barrisdale 86 E4
Barrmill 74 B5
Barrnacarry 79 K5
Barrock 105 H1
Barrow *Lancs.* 56 C6
Barrow *Rut.* 42 B4
Barrow *Shrop.* 39 F5
Barrow *Som.* 9 G1
Barrow *Suff.* 34 B2
Barrow Gurney 19 J5
Barrow Haven 59 G7
Barrow-in-Furness 55 F3
Barrow Nook 48 D2
Barrow Street 9 H1
Barrow upon Humber 59 G7
Barrow upon Soar 41 H4
Barrow upon Trent 41 F3
Barrowby 42 B2
Barrowden 42 C5
Barrowford 56 D6
Barry *Angus* 83 G4
Barry *V. of Glam.* 18 E5
Barsby 42 A4
Barsham 45 H6
Barskimming 67 J1
Barsloisnoch 73 G1
Barston 30 D1
Bartestree 28 E4
Barthol Chapel 91 G1
Barthomley 49 G7
Bartley 10 E3
Bartlow 33 J4
Barton *Cambs.* 33 H3
Barton *Ches.* 48 D7
Barton *Glos.* 30 B6
Barton *Lancs.* 55 J6
Barton *Lancs.* 48 C2
Barton *N.Yorks.* 62 D6
Barton *Torbay* 5 K4
Barton *Warks.* 30 C3
Barton Bendish 44 B5
Barton Common 45 H3
Barton End 20 B2
Barton Hartshorn 31 H5
Barton in Fabis 41 H2
Barton in the Beans 41 F5
Barton-le-Clay 32 D5
Barton-le-Street 58 D2
Barton-le-Willows 58 D3
Barton Mills 34 B1
Barton on Sea 10 D5
Barton-on-the-Heath 30 D5
Barton St. David 8 E1
Barton Seagrave 32 B1
Barton Stacey 21 H7
Barton Turf 45 H3
Barton-under-Needwood 40 D4
Barton-upon-Humber 59 G7
Barvas (Barabhas) 101 F2
Barway 33 J1
Barwell 41 G6
Barwhinnock 65 G5
Barwick 8 E3
Barwick in Elmet 57 J6
Barwinnock 64 D6
Baschurch 38 D3
Bascote 31 F2
Basford Green 49 J7
Bashall Eaves 56 B5
Bashall Town 56 C5
Bashley 10 D5
Basildon *Essex* 24 D3
Basildon *W.Berks.* 21 K4
Basingstoke 21 K6
Baslow 50 E5
Bason Bridge 19 G7
Bassaleg 19 F3
Bassenthwaite 60 D3
Basset's Cross 6 D5
Bassett 11 F3
Bassingbourn 33 G4
Bassingfield 41 J2
Bassingham 52 C6
Bassingthorpe 42 C3
Basta 108 E3
Baston 42 E4
Bastwick 45 J4
Batavaime 81 F4
Batchworth 22 D2
Batchworth Heath 22 D2
Batcombe *Dorset* 9 F4
Batcombe *Som.* 9 F1
Bate Heath 49 F5
Bath 20 A5
Bathampton 20 A5
Bathealton 7 J3
Batheaston 20 A5
Bathford 20 A5
Bathgate 75 H4
Bathley 51 K7
Bathpool *Cornw.* 4 C3
Bathpool *Som.* 8 B2
Batley 57 H7
Batsford 30 C5
Battersby 63 G6
Battersea 23 F4
Battisborough Cross 5 G6
Battisford 34 E3
Battisford Tye 34 E3
Battle *E.Suss.* 14 C6
Battle *Powys* 27 K5
Battlefield 38 E4
Battlesbridge 24 D2
Battlesden 32 C6
Battleton 7 H3
Battramsley 10 E5
Batt's Corner 22 B7
Bauds of Cullen 98 C4
Baugh 78 B3
Baughton 29 H4
Baughurst 21 J6
Baulds 90 E5
Baulking 21 G2
Baumber 53 F5
Baunton 20 D1
Baveney Wood 29 F1
Baverstock 10 B1
Bawburgh 45 F5
Bawdeswell 44 E3
Bawdrip 8 C1
Bawdsey 35 H4
Bawtry 51 J3
Baxenden 56 C7
Baxterley 40 E6
Baycliff 55 F2
Baydon 21 F4
Bayford *Herts.* 23 G1
Bayford *Som.* 9 G2
Bayfordbury 33 G7
Bayham Abbey 13 K3
Bayles 61 J2
Baylham 35 F3
Baynards Green 31 G6
Baysham 28 E6
Bayston Hill 38 D5
Baythorn End 34 B4
Bayton 29 F1
Beach 79 J2
Beachampton 31 J5
Beacharr 72 E6
Beachborough 15 G4
Beachley 19 J2
Beacon 7 K5
Beacon End 34 D6
Beacon Hill 12 B3
Beacon's Bottom 22 A2
Beaconsfield 22 C2
Beadlam 58 C1
Beadnell 71 H1
Beaford 6 D4
Beal *N.Yorks.* 58 B7
Beal *Northumb.* 77 J6
Bealach 80 A2
Beambridge 49 F7
Beamhurst 40 C2
Beaminster 8 D4
Beamish 62 D1
Beamsley 57 F4
Bean 23 J4
Beanacre 20 B5
Beanley 71 F2
Beaquoy 106 C5
Beardon 6 D7
Beare Green 22 E7
Bearley 30 C2
Bearnie 91 H1
Bearnock 88 B1
Bearnus 79 F3
Bearpark 62 D2
Bearsbridge 61 J1
Bearsden 74 D3
Bearsted 14 C2
Bearwood 10 B5
Beattock 69 F3
Beauchamp Roding 23 J1
Beauchief 51 F4
Beaudesert 30 C2
Beaufort 28 A7
Beaulieu 10 E4
Beauly 96 C7
Beaumaris (Biwmaris) 46 E5
Beaumont *Cumb.* 60 E1
Beaumont *Essex* 35 F6
Beausale 30 D1
Beauworth 11 G2
Beaworthy 6 C6
Beazley End 34 B6
Bebington 48 C4
Bebside 71 H5
Beccles 45 J6
Becconsall 55 H7
Beck Foot 61 H7
Beck Hole 63 K6
Beck Row 33 K1
Beck Side 55 F1
Beckbury 39 G5
Beckenham 23 G5
Beckermet 60 B6
Beckfoot *Cumb.* 60 C6
Beckfoot *Cumb.* 60 B2
Beckford 29 J5
Beckhampton 20 D5
Beckingham *Lincs.* 52 B7
Beckingham *Notts.* 51 K4
Beckington 20 A6
Beckley *E.Suss.* 14 D5
Beckley *Oxon.* 31 G7
Beckton 23 H3
Beckwithshaw 57 H4
Becontree 23 H3
Bedale 57 H1
Bedburn 62 C3
Bedchester 9 H3
Beddau 18 D3
Beddgelert 36 E1
Beddingham 13 H6
Beddington 23 G5
Beddington Corner 23 F5
Bedfield 35 G2
Bedford 32 D4
Bedgebury Cross 14 C4
Bedhampton 11 J4
Bedingfield 35 F2
Bedlington 71 H5
Bedlinog 18 D1
Bedminster 19 J4
Bedmond 22 E1
Bednall 40 B4
Bedol 48 B5
Bedrule 70 A2
Bedstone 28 C1
Bedwas 18 E3
Bedwellty 18 E1
Bedworth 41 F7
Beeby 41 J5
Beech *Hants.* 11 H1
Beech *Staffs.* 40 A2
Beech Hill 21 K5
Beechamwell 44 B5
Beechingstoke 20 D6
Beedon 21 H4
Beeford 59 H4
Beeley 50 E6
Beelsby 53 F2
Beenham 21 J5
Beer 8 B6
Beer Hackett 8 E3
Beercrocombe 8 C2
Beesands 5 J6
Beesby 53 H4
Beeson 5 J6
Beeston *Beds.* 32 E4
Beeston *Ches.* 48 E7
Beeston *Norf.* 44 D4
Beeston *Notts.* 41 H2
Beeston *W.Yorks.* 57 H6
Beeston Regis 45 F1
Beeston St. Lawrence 45 H3
Beeswing 65 J4
Beetham 55 H2
Beetley 44 D4
Began 19 F3
Begbroke 31 F7
Begelly 16 E4
Beggshill 90 D1
Beguildy 28 A1
Beighton *Norf.* 45 H5
Beighton *S.Yorks.* 51 G4
Beith 74 B5
Bekesbourne 15 G2
Belaugh 45 G4
Belbroughton 29 J1
Belchamp Otten 34 C4
Belchamp St. Paul 34 B4
Belchamp Walter 34 C4
Belchford 53 F5
Belford 77 K7
Belgrave 41 H5
Belhaven 76 E3
Belhelvie 91 H3
Belhinnie 90 C2
Bell Bar 23 F1
Bell Busk 56 E4
Bell End 29 J1
Bellabeg 90 B3
Belladrum 96 C7
Bellanoch 73 G1
Bellasize 58 E7
Bellaty 82 D2
Belleau 53 H5
Bellehiglash 89 J1
Bellerby 62 C7
Bellever 5 G3
Belliehill 83 G1
Bellingdon 22 C1
Bellingham 70 D5
Belloch 72 E7
Bellochantuy 72 E7
Bells Yew Green 13 K3
Bellshill *N.Lan.* 75 F5
Bellshill *Northumb.* 77 K7
Bellside 75 G5
Bellsquarry 75 J4
Belluton 19 K5
Belmaduthy 96 D6
Belmesthorpe 42 D4
Belmont *B'burn.* 49 F1
Belmont *Gt.Lon.* 23 F5
Belmont *Shet.* 108 E2
Belowda 3 G2
Belper 41 F1
Belper Lane End 41 F1
Belsay 71 G6
Belsford 5 H5
Belstead 35 F4
Belston 67 H1
Belstone 6 E6
Belstone Corner 6 E6
Belsyde 75 H3
Belthorn 56 C7
Beltinge 25 H5
Beltoft 52 B2
Belton *Leics.* 41 G3
Belton *Lincs.* 42 C2
Belton *N.Lincs.* 51 K2
Belton *Norf.* 45 J5
Belton *Rut.* 42 B5
Beltring 23 K7
Belvedere 23 H4
Belvoir 42 B2
Bembridge 11 H6
Bemersyde 76 D7
Bempton 59 H2
Ben Alder Cottage 81 F1
Ben Alder Lodge 88 C7
Benacre 45 K7
Benbecula (Baile a' Mhanaich) Airport 92 C6
Benbuie 68 C4
Benderloch 80 A4
Bendish 32 E6
Benenden 14 D4
Benfield 64 D4
Bengate 45 H3
Bengeo 33 G7
Benholm 83 K1
Beningbrough 58 B4
Benington *Herts.* 33 F6
Benington *Lincs.* 43 G1
Benington Sea End 43 H1
Benllech 46 D4
Benmore *Arg. & B.* 73 K2
Benmore *Stir.* 81 F5
Bennacott 4 C1
Bennan Cottage 65 G3
Benniworth 53 F4
Benover 14 C3
Benson 21 K2
Benthall *Northumb.* 71 H1
Benthall *Shrop.* 39 F5
Bentham 29 J7
Benthoul 91 G4
Bentley *E.Riding* 59 G6
Bentley *Hants.* 22 A7
Bentley *S.Yorks.* 51 H2
Bentley *Suff.* 35 F5
Bentley *Warks.* 40 E6
Bentley Heath 30 C1
Benton 6 E2
Benton Square 71 J6
Bentpath 69 J4
Bentworth 21 K7
Benvie 82 E4
Benville Lane 8 E4
Benwick 43 G7
Beoley 30 B2
Bepton 12 B5
Berden 33 H6
Bere Alston 4 E4
Bere Ferrers 4 E4
Bere Regis 9 H5
Berea 16 A2
Berepper 2 D6
Bergh Apton 45 H5
Berinsfield 21 J2
Berkeley 19 K2
Berkhamsted 22 C1
Berkley 20 B7
Berkswell 30 D1
Bermondsey 23 G4
Bernera 86 E2
Berners Roding 24 C1
Bernice 73 K1
Bernisdale 93 K6
Berrick Salome 21 K2
Berriedale 105 G6
Berriew (Aberriw) 38 A5
Berrington *Northumb.* 77 J6
Berrington *Shrop.* 38 E5
Berrow 19 F6
Berrow Green 29 G3
Berry Down Cross 6 D1
Berry Hill *Glos.* 28 E7
Berry Hill *Pembs.* 16 D1
Berry Pomeroy 5 J4
Berryhillock 98 D4
Berrynarbor 6 D1
Bersham 38 C1
Berstane 107 D6
Berwick 13 J6
Berwick Bassett 20 D4
Berwick Hill 71 G6
Berwick St. James 10 B1
Berwick St. John 9 J2
Berwick St. Leonard 9 J1
Berwick-upon-Tweed 77 H5
Bescar 48 C1
Besford *Shrop.* 38 E3
Besford *Worcs.* 29 J4
Bessacarr 51 J2
Bessels Leigh 21 H1
Bessingby 59 H3
Bessingham 45 F2
Best Beech Hill 13 K3
Besthorpe *Norf.* 44 E6
Besthorpe *Notts.* 52 B6
Beswick 59 G5
Betchworth 23 F6
Bethania *Cere.* 26 E2
Bethania *Gwyn.* 37 G1
Bethel *Gwyn.* 46 D6
Bethel *Gwyn.* 37 J1
Bethel *I.o.A.* 46 B5
Bethersden 14 E3
Bethesda *Gwyn.* 46 E6
Bethesda *Pembs.* 16 D3
Bethlehem 17 K2
Bethnal Green 23 G3
Betley 39 G1
Betsham 24 C4
Betteshanger 15 J2
Bettiscombe 8 C5
Bettisfield 38 D2
Betton *Shrop.* 38 C5
Betton *Shrop.* 39 F2
Bettws 19 F2
Bettws Bledrws 26 E3
Bettws Cedewain 38 A6
Bettws Evan 26 C4
Bettws Gwerfil Goch 37 K1
Bettws Newydd 19 G1
Bettws-y-crwyn 38 B7
Bettyhill 104 C2
Betws *Bridgend* 18 C3
Betws *Carmar.* 17 K3
Betws Disserth 28 A3
Betws Garmon 46 D7
Betws-y-coed 47 F7
Betws-yn-Rhos 47 H5
Beulah *Cere.* 26 B4
Beulah *Powys* 27 J3
Bevendean 13 G6
Bevercotes 51 K5
Beverley 59 G6
Beverstone 20 B2
Bevington 19 K2
Bewaldeth 60 D3
Bewcastle 70 A6
Bewdley 29 G1
Bewerley 57 G3
Bewholme 59 H5
Bewley Common 20 C5
Bexhill 14 C7
Bexley 23 H4
Bexleyheath 23 H4
Bexwell 44 A5
Beyton 34 D2
Beyton Green 34 D2
Bhalamus 100 E7
Bhaltos 100 C4
Bhatarsaigh (Vatersay) 84 B5
Biallaid 88 E5
Bibury 20 E1
Bicester 31 G6
Bickenhall 8 B3
Bickenhill 40 D7
Bicker 43 F2
Bickerstaffe 48 D2
Bickerton *Ches.* 48 E7
Bickerton *N.Yorks.* 57 K4
Bickford 40 A4
Bickham Bridge 5 H5
Bickham House 7 H7
Bickington *Devon* 6 D2
Bickington *Devon* 5 H3
Bickleigh *Devon* 5 F4
Bickleigh *Devon* 7 H5
Bickleton 6 D2
Bickley 23 H5
Bickley Moss 38 E1
Bickley Town 38 E1
Bicknacre 24 D1
Bicknoller 7 K2
Bicknor 14 D2
Bickton 10 C3
Bicton *Shrop.* 38 D4
Bicton *Shrop.* 38 B7
Bicton Heath 38 D4
Bidborough 23 J7
Biddenden 14 D4
Biddenham 32 D4
Biddestone 20 B4
Biddisham 19 G6
Biddlesden 31 H4
Biddlestone 70 E3
Biddulph 49 H7
Biddulph Moor 49 J7
Bideford 6 C3
Bidford-on-Avon 30 B3
Bidston 48 B3
Bielby 58 D5
Bieldside 91 G4
Bierley *I.o.W.* 11 G7
Bierley *W.Yorks.* 57 G6
Bierton 32 B7
Big Sand 94 D4
Bigbury 5 G6
Bigbury-on-Sea 5 G6
Bigby 52 D2
Bigert Mire 60 C7
Biggar *Cumb.* 54 E3
Biggar *S.Lan.* 75 J7
Biggin *Derbys.* 40 E1
Biggin *Derbys.* 50 D7
Biggin *N.Yorks.* 58 B6
Biggin Hill 23 H6
Biggings 109 A6
Biggleswade 32 E4
Bigholms 69 J5
Bighouse 104 D2
Bighton 11 H1
Biglands 60 D1
Bignor 12 C5
Bigrigg 60 B5
Bigton 109 C10
Bilberry 4 A4
Bilborough 41 H1
Bilbrook *Som.* 7 J1
Bilbrook *Staffs.* 40 A5
Bilbrough 58 B5
Bilbster 105 H3
Bildershaw 62 C4
Bildeston 34 D4
Billericay 24 C2
Billesdon 42 A5
Billesley 30 C3
Billholm 69 H4
Billingborough 42 E2
Billinge 48 E2
Billingford *Norf.* 35 F1
Billingford *Norf.* 44 E3
Billingham 63 F4
Billinghay 52 E7
Billingley 51 G2
Billingshurst 12 D4
Billingsley 39 G7
Billington *Beds.* 32 C6
Billington *Lancs.* 56 C6
Billockby 45 J4
Billy Row 62 C3
Bilsborrow 55 J5
Bilsby 53 H5
Bilsdean 77 F3
Bilsham 12 C6
Bilsington 15 F4
Bilsthorpe 51 J6
Bilston *Midloth.* 76 A4
Bilston *W.Mid.* 40 B6
Bilstone 41 F5
Bilting 15 F3
Bilton *E.Riding* 59 H6
Bilton *N.Yorks.* 57 K4
Bilton *N.Yorks.* 57 J4
Bilton *Northumb.* 71 H2
Bilton *Warks.* 31 F1
Bimbister 107 C6
Binbrook 53 F3
Bincombe 9 F6
Bindal 97 G3
Binegar 19 K7
Bines Green 12 E5
Binfield 22 B4
Binfield Heath 22 A4
Bingfield 70 E6
Bingham 42 A2
Bingham's Melcombe 9 G4
Bingley 57 G6
Binham 44 D2
Binley *Hants.* 21 H6
Binley *W.Mid.* 30 E1
Binniehill 75 G3
Binsoe 57 H2
Binstead 11 G5
Binsted *Hants.* 22 A7
Binsted *W.Suss.* 12 C6
Binton 30 C3
Bintree 44 E3
Binweston 38 B5
Birch *Essex* 34 D7
Birch *Gt.Man.* 49 H2
Birch Green 34 D7
Birch Heath 48 E6
Birch Vale 50 C4
Bircham Newton 44 B2
Bircham Tofts 44 B2
Birchanger 33 J6
Bircher 28 D2
Birchfield 96 B2
Birchgrove *Cardiff* 18 E3
Birchgrove *Swan.* 18 A2
Birchington 25 J5
Birchover 50 E6
Birchwood 49 F3
Bircotes 51 J3
Bird End 40 C6
Birdbrook 34 B4
Birdfield 73 H1
Birdham 12 B7
Birdingbury 31 F2
Birdlip 29 J7
Birdsall 58 E3
Birdsgreen 39 G7
Birdsmoor Gate 8 C4
Birdwell 51 F2
Birdwood 29 G7
Birgham 77 F7
Birichen 96 E2
Birkby 62 E6
Birkdale *Mersey.* 48 C1
Birkdale *N.Yorks.* 61 K6
Birkenhead 48 C4
Birkenhills 99 F6
Birkenshaw 57 H7
Birkhall 90 B5
Birkhill *Angus* 82 E4
Birkhill *Sc.Bord.* 76 D6
Birkhill *Sc.Bord.* 69 H2
Birkin 58 B7
Birkwood 75 G7
Birley 28 D3
Birley Carr 51 F3
Birling *Kent* 24 C5
Birling *Northumb.* 71 H3
Birling Gap 13 J7
Birlingham 29 J4
Birmingham 40 C7
Birmingham International Airport 40 D7
Birnam 82 B3
Birsay 106 B5
Birse 90 D5
Birsemore 90 D5
Birstall 41 H5
Birstall Smithies 57 H7
Birstwith 57 H4
Birthorpe 42 E2
Birtley *Here.* 28 C2
Birtley *Northumb.* 70 D6
Birtley *T. & W.* 62 D1
Birts Street 29 G5
Bisbrooke 42 B6
Bish Mill 7 F3
Bisham 22 B3
Bishampton 29 J3
Bishop Auckland 62 D3
Bishop Burton 59 F6
Bishop Middleham 62 E3
Bishop Monkton 57 J3
Bishop Norton 52 C3
Bishop Sutton 19 J6
Bishop Thornton 57 H3
Bishop Wilton 58 D4
Bishopbridge 52 D3
Bishopbriggs 74 E4
Bishopmill 97 K5
Bishops Cannings 20 D5
Bishop's Castle 38 C7
Bishop's Caundle 9 F3
Bishop's Cleeve 29 J6
Bishop's Frome 29 F4
Bishop's Green 33 K7
Bishop's Hull 8 B2
Bishop's Itchington 30 E3
Bishop's Lydeard 7 K3
Bishop's Nympton 7 F3
Bishop's Offley 39 G3
Bishop's Stortford 33 H6
Bishop's Sutton 11 H1
Bishop's Tachbrook 30 E2
Bishop's Tawton 6 D2
Bishop's Waltham 11 G3
Bishop's Wood 40 A5
Bishopsbourne 15 G2
Bishopsteignton 5 K3
Bishopstoke 11 F3
Bishopston 17 J6
Bishopstone *Bucks.* 32 B7
Bishopstone *E.Suss.* 13 H6
Bishopstone *Here.* 28 D4
Bishopstone *Swin.* 21 F3
Bishopstone *Wilts.* 10 B2
Bishopstrow 20 B7
Bishopswood 8 B3
Bishopsworth 19 J5
Bishopthorpe 58 B5
Bishopton *Darl.* 62 E4
Bishopton *Renf.* 74 C3
Bishton 19 G3
Bisley *Glos.* 20 C1
Bisley *Surr.* 22 C6
Bispham 55 G5
Bissoe 2 E4
Bisterne 10 C4
Bisterne Close 10 D4
Bitchfield 42 C3
Bittadon 6 D1
Bittaford 5 G5
Bittering 44 D4
Bitterley 28 E1
Bitterne 11 F3
Bitteswell 41 H7
Bitton 19 K5
Biwmaris (Beaumaris) 46 E5
Bix 22 A3
Bixter 109 C7
Blaby 41 H6
Black Bourton 21 F1
Black Callerton 71 G7
Black Clauchrie 67 G5
Black Corries Lodge 80 D2
Black Cross 3 G2
Black Dog 7 G5
Black Heddon 71 F6
Black Marsh 38 C6
Black Mount 80 D3
Black Notley 34 B6
Black Pill 17 K5
Black Torrington 6 C5
Blackacre 69 F4
Blackadder 77 G5
Blackawton 5 J5
Blackborough 7 J5
Blackborough End 44 A4
Blackboys 13 J4
Blackbraes *Aber.* 91 G3
Blackbraes *Falk.* 75 H3
Blackbrook 39 G2
Blackburn *Aber.* 91 G3
Blackburn *B'burn.* 56 B7
Blackburn *W.Loth.* 75 H4
Blackbushe 22 A6
Blackcastle 97 F6
Blackchambers 91 F3
Blackcraig *D. & G.* 64 E4
Blackcraig *D. & G.* 68 C5
Blackden Heath 49 G5
Blackdog 91 H3
Blackdown *Devon* 5 F3
Blackdown *Dorset* 8 C4
Blackfield 11 F4
Blackford *Aber.* 90 E1
Blackford *Cumb.* 69 J7
Blackford *P. & K.* 81 K7
Blackford *Som.* 9 F2
Blackford *Som.* 19 H7
Blackfordby 41 F4
Blackgang 11 F7
Blackhall 76 A3
Blackhall Colliery 63 F3
Blackhall Rocks 63 F3
Blackham 13 J3
Blackheath *Essex* 34 D6
Blackheath *Gt.Lon.* 23 G4
Blackheath *Suff.* 35 J1
Blackheath *Surr.* 22 D7
Blackheath *W.Mid.* 40 B7
Blackhill *Aber.* 99 J5
Blackhill *Aber.* 99 J6
Blackhillock 98 C6
Blackhills 97 K6
Blackland 20 D5
Blacklunans 82 C1
Blackmill 18 C3
Blackmoor *Hants.* 11 J1
Blackmoor *Som.* 7 K4
Blackmoor Gate 6 E1
Blackmore 24 C1
Blackmore End *Essex* 34 B5
Blackmore End *Herts.* 32 E7
Blackness *Aber.* 90 E5
Blackness *Falk.* 75 J3
Blackness *High.* 105 H5
Blacknest 22 A7
Blacko 56 D5
Blackpool 55 G6
Blackpool Airport 55 G6
Blackpool Gate 70 A6
Blackridge 75 G4
Blackrock *Arg. & B.* 72 B4
Blackrock *Mon.* 28 B7
Blackrod 49 F1
Blackshaw 69 F7
Blackshaw Head 56 E7
Blacksmith's Corner 34 E5
Blackstone 13 F5
Blackthorn 31 H7
Blackthorpe 34 D2
Blacktoft 58 E7
Blacktop 91 G4
Blacktown 19 F3
Blackwater *Cornw.* 2 E4
Blackwater *Hants.* 22 B6
Blackwater *I.o.W.* 11 G6
Blackwater *Suff.* 35 J1
Blackwaterfoot 66 D1
Blackwell *Darl.* 62 D5
Blackwell *Derbys.* 50 D5
Blackwell *Derbys.* 51 G7
Blackwell *Warks.* 30 D4
Blackwell *Worcs.* 29 J1
Blackwells End 29 G6
Blackwood *Caerp.* 18 E2
Blackwood *D. & G.* 68 E5
Blackwood *S.Lan.* 75 F6
Blackwood Hill 49 J7
Blacon 48 C6
Bladbean 15 G3
Blades 62 A7
Bladnoch 64 E5
Bladon 31 F7
Blaen Dyryn 27 J5
Blaen-y-coed 17 G2
Blaenannerch 26 B4
Blaenau Dolwyddelan 46 E7
Blaenau Ffestiniog 37 F1
Blaenavon 19 F1
Blaenawey 28 B7
Blaencwm 18 C1
Blaenffos 16 E1
Blaengarw 18 C2
Blaengweche 17 K3
Blaengwrach 18 B1
Blaengwynfi 18 B2
Blaenos 27 G5

Blaenpennal	27	F2
Blaenplwyf	26	E1
Blaenporth	26	B4
Blaenrhondda	18	C1
Blaenwaun	17	F2
Blagdon N.Som.	19	H6
Blagdon Torbay	5	J4
Blagdon Hill	8	B3
Blaich	87	G7
Blaina	19	F1
Blair	74	B6
Blair Atholl	81	K1
Blair Drummond	75	F1
Blairannaich	80	E7
Blairbuie	73	K3
Blairgowrie	82	C3
Blairhall	75	J2
Blairhoyle	81	H7
Blairhullichan	75	H1
Blairkip	74	D7
Blairlogie	75	G1
Blairmore Arg. & B.	73	K2
Blairmore High.	96	E1
Blairmore High.	102	D2
Blairnairn	74	B2
Blairnamarrow	89	K3
Blairpark	74	A5
Blairquhan	67	H3
Blairquhosh	74	D2
Blair's Ferry	73	H4
Blairshinnoch	98	E4
Blairuskinmore	81	F7
Blairvadach	74	A2
Blairydryne	91	F5
Blairythan Cottage	91	H1
Blaisdon	29	G7
Blake End	33	K6
Blakebrook	29	H1
Blakedown	29	H1
Blakelaw Sc.Bord.	77	F7
Blakelaw T. & W.	71	H7
Blakemere	28	C4
Blakeney Glos.	19	K1
Blakeney Norf.	44	E1
Blakenhall Ches.	39	G1
Blakenhall W.Mid.	40	B6
Blakeshall	40	A7
Blakesley	31	H3
Blanchland	61	K1
Bland Hill	57	H4
Blandford Camp	9	J4
Blandford Forum	9	H4
Blandford St. Mary	9	H4
Blanefield	74	D3
Blankney	52	D6
Blar a' Chaorainn	80	C1
Blargie	88	D5
Blarglas	74	B2
Blarmachfoldach	80	B1
Blarnalevoch	95	H2
Blashford	10	C4
Blaston	42	B6
Blathaisbhal	92	D4
Blatherwycke	42	C6
Blawith	55	F1
Blaxhall	35	H3
Blaxton	51	J2
Blaydon	71	G7
Bleadney	19	H7
Bleadon	19	G6
Bleak Hey Nook	50	C2
Blean	25	H5
Bleasby	42	A1
Bleatarn	61	J5
Blebocraigs	83	F6
Bleddfa	28	B2
Bledington	30	D6
Bledlow	22	A1
Bledlow Ridge	22	A2
Blencarn	61	H3
Blencogo	60	C2
Blencow	61	F3
Blendworth	11	J3
Blennerhasset	60	C2
Blervie Castle	97	H6
Bletchingdon	31	G7
Bletchingley	23	G6
Bletchley M.K.	32	B5
Bletchley Shrop.	39	F2
Bletherston	16	D2
Bletsoe	32	D3
Blewbury	21	J3
Blickling	45	F3
Blidworth	51	H7
Blindburn Aber.	91	H1
Blindburn Northumb.	70	D2
Blindcrake	60	C3
Blindley Heath	23	G7
Blisland	4	B3
Bliss Gate	29	G1
Blissford	10	C3
Blisworth	31	J3
Blithbury	40	C3
Blitterlees	60	C1
Blo Norton	34	E1
Blockley	30	C5
Blofield	45	H5
Blore	40	D1
Blossomfield	30	C1
Blount's Green	40	C2
Bloxham	31	F5
Bloxholm	52	D7
Bloxwich	40	B5
Bloxworth	9	H5
Blubberhouses	57	G4
Blue Anchor Cornw.	3	G3
Blue Anchor Som.	7	J1
Blue Bell Hill	24	D5
Bluewater	23	J4
Blundeston	45	K6
Blunham	32	E3
Blunsdon St. Andrew	20	E2
Bluntisham	33	G1
Blunts	4	D4
Blyborough	52	C3
Blyford	35	J1
Blymhill	40	A4
Blyth Northumb.	71	J5
Blyth Notts.	51	J4
Blyth Bridge	75	K6
Blythburgh	35	J1
Blythe Bridge	40	B1
Blythe Marsh	40	B1
Blyton	52	B3
Boarhills	83	G6
Boarhunt	11	H4
Boars Hill	21	H1
Boarshead	13	J3
Boarstall	31	H7
Boarzell	14	C5
Boasley Cross	6	D6
Boat o' Brig	98	B5
Boat of Garten	89	G3
Boath	96	C4
Bobbing	24	E5
Bobbington	40	A6
Bobbingworth	23	J1
Bocaddon	4	B5
Bochastle	81	H7
Bockhampton	21	G4
Docking	34	B6
Bocking Churchstreet	34	B6
Boconnoc	4	B4
Boddam Aber.	99	K6
Boddam Shet.	109	G9
Boddington	29	H6
Bodedern	46	B4
Bodelwyddan	47	J5
Bodenham Here.	28	E3
Bodenham Wilts.	10	C2
Bodenham Moor	28	E3
Bodesbeck	69	G3
Bodewryd	46	B3
Bodfari	47	J5
Bodffordd	46	C5
Bodfuan	36	C2
Bodham Street	45	F1
Bodiam	14	C5
Bodicote	31	F5
Bodieve	3	G1
Bodinnick	4	B5
Bodior	46	A5
Bodle Street Green	13	K5
Bodmin	4	A4
Bodney	44	C6
Bodorgan	46	B6
Bodsham Green	15	G3
Bodwen	4	A4
Bogallan	96	D6
Bogbain	96	E7
Bogbrae	91	J1
Bogbuie	96	C6
Bogend	74	B7
Bogfern	90	D4
Bogfields	90	D4
Bogfold	99	G5
Boghead Aber.	98	E5
Boghead E.Ayr.	68	B1
Boghead S.Lan.	75	F6
Boghole Farm	97	G6
Bogmoor	98	B4
Bogniebrae	98	D6
Bognor Regis	12	C7
Bograxie	91	F3
Bogroy	89	G2
Bogside	75	H1
Bogston	90	B4
Bogton	98	E5
Bogue	68	B5
Bohenie	87	J6
Bohortha	3	F5
Bohuntine	87	J6
Boirseam	93	F3
Bojewyan	2	A5
Bolam	62	C4
Bolberry	5	G7
Bold Heath	48	E4
Bolderwood	10	D4
Boldon	71	J7
Boldre	10	E5
Boldron	62	B5
Bole	51	K4
Bolehill	50	E7
Boleigh	2	B6
Boleside	76	C7
Bolfracks	81	K3
Bolgoed	17	K4
Bolham	7	H4
Bolham Water	7	K4
Bolingey	2	E3
Bollington	49	J5
Bolney	13	F4
Bolnhurst	32	D3
Bolshan	83	H2
Bolsover	51	G5
Bolsterstone	50	E3
Bolstone	28	E5
Boltby	57	K1
Bolter End	22	A2
Bolton Cumb.	61	H4
Bolton E.Loth.	76	D3
Bolton E.Riding	58	D4
Bolton Gt.Man.	49	G2
Bolton Northumb.	71	G2
Bolton Abbey	57	F4
Bolton Bridge	57	F4
Bolton by Bowland	56	C5
Bolton-le-Sands	55	H3
Bolton Low Houses	60	D2
Bolton-on-Swale	62	D7
Bolton Percy	58	B5
Bolton upon Dearne	51	G2
Boltonfellend	69	K7
Boltongate	60	D2
Bolventor	4	B3
Bombie	65	H5
Bomere Heath	38	D4
Bon-y-maen	17	K5
Bonar Bridge	96	D2
Bonawe	80	B4
Bonawe Quarries	80	B4
Bonby	52	D1
Boncath	17	F1
Bonchester Bridge	70	A2
Bonchurch	11	G7
Bondleigh	6	E5
Bonehill	40	D5
Bo'ness	75	H2
Bonhill	74	B3
Boningale	40	A5
Bonjedward	70	B1
Bonkle	75	G5
Bonnington	15	F4
Bonnybank	82	E7
Bonnybridge	75	G2
Bonnykelly	99	G5
Bonnyrigg	76	B4
Bonnyton Aber.	90	E1
Bonnyton Angus	83	G4
Bonnyton Angus	83	H2
Bonnyton Angus	82	E4
Bonsall	50	E7
Bont	28	C7
Bont Dolgadfan	37	H5
Bont-goch (Elerch)	37	F7
Bont Newydd	37	G3
Bontddu	37	F4
Bontnewydd	46	C6
Bontuchel	47	J7
Bonvilston	18	D4
Boohay	5	K5
Booker	22	B2
Booley	38	E3
Boor	94	E3
Boosbeck	63	H5
Boot	60	C6
Booth Wood	50	C1
Boothby Graffoe	52	C7
Boothby Pagnell	42	C2
Boothstown	49	G2
Boothtown	57	F7
Boothville	31	J2
Bootle Cumb.	54	E1
Bootle Mersey.	48	C3
Booton	45	F3
Boquhan	74	D2
Boraston	29	F1
Bordeaux	3	J5
Borden	24	E5
Bordley	56	E3
Bordon	11	J1
Boreham Essex	24	D1
Boreham Wilts.	20	B7
Boreham Street	13	K5
Borehamwood	22	E2
Boreland D. & G.	69	G4
Boreland D. & G.	64	D4
Boreland Stir.	81	G4
Boreraig	93	G6
Borgh W.Isles	92	E3
Borgh W.Isles	84	B4
Borghastan	100	D3
Borgie	103	J3
Borgue D. & G.	65	G6
Borgue High.	105	G6
Borley	34	C4
Bornais	84	C2
Borness	65	G6
Borough Green	23	K6
Boroughbridge	57	J3
Borras Head	48	C7
Borreraig	93	G6
Borrowash	41	G2
Borrowby N.Yorks.	57	K1
Borrowby N.Yorks.	63	J5
Borrowdale	60	D5
Borrowfield	91	G5
Borstal	24	D5
Borth	37	F7
Borth-y-Gest	36	E2
Borthwick	76	B5
Borthwickbrae	69	K2
Borthwickshiels	69	K2
Borve	93	K7
Borwick	55	J2
Bosavern	2	A5
Bosbury	29	F4
Boscastle	4	B1
Boscombe Bourne.	10	C5
Boscombe Wilts.	10	D1
Boscoppa	4	A5
Bosham	12	B6
Bosherston	16	C5
Bosley	49	J6
Bossall	58	D3
Bossiney	4	A2
Bossingham	15	G3
Bossington Hants.	10	E1
Bossington Som.	7	G1
Bostock Green	49	F6
Boston	43	G1
Boston Spa	57	K5
Boswinger	3	G4
Botallack	2	A5
Botany Bay	23	F2
Botarua	92	C4
Botcheston	41	G5
Botesdale	34	E1
Bothal	71	H5
Bothamsall	51	J5
Bothel	60	C3
Bothenhampton	8	D5
Bothwell	75	F5
Botley Bucks.	22	C1
Botley Hants.	11	G3
Botley Oxon.	21	H1
Botloe's Green	29	G6
Botolph Claydon	31	J6
Botolphs	12	E6
Bottacks	96	B5
Bottesford Leics.	42	B2
Bottesford N.Lincs.	52	C2
Bottisham	33	J2
Bottom Head	56	B3
Bottomcraig	82	E5
Botusfleming	4	E4
Botwnnog	36	B2
Bough Beech	23	H7
Boughrood	28	A5
Boughspring	19	J2
Boughton Norf.	44	A5
Boughton Northants.	31	J2
Boughton Notts.	51	J6
Boughton Aluph	15	F3
Boughton Green	14	C2
Boughton Lees	15	F3
Boughton Malherbe	14	D3
Boughton Street	15	F2
Boulby	63	J5
Bouldon	38	E7
Boulmer	71	H2
Boulston	16	C3
Boultenstone Hotel	90	C3
Boultham	52	C6
Bourn	33	G3
Bournbrook	40	C7
Bourne	42	D3
Bourne End Beds.	32	C4
Bourne End Bucks.	22	B3
Bourne End Herts.	22	D1
Bournebridge	23	J2
Bournemouth	10	B5
Bournemouth International Airport	10	C5
Bournes Green	20	C1
Bournheath	29	J1
Bournmoor	62	E1
Bournville	40	C1
Bourton Dorset	9	G1
Bourton N.Som.	19	G5
Bourton Oxon.	21	F3
Bourton Shrop.	38	E6
Bourton on Dunsmore	31	F1
Bourton-on-the-Hill	30	C5
Bourton-on-the-Water	30	C6
Bousd	78	D1
Boustead Hill	60	D1
Bouth	55	G1
Bouthwaite	57	G2
Bovain	81	G4
Boveney	22	C4
Boveridge	10	B3
Boverton	18	C5
Bovey Tracey	5	J3
Bovingdon	22	D1
Bovinger	22	D1
Bovington Camp	9	H6
Bow Devon	7	F5
Bow Devon	5	J5
Bow Ork.	107	C8
Bow Brickhill	32	C5
Bow of Fife	82	E6
Bow Street	37	F7
Bowbank	62	A4
Bowburn	62	E3
Bowcombe	11	F6
Bowd	7	K7
Bowden Devon	5	J6
Bowden Sc.Bord.	76	D7
Bowden Hill	20	C5
Bowdon	49	G4
Bower	70	C7
Bower Hinton	8	D3
Bowerchalke	10	B2
Bowerhill	20	C5
Bowermadden	105	H2
Bowers Gifford	24	D3
Bowershall	75	J1
Bowertower	105	H2
Bowes	62	A5
Bowgreave	55	H5
Bowhead Bridge	55	H1
Bowley	28	E3
Bowlhead Green	12	C3
Bowling	74	C3
Bowling Bank	38	C1
Bowlish	19	K7
Bowmanstead	60	E7
Bowmore	72	B5
Bowness-on-Solway	69	H7
Bowness-on-Windermere	61	F7
Bowsden	77	H6
Bowside Lodge	104	D2
Bowthorpe	45	F5
Bowtrees	75	H2
Box Glos.	20	B1
Box Wilts.	20	B5
Box End	32	D4
Boxbush	29	G7
Boxford Suff.	34	D4
Boxford W.Berks.	21	H4
Boxgrove	12	C6
Boxley	14	C2
Boxmoor	22	D1
Boxted Essex	34	D5
Boxted Suff.	34	C3
Boxted Cross	34	E5
Boxworth	33	G2
Boxworth End	33	G2
Boyden Gate	25	J5
Boydston	74	C7
Boylestone	40	D2
Boyndie	98	E4
Boynton	59	H3
Boysack	83	H3
Bozeat	32	C3
Braaid	54	C6
Braal Castle	105	G2
Brabling Green	35	G2
Brabourne	15	F3
Brabourne Lees	15	F3
Brabster	105	J2
Bracadale	85	J1
Braceborough	42	D4
Bracebridge	52	C6
Bracebridge Heath	52	C6
Braceby	42	D2
Bracewell	56	D5
Brachla	88	C1
Brackenber	61	J4
Brackenfield	51	F7
Brackens	99	F5
Bracklach	90	B2
Bracklamore	99	G5
Brackletter	87	H6
Brackley Arg. & B.	73	G2
Brackley High.	97	F6
Brackley Northants.	31	G5
Bracknell	22	B5
Braco	81	K7
Bracobrae	98	D5
Bracon Ash	45	F6
Bracora	86	D5
Bracorina	86	D5
Bradbourne	50	E7
Bradda	54	B6
Bradden	31	H4
Bradenham	22	B2
Bradenstoke	20	D3
Bradfield Devon	7	J5
Bradfield Essex	35	F5
Bradfield Norf.	45	G2
Bradfield W.Berks.	21	K4
Bradfield Combust	34	C3
Bradfield Green	49	F7
Bradfield Heath	35	F6
Bradfield St. Clare	34	D3
Bradfield St. George	34	D3
Bradford Devon	6	C5
Bradford Northumb.	77	K7
Bradford W.Yorks.	57	G6
Bradford Abbas	8	E3
Bradford Leigh	20	B5
Bradford-on-Avon	20	B5
Bradford-on-Tone	7	K3
Bradford Peverell	9	F5
Brading	11	H6
Bradley Derbys.	40	E1
Bradley Hants.	21	K7
Bradley N.E.Lincs.	53	F2
Bradley N.Yorks.	57	F1
Bradley Staffs.	40	A4
Bradley W.Mid.	40	B6
Bradley Green	29	J2
Bradley in the Moors	40	C1
Bradley Stoke	19	K3
Bradmore Notts.	41	H2
Bradmore W.Mid.	40	A6
Bradninch	7	J5
Bradnop	50	C7
Bradpole	8	D5
Bradshaw	49	G1
Bradstone	6	B7
Bradwall Green	49	G6
Bradwell Derbys.	50	D4
Bradwell Essex	34	C6
Bradwell M.K.	32	B5
Bradwell Norf.	45	K5
Bradwell Grove	21	F1
Bradwell-on-Sea	25	F1
Bradwell Waterside	25	F1
Bradworthy	6	B4
Brae D. & G.	65	J3
Brae High.	96	B1
Brae Shet.	109	C6
Braeantra	96	C4
Braedownie	89	K7
Braefoot	99	F6
Braegrum	82	B5
Braehead Moray	98	B6
Braehead Ork.	107	E7
Braehead Ork.	106	D3
Braehead S.Lan.	75	G7
Braehead S.Lan.	75	H5
Braehead of Lunan	83	H2
Braehoulland	108	B5
Braeleny	81	H6
Braemar	89	J5
Braemore High.	96	C1
Braemore High.	105	F5
Braemore High.	95	H4
Braenaloin	89	K5
Braes of Enzie	98	B5
Braes of Foss	81	J2
Braes of Ullapool	95	H2
Braeswick	106	F4
Braeval	81	G7
Brafferton Darl.	62	D4
Brafferton N.Yorks.	57	K2
Brafield-on-the-Green	32	B3
Bragar	100	E3
Bragbury End	33	F6
Bragleenbeg	80	A5
Braichmelyn	46	E6
Braides	55	H4
Braidwood	75	G6
Braigo	72	A4
Brailsford	40	E1
Braintree	34	B6
Braiseworth	35	F1
Braishfield	10	E2
Braithwaite Cumb.	60	D4
Braithwaite S.Yorks.	51	J1
Braithwell	51	H3
Bramber	12	E5
Brambletye	13	H3
Bramcote	41	H2
Bramdean	11	H2
Bramerton	45	G5
Bramfield Herts.	33	F7
Bramfield Suff.	35	H1
Bramford	35	F4
Bramhall	49	H4
Bramham	57	K5
Bramhope	57	H5
Bramley Hants.	21	K6
Bramley S.Yorks.	51	G3
Bramley Surr.	22	D7
Bramling	15	H2
Brampford Speke	7	H6
Brampton Cambs.	33	F1
Brampton Cumb.	70	A7
Brampton Cumb.	61	H4
Brampton Derbys.	51	F5
Brampton Lincs.	52	B5
Brampton Norf.	45	G3
Brampton S.Yorks.	51	G2
Brampton Suff.	45	J7
Brampton Abbotts	29	F6
Brampton Ash	42	A7
Brampton Bryan	28	C1
Brampton en le Morthen	51	G4
Bramshall	40	C2
Bramshaw	10	D3
Bramshill	22	A5
Bramshott	12	B3
Bramwell	8	D2
Bran End	33	K6
Branault	79	G1
Brancaster	44	B1
Brancaster Staithe	44	B1
Brancepeth	62	D3
Branchill	97	H6
Brand Green	29	G6
Branderburgh	97	K4
Brandesburton	59	H5
Brandeston	35	G2
Brandis Corner	6	C5
Brandiston	45	F3
Brandon Dur.	62	D3
Brandon Lincs.	42	C1
Brandon Northumb.	71	F2
Brandon Suff.	44	B7
Brandon Warks.	31	F1
Brandon Bank	44	A7
Brandon Creek	44	A6
Brandon Parva	44	E5
Brandsby	58	B2
Brandy Wharf	52	D3
Brane	2	A6
Branksome	10	B5
Branksome Park	10	B5
Bransby	52	B5
Branscombe	7	K7
Bransford	29	G3
Bransford Bridge	29	H3
Bransgore	10	C5
Branson's Cross	30	B1
Branston Leics.	42	B3
Branston Lincs.	52	D6
Branston Staffs.	40	E3
Branston Booths	52	D6
Branstone	11	G6
Brant Broughton	52	C7
Brantham	35	F5
Branthwaite Cumb.	60	D3
Branthwaite Cumb.	60	B4
Brantingham	59	F7
Branton Northumb.	71	F2
Branton S.Yorks.	51	J2
Brantwood	60	E7
Branxholm	69	K2
Branxholme	69	K2
Branxton	77	G7
Brassington	50	E7
Brasted	23	H6
Brasted Chart	23	H6
Brathens	90	E5
Bratoft	53	H6
Brattleby	52	C4
Bratton	20	C6
Bratton Clovelly	6	C6
Bratton Fleming	6	E2
Bratton Seymour	9	F2
Braughing	33	G6
Braunston Northants.	31	G2
Braunston Rut.	42	B5
Braunstone	41	H5
Braunton	6	C2
Brawby	58	D2
Brawdy	16	B3
Brawith	63	G6
Brawl	104	D2
Brawlbin	105	F3
Bray	22	C4
Bray Shop	4	D3
Bray Wick	22	B4
Braybrooke	42	A7
Brayford	6	E2
Brayshaw	56	C4
Brayton	58	C6
Brazacott	4	C1
Breach	15	G3
Breachwood Green	32	E6
Breacleit	100	D4
Breadsall	41	F2
Breadstone	20	A1
Breage	2	D6
Breakon	108	E2
Bream	19	K1
Breamore	10	C3
Brean	19	F6
Breanais	100	B5
Brearton	57	J3
Breascleit	100	E4
Brechfa	17	J1
Brechin	83	H1
Brecklate	66	A2
Breckles	44	D6
Brecon (Aberhonddu)	27	K6
Breconside	68	D3
Bredbury	49	J3
Brede	14	D6
Bredenbury	29	F3
Bredfield	35	G3
Bredgar	24	E5
Bredhurst	24	D5
Bredicot	29	J3
Bredon	29	J5
Bredon's Hardwick	29	J5
Bredon's Norton	29	J5
Bredwardine	28	C4
Breedon on the Hill	41	G3
Breibhig	101	G4
Breich	75	H4
Breighton	58	D6
Breinton	28	D4
Bremhill	20	C4
Brenachoille	80	B7
Brenchley	23	K7
Brendon Devon	7	F1
Brendon Devon	6	B4
Brenkley	71	H6
Brent	22	E3
Brent Eleigh	34	D4
Brent Knoll	19	G6
Brent Pelham	33	H5
Brentford	22	E4
Brentingby	42	A4
Brentwood	23	J2
Brenzett	15	F5
Breoch	65	H5
Brereton	40	C4
Brereton Green	49	G6
Brereton Heath	49	H6
Bressingham	44	E7
Bretabister	109	D7
Bretby	40	E3
Bretford	31	F1
Bretforton	30	B4
Bretherdale Head	61	G6
Bretherton	55	H7
Brettenham Norf.	44	D7
Brettenham Suff.	34	D3
Bretton	48	C6
Brewood	40	A5
Briach	97	H6
Briantspuddle	9	H5
Bricket Wood	22	E1
Bricklehampton	29	J4
Bride	54	D3
Bridekirk	60	C3
Bridell	26	A4
Bridestones	49	J6
Bridestowe	6	D7
Brideswell	90	D1
Bridford	7	G7
Bridge Cornw.	2	D4
Bridge Kent	15	G2
Bridge End Lincs.	42	E2
Bridge End Shet.	109	C9
Bridge Hewick	57	J2
Bridge o' Ess	90	D5
Bridge of Alford	90	D3
Bridge of Allan	75	F1
Bridge of Avon	89	J1
Bridge of Balgie	81	G3
Bridge of Bogendreip	90	E5
Bridge of Brewlands	82	C1
Bridge of Brown	89	J2
Bridge of Cally	82	C2
Bridge of Canny	90	E5
Bridge of Craigisla	82	D2
Bridge of Dee Aber.	89	J5
Bridge of Dee Aber.	90	E5
Bridge of Dee D. & G.	65	H4
Bridge of Don	91	H4
Bridge of Dun	83	H2
Bridge of Dye	90	E6
Bridge of Earn	82	C6
Bridge of Ericht	81	G2
Bridge of Feugh	90	E5
Bridge of Forss	105	F1
Bridge of Gairn	90	B5
Bridge of Gaur	81	G2
Bridge of Muchalls	91	G5
Bridge of Muick	90	B5
Bridge of Orchy	80	E4
Bridge of Tilt	81	K1
Bridge of Tynet	98	B4
Bridge of Walls	109	B7
Bridge of Weir	74	B4
Bridge Sollers	28	D4
Bridge Street	34	C4
Bridge Trafford	48	D5
Bridgefoot	33	H4
Bridgefoot Cambs.	60	B4
Bridgehampton	8	E2
Bridgemary	11	G4
Bridgemere	39	G1
Bridgend Aber.	90	D1
Bridgend Angus	83	G1
Bridgend Arg. & B.	72	B4
Bridgend Arg. & B.	73	G1
Bridgend (Pen-y-Bont ar Ogwr) Bridgend	18	C4
Bridgend Carmar.	17	J2
Bridgend Cumb.	61	F5
Bridgend Fife	82	E6
Bridgend Moray	90	B1
Bridgend P. & K.	82	C6
Bridgend W.Loth.	75	J3
Bridgend of Lintrathen	82	D2
Bridgerule	6	A5
Bridges	38	C6
Bridgeton	4	B4
Bridgetown Cornw.	6	B7
Bridgetown Som.	7	H2
Bridgeyate	19	K4
Bridgham	44	D7
Bridgnorth	39	G6
Bridgtown	40	B5
Bridgwater	8	B1
Bridlington	59	H3
Bridstow	28	E6
Brierfield	56	D6
Brierley Glos.	29	F7
Brierley Here.	28	D3
Brierley S.Yorks.	51	G1
Brierley Hill	40	B7
Brig o'Turk	81	G7
Brigehaugh	90	B1
Brigg	52	D2
Brigham Cumb.	60	B3
Brigham E.Riding	59	G4
Brighouse	57	G7
Brighstone	11	F6
Brightgate	50	E7
Brighthampton	21	G1
Brightling	13	K4
Brightlingsea	34	E7
Brighton B. & H.	13	G6
Brighton Cornw.	3	G3
Brightons	75	H3
Brightwalton	21	H4
Brightwell Oxon.	21	J2
Brightwell Suff.	35	G4
Brightwell Baldwin	21	K2
Brignall	62	B5
Brigsley	53	F2
Brigsteer	55	H1
Brigstock	42	C7
Brill Bucks.	31	H7
Brill Cornw.	2	E6
Brilley	28	B4
Brilley Mountain	28	B3
Brimfield	28	E2
Brimington	51	G5
Brimington Common	51	G5
Brimley	5	J3
Brimpsfield	29	J7
Brimpton	21	J5
Brimscombe	20	B1
Brimstage	48	C4
Brind	58	D6
Brindister Shet.	109	D9
Brindister Shet.	109	B7
Brindle	55	J7
Brindley Ford	49	H7
Brineton	40	A4
Bringhurst	42	B6
Brington	32	D1
Briningham	44	E2
Brinian	106	D5
Brinkhill	53	G5
Brinkley	33	K3
Brinklow	31	F1
Brinkworth	20	D3
Brinmore	88	D2
Brinscall	56	B7
Brinsley	41	G1
Brinsop	28	D4
Brinsworth	51	G4
Brinton	44	E2
Brisco	61	F1
Brisley	44	D3
Brislington	19	K4
Brisson	19	J4
Bristol	19	J4
Bristol International Airport	19	H5
Briston	44	E2
Britannia	56	D7
Britford	10	C2
Brithdir	37	G4
Brithem Bottom	7	J4
Briton Ferry (Llansawel)	18	A2
Britwell Salome	21	K2
Brixham	5	K5
Brixton	5	F5
Brixton Deverill	9	H1
Brixworth	31	J1
Brize Norton	21	F1
Broad Blunsdon	20	E2
Broad Campden	30	C5
Broad Chalke	10	B2
Broad Green Beds.	32	C4
Broad Green Essex	34	C6
Broad Green Worcs.	29	G3
Broad Haven	16	B3
Broad Hill	33	J1
Broad Hinton	20	E4
Broad Laying	21	H5
Broad Marston	30	C4
Broad Oak Cumb.	60	C7
Broad Oak E.Suss.	13	K4
Broad Oak Here.	28	D6
Broad Oak E.Suss.	14	D6
Broad Street	14	D2
Broad Street Green	24	E1
Broad Town	20	D4
Broadbottom	49	J3
Broadbridge	12	B6
Broadbridge Heath	12	E3
Broadclyst	7	H6
Broadford	86	C2
Broadford Bridge	12	D4
Broadgate	54	E1
Broadgroves	33	K7
Broadhaugh	69	K3
Broadheath Gt.Man.	49	G4
Broadheath Worcs.	29	F2
Broadhembury	7	K5
Broadhempston	5	J4
Broadholme	52	B5
Broadland Row	14	D6
Broadlay	17	G4
Broadmayne	9	G6
Broadmeadows	69	K1
Broadmere	21	K7
Broadnymett	7	F5
Broadoak Carmar.	17	J2
Broadoak Dorset	8	D5
Broadoak Kent	25	H5
Broadrashes	98	C5
Broadsea	99	H4
Broadstairs	25	K5
Broadstone Poole	10	B5
Broadstone Shrop.	38	E7
Broadstreet Common	19	G3
Broadwas	29	G3
Broadwater Herts.	33	F6

Place	Page	Grid
Broadwater *W.Suss.*	12	E6
Broadway *Carmar.*	17	G4
Broadway *Carmar.*	17	F3
Broadway *Pembs.*	16	B3
Broadway *Som.*	8	C3
Broadway *Suff.*	35	H1
Broadway *Worcs.*	30	B5
Broadwell *Glos.*	30	D6
Broadwell *Glos.*	28	E7
Broadwell *Oxon.*	21	F1
Broadwell *Warks.*	31	F2
Broadwell House	62	A1
Broadwey	9	F6
Broadwindsor	8	D4
Broadwoodkelly	6	E5
Broadwoodwidger	6	C7
Brobury	28	C4
Brochel	94	B7
Brochloch	67	K4
Brock	78	B3
Brockbridge	11	H3
Brockdish	35	G1
Brockenhurst	10	E4
Brockford Street	35	F2
Brockhall	31	H2
Brockham	22	E7
Brockhampton *Glos.*	30	B6
Brockhampton *Here.*	28	E5
Brockholes	50	D1
Brockhurst	13	H3
Brocklebank	60	E2
Brocklesby	52	E1
Brockley	19	H5
Brockley Green	34	C3
Brockton *Shrop.*	38	E6
Brockton *Shrop.*	39	G5
Brockton *Shrop.*	38	C5
Brockton *Shrop.*	38	C7
Brockweir	19	J1
Brockwood Park	11	H2
Brockworth	29	H7
Brocton	40	B4
Brodick	73	J7
Brodsworth	51	H2
Brogborough	32	C5
Brogyntyn	38	B2
Broken Cross *Ches.*	49	H5
Broken Cross *Ches.*	49	F5
Brokenborough	20	C3
Bromborough	48	C4
Brome	35	F1
Brome Street	35	F1
Bromeswell	35	G3
Bromfield *Cumb.*	60	C2
Bromfield *Shrop.*	28	D1
Bromham *Beds.*	32	D3
Bromham *Wilts.*	20	C5
Bromley	23	H5
Bromley Green	14	E4
Brompton *Med.*	24	D5
Brompton *N.Yorks.*	62	E7
Brompton *N.Yorks.*	59	F1
Brompton on Swale	62	D6
Brompton Ralph	7	J2
Brompton Regis	7	H2
Bromsash	29	F6
Bromsberrow Heath	29	G5
Bromsgrove	29	J1
Bromstead Heath	40	A4
Bromyard	29	F3
Bromyard Downs	29	F3
Bron-y-Gaer	17	G3
Bronaber	37	G2
Brongest	26	C4
Bronington	38	D2
Bronllys	28	A5
Bronnant	27	F2
Bronydd	28	B4
Bronygarth	38	B2
Brook *Carmar.*	17	F4
Brook *Hants.*	10	D3
Brook *Hants.*	10	E2
Brook *I.o.W.*	10	E6
Brook *Kent*	15	F3
Brook *Surr.*	12	C3
Brook Street *Essex*	23	J2
Brook Street *Kent*	14	E4
Brook Street *Suff.*	34	C4
Brook Street *W.Suss.*	13	G4
Brooke *Norf.*	45	G6
Brooke *Rut.*	42	B5
Brookend	19	J2
Brookhouse	55	J3
Brookhouse Green	49	H6
Brookland	14	E5
Brooklands	65	J3
Brookmans Park	23	F1
Brooks	38	A6
Brooks Green	12	E4
Brooksby	41	J4
Brookthorpe	29	H7
Brookwood	22	C6
Broom *Beds.*	32	E4
Broom *Warks.*	30	B3
Broom Hill	10	B4
Broom of Dalreach	82	B6
Broomcroft	38	E5
Broome *Norf.*	45	H6
Broome *Shrop.*	38	C7
Broome *Worcs.*	29	J1
Broome Wood	71	G2
Broomedge	49	G4
Broomer's Corner	12	E4
Broomfield *Aber.*	91	H1
Broomfield *Essex*	34	B7
Broomfield *Kent*	25	H5
Broomfield *Kent*	14	D2
Broomfield *Som.*	8	B1
Broomfleet	58	E7
Broomhaugh	71	F7
Broomhead	99	H4
Broomhill	71	H3
Broom's Green	29	G5
Brora	97	G1
Broseley	39	F5
Brotherlee	62	A3
Brotherton	57	K7
Brotton	63	H4
Broubster	105	F2
Brough *Cumb.*	61	J5
Brough *Derbys.*	50	D4
Brough *E.Riding*	59	F7
Brough *High.*	105	H1
Brough *Notts.*	52	B7
Brough *Ork.*	107	C6
Brough *Shet.*	109	E8
Brough *Shet.*	108	D5
Brough *Shet.*	109	G6
Brough *Shet.*	108	E5
Brough Lodge	108	E3
Brough Sowerby	61	J5
Broughall	38	E1
Brougham	61	G4
Broughton *Cambs.*	33	F1
Broughton *Flints.*	48	C6
Broughton *Hants.*	10	E1
Broughton *Lancs.*	55	J6
Broughton *M.K.*	32	B4
Broughton *N.Lincs.*	52	C2
Broughton *N.Yorks.*	58	D2
Broughton *N.Yorks.*	56	E4
Broughton *Northants.*	32	B1
Broughton *Ork.*	106	D3
Broughton *Oxon.*	31	G6
Broughton *Sc.Bord.*	75	K7
Broughton *V. of Glam.*	18	C4
Broughton Astley	41	H6
Broughton Beck	55	F1
Broughton Gifford	20	B5
Broughton Hackett	29	J3
Broughton in Furness	55	F1
Broughton Mills	60	D7
Broughton Moor	60	B3
Broughton Poggs	21	F1
Broughtown	106	F3
Broughty Ferry	83	F4
Browland	109	B7
Brown Candover	11	G1
Brown Edge *Lancs.*	48	C1
Brown Edge *Staffs.*	49	J7
Brown Lees	49	H7
Brownhill	99	G6
Brownhills *Fife*	83	G6
Brownhills *W.Mid.*	40	C5
Brownieside	71	G1
Brownlow Heath	49	H6
Brownshill Green	41	F7
Brownston	5	G5
Broxa	63	J3
Broxbourne	23	G1
Broxburn *E.Loth.*	76	E3
Broxburn *W.Loth.*	75	J3
Broxholme	52	C5
Broxted	33	J6
Broxton	48	D7
Broxwood	28	C3
Bru	101	F2
Bruachmary	97	F7
Bruan	105	J5
Bruar	81	J1
Bruera	48	D6
Bruichladdich	72	A4
Bruisyard	35	H2
Bruisyard Street	35	H2
Brund	50	D6
Brundall	45	H5
Brundish	35	G2
Brundish Street	35	G1
Bruntingthorpe	41	J7
Bruntland	90	C2
Brunton *Fife*	82	E5
Brunton *Northumb.*	71	H1
Brushford *Devon*	6	E5
Brushford *Som.*	7	H3
Bruton	9	F1
Bryanston	9	H4
Brydekirk	69	G6
Brymbo	48	B7
Brympton	8	E3
Bryn *Carmar.*	17	J4
Bryn *Gt.Man.*	48	E2
Bryn *N.P.T.*	18	B2
Bryn *Shrop.*	38	B7
Bryn-côch	18	A2
Bryn Gates	48	E2
Bryn-henllan	16	D1
Bryn-teg	46	C4
Bryn-y-maen	47	G5
Brynamman	27	G7
Brynberian	16	E1
Bryncae	18	C3
Bryncethin	18	C3
Bryncir	36	D1
Bryncroes	36	B2
Bryncrug	37	F5
Brynford	47	K5
Bryngwran	46	B5
Bryngwyn *Mon.*	19	G1
Bryngwyn *Powys*	28	A4
Brynhoffnant	26	C3
Brynmawr	28	A7
Brynmelyn	28	A1
Brynna	18	C3
Brynog	26	E3
Brynrefail *Gwyn.*	46	D6
Brynrefail *I.o.A.*	46	C4
Brynsadler	18	D3
Brynsiencyn	46	C6
Brynteg	48	C7
Buaile nam Bodach	84	C4
Bualintur	85	K2
Bualnaluib	94	E3
Bubbenhall	30	E1
Bubwith	58	D6
Buccleuch	69	J2
Buchan	65	H4
Buchanan Castle	74	C2
Buchanhaven	99	K6
Buchanty	82	A5
Buchlyvie	74	D1
Buckabank	60	E2
Buckby Wharf	31	H2
Buckden *Cambs.*	32	E2
Buckden *N.Yorks.*	56	E1
Buckenham	45	H5
Buckerell	7	K5
Buckfast	5	H4
Buckfastleigh	5	H4
Buckholm	76	C7
Buckhorn Weston	9	G2
Buckhurst Hill	23	H2
Buckie	98	C4
Buckies	105	G2
Buckingham	31	H5
Buckland *Bucks.*	32	B7
Buckland *Devon*	5	G6
Buckland *Glos.*	30	B5
Buckland *Herts.*	33	G5
Buckland *Kent*	15	J3
Buckland *Oxon.*	21	G2
Buckland *Surr.*	23	F6
Buckland Brewer	6	C3
Buckland Common	22	C1
Buckland Dinham	20	A6
Buckland Filleigh	6	C5
Buckland in the Moor	5	H3
Buckland Monachorum	4	E4
Buckland Newton	9	F4
Buckland St. Mary	8	B3
Buckland-tout-Saints	5	H6
Bucklebury	21	J4
Bucklerheads	83	F4
Bucklers Hard	11	F4
Bucklesham	35	G4
Buckley (Bwcle)	48	B6
Buckman Corner	12	D4
Buckminster	42	B3
Bucknall *Lincs.*	52	E6
Bucknall *Stoke*	40	B1
Bucknell *Oxon.*	31	G6
Bucknell *Shrop.*	28	C1
Buck's Cross	6	B3
Bucks Green	12	D3
Bucks Hill	22	D1
Bucks Horn Oak	22	B7
Buck's Mills	6	B3
Buckshorn	91	G4
Buckton *E.Riding*	59	H2
Buckton *Here.*	28	C1
Buckton *Northumb.*	77	J7
Buckworth	32	E1
Budbrooke	30	D2
Budby	51	J6
Buddon	83	G4
Bude	6	A5
Budlake	7	H5
Budleigh Salterton	7	J7
Budock Water	2	E5
Buerton	39	F1
Bugbrooke	31	H3
Bugle	4	A5
Bugthorpe	58	D4
Buildwas	39	F5
Builth Road	27	K3
Builth Wells	27	K3
Buirgh	93	F2
Bulby	42	D3
Buldoo	104	E2
Bulford	20	E7
Bulford Camp	20	E7
Bulkeley	48	E7
Bulkington *Warks.*	41	F7
Bulkington *Wilts.*	20	C6
Bulkworthy	6	B4
Bull Bay	46	C3
Bull Green	14	E4
Bulley	29	G7
Bullington	21	H7
Bullpot Farm	56	B1
Bull's Green	33	F7
Bullwood	73	K3
Bulmer *Essex*	34	C4
Bulmer *N.Yorks.*	58	C3
Bulmer Tye	34	C5
Bulphan	24	C3
Bulverhythe	14	C7
Bulwark	99	H6
Bulwell	41	H1
Bulwick	42	C6
Bumble's Green	23	H1
Bun Abhainn Eadarra	100	D7
Bun Loyne	87	J4
Bunarkaig	87	H6
Bunbury	48	E7
Bunchrew	96	D7
Bundalloch	86	E2
Buness	108	F2
Bunessan	78	E5
Bungay	45	H7
Bunlarie	73	F7
Bunloit	88	C2
Bunnahabhainn	72	C3
Bunny	41	H3
Buntait	87	K1
Buntingford	33	G6
Bunwell	45	F6
Bunwell Street	45	F6
Burbage *Derbys.*	50	C5
Burbage *Leics.*	41	G6
Burbage *Wilts.*	21	F5
Burchett's Green	22	B3
Burcombe	10	B1
Burcot	21	J2
Burcott	32	B6
Burdale	58	E3
Burdocks	12	D4
Bures	34	D5
Bures Green	34	D5
Burford	30	D7
Burgate	34	E1
Burgess Hill	13	G5
Burgh	35	G3
Burgh by Sands	60	E1
Burgh Castle	45	J5
Burgh Heath	23	F6
Burgh le Marsh	53	H6
Burgh next Aylsham	45	G3
Burgh on Bain	53	F4
Burgh St. Margaret	45	J4
Burgh St. Peter	45	J6
Burghclere	21	H5
Burghead	97	J5
Burghfield	21	K5
Burghfield Common	21	K5
Burghill	28	D4
Burghwallis	51	H1
Burham	24	D5
Buriton	11	J2
Burland	49	F7
Burlawn	3	G1
Burleigh	22	C5
Burlescombe	7	J4
Burleston	9	G5
Burley *Hants.*	10	D4
Burley *Rut.*	42	B4
Burley Gate	28	E4
Burley in Wharfedale	57	G5
Burley Street	10	D4
Burleydam	39	F1
Burlingjobb	28	B3
Burlow	13	J5
Burlton	38	D3
Burmarsh	15	G4
Burmington	30	D5
Burn	58	B7
Burn Farm	98	B7
Burn Naze	55	G5
Burn of Cambus	81	J7
Burnage	49	H3
Burnaston	40	E2
Burnby	58	E5
Burndell	12	C6
Burnend	99	G6
Burneside	61	G7
Burneston	57	J1
Burnett	19	K5
Burnfoot *High.*	104	D5
Burnfoot *P. & K.*	82	A7
Burnfoot *Sc.Bord.*	70	A2
Burnfoot *Sc.Bord.*	69	K2
Burnham *Bucks.*	22	C3
Burnham *N.Lincs.*	52	D1
Burnham Deepdale	44	C1
Burnham Green	33	F7
Burnham Market	44	C1
Burnham Norton	44	C1
Burnham-on-Crouch	25	F2
Burnham-on-Sea	19	G7
Burnham Overy	44	C1
Burnham Thorpe	44	C1
Burnhaven	99	K6
Burnhead *D. & G.*	67	K5
Burnhead *D. & G.*	68	D4
Burnhervie	91	F3
Burnhill Green	39	G5
Burnhope	62	C2
Burnhouse	74	B5
Burniston	63	K3
Burnley	56	D6
Burnmouth	77	H4
Burnopfield	62	C1
Burnsall	57	F3
Burnside *Aber.*	91	F3
Burnside *Angus*	83	G1
Burnside *E.Ayr.*	67	K2
Burnside *Fife*	82	C7
Burnside *Shet.*	108	B5
Burnside *W.Loth.*	75	J3
Burnside of Duntrune	83	F4
Burnstones	61	H1
Burnswark	69	G6
Burnt Houses	62	C4
Burnt Yates	57	H3
Burntcliff Top	49	J6
Burntisland	76	A2
Burnton *E.Ayr.*	67	J2
Burnton *E.Ayr.*	67	J3
Burntwood	40	C4
Burntwood Green	40	C5
Burpham *Surr.*	22	D6
Burpham *W.Suss.*	12	D6
Burradon *Northumb.*	6	D7
Burradon *T. & W.*	71	H6
Burrafirth	108	F1
Burraland	108	C5
Burras	2	D5
Burravoe *Shet.*	108	E5
Burravoe *Shet.*	109	C6
Burrells	61	H5
Burrelton	82	C4
Burridge	11	G3
Burrill	57	H1
Burringham	52	B2
Burrington *Devon*	6	E4
Burrington *Here.*	28	D1
Burrington *N.Som.*	19	H6
Burrough End	33	K3
Burrough Green	33	K3
Burrough on the Hill	42	A4
Burrow Bridge	8	C1
Burrowhill	22	C5
Burry Port	17	H4
Burscough	48	D1
Burscough Bridge	48	D1
Bursea	58	E6
Burshill	59	G5
Bursledon	11	F4
Burslem	40	A1
Burstall	35	F4
Burstock	8	D4
Burston *Norf.*	45	F7
Burston *Staffs.*	40	B2
Burstow	23	G7
Burstwick	59	J7
Burtersett	56	D1
Burtle	19	H7
Burton *Ches.*	48	C5
Burton *Ches.*	48	E6
Burton *Dorset*	10	C5
Burton *Dorset*	9	F5
Burton *Lincs.*	52	C5
Burton *Northumb.*	77	K7
Burton *Pembs.*	16	C4
Burton *Som.*	7	K1
Burton *Wilts.*	20	B4
Burton Agnes	59	H3
Burton Bradstock	8	D6
Burton Coggles	42	C3
Burton Fleming	59	G2
Burton Green *Warks.*	30	D1
Burton Green *Wrex.*	48	C7
Burton Hastings	41	G6
Burton-in-Kendal	55	J2
Burton in Lonsdale	56	B2
Burton Joyce	41	J1
Burton Latimer	32	C1
Burton Lazars	42	A4
Burton Leonard	57	J3
Burton on the Wolds	41	H3
Burton Overy	41	J6
Burton Pedwardine	42	E1
Burton Pidsea	59	J6
Burton Salmon	57	K7
Burton upon Stather	52	B1
Burton upon Trent	40	E3
Burtonwood	48	E3
Burwardsley	48	E7
Burwarton	39	F7
Burwash	13	K4
Burwash Common	13	K4
Burwash Weald	13	K4
Burwell *Cambs.*	33	J2
Burwell *Lincs.*	53	G5
Burwen	46	C3
Burwick *Ork.*	107	D9
Burwick *Shet.*	109	C8
Bury *Cambs.*	43	F7
Bury *Gt.Man.*	49	H1
Bury *Som.*	7	H3
Bury *W.Suss.*	12	D5
Bury Green	33	H6
Bury St. Edmunds	34	C2
Buryas Bridge	2	B6
Burythorpe	58	D3
Busbridge	22	C7
Busby *E.Renf.*	74	D5
Busby *P. & K.*	82	B5
Buscot	21	F2
Bush Bank	28	D3
Bush Crathie	89	K5
Bush Green	45	G7
Bushbury	40	B5
Bushby	41	J5
Bushey	22	E2
Bushey Heath	22	E2
Bushley	29	H5
Bushton	20	D4
Bussage	20	B1
Busta	109	C6
Butcher's Cross	13	J4
Butcher's Pasture	33	K6
Butcombe	19	J5
Buthill	97	J5
Butleigh	8	E1
Butleigh Wootton	8	E1
Butler's Cross	22	B1
Butler's Hill	41	H1
Butlers Marston	30	E3
Butley	35	H3
Butsfield	62	C2
Butt Green	49	F7
Butt Lane	49	H7
Butterburn	70	B6
Buttercrambe	58	D4
Butterknowle	62	C4
Butterleigh	7	H5
Butterley	51	G7
Buttermere *Cumb.*	60	C5
Buttermere *Wilts.*	21	G5
Butters Green	49	H7
Buttershaw	57	G7
Butterstone	82	B3
Butterton	50	C7
Butterwick *Lincs.*	43	G1
Butterwick *N.Yorks.*	59	F2
Butterwick *N.Yorks.*	58	D2
Buttington	38	B5
Buttonoak	29	G1
Buxhall	34	E3
Buxted	13	H4
Buxton *Derbys.*	50	C5
Buxton *Norf.*	45	G3
Buxton Heath	45	F3
Buxworth	50	C4
Bwcle (Buckley)	48	B6
Bwlch	28	A6
Bwlch-clawdd	17	G1
Bwlch-derwin	36	D1
Bwlch-llan	26	E3
Bwlch-y-cibau	38	A4
Bwlch-y-ddar	38	A3
Bwlch-y-ffridd	37	K6
Bwlch-y-groes	17	F1
Bwlch-y-sarnau	27	K1
Bwlchgwyn	48	B7
Bwlchnewydd	17	G2
Bwlchtocyn	36	C3
Byers Green	62	D3
Byfield	31	G3
Byfleet	22	D5
Byford	28	C4
Bygrave	33	F5
Byker	71	H7
Bylane End	4	C5
Bylchau	47	H6
Byley	49	G6
Bynea	17	J5
Byrness	70	C3
Bythorn	32	D1
Byton	28	C2
Byworth	12	C4

C

Place	Page	Grid
Cabharstadh	101	F5
Cabourne	52	E2
Cabrach *Arg. & B.*	72	C4
Cabrach *Moray*	90	B2
Cackle Street	14	D6
Cacrabank	69	J2
Cadbury	7	H5
Cadbury Barton	6	E4
Cadbury Heath	19	K4
Cadder	74	E3
Cadderlie	80	B4
Caddington	32	D7
Caddleton	79	J6
Caddonfoot	76	C7
Cade Street	13	K4
Cadeby *Leics.*	41	G5
Cadeby *S.Yorks.*	51	H2
Cadeleigh	7	H5
Cadgwith	2	E7
Cadham	82	D7
Cadishead	49	G3
Cadle	17	K5
Cadley	21	F5
Cadmore End	22	A2
Cadnam	10	E3
Cadney	52	D2
Cadole	48	B6
Cadover Bridge	5	F4
Cadoxton	18	E5
Cadoxton-Juxta-Neath	18	A2
Cae Ddafydd	37	F1
Caeathro	46	D6
Caehopkin	27	H7
Caen	105	F7
Caenby	52	D4
Caenby Corner	52	C4
Caer-Lan	27	H7
Caer Llan	19	H1
Caerau *Bridgend*	18	B2
Caerau *Cardiff*	18	E4
Caerdeon	37	F4
Caerfarchell	16	A2
Caerffyrddin (Carmarthen)	17	H3
Caergeiliog	46	B5
Caergwrle	48	C7
Caergybi (Holyhead)	46	A4
Caerhun	47	F5
Caerleon	19	G2
Caernarfon	46	C6
Caerphilly	18	E3
Caersws	37	K6
Caerwent	19	H2
Caerwys	47	K5
Caethle Farm	37	F6
Caggan	89	G3
Caio	17	K1
Cairinis	92	D6
Cairminis	93	F3
Cairnargat	90	C1
Cairnbaan	73	G1
Cairnbeathie	90	D4
Cairnbrogie	91	H2
Cairnbulg	99	J4
Cairncross	77	G4
Cairncurran	74	B4
Cairndoon	64	D7
Cairndow	80	C6
Cairness	99	J4
Cairney Lodge	82	E6
Cairneyhill	75	J2
Cairnhill *Aber.*	91	H2
Cairnhill *Aber.*	90	E1
Cairnie *Aber.*	91	G4
Cairnie *Aber.*	98	C6
Cairnorrie	99	G6
Cairnryan	64	A4
Cairnsmore	64	E4
Caister-on-Sea	45	K4
Caistor	52	E2
Caistor St. Edmund	45	G5
Caistron	70	E3
Cake Street	44	E6
Calanais (Callanish)	100	E4
Calbost	101	G6
Calbourne	11	F6
Calceby	53	G5
Calcot	21	K4
Calcott	25	H5
Caldarvan	74	C2
Caldback	108	F2
Caldbeck	60	E3
Caldbergh	57	F1
Caldecote *Cambs.*	33	G3
Caldecote *Cambs.*	42	E7
Caldecote *Herts.*	33	F5
Caldecote *Warks.*	41	F6
Caldecott *Northants.*	32	C2
Caldecott *Rut.*	42	B6
Calder Bridge	60	B6
Calder Mains	105	F3
Calder Vale	55	J5
Calderbank	75	F4
Calderbrook	49	J1
Caldercruix	75	G4
Calderglen	74	E5
Caldermill	74	E6
Caldhame	83	F3
Caldicot	19	H3
Caldwell *Derbys.*	40	E4
Caldwell *N.Yorks.*	62	C5
Caldy	48	B4
Caledrhydiau	26	D3
Calfsound	106	E4
Calgary	78	E2
Califer	97	H6
California *Falk.*	75	H3
California *Norf.*	45	K4
Calke	41	F3
Callakille	94	C6
Callaly	71	F3
Callander	81	H7
Callanish (Calanais)	100	E4
Callaughton	39	F6
Callerton Lane End	71	G7
Callestick	2	E3
Calligarry	86	C4
Callington	4	D4
Callisterhall	69	H5
Callow	28	D5
Callow End	29	H4
Callow Hill *Wilts.*	20	D3
Callow Hill *Worcs.*	29	G1
Callows Grave	28	E2
Calmore	10	E3
Calmsden	20	D1
Calne	20	C4
Calow	51	G5
Calrossie	96	E4
Calshot	11	F4
Calstock	4	E4
Calstone Wellington	20	D5
Calthorpe	45	F2
Calthwaite	61	F2
Calton *N.Yorks.*	56	E4
Calton *Staffs.*	50	D7
Calveley	48	E7
Calver	50	E5
Calver Hill	28	C4
Calverhall	39	F2
Calverleigh	7	H4
Calverley	57	H6
Calvert	31	H6
Calverton *M.K.*	31	J5
Calverton *Notts.*	41	J1
Calvine	81	K1
Calvo	60	C1
Cam	20	A2
Camasnacroise	79	K2
Camastianavaig	86	B1
Camasunary	86	B3
Camault Muir	96	C7
Camb	108	E3
Camber	14	E6
Camberley	22	B5
Camberwell	23	G4
Camblesforth	58	C7
Cambo	71	F5
Cambois	71	J5
Camborne	2	D4
Cambourne	33	G3
Cambridge *Cambs.*	33	H3
Cambridge *Glos.*	20	A1
Cambridge Airport	33	H3
Cambus	75	G1
Cambus o'May	90	C5
Cambusbarron	75	F1
Cambuskenneth	75	G1
Cambuslang	74	E4
Cambusnethan	75	G5
Camden	23	F3
Cameley	19	K6
Camelford	4	B2
Camelon	75	G2
Camelsdale	12	B3
Camer	24	C5
Cameron	74	B2
Camerory	89	H1
Camer's Green	29	G5
Camerton *B. & N.E.Som.*	19	K6
Camerton *Cumb.*	60	B3
Camghouran	81	G2
Camis Eskan	74	B2
Cammachmore	91	H5
Cammeringham	52	C4
Campbeltown	66	B2
Campbeltown (Machrihanish) Airport	66	A1
Camperdown	71	H6
Camphouse	79	G1
Campmuir	82	D4
Camps End	33	K4
Camps Heath	45	K6
Campsall	51	H1
Campsey Ash	35	H3
Campton	32	E5
Camptown	70	B2
Camquhart	73	H2
Camrose	16	C3
Camserney	81	K3
Camstraddan House	74	B1
Camus Croise	86	C3
Camus-luinie	87	F2
Camusnagaul *High.*	87	G1
Camusnagaul *High.*	95	G3
Camusrory	86	E5
Camusteel	94	D7
Camusterrach	94	D7
Camusurich	81	H4
Camusvrachan	81	H3
Canada	10	D3
Candacraig	90	B4
Candlesby	53	H6
Candy Mill	75	J6
Cane End	21	K4
Canewdon	24	E2
Canford Bottom	10	B4
Canford Cliffs	10	B6
Canford Magna	10	B5
Canisbay	105	J1
Cann	9	H2
Cann Common	9	H2
Cannard's Grave	19	K7
Cannich	87	K1
Cannington	8	B1
Cannock	40	B4
Cannock Wood	40	C4
Cannop	29	F7
Canon Bridge	28	D4
Canon Frome	29	F4
Canon Pyon	28	D4
Canonbie	69	J6
Canons Ashby	31	G3
Canon's Town	2	C5
Canterbury *Aber.*	98	D5
Canterbury *Kent*	15	H5
Cantley *Norf.*	45	H5
Cantley *S.Yorks.*	51	J2
Cantlop	38	E5
Canton	18	E4
Cantray	96	E7
Cantraydoune	96	E7
Cantraywood	96	E7
Cantsfield	56	B2
Canvey Island	24	D3
Canwell Hall	40	D5
Canwick	52	C6
Canworthy Water	4	C1
Caol	87	H7
Caolas *Arg. & B.*	78	B3
Caolas *W.Isles*	84	B5
Caolas Scalpaigh (Kyles Scalpay)	93	H2
Caolasnacon	80	C1
Capel *Kent*	23	K7
Capel *Surr.*	22	E7
Capel Bangor	37	F7
Capel Betws Lleucu	27	F3
Capel Carmel	36	A3
Capel Coch	46	C4
Capel Curig	47	F7
Capel Cynon	26	C4
Capel Dewi *Carmar.*	17	H2
Capel Dewi *Cere.*	37	F7
Capel Dewi *Cere.*	26	D3
Capel Garmon	47	G7
Capel Gwyn *Carmar.*	17	H2
Capel Gwyn *I.o.A.*	46	B5
Capel Gwynfe	27	G6
Capel Hendre	17	J3
Capel Isaac	17	J2
Capel Iwan	17	F1
Capel le Ferne	15	H4
Capel Parc	46	C4
Capel St. Andrew	35	H4
Capel St. Mary	34	E5
Capel St. Silin	26	E3
Capel Seion	27	F1
Capel Tygwydd	26	B4
Capel-y-ffin	28	B5
Capeluchaf	36	D1
Capelulo	47	F5
Capenhurst	48	C5
Capernwray	55	J2
Capheaton	71	F5
Caplaw	74	C5
Cappercleuch	69	H1
Capplegill	69	G3
Capstone	24	D5
Capton	5	J5
Caputh	82	B3
Car Colston	42	A1
Carbellow	68	B1
Carbeth	74	D3
Carbis Bay	2	C5
Carbost *High.*	93	K7
Carbost *High.*	85	J1
Carbrain	75	F3
Carbrooke	44	D5
Carburton	51	J5
Carcary	83	H2
Carclew	2	E5
Carco	68	C2
Carcroft	51	H2
Cardenden	76	A1
Cardeston	38	C4
Cardiff (Caerdydd)	18	E4
Cardiff International Airport	18	D5
Cardigan (Aberteifi)	26	A4
Cardington *Beds.*	32	D4
Cardington *Shrop.*	38	E6
Cardinham	4	B4
Cardno	99	H4
Cardoness	65	F5
Cardow	97	J7
Cardrona	76	A7
Cardross	74	B3
Cardurnock	60	C1
Careby	42	D4
Careston	83	G1
Carew	16	D4
Carew Cheriton	16	D4
Carew Newton	16	D4
Carey	28	E5
Carfrae	76	D4
Carfraemill	76	C5
Cargen	65	K3
Cargenbridge	65	K3
Cargill	82	C4
Cargo	60	E1
Cargo Fleet	63	G4
Cargreen	4	E4
Carham	77	F7
Carhampton	7	J1
Carharrack	2	E4
Carie *P. & K.*	81	G3
Carie *P. & K.*	81	H4
Carines	2	E3
Carisbrooke	11	F6
Carlabhagh (Carloway)	100	E4

Carland Cross 3 F3
Carlby 42 D4
Carlecotes 50 D2
Carleton Cumb. 61 F1
Carleton Lancs. 55 G5
Carleton N.Yorks. 56 E5
Carleton N.Yorks. 57 K7
Carleton Fishery 67 F5
Carleton Forehoe 44 E5
Carleton Rode 45 F6
Carlin How 63 J5
Carlingcott 19 K6
Carlisle 61 F1
Carlops 75 K5
Carloway (Carlabhagh) 100 E3
Carlton Beds. 32 C3
Carlton Cambs. 33 K3
Carlton Leics. 41 F5
Carlton N.Yorks. 58 C7
Carlton N.Yorks. 57 F1
Carlton N.Yorks. 58 C1
Carlton Notts. 41 J1
Carlton S.Yorks. 51 F2
Carlton Stock. 62 E4
Carlton Suff. 35 H2
Carlton W.Yorks. 57 J7
Carlton Colville 45 K6
Carlton Curlieu 41 J6
Carlton Husthwaite 57 K2
Carlton-in-Cleveland 63 G6
Carlton in Lindrick 51 H4
Carlton-le-Moorland 52 C7
Carlton Miniott 57 J1
Carlton-on-Trent 52 B6
Carlton Scroop 42 C1
Carluke 75 G5
Carlyon Bay 4 A5
Carmacoup 68 C1
Carmarthen (Caerfyrddin) 17 H3
Carmel Carmar. 17 J3
Carmel Flints. 47 K5
Carmel Gwyn. 46 C7
Carmel I.o.A. 46 B4
Carmont 91 G6
Carmore 96 E2
Carmunnock 74 E5
Carmyle 74 E4
Carmyllie 83 G3
Carn 72 A5
Carn Brea 2 D4
Carn Dearg 94 D4
Carnaby 59 H3
Carnach High. 87 G2
Carnach High. 95 G2
Carnassarie 79 K7
Carnbee 83 G7
Carnbo 82 B7
Carnduncan 72 A4
Carne 3 G5
Carnforth 55 H2
Carnhell Green 2 D5
Carnichal 99 H5
Carnmore 72 B6
Carno 37 J6
Carnoch High. 87 K1
Carnoch High. 95 J6
Carnoch High. 97 F7
Carnock 75 J2
Carnon Downs 2 E4
Carnousie 98 E5
Carnoustie 83 G4
Carnwath 75 H6
Carnyorth 2 A5
Carperby 62 B7
Carr Shield 61 K2
Carr Vale 51 G5
Carradale 73 G7
Carragrich 93 G2
Carrbridge 89 G2
Carrefour Selous 3 J6
Carreg-lefn 46 B4
Carrick Arg. & B. 73 K1
Carrick Arg. & B. 73 H2
Carrick Fife 83 F5
Carriden 75 J2
Carrine 66 A3
Carrington Gt.Man. 49 G3
Carrington Lincs. 53 G7
Carrington Midloth. 76 B4
Carroch 68 B4
Carrog 38 A1
Carroglen 81 J5
Carrol 97 F1
Carron Arg. & B. 73 H1
Carron Falk. 75 G2
Carron Moray 97 K7
Carron Bridge 75 F2
Carronbridge 68 D4
Carronshore 75 G2
Carrot 83 F3
Carrutherstown 69 G6
Carruthmuir 74 B4
Carrville 62 E2
Carry 73 H4
Carsaig 79 G5
Carscreugh 64 C4
Carse 73 F4
Carse of Ardersier 97 F6
Carsegowan 64 E5
Carseriggan 64 D4
Carsethorn 65 K5
Carsgoe 105 G2
Carshalton 23 F5
Carsington 50 E7
Carsluith 64 E5
Carsphairn 67 K4
Carstairs 75 H6
Carstairs Junction 75 H6
Carswell Marsh 21 G2
Carter's Clay 10 E2
Carterton 21 F1
Carterway Heads 62 B1
Carthew 4 A5
Carthorpe 57 J1
Cartington 71 F3
Cartmel 55 G1
Cartmel Fell 55 H1
Carway 17 H4
Cascob 28 B2
Cashel Farm 74 C1
Cashlie 81 F3
Cashmoor 9 J3
Casnewydd (Newport) Newport 19 G3
Cassencarie 64 E5
Cassington 31 F7
Cassop 62 E3
Castell Gorfod 17 F2
Castell Howell 26 D4
Castell-Nedd (Neath) 18 A2

Castell Newydd Emlyn (Newcastle Emlyn) 26 C4
Castell-y-bwch 19 F2
Castellau 18 D3
Cacterton 56 B2
Castle Acre 44 C4
Castle Ashby 32 B3
Castle Bolton 62 B7
Castle Bromwich 40 D7
Castle Bytham 42 C4
Castle Caereinion 38 A5
Castle Camps 33 K4
Castle Carrock 61 G1
Castle Cary 9 F1
Castle Combe 20 B4
Castle Donington 41 G3
Castle Douglas 65 H4
Castle Eaton 20 E2
Castle Eden 63 F3
Castle End 30 D1
Castle Frome 29 F4
Castle Gresley 40 E4
Castle Heaton 77 H6
Castle Hedingham 34 B5
Castle Hill 35 F4
Castle Kennedy 64 B5
Castle Leod 96 B6
Castle Levan 74 A3
Castle Madoc 27 K5
Castle Morris 16 C1
Castle O'er 69 H4
Castle Rising 44 A3
Castle Stuart 96 E7
Castlebay (Bagh a' Chaisteil) 84 B5
Castlebythe 16 D2
Castlecary 75 F3
Castlecraig High. 97 F5
Castlecraig Sc.Bord. 75 K6
Castlefairn 68 C5
Castleford 57 K7
Castlemartin 16 B5
Castlemilk D. & G. 69 G6
Castlemilk Glas. 74 E5
Castleside 62 B2
Castlethorpe 32 B4
Castleton Aber. 99 F5
Castleton Angus 82 E3
Castleton Arg. & B. 73 G2
Castleton Derbys. 50 D4
Castleton Gt.Man. 49 H1
Castleton N.Yorks. 63 H6
Castleton Newport 19 F3
Castleton Sc.Bord. 70 A4
Castletown High. 105 G2
Castletown High. 96 E7
Castletown I.o.M. 54 B7
Castletown T. & W. 62 E1
Castleweary 69 K3
Castlewigg 64 E6
Caston 44 D6
Castor 42 E6
Castramont 64 E4
Cat and Fiddle Inn 50 C5
Catbrain 19 J3
Catchall 2 B6
Catcleugh 70 C3
Catcliffe 51 G4
Catcott 8 C1
Caterham 23 G6
Catesby 31 G3
Catfield 45 H3
Catford 23 G4
Catforth 55 H6
Cathedine 28 A6
Catherington 11 H3
Catherton 29 F1
Catlow 56 D6
Catlowdy 69 K6
Catmore 21 H4
Caton Devon 5 H3
Caton Lancs. 55 J3
Cator Court 5 G3
Catrine 67 K1
Catsfield 14 C6
Catshill 29 J1
Cattadale 72 B5
Cattal 57 K4
Cattawade 35 F5
Catterall 55 J5
Catterick 62 D7
Catterick Camp 62 C7
Catterlen 61 F3
Catterline 91 G7
Catterton 58 B5
Catthorpe 31 G1
Cattistock 8 E4
Catton N.Yorks. 57 J2
Catton Norf. 45 G4
Catton Northumb. 61 K1
Catwick 59 H5
Catworth 32 D1
Caudworthy 4 C1
Caulcott 31 G6
Cauldcots 83 H3
Cauldhame Stir. 74 E1
Cauldhame Stir. 81 K7
Cauldon 40 C1
Caulkerbush 65 K5
Caulside 69 K5
Caundle Marsh 9 F3
Caunsall 40 A7
Caunton 51 K6
Causeway End D. & G. 64 E4
Causeway End Essex 33 K7
Causewayhead Cumb. 60 C1
Causewayhead Stir. 75 G1
Causey Park 71 G4
Causeyend 91 H3
Cautley 61 H7
Cavendish 34 C4
Cavenham 34 B2
Caversfield 31 G6
Caversham 22 A4
Caverswall 40 B1
Cawdor 97 F6
Cawkwell 53 F5
Cawood 58 B6
Cawsand 4 E5
Cawston 45 F3
Cawthorne 50 E2
Cawthorpe 42 D3
Cawton 58 C2
Caxton 33 G3

Caxton Gibbet 33 F3
Caynham 28 E1
Caythorpe Lincs. 42 C1
Caythorpe Notts. 41 J1
Cayton 59 G1
Ceallan 92 D6
Ceann a' Bhaigh W.Isles 92 C5
Ceann a' Bhaigh W.Isles 93 F3
Ceann Loch Shiphoirt 100 E6
Cearsiadar 101 F5
Ceathramh Meadhanach 92 C4
Cedig 37 J3
Cefn-brith 47 H7
Cefn Bycharn (Newbridge) 19 F2
Cefn-caer-Ferch 36 D1
Cefn Cantref 27 K6
Cefn Coch 47 K7
Cefn-coch 38 A3
Cefn-coed-y-cymmer 18 D1
Cefn Cribwr 18 B3
Cefn Cross 18 B3
Cefn-ddwysarn 37 J1
Cefn Einion 38 B7
Cefn-gorwydd 27 J4
Cefn-gwyn 38 A7
Cefn Hengoed 18 E2
Cefn-mawr 38 B1
Cefn-y-bedd 48 C7
Cefn-y-pant 17 F2
Cefndeuddwr 37 G3
Cefneithin 17 J3
Cegidfa (Guilsfield) 38 B4
Ceidio 46 C4
Ceidio Fawr 36 B2
Ceinewydd (New Quay) 26 C3
Ceint 46 C5
Cellan 27 F4
Cellardyke 83 G7
Cellarhead 40 B1
Cemaes 46 B3
Cemmaes 37 H5
Cemmaes Road (Glantwymyn) 37 H5
Cenarth 26 B4
Cennin 36 D1
Ceos 101 F5
Ceres 82 E6
Cerne Abbas 9 F4
Cerney Wick 20 D2
Cerrigceinwen 46 C5
Cerrigydrudion 37 J1
Cessford 70 C1
Chaceley 29 H5
Chacewater 2 E4
Chackmore 31 H5
Chacombe 31 F4
Chad Valley 40 C7
Chadderton 49 J2
Chaddesden 41 F2
Chaddesley Corbett 29 H1
Chaddleworth 21 H4
Chadlington 30 E6
Chadshunt 30 E3
Chadwell 42 A3
Chadwell St. Mary 24 C4
Chadwick End 30 D1
Chaffcombe 8 C3
Chagford 7 F7
Chailey 13 G5
Chainhurst 14 C3
Chalbury Common 10 B4
Chaldon 23 G6
Chaldon Herring or East Chaldon 9 G6
Chale 11 F7
Chale Green 11 F7
Chalfont Common 22 D2
Chalfont St. Giles 22 C2
Chalfont St. Peter 22 D2
Chalford 20 B1
Chalgrove 21 K2
Chalk 24 C4
Challacombe 6 E1
Challoch 64 D4
Challock 15 F2
Chalmington 8 E4
Chalton Beds. 32 D6
Chalton Hants. 11 J3
Chalvington 13 J6
Champany 75 J3
Chandler's Cross 22 D2
Chandler's Ford 11 F2
Channerwick 109 D10
Chantry Som. 20 A7
Chantry Suff. 35 F4
Chapel 76 A1
Chapel Allerton Som. 19 H6
Chapel Allerton W.Yorks. 57 J6
Chapel Amble 3 G1
Chapel Brampton 31 J2
Chapel Chorlton 40 A2
Chapel Cross 13 K4
Chapel-en-le-Frith 50 C4
Chapel End 41 F6
Chapel Fields 30 E1
Chapel Haddlesey 58 B7
Chapel Hill Aber. 91 J1
Chapel Hill Lincs. 53 F7
Chapel Hill Mon. 19 J1
Chapel Lawn 28 C1
Chapel-le-Dale 56 C2
Chapel of Garioch 91 F2
Chapel Rossan 64 B6
Chapel Row 21 J5
Chapel St. Leonards 53 J5
Chapel Stile 60 E6
Chapel Town 3 F3
Chapelbank 82 B6
Chapeldonan 67 F3
Chapelhall 75 F4
Chapelhill High. 97 F4
Chapelhill P. & K. 82 B5
Chapelhill P. & K. 82 B4
Chapelknowe 69 J6
Chapelton Aber. 91 G5
Chapelton Angus 83 H3
Chapelton S.Lan. 74 E6
Chapeltown B'burn. 49 G1
Chapeltown Cumb. 69 K6
Chapeltown Moray 89 K2
Chapeltown S.Yorks. 51 F3
Chapmans Well 6 B6
Chapmanslade 20 B7

Chapmore End 33 G7
Chappel 34 C6
Chard 8 C4
Chard Junction 8 C4
Chardstock 8 C4
Charfield 20 A2
Charing 14 E3
Charing Heath 14 E3
Charingworth 30 C4
Charlbury 30 E7
Charlcombe 20 A5
Charlcutt 20 C4
Charlecote 30 D3
Charles 6 E2
Charles Tye 34 E3
Charlesfield 70 A1
Charleshill 22 B7
Charleston 82 E3
Charlestown Aber. 91 H4
Charlestown Aberdeen 99 H4
Charlestown Cornw. 4 A5
Charlestown Dorset 9 F7
Charlestown Fife 75 J2
Charlestown High. 94 E4
Charlestown High. 96 E7
Charlestown of Aberlour (Aberlour) 97 K7
Charlesworth 50 C3
Charleton 83 F7
Charlinch 8 B1
Charlton Gt.Lon. 23 H4
Charlton Hants. 21 G7
Charlton Herts. 32 E6
Charlton Northants. 31 G5
Charlton Northumb. 70 D5
Charlton Oxon. 19 K6
Charlton Som. 19 K6
Charlton W.Suss. 12 B5
Charlton Wilts. 9 J2
Charlton Wilts. 20 C3
Charlton Wilts. 20 E6
Charlton Worcs. 30 B4
Charlton Abbots 30 B6
Charlton Adam 8 E2
Charlton-All-Saints 10 C2
Charlton Horethorne 9 F2
Charlton Kings 29 J6
Charlton Mackrell 8 E2
Charlton Marshall 9 H4
Charlton Musgrove 9 G2
Charlton-on-Otmoor 31 G7
Charlwood 23 F7
Charminster 9 F5
Charmouth 8 C5
Charndon 31 H6
Charney Bassett 21 G2
Charnock Richard 48 E1
Charsfield 35 G3
Chart Corner 14 C3
Chart Sutton 14 D3
Charter Alley 21 K6
Charterhouse 19 H6
Charterville Allotments 30 E7
Chartham 15 G2
Chartham Hatch 15 F2
Chartridge 22 C1
Charwelton 31 G3
Chase End Street 29 G5
Chase Terrace 40 C5
Chasetown 40 C5
Chastleton 30 D6
Chasty 6 B5
Chatburn 56 C5
Chatcull 39 G2
Chatham 24 D5
Chathill 71 G1
Chattenden 24 D4
Chatteris 43 G7
Chattisham 34 E4
Chatto 70 C2
Chatton 71 F1
Chawleigh 7 F4
Chawley 21 H1
Chawston 32 E3
Chawton 11 J1
Cheadle Gt.Man. 49 H4
Cheadle Staffs. 40 C1
Cheadle Hulme 49 H4
Cheam 23 F5
Cheapside 22 C5
Chearsley 22 A1
Chebsey 40 A3
Checkendon 21 K3
Checkley Ches. 39 G1
Checkley Here. 28 E5
Checkley Staffs. 40 C2
Chedburgh 34 B3
Cheddar 19 H6
Cheddington 32 C7
Cheddleton 40 C1
Cheddon Fitzpaine 8 B2
Chedglow 20 C2
Chedgrave 45 H6
Chedington 8 D4
Chediston 35 H1
Chedworth 30 B7
Chedzoy 8 C1
Cheeklaw 77 F5
Cheesden 49 H1
Cheeseman's Green 15 F4
Cheetham Hill 49 H2
Cheldon 7 F4
Chelford 49 H5
Chellaston 41 F2
Chelmarsh 39 G7
Chelmondiston 35 G5
Chelmorton 50 D6
Chelmsford 24 D1
Chelsfield 23 H5
Chelsham 23 G6
Chelsworth 34 D4
Cheltenham 29 J6
Chelveston 32 C2
Chelvey 19 H5
Chelwood 19 K5
Chelwood Gate 13 H4
Cheney Longville 38 D7
Chenies 22 D2
Chepstow 19 J2
Cherhill 20 D4
Cherington Glos. 20 C2
Cherington Warks. 30 D5
Cheriton Devon 7 F1
Cheriton Hants. 11 G2
Cheriton Kent 15 H4
Cheriton Pembs. 16 C5
Cheriton Swan. 17 H5

Cheriton Bishop 7 F6
Cheriton Cross 7 F6
Cheriton Fitzpaine 7 G5
Cherrington 39 F4
Cherry Burton 59 F5
Cherry Hinton 33 H3
Cherry Willingham 52 D5
Chertsey 22 D5
Cheselbourne 9 G5
Chesham 22 C1
Chesham Bois 22 C2
Cheshunt 23 G1
Cheslyn Hay 40 B5
Chessington 22 E5
Chester 48 D6
Chester-le-Street 62 D1
Chesterblade 19 K7
Chesterfield Derbys. 51 F5
Chesterfield Staffs. 40 D5
Chesters Sc.Bord. 70 B2
Chesters Sc.Bord. 70 B2
Chesterton Cambs. 33 H3
Chesterton Cambs. 42 E6
Chesterton Oxon. 31 G6
Chesterton Shrop. 39 G6
Chesterton Staffs. 40 A1
Chesterton Green 30 E3
Chestfield 25 H5
Cheswardine 39 G3
Cheswick 77 J6
Chetnole 9 F4
Chettiscombe 7 H4
Chettisham 43 J7
Chettle 9 J3
Chetton 39 F6
Chetwode 31 H6
Chetwynd Aston 39 G4
Cheveley 33 K2
Chevening 23 H6
Cheverell's Green 32 D7
Chevington 34 B3
Chevington Drift 71 H4
Chevithorne 7 H4
Chew Magna 19 J5
Chew Stoke 19 J5
Chewton Keynsham 19 K5
Chewton Mendip 19 J6
Chicheley 32 C4
Chichester 12 B6
Chickerell 9 F6
Chickering 35 G1
Chicklade 9 J1
Chickney 33 J6
Chicksands 32 E5
Chidden 11 H3
Chiddingfold 12 C3
Chiddingly 13 J5
Chiddingstone 23 H7
Chiddingstone Causeway 23 H7
Chiddingstone Hoath 23 H7
Chideock 8 D5
Chidham 11 J4
Chieveley 21 H4
Chignall St. James 24 C1
Chignall Smealy 33 K7
Chigwell 23 H2
Chigwell Row 23 H2
Chilbolton 21 G7
Chilcomb 11 G2
Chilcombe 8 E5
Chilcompton 19 K6
Chilcote 40 E4
Child Okeford 9 H3
Childer Thornton 48 C5
Childerditch 24 C3
Childrey 21 G3
Child's Ercall 39 F3
Childswickham 30 B5
Childwall 48 D4
Childwick Green 32 E7
Chilfrome 8 E5
Chilgrove 12 B5
Chilham 15 F2
Chillaton 6 C7
Chillenden 15 H2
Chillerton 11 F6
Chillesford 35 H3
Chillingham 71 F1
Chillington Devon 5 H6
Chillington Som. 8 C3
Chilmark 9 J1
Chilson 30 E7
Chilsworthy Cornw. 4 E3
Chilsworthy Devon 6 B5
Chilthorne Domer 8 E3
Chilton Bucks. 31 H7
Chilton Dur. 62 D3
Chilton Oxon. 21 H3
Chilton Candover 11 G1
Chilton Cantelo 8 E2
Chilton Foliat 21 G4
Chilton Polden 8 C1
Chilton Street 34 B4
Chilton Trinity 8 B1
Chilvers Coton 41 F6
Chilwell 41 H2
Chilworth Hants. 11 F3
Chilworth Surr. 22 D7
Chimney 21 G1
Chineham 21 K6
Chingford 23 G2
Chinley 50 C4
Chinley Head 50 C4
Chinnor 22 A1
Chipchase Castle 70 D6
Chipley Park 7 K3
Chipnall 39 G2
Chippenham Cambs. 33 K2
Chippenham Wilts. 20 C4
Chipperfield 22 D1
Chipping Herts. 33 G5
Chipping Lancs. 56 B5
Chipping Campden 30 C5
Chipping Hill 34 C7
Chipping Norton 30 E6
Chipping Ongar 23 J1
Chipping Sodbury 20 A3
Chipping Warden 31 F4
Chipstable 7 J3
Chipstead Kent 23 H6
Chipstead Surr. 23 F6
Chirbury 38 B6
Chirk 38 B2
Chirmorrie 64 C3
Chirnside 77 G5
Chirnsidebridge 77 G5
Chirton 20 D6
Chisbury 21 F5
Chiscan 66 A2
Chiselborough 8 D3
Chiseldon 20 E3

Chislehampton 21 J2
Chislehurst 23 H4
Chislet 25 J5
Chiswell Green 22 E1
Chiswick 23 F4
Chisworth 49 J3
Chithurst 12 B4
Chittering 33 H2
Chitterne 20 C7
Chittlehamholt 6 E3
Chittlehampton 6 E3
Chittoe 20 C5
Chivelstone 5 H7
Chobham 22 C5
Choicelee 77 F5
Cholderton 21 F7
Cholesbury 22 C1
Chollerford 70 E6
Chollerton 70 E6
Cholsey 21 J3
Cholstrey 28 D3
Cholwell B. & N.E.Som. 19 K6
Cholwell Devon 4 E3
Chop Gate 63 G6
Chopwell 62 C1
Chorley Ches. 48 E7
Chorley Lancs. 48 E1
Chorley Shrop. 39 F7
Chorley Staffs. 40 C4
Chorleywood 22 D2
Chorlton 49 G7
Chorlton-cum-Hardy 49 H3
Chorlton Lane 38 D1
Chowley 48 D7
Chrishall 33 H5
Chrishall Grange 33 H4
Chrisswell 74 A3
Christchurch Cambs. 43 H6
Christchurch Dorset 10 C5
Christchurch Glos. 28 E7
Christchurch Newport 19 G3
Christian Malford 20 C4
Christleton 48 D6
Christmas Common 22 A2
Christon 19 G6
Christon Bank 71 H1
Christow 7 G7
Chryston 74 E3
Chudleigh 5 J3
Chudleigh Knighton 5 J3
Chulmleigh 6 E4
Chunal 50 C3
Church 56 C7
Church Aston 39 G4
Church Brampton 31 J2
Church Broughton 40 E2
Church Common 35 H3
Church Crookham 22 B6
Church Eaton 40 A4
Church End Beds. 32 E5
Church End Beds. 32 C6
Church End Beds. 32 E5
Church End Cambs. 43 G5
Church End Cambs. 33 H3
Church End Cambs. 33 G1
Church End E.Riding 59 G4
Church End Essex 33 J4
Church End Essex 34 B6
Church End Hants. 21 K6
Church End Herts. 32 E7
Church End Lincs. 43 F2
Church End Lincs. 53 H3
Church End Warks. 40 E6
Church End Wilts. 20 D4
Church Enstone 30 E6
Church Fenton 58 B6
Church Green 7 K6
Church Gresley 40 E4
Church Hanborough 31 F7
Church Houses 63 H7
Church Knowle 9 J6
Church Langley 23 H1
Church Langton 42 A6
Church Lawford 31 F1
Church Lawton 49 H7
Church Leigh 40 C2
Church Lench 30 B3
Church Minshull 49 F6
Church Norton 12 B7
Church Preen 38 E6
Church Pulverbatch 38 D5
Church Stoke 38 B6
Church Stowe 31 H3
Church Street 24 D4
Church Stretton 38 D6
Church Village 18 D3
Church Warsop 51 H6
Churcham 29 G7
Churchdown 29 H6
Churchend Essex 25 G2
Churchend Essex 33 K6
Churchend S.Glos. 20 A2
Churchgate 23 G1
Churchgate Street 33 H7
Churchill N.Som. 19 H6
Churchill Oxon. 30 D6
Churchill Worcs. 29 J3
Churchill Worcs. 29 H1
Churchingford 7 K4
Churchover 41 H7
Churchstanton 7 K4
Churchstow 5 H6
Churchthorpe 53 G3
Churchtown Devon 6 E1
Churchtown I.o.M. 54 D4
Churchtown Lancs. 55 H5
Churchtown Mersey. 48 C1
Churnsike Lodge 70 B6
Churston Ferrers 5 K5
Churt 12 B3
Churton 48 D7
Churwell 57 H7
Chute Cadley 21 G6
Chute Standen 21 G6
Chwilog 36 D2
Chwitffordd (Whitford) 47 K5
Chyandour 2 B5
Cilan Uchaf 36 C3
Cilcain 47 K6
Cilcennin 26 E2
Cilfrew 18 A1
Cilfynydd 18 D2
Cilgerran 26 A4
Cilgwyn Carmar. 27 G6
Cilgwyn Pembs. 16 D1

Ciliau-Aeron 26 E3
Cille Bhrighde 84 C3
Cille Pheadair 84 C3
Cilmery 27 K3
Cilrhedyn 17 F1
Cilrhedyn Bridge 16 D1
Ciltalgarth 37 H1
Cilwendeg 17 F1
Cilybebyll 18 A1
Cilycwm 27 G4
Cinderford 29 F7
Cippyn 26 A4
Cirbhig 100 D3
Cirencester 20 D1
City Dulas 46 C4
City of London 23 G4
City of Westminster 23 F4
Clabhach 78 C2
Clachaig 84 C3
Clachan Arg. & B. 80 C6
Clachan Arg. & B. 79 G2
Clachan Arg. & B. 73 F5
Clachan High. 86 B1
Clachan W.Isles 92 C7
Clachan of Campsie 74 E3
Clachan of Glendaruel 73 J2
Clachan-Seil 79 J6
Clachan Strachur 80 C7
Clachandhu 79 F4
Clachaneasy 64 D3
Clachanmore 64 A6
Clachanturn 89 K5
Clachbreck 73 F3
Clachnabrain 82 E1
Clachnaharry 96 D7
Clachtoll 102 C6
Clackmannan 75 H1
Clacton-on-Sea 35 F7
Cladach a' Chaolais 92 C5
Cladach Chircebost 92 C5
Cladich 80 B5
Claggan High. 87 H7
Claggan High. 79 J3
Claigan 93 H6
Claines 29 H3
Clandown 19 K6
Clanfield Hants. 11 J3
Clanfield Oxon. 21 F1
Clannaborough Barton 7 F5
Clanville 21 G7
Claonaig 73 G5
Claonairigh 80 B7
Claonel 96 C1
Clap Gate 57 J5
Clapgate 10 B4
Clapham Beds. 32 D3
Clapham Gt.Lon. 23 F4
Clapham N.Yorks. 56 C3
Clapham W.Suss. 12 D6
Clapham Hill 25 H5
Clappers 77 H5
Clappersgate 60 E6
Clapton 8 D4
Clapton-in-Gordano 19 H4
Clapton-on-the-Hill 30 C7
Clapworthy 6 E3
Clarach 37 F7
Clarbeston 16 D2
Clarbeston Road 16 D2
Clarborough 51 K4
Clardon 105 G2
Clare 34 B4
Clarebrand 65 H4
Clarencefield 69 F7
Clareton 57 J4
Clarilaw 70 A2
Clarkston 74 D5
Clashban 96 D2
Clashcoig 96 D2
Clashgour 80 D3
Clashindarroch 90 C1
Clashmore 96 E2
Clashnessie 102 C5
Clashnoir 89 K2
Clathy 82 A5
Clatt 90 D2
Clatter 37 J6
Clatterford End 23 J1
Clatterin Brig 90 E7
Clatteringshaws 65 F3
Clatworthy 7 J2
Claughton Lancs. 55 J3
Claughton Lancs. 55 J5
Claverdon 30 C2
Claverham 19 H5
Clavering 33 H5
Claverley 39 G6
Claverton 20 A5
Clawdd-newydd 47 J7
Clawfin 67 K3
Clawthorpe 55 J2
Clawton 6 B6
Claxby Lincs. 53 H5
Claxby Lincs. 52 E3
Claxby Pluckacre 53 G6
Claxton N.Yorks. 58 C3
Claxton Norf. 45 H5
Clay Common 45 J7
Clay Coton 31 G1
Clay Cross 51 F6
Clay of Allan 97 F4
Claybrooke Magna 41 G7
Claybrooke Parva 41 G7
Claydene 23 H7
Claydon Oxon. 31 F3
Claydon Suff. 35 F4
Claygate Kent 14 C3
Claygate Surr. 22 E5
Claygate Cross 23 K6
Clayhanger Devon 7 J3
Clayhanger W.Mid. 40 C5
Clayhidon 7 K4
Clayock 105 G3
Claypole 42 B1
Claythorpe 53 H5
Clayton S.Yorks. 51 G2
Clayton Staffs. 40 A1
Clayton W.Suss. 13 G5
Clayton W.Yorks. 57 G6
Clayton-le-Moors 56 C6
Clayton-le-Woods 55 J7
Clayton West 50 E1
Clayworth 51 K4
Cleadale 85 K6
Cleadon 71 J7
Clearbrook 5 F4
Clearwell 19 J1
Cleasby 62 D5
Cleat 107 D9
Cleatlam 62 C5
Cleatop 56 D3

Cleator 60 B5
Cleator Moor 60 B5
Cleckheaton 57 G7
Cleedownton 38 E7
Clee St. Margaret 38 E7
Cleehill 28 E1
Cleethorpes 53 G2
Cleeton St. Mary 29 F1
Cleeve N.Som. 19 H5
Cleeve Oxon. 21 K3
Cleeve Hill 29 J6
Cleeve Prior 30 B4
Cleghorn 75 H6
Clehonger 28 D5
Cleigh 79 K5
Cleish 75 J1
Cleland 75 F5
Clench Common 20 E5
Clenchwarton 43 J3
Clent 29 J1
Cleobury Mortimer 29 F1
Cleobury North 39 F7
Clephanton 97 F6
Clerklands 70 A1
Clestrain 107 C7
Cleuch Head 70 A2
Cleughbrae 69 F6
Clevancy 20 D4
Clevedon 19 H4
Cleveland Tontine 63 F7
Cleveleys 55 G5
Clevelode 29 H4
Cleverton 20 C3
Clewer 19 H6
Clewer Village 22 C4
Cley next the Sea 44 E1
Cliburn 61 G4
Cliddesden 21 K7
Cliff Carmar. 17 G4
Cliff High. 79 H1
Cliff End 14 D6
Cliffe Med. 24 D4
Cliffe N.Yorks. 58 C6
Cliffe Woods 24 D4
Clifford Here. 28 B4
Clifford W.Yorks. 57 K5
Clifford Chambers 30 C3
Clifford's Mesne 29 G6
Cliffs End 25 K5
Clifton Beds. 32 E5
Clifton Bristol 19 J4
Clifton Cumb. 61 G4
Clifton Derbys. 40 D1
Clifton Lancs. 55 H6
Clifton Northumb. 71 H5
Clifton Nott. 41 H2
Clifton Oxon. 31 F5
Clifton Stir. 80 E4
Clifton Worcs. 29 H4
Clifton Campville 40 E4
Clifton Hampden 21 J2
Clifton Reynes 32 C3
Clifton upon Dunsmore 31 G1
Clifton upon Teme 29 G2
Cliftonville 25 K4
Climping 12 D6
Climpy 75 H5
Clint 57 H4
Clint Green 44 E4
Clinterty 91 G3
Clintmains 76 E7
Clippesby 45 J4
Clipsham 42 C4
Clipston Northants. 42 A7
Clipston Notts. 41 J2
Clipstone 51 H6
Clitheroe 56 C5
Clive 38 E3
Clivocast 108 F2
Clocaenog 47 J7
Clochan 98 C4
Clochtow 91 J1
Clock Face 48 E3
Clockhill 99 G6
Cloddach 97 J6
Clodock 28 C6
Cloford 20 A1
Cloichran 81 H4
Clola 99 J6
Clonrae 68 D4
Clophill 32 D5
Clopton 32 D1
Clopton Green 34 B3
Close Clark 54 B6
Closeburn 68 D4
Closworth 8 E3
Clothall 33 F5
Clothan 108 D4
Clotton 48 E6
Clough Cumb. 61 J7
Clough Gt.Man. 49 J1
Clough Foot 56 E7
Cloughton 63 K3
Cloughton Newlands 63 K3
Clounlaid 79 J2
Clousta 109 C7
Clouston 107 C6
Clova Aber. 90 C2
Clova Angus 90 B7
Clove Lodge 62 A5
Clovelly 6 B3
Clovelly Cross 6 B3
Clovenfords 76 C7
Clovenstone 91 F3
Cloverhill 91 H3
Cloves 97 J5
Clovullin 80 B1
Clowne 51 G5
Clows Top 29 G1
Cloyntie 67 H3
Cluanach 72 B5
Clubworthy 4 C1
Cluer 93 G2
Clun 38 B7
Clunas 97 F7
Clunbury 38 C7
Clune High. 88 E2
Clune Moray 98 D4
Clunes 87 H6
Clungunford 28 C1
Clunie Aber. 98 E5
Clunie P.&K. 82 C3
Clunton 38 C7
Cluny 76 A1
Clutton B.&N.E.Som. 19 K6
Clutton Ches. 48 D7
Clwt-y-bont 46 D6
Clydach Mon. 28 B7
Clydach Swan. 17 K4
Clydach Vale 18 C2
Clydebank 74 D4
Clydey 17 F1

Clyffe Pypard 20 D4
Clynder 74 A2
Clynderwen 16 E3
Clynelish 97 F1
Clynfyw 17 F1
Clynnog-fawr 36 D1
Clyro 28 B4
Clyst Honiton 7 H6
Clyst Hydon 7 J5
Clyst St. George 7 H7
Clyst St. Lawrence 7 J5
Clyst St. Mary 7 H6
Cnewr 27 H6
Cnoc 101 G4
Cnwch Coch 27 F1
Coachford 98 C6
Coad's Green 4 C3
Coal Aston 51 F5
Coalbrookdale 39 F5
Coalbrookvale 18 E1
Coalburn 75 G7
Coalburns 71 G7
Coalcleugh 61 K2
Coaley 20 A1
Coalpit Heath 19 K3
Coalpit Hill 49 H7
Coalport 39 G5
Coalsnaughton 75 H1
Coaltown of Balgonie 76 B1
Coaltown of Wemyss 76 B1
Coalville 41 G4
Coast 95 F2
Coat 8 D2
Coatbridge 75 F4
Coate Swin. 20 E3
Coate Wilts. 20 D5
Coates Cambs. 43 G6
Coates Glos. 20 C1
Coates Lincs. 52 C4
Coates W.Suss. 12 C5
Coatham 63 G4
Coatham Mundeville 62 D4
Cobairdy 98 D6
Cobbaton 6 E3
Coberley 29 J7
Cobham Kent 24 C5
Cobham Surr. 22 E6
Cobleland 74 D1
Cobler's Green 33 K7
Cobnash 28 D2
Coburty 99 H4
Cochno 74 C3
Cock Alley 51 G6
Cock Bridge 89 K4
Cock Clarks 24 E1
Cockayne 63 H7
Cockayne Hatley 33 F4
Cockburnspath 77 F3
Cockenzie and Port Seton 76 C3
Cockerham 55 H4
Cockermouth 60 C3
Cockernhoe 32 E6
Cockett 17 K5
Cockfield Dur. 62 C4
Cockfield Suff. 34 D3
Cockfosters 23 F2
Cocking 12 B5
Cockington 5 J4
Cocklake 19 H7
Cockley Beck 60 D6
Cockley Cley 44 B5
Cockpole Green 22 A3
Cockshutt 38 D3
Cockthorpe 44 D1
Cockwood 7 H7
Codda 4 B3
Coddenham 35 F3
Coddington Ches. 48 D7
Coddington Here. 29 G4
Coddington Notts. 52 B7
Codford St. Mary 9 J1
Codford St. Peter 20 C7
Codicote 33 F7
Codmore Hill 12 D5
Codnor 41 G1
Codrington 20 A4
Codsall 40 A5
Codsall Wood 40 A5
Coed Morgan 28 C7
Coed-y-paen 19 G2
Coed-yr-ynys 28 A6
Coed Ystumgwern 36 E3
Coedcae 19 F1
Coedely 18 D3
Coedkernew 19 F3
Coedpoeth 48 B7
Coelbren 27 H7
Coffinswell 5 J4
Cofton Hackett 30 B1
Cogan 18 E4
Cogenhoe 32 B2
Coggeshall 34 C6
Coggeshall Hamlet 34 C6
Coggins Mill 13 J4
Cóig Peighinnean W.Isles 101 F2
Cóig Peighinnean W.Isles 101 H1
Coilantogle 81 G7
Coileitir 80 C3
Coilessan 80 D7
Coillaig 80 B5
Coille Mhorgil 87 H4
Coille-righ 87 F2
Coillore 85 J1
Coity 18 C3
Col 101 G3
Colaboll 103 H7
Colan 3 F2
Colaton Raleigh 7 J7
Colbost 93 H7
Colbury 10 E3
Colby Cumb. 61 H4
Colby I.o.M. 54 B6
Colby Norf. 45 G2
Colchester 34 D6
Colcot 18 E5
Cold Ash 21 J5
Cold Ashby 31 H1
Cold Ashton 20 A4
Cold Aston 30 C6
Cold Blow 16 E3
Cold Brayfield 32 C3
Cold Chapel 68 E1
Cold Hanworth 52 D4
Cold Hesledon 63 F2
Cold Higham 31 H3
Cold Kirby 58 B1
Cold Newton 42 A5
Cold Norton 24 E1
Cold Overton 42 B5
Coldbackie 103 J2
Coldblow 23 J4
Coldean 13 G6
Coldeast 5 J3

Colden Common 11 F2
Coldfair Green 35 J2
Coldham 43 H5
Coldharbour 22 E7
Coldingham 77 G4
Coldrain 82 B7
Coldred 15 H3
Coldrey 22 A7
Coldridge 6 E5
Coldrife 71 F4
Coldstream 77 G7
Coldwaltham 12 D5
Coldwells 99 K6
Cole 9 F1
Cole Green 33 F7
Colebatch 38 C7
Colebrook 7 J5
Colebrooke 7 F5
Coleby Lincs. 52 C6
Coleby N.Lincs. 52 C1
Coleford Devon 7 F5
Coleford Glos. 28 E7
Coleford Som. 19 K7
Colehill 10 B4
Coleman's Hatch 13 H3
Colemere 38 D2
Colemore 11 J1
Colenden 82 C5
Coleorton 41 G4
Colerne 20 B4
Cole's Cross 5 H6
Colesbourne 30 B7
Colesden 32 E3
Coleshill Bucks. 22 C2
Coleshill Oxon. 21 F2
Coleshill Warks. 40 E7
Colestocks 7 J5
Colfin 64 A5
Colgate 13 F3
Colgrain 74 B2
Colinsburgh 83 F7
Colinton 76 A4
Colintraive 73 J3
Colkirk 44 D3
Collace 82 D4
Collafirth Shet. 109 D6
Collafirth Shet. 108 C4
Collamoor Head 4 B1
Collaton St. Mary 5 J4
Collessie 82 D6
Colleton Mills 6 E4
Collett's Green 29 H3
Collier Row 23 J2
Collier Street 14 C3
Collier's End 33 G6
Colliery Row 62 E1
Colliston 91 J2
Collin 69 F6
Collingbourne Ducis 21 F6
Collingbourne Kingston 21 F6
Collingham Notts. 52 B6
Collingham W.Yorks. 57 J5
Collington 29 F2
Collingtree 31 J3
Collins Green 48 E3
Colliston 83 H3
Colliton 7 J5
Collmuir 90 D4
Collycroft 41 F7
Collynie 91 G1
Collyweston 42 D5
Colmonell 67 F5
Colmworth 32 E3
Coln Rogers 20 D1
Coln St. Aldwyns 20 E1
Coln St. Dennis 30 B7
Colnabaichin 89 K4
Colnbrook 22 D4
Colne Cambs. 33 G1
Colne Lancs. 56 D5
Colne Engaine 34 C5
Colney 45 F5
Colney Heath 23 F1
Colney Street 22 E1
Colonsay 72 B1
Colpy 90 E1
Colquhar 76 B6
Colsterdale 57 G1
Colsterworth 42 C3
Colston Bassett 42 A2
Coltfield 97 J5
Coltishall 45 G4
Colton Cumb. 55 G1
Colton N.Yorks. 58 B5
Colton Norf. 45 F4
Colton Staffs. 40 C3
Colva 28 B3
Colvend 65 J5
Colvister 108 E3
Colwall Green 29 G4
Colwall Stone 29 G4
Colwell 70 E6
Colwich 40 C3
Colwick 41 J1
Colwinston 18 C4
Colworth 12 C6
Colwyn Bay (Bae Colwyn) 47 G5
Colyford 8 B5
Colyton 8 B5
Combe Here. 28 C2
Combe Oxon. 31 F7
Combe W.Berks. 21 G5
Combe Cross 5 H3
Combe Down 20 A5
Combe Florey 7 K2
Combe Hay 20 A5
Combe Martin 6 D1
Combe Raleigh 7 K5
Combe St. Nicholas 8 B3
Combeinteignhead 5 K3
Comberbach 49 F5
Comberford 40 D5
Comberton Cambs. 33 G3
Comberton Here. 28 D2
Combpyne 8 B5
Combrook 30 E3
Combs Derbys. 50 C5
Combs Suff. 34 E3
Combs Ford 34 E3
Combwich 19 F7
Comer 90 E4
Commercial End 33 J2
Commins Coch 37 H5
Common Edge 55 G6
Common Moor 4 C4
Common Side 51 F5
Commondale 63 H5
Commonside 40 E1
Compstall 49 J3
Compton Devon 5 J4
Compton Hants. 11 F2
Compton Surr. 22 C7
Compton W.Berks. 21 J4

Compton W.Suss. 11 J3
Compton Abbas 9 H3
Compton Abdale 30 B7
Compton Bassett 20 D4
Compton Beauchamp 21 F3
Compton Bishop 19 G6
Compton Chamberlayne 10 B2
Compton Dando 19 K5
Compton Dundon 8 D1
Compton Martin 19 J6
Compton Pauncefoot 9 F2
Compton Valence 8 E5
Comra 88 C5
Comrie 81 J5
Conchra Arg. & B. 73 J2
Conchra High. 86 E2
Concraigie 82 C3
Conder Green 55 H4
Conderton 29 J5
Condicote 30 C6
Condorrat 75 F3
Condover 38 D5
Coney Weston 34 D1
Coneyhurst 12 E4
Coneysthorpe 58 D2
Coneythorpe 57 J4
Conford 12 B3
Congash 89 H2
Congdon's Shop 4 C3
Congerstone 41 F5
Congham 44 B3
Congleton 49 H6
Congresbury 19 H5
Conicavel 97 G6
Coningsby 53 F7
Conington Cambs. 42 E7
Conington Cambs. 33 G2
Conisbrough 51 H3
Conisby 72 A4
Conisholme 53 H3
Coniston Cumb. 60 E7
Coniston E.Riding 59 H6
Coniston Cold 56 E4
Conistone 56 E3
Conland 98 E6
Connah's Quay 48 B6
Connel 80 A4
Connel Park 68 B2
Connor Downs 2 C5
Conon Bridge 96 C6
Cononish 80 E5
Cononley 56 E5
Cononsyth 83 G3
Consall 40 B1
Consett 62 C1
Constable Burton 62 C7
Constantine 2 E6
Contin 96 B6
Contlaw 91 G4
Contullich 96 D4
Conwy 47 F5
Conyer 25 F5
Cooden 14 C7
Coodham 74 B7
Cookbury 6 C5
Cookham 22 B3
Cookham Dean 22 B3
Cookham Rise 22 B3
Cookhill 30 B3
Cookley Suff. 35 H1
Cookley Worcs. 40 A7
Cookley Green 21 K3
Cookney 91 G5
Cooksbridge 13 H5
Cookshill 40 B1
Cooksmill Green 24 C1
Cookston 91 H1
Coolham 12 E4
Cooling 24 D4
Coombe Cornw. 3 G3
Coombe Cornw. 6 A4
Coombe Cornw. 2 D4
Coombe Devon 5 H6
Coombe Devon 7 G7
Coombe Bissett 10 C2
Coombe Hill 29 H6
Coombe Keynes 9 H6
Coombes 12 E6
Coombes Moor 28 C2
Cooper's Corner E.Suss. 14 C5
Cooper's Corner Kent 23 H7
Cooper's Hill 22 C4
Coopersale Common 23 H1
Cootham 12 D5
Cop Street 15 H2
Copdock 35 F4
Copford Green 34 D6
Copgrove 57 J3
Copister 108 D5
Cople 32 E4
Copley 62 B4
Coplow Dale 50 D5
Copmanthorpe 58 B5
Coppathorne 6 A5
Coppenhall 40 B4
Coppenhall Moss 49 G7
Coppingford 32 E1
Copplestone 7 F5
Coppull 48 E1
Coppull Moor 48 E1
Copsale 12 E4
Copster Green 56 B6
Copston Magna 41 G7
Copt Heath 30 C1
Copt Hewick 57 J2
Copt Oak 41 G4
Copthorne 13 G3
Copy Lake 6 E4
Copythorne 10 E3
Coralhill 99 J4
Corbiegoe 105 J4
Corbridge 70 E7
Corby 42 B7
Corby Glen 42 D3
Cordach 90 E5
Coreley 29 F1
Corfcott Green 6 B6
Corfe 8 B3
Corfe Castle 9 J6
Corfe Mullen 9 J5
Corfton 38 D7
Corgarff 89 K4
Corhampton 11 H2
Corley 40 E7
Corley Ash 40 E7
Corley Moor 40 E7
Cornabus 72 B6
Corney 60 C7
Cornforth 62 E3
Cornhill 98 D5
Cornhill on Tweed 77 G7
Cornholme 56 E7

Cornish Hall End 33 K5
Cornquoy 107 E7
Cornriggs 61 K2
Cornsay 62 C2
Cornsay Colliery 62 C2
Corntown High. 96 C6
Corntown V. of Glam. 18 C4
Cornwell 30 D6
Cornwood 5 G5
Cornworthy 5 J5
Corpach 87 H7
Corpusty 45 F3
Corrachree 90 C4
Corran Arg. & B. 74 A1
Corran High. 86 E4
Corran High. 80 B1
Corranbuie 73 G4
Corranmore 79 J7
Corrany 54 D5
Corrie 73 J6
Corrie Common 69 H5
Corriechrevie 73 F5
Corriecravie 66 D1
Corrielorne 79 K6
Corrievorrie 88 E2
Corrimony 87 K1
Corringham Lincs. 52 B3
Corringham Thur. 24 D3
Corris 37 G5
Corris Uchaf 37 G5
Corrlarrach 87 F7
Corrour Shooting Lodge 81 F1
Corrow 80 C7
Corry 86 C2
Corrychurrachan 80 B1
Corrykinloch 103 F6
Corrylach 66 B1
Corrymuckloch 81 K4
Corscombe 8 E4
Corse Aber. 98 E6
Corse Glos. 29 G6
Corse Lawn 29 H5
Corse of Kinnoir 98 D6
Corsebank 68 D2
Corsehill 69 G5
Corsewall 64 A4
Corsham 20 B4
Corsindae 90 E4
Corsley 20 B7
Corsley Heath 20 B7
Corsock 65 H3
Corston B. & N.E.Som. 19 K5
Corston Wilts. 20 C3
Corstorphine 75 K3
Cortachy 82 E2
Corton Suff. 45 K6
Corton Wilts. 20 C7
Corton Denham 9 F2
Coruna (Corunna) 92 D5
Corunna (Córúna) 92 D5
Corwar House 67 G5
Corwen 37 K1
Coryton Devon 6 C7
Coryton Thur. 24 D3
Cosby 41 H6
Coseley 40 B6
Cosford 39 G5
Cosgrove 31 J4
Cosham 11 H4
Cosheston 16 D4
Coshieville 81 J3
Cossall 41 G1
Cossington Leics. 41 J4
Cossington Som. 19 G7
Costa 106 C5
Costessey 45 F4
Costock 41 H3
Coston Leics. 42 B3
Coston Norf. 44 E5
Cote Oxon. 21 G1
Cote Som. 19 G6
Cotebrook 48 E6
Cotehill 61 F1
Cotes Cumb. 55 H1
Cotes Leics. 41 H3
Cotes Staffs. 40 A2
Cotesbach 41 H7
Cotgrave 41 J2
Cotham 42 A1
Cothelstone 7 K2
Cothercott 38 D5
Cotheridge 29 G3
Cotherstone 62 B5
Cothill 21 H2
Cotleigh 8 B4
Coton Cambs. 33 H3
Coton Northants. 31 H1
Coton Staffs. 40 D5
Coton Staffs. 40 A2
Coton Clanford 40 A3
Coton in the Clay 40 D3
Coton in the Elms 40 E4
Cott 5 H4
Cottam E.Riding 59 F3
Cottam Lancs. 55 H6
Cottam Notts. 52 B4
Cottartown 89 H1
Cottenham 33 H2
Cotterdale 61 K7
Cottered 33 G6
Cotteridge 40 C7
Cotterstock 42 D6
Cottesbrooke 31 J1
Cottesmore 42 C4
Cottingham E.Riding 59 G6
Cottingham Northants. 42 B6
Cottisford 31 G5
Cotton Suff. 34 E2
Cottown Aber. 90 D2
Cottown Aber. 99 G6
Cottown Aber. 99 F6
Cotwalton 40 B2
Couch's Mill 4 B5
Coughton Here. 28 E6
Coughton Warks. 30 B2
Cougie 87 J2
Coulaghailtro 72 E5
Coulags 95 F7
Coulby Newham 63 G5
Coulderton 60 A6
Coull 90 D4
Coulport 74 A2
Coulsdon 23 F6
Coulston 20 C6
Coulter 75 J7
Coultershaw Bridge 12 C5
Coultings 19 F7
Coulton 58 C2
Coultra 82 E5
Cound 38 E5

Coundon 62 D3
Coundon Grange 62 D4
Countersett 56 E1
Countess 20 E7
Countess Wear 7 H6
Countesthorpe 41 H6
Countisbury 7 F1
County Oak 13 F3
Coupar Angus 82 D3
Coupland Cumb. 61 J5
Coupland Northumb. 77 H7
Cour 73 G6
Court-at-Street 15 F4
Court Barton 7 G6
Court Henry 17 J2
Court House Green 41 F7
Courteenhall 31 J3
Courtsend 25 G2
Courtway 8 B1
Cousland 76 B4
Cousley Wood 13 K3
Coustonn 73 J3
Cove Arg. & B. 74 A2
Cove Devon 7 H4
Cove Hants. 22 B6
Cove High. 94 E2
Cove Sc.Bord. 77 F3
Cove Bay 91 H4
Covehithe 45 K7
Coven 40 B5
Coveney 43 H7
Covenham St. Bartholomew 53 G3
Covenham St. Mary 53 G3
Coventry 30 E1
Coverack 2 E7
Coverham 57 F1
Covesea 97 J4
Covington Cambs. 32 D1
Covington S.Lan. 75 H7
Cowan Bridge 56 B2
Cowbeech 13 K5
Cowbit 43 F4
Cowbridge 18 D4
Cowden 23 H7
Cowden Pound 23 H7
Cowdenbeath 75 K1
Cowes 11 F5
Cowesby 63 F7
Cowfold 13 F4
Cowgill 56 C1
Cowie Aber. 91 G6
Cowie Stir. 75 G2
Cowlam Manor 59 F3
Cowley Devon 7 H6
Cowley Glos. 29 J7
Cowley Gt.Lon. 22 D3
Cowley Oxon. 21 J1
Cowling N.Yorks. 56 E5
Cowling N.Yorks. 57 H1
Cowlinge 34 B3
Cowmes 50 D1
Cowpen 71 H5
Cowpen Bewley 63 F4
Cowplain 11 H3
Cowshill 61 K2
Cowthorpe 57 K4
Cox Common 45 H7
Coxbank 39 F1
Coxbench 41 F1
Coxheath 14 C2
Coxhoe 62 E3
Coxley 19 J7
Coxtie Green 23 J2
Coxwold 58 B2
Coychurch 18 C4
Coylet 73 K2
Coylton 67 J2
Coylumbridge 89 G3
Coynach 90 C4
Coynachie 90 C1
Coytrahen 18 B3
Crabbet Park 13 G3
Crabbs Cross 30 B2
Crabtree Plym. 5 F5
Crabtree W.Suss. 13 F4
Crackaig 72 D4
Crackenthorpe 61 H4
Crackington 4 B1
Crackington Haven 4 B1
Cracklybank 39 G4
Crackpot 62 A7
Cracoe 56 E3
Craddock 7 K2
Cradhlastadh 100 C4
Cradley Here. 29 G4
Cradley W.Mid. 40 B7
Crafthole 4 D5
Cragg 57 F7
Craggan Moray 89 H1
Craggan P.&K. 81 K6
Cragganruar 81 H3
Craggie High. 88 E1
Craggie High. 104 D6
Craghead 62 D1
Craibstone Aberdeen 91 G3
Craibstone Moray 98 C5
Craichie 83 F3
Craig Arg. & B. 80 B4
Craig Arg. & B. 79 G5
Craig D. & G. 65 G4
Craig High. 94 D5
Craig High. 95 G7
Craig S.Ayr. 67 H3
Craig-cefn-parc 17 K4
Craig-y-nos 27 H7
Craigans 73 H1
Craigbeg 88 B6
Craigcleuch 69 J5
Craigculter 99 H5
Craigdallie 82 D5
Craigdam 91 G1
Craigdarroch D. & G. 68 C4
Craigdarroch E.Ayr. 68 B3
Craigdhu D. & G. 64 D6
Craigdhu High. 96 B7
Craigearn 91 F3
Craigellachie 97 K7
Craigencallie 65 F3
Craigend Moray 97 J6
Craigend P.&K. 82 C5
Craigendive 73 J2
Craigendoran 74 B2
Craigends 74 C4
Craigengillan 67 J3
Craigenputtock 68 C4
Craigens 72 A4
Craigglas 73 G1
Craighall 83 F6
Craighat 74 C2
Craighead Fife 83 H7
Craighead High. 96 E5
Craighlaw 64 D4

Craighouse 72 D4
Craigie Aber. 91 H3
Craigie P.&K. 82 C3
Craigie S.Ayr. 74 C7
Craigie Brae 91 G1
Craigieburn 69 G3
Craigieholm 82 C4
Craiglockhart 76 A3
Craiglug 91 G5
Craigmaud 99 G5
Craigmillar 76 A3
Craigmore 73 K4
Craigmyle House 90 E4
Craignafeoch 73 H3
Craignant 38 B2
Craignavie 81 G4
Craigneil 67 F5
Craignure 79 J4
Craigo 83 H1
Craigoch 67 H3
Craigow 82 B7
Craigrothie 82 E6
Craigroy 97 J6
Craigroy Farm 82 E6
Craigruie 81 G5
Craigsanquhar 82 E6
Craigton Aberdeen
Craigton Angus 83 G4
Craigton Angus 82 E2
Craigton Stir. 74 E2
Craigtown 104 D3
Craik Aber. 90 C2
Craik Sc.Bord. 69 J3
Crail 83 H7
Crailing 70 B1
Crailinghall 70 B1
Crakehill 57 K2
Crakemarsh 40 C2
Crambe 58 D3
Cramlington 71 H6
Cramond 75 K3
Cranage 49 G6
Cranberry 40 A2
Cranborne 10 B3
Cranbourne 22 C4
Cranbrook 14 C4
Cranbrook Common 14 C4
Cranfield 32 C4
Cranford Devon 6 B3
Cranford Gt.Lon. 22 E4
Cranford St. Andrew 32 C1
Cranford St. John 32 C1
Cranham Glos. 29 H7
Cranham Gt.Lon. 23 J3
Crank 48 E2
Cranleigh 12 D3
Cranmer Green 34 E1
Cranmore I.o.W. 11 F5
Cranmore Som. 19 K7
Cranna 98 E5
Crannach 98 C5
Cranoe 42 A6
Cransford 35 H2
Cranshaws 76 E4
Cranstal 54 D3
Crantock 2 E2
Cranwell 42 D1
Cranwich 44 B6
Cranworth 44 D5
Craobh Haven 79 J7
Crapstone 5 F4
Crarae 73 H1
Crask Inn 103 H6
Crask of Aigas 96 B7
Craster 71 H1
Craswall 28 B5
Cratfield 35 H1
Crathes 91 F5
Crathie Aber. 89 K5
Crathie High. 88 C5
Crathorne 63 F6
Craven Arms 38 D7
Craw 73 G6
Crawcrook 71 G7
Crawford Lancs. 48 D2
Crawford S.Lan. 68 E1
Crawfordjohn 68 D1
Crawfordton 68 C4
Crawick 68 C2
Crawley Hants. 11 F1
Crawley Oxon. 30 E7
Crawley W.Suss. 13 F3
Crawley Down 13 G3
Crawleyside 62 A2
Crawshawbooth 56 D7
Crawton 91 G7
Crawyn 54 C4
Cray N.Yorks. 56 E2
Cray P.&K. 82 C1
Cray Powys 27 H6
Crayford 23 J4
Crayke 58 B2
Crays Hill 24 D2
Cray's Pond 21 K3
Crazies Hill 22 A3
Creacombe 7 G4
Creag Ghoraidh 92 D7
Creagbheitheachain 80 A1
Creaton 31 J1
Creca 69 H6
Credenhill 28 D4
Crediton 7 G5
Creech Heathfield 8 B2
Creech St. Michael 8 B2
Creed 3 G4
Creedy Park 7 G5
Creekmouth 23 H3
Creeting St. Mary 34 E3
Creeton 42 D3
Creetown 64 E5
Creggans 80 B7
Cregneash 54 A7
Cregrina 28 A3
Creich 82 E5
Creigiau 18 D3
Crelevan 87 K1
Cremyll 4 E5
Cressage 38 E5
Cresselly 16 D4
Cressing 34 B6
Cresswell Northumb. 71 H4
Cresswell Staffs. 40 B2
Cresswell Quay 16 D4
Creswell 51 H5
Cretingham 35 G3
Cretshengan 73 F4
Crewe Ches. 49 G7
Crewe Ches. 48 D7
Crewgreen 38 C4
Crewkerne 8 D4
Crewton 41 F2
Crianlarich 80 E5
Cribbs Causeway 19 J3
Cribyn 26 E3

Criccieth	36	D2	Crossaig	73	G5	Culham	21	J2	Cynwyl Elfed	17	G2	Dargate	25	G5	Denston	34	B3	Dockenfield	22	B7
Crich	51	F7	Crossapol	78	C2	Culindrach	73	H5				Dargues	70	D4	Denstone	40	C1	Docking	44	B2
Crich Carr	51	F7	Crossapoll	78	A3	Culkein	102	C5	**D**			Darite	4	C4	Dent	56	C1	Docklow	28	E3
Crichie	99	H6	Crossbush	12	D6	Culkerton	20	C2	Dabton	68	D4	Darlaston	40	B6	Denton Cambs.	42	E7	Dockray	60	E4
Crichton	76	B4	Crosscanonby	60	B3	Cullachie	89	G2	Daccombe	5	K4	Darley	57	H4	Denton Darl.	62	D5	Doddinghurst	23	J2
Crick Mon.	19	H3	Crossdale Street	45	G2	Cullen	98	D4	Dacre Cumb.	61	F4	Darley Dale	50	E6	Denton E.Suss.	13	H6	Doddington	43	G6
Crick Northants.	31	G1	Crossens	55	G7	Cullercoats	71	J6	Dacre N.Yorks.	57	G3	Darlingscott	30	D4	Denton Gt.Man.	49	J3	Cambs.		
Crickadarn	27	K4	Crossford D. & G.	68	D5	Cullicudden	96	D5	Dacre Banks	57	G3	Darlington	62	D5	Denton Kent	15	H3	Doddington Kent	14	E2
Cricket Malherbie	8	C3	Crossford Fife	75	J2	Culligran	95	K7	Daddry Shield	61	K3	Darliston	38	E2	Denton Lincs.	42	B2	Doddington Lincs.	52	C5
Cricket St. Thomas	8	C4	Crossford S.Lan.	75	G6	Cullingworth	57	F6	Dadford	31	H5	Darlton	51	K5	Denton N.Yorks.	57	G5	Doddington	77	H7
Crickheath	38	B3	Crossgate	43	F3	Cullipool	79	J6	Dadlington	41	G6	Darnabo	99	F6	Denton Norf.	45	G7	Northumb.		
Crickhowell	28	B7	Crossgatehall	76	B4	Culloch	81	J6	Dafen	17	J4	Darnall	51	F4	Denton Northants.	32	B3	Doddington Shrop.	28	E1
Cricklade	20	D2	Crossgates Fife	75	K2	Culloden	96	E7	Daffy Green	44	D5	Darnconner	67	K1	Denton Oxon.	21	J1	Doddiscombsleigh	7	G7
Cridling Stubbs	58	B7	Crossgates P. & K.	82	B5	Cullompton	7	J5	Dagenham	23	H3	Darnford	91	F5	Denton	77	H7	Dodford	31	H2
Crieff	81	K5	Crossgates Powys	27	K2	Culmaily	97	F2	Daggons	10	C3	Darngarroch	65	G4	Northumb.			Northants.		
Criggion	38	B4	Crossgill	55	J3	Culmalzie	64	D5	Daglingworth	20	C1	Darnick	76	D7	Denver	44	A5	Dodford Worcs.	29	J1
Crigglestone	51	F1	Crosshands	74	C7	Culmington	38	D7	Dagnall	32	C7	Darowen	37	H5	Denvilles	11	J4	Dodington S.Glos.	20	A3
Crimdon Park	63	F3	Crosshill Fife	75	K1	Culmstock	7	J4	Dail	80	B4	Darra	99	F6	Denwick	71	H2	Dodington Som.	7	K1
Crimond	99	J5	Crosshill S.Ayr.	67	H3	Culnacraig	95	G1	Dail Beag	100	E3	Darras Hall	71	G6	Deopham	44	E5	Dodington Ash	20	A4
Crimonmogate	99	J5	Crosshouse	74	B7	Culnadalloch	80	A4	Dail Bho Dheas	101	G1	Darrington	51	G1	Deopham Green	44	E6	Dodleston	48	C6
Crimplesham	44	A5	Crosskeys	19	F2	Culnaknock	94	B5	Dail Bho Thuath	101	G1	Darsham	35	J2	Depden	34	B3	Dodworth	51	F2
Crinan	73	F1	Crosskirk	105	F1	Culnamean	85	K2	Dail Mòr	100	E3	Dartfield	99	J5	Deptford Gt.Lon.	23	G4	Doe Lea	51	G6
Cringleford	45	F5	Crosslanes Cornw.	2	D6	Culpho	35	G4	Dailly	67	G3	Dartford	23	J4	Deptford Wilts.	10	B1	Dog Village	7	H6
Cringletie	76	A6	Crosslanes Shrop.	38	C4	Culquhirk	64	E5	Dailnamac	80	A4	Dartington	5	H4	Derby	41	F2	Dogdyke	53	F7
Crinow	16	E3	Crosslee Renf.	74	C4	Culrain	96	C2	Dairsie or	83	F6	Dartmeet	5	G3	Derbyhaven	54	B7	Dogmersfield	22	A6
Cripplesease	2	B5	Crosslee Sc.Bord.	69	J2	Culross	75	H2	Osnaburgh			Dartmouth	5	J5	Dererach	79	G5	Dol Fawr	37	H5
Cripp's Corner	14	C5	Crosslet	74	C3	Culroy	67	H2	Dalabrog	84	C2	Darton	51	F2	Deri	18	E1	Dol-gran	17	H1
Crix	34	B7	Crossmichael	65	H4	Culsh	90	B5	Dalavich	80	A6	Darvel	74	D7	Derringstone	15	G3	Dolanog	37	K4
Croalchapel	68	E4	Crossmoor	55	H6	Culshabbin	64	D5	Dalballoch	88	D5	Darwell Hole	13	K5	Derrington	40	A3	Dolau	28	A2
Croasdale	60	B5	Crossroads Aber.	91	F5	Culswick	109	B8	Dalbeattie	65	J4	Darwen	56	B7	Derry	81	H5	Dolbenmaen	36	E1
Crock Street	8	C3	Crossroads E.Ayr.	74	C7	Culter Allers Farm	75	J7	Dalblair	68	B2	Datchet	22	C4	Derry Hill	20	C4	Dolfach	27	J1
Crockenhill	23	J5	Crossway Mon.	28	D7	Cultercullen	91	H2	Dalbog	90	D7	Datchworth	33	F7	Derrythorpe	52	B2	Dolfor	38	A7
Crockernwell	7	F6	Crossway Powys	27	K3	Cults Aber.	90	D1	Dalbreck	104	C7	Datchworth Green	33	F7	Dersingham	44	A2	Dolgarreg	27	G5
Crockerton	20	B7	Crossway Green	29	H2	Cults Aberdeen	91	G4	Dalby	54	B6	Daubhill	49	G2	Dervaig	79	F2	Dolgarrog	47	F6
Crocketford or	65	J3	Crossways Dorset	9	G6	Cults D. & G.	64	E6	Dalcairnie	67	J3	Daugh of	97	K7	Derwen	47	J7	Dolgellau	37	G4
Ninemile Bar			Crossways Glos.	28	E7	Cultybraggan	81	J6	Dalchalloch	81	J1	Kinermony			Derwenlas	37	G6	Dolgoch	37	F5
Crockey Hill	58	C5	Crosswell	16	E1	Camp			Dalchalm	97	G1	Dauntsey	20	C3	Derwydd	17	K3	Doll	97	F1
Crockham Hill	23	H6	Crosthwaite	61	F7	Culverhouse Cross	18	E4	Dalchenna	80	B7	Dava	89	H1	Derybruich	73	H3	Dollar	75	H1
Crockhurst Street	23	K7	Croston	48	D1	Culverstone Green	24	C5	Dalchirach	89	J1	Davaar	66	B2	Desborough	42	B7	Dollarbeg	75	H1
Crockleford Heath	34	E6	Crostwick	45	G4	Culverthorpe	42	D1	Dalchork	103	H7	Davan	90	C4	Desford	41	G5	Dolleycanney	28	A4
Croes Hywel	28	C7	Crostwight	45	H2	Culvie	98	D5	Dalchreichart	87	J3	Davenham	49	F5	Detchant	77	J7	Dolphinholme	55	J4
Croes-lan	26	C4	Crouch	23	K6	Culworth	31	G4	Dalchruin	81	J6	Daventry	31	G2	Detling	14	C2	Dolphinton	75	K6
Croes-y-mwyalch	19	G2	Crouch Hill	9	G3	Cumberhead	75	F7	Dalcross	96	E7	Davidston	4	B2	Deuddwr	38	B4	Dolton	6	D4
Croes y pant	19	G1	Croughton	31	G5	Cumbernauld	75	F3	Dalderby	53	F6	Davington	69	H3	Deunant	47	H6	Dolwen Conwy	47	G5
Croesau Bach	38	B3	Crovie	99	G4	Cumberworth	53	J5	Daldownie	89	K4	Daviot Aber.	91	F2	Deuxhill	39	F7	Dolwen Powys	37	J5
Croeserw	18	B2	Crow	10	C4	Cuminestown	99	G5	Dale Derbys.	41	G2	Daviot High.	88	E1	Devauden	19	H2	Dolwyddelan	47	F7
Croesgoch	16	B2	Crow Hill	29	F6	Cumloden	64	E4	Dale Pembs.	16	B4	Davoch of Grange	98	C5	Devil's Bridge	27	G1	Dolybont	37	F7
Croesor	37	F1	Crowan	2	D5	Cummersdale	60	E1	Dale Head	61	F5	Dawley	39	F5	(Pontarfynach)			Dolyhir	28	B3
Croespenmaen	18	E2	Crowborough	13	J3	Cummertrees	69	G7	Dale of Walls	109	A7	Dawlish	5	K3	Devizes	20	D5	Domgay	38	B4
Croesyceiliog	17	H3	Crowcombe	7	K2	Cummingstown	97	J5	Dale Park	12	C6	Dawn	47	G6	Devonport	4	E5	Doncaster	51	H2
Carmar.			Crowdecote	50	D6	Cumnock	67	K1	Dalehouse	63	J5	Daws Heath	24	E3	Devonside	75	H1	Donhead St.	9	J2
Croesyceiliog	19	G2	Crowdhill	11	F2	Cumnor	21	H1	Dalelia	79	J1	Dawsmere	43	H2	Devoran	2	E5	Andrew		
Torfaen			Crowfield	31	H4	Cumrew	61	G1	Daless	89	F1	Daylesford	30	D6	Dewar	76	B6	Donhead St. Mary	9	J2
Croft Leics.	41	H6	Northants.			Cumrue	69	F5	Dalestie	89	J3	Ddôl	47	K5	Dewlish	9	G5	Donibristle	75	K2
Croft Lincs.	53	J6	Crowfield Suff.	35	F3	Cumstoun	65	G5	Dalfad	90	B4	Deadwaters	75	F6	Dewsall Court	28	D5	Doniford	7	J1
Croft Warr.	49	F3	Crowhurst E.Suss.	14	C6	Cumwhinton	61	F1	Dalganachan	105	F4	Deal	15	J2	Dewsbury	57	H7	Donington	12	E5
Croft-on-Tees	62	D5	Crowhurst Surr.	23	G7	Cumwhitton	61	G1	Dalgarven	74	A6	Deal Hall	25	G2	Dhiseig	79	F4	Donington le Heath	41	G4
Crofthead	69	J6	Crowhurst Lane	23	G7	Cundall	57	K2	Dalgety Bay	75	K2	Dean Cumb.	60	B4	Dhoon	54	D5	Donington on Bain	53	F4
Croftmore	81	K1	End			Cunninghamhead	74	B6	Dalgig	67	K2	Dean Devon	5	H4	Dhoor	54	D4	Donisthorpe	41	F4
Crofton W.Yorks.	51	F1	Crowland Lincs.	43	F4	Cunnister	108	E3	Dalginross	81	J5	Dean Dorset	9	J3	Dhowin	54	D3	Donkey Town	22	C5
Crofton Wilts.	21	F5	Crowland Suff.	34	E1	Cunnoquhie	82	E6	Dalgonar	68	C3	Dean Hants.	11	G3	Duhallow	88	C2	Donnington Glos.	30	C6
Crofts	65	H3	Crowlas	2	C5	Cupar	82	E6	Dalguise	82	A3	Dean Oxon.	30	E6	Dial Post	12	E5	Donnington Here.	29	G5
Crofts of	105	G5	Crowle N.Lincs.	51	K1	Cupar Muir	82	E6	Dalhalvaig	104	D3	Dean Som.	19	K7	Dibden	11	F4	Donnington Shrop.	38	E5
Benachielt			Crowle Worcs.	29	J3	Curbar	50	E5	Dalham	34	B2	Dean Bank	62	D3	Dibden Purlieu	11	F4	Donnington	39	G4
Crofts of Buinach	97	J6	Crowle Green	29	J3	Curbridge Hants.	11	G3	Daligan	74	B2	Dean Prior	5	H4	Dickleburgh	45	F7	Tel. & W.		
Crofts of Haddo	91	G1	Crowmarsh Gifford	21	K3	Curbridge Oxon.	21	G1	Dalivaddy	66	A2	Dean Row	49	H4	Didbrook	30	B5	Donnington	21	H5
Crofty	17	J5	Crownhill	4	E5	Curdridge	11	G3	Daljarrock	67	F5	Dean Street	14	C2	Didcot	21	J3	W.Berks.		
Crogen	37	K2	Crownthorpe	44	E5	Curdworth	40	D6	Dalkeith	76	B4	Deanburnhaugh	69	J2	Diddington	32	E2	Donnington	12	B6
Croggan	79	J5	Crowntown	2	D5	Curland	8	B3	Dallas	97	J6	Deane	21	J7	Diddlebury	38	E7	W.Suss.		
Croglin	61	G2	Crows-an-wra	2	A6	Curload	8	C2	Dallaschyle	97	F7	Deanland	9	J3	Didley	28	D5	Donyatt	8	C3
Croick High.	96	B2	Crowthorne	22	B5	Curridge	21	H4	Dallash	64	E4	Deanscales	60	B4	Didling	12	B5	Dorchester Dorset	9	F5
Croick High.	104	D3	Crowton	48	E5	Currie	75	K4	Dallinghoo	35	G3	Deanshanger	31	J4	Didmarton	20	B3	Dorchester Oxon.	21	J2
Croig	79	F2	Croxall	40	D4	Curry Mallet	8	C2	Dallington E.Suss.	13	K5	Deanston	81	J7	Didsbury	49	H3	Dordon	40	E5
Crois Dughaill	84	C3	Croxdale	62	D3	Curry Rivel	8	C2	Dallington	31	J2	Dearham	60	B3	Didworthy	5	G4	Dore	51	F4
Croit e Caley	54	B6	Croxden	40	C2	Curteis' Corner	14	D4	Northants.			Debach	35	G3	Digby	52	D7	Dores	88	C1
Cromarty	96	E5	Croxley Green	22	D2	Curtisden Green	14	C3	Dalmadilly	91	F3	Debate	69	H5	Digg	93	K5	Dorket Head	41	H1
Crombie Mill	83	G3	Croxton Cambs.	33	F3	Cury	2	D6	Dalmally	80	C5	Debden	33	J5	Diggle	50	C2	Dorking	22	E7
Cromblet	91	F1	Croxton N.Lincs.	52	E1	Cushnie	99	F4	Dalmarnock	82	A3	Debden Green	33	J5	Digmoor	48	D2	Dormans Park	23	G7
Cromdale	89	H2	Croxton Norf.	44	C7	Cushuish	7	K2	Dalmary	74	D1	Debenham	35	F2	Digswell	33	F7	Dormansland	23	H7
Cromer Herts.	33	F6	Croxton Staffs.	39	G2	Cusop	28	B4	Dalmellington	67	J3	Deddington	31	F5	Dihewyd	26	D3	Dormanstown	63	G4
Cromer Norf.	45	G1	Croxton Green	48	E7	Cutcloy	64	E7	Dalmeny	75	K3	Dedham	34	E5	Dildawn	65	H5	Dormington	28	E4
Cromer Hyde	33	F7	Croxton Kerrial	42	B3	Cutcombe	7	H2	Dalmichy	103	H7	Deecastle	90	C5	Dilham	45	H3	Dorney	22	C4
Cromford	50	E7	Croxtonbank	39	G2	Cuthill	96	E3	Dalmigavie	88	E3	Deene	42	C6	Dilhorne	40	B1	Dornie	86	E2
Cromhall	19	K2	Croy High.	96	E7	Cutnall Green	29	H2	Dalmore	96	D5	Deenethorpe	42	C6	Dilston	70	E7	Dornoch	96	E3
Cromhall Common	19	K3	Croy N.Lan.	75	F3	Cutsdean	30	B5	Dalmunzie Hotel	89	H7	Deepcar	50	E3	Dilton Marsh	20	B6	Dornock	69	H7
Crompton Fold	49	J2	Croyde	6	C2	Cutthorpe	51	F5	Dalnabreck	79	J1	Deepcut	22	C6	Dilwyn	28	D3	Dorrery	105	F3
Cromwell	52	B6	Croydon Cambs.	33	G4	Cutts	109	D9	Dalnacarn	82	B1	Deepdale Cumb.	56	C1	Dilwyn Common	28	D3	Dorridge	30	C1
Cronberry	68	B1	Croydon Gt.Lon.	23	G5	Cuttyhill	99	J5	Dalnaglar Castle	82	C1	Deepdale N.Yorks.	56	D2	Dinas Carmar.	17	F1	Dorrington Lincs.	52	D7
Crondall	22	A7	Cruach	72	B5	Cuxham	21	K2	Dalnaha	79	H5	Deeping Gate	42	E5	Dinas Gwyn.	46	C7	Dorrington Shrop.	38	D5
Cronk-y-Voddy	54	C5	Cruchie	98	D6	Cuxton	24	D5	Dalnahaitnach	89	F3	Deeping St. James	42	E5	Dinas Gwyn.	36	B2	Dorsell	90	D3
Cronton	48	D4	Cruckmeole	38	D5	Cuxwold	52	E2	Dalnamain	96	E2	Deeping St.	43	F4	Dinas Cross	16	D1	Dorsington	30	C3
Crook Cumb.	61	F7	Cruckton	38	D4	Cwm B.Gwent	18	E1	Dalnatrat	80	A2	Nicholas			Pembs.			Dorstone	28	C4
Crook Dur.	62	C3	Cruden Bay	91	J1	Cwm Denb.	47	J5	Dalnavie	96	D4	Deerhill	98	C5	Dinas Dinlle	46	C7	Dorton	31	H7
Crook of Devon	82	B7	Crudgington	39	F4	Cwm-Cewydd	37	H4	Dalness	80	C2	Deerhurst	29	H6	Dinas-Mawddwy	37	H4	Dorusduain	87	F2
Crookedholm	74	C7	Crudwell	20	C2	Cwm Ffrwd-oer	19	F1	Dalnessie	103	J7	Defford	29	J4	Dinas Powys	18	E4	Dosthill	40	E5
Crookham	77	H7	Crug	28	A1	Cwm Gwaun	16	D1	Dalnigap	64	B3	Defynnog	27	J6	Dinbych (Denbigh)	47	J6	Dotland	62	A1
Northumb.			Crugmeer	3	G1	Cwm Irfon	27	H4	Dalqueich	82	B7	Deganwy	46	E5	Dinbych-y-Pysgod	16	E4	Dottery	8	D5
Crookham	21	J5	Crugybar	17	K1	Cwm-Llinau	37	H5	Dalreoch	67	F5	Degnish	79	J6	(Tenby)			Doublebois	4	B4
W.Berks.			Crulabhig	100	D4	Cwm-Morgan	17	F1	Dalriech	81	J4	Deighton N.Yorks.	62	E6	Dinder	19	J7	Dougalston	74	D3
Crookham Village	22	A6	Crumlin	19	F2	Cwm-parc	18	C2	Dalroy	96	E7	Deighton York	58	C5	Dinedor	28	E5	Dougarie	73	G7
Crooklands	55	J1	Crundale Kent	15	F3	Cwm-twrch Isaf	27	G7	Dalrulzian	82	C2	Deiniolen	46	D6	Dingestow	28	D7	Doughton	20	B2
Cropredy	31	F4	Crundale Pembs.	16	C3	Cwm-y-glo	46	D6	Dalry	74	A6	Delabole	4	A2	Dingley	42	A7	Douglas I.o.M.	54	C6
Cropston	41	H4	Crutherland	74	E5	Cwm-yr-Eglwys	16	D1	Dalrymple	67	H2	Delamere	48	E6	Dingwall	96	C6	Douglas S.Lan.	75	G7
Cropthorne	29	J4	Cruwys Morchard	7	G4	Cwmafan	18	A2	Dalserf	75	F5	Delavorar	89	J3	Dinlabyre	70	A4	Douglas and	83	F4
Cropton	58	D1	Crux Easton	21	H6	Cwmaman	18	D2	Dalshangan	67	K5	Delfrigs	91	H2	Dinnet	90	C5	Angus		
Cropwell Bishop	41	J2	Crwbin	17	H3	Cwmann	26	E4	Dalskairth	65	K3	Dell Lodge	89	H3	Dinnington	51	H4	Douglas Hall	65	J5
Cropwell Butler	41	J2	Cryers Hill	22	B2	Cwmbach Carmar.	17	F2	Dalston	60	E1	Delliefure	89	H1	S.Yorks.			Douglas Water	75	G7
Cros	101	G1	Crymlyn	46	E5	Cwmbach Powys	28	A5	Dalswinton	68	E5	Delnabo	89	J3	Dinnington Som.	8	D3	Douglastown	83	F3
Crosbie	74	A6	Crymych	16	E1	Cwmbach Powys	27	K3	Daltomach	88	E2	Delny	96	E4	Dinnington	71	H6	Doulting	19	K7
Crosbost	101	F5	Crynant	18	A1	Cwmbach R.C.T.	18	D1	Dalton D. & G.	69	G6	Delph	49	J2	T. & W.			Dounby	106	B5
Crosby Cumb.	60	B3	Crystal Palace	23	G4	Cwmbelan	37	J7	Dalton Lancs.	48	D2	Delphorrie	90	C3	Dinorwic	46	D6	Doune Arg. & B.	74	B1
Crosby I.o.M.	54	C6	Cuaig	94	D6	Cwmbran	19	F2	Dalton N.Yorks.	57	K2	Delves	62	C2	Dinton Bucks.	31	J7	Doune Arg. & B.	80	E6
Crosby Mersey.	48	C3	Cubbington	30	E2	Cwmbrwyno	37	G7	Dalton N.Yorks.	62	C6	Delvine	82	C3	Dinton Wilts.	10	B1	Doune High.	89	J1
Crosby N.Lincs.	52	B1	Cubert	2	E3	Cwmcarn	19	F1	Dalton Northumb.	71	G6	Dembleby	42	D2	Dinvin	64	A5	Doune High.	96	B1
Crosby Court	62	E7	Cublington	32	B6	Cwmcarvan	19	H1	Dalton Northumb.	62	A1	Denaby	51	G3	Dinworthy	6	B4	Doune Stir.	81	J7
Crosby Garrett	61	H5	Cuckfield	13	G4	Cwmcoy	26	B4	Dalton S.Yorks.	51	G3	Denaby Main	51	G3	Dippen Arg. & B.	73	G6	Dounepark	99	F4
Crosby	61	H5	Cucklington	9	G2	Cwmdare	18	C1	Dalton-in-Furness	55	F2	Denbigh (Dinbych)	47	J6	Dippen N.Ayr.	66	E1	Douneside	90	C4
Ravensworth			Cuckney	51	H5	Cwmdu Carmar.	17	K1	Dalton-le-Dale	63	F2	Denbury	5	J4	Dippenhall	22	B7	Dounie High.	96	D3
Croscombe	19	J7	Cuckoo's Nest	48	C6	Cwmdu Powys	28	A6	Dalton-on-Tees	62	D6	Denby	41	F1	Dipple Moray	98	B5	Dounie High.	96	D2
Cross	19	H6	Cuddesdon	21	J1	Cwmduad	17	G1	Dalton Piercy	63	F3	Denby Dale	50	E2	Dipple S.Ayr.	67	F4	Dounreay	104	E2
Cross Ash	28	D7	Cuddington Bucks.	31	J7	Cwmfelin Boeth	16	E3	Daltote	73	F2	Denchworth	21	G2	Diptford	5	H5	Dousland	5	F4
Cross-at-Hand	14	C3	Cuddington Ches.	49	F5	Cwmfelin Mynach	17	F2	Daltra	97	G6	Dendron	55	F2	Dipton	62	C1	Dovaston	38	C3
Cross Foxes Inn	37	G4	Cuddington Heath	38	D1	Cwmfelinfach	18	E2	Dalveich	81	H5	Denend	90	D1	Dirdhu	89	H2	Dove Holes	50	C5
Cross Gates	57	J6	Cuddy Hill	55	H6	Cwmffrwd	17	H3	Dalvennan	88	D1	Dengie	25	F1	Dirleton	76	D2	Dovenby	60	B3
Cross Green	6	B7	Cudham	23	H5	Cwmgiedd	27	G7	Dalvourn	88	D1	Denham Bucks.	22	D3	Discoed	28	B2	Dover	15	J3
Devon			Cudliptown	5	F3	Cwmgors	27	G7	Dalwhinnie	88	D6	Denham Suff.	35	F1	Diseworth	41	G3	Dovercourt	35	G6
Cross Green Suff.	34	D3	Cudworth S.Yorks.	51	F2	Cwmgwrach	18	B1	Dalwood	8	B4	Denham Suff.	34	B2	Dishes	106	F5	Doverdale	29	H2
Cross Green Suff.	34	C3	Cudworth Som.	8	C3	Cwmisfael	17	H3	Damerham	10	C3	Denham Green	22	D3	Dishforth	57	J2	Doveridge	40	D2
Cross Hands	17	J3	Cuffley	23	G1	Cwmllyfri	17	G3	Damgate	45	J5	Denhead Aber.	91	F3	Disley	49	J4	Doversgreen	23	F7
Carmar.			Cuidhaseadair	101	H2	Cwmllynfell	27	G7	Damnaglaur	64	B7	Denhead Aber.	99	H5	Diss	45	F7	Dowally	82	B3
Cross Hands	16	D3	Cuidhir	84	B4	Cwmpengraig	17	G1	Damside	82	A6	Denhead Dundee	83	F4	Disserth	27	K3	Dowdeswell	30	B6
Pembs.			Cuidhtinis	93	F3	Cwmsymlog	37	F7	Danbury	24	D1	Denhead Fife	83	F6	Distington	60	B4	Dowhill	67	G3
Cross Hill	41	G1	Cuidrach	93	J6	Cwmtillery	19	F1	Danby	63	J6	Denhead of	83	G3	Ditcheat	9	F1	Dowland	6	D4
Cross Hills	57	F5	Cuil-uaine	80	A4	Cwmyoy	28	C6	Danby Wiske	62	E7	Arbirlot			Ditchingham	45	H6	Dowlands	8	B5
Cross Houses	38	E5	Cuilmuich	73	K1	Cwmystwyth	27	G1	Dandaleith	97	K7	Denholm	70	A2	Ditchley	30	E6	Dowlish Wake	8	C3
Cross in Hand	13	J4	Culag	74	B1	Cwrt	37	F5	Danderhall	76	B4	Denholme	57	F6	Ditchling	13	G5	Down Ampney	20	E2
Cross Inn Cere.	26	C3	Culbo	96	D5	Cwrt-newydd	26	D4	Dane Bank	49	J3	Denholme Clough	57	F6	Ditteridge	20	B5	Down End	19	G2
Cross Inn Cere.	26	E2	Culbokie	96	D6	Cwrt-y-gollen	28	B7	Dane End	33	G6	Denio	36	C2	Dittisham	5	J5	Down Hatherley	29	H6
Cross Inn R.C.T.	18	D3	Culbone	7	G1	Cydwelli (Kidwelly)	17	H4	Dane Hills	41	H5	Denmead	11	H3	Ditton Halton	48	D4	Down St. Mary	7	F5
Cross Keys	20	B4	Culburnie	96	B7	Cyffylliog	47	J7	Danebridge	49	J6	Denmill	91	G3	Ditton Kent	14	C2	Down Thomas	5	F6
Cross Lane Head	39	G6	Culcabock	96	D7	Cyfronydd	38	A5	Danehill	13	H4	Denmoss	98	E6	Ditton Green	33	K3	Downderry	4	D5
Cross Lanes	2	E4	Culcharan	80	A4	Cymmer N.P.T.	18	B2	Danemoor	51	G6	Dennington	35	G2	Ditton Priors	39	F7	Downe	23	H5
Cornw.			Culcharry	97	F6	Cymmer R.C.T.	18	D2	Green			Denny	75	G2	Dixton Glos.	29	J5	Downend I.o.W.	11	G6
Cross Lanes	58	B3	Culcheth	49	F3	Cynghordy	27	H5	Danesmoor	51	G6	Dennyloanhead	75	G2	Dixton Mon.	28	E7	Downend S.Glos.	19	K4
N.Yorks.			Culdrain	90	D1	Cynheidre	17	H4	Danestone	91	H3	Denshaw	49	J1	Dobcross	49	J2	Downend W.Berks.	21	H4
Cross Lanes Wrex.	38	C1	Culduie	94	D7	Cynwyd	37	K1	Daniel's Water	14	E3	Denside	91	G5	Dobwalls	4	C4			
Cross o' the Hands	40	E1	Culford	34	C2				Danskine	76	D4				Doc Penfro	16	C4			
Cross of Jackson	91	F1	Culfordheath	34	C1				Darby Green	22	B5				(Pembroke Dock)					
Cross Street	35	F1	Culgaith	61	H4				Darenth	23	J4				Doccombe	7	F7			
			Culgower	104	E7				Daresbury	48	E4				Dochgarroch	96	D7			
									Darfield	51	G2									

Downfield 82 E4
Downfields 33 J1
Downgate 4 D3
Downham Essex 24 D2
Downham Lancs. 56 C5
Downham Northumb. 77 G7
Downham Market 44 A5
Downhead Cornw. 4 C2
Downhead Som. 19 K7
Downholland Cross 48 C2
Downholme 62 C7
Downies 91 H5
Downing 47 K5
Downley 22 B2
Downside N.Som. 19 H5
Downside Som. 19 K7
Downside Surr. 22 E6
Downton Devon 6 D7
Downton Devon 5 J5
Downton Hants. 10 D5
Downton Wilts. 10 C2
Downton on the Rock 28 D1
Dowsby 42 E2
Dowthwaitehead 60 E4
Doynton 20 A4
Draethen 19 F3
Draffan 75 F6
Drakeland Corner 5 F5
Drakes Broughton 29 J4
Drakes Cross 30 B1
Draughton N.Yorks. 57 F4
Draughton Northants. 31 J1
Drax 58 C7
Draycote 31 F1
Draycott Derbys. 41 G2
Draycott Glos. 30 C5
Draycott Som. 19 H6
Draycott Worcs. 29 H4
Draycott in the Clay 40 D3
Draycott in the Moors 40 B2
Drayton Leics. 42 B6
Drayton Lincs. 43 F2
Drayton Norf. 45 F4
Drayton Oxon. 31 F4
Drayton Oxon. 21 H2
Drayton Ports. 11 H4
Drayton Som. 8 D2
Drayton Worcs. 29 J1
Drayton Bassett 40 D5
Drayton Beauchamp 32 C7
Drayton Parslow 32 B6
Drayton St. Leonard 21 J2
Dre-fach 26 E4
Drebley 57 F4
Dreemskerry 54 D4
Dreenhill 16 C3
Drefach Carmar. 17 G1
Drefach Carmar. 17 J3
Dreghorn 74 B7
Drellingore 15 H3
Drem 76 D3
Drewsteignton 7 F6
Driby 53 G5
Driffield E.Riding 59 G4
Driffield Glos. 20 D2
Drigg 60 B7
Drighlington 57 H7
Drimfern 80 B6
Drimlee 80 C6
Drimnin 79 G2
Drimore 84 C1
Drimpton 8 D4
Drimsynie 80 C7
Drimvore 73 G1
Drinan 86 B3
Drinkstone 34 D2
Drinkstone Green 34 D3
Drishaig 80 A6
Drissaig 80 C6
Drointon 40 C3
Droitwich 29 H2
Dron 82 C6
Dronfield 51 F5
Dronfield Woodhouse 51 F5
Drongan 67 J2
Dronley 82 E4
Dropmore 22 C3
Droxford 11 H3
Droylsden 49 J3
Druid 37 K1
Druidston 16 B3
Druimarbin 80 B1
Druimavuic 80 B3
Druimdrishaig 73 F3
Druimindarroch 86 C6
Druimkinnerras 96 B7
Drum Arg. & B. 73 H3
Drum P. & K. 82 B7
Drumachloy 73 J4
Drumbeg 102 D5
Drumblade 98 D6
Drumblair 98 E6
Drumbuie D. & G. 68 C2
Drumbuie High. 86 D1
Drumburgh 60 D1
Drumchapel 74 D3
Drumchardine 96 C7
Drumchork 94 E3
Drumclog 74 E7
Drumdelgie 98 C6
Drumderfit 96 D6
Drumeldrie 83 F7
Drumelzier 75 K7
Drumfearn 86 C3
Drumfern 87 F7
Drumgarve 66 B1
Drumgley 83 F3
Drumguish 88 E5
Drumhead 90 E5
Drumin 89 J1
Drumine 96 E6
Drumjohn 67 K4
Drumlamford House 64 C3
Drumlasie 90 E4
Drumlemble 66 A2
Drumlithie 91 F6
Drummond High. 96 D5
Drummond Stir. 81 H7
Drummore 64 B7
Drummuir Castle 98 B6
Drumnadrochit 88 C1
Drumnagorrach 98 D5
Drumnatorran 79 K1
Drumoak 91 F5
Drumore 66 B1
Drumour 82 A3
Drumrash 65 G3
Drumrunie 95 H1
Drums 91 H2
Drumsturdy 83 F4
Drumuie 93 K7
Drumuillie 89 G2
Drumvaich 81 H7
Drumwhindle 91 H1
Drumwhirn 68 C5
Drunkendub 83 H3
Drury 48 B6
Drws-y-nant 37 H3
Dry Doddington 42 B1
Dry Drayton 33 G2
Dry Harbour 94 C6
Dry Sandford 21 H2
Dry Street 24 C3
Drybeck 61 H5
Drybridge Moray 98 C4
Drybridge N.Ayr. 74 B7
Drybrook 29 F7
Drygrange 76 D7
Dryhope 69 H1
Drymen 74 C2
Drymuir 99 H6
Drynoch 85 K1
Dryslwyn 17 J2
Dryton 38 E5
Duachy 79 K5
Dubford 99 F4
Dubhchladach 73 G4
Dubheads 82 A5
Dubton 83 G2
Duchal 74 B4
Duchally 103 F7
Duchray 74 C1
Duck End 33 K6
Duckington 48 D7
Ducklington 21 G1
Duck's Cross 32 E3
Duddenhoe End 33 H5
Duddingston 76 A3
Duddington 42 C5
Duddleswell 13 H4
Duddo 77 H6
Duddon 48 E6
Duddon Bridge 54 E1
Dudleston Heath 38 C2
Dudley T. & W. 71 H6
Dudley W.Mid. 40 B6
Dudley Hill 57 G6
Dudley Port 40 B6
Dudsbury 10 B5
Duffield 41 F1
Duffryn 18 B2
Dufftown 98 B6
Duffus 97 J5
Dufton 61 H4
Duggleby 58 E3
Duiar 89 J1
Duible 104 E6
Duiletter 80 C5
Duinish 81 H1
Duirinish 86 D1
Duisdealmor 86 D3
Duisky 87 G7
Dukestown 28 A7
Dukinfield 49 J3
Dulas 46 C4
Dulax 90 B3
Dulcote 19 J7
Dulford 7 J5
Dull 81 K3
Dullatur 75 F3
Dullingham 33 K3
Dulnain Bridge 89 G2
Duloe Beds. 32 E2
Duloe Cornw. 4 C5
Dulsie 97 G7
Dulverton 7 H3
Dulwich 23 G4
Dumbarton 74 C3
Dumbleton 30 B5
Dumcrieff 69 G3
Dumeath 90 C1
Dumfin 74 B2
Dumfries 65 K3
Dumgoyne 74 D2
Dummer 21 J7
Dun 83 H2
Dunach 79 K5
Dunalastair 81 J2
Dunan Arg. & B. 73 K3
Dunan High. 86 B2
Dunans 73 J1
Dunball 19 G7
Dunbar 76 E3
Dunbeath 105 G6
Dunbeg 79 K4
Dunblane 81 J7
Dunbog 82 D6
Duncanston Aber. 90 D2
Duncanston High. 96 C6
Dunchideock 7 G7
Dunchurch 31 F1
Duncote 31 H3
Duncow 68 E5
Duncraggan 81 G7
Duncrievie 82 C7
Duncroist 81 G4
Duncrub 82 B6
Duncryne 74 C2
Duncton 12 C5
Dundee 83 F4
Dundee Airport 82 E5
Dundon 8 D1
Dundonald 74 B7
Dundonnell 95 G3
Dundraw 60 D2
Dundreggan 87 K3
Dundrennan 65 H6
Dundry 19 J5
Dunearn 76 A2
Dunecht 91 F4
Dunfermline 75 J2
Dunfield 20 E2
Dunford Bridge 50 D2
Dungavel 74 E7
Dunham 52 B5
Dunham-on-the-Hill 48 D5
Dunham Town 49 G4
Dunhampton 29 H2
Dunholme 52 D5
Dunino 83 G6
Dunipace 75 G2
Dunira 81 J5
Dunkeld 82 B3
Dunkerton 20 A6
Dunkeswell 7 K5
Dunkeswick 57 J5
Dunkirk 15 F2
Dunk's Green 23 K6
Dunlappie 83 G1
Dunley 29 G2
Dunlop 74 C6
Dunloskin 73 K3
Dunmere 4 A4
Dunmore Arg. & B. 73 F4
Dunmore Falk. 75 G2
Dunn 105 G3
Dunnabie 69 H5
Dunnet 105 H1
Dunnichen 83 G3
Dunning 82 B6
Dunnington E.Riding 59 H4
Dunnington Warks. 30 B3
Dunnington York 58 C4
Dunnockshaw 56 D7
Dunoon 73 K3
Dunragit 64 B5
Dunrostan 73 F2
Duns 77 F5
Duns Tew 31 F6
Dunsby 42 E3
Dunscore 68 D5
Dunscroft 51 J2
Dunsdale 63 H5
Dunsden Green 22 A4
Dunsfold 12 D3
Dunsford 7 G7
Dunshelt 82 D6
Dunsinnan 82 C4
Dunsland Cross 6 C5
Dunsley 63 K5
Dunsmore 22 B1
Dunsop Bridge 56 B4
Dunstable 32 D6
Dunstall 40 D3
Dunstall Green 34 B2
Dunstan 71 H1
Dunster 7 H1
Dunston Lincs. 52 D6
Dunston Norf. 45 G5
Dunston Staffs. 40 B4
Dunston T. & W. 71 H7
Dunstone Devon 5 H6
Dunstone Devon 5 H3
Dunstone Devon 5 F5
Dunsville 51 J2
Dunswell 59 G6
Dunsyre 75 J6
Dunterton 4 D3
Duntisbourne Abbots 20 C1
Duntisbourne Leer 20 C1
Duntisbourne Rouse 20 C1
Duntish 9 F4
Duntocher 74 C3
Dunton Beds. 33 F4
Dunton Bucks. 32 B6
Dunton Norf. 44 C2
Dunton Bassett 41 H6
Dunton Green 23 J6
Dunton Wayletts 24 C3
Duntulm 93 K4
Dunure 67 G2
Dunure Mains 67 G2
Dunvant 17 J5
Dunvegan 93 H7
Dunwich 35 J1
Dura 83 F6
Durdar 61 F1
Durgates 13 K3
Durham 62 D2
Durinemast 79 H2
Durisdeer 68 D3
Durleigh 8 B1
Durley Hants. 11 G3
Durley Wilts. 21 F5
Durnamuck 95 G2
Durness 103 F2
Durno 91 F2
Duror 80 A2
Durran Arg. & B. 80 A7
Durran High. 105 G2
Durrington W.Suss. 12 E6
Durrington Wilts. 20 E7
Dursley 20 A2
Durston 8 B2
Durweston 9 H4
Dury 109 D6
Duston 31 J2
Duthil 89 G2
Dutlas 28 B1
Duton Hill 33 K6
Dutton 48 E5
Duxford 33 H4
Dwygyfylchi 47 F5
Dwyran 46 C6
Dyce 91 G3
Dyfatty 17 H4
Dyffryn Bridgend 18 B2
Dyffryn (Valley) I.o.A. 46 A5
Dyffryn Pembs. 16 C1
Dyffryn Ardudwy 36 E3
Dyffryn Castell 37 G7
Dyffryn Ceidrych 27 G6
Dyffryn Cellwen 27 H7
Dyke Devon 6 B3
Dyke Lincs. 42 E3
Dyke Moray 97 G6
Dykehead Angus 82 E1
Dykehead N.Lan. 75 G5
Dykehead Stir. 74 D1
Dykelands 83 J1
Dykends 82 D2
Dykeside 99 F6
Dylife 37 H6
Dymchurch 15 F5
Dymock 29 G5
Dyrham 20 A4
Dysart 76 B1
Dyserth 47 J5

E

Eadar dha Fhadhail 100 C4
Eagland Hill 55 H5
Eagle 52 B6
Eaglescliffe 63 F5
Eaglesfield Cumb. 60 B4
Eaglesfield D. & G. 69 H6
Eaglesham 74 D5
Eaglethorpe 42 D6
Eagley 49 G1
Eairy 54 C6
Eakley 32 B3
Eakring 51 J6
Ealand 51 K1
Ealing 22 E3
Eamont Bridge 61 G4
Earby 56 E5
Earcroft 56 B7
Eardington 39 G6
Eardisland 28 D3
Eardisley 28 C4
Eardiston Shrop. 38 C3
Eardiston Worcs. 29 F2
Earith 33 G1
Earl Shilton 41 G6
Earl Soham 35 G2
Earl Sterndale 50 C6
Earl Stonham 35 F3
Earle 70 E1
Earlestown 48 E3
Earley 22 A4
Earlham 45 F5
Earlish 93 J5
Earls Barton 32 B2
Earls Colne 34 C6
Earl's Common 29 J3
Earl's Croome 29 H4
Earl's Green 34 E2
Earlsdon 30 E1
Earlsferry 83 F7
Earlsford 91 G1
Earlston 76 D7
Earlswood Mon. 19 H2
Earlswood Warks. 30 C1
Earnley 12 B7
Earsairidh 84 C5
Earsdon 71 J6
Earsdon Moor 71 G4
Earsham 45 H7
Earswick 58 C4
Eartham 12 C6
Earthcott Green 19 K3
Easby 63 G6
Easdale 79 J6
Easebourne 12 B4
Easenhall 31 F1
Eashing 22 C7
Easington Bucks. 21 K1
Easington Dur. 63 F2
Easington E.Riding 53 H1
Easington Northumb. 77 K7
Easington Oxon. 21 K2
Easington R. & C. 63 J5
Easington Colliery 63 F2
Easington Lane 62 E2
Easingwold 58 B3
Easole Street 15 H2
Eassie and Nevay 82 E3
East Aberthaw 18 D5
East Allington 5 H6
East Anstey 7 G3
East Appleton 62 D7
East Ardsley 57 J7
East Ashey 11 G6
East Ashling 12 B6
East Auchronie 91 G4
East Ayton 59 F1
East Barkwith 52 E4
East Barming 14 C2
East Barnby 63 K5
East Barnet 23 F2
East Barsham 44 D2
East Beckham 45 F2
East Bedfont 22 D4
East Bergholt 34 E5
East Bilney 44 D4
East Blatchington 13 H7
East Boldon 71 J7
East Boldre 10 E4
East Bolton 71 G2
East Bradenham 44 D5
East Brent 19 G6
East Bridge 35 J2
East Bridgford 41 J1
East Brora 97 F1
East Buckland 6 E2
East Budleigh 7 J7
East Burrafirth 109 C7
East Burton 9 H6
East Cairnbeg 91 F7
East Calder 75 J4
East Carleton 45 F5
East Carlton 42 B7
East Chaldon or Chaldon Herring 9 G6
East Challow 21 G3
East Charleton 5 H6
East Chelborough 8 E4
East Chiltington 13 G5
East Chinnock 8 D3
East Chisenbury 20 E6
East Clandon 22 D6
East Claydon 31 J6
East Clyth 105 H5
East Coker 8 E3
East Combe 7 K2
East Cornworthy 5 J5
East Cottingwith 58 D5
East Cowes 11 G5
East Cowick 58 C7
East Cowton 62 E6
East Cranmore 19 K7
East Creech 9 J6
East Croachy 88 D2
East Darlochan 66 A1
East Davoch 90 C4
East Dean E.Suss. 13 J7
East Dean Hants. 10 D2
East Dean W.Suss. 12 C5
East Dereham 44 D4
East Down 6 E1
East Drayton 51 K5
East End Hants. 21 H5
East End Hants. 10 E5
East End Herts. 33 H6
East End Kent 14 D4
East End N.Som. 19 H4
East End Oxon. 30 E7
East End Poole 9 J5
East End Suff. 35 F5
East Farleigh 14 C2
East Farndon 42 A7
East Ferry 52 B3
East Fortune 76 D3
East Garston 21 G4
East Ginge 21 H3
East Goscote 41 J4
East Grafton 21 F5
East Grimstead 10 D2
East Grinstead 13 G3
East Guldeford 14 E5
East Haddon 31 H2
East Hagbourne 21 J3
East Halton 52 E1
East Ham 23 H3
East Hanney 21 H2
East Hanningfield 24 D1
East Hardwick 51 G1
East Harling 44 D7
East Harlsey 63 F7
East Harptree 19 J6
East Hartford 71 H6
East Harting 11 J3
East Hatch 9 J2
East Hatley 33 F3
East Hauxwell 62 C7
East Haven 83 G4
East Heckington 42 E1
East Hedleyhope 62 C2
East Helmsdale 105 F7
East Hendred 21 H3
East Heslerton 59 F2
East Hoathly 13 J5
East Horndon 24 C3
East Horrington 19 J7
East Horsley 22 D6
East Horton 77 J7
East Huntspill 19 G7
East Hyde 32 E7
East Ilsley 21 H3
East Keal 53 G6
East Kennett 20 E5
East Keswick 57 J5
East Kilbride 74 E5
East Kirkby 53 G6
East Knapton 58 E2
East Knighton 9 H6
East Knoyle 9 H1
East Lambrook 8 D3
East Langdon 15 J3
East Langton 42 A6
East Langwell 96 E1
East Lavant 12 B6
East Lavington 12 C5
East Layton 62 C5
East Leake 41 H3
East Learmouth 77 G7
East Learney 90 E4
East Leigh 7 F5
East Lexham 44 C4
East Lilburn 71 F1
East Linton 76 D3
East Liss 11 J2
East Looe 4 C5
East Lound 51 K3
East Lulworth 9 H6
East Lutton 59 F3
East Lydford 8 E1
East Mains 90 E5
East Malling 14 C2
East March 83 F4
East Marden 12 B5
East Markham 51 K5
East Marton 56 E4
East Meon 11 H2
East Mere 7 H4
East Mersea 34 E7
East Mey 105 J1
East Midlands International Airport 41 G3
East Molesey 22 E5
East Morden 9 J5
East Morton 57 F5
East Ness 58 C2
East Norton 42 A5
East Oakley 21 J7
East Ogwell 5 J3
East Orchard 9 H3
East Ord 77 H5
East Panson 6 B6
East Peckham 23 K7
East Pennard 8 E1
East Portlemouth 5 H7
East Prawle 5 H7
East Preston 12 D6
East Putford 6 B4
East Quantoxhead 7 K1
East Rainton 62 E2
East Ravendale 53 F3
East Raynham 44 C3
East Rigton 57 J5
East Rolstone 19 G5
East Rounton 63 F6
East Rudham 44 C3
East Runton 45 F1
East Ruston 45 H3
East Saltoun 76 C4
East Shefford 21 G4
East Sleekburn 71 H5
East Somerton 45 J4
East Stockwith 51 K3
East Stoke Dorset 9 H6
East Stoke Notts. 42 A1
East Stour 9 G2
East Stourmouth 25 J5
East Stratton 11 G1
East Studdal 15 J3
East Suisnish 86 B1
East Taphouse 4 B4
East-the-Water 6 C3
East Thirston 71 G4
East Tilbury 24 C4
East Tisted 11 J1
East Torrington 52 E4
East Tuddenham 44 E4
East Tytherley 10 D2
East Tytherton 20 C4
East Village 7 G5
East Wall 38 E6
East Walton 44 B4
East Wellow 10 E2
East Wemyss 76 B1
East Whitburn 75 H4
East Wickham 23 H4
East Williamston 16 D4
East Winch 44 A4
East Wittering 12 B7
East Witton 57 G1
East Woodhay 21 H5
East Worldham 11 J1
East Worlington 7 F4
East Youlstone 6 A4
Eastbourne Darl. 62 E5
Eastbourne E.Suss. 13 K7
Eastburn 59 F4
Eastbury Herts. 22 E2
Eastbury W.Berks. 21 G4
Eastby 57 F4
Eastchurch 25 F4
Eastcombe 20 B1
Eastcote Gt.Lon. 22 E3
Eastcote Northants. 31 H3
Eastcote W.Mid. 30 C1
Eastcott Cornw. 6 A4
Eastcott Wilts. 20 D6
Eastcourt 20 C2
Eastend 30 E6
Easter Ardross 96 D4
Easter Balmoral 89 K5
Easter Boleskine 88 C2
Easter Borland 81 H7
Easter Brae 96 D5
Easter Buckieburn 75 F2
Easter Compton 19 J3
Easter Drummond 88 B3
Easter Dullater 81 G7
Easter Ellister 72 A5
Easter Fearn 96 D3
Easter Galcantray 97 F7
Easter Howlaws 77 F6
Easter Kinkell 96 C6
Easter Knox 83 G3
Easter Lednathie 82 E1
Easter Moniack 96 C7
Easter Ord 91 G4
Easter Poldar 74 E1
Easter Quarff 109 D9
Easter Skeld 109 C8
Easter Suddie 96 D6
Easter Tulloch 91 F7
Easter Whyntie 98 E4
Eastergate 12 C6
Easterton 20 D6
Eastertown 19 G6
Eastfield N.Lan. 75 G4
Eastfield N.Yorks. 59 G1
Eastfield Hall 71 H3
Eastgate Dur. 62 A3
Eastgate Lincs. 42 E4
Eastgate Norf. 45 F3
Eastham 48 C4
Easthampstead 22 B5
Eastheath 22 B5
Easthope 38 E6
Easthorpe Essex 34 D6
Easthorpe Leics. 42 B2
Easthorpe Notts. 51 K7
Easthouses 76 B4
Eastington Devon 7 F5
Eastington Glos. 30 C7
Eastington Glos. 20 A1
Eastleach Martin 21 F1
Eastleach Turville 21 F1
Eastleigh Devon 6 C3
Eastleigh Hants. 11 F3
Eastling 14 E2
Eastney 11 H5
Eastnor 29 G5
Eastoft 52 B1
Eastoke 11 J5
Easton Cambs. 32 E1
Easton Cumb. 69 K6
Easton Cumb. 60 D1
Easton Devon 7 F7
Easton Dorset 9 F7
Easton Hants. 11 G1
Easton I.o.W. 10 E6
Easton Lincs. 42 C3
Easton Norf. 45 F4
Easton Som. 19 J7
Easton Suff. 35 G3
Easton Wilts. 20 B4
Easton Grey 20 B3
Easton-in-Gordano 19 J4
Easton Maudit 32 B3
Easton on the Hill 42 D5
Easton Royal 21 F5
Eastrea 43 F6
Eastriggs 69 H7
Eastrington 58 D6
Eastry 15 H2
Eastside 107 D8
Eastville 53 H7
Eastwell 42 A3
Eastwick 33 H7
Eastwood Notts. 41 G1
Eastwood S'end 24 E3
Eastwood W.Yorks. 56 E7
Eathorpe 30 E2
Eaton Ches. 49 H6
Eaton Ches. 48 E6
Eaton Leics. 42 A3
Eaton Norf. 45 G5
Eaton Notts. 51 K5
Eaton Oxon. 21 H1
Eaton Shrop. 38 E6
Eaton Shrop. 38 C7
Eaton Bishop 28 D5
Eaton Bray 32 C6
Eaton Constantine 38 E5
Eaton Ford 32 E3
Eaton Green 32 C6
Eaton Hall 48 D6
Eaton Hastings 21 F2
Eaton Socon 32 E3
Eaton upon Tern 39 F3
Eavestone 57 H3
Ebberston 59 F1
Ebbesborne Wake 9 J2
Ebbw Vale 18 E1
Ebchester 62 C1
Ebford 7 H7
Ebrington 30 C4
Ecchinswell 21 J6
Ecclaw 77 F4
Ecclefechan 69 G6
Eccles Gt.Man. 49 G3
Eccles Kent 24 D5
Eccles Sc.Bord. 77 F6
Eccles Road 44 E6
Ecclesfield 51 F3
Ecclesgreig 83 J1
Eccleshall 40 A3
Ecclesmachan 75 J3
Eccleston Ches. 48 D6
Eccleston Lancs. 48 E1
Eccleston Mersey. 48 D3
Eccup 57 H5
Echt 91 F4
Eckford 70 C1
Eckington Derbys. 51 G5
Eckington Worcs. 29 J4
Ecton Northants. 32 B2
Ecton Staffs. 50 C7
Edale 50 D4
Edburton 13 F5
Edderside 60 C2
Edderton 96 E3
Eddington 21 G5
Eddleston 76 A6
Eddlewood 75 F5
Eden Park 23 G5
Edenbridge 23 H7
Edendonich 80 C5
Edenfield 49 H1
Edenhall 61 G3
Edenham 42 D3
Edensor 50 E6
Edentaggart 74 B1
Edenthorpe 51 J2
Edern 36 B2
Edgarley 8 E1
Edgbaston 40 C7
Edgcott 31 H6
Edgcumbe 2 E5
Edge Glos. 20 B1
Edge Shrop. 38 C5
Edge End 28 E7
Edgebolton 38 E3
Edgefield 45 F2
Edgeley 38 E1
Edgerley 38 C4
Edgeworth 20 C1
Edginswell 5 J4
Edgmond 39 G4
Edgmond Marsh 39 G3
Edgton 38 C7
Edgware 23 F2
Edgworth 49 G1
Edial 40 C5
Edinample 81 H5
Edinbanchory 90 C3
Edinbane 93 J6
Edinbarnet 74 D3
Edinburgh 76 A3
Edinburgh Airport 75 K3
Edinchip 81 G5
Edingale 40 E4
Edingley 51 J7
Edingthorpe 45 H2
Edington Som. 8 C1
Edington Wilts. 20 C6
Edintore 98 C6
Edinvale 97 J6
Edistone 6 A3
Edith Weston 42 C5
Edithmead 19 G7
Edlaston 40 D1
Edlesborough 32 C7
Edlingham 71 G3
Edlington 53 F5
Edmondsham 10 B3
Edmondsley 62 D2
Edmondthorpe 42 B4
Edmonstone 106 E5
Edmonton 23 G2
Edmundbyers 62 B1
Ednam 77 F7
Ednaston 40 E1
Edney Common 24 C1
Edra 81 F6
Edradynate 81 K2
Edrom 77 G5
Edstaston 38 E2
Edstone 30 C2
Edvin Loach 29 F3
Edwalton 41 H2
Edwardstone 34 D4
Edwinsford 17 K1
Edwinstowe 51 J6
Edworth 33 F4
Edwyn Ralph 29 F3
Edzell 83 G1
Efail Isaf 18 D3
Efailnewydd 36 C2
Efailwen 16 E2
Efenechtyd 47 K7
Effingham 22 E6
Effirth 109 C7
Efford 7 G5
Egbury 21 H6
Egdean 12 C4
Egerton Gt.Man. 49 G1
Egerton Kent 14 E3
Egerton Forstal 14 D3
Egerton Green 48 E7
Egg Buckland 5 F5
Eggerness 64 E6
Eggesford Barton 6 E4
Eggington 32 C6
Egginton 40 E3
Egglescliffe 63 F5
Eggleston 62 B4
Egham 22 D4
Egleton 42 B5
Eglingham 71 G2
Egloshayle 4 A3
Egloskerry 4 C2
Eglwys-Brewis 18 D5
Eglwys Cross 38 D1
Eglwys Fach 37 F6
Eglwysbach 47 G5
Eglwyswrw 16 E1
Egmanton 51 K6
Egmere 44 D2
Egremont 60 B5
Egton 63 K6
Egton Bridge 63 K6
Egypt 21 H7
Eight Ash Green 34 D6
Eignaig 79 J3
Eil 89 F3
Eilanreach 86 E3
Eilean Darach 95 H3
Eilean Iarmain (Isleornsay) 86 C3
Einacleit 100 D5
Eisgean 101 F6
Eisingrug 37 F2
Eisteddfa Gurig 37 G7
Elan Village 27 J2
Elberton 19 J3
Elburton 5 F5
Elcho 82 C5
Elcombe 20 E3
Eldernell 43 G6
Eldersfield 29 H5
Elderslie 74 C4
Eldrick 67 G5
Eldroth 56 C3
Eldwick 57 G5
Elerch (Bont-goch) 37 F7
Elford Northumb. 77 K7
Elford Staffs. 40 D4
Elgin 97 K5
Elgol 86 B3
Elham 15 G3
Elie 83 F7
Elilaw 70 E3
Elim 46 B4
Eling 10 E3
Eliock 68 D3
Elishader 94 B5
Elishaw 70 D4
Elkesley 51 J5
Elkstone 29 J7
Elland 57 G7
Ellary 73 F3
Ellastone 40 D1
Ellemford 77 F4
Ellenborough 60 B3
Ellenhall 40 A3
Ellen's Green 12 D3
Ellerbeck 63 F7
Ellerby 63 J5
Ellerdine Heath 39 F3
Elleric 80 B3
Ellerker 59 F7
Ellerton E.Riding 58 D5
Ellerton N.Yorks. 62 D7
Ellerton Shrop. 39 G3
Ellesborough 22 B1
Ellesmere 38 C2
Ellesmere Port 48 C5
Ellingham Hants. 10 C4
Ellingham Norf. 45 H6
Ellingham Northumb. 71 G1
Ellingstring 57 G1
Ellington Cambs. 32 E1
Ellington Northumb. 71 H4
Ellisfield 21 K7
Ellistown 41 G4
Ellon 91 H1
Ellonby 61 F3
Ellough 45 J7
Elloughton 59 F7
Ellwood 19 J1
Elm 43 H5
Elm Park 23 J3
Elmbridge 29 J2
Elmdon Essex 33 H5
Elmdon W.Mid. 40 D7
Elmdon Heath 40 D7
Elmesthorpe 41 G6
Elmhurst 40 D4
Elmley Castle 29 J4

Elmley Lovett 29 H2
Elmore 29 G7
Elmore Back 29 G7
Elmscott 6 A3
Elmsett 34 E4
Elmstead Markct 34 E6
Elmstone 25 J5
Elmstone Hardwicke 29 J6
Elmswell E.Riding 59 F4
Elmswell Suff. 34 E2
Elmton 51 H5
Elphin 102 E7
Elphinstone 76 B3
Elrick Aber. 91 G4
Elrick Moray 90 C2
Elrig 64 D6
Elsdon 70 E4
Elsecar 51 F2
Elsenham 33 J6
Elsfield 21 J1
Elsham 52 D1
Elsing 44 E4
Elslack 56 E5
Elson 38 C2
Elsrickle 75 J6
Elstead 22 C7
Elsted 12 B5
Elsthorpe 42 D4
Elstob 62 E4
Elston Lancs. 55 J6
Elston Notts. 42 A1
Elstone 6 E4
Elstow 32 D4
Elstree 22 E2
Elstronwick 59 J6
Elswick 55 H6
Elsworth 33 G2
Elterwater 60 E7
Eltham 23 H4
Eltisley 33 F3
Elton Cambs. 42 D6
Elton Ches. 48 D5
Elton Derbys. 50 E6
Elton Glos. 29 G7
Elton Here. 28 D1
Elton Notts. 42 A2
Elton Stock. 63 F5
Elvanfoot 68 E2
Elvaston 41 G2
Elveden 34 C1
Elvingston 76 C3
Elvington Kent 15 H2
Elvington York 58 D5
Elwick Hart. 63 F3
Elwick Northumb. 77 K7
Elworth 49 G6
Elworthy 7 J2
Ely Cambs. 33 J1
Ely Cardiff 18 E4
Emberton 32 B4
Embleton Cumb. 60 C3
Embleton Northumb. 71 H1
Embo 97 F2
Embo Street 97 F2
Emborough 19 K6
Embsay 57 F4
Emery Down 10 D4
Emley 50 E1
Emmer Green 22 A4
Emmington 22 A1
Emneth 43 H5
Emneth Hungate 43 J5
Empingham 42 C5
Empshott 11 J1
Emsworth 11 J4
Enborne 21 H5
Enchmarsh 38 E6
Enderby 41 H6
Endmoor 55 J1
Endon 49 J7
Enfield 23 G2
Enford 20 E6
Engine Common 19 K3
Englefield 21 K4
Englefield Green 22 C4
Englesea-brook 49 G7
English Bicknor 28 E7
English Frankton 38 D3
Englishcombe 20 A5
Enham Alamein 21 G7
Enmore 8 B1
Ennerdale Bridge 60 B5
Ennochdhu 82 B1
Ensay 78 E3
Ensdon 38 D4
Ensis 6 D3
Enstone 30 E6
Enterkinfoot 68 D3
Enterpen 63 F6
Enville 40 A7
Eolaigearraidh 84 C4
Eorabus 78 E3
Eorodal 101 H1
Eoropaidh 101 H1
Epperstone 41 J1
Epping 23 H1
Epping Green Essex 23 H1
Epping Green Herts. 23 F1
Epping Upland 23 H1
Eppleby 62 C5
Eppleworth 59 G6
Epsom 23 F5
Epwell 30 E4
Epworth 51 K2
Erbistock 38 C1
Erbusaig 86 D2
Erchless Castle 96 B7
Erdington 40 D6
Eredine 80 A7
Eriboll 103 G3
Ericstane 69 F2
Eridge Green 13 J3
Eriff 67 K3
Erines 73 G3
Eriswell 34 B1
Erith 23 J4
Erlestoke 20 C6
Ermington 5 G5
Erpingham 45 F2
Errogie 88 C2
Errol 82 D5
Errollston 91 J1
Erskine 74 C3
Ervie 64 A4
Erwarton 35 G5
Erwood 27 K4
Eryholme 62 D6
Eryrys 48 B7
Escart 73 G4
Escart Farm 73 G5
Escomb 62 C4
Escrick 58 C5
Esgair 67 G2
Esgairgeiliog 37 G5
Esh 62 C2

Esh Winning 62 C2
Esher 22 E5
Eshott 71 H4
Eshton 56 E4
Eskadale 88 B1
Eskbank 76 R4
Eskdale Green 60 C6
Eskdalemuir 69 H4
Eskham 53 G3
Esknish 72 B4
Espley Hall 71 G4
Esprick 55 H6
Essendine 42 D4
Essendon 23 F1
Essich 88 D1
Essington 40 B5
Esslemont 91 H2
Eston 63 G5
Etal 77 H7
Etchilhampton 20 D5
Etchingham 14 C5
Etchinghill Kent 15 G4
Etchinghill Staffs. 40 C4
Ethie Mains 83 H3
Eton 22 C4
Eton Wick 22 C4
Etteridge 88 D5
Ettersgill 61 K4
Ettingshall 40 B6
Ettington 30 D4
Etton E.Riding 59 F5
Etton Peter. 42 E5
Ettrick 69 H2
Ettrickbridge 69 J1
Ettrickhill 69 H2
Etwall 40 E2
Eurach 79 K7
Euston 34 C1
Euxton 48 E1
Evanton 96 D5
Evedon 42 D1
Evelix 96 E2
Evenjobb 28 B2
Evenley 31 G5
Evenlode 30 D6
Evenwood 62 C4
Everbay 106 F5
Evercreech 9 F1
Everdon 31 G3
Everingham 58 E5
Everleigh 21 F6
Everley High. 105 J2
Everley N.Yorks. 59 F1
Eversholt 32 C5
Evershot 8 E4
Eversley 22 A5
Eversley Cross 22 A5
Everthorpe 59 F6
Everton Beds. 33 F3
Everton Hants. 10 D5
Everton Notts. 51 J3
Evertown 69 J6
Evesbatch 29 F4
Evesham 30 B4
Evie 106 C5
Evington 41 J5
Ewart Newtown 77 H7
Ewden Village 50 E3
Ewell 23 F5
Ewell Minnis 15 H3
Ewelme 21 K2
Ewen 20 D2
Ewenny 18 C4
Ewerby 42 E1
Ewerby Thorpe 42 E1
Ewhurst E.Suss. 14 C5
Ewhurst Surr. 22 D7
Ewhurst Green 12 D3
Ewloe 48 B6
Ewood 56 B7
Eworthy 6 C6
Ewshot 22 B7
Ewyas Harold 28 C6
Exbourne 6 E5
Exbury 11 F4
Exebridge 7 H3
Exelby 57 H1
Exeter 7 H6
Exeter Airport 7 H6
Exford 7 G2
Exfords Green 38 D5
Exhall Warks. 30 C3
Exhall Warks. 41 F7
Exlade Street 21 K3
Exminster 7 H7
Exmouth 7 J7
Exnaboe 109 G10
Exning 33 K2
Exton Devon 7 H7
Exton Hants. 11 H2
Exton Rut. 42 C4
Exton Som. 7 H2
Exwick 7 H6
Eyam 50 E5
Eydon 31 G3
Eye Here. 28 D2
Eye Peter. 43 F5
Eye Suff. 35 F1
Eye Green 43 F5
Eyemouth 77 H4
Eyeworth 33 F4
Eyhorne Street 14 D2
Eyke 35 H3
Eynesbury 32 E3
Eynort 85 J2
Eynsford 23 J5
Eynsham 21 H1
Eype 8 D5
Eyre 93 K6
Eythorne 15 H3
Eyton Here. 28 D2
Eyton Shrop. 38 C7
Eyton Wrex. 38 C1
Eyton upon the Weald Moors 39 F4
Eywood 28 C3

F
Faccombe 21 G6
Faceby 63 F6
Fachwen 46 D6
Faddiley 48 E7
Fadmoor 58 C1
Faebait 96 B6
Faifley 74 D3
Fail 67 J1
Failand 19 J4
Failford 67 J1
Failsworth 49 H2
Fain 95 H4
Fair Oak Hants. 11 F3
Fair Oak Hants. 21 J5
Fairbourne 37 F4
Fairburn 57 K7
Fairfield Derbys. 50 C5
Fairfield Worcs. 29 J1
Fairford 20 E1
Fairgirth 65 J5
Fairholm 75 F5

Fairley 91 G4
Fairlie 74 A5
Fairlight 14 D6
Fairlight Cove 14 D6
Fairmile 7 J6
Fairmilehead 76 A4
Fairnington 70 B1
Fairoak 39 G2
Fairseat 14 C2
Fairstead Essex 34 B7
Fairstead Norf. 45 G3
Fairwarp 13 H4
Fairy Cross 6 C3
Fairyhill 17 H5
Fakenham 44 D3
Fala 76 C4
Fala Dam 76 C4
Falahill 76 B5
Faldingworth 52 D4
Falfield Fife 83 F7
Falfield S.Glos. 19 K2
Falkenham 35 G5
Falkirk 75 G3
Falkland 82 D7
Falla 70 C2
Fallgate 51 F6
Fallin 75 G1
Falmer 13 G6
Falmouth 3 F5
Falsgrave 59 G1
Falstone 70 C5
Fanagmore 102 D3
Fanans 80 B5
Fancott 32 D6
Fangdale Beck 63 G7
Fangfoss 58 D4
Fanmore 79 F3
Fans 76 E6
Far Cotton 31 J3
Far Forest 29 G1
Far Gearstones 56 C1
Farcet 43 F6
Farden 28 E1
Fareham 11 G4
Farewell 40 C4
Farforth 53 G5
Faringdon 21 F2
Farington 55 J7
Farlam 61 G1
Farlary 96 E1
Farleigh N.Som. 19 H5
Farleigh Surr. 23 G5
Farleigh Hungerford 20 A6
Farleigh Wallop 21 K7
Farlesthorpe 53 H5
Farleton 55 J1
Farley Shrop. 38 C5
Farley Wilts. 10 D2
Farley Wilts. 10 D2
Farley Green 22 D7
Farley Hill 22 A5
Farleys End 29 G7
Farlington 58 C3
Farlow 39 F7
Farmborough 19 K5
Farmcote 30 B6
Farmington 30 C7
Farmoor 21 H1
Farmtown 98 D5
Farnborough Gt.Lon. 23 H5
Farnborough Hants. 22 B6
Farnborough W.Berks. 21 H3
Farnborough Warks. 31 F3
Farnborough Green 22 B6
Farncombe 22 C7
Farndish 32 C2
Farndon Ches. 48 D7
Farndon Notts. 51 K7
Farnell 83 H2
Farnham Dorset 9 J3
Farnham Essex 33 H6
Farnham N.Yorks. 57 J3
Farnham Suff. 35 H3
Farnham Surr. 22 B7
Farnham Common 22 C3
Farnham Green 33 H6
Farnham Royal 22 C3
Farningham 23 J5
Farnley 57 H5
Farnley Tyas 50 D1
Farnsfield 51 J7
Farnworth Gt.Man. 49 G2
Farnworth Halton 48 E4
Farr High. 104 C2
Farr High. 88 D1
Farr High. 89 F4
Farr House 88 D1
Farraline 88 C2
Farrington Gurney 19 K6
Farsley 57 H6
Farthinghoe 31 G5
Farthingloe 15 H3
Farthingstone 31 H3
Farway 7 K6
Fasag 94 E6
Fasagrianach 95 H3
Fascadale 86 B7
Faslane 74 A2
Fasnacloich 80 B3
Fasnakyle 87 K2
Fassfern 87 G7
Fatfield 62 E1
Fattahead 98 E5
Faugh 61 G1
Fauldhouse 75 H4
Faulkbourne 34 B7
Faulkland 20 A6
Fauls 38 E2
Faversham 25 G5
Favillar 89 K1
Fawdington 57 K2
Fawdon 50 C6
Fawfieldhead 50 C6
Fawkham Green 23 J5
Fawler 30 E7
Fawley Bucks. 22 A3
Fawley Hants. 11 F4
Fawley W.Berks. 21 G3
Fawley Chapel 28 E6
Fawsyde 91 G7
Faxfleet 58 E7
Faxton 31 J1
Faygate 13 F3
Fazeley 40 E5
Fearby 57 G1
Fearn 97 F4
Fearnan 81 J3
Fearnbeg 94 D6
Fearnhead 49 F3
Fearnmore 94 D5
Fearnoch Arg. & B. 73 J3
Fearnoch Arg. & B. 73 J2
Featherstone Staffs. 40 B5

Featherstone W.Yorks. 51 G1
Featherstone Castle 70 B7
Feckenham 30 B2
Feering 34 C6
Feetham 62 A7
Feith-hill 98 E6
Feizor 56 C3
Felbridge 13 G3
Felbrigg 45 G2
Felcourt 23 G7
Felden 22 D1
Felindre Carmar. 27 G6
Felindre Carmar. 17 J2
Felindre Carmar. 17 G1
Felindre Powys 38 A7
Felindre Swan. 17 K4
Felinfach 27 K5
Felinfoel 17 J4
Felingwmuchaf 17 J2
Felixkirk 57 K1
Felixstowe 35 G5
Felixstowe Ferry 35 H5
Felkington 77 H6
Felldownhead 6 B7
Felling 71 H7
Fellonmore 79 H5
Felmersham 32 C3
Felmingham 45 G3
Felpham 12 C7
Felsham 34 D3
Felsted 33 K6
Feltham 22 E4
Felthorpe 45 F4
Felton Here. 28 E4
Felton N.Som. 19 J5
Felton Northumb. 71 G3
Felton Butler 38 C4
Feltwell 44 B7
Fen Ditton 33 H3
Fen Drayton 33 G2
Fen End 30 D1
Fen Street 34 D1
Fence 56 D6
Fence Houses 62 E1
Fencott 31 G7
Fendike Corner 53 H6
Fenhouses 43 F1
Feniscowles 56 B7
Feniton 7 K6
Fenny Bentley 50 D7
Fenny Bridges 7 K6
Fenny Compton 31 F3
Fenny Drayton 41 F6
Fenny Stratford 32 B5
Fenrother 71 G4
Fenstanton 33 G2
Fenton Cambs. 33 G1
Fenton Lincs. 52 B5
Fenton Lincs. 52 B7
Fenton Northumb. 77 H7
Fenton Stoke 40 A1
Fenwick E.Ayr. 74 C6
Fenwick Northumb. 71 F6
Fenwick Northumb. 77 J6
Fenwick S.Yorks. 51 H1
Feochaig 66 B2
Feock 3 F5
Feolin 72 D4
Feolin Ferry 72 C4
Feorlan 66 A3
Feorlin 73 H1
Feriniquarrie 93 G6
Fern 83 F1
Ferndale 18 C2
Ferndown 10 B4
Ferness 97 G7
Fernham 21 F2
Fernhill Heath 29 H3
Fernhurst 12 B4
Fernie 82 E6
Fernilea 85 J1
Fernilee 50 C5
Fernybank 90 D7
Ferrensby 57 J3
Ferring 12 D6
Ferrybridge 57 K7
Ferryden 83 J2
Ferryhill 62 D3
Ferryside 17 G3
Fersfield 44 E7
Fersit 87 K7
Ferwig 26 A4
Feshiebridge 89 F4
Fetcham 22 E6
Fetterangus 99 H5
Fettercairn 90 E7
Fetternear House 91 F3
Feus of Caldhame 83 H1
Fewcott 31 G6
Fewston 57 G4
Ffair-Rhos 27 G2
Ffairfach 17 K2
Ffarmers 27 F4
Ffawyddog 28 B7
Ffestiniog 37 G1
Ffordd-las 47 K6
Fforest 17 J4
Fforest-fach 17 K5
Ffos-y-ffin 26 D2
Ffostrasol 26 C4
Ffridd Uchaf 46 D7
Ffrith 48 B7
Ffrwdgrech 27 K6
Ffynnon-ddrain 17 H2
Ffynnon Taf (Taff's Well) 18 E3
Ffynnongroyw 47 K4
Fibhig 100 E3
Fichlie 90 C3
Fidden 78 E5
Fiddington Glos. 29 J5
Fiddington Som. 19 F7
Fiddleford 9 H3
Fiddler's Green 28 E5
Fiddlers Hamlet 23 H1
Field 40 C2
Field Broughton 55 G1
Field Dalling 44 E2
Field Head 41 G5
Fife Keith 98 C5
Fifehead Magdalen 9 G2
Fifehead Neville 9 G3
Fifield Oxon. 30 D7
Fifield W. & M. 22 C4
Fifield Bavant 10 B2
Figheldean 20 E7
Filby 45 J4
Filey 59 H2
Filgrave 32 B4
Filkins 21 F1
Filleigh Devon 6 E3
Filleigh Devon 7 F4
Fillingham 52 C4
Fillongley 40 E7
Filmore Hill 11 H2
Filton 19 J4
Fimber 59 F3

Finavon 83 F2
Fincham 44 A5
Finchampstead 22 A5
Finchdean 11 J3
Finchingfield 33 K5
Finchley 23 F2
Findern 41 F2
Findhorn 97 H5
Findhorn Bridge 89 F2
Findo Gask 82 B5
Findochty 98 C4
Findon Aber. 91 H5
Findon W.Suss. 12 E6
Findon Mains 96 D5
Findrassie 97 J5
Findron 89 J3
Finedon 32 C1
Fingal Street 35 G2
Fingask 91 F2
Fingerpost 29 G1
Fingest 22 A2
Finghall 62 C7
Fingland Cumb. 60 D1
Fingland D. & G. 69 H3
Fingland D. & G. 68 C2
Finglesham 15 J2
Fingringhoe 34 E7
Finlarig 81 G4
Finmere 31 H5
Finnart Arg. & B. 74 A1
Finnart P. & K. 81 G3
Finningham 34 E2
Finningley 51 J3
Finnygaud 98 E5
Finsbury 23 G3
Finstall 29 J1
Finsthwaite 55 G1
Finstock 30 E7
Finstown 107 C6
Fintry Aber. 99 F5
Fintry Stir. 74 E2
Finzean 90 D5
Fionnphort 78 E5
Fir Tree 62 C3
Fir Vale 51 F4
Firbank 61 H7
Firbeck 51 H4
Firby N.Yorks. 58 D3
Firby N.Yorks. 57 H1
Firgrove 49 J1
Firs Road 10 D1
Firsby 53 H6
Firth 108 D5
Fishbourne I.o.W. 11 G5
Fishbourne W.Suss. 12 B6
Fishburn 62 E3
Fisherford 90 E1
Fisher's Pond 11 F2
Fisher's Row 55 H5
Fisherstreet 12 C3
Fisherton High. 96 E6
Fisherton S.Ayr. 67 G2
Fisherton de la Mere 10 B1
Fishguard (Abergwaun) 16 C1
Fishlake 51 J1
Fishleigh Barton 6 D3
Fishnish 79 H3
Fishpond Bottom 8 C5
Fishponds 19 K4
Fishpool 49 H1
Fishtoft 43 G1
Fishtoft Drove 43 G1
Fishtown of Usan 83 J2
Fishwick Lancs. 55 J6
Fishwick Sc.Bord. 77 H5
Fiskerton Lincs. 52 D5
Fiskerton Notts. 51 K7
Fittleton 20 E6
Fittleworth 12 D5
Fitton End 43 H4
Fitz 38 D4
Fitzhead 7 K3
Fitzwilliam 51 G1
Fiunary 79 H3
Five Ash Down 13 H4
Five Ashes 13 J4
Five Bridges 29 F4
Five Oak Green 23 K7
Five Oaks Chan.I. 3 K7
Five Oaks W.Suss. 12 D4
Five Roads 17 H4
Five Turnings 28 B1
Five Wents 14 D2
Fivehead 8 C2
Fivelanes 4 C2
Flackwell Heath 22 B3
Fladbury 29 J4
Fladdabister 109 D9
Flagg 50 D6
Flamborough 59 J2
Flamstead 32 D7
Flamstead End 23 G1
Flansham 12 C6
Flasby 56 E4
Flash 50 C6
Flashader 93 J6
Flask Inn 63 J2
Flaunden 22 D1
Flawborough 42 A1
Flawith 57 K3
Flax Bourton 19 J5
Flaxby 57 J4
Flaxley 29 F7
Flaxpool 7 K2
Flaxton 58 C3
Fleckney 41 J6
Flecknoe 31 G2
Fleet Hants. 22 B6
Fleet Lincs. 43 G3
Fleet Hargate 43 G3
Fleetwood 55 G5
Flemington 74 E5
Flempton 34 C2
Fleoideabhagh 93 F3
Fletchertown 60 D2
Fletching 13 H4
Flete 5 G5
Fleuchats 90 B4
Fleur-de-lis 18 E2
Flexbury 6 A5
Flexford 22 C6
Flimby 60 B3
Flimwell 14 C4
Flint (Y Fflint) 48 B5
Flint Cross 33 H4
Flint Mountain 48 B5
Flinton 59 J6
Flishinghurst 14 C4
Flitcham 44 B3
Flitton 32 D5
Flitwick 32 D5
Flixborough 52 B1
Flixton Gt.Man. 49 G3
Flixton N.Yorks. 59 G2

Flixton Suff. 45 H7
Flockton 50 E1
Flockton Green 50 E1
Flodden 77 H7
Flodigarry 93 K4
Flookburgh 55 G2
Floors 98 C5
Flordon 45 F6
Flore 31 H2
Flotterton 71 F3
Flowton 34 E4
Flushing Aber. 99 J6
Flushing Cornw. 3 F5
Flyford Flavell 29 J3
Fobbing 24 D3
Fochabers 98 B5
Fochriw 18 E1
Fockerby 52 B1
Fodderletter 89 J2
Fodderty 96 C6
Foddington 8 E2
Foel 37 J4
Foffarty 83 F3
Foggathorpe 58 D6
Fogo 77 F6
Fogorig 77 F6
Foindle 102 D4
Fola 82 C1
Fole 40 C2
Foleshill 41 F7
Folke 9 F3
Folkestone 15 H4
Folkingham 42 D2
Folkington 13 J6
Folksworth 42 E7
Folkton 59 G2
Folla Rule 91 F1
Follifoot 57 J4
Folly Dorset 9 G4
Folly Pembs. 16 C2
Folly Gate 6 D6
Fonthill Bishop 9 J1
Fonthill Gifford 9 J1
Fontmell Magna 9 H3
Fontwell 12 C6
Foolow 50 D5
Foots Cray 23 H4
Forbestown 90 B3
Force Forge 60 E7
Forcett 62 C5
Forches Cross 7 F5
Ford Arg. & B. 79 K7
Ford Bucks. 22 A1
Ford Devon 5 G5
Ford Devon 6 C3
Ford Devon 5 H6
Ford Glos. 30 B6
Ford Mersey. 48 C2
Ford Midloth. 76 B4
Ford Northumb. 77 H7
Ford Pembs. 16 C2
Ford Shrop. 38 D4
Ford Som. 7 J3
Ford W.Suss. 12 C6
Ford Wilts. 20 B4
Ford End 33 K7
Ford Street 7 K4
Fordcombe 23 J7
Fordell 75 K2
Forden 38 B5
Forder Green 5 H4
Fordham Cambs. 33 K1
Fordham Essex 34 D6
Fordham Norf. 44 A6
Fordham Abbey 33 K2
Fordingbridge 10 C3
Fordon 59 G2
Fordoun 91 F7
Fordstreet 34 D6
Fordwells 30 E7
Fordwich 15 G2
Fordyce 98 D4
Forebrae 82 A5
Foreland 72 A4
Forest Gate 23 H3
Forest Green 22 E7
Forest Hall Cumb. 61 G6
Forest Hall T. & W. 71 H7
Forest Head 61 G1
Forest Hill 21 J1
Forest-in-Teesdale 61 K3
Forest Lodge Arg. & B. 80 D3
Forest Lodge P. & K. 89 G7
Forest Mill 75 H1
Forest Row 13 H3
Forest Town 51 H6
Forestburn Gate 71 F4
Forestside 11 J3
Forfar 83 F2
Forgandenny 82 B6
Forgie 98 B5
Forgorig 77 F6
Formby 48 B2
Forncett End 45 F6
Forncett St. Mary 45 F6
Forncett St. Peter 45 F6
Forneth 82 B3
Fornham All Saints 34 C2
Fornham St. Martin 34 C2
Fornighty 97 G6
Forres 97 H6
Forrest 75 G4
Forrest Lodge 67 K5
Forsbrook 40 B1
Forse 105 H5
Forsie 105 F2
Forsinain 104 E4
Forsinard 104 D4
Forston 9 F5
Fort Augustus 87 K4
Fort George 96 E6
Fort William 87 H7
Forter 82 C1
Forteviot 82 B6
Forth 75 H5
Forthampton 29 H5
Fortingall 81 J3
Forton Hants. 21 H7
Forton Lancs. 55 H4
Forton Shrop. 38 D4
Forton Som. 8 C4
Forton Staffs. 39 G3
Fortrie 98 E6
Fortrose 96 E6
Fortuneswell 9 F7
Forty Green 22 C2
Forty Hill 23 G2
Forward Green 34 E3
Fosbury 21 G6
Foscot 30 D6
Fosdyke 43 G2
Foss 81 J2
Foss Cross 20 D1
Fossdale 61 K7
Fossebridge 30 B7
Foster Street 23 H1
Foster's Booth 31 H3
Foston Derbys. 40 D2
Foston Leics. 41 J6
Foston Lincs. 42 B1

Foston N.Yorks. 58 C3
Foston on the Wolds 59 H4
Fotherby 53 G3
Fotheringhay 42 D6
Foubister 107 E7
Foul Mile 13 K5
Foulbog 69 H3
Foulden Norf. 44 B6
Foulden Sc.Bord. 77 H5
Foulridge 56 D5
Foulsham 44 E3
Foulzie 99 F4
Fountainhall 76 C6
Four Ashes Staffs. 40 B7
Four Ashes Suff. 34 D1
Four Crosses Denb. 37 K1
Four Crosses Powys 38 B4
Four Crosses Powys 37 K5
Four Crosses Staffs. 40 B5
Four Elms 23 H7
Four Forks 8 B1
Four Gotes 43 H4
Four Lanes 2 D5
Four Marks 11 H1
Four Mile Bridge 46 A5
Four Oaks E.Suss. 14 D5
Four Oaks W.Mid. 40 D6
Four Oaks W.Mid. 40 D7
Four Roads 17 H4
Four Throws 14 C5
Fourlane Ends 51 F7
Fourlanes End 49 H7
Fourpenny 96 E2
Fourstones 70 D7
Fovant 10 B2
Foveran House 91 H2
Fowey 4 B5
Fowlis 82 E4
Fowlis Wester 82 A5
Fowlmere 33 H4
Fownhope 28 E5
Fox Lane 22 B6
Fox Street 34 E6
Foxcote 30 B7
Foxdale 54 B6
Foxearth 34 C4
Foxfield 55 F1
Foxham 20 C4
Foxhole Cornw. 3 G3
Foxhole High. 88 C1
Foxholes 59 G2
Foxhunt Green 13 J5
Foxley Here. 28 D4
Foxley Norf. 44 E3
Foxley Northants. 31 H3
Foxley Wilts. 20 B3
Foxt 40 C1
Foxton Cambs. 33 H4
Foxton Dur. 62 E4
Foxton Leics. 42 A6
Foxup 56 D2
Foxwist Green 49 F6
Foy 28 E6
Foyers 88 B2
Fraddam 2 C5
Fraddon 3 G3
Fradley 40 D4
Fradswell 40 B2
Fraisthorpe 59 H4
Framfield 13 H4
Framingham Earl 45 G5
Framingham Pigot 45 G5
Framlingham 35 G2
Frampton Dorset 9 F5
Frampton Lincs. 43 G2
Frampton Cotterell 19 K3
Frampton Mansell 20 C1
Frampton on Severn 20 A1
Frampton West End 43 G1
Framsden 35 G3
Framwellgate Moor 62 D2
Franche 29 H1
Frankby 48 B4
Frankley 40 B7
Frankton 31 F1
Frant 13 J3
Fraserburgh 99 H4
Frating 34 E6
Fratton 11 H4
Freathy 4 D5
Freckenham 33 K1
Freckleton 55 H7
Freeby 42 B3
Freefolk 21 H7
Freeland 31 F7
Freemantle 11 F3
Freester 109 D7
Freethorpe 45 J5
Freethorpe Common 45 J5
Freiston 43 G1
Freiston Shore 43 G1
Fremington Devon 6 D2
Fremington N.Yorks. 62 B7
Frenchay 19 K4
Frenchbeer 6 E7
Frendraught 98 E6
Frenich 81 F7
Frensham 22 B7
Fresgoe 104 E2
Freshfield 48 B2
Freshford 20 A5
Freshwater 10 E6
Freshwater East 16 D5
Fressingfield 35 G1
Freston 35 F5
Freswick 105 J2
Frettenham 45 G4
Freuchie 82 D7
Freystrop Cross 16 C3
Friars Carse 68 E5
Friar's Gate 13 H3
Friarton 82 C5
Friday Bridge 43 H5
Friday Street E.Suss. 13 K6
Friday Street Surr. 22 E7
Fridaythorpe 58 E4
Friern Barnet 23 F2
Friesthorpe 52 D4
Frieston 42 C1
Frieth 22 A2
Frilford 21 H2
Frilsham 21 J4
Frimley 22 B6
Frimley Green 22 B6
Frindsbury 24 D5

Name	Page	Grid
Fring	44	B2
Fringford	31	H6
Frinsted	14	D2
Frinton-on-Sea	35	G7
Friockheim	83	G3
Friog	37	F4
Frisby on the Wreake	41	J4
Friskney	53	H7
Friskney Eaudyke	53	H7
Friston E.Suss.	13	J7
Friston Suff.	35	J3
Fritchley	51	F7
Frith	14	E2
Frith Bank	43	G1
Frith Common	29	F2
Fritham	10	D3
Frithelstock	6	C4
Frithelstock Stone	6	C4
Frithville	53	G7
Frittenden	14	D3
Fritton Norf.	45	G6
Fritton Norf.	45	J5
Fritwell	31	G6
Frizington	60	B5
Frocester	20	A1
Frochas	38	B4
Frodesley	38	E5
Frodingham	52	B1
Frodsham	48	E5
Frog End	33	H3
Frog Pool	29	G2
Frogden	70	C1
Froggatt	50	E5
Froghall	40	C1
Frogham	10	C3
Frogmore Devon	5	H6
Frogmore Hants.	22	B6
Frogmore Herts.	22	E1
Frolesworth	41	H6
Frome	20	A7
Frome Market	20	B6
Frome St. Quentin	8	E4
Fromes Hill	29	F4
Fron Gwyn.	36	C2
Fron Powys	38	B5
Fron Powys	27	K2
Fron-goch	37	J2
Froncysyllte	38	B1
Frostenden	45	J7
Frosterley	62	B3
Froxfield	21	F5
Froxfield Green	11	J2
Fryerning	24	C1
Fryton	58	C2
Fugglestone St. Peter	10	C1
Fulbeck	52	C7
Fulbourn	33	J3
Fulbrook	30	D7
Fulford Som.	8	B2
Fulford Staffs.	40	B2
Fulford York	58	C5
Fulham	23	F4
Fulking	13	F5
Full Sutton	58	D4
Fuller Street	34	B7
Fuller's Moor	48	D7
Fullerton	10	E1
Fulletby	53	F5
Fullwood	74	C6
Fulmer	22	C3
Fulmodeston	44	D2
Fulnetby	52	E5
Fulready	30	D4
Fulstow	53	G3
Fulwell Oxon.	30	E6
Fulwell T. & W.	62	E1
Fulwood Lancs.	55	J6
Fulwood S.Yorks.	51	F4
Fundenhall	45	F6
Funtington	12	B6
Funtley	11	G4
Funzie	108	F4
Furley	8	B3
Furnace Arg. & B.	80	B7
Furnace Cere.	37	F6
Furnace High.	95	F4
Furness Vale	50	C4
Furneux Pelham	33	H6
Furze Platt	22	B3
Furzehill	7	F1
Fyfett	8	B3
Fyfield Essex	23	J1
Fyfield Glos.	21	F1
Fyfield Hants.	21	F7
Fyfield Oxon.	21	H2
Fyfield Wilts.	20	E5
Fylingthorpe	63	J2
Fyvie	91	F1

G

Name	Page	Grid
Gabhsunn Bho Dheas	101	G2
Gabhsunn Bho Thuath	101	G2
Gablon	96	E2
Gabroc Hill	74	C5
Gaddesby	41	J4
Gaddesden Row	32	D7
Gaer Newport	19	F3
Gaer Powys	28	A6
Gaerllwyd	19	H2
Gaerwen	46	C5
Gagingwell	31	F6
Gaich	89	H2
Gaick	88	D1
Gaick Lodge	88	E6
Gailey	40	B4
Gainford	62	C5
Gainsborough	52	B3
Gairloch	94	E4
Gairlochy	87	H6
Gairney Bank	75	K1
Gairnshiel Lodge	89	K4
Gaitsgill	60	E2
Galabank	76	C6
Galashiels	76	C7
Galdenoch	64	B4
Galgate	55	H4
Galhampton	9	F2
Gallanach	79	K5
Gallantry Bank	48	E7
Gallatown	76	A1
Gallchoille	73	F2
Gallery	83	H1
Galley Common	41	F6
Galleyend	24	D1
Galleywood	24	D1
Gallowfauld	83	F3
Gallows Green	21	K4
Gallowstree Common		
Gallowstree Elm	40	A7
Gallt Melyd (Meliden)	47	J4
Galltair	86	E3
Galmisdale	85	K6
Galmpton Devon	5	G6
Galmpton Torbay	5	J5
Galphay	57	H2
Galston	74	D7
Galtrigill	93	G6
Gamble's Green	34	B7
Gamblesby	61	H3
Gamelsby	60	D1
Gamlingay	33	F3
Gammaton Moor	6	C3
Gammersgill	57	F1
Gamrie	99	F4
Gamston Notts.	51	K5
Gamston Notts.	41	J2
Ganarew	28	E7
Ganllwyd	37	G3
Gannochy	90	E7
Ganstead	59	H6
Ganthorpe	58	C2
Ganton	59	F2
Goadhail	79	H4
Gara Bridge	5	H5
Garabal	80	E6
Garadheancal	95	F1
Garbat	96	B5
Garbhallt	73	J1
Garboldisham	44	E7
Garden	74	D1
Garden City	48	C6
Gardenstown	99	F4
Garderhouse	109	C8
Gardham	59	F5
Gare Hill	20	A7
Garelochhead	74	A1
Garford	21	H2
Garforth	57	K6
Gargrave	56	E4
Gargunnock	75	F1
Gariob	73	F2
Garlies Castle	64	E4
Garlieston	64	E6
Garlogie	91	F4
Garmond	99	G5
Garmony	79	H3
Garmouth	98	B4
Garnant	17	K3
Garndolbenmaen	36	D1
Garneddwen	37	G5
Garnett Bridge	61	G7
Garnswllt	17	K4
Garrabost	101	H4
Garrachra	73	J2
Garralburn	98	C5
Garras	2	D6
Garreg	37	F1
Garreg Bank	38	B4
Garrick	81	K6
Garrigill	61	J2
Garroch	67	K5
Garrochty	73	J5
Garros	94	B5
Garrow	81	K4
Garryhorn	67	K4
Garrynahine (Gearraidh na h-Aibhne)	100	E4
Garsdale Head	61	J7
Garsdon	20	C3
Garshall Green	40	B2
Garsington	21	J1
Garstang	55	H5
Garston	48	D4
Garswood	48	E3
Gartachoil	74	D1
Gartally	88	B1
Gartavaich	73	G5
Gartbreck	72	A5
Gartcosh	74	E4
Garth Bridgend	18	B2
Garth Gwyn.	46	D5
Garth I.o.M.	54	C6
Garth Powys	27	J4
Garth Shet.	109	B7
Garth Wrex.	38	B1
Garthbrengy	27	K5
Gartheli	26	E3
Garthmyl	38	A6
Garthorpe Leics.	42	B3
Garthorpe N.Lincs.	52	B1
Garths	61	G2
Garthynty	27	G4
Gartincaber	81	J7
Gartly	90	D1
Gartmore	74	D1
Gartnagrenach	73	F5
Gartnatra	72	B5
Gartness	74	D2
Gartocharn	74	C2
Garton	59	J6
Garton-on-the-Wolds	59	F3
Gartymore	105	F7
Garvald	76	D3
Garvamore	88	C5
Garvan	87	F7
Garvard	72	B1
Garve	95	K5
Garveld	66	A3
Garvestone	44	E5
Garvie	73	J2
Garvock Aber.	91	F7
Garvock Inclyde	74	A3
Garvock P.& K.	82	B6
Garwald	69	H3
Garwaldwaterfoot	69	H3
Garway	28	D6
Garway Hill	28	D6
Gask Aber.	99	F6
Gask Aber.	99	F6
Gask P.& K.	82	A6
Gaskan	86	E7
Gass	67	J3
Gastard	20	B5
Gasthorpe	44	D7
Gatcombe	11	F6
Gate Burton	52	B4
Gate Helmsley	58	C4
Gate House	72	D3
Gateacre	48	D4
Gatebeck	55	J1
Gateford	51	H4
Gateforth	58	B7
Gatehead	74	B7
Gatehouse	72	B7
Gatehouse of Fleet	65	G5
Gatelawbridge	68	E4
Gateley	44	D3
Gatenby	57	J1
Gateshaw	70	C1
Gateshead	71	H7
Gatesheath	48	D6
Gateside Aber.	90	E3
Gateside Angus	83	F3
Gateside Fife	82	C7
Gateside N.Ayr.	74	B5
Gateslack	68	D3
Gathurst	48	E2
Gatley	49	H4
Gattonside	76	D7
Gatwick (London) Airport	23	F7
Gaufron	27	J2
Gaulby	41	J5
Gauldry	82	E5
Gaunt's Common	10	B4
Gautby	52	E5
Gavinton	77	F5
Gawber	51	F2
Gawcott	31	H5
Gawsworth	49	H6
Gawthrop	56	B1
Gawthwaite	55	F1
Gay Street	12	D4
Gaydon	30	E3
Gayhurst	32	B4
Gayles	62	C6
Gayton Mersey.	48	B4
Gayton Norf.	44	B4
Gayton Northants.	31	J3
Gayton Staffs.	40	B3
Gayton le Marsh	53	H4
Gayton le Wold	53	F4
Gayton Thorpe	44	B4
Gaywood	44	A3
Gazeley	34	B2
Geanies House	97	F4
Gearach	72	A5
Gearnsary	104	C5
Gearradh	80	A1
Gearraidh Bhailteas	84	C2
Gearraidh Bhaird	101	F5
Gearraidh na h-Aibhne (Garrynahine)	100	E4
Gearraidh na Monadh	84	C3
Gearrannan	100	D3
Geary	93	H5
Gedding	34	D3
Geddington	42	B7
Gedgrave Hall	35	J4
Gedling	41	J1
Gedney	43	H3
Gedney Broadgate	43	H3
Gedney Drove End	43	H3
Gedney Dyke	43	H3
Gedney Hill	43	G4
Gee Cross	49	J3
Geirinnis	92	C7
Geisiadar	100	D4
Geldeston	45	H6
Gell Conwy	47	G6
Gell Gwyn.	36	D2
Gelli Gynan	47	K7
Gelligaer	18	E2
Gellilydan	37	F2
Gellioedd	37	J1
Gelly	16	D3
Gellyburn	82	B4
Gellywen	17	F2
Gelston	65	H5
Gembling	59	H4
Gemmil	79	J7
Genoch	64	B5
Genoch Square	64	B5
Gentleshaw	40	C4
George Green	22	D3
George Nympton	7	F3
Georgeham	6	C2
Georgetown	74	C4
Gerlan	46	E6
Germansweek	6	C6
Germoe	2	C6
Gerrans	3	F5
Gerrards Cross	22	C3
Gerston	105	G3
Gestingthorpe	34	C5
Geuffordd	38	B4
Geufron	37	H7
Gibbshill	65	H3
Gibraltar	53	J7
Gidea Park	23	J3
Gidleigh	6	E7
Giffnock	74	D5
Gifford	76	D4
Giffordland	74	A6
Giggleswick	56	D3
Gilberdyke	58	E7
Gilchriston	76	C4
Gilcrux	60	C3
Gildersome	57	H7
Gildingwells	51	H4
Gileston	18	D5
Gilfach	18	E2
Gilfach Goch	18	C3
Gilfachrheda	26	D3
Gilgarran	60	B4
Gillamoor	63	H7
Gillan	93	H5
Gillenbie	69	G5
Gillfoot	65	K3
Gilling East	58	C2
Gilling West	62	C6
Gillingham Dorset	9	H2
Gillingham Med.	24	D5
Gillingham Norf.	45	J6
Gillivoan	105	G5
Gillock	105	H3
Gillow Heath	49	H7
Gills	105	J1
Gill's Green	14	C4
Gilmanscleuch	69	J1
Gilmerton Edin.	76	A4
Gilmerton P.& K.	81	K5
Gilmilnscroft	67	K1
Gilmonby	62	A5
Gilmorton	41	H7
Gilsland	70	B7
Gilsland Spa	70	B7
Gilston	76	C5
Gilston Park	33	H7
Gilwern	28	B7
Gimingham	45	G2
Giosla	100	D5
Gipping	34	E2
Gipsey Bridge	43	F1
Girlsta	109	D7
Girsby	62	E6
Girtford	32	E4
Girthon	65	G5
Girton Cambs.	33	H2
Girton Notts.	52	B6
Girvan	67	F4
Gisburn	56	D5
Gisleham	45	K7
Gislingham	34	E1
Gissing	45	F7
Gittisham	7	K6
Givons Grove	22	E6
Glackour	95	H3
Gladestry	28	B3
Gladsmuir	76	C3
Glaic	73	J3
Glais	18	A1
Glaisdale	63	J6
Glaister	73	H7
Glame	94	B7
Glamis	82	E3
Glan Conwy	47	G7
Glan-Dwyfach	36	D1
Glan Honddu	27	K5
Glan-y-don	47	K5
Glan-y-llyn	18	E3
Glan-yr-afon Gwyn.	37	J1
Glan-yr-afon Gwyn.	37	K1
Glanaber Terrace	37	G1
Glanadda	46	D5
Glanaman	17	K3
Glanbran	27	G5
Glanderston	90	D2
Glandford	44	E1
Glandwr B.Gwent	19	F1
Glandwr Pembs.	16	E2
Glangrwyne	28	B7
Glanllynfi	18	B2
Glanmule	38	A6
Glanrhyd	26	A4
Glanton	71	F2
Glantwymyn (Cemmaes Road)	37	H5
Glanvilles Wootton	9	F4
Glapthorn	42	D7
Glapwell	51	G6
Glasahoile	81	F7
Glasbury	28	A5
Glaschoil	89	H1
Glascoed	19	G1
Glascorrie	90	B5
Glascote	40	E5
Glascwm	28	A3
Glasdrum	80	B3
Glasfryn	47	H7
Glasgow	74	D4
Glasgow Airport	74	C4
Glashmore	91	F4
Glasinfryn	46	D6
Glasnacardoch	86	C5
Glasnakille	86	B3
Glaspant	17	F1
Glaspwll	37	G6
Glassburn	87	K1
Glassel	90	E5
Glassenbury	14	C4
Glasserton	64	E7
Glassford	75	F6
Glasshouse Hill	29	G6
Glasshouses	57	G3
Glassingall	81	J7
Glasslie	82	D7
Glasson Cumb.	69	H7
Glasson Lancs.	55	H4
Glassonby	61	G3
Glasterlaw	83	G2
Glaston	42	B5
Glastonbury	8	D1
Glatton	42	E7
Gleadless	51	F4
Gleadsmoss	49	H6
Gleann Ghrabhair	101	F5
Gleann Tholastaidh	101	H3
Gleaston	55	F2
Glecknabae	73	J4
Gledhow	57	J6
Gledrid	38	B2
Glemsford	34	C4
Glen D. & G.	65	J3
Glen D. & G.	65	F5
Glen Auldyn	54	D4
Glen Parva	41	H6
Glen Trool Lodge	67	J5
Glen Vine	54	C6
Glenae	68	E5
Glenaladale	86	E7
Glenald	74	A1
Glenamachrie	80	A5
Glenapp Castle	66	E5
Glenarm	82	E1
Glenbarr	72	E7
Glenbatrick	72	D3
Glenbeg High.	95	K3
Glenbeg High.	89	H2
Glenbeg High.	79	G1
Glenbeich	81	H5
Glenbervie Aber.	91	F6
Glenbervie Falk.	75	G2
Glenboig	75	F4
Glenborrodale	79	H1
Glenbranter	73	K1
Glenbreck	69	F1
Glenbrittle	85	K2
Glenbuck	68	C1
Glenbyre	79	G5
Glencaple	65	K4
Glencarse	82	C5
Glencat	90	D5
Glenceitlein	80	C3
Glencloy	73	J7
Glencoe	80	C2
Glenconglass	89	J2
Glencraig	75	K1
Glencripesdale	79	H2
Glencrosh	68	C5
Glencruitten	79	K5
Glencuie	90	C3
Glendearg D. & G.	69	J3
Glendearg Sc.Bord.	76	D7
Glendessary	87	F5
Glendevon	82	A7
Glendoebeg	88	B4
Glendoick	82	D5
Glendoll Lodge	89	K7
Glendoune	67	F4
Glendrissaig	67	F4
Glenduckie	82	D6
Glenduisk	67	G5
Glendye Lodge	90	E6
Gleneagles Hotel	82	A6
Gleneagles House	82	A6
Glenearn	82	C6
Glenegedale	72	B5
Glenelg	86	E3
Glenfarg	82	C6
Glenfeochan	79	K5
Glenfield	41	H5
Glenfinnan	86	E6
Glenfoot	82	C6
Glengalmadale	79	K2
Glengap	65	G5
Glengarnock	74	B5
Glengarrisdale	72	E1
Glengennet	67	G4
Glengolly	105	G2
Glengorm Castle	79	F2
Glengrasco	93	K7
Glengyle	80	E6
Glenhead	82	D1
Glenhead Farm	82	D1
Glenhurich	79	K1
Glenkerry	69	H2
Glenkiln	73	J7
Glenkin	73	K3
Glenkindie	90	C3
Glenlair	65	H3
Glenlatterach	97	K6
Glenlean	73	J2
Glenlee Angus	90	C6
Glenlee D. & G.	68	B5
Glenlichorn	81	J6
Glenlivet	89	J2
Glenlochar	65	H4
Glenluce	64	B5
Glenmallan	74	A1
Glenmanna	68	C3
Glenmavis	75	F4
Glenmaye	54	B5
Glenmeanie	95	J6
Glenmore Arg. & B.	73	J3
Glenmore High.	93	K7
Glenmore Lodge	89	G4
Glenmoy	83	F1
Glenmuick	103	F7
Glennoe	80	B4
Glenochar	68	E2
Glenogil	83	F1
Glenprosen Village	82	E1
Glenquiech	83	F1
Glenramskill	66	B2
Glenrazie	64	D4
Glenridding	60	E5
Glenrisdell	73	G5
Glenrossal	96	B1
Glenrothes	82	D7
Glensanda	79	K3
Glensaugh	90	E7
Glensgaich	96	B5
Glenshalg	90	D4
Glenshellish	73	K1
Glensluain	73	J1
Glentaggart	68	D1
Glentham	52	D3
Glenton	90	E2
Glentress	76	A7
Glentrool	64	D3
Glentruan	54	D3
Glentworth	52	C4
Glenuachdarach	93	K6
Glenuig	86	C7
Glenure	80	B3
Glenurquhart	96	E5
Glenwhilly	64	B3
Glespin	68	D1
Gletness	109	D7
Glewstone	28	E6
Glinton	42	E5
Glooston	42	A6
Glororum	77	K7
Glossop	50	C3
Gloster Hill	71	H3
Gloucester	29	H7
Gloup	108	E2
Gloweth	2	E4
Glusburn	57	F5
Gluss	108	C5
Glympton	31	F6
Glyn	47	F7
Glyn Ceiriog	38	B2
Glyn-Cywarch	37	F2
Glynarthen	26	C4
Glyncoch	18	D2
Glyncorrwg	18	B2
Glynde	13	H6
Glyndebourne	13	H5
Glyndyfrdwy	38	A1
Glynneath	18	B1
Glynogwr	18	C3
Glyntaff	18	D3
Glynteg	17	G1
Gnosall	40	A3
Gnosall Heath	40	A4
Goadby	42	A6
Goadby Marwood	42	A3
Goatacre	20	D4
Goatfield	80	B7
Goathill	9	F3
Goathland	63	K6
Goathurst	8	B1
Gobernuisgeach	104	E5
Gobhaig	100	C7
Gobowen	38	B2
Godalming	22	C7
Godford Cross	7	K5
Godmanchester	33	F1
Godmanstone	9	F5
Godmersham	15	F2
Godolphin Cross	2	D5
Godor	38	B4
Godre'r-graig	18	A1
Godshill Hants.	10	C3
Godshill I.o.W.	11	G6
Godstone	23	G6
Goetre	19	G1
Goff's Oak	23	G1
Gogar	75	K3
Gogarth	47	F4
Goginan	37	F7
Goirtean a' Chladaich	87	G7
Goirtein	73	H2
Golan	36	E1
Golant	4	B5
Golberdon	4	D3
Golborne	49	F3
Golcar	50	D1
Gold Hill	43	J6
Goldcliff	19	G3
Golden Cross	13	J5
Golden Green	23	K7
Golden Grove	17	J3
Golden Pot	22	A7
Golden Valley	29	J6
Goldenhill	49	H7
Golders Green	23	F3
Goldhanger	24	E1
Goldielea	65	K3
Golding	38	E5
Goldington	32	D3
Goldsborough N.Yorks.	57	J4
Goldsborough N.Yorks.	63	K5
Goldsithney	2	C5
Goldthorpe	51	G2
Goldworthy	6	B3
Gollanfield	97	F6
Golspie	97	F2
Golval	104	D2
Gomeldon	10	C1
Gomersal	57	H7
Gometra House	78	E3
Gomshall	22	D7
Gonachan Cottage	74	E2
Gonalston	41	J1
Gonfirth	109	C6
Good Easter	33	K7
Gooderstone	44	B5
Goodleigh	6	E2
Goodmanham	58	E5
Goodnestone Kent	15	H2
Goodnestone Kent	25	G5
Goodrich	28	E7
Goodwick (Wdig)	16	C1
Goodworth Clatford	21	G7
Goodyers End	41	F7
Goole	58	D7
Goonbell	2	E4
Goonhavern	2	E3
Goose Green	23	K6
Gooseham	6	A4
Goosewell	5	F5
Goosey	21	G2
Goosnargh	55	J6
Goostrey	49	G5
Gorcott Hill	30	B2
Gordding	46	E5
Gordon	76	E6
Gordonbush	97	F1
Gordonsnargh	97	J5
Gordonstoun	98	D5
Gordonstown Aber.	91	F1
Gordonstown Aber.	98	D5
Gore Cross	20	D6
Gore Street	25	J5
Gorebridge	76	B4
Gorefield	43	H4
Gorey	3	K7
Goring	21	K3
Goring-by-Sea	12	E6
Gorleston on Sea	45	K5
Gorllwyn	17	G1
Gornalwood	40	B6
Gorrachie	99	F5
Gorran Churchtown	3	G4
Gorran Haven	4	A6
Gors	27	F1
Gorsedd	47	K5
Gorseinon	17	J5
Gorseness	107	D6
Gorsgoch	26	D3
Gorslas	17	J3
Gorsley	29	F6
Gorsley Common	29	F6
Gorstan	95	K5
Gorstanvorran	86	E7
Gorten	79	J4
Gortenbuie	79	G4
Gorteneorn	79	H1
Gorton Gt.Man.	49	H3
Gosbeck	35	F3
Gosberton	43	F2
Goseley Dale	41	F3
Gosfield	34	B6
Gosforth Cumb.	60	B6
Gosforth T. & W.	71	H7
Gosmore	32	E6
Gospel End	40	B6
Gosport	11	H5
Gossabrough	108	E4
Gossops Green	13	F3
Goswick	77	J6
Gotham	41	H2
Gotherington	29	J6
Gott	109	D8
Goudhurst	14	C4
Goulceby	53	F5
Gourdas	99	F6
Gourdon	91	G7
Gourock	74	A3
Govan	74	D4
Goveton	5	H6
Govilon	28	B7
Gowanhill	99	J4
Gowdall	58	C7
Gowerton	17	J6
Gowkhall	75	J2
Gowthorpe	58	D4
Goxhill E.Riding	59	H5
Goxhill N.Lincs.	59	H7
Goytre	18	A3
Grabhair	101	F6
Gradbach	49	J6
Grade	2	E7
Graffham	12	C5
Grafham Cambs.	32	E2
Grafham Surr.	22	D7
Grafton Here.	28	D5
Grafton N.Yorks.	57	K3
Grafton Oxon.	21	F1
Grafton Shrop.	38	D4
Grafton Worcs.	28	E2
Grafton Flyford	29	J3
Grafton Regis	31	J4
Grafton Underwood	42	C7
Grafty Green	14	D3
Graianrhyd	48	B7
Graig Conwy	47	G5
Graig Denb.	47	J5
Graig-fechan	47	K7
Graig Penllyn	18	C4
Grain	24	E4
Grainel	72	A4
Grainhow	99	G6
Grainsby	53	F3
Grainthorpe	53	G3
Graiselound	51	K3
Grampound	3	G4
Grampound Road	3	G3
Gramsdal	92	D6
Granborough	31	J6
Granby	42	A2
Grandborough	31	F2
Grandtully	82	A2
Grange Cumb.	60	D5
Grange High.	87	K1
Grange Med.	24	D5
Grange N.Yorks.	63	G7
Grange P.& K.	82	C5
Grange Crossroads	98	C5
Grange Hall	97	H5
Grange Hill	23	H2
Grange Moor	50	E1
Grange of Lindores	82	D6
Grange-over-Sands	55	H2
Grange Villa	62	D1
Grangemill	50	E7
Grangemouth	75	H2
Grangemuir	83	G7
Grangeston	67	G4
Grangetown Cardiff	18	E4
Grangetown R. & C.	63	G4
Granish	89	G3
Gransmoor	59	H4
Granston	16	B1
Grantchester	33	H3
Grantham	42	C2
Grantley	57	H2
Grantlodge	91	F3
Granton House	69	F3
Grantown-on-Spey	89	H2
Grantshouse	77	G4
Grappenhall	49	F4
Grasby	52	D2
Grasmere	60	E6
Grasscroft	49	J2
Grassendale	48	C4
Grassholme	62	A4
Grassington	57	F3
Grassmoor	51	G6
Grassthorpe	51	K6
Grateley	21	F7
Gratwich	40	C2
Graveley Cambs.	33	F2
Graveley Herts.	33	F6
Gravelly Hill	40	D6
Gravels	38	C5
Graven	108	D5
Graveney	25	G5
Gravesend	24	C4
Grayingham	52	C3
Grayrigg	61	G7
Grays	24	C4
Grayshott	12	B3
Grayswood	12	C3
Grazeley	22	A5
Greasbrough	51	G3
Greasby	48	B4
Great Abington	33	J4
Great Addington	32	C1
Great Alne	30	C3
Great Altcar	48	C2
Great Amwell	33	G7
Great Asby	61	H5
Great Ashfield	34	D2
Great Ayton	63	G5
Great Baddow	24	D1
Great Bardfield	33	K5
Great Barford	32	E3
Great Barr	40	C6
Great Barrington	30	D7
Great Barrow	48	D6
Great Barton	34	C2
Great Barugh	58	D2
Great Bavington	70	E5
Great Bealings	35	G4
Great Bedwyn	21	F5
Great Bentley	35	F6
Great Billing	32	B2
Great Bircham	44	B2
Great Blakenham	35	F4
Great Bolas	39	F3
Great Bookham	22	E6
Great Bourton	31	F4
Great Bowden	42	A7
Great Bradley	33	K3
Great Braxted	34	C7
Great Bricett	34	E3
Great Brickhill	32	C5
Great Bridgeford	40	A3
Great Brington	31	H2
Great Bromley	34	E6
Great Broughton Cumb.	60	B3
Great Broughton N.Yorks.	63	G6
Great Budworth	49	F5
Great Burdon	62	E5
Great Burstead	24	C2
Great Busby	63	G6
Great Canfield	33	J7
Great Canney	24	E1
Great Carlton	53	H4
Great Casterton	42	D5
Great Chart	14	E3
Great Chatwell	39	G4
Great Chesterford	33	J4
Great Cheverell	20	C6
Great Chishill	33	H5
Great Clacton	35	F7
Great Clifton	60	B4
Great Coates	53	F2
Great Comberton	29	J4
Great Corby	61	F1
Great Cornard	34	C4
Great Cowden	59	J5
Great Coxwell	21	F2
Great Crakehall	57	H1
Great Cransley	32	B1
Great Cressingham	44	C5
Great Crosby	48	C2
Great Cubley	40	D2
Great Dalby	42	A4
Great Doddington	32	B2
Great Dunham	44	C4
Great Dunmow	33	K6
Great Durnford	10	C1
Great Easton Essex	33	K6
Great Easton Leics.	42	B6
Great Eccleston	55	H5
Great Edstone	58	D1
Great Ellingham	44	E6
Great Elm	20	A7
Great Eversden	33	G3
Great Fencote	62	D7
Great Finborough	34	E3
Great Fransham	44	C4
Great Gaddesden	32	D7
Great Gidding	42	E7
Great Givendale	58	E4
Great Glemham	35	H2
Great Glen	41	J6
Great Gonerby	42	B2
Great Gransden	33	F3
Great Green Suff.	45	G7
Great Green Suff.	34	D3
Great Habton	58	D2
Great Hale	42	E1
Great Hallingbury	33	J7
Great Harrowden	32	B1
Great Harwood	56	C6
Great Haseley	21	K1
Great Hatfield	59	H5
Great Haywood	40	C3
Great Heath	41	F7
Great Heck	58	B7
Great Henny	34	C5
Great Hinton	20	C6
Great Hockham	44	D6
Great Holland	35	G6
Great Horkesley	34	D5
Great Hormead	33	H5
Great Horwood	31	J5
Great Houghton Northants.	31	J3
Great Houghton S.Yorks.	51	G2
Great Hucklow	50	D5
Great Kelk	59	H4
Great Kimble	22	B1
Great Kingshill	22	B2
Great Langton	62	D7
Great Leighs	34	B7
Great Limber	52	E2

Great Linford 32 B4
Great Livermere 34 C1
Great Longstone 50 E5
Great Lumley 62 D2
Great Lyth 38 D5
Great Malvern 29 G4
Great Maplestead 34 C5
Great Marton 55 G6
Great Massingham 44 B3
Great Melton 45 F5
Great Milton 21 K1
Great Missenden 22 B1
Great Mitton 56 C6
Great Mongeham 15 J2
Great Moulton 45 F6
Great Munden 33 G6
Great Musgrave 61 J5
Great Ness 38 C4
Great Notley 34 B6
Great Oak 28 C7
Great Oakley *Essex* 35 F6
Great Oakley *Northants.* 42 B7
Great Offley 32 E6
Great Ormside 61 J5
Great Orton 60 E1
Great Ouseburn 57 K3
Great Oxendon 42 A7
Great Oxney Green 24 C1
Great Palgrave 44 C4
Great Parndon 23 H1
Great Paxton 33 F2
Great Plumpton 55 G6
Great Plumstead 45 G5
Great Ponton 42 C2
Great Preston 57 J7
Great Raveley 43 F7
Great Rissington 30 C7
Great Rollright 30 E5
Great Ryburgh 44 D3
Great Ryle 71 F2
Great Ryton 38 D5
Great Saling 33 K6
Great Salkeld 61 G3
Great Sampford 33 K5
Great Sankey 48 E4
Great Saxham 34 B2
Great Shefford 21 G4
Great Shelford 33 H3
Great Smeaton 62 E6
Great Snoring 44 D2
Great Somerford 20 C3
Great Stainton 62 E4
Great Stambridge 24 E2
Great Staughton 32 E2
Great Steeping 53 H6
Great Stonar 15 J2
Great Strickland 61 G4
Great Stukeley 33 F1
Great Sturton 53 F5
Great Sutton *Ches.* 48 C5
Great Sutton *Shrop.* 38 E7
Great Swinburne 70 E6
Great Tew 30 E6
Great Tey 34 C6
Great Thurlow 33 K4
Great Torrington 6 D4
Great Tosson 71 F3
Great Totham *Essex* 34 C7
Great Totham *Essex* 34 C7
Great Urswick 55 F2
Great Wakering 25 F3
Great Waldingfield 34 D4
Great Walsingham 44 D2
Great Waltham 33 K7
Great Warley 23 J2
Great Washbourne 29 J5
Great Welnetham 34 C3
Great Wenham 34 E5
Great Whittington 71 F6
Great Wigborough 34 D7
Great Wilbraham 33 J3
Great Wishford 10 B1
Great Witcombe 29 J7
Great Witley 29 G2
Great Wolford 30 D5
Great Wratting 33 K4
Great Wymondley 33 F6
Great Wyrley 40 B5
Great Wytheford 38 E4
Great Yarmouth 45 K5
Great Yeldham 34 B5
Greatford 42 D4
Greatgate 40 C1
Greatham *Hants.* 11 J1
Greatham *Hart.* 63 F4
Greatham *W.Suss.* 12 D5
Greatstone-on-Sea 15 F5
Greatworth 31 G4
Green End *Beds.* 32 E3
Green End *Herts.* 33 G6
Green Hammerton 57 K4
Green Ore 19 J6
Green Street 22 E1
Green Street Green *Gt.Lon.* 23 H5
Green Street Green *Kent* 23 J4
Green Tye 33 H7
Greenburn 83 F4
Greencroft 62 C2
Greendams 90 E5
Greendykes 71 F1
Greenfield *Beds.* 32 D5
Greenfield (Maes-Glas) *Flints.* 47 K5
Greenfield *Gt.Man.* 50 C2
Greenfield *High.* 87 J4
Greenfield *Oxon.* 22 A2
Greenford 22 E3
Greengairs 75 F3
Greenhalgh 55 H6
Greenhall 90 E2
Greenham *Som.* 7 J3
Greenham *W.Berks.* 21 H5
Greenhaugh 70 C5
Greenhead 70 B7
Greenheads 91 J1
Greenhill *Gt.Lon.* 22 E3
Greenhill *High.* 97 G1
Greenhill *S.Yorks.* 51 F4
Greenhithe 23 J4
Greenholm 74 D7
Greenholme 61 G6
Greenhow Hill 57 G3
Greenigo 107 D7
Greenland 105 H2
Greenlands 22 A3
Greenlaw *Aber.* 98 E5
Greenlaw *Sc.Bord.* 77 F6
Greenloaning 81 K7
Greenmount 49 G1
Greenmyre 91 G1
Greenock 74 A3
Greenodd 55 G1
Greens Norton 31 H3
Greenscares 81 J6
Greenside 71 G7
Greenstead Green 34 C6
Greensted 23 J1
Greenway *Pembs.* 16 D1
Greenway *Som.* 8 C2
Greenwich *Gt.Lon.* 23 G4
Greenwich *Gt.Lon.* 23 G4
Greet 30 B5
Greete 28 E1
Greetham *Lincs.* 53 G5
Greetham *Rut.* 42 C4
Greetland 57 F7
Greinetobht 92 D4
Greinton 8 D1
Grenaby 54 B6
Grendon *Northants.* 32 B2
Grendon *Warks.* 40 E6
Grendon Common 40 E6
Grendon Green 28 E3
Grendon Underwood 31 H6
Grenoside 51 F3
Greosabhagh 93 G2
Gresford 48 C7
Gresham 45 F2
Greshornish 93 J6
Gressenhall 44 D4
Gressingham 55 J2
Greta Bridge 62 B5
Gretna 69 J7
Gretna Green 69 J7
Gretton *Glos.* 30 B5
Gretton *Northants.* 42 C6
Gretton *Shrop.* 38 E6
Grewelthorpe 57 H2
Greygarth 57 G2
Greylake 8 C1
Greys Green 22 A3
Greysouthen 60 B4
Greystoke 61 F3
Greystone *Aber.* 89 K5
Greystone *Angus* 83 G3
Greystone *Lancs.* 56 D5
Greywell 22 A6
Griais 101 G3
Gribthorpe 58 D6
Gribton 68 E5
Gridley Corner 6 B6
Griff 41 F7
Griffithstown 19 F2
Grigadale 79 F1
Grigghall 61 F7
Grimeford Village 49 F1
Grimethorpe 51 G2
Griminis 92 C6
Grimister 108 D3
Grimley 29 H2
Grimmet 67 H2
Grimness 107 D8
Grimoldby 53 G4
Grimpo 38 C3
Grimsargh 55 J6
Grimsbury 31 F4
Grimsby 53 F2
Grimscote 31 H3
Grimscott 6 A5
Grimsiadar 101 G5
Grimsthorpe 42 D3
Grimston *Leics.* 41 J3
Grimston *Norf.* 44 B3
Grimstone 9 F5
Grindale 59 H2
Grindiscol 109 D9
Grindle 39 G5
Grindleford 50 E5
Grindleton 56 C5
Grindley 40 C3
Grindlow 50 D5
Grindon *Northumb.* 77 H6
Grindon *Staffs.* 50 C7
Gringley on the Hill 51 K3
Grinsdale 60 E1
Grinshill 38 E3
Grinton 62 B7
Griomarstaidh 100 E4
Grishipoll 78 C2
Gristhorpe 59 G1
Griston 44 D6
Gritley 107 E7
Grittenham 20 D3
Grittleton 20 B3
Grizebeck 55 F1
Grizedale 60 E7
Grobister 106 F5
Groby 41 H5
Groes 47 J6
Groes-faen 18 D3
Groes-lwyd 38 B4
Groesffordd 36 B2
Groesffordd Marli 47 J5
Groeslon 46 C7
Grogport 73 G6
Groigearraidh 84 C1
Gromford 35 H3
Gronant 47 J4
Groombridge 13 J3
Grosmont *Mon.* 28 D6
Grosmont *N.Yorks.* 63 K6
Grotaig 88 B2
Groton 34 D4
Groundistone Heights 69 K2
Grouville 3 K7
Grove *Dorset* 9 F7
Grove *Kent* 25 J5
Grove *Notts.* 51 K5
Grove *Oxon.* 21 H2
Grove Park 23 H4
Grovesend 17 J4
Gruids 96 C1
Gruinart Flats 72 A4
Gruline 79 G4
Grundcruie 82 B5
Grundisburgh 35 G3
Gruting 109 B8
Grutness 109 G10
Gualachulain 80 C3
Guardbridge 83 F6
Guarlford 29 H4
Guay 82 B3
Gubbergill 60 B7
Guernsey Airport 3 H5
Guestling Green 14 D6
Guestling Thorn 14 D6
Guestwick 44 E3
Guide Post 71 H5
Guilden Morden 33 F4
Guilden Sutton 48 D6
Guildford 22 C7
Guildtown 82 C4
Guilsborough 31 H1
Guilsfield (Cegidfa) 38 B4
Guisborough 63 H5
Guiseley 57 G5
Guist 44 D3
Guith 106 E4
Guiting Power 30 B6
Gulberwick 109 D9
Gullane 76 C2
Gulval 2 B5
Gulworthy 4 E3
Gumfreston 16 E4
Gumley 41 J7
Gunby *E.Riding* 58 D6
Gunby *Lincs.* 42 C3
Gundleton 11 H1
Gunn 6 E2
Gunnerside 62 A7
Gunnerton 70 E6
Gunness 52 B1
Gunnislake 4 E3
Gunnista 109 D8
Gunter's Bridge 12 C4
Gunthorpe *Norf.* 44 E2
Gunthorpe *Notts.* 41 J1
Gunville 11 F6
Gunwalloe 2 D6
Gurnard 11 F5
Gurney Slade 19 K7
Gurnos 18 A1
Gussage All Saints 10 B3
Gussage St. Michael 9 J3
Guston 15 J3
Gutcher 108 E3
Guthrie 83 G2
Guyhirn 43 G5
Guynd 83 G3
Guy's Head 43 H3
Guy's Marsh 9 H2
Guyzance 71 H3
Gwaelod-y-garth 18 E3
Gwaenysgor 47 J4
Gwaithla 28 B3
Gwalchmai 46 B5
Gwaun-Cae-Gurwen 27 G7
Gwaynynog 47 J6
Gwbert 26 A4
Gweek 2 E6
Gwehelog 19 G1
Gwenddwr 27 K4
Gwennap 2 E4
Gwenter 2 E7
Gwernaffield 48 B6
Gwernesney 19 H1
Gwernogle 17 J1
Gwernymynydd 48 B6
Gwersyllt 48 C7
Gwespyr 47 K4
Gwinear 2 C5
Gwithian 2 C4
Gwyddelwern 37 K1
Gwyddgrug 17 H1
Gwystre 27 K2
Gwytherin 47 G6
Gyfelia 38 C1
Gyffin 47 F5
Gyre 107 C7
Gyrn Goch 36 D1

H

Habberley 38 C5
Habrough 52 E1
Haccombe 5 J3
Hacconby 42 E3
Haceby 42 D2
Hacheston 35 H3
Hackenthorpe 51 G4
Hackford 44 E5
Hackforth 62 D7
Hackland 106 C5
Hackleton 32 B3
Hacklinge 15 J2
Hackness *N.Yorks.* 63 J3
Hackness *Ork.* 107 C8
Hackney 23 G3
Hackthorn 52 C4
Hackthorpe 61 G4
Hadden 77 F7
Haddenham *Bucks.* 22 A1
Haddenham *Cambs.* 33 H1
Haddington *E.Loth.* 76 D3
Haddington *Lincs.* 52 C6
Haddiscoe 45 J6
Haddon 42 E6
Hademore 40 D5
Hadfield 50 C3
Hadham Cross 33 H7
Hadham Ford 33 H6
Hadleigh *Essex* 24 E3
Hadleigh *Suff.* 34 E4
Hadley 39 F4
Hadley End 40 D3
Hadley Wood 23 F2
Hadlow 23 K7
Hadlow Down 13 J4
Hadnall 38 E3
Hadstock 33 J4
Hadzor 29 J2
Haffenden Quarter 14 D3
Hafod-Dinbych 47 G7
Hafodunos 47 G6
Haggate 56 D6
Haggbeck 69 K6
Haggs 75 F3
Hagley *Here.* 28 E4
Hagley *Worcs.* 40 B7
Hagnaby 53 G6
Hagworthingham 53 G6
Haigh 49 F2
Haighton Green 55 J6
Hail Weston 32 E2
Haile 60 B6
Hailes 30 B5
Hailey *Herts.* 33 G7
Hailey *Oxon.* 21 K3
Hailey *Oxon.* 30 E7
Hailsham 13 J6
Haimer 105 G2
Hainault 23 H2
Hainford 45 G4
Hainton 52 E4
Haisthorpe 59 H3
Halam 51 J7
Halbeath 75 K2
Halberton 7 J4
Halcro 105 H2
Hale *Gt.Man.* 49 G4
Hale *Hants.* 10 C3
Hale *Surr.* 22 B7
Hale Bank 48 D4
Hale Street 23 K7
Halebarns 49 G4
Hales *Norf.* 45 H6
Hales *Staffs.* 39 G2
Hales Place 15 G2
Halesowen 40 B7
Halesworth 35 H1
Halewood 48 D4
Half Way Inn 7 J6
Halford *Shrop.* 38 D7
Halford *Warks.* 30 D4
Halfpenny Green 40 A6
Halfway *Carmar.* 17 K1
Halfway *Powys* 27 H5
Halfway *S.Yorks.* 51 G4
Halfway *W.Berks.* 21 H5
Halfway House 38 C4
Halfway Houses 25 F4
Halghton Mill 38 D1
Halifax 57 F7
Halistra 93 H6
Halkirk 105 G3
Halkyn 48 B5
Hall 74 C5
Hall Dunnerdale 60 D7
Hall Green 40 D7
Hall of the Forest 38 B7
Halland 13 J5
Hallaton 42 A6
Hallatrow 19 K6
Hallbankgate 61 G1
Hallen 19 J4
Hallin 93 H6
Halling 24 D5
Hallington *Lincs.* 53 G4
Hallington *Northumb.* 70 E6
Halloughton 51 J7
Hallow 29 H3
Hallow Heath 29 H3
Hallrule 70 A2
Halls 76 E3
Hall's Green 33 F6
Hall's Tenement 61 G1
Hallsands 5 J7
Hallworthy 4 B2
Halmer End 39 G1
Halmore 19 K1
Halmyre Mains 75 K6
Halnaker 12 C6
Halsall 48 C1
Halse *Northants.* 31 G4
Halse *Som.* 7 K3
Halsetown 2 C5
Halsham 59 J7
Halsinger 6 D2
Halstead *Essex* 34 C5
Halstead *Kent* 23 H5
Halstead *Leics.* 42 A5
Halstock 8 E4
Haltham 53 F6
Haltoft End 43 G1
Halton *Bucks.* 32 B7
Halton *Halton* 48 E4
Halton *Lancs.* 55 J3
Halton *Northumb.* 71 F7
Halton *Wrex.* 38 C2
Halton East 57 F4
Halton Gill 56 D2
Halton Holegate 53 H6
Halton Lea Gate 61 H1
Halton West 56 D4
Haltwhistle 70 C7
Halvergate 45 J5
Halwell 5 H5
Halwill 6 C6
Halwill Junction 6 C6
Ham *Glos.* 19 K2
Ham *Gt.Lon.* 22 E4
Ham *High.* 105 H1
Ham *Kent* 15 J2
Ham *Shet.* 108 B1
Ham *Som.* 8 B2
Ham *Wilts.* 21 G5
Ham Green *N.Som.* 19 J4
Ham Green *Worcs.* 30 B2
Ham Hill 24 C5
Ham Street 8 E1
Hamble-le-Rice 11 F4
Hambleden 22 A3
Hambledon *Hants.* 11 H3
Hambledon *Surr.* 12 C3
Hambleton *Lancs.* 55 G5
Hambleton *N.Yorks.* 58 B6
Hambleton Moss Side 55 G5
Hambridge 8 C2
Hambrook *S.Glos.* 19 K4
Hambrook *W.Suss.* 11 J4
Hameringham 53 G6
Hamerton 32 E1
Hamilton 75 F5
Hamlet 7 K6
Hammer 12 B3
Hammerpot 12 D6
Hammersmith & Fulham 22 E4
Hammerwich 40 C5
Hammerwood 13 H3
Hammond Street 23 G1
Hammoon 9 H3
Hamnavoe *Shet.* 109 C9
Hamnavoe *Shet.* 108 D4
Hamnavoe *Shet.* 108 B4
Hamnavoe *Shet.* 108 D5
Hampden Park 13 K6
Hampnett 30 C7
Hampole 51 H2
Hampreston 10 B5
Hampstead 23 F3
Hampstead Norreys 21 J4
Hampsthwaite 57 H4
Hampton *Gt.Lon.* 22 E5
Hampton *Shrop.* 39 G7
Hampton *Worcs.* 30 B4
Hampton Bishop 28 E5
Hampton Heath 38 D1
Hampton in Arden 40 E7
Hampton Lovett 29 H2
Hampton Lucy 30 D3
Hampton on the Hill 30 D2
Hampton Poyle 31 G7
Hamptworth 10 D2
Hamsey 13 H5
Hamstall Ridware 40 D4
Hamstead *I.o.W.* 11 F5
Hamstead *W.Mid.* 40 C6
Hamstead Marshall 21 H5
Hamsterley *Dur.* 62 C3
Hamsterley *Dur.* 62 C1
Hamstreet 15 F4
Hamworthy 9 J5
Hanbury *Staffs.* 40 D3
Hanbury *Worcs.* 29 J2
Hanbury Woodend 40 D3
Hanchurch 40 A1
Handbridge 48 D6
Handcross 13 F4
Handforth 49 H4
Handley 48 D7
Handsacre 40 C4
Handsworth *S.Yorks.* 51 G4
Handsworth *W.Mid.* 40 C6
Handy Cross 22 B2
Hanford 40 A1
Hanging Bridge 40 D1
Hanging Langford 10 B1
Hangingshaw 69 G5
Hangleton 13 F6
Hanham 19 K4
Hankelow 39 F1
Hankerton 20 C2
Hankham 13 K6
Hanley 40 A1
Hanley Castle 29 H4
Hanley Child 29 F2
Hanley Swan 29 H4
Hanley William 29 F2
Hanlith 56 E3
Hanmer 38 D2
Hannah 53 H5
Hannington *Hants.* 21 J6
Hannington *Northants.* 32 B1
Hannington *Swin.* 20 E2
Hannington Wick 20 E2
Hanslope 32 B4
Hanthorpe 42 D3
Hanwell *Gt.Lon.* 22 E4
Hanwell *Oxon.* 31 F4
Hanwood 38 D5
Hanworth *Gt.Lon.* 22 E4
Hanworth *Norf.* 45 F2
Happisburgh 45 H2
Happisburgh Common 45 H3
Hapsford 48 D5
Hapton *Lancs.* 56 C6
Hapton *Norf.* 45 F6
Harberton 5 H5
Harbertonford 5 H5
Harbledown 15 G2
Harborne 40 C7
Harborough Magna 31 F1
Harbottle 70 E3
Harbourneford 5 H4
Harbridge 10 C3
Harburn 75 J4
Harbury 30 E3
Harby *Leics.* 42 A2
Harby *Notts.* 52 B5
Harcombe 7 K6
Harden 57 F6
Hardenhuish 20 C4
Hardgate 91 F4
Hardham 12 D5
Hardingham 44 E5
Hardings Wood 49 H7
Hardingstone 31 J3
Hardington 20 A6
Hardington Mandeville 8 E3
Hardington Marsh 8 E4
Hardley 11 F4
Hardley Street 45 H5
Hardmead 32 C4
Hardraw 61 K7
Hardstoft 51 G6
Hardway *Hants.* 11 H4
Hardway *Som.* 9 G1
Hardwick *Bucks.* 32 B7
Hardwick *Cambs.* 33 G3
Hardwick *Norf.* 45 G6
Hardwick *Northants.* 32 B2
Hardwick *Oxon.* 21 G1
Hardwick *Oxon.* 31 G6
Hardwick Village 51 J5
Hardwicke *Glos.* 29 J6
Hardwicke *Glos.* 29 G7
Hardwicke *Here.* 28 B4
Hardy's Green 34 D7
Hare Green 34 E6
Hare Hatch 22 B4
Hare Street *Herts.* 33 G6
Hare Street *Herts.* 33 G6
Hareby 53 G6
Hareden 56 B4
Harefield 22 D2
Harehills 57 J6
Harelaw 75 H6
Haresceugh 61 H2
Harescombe 29 H7
Haresfield 29 H7
Hareshaw 74 E6
Harewood 57 J5
Harewood End 28 E6
Harford 5 G5
Hargate 45 F6
Hargrave *Ches.* 48 D6
Hargrave *Northants.* 32 D1
Hargrave *Suff.* 34 B3
Haringey 23 G3
Harker 69 J7
Harkstead 35 F5
Harlaston 40 E4
Harlaxton 42 B2
Harle Syke 56 D6
Harlech 36 E2
Harlesden 23 F3
Harleston *Norf.* 45 G7
Harleston *Suff.* 34 E3
Harlestone 31 J2
Harley 38 E5
Harleyholm 75 H7
Harlington 32 D5
Harlosh 93 H7
Harlow 33 H7
Harlow Hill 71 F7
Harlthorpe 58 D6
Harlton 33 G3
Harman's Cross 9 J6
Harmby 62 C7
Harmer Green 33 F7
Harmer Hill 38 D3
Harmondsworth 22 D4
Harmston 52 C6
Harnham 10 C2
Harnhill 20 D1
Harold Hill 23 J2
Harold Wood 23 J2
Haroldston West 16 B3
Haroldswick 108 F1
Harome 58 C1
Harpenden 32 E7
Harpford 7 J6
Harpham 59 G3
Harpley *Norf.* 44 B3
Harpley *Worcs.* 29 F2
Harpole 31 H2
Harprigg 56 B1
Harpsdale 105 G3
Harpsden 22 A3
Harpswell 52 C3
Harpur Hill 50 C5
Harpurhey 49 H2
Harrapool 86 C2
Harrietfield 82 A4
Harrietsham 14 D2
Harrington *Lincs.* 53 G5
Harrington *Northants.* 31 J1
Harringworth 42 C6
Harris 85 J5
Harriseahead 49 H7
Harrogate 57 J4
Harrold 32 C3
Harrow *Gt.Lon.* 22 E3
Harrow *High.* 105 H1
Harrow on the Hill 22 E3
Harrow Weald 22 E2
Harrowbarrow 4 E3
Harrowden 32 D4
Harston *Cambs.* 33 H3
Harston *Leics.* 42 B2
Hart 63 F3
Hartburn *Northumb.* 71 F5
Hartburn *Stock.* 63 F5
Hartest 34 C3
Hartfield *E.Suss.* 13 H3
Hartfield *High.* 94 D7
Hartford *Cambs.* 33 F1
Hartford *Ches.* 49 F5
Hartford End 33 K7
Hartfordbridge 22 A6
Harthill *Ches.* 48 D7
Harthill *N.Lan.* 75 H4
Harthill *S.Yorks.* 51 G4
Hartington 50 D6
Hartland 6 A3
Hartland Quay 6 A3
Hartlebury 29 H1
Hartlepool 63 G3
Hartley *Cumb.* 61 J6
Hartley *Kent* 24 C5
Hartley *Kent* 14 C4
Hartley *Northumb.* 71 J6
Hartley Wespall 22 A6
Hartley Wintney 22 A6
Hartlip 24 E5
Harton *N.Yorks.* 58 D3
Harton *Shrop.* 38 D7
Harton *T.& W.* 71 J7
Hartpury 29 G6
Hartrigge 70 B1
Hartshill 41 F6
Hartshorne 41 F3
Hartsop 61 F5
Hartwell *Bucks.* 31 J7
Hartwell *E.Suss.* 13 H3
Hartwell *Northants.* 31 J4
Hartwood 75 G5
Harvel 24 C5
Harvington *Worcs.* 30 B4
Harvington *Worcs.* 29 H1
Harwell *Notts.* 51 J3
Harwell *Oxon.* 21 H3
Harwich 35 G5
Harwood *Dur.* 61 K3
Harwood *Gt.Man.* 49 G1
Harwood Dale 63 J3
Harwood on Teviot 69 K3
Harworth 51 J3
Hasbury 40 B7
Hascombe 12 C3
Haselbech 31 J1
Haselbury Plucknett 8 D3
Haseley 30 D2
Haselor 30 C3
Hasfield 29 H6
Hasguard 16 B4
Haskayne 48 C2
Hasketon 35 G3
Hasland 51 F6
Haslemere 12 C3
Haslingden 56 C7
Haslingden Grane 56 C7
Haslingfield 33 H3
Haslington 49 G7
Hassall 49 G7
Hassall Green 49 G7
Hassell Street 15 F3
Hassendean 70 A1
Hassingham 45 H5
Hassocks 13 F5
Hassop 50 E5
Haster 105 J3
Hastigrow 105 H2
Hastingleigh 15 F3
Hastings 14 D7
Hastingwood 23 H1
Hastoe 22 C1
Haswell 62 E2
Hatch *Beds.* 32 E4
Hatch *Hants.* 21 K6
Hatch Beauchamp 8 B2
Hatch End 22 E2
Hatch Green 8 B3
Hatching Green 32 E7
Hatchmere 48 E5
Hatcliffe 53 F2
Hatfield *Here.* 28 E3
Hatfield *Herts.* 23 F1
Hatfield *S.Yorks.* 51 J2
Hatfield Broad Oak 33 J7
Hatfield Heath 33 J7
Hatfield Hyde 33 F7
Hatfield Peverel 34 B7
Hatfield Woodhouse 51 J2
Hatford 21 G2
Hatherden 21 G6
Hatherleigh 6 D5
Hathern 41 G3
Hatherop 20 E1
Hathersage 50 E4
Hatherton *Ches.* 39 F1
Hatherton *Staffs.* 40 B4
Hatley St. George 33 F3
Hatt 4 D4
Hattingley 11 H1
Hatton *Aber.* 91 J1
Hatton *Derbys.* 40 E3
Hatton *Gt.Lon.* 22 D4
Hatton *Lincs.* 52 E5
Hatton *Shrop.* 38 D6
Hatton *Warks.* 30 D2
Hatton *Warr.* 48 E4
Hatton Castle 99 F6
Hatton Heath 48 D6
Hatton of Fintray 91 G3
Hattoncrook 91 G2
Haugh Head 71 F1
Haugh of Glass 90 C1
Haugh of Urr 65 J4
Haugham 53 G4
Haughhead 74 E3
Haughley 34 E2
Haughley Green 34 E2
Haughley New Street 34 E2
Haughs 98 D6
Haughton *Notts.* 51 J5
Haughton *Shrop.* 39 F6
Haughton *Shrop.* 38 E4
Haughton *Shrop.* 38 C3
Haughton *Staffs.* 40 A3
Haughton Green 49 J3
Haughton Le Skerne 62 E5
Haughton Moss 48 E7
Haultwick 33 G6
Haunn 84 C3
Haunton 40 E4
Hauxley 71 H3
Hauxton 33 H3
Havant 11 J4
Haven 28 D3
Haven Side 59 K7
Havenstreet 11 G5
Haverfordwest (Hwlffordd) 16 C3
Haverhill 33 K4
Haverigg 54 E2
Havering 23 J3
Havering-atte-Bower 23 J2
Haversham 32 B4
Haverthwaite 55 G1
Haverton Hill 63 F4
Hawarden 48 C6
Hawbridge 29 J4
Hawbush Green 34 B7
Hawcoat 55 F2
Hawen 26 C4
Hawes 56 D1
Hawford 29 H2
Hawick 70 A2
Hawkchurch 8 C4
Hawkedon 34 B3
Hawkenbury 13 J3
Hawkeridge 20 B6
Hawkerland 7 J7
Hawkes End 41 F7
Hawkesbury 20 A3
Hawkesbury Upton 20 A3
Hawkhill 71 H2
Hawkhurst 14 C4
Hawkinge 15 H3
Hawkley 11 J2
Hawkridge 7 G2
Hawkshead 60 E7
Hawksland 75 G7
Hawkswick 56 E2
Hawksworth *Notts.* 42 A1
Hawksworth *W.Yorks.* 57 G5
Hawkwell *Essex* 24 E2
Hawkwell *Northumb.* 71 F6
Hawley *Hants.* 22 B6
Hawley *Kent* 23 J4
Hawling 30 B6
Hawnby 63 G7
Haworth 57 F6
Hawstead 34 C3
Hawthorn *Dur.* 63 F2
Hawthorn *Wilts.* 20 B5
Hawthorn Hill *Brack.F.* 22 B4
Hawthorn Hill *Lincs.* 53 F7
Hawthorpe 42 D3
Hawton 51 K7
Haxby 58 C4
Haxey 51 K3
Haxted 23 H7
Hay Mills 40 D7
Hay-on-Wye 28 B4
Hay Street 33 G6
Haydock 48 E3
Haydon 9 F3
Haydon Bridge 70 D7
Haydon Wick 20 E3
Haye 4 D4
Hayes *Gt.Lon.* 22 D3
Hayes *Gt.Lon.* 23 H5
Hayfield *Arg. & B.* 80 B5
Hayfield *Derbys.* 50 C4
Hayfield *High.* 105 G2
Hayhillock 83 G3
Haylands 11 G5
Hayle 2 C5
Haynes 32 E4
Haynes Church End 32 D4
Hayscastle 16 B2
Hayscastle Cross 16 C2
Hayton *Cumb.* 61 G1
Hayton *Cumb.* 60 C2
Hayton *E.Riding* 58 E5
Hayton *Notts.* 51 K4
Hayton's Bent 38 E7
Haytor Vale 5 H3
Haywards Heath 13 G4
Haywood Oaks 51 J7
Hazel End 33 H6
Hazel Grove 49 J4
Hazelbank *Arg. & B.* 80 B7
Hazelbank *S.Lan.* 75 G6
Hazelbury Bryan 9 G4
Hazeleigh 24 E1
Hazeley 22 A6
Hazelhead 91 G4
Hazelside 68 D1
Hazelslade 40 C4
Hazelton Walls 82 E5
Hazelwood *Derbys.* 41 F1
Hazelwood *Gt.Lon.* 23 H5
Hazlefield 65 H6
Hazlemere 22 B2
Hazlerigg 71 H6
Hazleton 30 B7
Heacham 44 A2
Head Bridge 6 E4
Headbourne Worthy 11 F1
Headcorn 14 D3
Headington 21 J1
Headlam 62 C5
Headless Cross 30 B2
Headley *Hants.* 12 B3
Headley *Hants.* 21 J5
Headley *Surr.* 23 F6
Headley Down 12 B3
Headon 51 K5
Heads Nook 61 F1
Heage 51 F7
Healaugh *N.Yorks.* 62 B7
Healaugh *N.Yorks.* 58 B5
Heald Green 49 H4

Heale 6 E1
Healey *Lancs.* 49 H1
Healey *N.Yorks.* 57 G1
Healey *Northumb.* 62 B1
Healeyfield 62 B2
Healing 53 F1
Heamoor 2 B5
Heanish 78 B3
Heanor 41 G1
Heanton 6 D2
Punchardon
Heanton Satchville 6 D4
Heapham 52 B4
Hearthstane 69 G1
Heasley Mill 7 F2
Heast 86 C3
Heath 51 G6
Heath and Reach 32 C6
Heath End *Hants.* 21 J5
Heath End *Surr.* 22 B7
Heath Hayes 40 C4
Heath Hill 39 G4
Heath House 19 H7
Heath Town 40 B6
Heathcot 91 G4
Heathcote *Derbys.* 50 D6
Heathcote *Shrop.* 39 F3
Heather 41 F4
Heathfield *Devon* 5 J3
Heathfield *E.Suss.* 13 J4
Heathfield *Som.* 7 K3
Heathton 40 A6
Heatley 49 G4
Heaton *Lancs.* 55 H3
Heaton *Staffs.* 49 J6
Heaton *T. & W.* 71 H7
Heaton Moor 49 H3
Heaverham 23 J6
Heaviley 49 J4
Hebburn 71 J7
Hebden 57 F3
Hebden Bridge 56 E7
Hebden Green 49 F6
Hebing End 33 G6
Hebron *Carmar.* 16 E2
Hebron *Northumb.* 71 G5
Heck 69 F5
Heckfield 22 A5
Heckfield Green 35 F1
Heckfordbridge 34 D6
Heckingham 45 H6
Heckington 42 E1
Heckmondwike 57 H7
Heddington 20 C5
Heddle 107 C6
Heddon-on-the-
Wall 71 G7
Hedenham 45 H6
Hedge End 11 F3
Hedgerley 22 C3
Hedging 8 B2
Hedley on the Hill 62 B1
Hednesford 40 C4
Hedon 59 H7
Hedsor 22 C3
Heeley 51 F4
Heglibister 109 C7
Heighington *Darl.* 62 D4
Heighington 52 D6
Lincs.
Heights of Brae 96 C5
Heilam 103 G2
Heithat 69 G5
Heiton 77 F7
Hele *Devon* 6 D1
Hele *Devon* 7 H5
Hele Bridge 6 D5
Hele Lane 7 F4
Helebridge 6 A5
Helensburgh 74 A2
Helford 2 E6
Helhoughton 44 C3
Helions Bumpstead 33 K4
Helland 4 A3
Hellandbridge 4 A3
Hellesdon 45 F4
Hellidon 31 G3
Hellifield 56 D4
Hellingly 13 J5
Hellington 45 H5
Hellister 109 C8
Helmdon 31 G4
Helmingham 35 F3
Helmsdale 105 F7
Helmshore 56 C7
Helmsley 58 C1
Helperby 57 K2
Helperthorpe 59 F2
Helpringham 42 E1
Helpston 42 E5
Helsby 48 D5
Helston 2 D6
Helstone 4 A2
Helton 61 G4
Helwith Bridge 56 D3
Hemblington 45 H4
Hemborough Post 5 J5
Hemel Hempstead 22 D1
Hemingbrough 58 C6
Hemingby 53 F5
Hemingford 33 F1
Abbots
Hemingford Grey 33 F1
Hemingstone 35 F3
Hemington *Leics.* 41 G3
Hemington 42 D7
Northants.
Hemington *Som.* 20 A6
Hemley 35 G4
Hemlington 63 F5
Hempholme 59 G5
Hempnall 45 G6
Hempnall Green 45 G6
Hempriggs 97 J5
Hempriggs House 105 J4
Hempstead *Essex* 33 K5
Hempstead *Norf.* 45 J3
Hempstead *Norf.* 45 F2
Hempsted 29 H7
Hempton *Norf.* 44 D3
Hempton *Oxon.* 31 F5
Hemsby 45 J4
Hemswell 52 C3
Hemsworth 51 G1
Hemyock 7 K4
Henbury *Bristol* 19 J4
Henbury *Ches.* 49 H5
Henderland 65 J3
Hendersyde Park 77 F7
Hendon *Gt.Lon.* 23 F3
Hendon *T. & W.* 62 E1
Hendy 17 J4
Heneglwys 46 C5
Henfield 13 F5
Henford 6 B6

Hengherst 14 E4
Hengoed *Caerp.* 18 E2
Hengoed *Powys* 28 B3
Hengoed *Shrop.* 38 B2
Hengrave 34 C2
Henham 33 J6
Heniarth 38 A5
Henlade 8 B2
Henley *Shrop.* 28 E1
Henley *Som.* 8 D1
Henley *Suff.* 35 F3
Henley *W.Suss.* 12 B4
Henley Corner 8 D1
Henley-in-Arden 30 C2
Henley-on-Thames 22 A3
Henley Park 22 C6
Henley's Down 14 C6
Henllan *Carmar.* 17 G1
Henllan *Denb.* 47 J6
Henllan Amgoed 16 E2
Henllys 19 F2
Henlow 32 E5
Hennock 7 G7
Henny Street 34 C5
Henryd 47 F5
Henry's Moat 16 D2
Hensall 58 B7
Henshaw 70 C7
Hensingham 60 A5
Henstead 45 J7
Hensting 11 F2
Henstridge 9 G3
Henstridge Ash 9 G2
Henstridge Marsh 9 G2
Henton *Oxon.* 22 A1
Henton *Som.* 19 H7
Henwick 29 H3
Henwood 4 C3
Heogan 109 D8
Heol-ddu 17 J3
Heol Lly Goden 28 A6
Heol Senni 27 J6
Heol-y-Cyw 18 C3
Hepburn 71 F1
Hepple 70 E3
Hepscott 71 H5
Heptonstall 56 E7
Hepworth *Suff.* 34 D1
Hepworth 50 D2
W.Yorks.
Herbrandston 16 B4
Herdicott 6 B6
Hereford 28 E4
Heriot 76 B5
Hermiston 75 K3
Hermitage *D. & G.* 65 J4
Hermitage *Dorset* 9 F4
Hermitage 70 A4
Sc.Bord.
Hermitage 21 J4
W.Berks.
Hermitage *W.Suss.* 11 J4
Hermon *Carmar.* 17 G1
Hermon *I.o.A.* 46 B6
Hermon *Pembs.* 17 F1
Herne 25 H5
Herne Bay 25 H5
Herne Common 25 H5
Herner 6 D3
Hernhill 25 G5
Herodsfoot 4 C4
Herongate 24 C2
Heron's Ghyll 13 H4
Heronsgate 22 D2
Herriard 21 K7
Herringfleet 45 J6
Herring's Green 32 D4
Herringswell 34 B2
Herrington 62 E1
Hersden 25 H5
Hersham *Cornw.* 6 A5
Hersham *Surr.* 22 E5
Herstmonceux 13 K5
Herston *Dorset* 10 B7
Herston *Ork.* 107 D8
Hertford 33 G7
Hertford Heath 33 G7
Hertingfordbury 33 G7
Hesket Newmarket 60 E3
Hesketh Bank 55 H7
Hesketh Lane 56 B5
Heskin Green 48 E1
Hesleden 63 F3
Hesleyside 70 D5
Heslington 58 C4
Hessay 58 B4
Hessenford 4 D5
Hessett 34 D2
Hessle 59 G7
Hest Bank 55 H3
Heston 22 E4
Heswall 48 B4
Hethe 31 G6
Hetherington 70 D6
Hethersett 45 F5
Hethersgill 69 K7
Hethpool 70 D1
Hett 62 D3
Hetton 56 E4
Hetton-le-Hole 62 E2
Heugh 71 F6
Heugh-head *Aber.* 90 B3
Heugh-head *Aber.* 90 D5
Heveningham 35 H1
Hever 23 H7
Heversham 55 H1
Hevingham 45 F3
Hewas Water 3 G4
Hewell Grange 30 B2
Hewell Lane 30 B2
Hewelsfield 19 J1
Hewelsfield 19 J1
Common
Hewish *N.Som.* 19 G5
Hewish *Som.* 8 D4
Hewton 6 D6
Hexham 70 E7
Hextable 23 J4
Hexton 32 E5
Hexworthy 5 G3
Heybridge *Essex* 24 C2
Heybridge *Essex* 24 E1
Heybridge Basin 24 E1
Heybrook Bay 5 F6
Heydon *Cambs.* 33 H4
Heydon *Norf.* 45 F3
Heydour 42 D2
Heylipoll 78 A3
Heylor 108 B4
Heysham 55 H3
Heyshaw 57 G3
Heyshott 12 B5
Heyside 49 J2
Heytesbury 20 C7
Heythrop 30 E6
Heywood *Gt.Man.* 49 H1
Heywood *Wilts.* 20 B6
Hibaldstow 52 C2
Hickleton 51 G2

Hickling *Norf.* 45 J3
Hickling *Notts.* 41 J3
Hickling Green 45 J3
Hickling Heath 45 J3
Hickstead 13 F4
Hidcote Boyce 30 C4
High Ackworth 51 G1
High Balantyre 80 B6
High Beach 23 H2
High Bentham 56 B3
High Birkwith 56 D2
High Blantyre 74 E5
High Bonnybridge 75 G3
High Borgue 65 G5
High Bradfield 50 E3
High Bray 6 E2
High Brooms 23 J7
High Bullen 6 D3
High Burton 57 H1
High Buston 71 H3
High Callerton 71 G6
High Catton 58 D4
High Cogges 21 G1
High Coniscliffe 62 D5
High Cross *Hants.* 11 J2
High Cross *Herts.* 33 G7
High Cross Bank 40 E4
High Easter 33 K7
High Ellington 57 G1
High Ercall 38 E4
High Etherley 62 C4
High Garrett 34 B6
High Gate 56 E7
High Grange 62 C3
High Green *Norf.* 45 F5
High Green 51 F3
S.Yorks.
High Green *Worcs.* 29 H4
High Halden 14 D4
High Halstow 24 D4
High Ham 8 D1
High Harrington 60 B4
High Harrogate 57 J4
High Hatton 39 F3
High Hawsker 63 J2
High Heath 39 F3
High Hesket 61 F2
High Hoyland 50 E1
High Hunsley 59 F6
High Hurstwood 13 H4
High Hutton 58 D3
High Ireby 60 D3
High Kilburn 58 B1
High Lane *Derbys.* 41 G1
High Lane *Worcs.* 29 F2
High Laver 23 J1
High Legh 49 G4
High Leven 63 F5
High Littleton 19 K6
High Lorton 60 C4
High Melton 51 H2
High Newton 55 H1
High Newton by-
the-Sea 71 H1
High Nibthwaite 60 D7
High Offley 39 G3
High Ongar 23 J1
High Onn 40 A4
High Risby 52 C1
High Roding 33 K7
High Salvington 12 E6
High Shaw 61 K7
High Spen 71 G7
High Street *Cornw.* 3 G3
High Street *Kent* 14 C4
High Street *Suff.* 35 J3
High Street Green 34 E3
High Toynton 53 F6
High Trewhitt 71 F3
High Wollaston 19 J2
High Wray 60 E7
High Wych 33 H7
High Wycombe 22 B2
Higham *Derbys.* 51 F7
Higham *Kent* 24 D4
Higham *Lancs.* 56 D6
Higham *Suff.* 34 E5
Higham *Suff.* 34 B2
Higham Dykes 71 G6
Higham Ferrers 32 C2
Higham Gobion 32 E5
Higham on the Hill 41 F6
Higham Wood 23 K7
Highampton 6 C5
Highbridge 19 G7
Highbrook 13 G3
Highburton 50 D1
Highbury 19 K7
Highbury Vale 41 H1
Highclere 21 H5
Highcliffe 10 D5
Higher Ansty 9 G4
Higher Ashton 7 G7
Higher Ballam 55 G6
Higher Blackley 49 H2
Higher Brixham 5 K5
Higher Cheriton 7 J5
Higher Gabwell 5 K4
Higher Green 49 G2
Higher Kingcombe 8 E5
Higher Tale 7 J5
Higher Thrushgill 56 B3
Higher Town 2 C1
Higher Walreddon 4 E3
Higher Walton 55 J7
Lancs.
Higher Walton 48 E4
Warr.
Higher Whatcombe 9 H4
Higher Whitley 49 F4
Higher Wych 38 D1
Highfield *E.Riding* 58 D6
Highfield *N.Ayr.* 74 B5
Highfield *T. & W.* 62 C1
Highfields 33 G3
Highgreen Manor 70 D4
Highlane *Ches.* 49 H6
Highlane *Derbys.* 51 G4
Highlaws 60 C2
Highleadon 29 G6
Highleigh 12 B7
Highley 39 G7
Highmead 26 E4
Highmoor Cross 21 K3
Highmoor Hill 19 H3
Highnam 29 G7
Highstead 25 J5
Highsted 25 F5
Highstreet Green 34 B5
Hightae 69 F6
Hightown *Ches.* 49 H6
Hightown *Mersey.* 48 B2
Highway 20 D4
Highweek 5 J3
Highworth 20 E2
Hilborough 44 C5
Hilcott 20 E6

Hilden Park 23 J7
Hildenborough 23 J7
Hildersham 33 J4
Hilderstone 40 B2
Hilderthorpe 59 H3
Hilfield 9 F4
Hilgay 44 A6
Hill 19 K2
Hill Brow 11 J2
Hill Chorlton 39 G2
Hill Dyke 43 G1
Hill End *Dur.* 62 B3
Hill End *Fife* 75 J1
Hill End *N.Yorks.* 57 F4
Hill Head 11 G4
Hill of Beath 75 K1
Hill of Fearn 97 F4
Hill Ridware 40 C4
Hill Top *Hants.* 11 F4
Hill Top *W.Yorks.* 51 F1
Hill View 9 J5
Hillam 58 B7
Hillbeck 61 J5
Hillberry 54 C5
Hillborough 25 J5
Hillbrae *Aber.* 98 E6
Hillbrae *Aber.* 91 F2
Hillbrae *Aber.* 91 G1
Hillend *Aber.* 98 C6
Hillend *Fife* 75 K2
Hillend *Midloth.* 76 A4
Hillesden 31 H6
Hillesley 20 A3
Hillfarrance 7 K3
Hillhead 5 K5
Hillhead of 99 H5
Auchentumb
Hillhead of 99 J6
Cocklaw
Hilliard's Cross 40 D4
Hilliclay 105 G2
Hillingdon 22 D3
Hillington 44 B3
Hillmorton 31 G1
Hillockhead *Aber.* 90 B4
Hillockhead *Aber.* 90 C3
Hillowton 65 H4
Hillpound 11 G3
Hills Town 51 G6
Hillsford Bridge 7 F1
Hillside *Aber.* 91 H5
Hillside *Angus* 83 J1
Hillside *Moray* 97 J5
Hillside *Shet.* 109 D6
Hillswick 108 B5
Hillway 11 H6
Hillwell 109 F9
Hilmarton 20 D4
Hilperton 20 B6
Hilsea 11 H4
Hilton *Cambs.* 33 F2
Hilton *Cumb.* 61 J4
Hilton *Derbys.* 40 E2
Hilton *Dorset* 9 G4
Hilton *Dur.* 62 C4
Hilton *High.* 97 G3
Hilton *Shrop.* 39 G6
Hilton *Stock.* 63 F5
Hilton Croft 91 H1
Hilton of Cadboll 97 F4
Hilton of Delnies 97 F6
Himbleton 29 J3
Himley 40 A6
Hincaster 55 J1
Hinckley 41 G6
Hinderclay 34 E1
Hinderwell 63 J5
Hindford 38 C2
Hindhead 12 B3
Hindley 49 F2
Hindley Green 49 F2
Hindlip 29 H3
Hindolveston 44 E3
Hindon 9 J1
Hindringham 44 D2
Hingham 44 E5
Hinstock 39 F3
Hintlesham 34 E4
Hinton *Hants.* 10 D5
Hinton *Here.* 28 C5
Hinton *Northants.* 31 G3
Hinton *S.Glos.* 20 A4
Hinton *Shrop.* 38 D5
Hinton Admiral 10 D5
Hinton Ampner 11 G2
Hinton Blewett 19 J6
Hinton 20 A6
Charterhouse
Hinton-in-the-
Hedges 31 G5
Hinton Martell 10 B4
Hinton on the 30 B4
Green
Hinton Parva 21 F3
Hinton St. George 8 D3
Hinton St. Mary 9 G3
Hinton Waldrist 21 G2
Hints *Shrop.* 29 F1
Hints *Staffs.* 40 D5
Hinwick 32 C2
Hinxhill 15 F3
Hinxton 33 H4
Hinxworth 33 F4
Hipperholme 57 G7
Hirn 91 F4
Hirnant 37 K3
Hirst 71 H5
Hirst Courtney 58 C7
Hirwaen 47 K6
Hirwaun 18 C1
Hiscott 6 D3
Histon 33 H2
Hitcham *Bucks.* 22 C3
Hitcham *Suff.* 34 D3
Hitchin 32 E6
Hither Green 23 G4
Hittisleigh 7 F6
Hixon 40 C3
Hoaden 25 J5
Hoaldalbert 28 C6
Hoar Cross 40 D3
Hoarwithy 28 E6
Hoath 25 H5
Hobarris 28 C1
Hobbister 107 C7
Hobbs Lots Bridge 43 G5
Hobkirk 70 A2
Hobland Hall 45 K5
Hobson 62 C1
Hoby 41 J4
Hockering 44 E4
Hockerton 51 K7
Hockley 24 E2
Hockley Heath 30 C1
Hockliffe 32 C6
Hockwold cum 44 B7
Wilton
Hockworthy 7 J4
Hoddesdon 23 G1

Hoddlesden 56 C7
Hodgeston 16 D5
Hodnet 39 F3
Hodthorpe 51 H5
Hoe 44 D4
Hoe Gate 11 H3
Hoff 61 H5
Hoffleet Stow 43 F2
Hoggeston 32 B6
Hoggie 98 D4
Hogha Gearraidh 92 C5
Hoghton 56 B7
Hognaston 50 E7
Hogsthorpe 53 J5
Holbeach 43 G3
Holbeach Bank 43 G3
Holbeach Clough 43 G3
Holbeach Drove 43 G4
Holbeach Hurn 43 G3
Holbeach St. Johns 43 G4
Holbeach St. Marks 43 G2
Holbeach St. 43 H2
Matthew
Holbeck 51 H5
Holberrow Green 30 B3
Holbeton 5 G5
Holborough 24 D5
Holbrook *Derbys.* 41 F1
Holbrook *Suff.* 35 F5
Holburn 77 J7
Holbury 11 F4
Holcombe *Devon* 5 K3
Holcombe *Som.* 19 K7
Holcombe Rogus 7 J4
Holcot 31 J2
Holden 56 C5
Holdenby 31 H2
Holdenhurst 10 C5
Holdgate 38 E7
Holdingham 42 D1
Holditch 8 C4
Hole-in-the-Wall 29 F6
Hole Park 14 D4
Hole Street 12 E5
Holford 7 K1
Holker 55 G2
Holkham 44 C1
Hollacombe 6 B5
Devon
Hollacombe 6 E4
Devon
Holland *Ork.* 106 F5
Holland *Ork.* 106 F5
Holland *Surr.* 23 H6
Holland-on-Sea 35 F7
Hollandstoun 106 G2
Hollee 69 H7
Hollesley 35 H4
Hollingbourne 14 D2
Hollingbury 13 G6
Hollington *Derbys.* 40 E2
Hollington *E.Suss.* 14 C6
Hollington *Staffs.* 40 C2
Hollingworth 50 C3
Hollins 49 H2
Hollins Green 49 F3
Hollinsclough 50 C6
Hollinwood 39 G5
Holloway 51 F7
Hollowell 31 H1
Holly End 43 J5
Holly Green 29 H4
Hollybush *Caerp.* 18 E1
Hollybush *E.Ayr.* 67 H2
Hollybush *Worcs.* 29 G5
Hollym 59 K7
Holm 69 H4
Holm of 68 D4
Drumlanrig
Holmbury St. Mary 22 E7
Holmbush *Cornw.* 4 A5
Holmbush *W.Suss.* 13 F3
Holme *Cambs.* 42 E7
Holme *Cumb.* 55 J2
Holme *Notts.* 52 B7
Holme *W.Yorks.* 50 D2
Holme Chapel 56 D7
Holme Hale 44 C5
Holme Lacy 28 E5
Holme Marsh 28 C3
Holme next the 44 B1
Sea
Holme-on- 58 E6
Spalding-Moor
Holme on the 59 F5
Wolds
Holme Pierrepont 41 J2
Holmebridge 9 H6
Holmer 28 E4
Holmer Green 22 C2
Holmes Chapel 49 G6
Holme's Hill 13 J5
Holmesfield 51 F5
Holmeswood 48 D1
Holmewood 51 G6
Holmfield 57 F7
Holmfirth 50 D2
Holmhead *D. & G.* 68 C5
Holmhead *E.Ayr.* 67 K1
Holmpton 59 K7
Holmrook 60 B6
Holmsgarth 109 D8
Holmside 62 D2
Holmston 67 H1
Holmwrangle 61 G2
Holne 5 H4
Holnest 9 F4
Holsworthy 6 B5
Holsworthy Beacon 6 B5
Holt *Dorset* 10 B4
Holt *Norf.* 44 E2
Holt *Wilts.* 20 B5
Holt *Worcs.* 29 H2
Holt *Wrex.* 48 D7
Holt End *Hants.* 11 H1
Holt End *Worcs.* 30 B2
Holt Fleet 29 H2
Holt Heath *Dorset* 10 B4
Holt Heath *Worcs.* 29 H2
Holtby 58 C4
Holton *Oxon.* 21 K1
Holton *Som.* 9 F2
Holton *Suff.* 35 H1
Holton cum 52 E4
Beckering
Holton le Clay 53 F2
Holton le Moor 52 D3
Holton St. Mary 34 E5
Holtspur 22 C2
Holtye Common 13 H3
Holwell *Dorset* 9 F3
Holwell *Herts.* 32 E5
Holwell *Leics.* 42 A3
Holwell *Oxon.* 21 F1
Holwell *Som.* 20 A7
Holwick 62 A4
Holworth 9 G6

Holy Cross 29 J1
Holy Island 77 K6
Holybourne 22 A7
Holyhead 46 A4
(Caergybi)
Holymoorside 51 F6
Holyport 22 B4
Holystone 70 E3
Holytown 75 F4
Holywell *Cambs.* 33 G1
Holywell *Cornw.* 2 E3
Holywell *Dorset* 8 E4
Holywell *E.Suss.* 13 J7
Holywell 47 K5
(Treffynnon)
Flints.
Holywell Green 50 C1
Holywell Lake 7 K3
Holywell Row 34 B1
Holywood 68 E5
Hom Green 28 E6
Homer 39 F5
Homersfield 45 G7
Homington 10 C2
Honey Hill 25 H5
Honey Tye 34 D5
Honeyborough 16 C4
Honeybourne 30 C4
Honeychurch 6 E5
Honiley 30 D1
Honing 45 H3
Honingham 45 F4
Honington *Lincs.* 42 C1
Honington *Suff.* 34 D1
Honington *Warks.* 30 D4
Honiton 7 K5
Honley 50 D1
Hoo *Med.* 24 D4
Hoo *Suff.* 35 G3
Hooe *E.Suss.* 13 K6
Hooe *Plym.* 5 F5
Hooe Common 13 K5
Hook *E.Riding* 58 D7
Hook *Gt.Lon.* 22 E5
Hook *Hants.* 22 A6
Hook *Pembs.* 16 C3
Hook *Wilts.* 20 D3
Hook-a-Gate 38 D5
Hook Green *Kent* 13 K3
Hook Green *Kent* 24 C5
Hook Green *Kent* 24 C4
Hook Norton 30 E5
Hooke 8 E4
Hookgate 39 G2
Hookway 7 G6
Hookwood 23 F7
Hoole 48 D6
Hooley 23 F6
Hooton 48 C5
Hooton Levitt 51 H3
Hooton Pagnell 51 G2
Hooton Roberts 51 G3
Hopcrofts Holt 31 F6
Hope *Derbys.* 50 D4
Hope *Devon* 5 G7
Hope *Flints.* 48 C7
Hope *Powys* 38 B5
Hope *Shrop.* 38 C5
Hope Bagot 28 E1
Hope Bowdler 38 D6
Hope End Green 33 J7
Hope Mansell 29 F7
Hope under 28 E3
Dinmore
Hopehouse 69 H2
Hopeman 97 J5
Hope's Green 24 D3
Hopesay 38 C7
Hopkinstown 18 D2
Hopton *Derbys.* 50 E7
Hopton *Norf.* 45 K5
Hopton *Shrop.* 38 E3
Hopton *Staffs.* 40 B3
Hopton *Suff.* 34 D1
Hopton Cangeford 38 E7
Hopton Castle 28 C1
Hopton Wafers 29 F1
Hoptonheath 28 C1
Hopwas 40 D5
Hopwood 30 B1
Horam 13 J5
Horbling 42 E2
Horbury 50 E1
Horden 63 F2
Horderley 38 D7
Hordle 10 D5
Hordley 38 C2
Horeb *Carmar.* 17 H4
Horeb *Cere.* 26 C4
Horfield 19 J4
Horham 35 G1
Horkesley Heath 34 D6
Horkstow 52 C1
Horley *Oxon.* 31 F4
Horley *Surr.* 23 F7
Horn Hill 22 D2
Hornblotton Green 8 E1
Hornby *Lancs.* 55 J3
Hornby *N.Yorks.* 62 D7
Hornby *N.Yorks.* 62 E6
Horncastle 53 F6
Hornchurch 23 J3
Horncliffe 77 H5
Horndean *Hants.* 11 J3
Horndean 77 G6
Sc.Bord.
Horndon 6 D7
Horndon on the 24 C3
Hill
Horne 23 G7
Horniehaugh 83 F1
Horning 45 H4
Horninghold 42 B6
Horningsea 33 H2
Horningsham 20 B7
Horningtoft 44 D3
Horns Cross 6 B3
Devon
Horns Cross 14 D5
E.Suss.
Hornsby 61 G2
Hornsby Gate 61 G1
Hornsea 59 J5
Hornsey 23 G3
Hornton 30 E4
Horrabridge 5 F4
Horridge 5 H3
Horringer 34 C2
Horse Bridge 49 J7
Horsebridge *Devon* 4 E3
Horsebridge 10 E1
Hants.
Horsebrook 40 A4
Horsehay 39 F5
Horseheath 33 K4
Horsehouse 57 F1
Horsell 22 C6

Horseman's Green 38 D1
Horseway 43 H7
Horsey 45 J3
Horsford 45 F4
Horsforth 57 H6
Horsham *W.Suss.* 12 E3
Horsham *Worcs.* 29 G3
Horsham St. Faith 45 G4
Horsington *Lincs.* 52 E6
Horsington *Som.* 9 F2
Horsley *Derbys.* 41 F1
Horsley *Glos.* 20 B2
Horsley 71 F7
Northumb.
Horsley 70 D4
Northumb.
Horsley Cross 35 F6
Horsley 41 F1
Woodhouse
Horsleycross Street 35 F6
Horsmonden 14 C3
Horspath 21 J1
Horstead 45 G4
Horsted Keynes 13 G4
Horton *Bucks.* 32 C7
Horton *Dorset* 10 B4
Horton *Lancs.* 56 D4
Horton *Northants.* 32 B3
Horton *S.Glos.* 20 A3
Horton *Som.* 8 C3
Horton *Staffs.* 49 J7
Horton *Swan.* 17 H6
Horton *W. & M.* 22 D4
Horton *Wilts.* 20 D5
Horton Cross 8 C3
Horton-cum-
Studley 31 G7
Horton Grange 71 G6
Horton Green 38 D1
Horton Heath 11 F3
Horton in 56 D2
Ribblesdale
Horton Inn 10 B4
Horton Kirby 23 J5
Horwich 49 F1
Horwich End 50 C4
Horwood 6 D3
Hose 42 A3
Hoses 60 D7
Hosh 81 K5
Hosta 92 C4
Hoswick 109 D10
Hotham 58 E6
Hothfield 14 E3
Hoton 41 H3
Houbie 108 F3
Hough 49 G7
Hough Green 48 D4
Hough-on-the-Hill 42 C1
Hougham 42 B1
Houghton *Cambs.* 33 F1
Houghton *Cumb.* 61 F1
Houghton *Devon* 5 G6
Houghton *Hants.* 10 E1
Houghton *Pembs.* 16 C4
Houghton *W.Suss.* 12 D5
Houghton Bank 62 D4
Houghton 32 D4
Conquest
Houghton-le-Side 62 D4
Houghton le 62 E2
Spring
Houghton on the 41 J5
Hill
Houghton Regis 32 D6
Houghton St. Giles 44 D2
Houlsyke 63 J6
Hound 11 F4
Hound Green 22 A6
Houndslow 76 E6
Houndwood 77 G4
Hounsdown 10 E3
Hounslow 22 E4
Hounslow Green 33 K7
Househill 97 F6
Housetter 108 C4
Houston 74 C4
Houstry 105 G5
Houstry of Dunn 105 H3
Houton 107 C7
Hove 13 F6
Hoveringham 41 J1
Hoveton 45 H4
Hovingham 58 C2
How 61 G1
How Caple 29 F5
How End 32 D4
How Man 60 A5
Howden 58 D7
Howden-le-Wear 62 C3
Howe *Cumb.* 55 H1
Howe *High.* 105 J2
Howe *N.Yorks.* 57 J1
Howe *Norf.* 45 G5
Howe Green 24 D1
Howe of Teuchar 99 F6
Howe Street *Essex* 33 K7
Howe Street *Essex* 33 K5
Howell 42 E1
Howey 27 K3
Howgate 76 A5
Howgill 57 F4
Howick 71 H2
Howle 39 F3
Howlett End 33 J5
Howley 8 B4
Hownam 70 C2
Hownam Mains 70 C1
Howpasley 69 J3
Howsham *N.Lincs.* 52 D2
Howsham *N.Yorks.* 58 D3
Howtel 77 G7
Howton 28 D6
Howwood 74 C4
Hoxa 107 D8
Hoxne 35 F1
Hoy 105 H2
Hoylake 48 B4
Hoyland 51 F2
Hoyland Swaine 50 E2
Hubberholme 56 E2
Hubbert's Bridge 43 F1
Huby *N.Yorks.* 57 H5
Huby *N.Yorks.* 58 B3
Hucclecote 29 H7
Hucking 14 D2
Hucknall 41 H1
Huddersfield 50 D1
Huddington 29 J3
Hudscott 6 E3
Hudswell 62 C7
Huggate 58 E4
Hugglescote 41 G4
Hugh Town 2 C1
Hughenden Valley 22 B2
Hughley 38 E6
Hugmore 48 C7
Huish *Devon* 6 D4
Huish *Wilts.* 20 E5

Huish Champflower 7 J3
Huish Episcopi 8 D2
Huisinis 100 B6
Hulcott 32 B7
Hulland 40 E1
Hullavington 20 B3
Hullbridge 24 E2
Hulme End 50 D7
Hulme Walfield 49 H6
Hulver Street 45 J7
Humber 28 E3
Humberside International Airport 52 E2
Humberston 53 G2
Humberstone 41 J5
Humbie 76 C4
Humbleton *E.Riding* 59 J6
Humbleton *Northumb.* 70 E1
Humby 42 D2
Hume 77 F6
Humehall 77 F6
Humshaugh 70 E6
Huna 105 J1
Huncoat 56 C6
Huncote 41 H6
Hundalee 70 B2
Hunderthwaite 62 A4
Hundleby 53 G6
Hundleton 16 C4
Hundon 34 B4
Hundred Acres 11 G3
Hundred End 55 H7
Hundred House 28 A3
Hungarton 41 J5
Hungerford *Hants.* 10 C3
Hungerford *W.Berks.* 21 G5
Hungerford Newtown 21 G4
Hunglader 93 J4
Hunmanby 59 H2
Hunningham 30 E2
Hunny Hill 11 F6
Hunsdon 33 H7
Hunsingore 57 K4
Hunsonby 61 G3
Hunspow 105 H1
Hunstanton 44 A1
Hunstanworth 62 A2
Hunston *Suff.* 34 D2
Hunston *W.Suss.* 12 B6
Hunstrete 19 K5
Hunt End 30 B2
Hunt House 63 K7
Huntercombe End 21 K3
Hunters Forstal 25 H5
Hunter's Inn 6 E1
Hunter's Quay 73 K3
Hunterston 73 K5
Huntford 70 B3
Huntingdon 33 F1
Huntingfield 35 H1
Huntingford 9 H1
Huntington *Here.* 28 B3
Huntington *Staffs.* 40 B4
Huntington *York* 58 C4
Huntingtower 82 B5
Huntley 29 G7
Huntly 98 D6
Huntlywood 76 E6
Hunton *Hants.* 11 F1
Hunton *Kent* 14 C3
Hunton *N.Yorks.* 62 C7
Hunton Bridge 22 D1
Hunt's Cross 48 D4
Huntsham 7 J3
Huntshaw Cross 6 D3
Huntspill 19 G7
Huntworth 8 C1
Hunwick 62 C3
Hunworth 44 E2
Hurdsfield 49 J5
Hurley *W. & M.* 22 B3
Hurley *Warks.* 40 E6
Hurley Bottom 22 B3
Hurlford 74 C7
Hurliness 107 B9
Hurn 10 C5
Hursley 11 F2
Hurst *Gt.Man.* 49 J2
Hurst *N.Yorks.* 62 B6
Hurst *W'ham* 22 A4
Hurst Green *E.Suss.* 14 C5
Hurst Green *Lancs.* 56 B6
Hurst Green *Surr.* 23 G6
Hurstbourne Priors 21 H7
Hurstbourne Tarrant 21 G6
Hurstpierpoint 13 F5
Hurstway Common 28 B4
Hurstwood 56 D6
Hurtmore 22 C7
Hurworth-on-Tees 62 E5
Hury 62 A4
Husabost 93 H6
Husbands Bosworth 41 J7
Husborne Crawley 32 C5
Husthwaite 58 B2
Huthwaite 51 G7
Huttoft 53 J5
Hutton *Cumb.* 61 F4
Hutton *Essex* 24 C2
Hutton *Lancs.* 55 H7
Hutton *N.Som.* 19 G6
Hutton *Sc.Bord.* 77 H5
Hutton Bonville 62 E6
Hutton Buscel 59 F1
Hutton Conyers 57 J2
Hutton Cranswick 59 G4
Hutton End 61 F3
Hutton Henry 63 F3
Hutton-le-Hole 63 J7
Hutton Magna 62 C5
Hutton Roof *Cumb.* 55 J2
Hutton Roof *Cumb.* 60 E3
Hutton Rudby 63 F6
Hutton Sessay 57 K2
Hutton Wandesley 58 B4
Huxley 48 E6
Huxter *Shet.* 109 C7
Huxter *Shet.* 109 E6
Huyton 48 D3
Hwlffordd (Haverfordwest) 16 C3
Hycemoor 54 D1
Hyde *Glos.* 20 B1
Hyde *Gt.Man.* 49 J3
Hyde Heath 22 C1
Hyde Lea 40 B4
Hydestile 22 C7
Hyndford Bridge 75 H6
Hyndlee 70 A3
Hynish 78 A4
Hyssington 38 C6
Hythe *Hants.* 11 F4
Hythe *Kent* 15 G4
Hythe End 22 D4
Hythie 99 J5
Hyton 54 D1

I

Ianstown 98 C4
Ibberton 9 G4
Ible 50 E7
Ibsley 10 C4
Ibstock 41 G4
Ibstone 22 A2
Ibthorpe 21 G6
Ibworth 21 J6
Icelton 19 G5
Ickburgh 44 C6
Ickenham 22 D3
Ickford 21 K1
Ickham 15 H2
Ickleford 32 E5
Icklesham 14 D6
Ickleton 33 H4
Icklingham 34 B1
Ickwell Green 32 E4
Icomb 30 D6
Idbury 30 D6
Iddesleigh 6 D5
Ide 7 H6
Ide Hill 23 H6
Ideford 5 J3
Iden 14 E5
Iden Green *Kent* 14 C4
Iden Green *Kent* 14 D4
Idlicote 30 D4
Idmiston 10 C1
Idridgehay 40 E1
Idrigil 93 J5
Idstone 21 F3
Idvies 83 G3
Iffley 21 J1
Ifield or Singlewell *Kent* 24 C4
Ifield *W.Suss.* 13 F3
Ifieldwood 13 F3
Ifold 12 D3
Iford 13 H6
Ifton Heath 38 C2
Ightfield 38 E2
Ightham 23 J6
Iken 35 J3
Ilam 50 D7
Ilchester 8 E2
Ilderton 71 F1
Ilford 23 H3
Ilfracombe 6 D1
Ilkeston 41 G1
Ilketshall St. Andrew 45 H7
Ilketshall St. Lawrence 45 H7
Ilketshall St. Margaret 45 H7
Ilkley 57 G5
Illey 40 B7
Illington 44 D7
Illingworth 57 F7
Illogan 2 D4
Illston on the Hill 42 A6
Ilmer 22 A1
Ilmington 30 D4
Ilminster 8 C3
Ilsington 5 H3
Ilston 17 J5
Ilton *N.Yorks.* 57 G2
Ilton *Som.* 8 C3
Imachar 73 G6
Immeroin 81 G6
Immingham 52 E1
Immingham Dock 53 F1
Impington 33 H2
Ince 48 D5
Ince Blundell 48 C2
Ince-in-Makerfield 48 E2
Inch of Arnhall 90 E7
Inchbare 83 H1
Inchberry 98 B5
Inchbraoch 83 J2
Inchgrundle 90 C7
Inchindown 96 D4
Inchinnan 74 C4
Inchkinloch 103 J4
Inchlaggan 87 H4
Inchlumpie 96 C4
Inchmarlo 90 E5
Inchnabobart 90 B6
Inchnacardoch Hotel 87 K3
Inchnadamph 102 E6
Inchock 83 H3
Inchrory 89 J4
Inchture 82 D5
Inchvuilt 87 J1
Inchyra 82 C6
Indian Queens 3 G3
Inerval 72 B6
Ingatestone 24 C1
Ingbirchworth 50 E2
Ingerthorpe 57 H3
Ingestre 40 B3
Ingham *Lincs.* 52 C4
Ingham *Norf.* 45 H3
Ingham *Suff.* 34 C1
Ingleby *Derbys.* 41 F3
Ingleby *Lincs.* 52 B5
Ingleby Arncliffe 63 F6
Ingleby Barwick 63 F5
Ingleby Cross 63 F6
Ingleby Greenhow 63 G6
Inglesbatch 19 K5
Inglesham 21 F2
Ingleton *Dur.* 62 C4
Ingleton *N.Yorks.* 56 B2
Inglewhite 55 J5
Ingmire Hall 61 H7
Ingoe 71 F6
Ingoldisthorpe 44 A2
Ingoldmells 53 J6
Ingoldsby 42 D2
Ingon 30 D3
Ingram 71 F2
Ingrave 24 C2
Ingrow 57 F6
Ings 61 F7
Ingst 19 J3
Ingworth 45 F3
Inistrynich 80 C5
Injebreck 54 C5
Inkberrow 30 B3
Inkhorn 91 H1
Inkpen 21 G5
Inkstack 105 H1
Innellan 73 K4
Innergellie 83 G7
Innerleithen 76 B7
Innerleven 82 E7
Innermessan 64 A4
Innerwick *E.Loth.* 77 F3
Innerwick *P. & K.* 81 G3
Inninbeg 79 J3
Innsworth 29 H6
Insch 90 E2
Insh 89 F4
Inshore 103 F2
Inskip 55 H6
Instow 6 C2
Intake 51 F4
Intwood 45 F5
Inver *Aber.* 89 K5
Inver *Arg. & B.* 80 A3
Inver *High.* 97 F3
Inver *High.* 105 G5
Inver *P. & K.* 82 B3
Inver Mallie 87 H6
Inverailort 86 D6
Inveralligin 94 E6
Inverallochy 99 J4
Inveran 96 C2
Inveraray 80 B7
Inverardoch Mains 81 J7
Inverardran 80 E5
Inverarish 86 B1
Inverarity 83 F3
Inverarnan 80 E6
Inverasdale 94 E3
Inverbain 94 D6
Inverbeg 74 B1
Inverbervie 91 G7
Inverbroom 95 H3
Inverbrough 89 F2
Invercassley 96 B1
Inverchaolain 73 J3
Invercharnan 80 C3
Inverchorachan 80 D6
Inverchoran 95 J6
Invercreran 80 B3
Inverdruie 89 G3
Inverebrie 91 H1
Invereen 89 F1
Invererne 97 H5
Inveresk 76 B3
Inverey 89 H6
Inverfarigaig 88 C2
Invergarry 87 K4
Invergelder 89 K5
Invergeldie 81 J5
Invergloy 87 J6
Invergordon 96 E5
Invergowrie 82 E4
Inverguseran 86 D4
Inverhadden 81 H2
Inverharroch 90 B1
Inverherive 80 E5
Inverhope 103 G2
Inverie 86 D4
Inverinan 80 A6
Inverinate 87 F2
Inverkeilor 83 H3
Inverkeithing 75 K2
Inverkeithny 98 E6
Inverkip 74 A3
Inverkirkaig 102 C7
Inverlael 95 H3
Inverlauren 74 B2
Inverliever 79 K7
Inverliver 80 B4
Inverlochlarig 81 F6
Inverlochy 80 C5
Inverlussa 72 E2
Invermay 82 B6
Invermoriston 88 B3
Invernaver 104 C2
Inverneil 73 G2
Inverness 96 D7
Inverness Airport 96 E6
Invernettie 99 K6
Invernoaden 73 K1
Inveroran Hotel 80 D3
Inverquharity 83 F2
Inverquhomery 99 J6
Inverroy 87 J6
Inversanda 80 A2
Invershiel 87 F3
Inversnaid Hotel 80 E7
Invertrossachs 81 G7
Inverugie 99 K6
Inveruglas 80 E7
Inveruglass 89 F4
Inverurie 91 F2
Invervar 81 H3
Invervegain 73 J3
Invery House 90 E5
Inverythan 99 F6
Inwardleigh 6 D6
Inworth 34 C7
Iochdar 92 C7
Iping 12 B4
Ipplepen 5 J4
Ipsden 21 K3
Ipstones 50 C7
Ipswich 35 F4
Irby 48 B4
Irby in the Marsh 53 H6
Irby upon Humber 52 E2
Irchester 32 C2
Ireby *Cumb.* 60 D3
Ireby *Lancs.* 56 B2
Ireland *Ork.* 107 C7
Ireland *Shet.* 109 C10
Ireleth 55 F2
Ireshopeburn 61 K3
Irlam 49 G3
Irnham 42 D3
Iron Acton 19 K3
Iron Cross 30 B3
Ironbridge 39 F5
Ironside 99 G5
Ironville 51 G7
Irstead 45 H3
Irthington 69 K7
Irthlingborough 32 C1
Irton 59 G1
Irvine 74 B7
Isauld 104 E2
Isbister *Ork.* 107 C6
Isbister *Ork.* 106 B5
Isbister *Shet.* 109 E6
Isbister *Shet.* 108 C3
Isfield 13 H5
Isham 32 B1
Ishriff 79 H4
Islay Airport 72 B5
Islay House 72 B4
Isle Abbotts 8 C2
Isle Brewers 8 C2
Isle of Man Airport 54 B7
Isle of Whithorn 64 E7
Isleham 33 K1
Isleornsay (Eilean Iarmain) 86 C3
Islesburgh 109 C6
Isleworth 22 E4
Isley Walton 41 G3
Islibhig 100 B5
Islington 23 G3
Islip *Northants.* 32 C1
Islip *Oxon.* 31 G7
Isombridge 39 F4
Istead Rise 24 C5
Itchen 11 F3
Itchen Abbas 11 G1
Itchen Stoke 11 G1
Itchingfield 12 E4
Itchington 19 K3
Itteringham 45 F2
Itton 6 E6
Itton Common 19 H2
Ivegill 61 F2
Ivelet 62 A7
Iver 22 D3
Iver Heath 22 D3
Iveston 62 C1
Ivinghoe 32 C7
Ivinghoe Aston 32 C7
Ivington 28 D3
Ivington Green 28 D3
Ivy Hatch 23 J6
Ivy Todd 44 C5
Ivybridge 5 G5
Ivychurch 15 F5
Iwade 25 F5
Iwerne Courtney (Shroton) 9 H3
Iwerne Minster 9 H3
Ixworth 34 D1
Ixworth Thorpe 34 D1

J

Jack Hill 57 G4
Jackstown 91 F1
Jackton 74 D5
Jacobstow 4 B1
Jacobstowe 6 D5
Jameston 16 D5
Jamestown *D. & G.* 69 J4
Jamestown *High.* 96 B6
Jamestown *W.Dun.* 74 B2
Janefield 96 E6
Janetstown 105 F2
Jarrow 71 J7
Jarvis Brook 13 J4
Jasper's Green 34 B6
Jawcraig 75 G3
Jayes Park 22 E7
Jaywick 35 F7
Jedburgh 70 B1
Jeffreyston 16 D4
Jemimaville 96 E5
Jersay 75 G4
Jersey Airport 3 J7
Jerviswood 75 G6
Jesmond 71 H7
Jevington 13 J6
Jodrell Bank 49 G5
John o' Groats 105 J1
Johnby 61 F3
John's Cross 14 C5
Johnshaven 83 J1
Johnston 16 C3
Johnston Mains 83 J1
Johnstone 74 C4
Johnstone Castle 74 C4
Johnstonebridge 69 F4
Johnstown *Carmar.* 17 G3
Johnstown *Wrex.* 38 C1
Joppa *Edin.* 76 B3
Joppa *S.Ayr.* 67 J2
Jordans 22 C2
Jordanston 16 C1
Jordanstone 82 D3
Jump 51 F2
Juniper Green 75 K4
Jura House 72 C4
Jurby East 54 C4
Jurby West 54 C4

K

Kaber 61 J5
Kaimes 76 A4
Kames *Arg. & B.* 73 H3
Kames *Arg. & B.* 79 K6
Kames *E.Ayr.* 68 B1
Kea 3 F4
Keadby 52 B1
Keal Cotes 53 G6
Kearsley 49 G2
Kearstwick 56 B1
Kearton 62 B7
Kearvaig 102 E1
Keasden 56 C3
Kebholes 98 E5
Keckwick 48 E4
Keddington 53 G4
Kedington 34 B4
Kedleston 41 F1
Keelby 52 E2
Keele 40 A1
Keeley Green 32 D4
Keeres Green 33 J7
Keeston 16 C3
Keevil 20 C6
Kegworth 41 G3
Kehelland 2 D4
Keig 90 E3
Keighley 57 F5
Keil *Arg. & B.* 66 A3
Keil *High.* 80 A2
Keilhill 99 F5
Keillmore 72 E2
Keillor 82 D3
Keillour 82 A5
Keills 72 C4
Keils 72 D4
Keinton Mandeville 8 E1
Keir House 75 F1
Keir Mill 68 D4
Keisby 42 D3
Keisley 61 J4
Keiss 105 J2
Keith 98 C5
Keithick 82 D4
Keithmore 90 B1
Keithock 83 H1
Kelbrook 56 E5
Kelby 42 D1
Keld *Cumb.* 61 G5
Keld *N.Yorks.* 61 K6
Keldholme 58 D1
Keldy Castle 63 J7
Kelfield *N.Lincs.* 52 B2
Kelfield *N.Yorks.* 58 B6
Kelham 51 K7
Kellan 79 G3
Kellas *Angus* 83 F4
Kellas *Moray* 97 J6
Kellaton 5 J7
Kelleth 61 H6
Kelleythorpe 59 G4
Kelling 44 E1
Kellington 58 B7
Kelloe 62 E3
Kelloholm 68 C2
Kelly *Cornw.* 4 A3
Kelly *Devon* 6 B7
Kelly Bray 4 D3
Kelmarsh 31 J1
Kelmscott 21 F2
Kelsale 35 H2
Kelsall 48 E6
Kelsay 72 A2
Kelshall 33 G5
Kelsick 60 C1
Kelso 77 F7
Kelstedge 51 F6
Kelstern 53 F3
Kelston 19 K5
Keltneyburn 81 J3
Kelton 65 K3
Kelton Hill or Rhonehouse 65 H5
Kelty 75 K1
Kelvedon 34 C7
Kelvedon Hatch 23 J2
Kelynack 2 A5
Kemback 83 F6
Kemberton 39 G5
Kemble 20 C2
Kemerton 29 J5
Kemeys Commander 19 G1
Kemeys Inferior 19 G2
Kemnay 91 F3
Kemp Town 13 G6
Kempley 29 F6
Kempley Green 29 F6
Kempsey 29 H4
Kempsford 20 E2
Kempshott 21 K7
Kempston 32 D4
Kempston Church End 32 D4
Kempston Hardwick 32 D4
Kempton 38 C7
Kemsing 23 J6
Kemsley 25 F5
Kenardington 14 E4
Kenchester 28 D4
Kencott 21 F1
Kendal 61 G7
Kenderchurch 28 D6
Kenfig 18 B3
Kenfig Hill 18 B3
Kenilworth 30 D1
Kenknock *P. & K.* 81 G3
Kenknock *Stir.* 81 F4
Kenley *Gt.Lon.* 23 G6
Kenley *Shrop.* 38 E5
Kenmore *Arg. & B.* 80 B7
Kenmore *High.* 94 D6
Kenmore *P. & K.* 81 J3
Kenmore *W.Isles* 100 E7
Kenn *Devon* 7 H7
Kenn *N.Som.* 19 H5
Kennacraig 73 G4
Kennards House 4 C2
Kennavay 93 H2
Kennerleigh 7 G5
Kennerty 90 E5
Kennet 75 H1
Kennethmont 90 D2
Kennett 33 K2
Kennford 7 H7
Kenninghall 44 E7
Kennington *Kent* 15 F3
Kennington *Oxon.* 21 J1
Kennoway 82 E7
Kennyhill 33 K1
Kennythorpe 58 D3
Kensaleyre 93 K6
Kensington & Chelsea 23 F4
Kensworth 32 D7
Kensworth Common 32 D7
Kent Street *E.Suss.* 14 C6
Kent Street *Kent* 23 K6
Kentallen 80 B2
Kentchurch 28 D6
Kentford 34 B2
Kentisbeare 7 J5
Kentisbury 6 E1
Kentisbury Ford 6 E1
Kentmere 61 F6
Kenton *Devon* 7 H7
Kenton *Suff.* 35 F2
Kenton *T. & W.* 71 H7
Kentra 79 H1
Kents Bank 55 H2
Kent's Green 29 G6
Kent's Oak 10 E2
Kenwick 38 D2
Kenwyn 3 F4
Kenyon 49 F3
Keoldale 103 F2
Keppanach 80 B1
Keppoch *Arg. & B.* 74 B3
Keppoch *High.* 86 E2
Keprigan 66 A2
Kepwick 63 F7
Keresley 41 F7
Kerne Bridge 28 E7
Kerridge 49 J5
Kerris 2 B6
Kerry 38 A7
Kerrycroy 73 K4
Kerry's Gate 28 C5
Kerrysdale 94 E4
Kersall 51 K6
Kersey 34 E4
Kershopefoot 69 K5
Kerswell 7 J5
Kerswell Green 29 H4
Kesgrave 35 G4
Kessingland 45 K7
Kessingland Beach 45 K7
Kestle Mill 3 F3
Keston 23 H5
Keswick *Cumb.* 60 D4
Keswick *Norf.* 45 G5
Keswick *Norf.* 45 H2
Ketsby 53 G5
Kettering 32 B1
Ketteringham 45 F5
Kettins 82 D4
Kettlebaston 34 D4
Kettlebridge 82 E7
Kettlebrook 40 E5
Kettleburgh 35 G3
Kettleholm 69 G6
Kettleness 63 K5
Kettleshulme 49 J5
Kettlesing 57 H4
Kettlesing Bottom 57 H4
Kettlestone 44 D2
Kettlethorpe 52 B5
Kettletoft 106 F4
Kettlewell 56 E2
Ketton 42 C5
Kew 22 E4
Kewstoke 19 G5
Kexbrough 51 F2
Kexby *Lincs.* 52 B4
Kexby *York* 58 D4
Key Green 49 H6
Keyham 41 J5
Keyhaven 10 E5
Keyingham 59 J7
Keymer 13 G5
Keynsham 19 K5
Key's Toft 53 H7
Keysoe 32 D2
Keysoe Row 32 D2
Keyston 32 D1
Keyworth 41 J2
Kibblesworth 62 D1
Kibworth Beauchamp 41 J6
Kibworth Harcourt 41 J6
Kidbrooke 23 H4
Kiddal Lane End 57 J6
Kiddemore Green 40 A5
Kidderminster 29 H1
Kiddington 31 F6
Kidlington 31 F7
Kidmore End 21 K4
Kidsdale 64 E7
Kidsgrove 49 H7
Kidstones 56 E1
Kidwelly (Cydweli) 17 H4
Kiel Crofts 80 A4
Kielder 70 B4
Kilbarchan 74 C4
Kilbeg 86 C4
Kilberry 73 F4
Kilbirnie 74 B5
Kilblaan 80 C6
Kilbraur 104 D7
Kilbrennan 79 F3
Kilbride *Arg. & B.* 79 K5
Kilbride *Arg. & B.* 73 J4
Kilbride *High.* 86 B2
Kilbride Farm 73 H4
Kilbridemore 73 J1
Kilburn *Derbys.* 41 F1
Kilburn *N.Yorks.* 58 B2
Kilby 41 J6
Kilchattan *Arg. & B.* 73 K5
Kilchenzie 66 A1
Kilcheran 79 K4
Kilchiaran 72 A5
Kilchoan *Arg. & B.* 79 J6
Kilchoan *High.* 79 F1
Kilchoman 72 A4
Kilchrenan 80 B5
Kilchrist 66 A2
Kilconquhar 83 F7
Kilcot 29 F6
Kilcoy 96 C6
Kilcreggan 74 A2
Kildale 63 H6
Kildary 96 E4
Kildavie 66 B2
Kildermorie Lodge 96 C4
Kildonan 66 E1
Kildonan Lodge 104 E6
Kildonnan 85 K6
Kildrochet House 64 A5
Kildrummy 90 C3
Kildwick 57 F5
Kilfinan 73 H3
Kilfinnan 87 J5
Kilgetty 16 E4
Kilgwrrwg Common 19 H2
Kilham *E.Riding* 59 G3
Kilham *Northumb.* 77 G7
Kilkenneth 78 A3
Kilkenny 30 B7
Kilkerran *Arg. & B.* 66 B2
Kilkerran *S.Ayr.* 67 H3
Kilkhampton 6 A4
Killamarsh 51 G4
Killay 17 K5
Killbeg 79 H3
Killean *Arg. & B.* 72 E6
Killean *Arg. & B.* 80 B7
Killearn 74 D2
Killellan 66 A2
Killen 96 D6
Killerby 62 C4
Killichonan 81 G2
Killiechanate 87 J6
Killiechronan 79 G3
Killiecrankie 82 A1
Killiehuntly 88 E5
Killiemor 79 F4
Killilan 87 F1
Killimster 105 J3
Killin *High.* 97 F1
Killin *Stir.* 81 G4
Killinallan 72 B3
Killinghall 57 H4
Killington 56 B1
Killingworth 71 H6
Killochyett 76 C6
Killocraw 66 A1
Killunaig 79 F5
Killundine 79 G3
Kilmacolm 74 B4
Kilmaha 80 A7
Kilmahog 81 H7
Kilmalieu 79 K2
Kilmaluag 93 K4
Kilmany 82 E5
Kilmarie 86 B3
Kilmarnock 74 C7
Kilmartin 73 G1
Kilmaurs 74 C6
Kilmelford 79 K6
Kilmersdon 19 K6
Kilmeston 11 G2
Kilmichael 66 A1
Kilmichael Glassary 73 G1
Kilmichael of Inverlussa 73 F2
Kilmington *Devon* 8 B5
Kilmington *Wilts.* 9 G1
Kilmington Street 9 G1
Kilmorack 96 B7
Kilmore *Arg. & B.* 79 K5
Kilmore *High.* 86 C4
Kilmory *Arg. & B.* 73 F2
Kilmory *Arg. & B.* 73 F3
Kilmory *High.* 85 J4
Kilmory *High.* 79 G1
Kilmote 104 E7
Kilmuir *High.* 93 H7
Kilmuir *High.* 96 D7
Kilmuir *High.* 96 E4
Kilmuir *High.* 93 J4
Kilmun 73 K2
Kilmux 82 E7
Kiln Green 22 B4
Kiln Pit Hill 62 B1
Kilnave 72 A3
Kilncadzow 75 G6
Kilndown 14 C4
Kilnhurst 51 G3
Kilninian 79 F3
Kilninver 79 K5
Kilnsea 53 H1
Kilnsey 56 E3
Kilnwick 59 G5
Kiloran 72 B1
Kilpatrick 66 D1
Kilpeck 28 D5
Kilphedir 104 E7
Kilpin 58 D7
Kilrenny 83 G7
Kilsby 31 G1
Kilspindie 82 D5
Kilstay 64 B7
Kilsyth 75 F3
Kiltarlity 96 C7
Kilton *R. & C.* 63 H5
Kilton *Som.* 7 K1
Kiltyrie 81 H4
Kilvaxter 93 J5
Kilve 7 K1
Kilverstone 44 C7
Kilvington 42 B1
Kilwinning 74 B6
Kimberley *Norf.* 44 E5
Kimberley *Notts.* 41 H1
Kimble Wick 22 B1
Kimblesworth 62 D2
Kimbolton *Cambs.* 32 E2
Kimbolton *Here.* 28 E2
Kimcote 41 H7
Kimmeridge 9 J7
Kimmerston 77 H7
Kimpton *Hants.* 21 F7
Kimpton *Herts.* 32 E7
Kinaldy 83 G6
Kinblethmont 83 H3
Kinbrace 104 D5
Kinbreack 87 G5
Kinbuck 81 J7
Kincaldrum 83 F3
Kincaple 83 F6
Kincardine *Fife* 75 H2
Kincardine *High.* 96 D3
Kincardine O'Neil 90 D5
Kinclaven 82 C4
Kincorth 91 H4
Kincraig *Aber.* 91 H2
Kincraig *High.* 89 F4
Kincraigie 82 A3
Kindallachan 82 A3
Kindrogan Field Centre 82 B1
Kinellar 91 G3
Kineton *Glos.* 30 B6
Kineton *Warks.* 30 E3
Kineton Green 40 D7
Kinfauns 82 C5
King Sterndale 50 C5
Kingarth 73 J5
Kingcoed 19 H1
Kingerby 52 D3
Kingham 30 D6
Kingholm Quay 65 K3
Kinghorn 76 A2
Kinglassie 76 A1
Kingoodie 82 E5
King's Bromley 40 D4
Kings Caple 28 E6
King's Cliffe 42 D6
King's Coughton 30 B3
King's Green 29 G5
Kings Heath 40 C7
King's Hill 40 B6
Kings Langley 22 D1
King's Lynn 44 A3
Kings Meaburn 61 H4
King's Mills 3 H5
Kings Muir 76 A7
King's Newton 41 F3
King's Norton *Leics.* 41 J5
King's Norton *W.Mid.* 30 B1
King's Nympton 6 E4
King's Pyon 28 D3
Kings Ripton 33 F1
King's Somborne 10 E1
King's Stag 9 G3
King's Stanley 20 B1
King's Sutton 31 F5
King's Walden 32 E6
Kings Worthy 11 F1
Kingsand 4 E5
Kingsbarns 83 G6
Kingsbridge *Devon* 5 H6
Kingsbridge *Som.* 7 H2
Kingsburgh 93 J6
Kingsbury *Gt.Lon.* 22 E3
Kingsbury *Warks.* 40 E6
Kingsbury Episcopi 8 D2
Kingscavil 75 J3
Kingsclere 21 J6
Kingscote 20 B2
Kingscott 6 D4
Kingscross 66 E1
Kingsdale 82 E7
Kingsdon 8 E2
Kingsdown 15 J3
Kingseat 75 K1
Kingsey 22 A1
Kingsfold *Pembs.* 16 C5
Kingsfold *W.Suss.* 12 E3
Kingsford *Aber.* 99 F6
Kingsford *Aber.* 90 D3
Kingsford *Aberdeen* 91 G4
Kingsford *E.Ayr.* 74 C6
Kingsford *Worcs.* 40 A7
Kingsforth 52 D1
Kingsgate 25 K4
Kingsheanton 6 D2
Kingshouse 81 G5
Kingshouse Hotel 80 D2
Kingskerswell 5 J4
Kingskettle 82 E7
Kingsland *Here.* 28 D2
Kingsland *I.o.A.* 46 A4
Kingsley *Ches.* 48 E5
Kingsley *Hants.* 11 J1
Kingsley *Staffs.* 40 C1
Kingsley Green 12 B3
Kingsmuir 83 F3
Kingsnorth 15 F4
Kingsnorth Power Station 24 E4

Place	Page	Ref
Kingstanding	40	C6
Kingsteignton	5	J3
Kingsteps	97	G6
Kingsthorne	28	E5
Kingsthorpe	31	J2
Kingston Cambs.	33	G3
Kingston Devon	5	G6
Kingston Dorset	9	G4
Kingston Dorset	9	J7
Kingston E.Loth.	76	D2
Kingston Hants.	10	C4
Kingston I.o.W.	11	F6
Kingston Kent	15	G2
Kingston Moray	98	B4
Kingston W.Suss.	12	D6
Kingston Bagpuize	21	H2
Kingston by Sea	13	F6
Kingston Deverill	9	H1
Kingston Lisle	21	G3
Kingston near Lewes	13	G6
Kingston on Soar	41	H3
Kingston Russell	8	E5
Kingston St. Mary	8	B2
Kingston Seymour	19	G5
Kingston Upon Hull	59	H7
Kingston upon Thames	22	E4
Kingston Warren	21	G3
Kingstone Here.	28	D5
Kingstone Som.	8	C3
Kingstone Staffs.	40	C3
Kingstown	60	E1
Kingswear	5	J5
Kingswell	74	D6
Kingswells	91	G4
Kingswinford	40	A7
Kingswood Bucks.	31	H7
Kingswood Glos.	20	A2
Kingswood Here.	28	B3
Kingswood Kent	14	D2
Kingswood Powys	38	B5
Kingswood S.Glos.	19	K4
Kingswood Surr.	23	F6
Kingswood Warks.	30	C1
Kingthorpe	52	E5
Kington Here.	28	B3
Kington Worcs.	29	J3
Kington Langley	20	C4
Kington Magna	9	G2
Kington St. Michael	20	B4
Kingussie	88	E4
Kingweston	8	E1
Kinharrachie	91	H1
Kinharvie	65	K4
Kinkell	74	E3
Kinkell Bridge	82	A6
Kinknockie	99	J6
Kinlet	39	G7
Kinloch Fife	82	D6
Kinloch High.	103	F5
Kinloch High.	79	H2
Kinloch High.	85	K5
Kinloch High.	96	C4
Kinloch P. & K.	82	D3
Kinloch P. & K.	82	C3
Kinloch Hourn	87	F4
Kinloch Laggan	88	C6
Kinloch Rannoch	81	H2
Kinlochan	79	K1
Kinlochard	81	F7
Kinlochbeoraid	86	E6
Kinlochbervie	102	E3
Kinlocheil	87	F7
Kinlochetive	80	C3
Kinlochewe	95	G5
Kinlochlaich	80	A3
Kinlochleven	80	C1
Kinlochmoidart	86	D7
Kinlochmorar	86	E5
Kinlochmore	80	C1
Kinlochspelve	79	H5
Kinloss	97	H5
Kinmel Bay (Bae Cinmel)	47	H4
Kinmuck	91	G3
Kinnadie	99	H6
Kinnaird	82	D5
Kinneff	91	G7
Kinnelhead	69	F3
Kinnell Angus	83	H2
Kinnell Stir.	81	G4
Kinnerley	38	C3
Kinnersley Here.	28	C4
Kinnersley Worcs.	29	H4
Kinnerton	28	B2
Kinnesswood	82	C7
Kinnettles	83	F3
Kinninvie	62	B4
Kinnordy	82	E2
Kinoulton	41	J2
Kinrara	89	F4
Kinrossie	82	C4
Kinsbourne Green	32	E7
Kinsham	28	C2
Kinsley	51	G1
Kinson	10	B5
Kintarvie	100	E6
Kintbury	21	G5
Kintessack	97	G5
Kintillo	82	C6
Kintocher	90	D4
Kinton Here.	28	D1
Kinton Shrop.	38	C4
Kintore	91	F3
Kintour	72	C5
Kintra Arg. & B.	72	B6
Kintra Arg. & B.	78	E5
Kintradwell	97	G1
Kintraw	79	K7
Kinuachdrachd	73	F1
Kinveachy	89	G3
Kinver	40	A7
Kiplaw Croft	91	J1
Kiplin	62	D7
Kiplingcotes	59	F5
Kipp	81	G6
Kippax	57	K6
Kippen P. & K.	82	B5
Kippen Stir.	74	E1
Kippenross House	81	J7
Kippford or Scaur	65	J5
Kipping's Cross	23	K7
Kirbister Ork.	107	C7
Kirbister Ork.	106	F5
Kirbuster	106	B5
Kirby Bedon	45	G5
Kirby Cane	45	H6
Kirby Corner	30	D1
Kirby Cross	35	G7
Kirby Grindalythe	59	F3
Kirby Hill N.Yorks.	62	C6
Kirby Hill N.Yorks.	57	J3
Kirby le Soken	35	G1
Kirby Misperton	58	D2
Kirby Muxloe	41	H5
Kirby Row	45	H6
Kirby Sigston	63	F7
Kirby Underdale	58	E4
Kirby Wiske	57	J1
Kirdford	12	D4
Kirk	105	H3
Kirk Bramwith	51	J1
Kirk Deighton	57	J4
Kirk Ella	59	G7
Kirk Hallam	41	G1
Kirk Hammerton	57	K4
Kirk Ireton	50	E7
Kirk Langley	40	E2
Kirk Merrington	62	D3
Kirk Michael	54	C4
Kirk of Shotts	75	G4
Kirk Sandall	51	J2
Kirk Smeaton	51	H1
Kirk Yetholm	70	D1
Kirkabister	109	D9
Kirkandrews	65	G6
Kirkandrews-upon-Eden	60	E1
Kirkbampton	60	E1
Kirkbean	65	K5
Kirkbride	60	D1
Kirkbridge	62	D7
Kirkbuddo	83	G3
Kirkburn E.Riding	59	F4
Kirkburn Sc.Bord.	76	A7
Kirkburton	50	D1
Kirkby Lincs.	52	D3
Kirkby Mersey.	48	D3
Kirkby N.Yorks.	63	G6
Kirkby Fleetham	62	D7
Kirkby Green	52	D7
Kirkby in Ashfield	51	G7
Kirkby la Thorpe	42	E1
Kirkby Lonsdale	56	B2
Kirkby Malham	56	D3
Kirkby Mallory	41	G5
Kirkby Malzeard	57	H2
Kirkby Mills	58	D1
Kirkby on Bain	53	F6
Kirkby Overblow	57	J5
Kirkby Stephen	61	J6
Kirkby Thore	61	H4
Kirkby Underwood	42	D3
Kirkby Wharfe	58	B5
Kirkbymoorside	58	C1
Kirkcaldy	76	A1
Kirkcambeck	70	A7
Kirkcolm	64	A4
Kirkconnel	68	C2
Kirkconnell	65	K4
Kirkcowan	64	D4
Kirkcudbright	65	G5
Kirkdale House	65	F5
Kirkdean	75	K6
Kirkfieldbank	75	G6
Kirkgunzeon	65	J4
Kirkham Lancs.	55	H6
Kirkham N.Yorks.	58	D3
Kirkhamgate	57	H7
Kirkharle	71	F5
Kirkhaugh	61	H2
Kirkheaton Northumb.	71	F6
Kirkheaton W.Yorks.	50	D1
Kirkhill Angus	83	H1
Kirkhill High.	96	C7
Kirkhill Moray	98	B5
Kirkhope	69	J1
Kirkibost High.	86	B3
Kirkibost W.Isles	100	D4
Kirkinch	82	E3
Kirkinner	64	E5
Kirkintilloch	74	E3
Kirkland Cumb.	61	H3
Kirkland Cumb.	60	C5
Kirkland D. & G.	68	D4
Kirkland D. & G.	68	C2
Kirkland D. & G.	69	F5
Kirkland of Longcastle	64	D6
Kirkleatham	63	G4
Kirklevington	63	F5
Kirkley	45	K6
Kirklington N.Yorks.	57	J1
Kirklington Notts.	51	J7
Kirklinton	69	K7
Kirkliston	75	K3
Kirkmaiden	64	B7
Kirkmichael P. & K.	82	B1
Kirkmichael S.Ayr.	67	H3
Kirkmuirhill	75	F6
Kirknewton Northumb.	70	E1
Kirknewton W.Loth.	75	K4
Kirkney	90	D1
Kirkoswald Cumb.	61	G2
Kirkoswald S.Ayr.	67	G3
Kirkpatrick Durham	65	H3
Kirkpatrick-Fleming	69	H6
Kirksanton	54	E1
Kirkstall	57	H6
Kirkstead	52	E6
Kirkstile Aber.	90	D1
Kirkstile D. & G.	69	J4
Kirkton Aber.	90	E2
Kirkton Aber.	98	E5
Kirkton Aber.	90	E3
Kirkton Angus	82	E3
Kirkton Arg. & B.	79	J7
Kirkton D. & G.	68	E5
Kirkton Fife	82	E5
Kirkton High.	96	E2
Kirkton High.	96	E6
Kirkton High.	104	D2
Kirkton High.	86	E2
Kirkton P. & K.	82	A6
Kirkton Sc.Bord.	70	A2
Kirkton Manor	76	A7
Kirkton of Airlie	82	E2
Kirkton of Auchterhouse	82	E4
Kirkton of Barevan	97	F7
Kirkton of Bourtie	91	G2
Kirkton of Collace	82	C4
Kirkton of Craig	83	J2
Kirkton of Culsalmond	90	E1
Kirkton of Durris	91	F5
Kirkton of Glenbuchat	90	B3
Kirkton of Glenisla	82	D1
Kirkton of Kingoldrum	82	E2
Kirkton of Lethendy	82	C3
Kirkton of Logie Buchan	91	H2
Kirkton of Maryculter	91	G5
Kirkton of Menmuir	83	G1
Kirkton of Monikie	83	G4
Kirkton of Rayne	90	E1
Kirkton of Skene	91	G4
Kirkton of Strathmartine	82	E4
Kirkton of Tealing	83	F4
Kirktonhill	83	H1
Kirktown	99	J5
Kirktown of Alvah	98	E5
Kirktown of Auchterless	99	F6
Kirktown of Deskford	98	D4
Kirktown of Fetteresso	91	G6
Kirktown of Slains	91	J2
Kirkwall	107	D7
Kirkwall Airport	107	D7
Kirkwhelpington	70	E5
Kirmington	52	E1
Kirmond le Mire	52	E3
Kirn	73	K3
Kirriemuir	82	E2
Kirstead Green	45	G6
Kirtlebridge	69	H6
Kirtling	33	K3
Kirtling Green	33	K3
Kirtlington	31	F7
Kirtomy	104	C2
Kirton Lincs.	43	G2
Kirton Notts.	51	J6
Kirton Suff.	35	G5
Kirton End	43	F1
Kirton Holme	43	F1
Kirton in Lindsey	52	C3
Kiscadale	66	E1
Kislingbury	31	H3
Kismeldon Bridge	6	B4
Kites Hardwick	31	F2
Kitley	5	F5
Kittisford	7	J3
Kitwood	11	H1
Kiveton Park	51	G4
Klibreck	103	H5
Knabbygates	98	D5
Knaith	52	B4
Knap Corner	9	H2
Knaphill	22	C6
Knapp P. & K.	82	D4
Knapp Som.	8	C2
Knapton Norf.	45	H2
Knapton York	58	B4
Knapton Green	28	D3
Knapwell	33	G2
Knaresborough	57	J4
Knarsdale	61	H1
Knaven	99	G6
Knayton	57	K1
Knebworth	33	F7
Knedlington	58	D7
Kneesall	51	K6
Kneesworth	33	G4
Kneeton	42	A1
Knelston	17	H6
Knenhall	40	B2
Knettishall	44	D7
Knightacott	6	E2
Knightcote	31	F3
Knightcott	19	G6
Knighton Devon	5	F6
Knighton Leic.	41	J5
Knighton Powys	28	B1
Knighton Som.	7	K1
Knighton Staffs.	39	G3
Knighton Staffs.	39	G2
Knighton Wilts.	21	F4
Knightwick	29	G3
Knill	28	B2
Knipoch	79	K5
Knipton	42	B2
Knitsley	62	C2
Kniveton	50	E7
Knock Arg. & B.	79	G4
Knock Cumb.	61	H4
Knock Moray	98	D5
Knock of Auchnahannet	89	H1
Knockalava	73	H1
Knockally	105	G6
Knockaloe Moar	54	B5
Knockan	102	E7
Knockandhu	89	K2
Knockando	97	J7
Knockbain	96	D6
Knockban	95	J5
Knockbreck	96	C3
Knockbrex	65	F6
Knockdamph	95	J2
Knockdee	105	G2
Knockdow	73	K3
Knockdown	20	B3
Knockenkelly	66	E1
Knockentiber	74	C7
Knockfin	87	J2
Knockgray	67	K4
Knockholt	23	H6
Knockholt Pound	23	H6
Knockin	38	C3
Knocklearn	65	H3
Knocknaha	66	A2
Knocknain	66	C7
Knocknalling	67	K5
Knockrome	72	D3
Knocksharry	54	B5
Knockville	64	D3
Knockvologan	78	E6
Knodishall	35	J2
Knolls Green	49	H5
Knolton	38	C2
Knook	20	C7
Knossington	42	B5
Knott End-on-Sea	55	G5
Knotting	32	D2
Knotting Green	32	D2
Knottingley	58	B7
Knotty Ash	48	D3
Knotty Green	22	C2
Knowbury	28	E1
Knowe	64	D3
Knowes of Elrick	98	E5
Knowesgate	70	E5
Knoweside	67	G2
Knowetownhead	70	A2
Knowhead	99	H5
Knowl Green	34	B4
Knowl Hill	22	B4
Knowl Wall	40	A2
Knowle Bristol	19	K4
Knowle Devon	7	F5
Knowle Devon	6	C2
Knowle Devon	7	F5
Knowle Shrop.	28	E1
Knowle W.Mid.	30	C1
Knowle Green	56	B6
Knowle Hall	19	G7
Knowlton Dorset	10	B3
Knowlton Kent	15	H2
Knowsley	48	D3
Knowstone	7	G3
Knucklas	28	B1
Knutsford	49	G5
Knypersley	49	H7
Kuggar	2	E7
Kyle of Lochalsh	86	D2
Kyleakin	86	D2
Kylerhea	86	D2
Kyles Scalpay (Caolas Scalpaigh)	93	H2
Kylesbeg	86	C7
Kylesknoydart	86	E5
Kylesmorar	86	E5
Kylestrome	102	E5
Kyloag	96	D2
Kynnersley	39	F4
Kyre Park	29	F2

L

Place	Page	Ref
L.Islet	3	J5
Labost	100	E3
Lacasaigh	101	F5
Lacasdal (Laxdale)	101	G4
Laceby	53	F2
Lacey Green	22	B1
Lach Dennis	49	G5
Lackford	34	B1
Lacock	20	C5
Ladbroke	31	F3
Laddingford	23	K7
Lade Bank	53	G7
Ladock	3	F3
Lady Hall	54	E1
Ladybank	82	D6
Ladycross	6	B7
Ladyfield	80	B6
Ladykirk	77	G6
Lady's Green	34	B3
Ladysford	99	H4
Laga	79	H1
Lagalochan	79	K6
Lagavulin	72	C6
Lagg Arg. & B.	72	D3
Lagg N.Ayr.	66	D1
Lagg S.Ayr.	67	G2
Laggan Arg. & B.	72	A5
Laggan High.	87	J5
Laggan High.	88	D5
Laggan Moray	90	B1
Laggan Stir.	81	G6
Lagganulva	79	F3
Lagganvoulin	89	J3
Laglingarten	80	C7
Lagnalean	96	D7
Lagrae	68	C2
Laguna	82	C4
Laid	103	G3
Laide	94	E2
Laig	85	K6
Laight	68	B2
Lainchoil	89	H3
Laindon	24	C3
Lair	82	C1
Lairg	96	C1
Lairg Lodge	96	C1
Lairigmor	80	C1
Laithers	98	E6
Laithes	61	F3
Lake	10	C1
Lakenham	45	G5
Lakenheath	44	B7
Lakesend	43	J6
Lakeside	55	G1
Laleham	22	D5
Laleston	18	B4
Lamancha	76	A5
Lamarsh	34	C5
Lamas	45	G3
Lamb Corner	34	E5
Lamberhurst	13	K3
Lamberhurst Quarter	13	K3
Lamberton	77	H5
Lambeth	23	F4
Lambfell Moar	54	B5
Lambley Northumb.	61	H1
Lambley Notts.	41	J1
Lambourn	21	G4
Lambourn Woodlands	21	G4
Lambourne End	23	H2
Lambs Green	13	F3
Lambston	16	C3
Lamellion	4	C4
Lamerton	4	E3
Lamesley	62	D1
Lamington High.	96	E4
Lamington S.Lan.	75	H7
Lamlash	73	J7
Lamloch	67	K4
Lamonby	61	F3
Lamorran	3	F4
Lampert	70	B6
Lampeter	26	E4
Lampeter Velfrey	16	E3
Lamphey	16	D4
Lamplugh	60	B4
Lamport	31	J1
Lamyatt	9	F1
Lana	6	B6
Lanark	75	G6
Lancaster	55	H3
Lanchester	62	C2
Lancing	12	E6
Landbeach	33	H2
Landcross	6	C3
Landerberry	91	F4
Landewednack	2	E7
Landford	10	D3
Landimore	17	H5
Landkey	6	D2
Landore	17	K5
Landscove	5	H4
Landshipping	16	D3
Landulph	4	E4
Landywood	40	B5
Lane-end	4	A4
Lane End Bucks.	22	B2
Lane End Cumb.	60	C7
Lane End Derbys.	51	G6
Lane End Dorset	9	H5
Lane End Kent	23	J4
Lane Green	40	A5
Lane Head Dur.	62	C5
Lane Head Gt.Man.	49	F3
Lane Head W.Yorks.	50	D2
Laneast	4	C2
Laneham	52	B5
Lanehead	70	C5
Laneshawbridge	56	E5
Langais	92	D5
Langamull	78	E2
Langar	42	A2
Langbank	74	B3
Langbar	57	F4
Langcliffe	56	D3
Langdale End	63	J3
Langdon	4	C1
Langdon Beck	61	K3
Langdon Hills	24	C3
Langdon House	5	K3
Langdyke	82	E7
Langenhoe	34	E7
Langford Beds.	32	E4
Langford Devon	7	J5
Langford Essex	24	E1
Langford Notts.	52	B7
Langford Oxon.	21	F1
Langford Budville	7	K3
Langham Essex	34	E5
Langham Norf.	44	E1
Langham Rut.	42	B4
Langham Suff.	34	D2
Langham Moor	34	E5
Langho	56	B6
Langholm	69	J5
Langlands	65	G5
Langlee	70	B2
Langleeford	70	E1
Langley Ches.	49	J5
Langley Derbys.	41	G1
Langley Essex	33	H5
Langley Hants.	11	F4
Langley Herts.	33	F6
Langley Kent	14	D2
Langley Slo.	22	D4
Langley W.Suss.	12	B4
Langley Warks.	30	C2
Langley Burrell	20	C4
Langley Green	40	E2
Langley Heath	14	D2
Langley Marsh	7	J3
Langley Mill	41	G1
Langley Moor	62	D2
Langley Park	62	D2
Langley Street	45	H5
Langney	13	K6
Langold	51	H4
Langore	6	B7
Langport	8	D2
Langrick	43	F1
Langridge B. & N.E.Som.	20	A5
Langridge Devon	6	D3
Langridgeford	6	D3
Langrigg	60	C2
Langrish	11	J2
Langriville	43	F1
Langsett	50	E2
Langshaw	76	D7
Langshawburn	69	H3
Langside	81	J6
Langskaill	106	D3
Langstone	11	J4
Langthorne	62	D7
Langthorpe	57	J3
Langthwaite	62	B7
Langtoft E.Riding	59	G3
Langtoft Lincs.	42	E4
Langton Dur.	62	C5
Langton Lincs.	53	G5
Langton Lincs.	53	F6
Langton N.Yorks.	58	E3
Langton by Wragby	52	E5
Langton Green	13	J3
Langton Herring	9	F6
Langton Long Blandford	9	J4
Langton Matravers	10	B7
Langtree	6	C4
Langwathby	61	G3
Langwell	96	B1
Langwell House	105	G6
Langworth	52	D5
Lanivery	4	A5
Lanivet	4	A4
Lanlivery	4	A5
Lanner	2	E4
Lanreath	4	B5
Lansallos	4	B5
Lansdown	20	A5
Lanteglos	4	A2
Lanton Northumb.	77	H7
Lanton Sc.Bord.	70	B1
Lapford	7	F5
Laphroaig	72	B6
Lapley	40	A4
Lapworth	30	C1
Larach na Gaibhre	73	F4
Larachbeg	79	H3
Larbert	75	G2
Larden Green	48	E7
Largie	90	E1
Largiemore	73	H2
Largoward	83	F7
Largs	74	A5
Largue	98	E6
Largybaan	66	A2
Largybeg	66	E1
Largymeanoch	66	E1
Largymore	66	E1
Lark Hall	33	J3
Larkhall	75	F5
Larkhill	20	E7
Larling	44	D7
Larriston	70	A4
Lartington	62	B5
Lary	90	B4
Lasborough	20	B2
Lasham	21	K7
Lashenden	14	D3
Lassington	29	G6
Lassintullich	81	J2
Lassodie	75	K1
Lasswade	76	B4
Lastingham	63	J7
Latchingdon	24	E1
Latchley	4	E3
Lately Common	49	F3
Latheron	105	G5
Latheronwheel	105	G5
Lathockar	83	F6
Lathones	83	F7
Latimer	22	D2
Latteridge	19	K3
Lattiford	9	F2
Latton	20	D2
Lauchentyre	65	F5
Lauchintilly	91	F3
Lauder	76	D6
Laugharne	17	G3
Laughterton	52	B5
Laughton E.Suss.	13	J5
Laughton Leics.	41	J7
Laughton Lincs.	42	D2
Laughton Lincs.	52	B3
Laughton en le Morthen	51	H4
Launcells	6	A5
Launcells Cross	6	A5
Launceston	6	B7
Launde Abbey	42	B5
Launton	31	H6
Laurencekirk	91	F7
Laurieston D. & G.	65	G4
Laurieston Falk.	75	H3
Lavendon	32	C3
Lavenham	34	D4
Laverhay	69	G4
Lavernock	18	E5
Laversdale	69	K7
Laverstock	10	C1
Laverstoke	21	H7
Laverton Glos.	30	B5
Laverton N.Yorks.	57	H2
Laverton Som.	20	A6
Lavister	48	C7
Law	75	G5
Lawers P. & K.	81	J5
Lawers P. & K.	81	H4
Lawford	34	E5
Lawhitton	6	B7
Lawkland	56	C3
Lawley	39	F5
Lawnhead	40	A3
Lawrenny	16	D4
Laws	83	F4
Lawshall	34	C3
Lawton	28	D3
Laxdale (Lacasdal)	101	G4
Laxey	54	D5
Laxfield	35	G1
Laxfirth Shet.	109	D7
Laxfirth Shet.	109	D8
Laxford Bridge	102	E4
Laxo	109	D6
Laxton E.Riding	58	D7
Laxton Northants.	42	C6
Laxton Notts.	51	K6
Laycock	57	F5
Layer Breton	34	D7
Layer de la Haye	34	D7
Layer Marney	34	D7
Layham	34	E4
Laytham	58	D6
Lazenby	63	G4
Lazonby	61	G3
Lea Derbys.	51	F7
Lea Here.	29	F6
Lea Lincs.	52	B4
Lea Shrop.	38	C7
Lea Shrop.	38	D5
Lea Wilts.	20	C3
Lea Marston	40	E6
Lea Town	55	H6
Lea Yeat	56	C1
Leac a' Li	93	G2
Leachd	73	J1
Leachkin	96	D7
Leadburn	76	A5
Leaden Roding	33	J7
Leadenham	52	C7
Leadgate Cumb.	61	J2
Leadgate Dur.	62	C1
Leadgate T. & W.	62	C1
Leadhills	68	D2
Leafield	30	E7
Leagrave	32	D6
Leake Common Side	53	G7
Leake Hurn's End	43	H1
Lealands	13	J5
Lealholm	63	J6
Lealt Arg. & B.	72	E1
Lealt High.	94	B5
Leamington Hastings	31	F2
Leanach Arg. & B.	73	J1
Leanach High.	96	E7
Leanaig	96	C6
Leanoch	97	J6
Leargybreck	72	D3
Leasgill	55	H1
Leasingham	42	D1
Leask	91	J1
Leatherhead	22	E6
Leathley	57	H5
Leaton	38	D4
Leaveland	15	F2
Leavenheath	34	D5
Leavening	58	D3
Leaves Green	23	H5
Lebberston	59	G1
Lechlade	21	F2
Leck	56	B2
Leckford	10	E1
Leckfurin	104	C3
Leckgruinart	72	A4
Leckhampstead Bucks.	31	J5
Leckhampstead W.Berks.	21	H4
Leckhampton	29	J7
Leckie High.	95	G5
Leckie Stir.	74	E1
Leckmelm	95	H2
Leckroy	87	K5
Leckuary	73	G1
Leckwith	18	E4
Leconfield	59	G5
Ledaig	80	A4
Ledard	81	F7
Ledbeg	102	E7
Ledburn	32	C6
Ledbury	29	G5
Ledcharrie	81	G5
Ledgemoor	28	D3
Ledicot	28	D2
Ledmore Arg. & B.	79	G3
Ledmore High.	102	E7
Lednagullin	104	C2
Ledsham Ches.	48	C5
Ledsham W.Yorks.	57	K7
Ledston	57	K7
Ledstone	5	H6
Ledwell	31	F6
Lee Arg. & B.	79	F5
Lee Devon	6	C1
Lee Hants.	10	E3
Lee Lancs.	55	J4
Lee Shrop.	38	D2
Lee Brockhurst	38	E3
Lee Clump	22	C1
Lee Mill Bridge	5	F5
Lee Moor	5	F4
Lee-on-the-Solent	11	G4
Leebotten	109	D10
Leebotwood	38	D6
Leece	55	F3
Leeds Kent	14	D2
Leeds W.Yorks.	57	H6
Leeds Bradford International Airport	57	H5
Leedstown	2	D5
Leegomery	39	F4
Leek	49	J7
Leek Wootton	30	D2
Leeming N.Yorks.	57	H1
Leeming W.Yorks.	57	F6
Leeming Bar	62	D7
Lees Derbys.	40	E2
Lees Gt.Man.	49	J2
Leeswood	48	B7
Legars	77	F6
Legbourne	53	G4
Legerwood	76	D6
Legsby	52	E4
Leicester	41	H5
Leideag	84	B5
Leigh Dorset	9	F4
Leigh Glos.	29	H6
Leigh Gt.Man.	49	F2
Leigh Kent	23	J7
Leigh Shrop.	38	C5
Leigh Surr.	23	F7
Leigh Wilts.	20	D2
Leigh Worcs.	29	G3
Leigh Beck	24	E3
Leigh Common	9	G2
Leigh Delamere	20	B4
Leigh Green	14	E4
Leigh Sinton	29	G3
Leigh upon Mendip	19	K7
Leigh Woods	19	J4
Leighterton	20	B2
Leighton N.Yorks.	57	G2
Leighton Powys	38	B5
Leighton Shrop.	39	F5
Leighton Som.	20	A7
Leighton Bromswold	32	E1
Leighton Buzzard	32	C6
Leinthall Earls	28	D2
Leinthall Starkes	28	D2
Leintwardine	28	D1
Leire	41	H7
Leirinmore	103	G2
Leiston	35	J2
Leitfie	82	D3
Leith	76	A3
Leitholm	77	F6
Lelant	2	C5
Lelley	59	J6
Lem Hill	29	G1
Lemington	71	G7
Lemnas	99	G4
Lempitlaw	77	F7
Lemsford	33	F7
Lenchwick	30	B4
Lendalfoot	67	F5
Lendrick Lodge	81	G7
Lenham	14	D2
Lenham Heath	14	E3
Lenie	88	C2
Lenimore	73	G6
Lennel	77	G6
Lennox Plunton	65	G5
Lennoxtown	74	E3
Lenton	42	D2
Lenwade	44	E4
Lenzie	74	E3
Leoch	82	E4
Leochel-Cushnie	90	D3
Leominster	28	D3
Leonard Stanley	20	B1
Leorin	72	B6
Lepe	11	F5
Lephinchapel	73	H1
Lephinmore	73	H1
Leppington	58	D3
Lepton	50	E1
Lerags	79	K5
Lerryn	4	B5
Lerwick	109	D8
Lesbury	71	H2
Leschangie	91	F3
Lescrow	4	B5
Leslie Aber.	90	D2
Leslie Fife	82	D7
Lesmahagow	75	G7
Lesnewth	4	B1
Lessendrum	98	D6
Lessingham	45	H3
Lessonhall	60	D1
Leswalt	64	A4
Letchmore Heath	22	E2
Letchworth	33	F5
Letcombe Bassett	21	G3
Letcombe Regis	21	G3
Leth Meadhanach	84	C3
Letham Angus	83	G3
Letham Fife	82	E6
Lethanhill	67	J2
Lethenty	99	G6
Letheringham	35	G3
Letheringsett	44	E2
Lettaford	7	F7
Letter Finlay	87	J5
Letterewe	95	F4
Letterfearn	86	E2
Lettermorar	86	D6
Lettermore Arg. & B.	79	G3
Lettermore High.	103	J3
Letters	95	H3
Lettershaws	68	D1
Letterston	16	C2
Lettoch High.	89	H3
Lettoch High.	89	H1
Letton Here.	28	C4
Letton Here.	28	C1
Letty Green	33	F7
Letwell	51	H4
Leuchars	83	F5
Leumrabhagh	101	F6
Levedale	40	A4
Leven E.Riding	59	H5
Leven Fife	82	E7
Levencorroch	66	E1
Levenhall	76	B3
Levens	55	H1
Levenshulme	49	H3
Levenwick	109	D10
Leverburgh (An t-Òb)	93	F3
Leverington	43	H4
Leverstock Green	22	D1
Leverton	43	G1
Leverton Outgate	43	G1
Levington	35	G5
Levisham	63	K7
Levishie	88	B3
Lew	21	G1
Lewannick	4	C2
Lewdown	6	C7
Lewes	13	H5
Leweston	16	C2
Lewisham	23	G4

Lewiston	88	C2
Lewknor	22	A2
Leworthy	6	E2
Lewtrenchard	6	C7
Ley Aber.	90	D3
Ley Cornw.	4	B4
Ley Green	32	F6
Ley Sc.Bord.	76	C7
Leybourne	23	K6
Leyburn	62	C7
Leycett	39	G1
Leyland	55	J7
Leylodge	91	F3
Leys Aber.	99	J5
Leys Aber.	90	C4
Leys P. & K.	82	D4
Leys of Cossans	82	E3
Leysdown-on-Sea	25	G4
Leysmill	83	H3
Leysters	28	E2
Leyton	23	G3
Lezant	4	D3
Lhanbryde	97	K5
Liatrie	87	J1
Libanus	27	J6
Libberton	75	H6
Liberton	76	A4
Liceasto	93	G2
Lichfield	40	D5
Lickey	29	J1
Lickey End	29	J1
Lickfold	12	C4
Liddel	107	D9
Liddesdale	79	J2
Liddington	21	F3
Lidgate Derbys.	51	F5
Lidgate Suff.	34	B3
Lidlington	32	C5
Lidsing	24	D5
Lidstone	30	E6
Lienassie	87	F2
Lieurary	105	F2
Liff	82	E4
Lifton	6	B7
Liftondown	6	B7
Lighthorne	30	E3
Lightwater	22	C5
Lightwood	40	B1
Lightwood Green Ches.	39	F1
Lightwood Green Wrex.	38	C1
Lilbourne	31	G1
Lilburn Tower	71	F1
Lilleshall	39	G4
Lilley Herts.	32	E6
Lilley W.Berks.	21	H4
Lilliesleaf	70	A1
Lillingstone Dayrell	31	J5
Lillingstone Lovell	31	J4
Lillington	9	F3
Lilliput	10	B5
Lilstock	7	K1
Limbrick	49	F1
Limbury	32	D6
Limefield	49	H1
Limehillock	98	D5
Limekilnburn	75	F5
Limekilns	75	J2
Limerigg	75	G3
Limerstone	11	F6
Limington	8	E2
Limpenhoe	45	H5
Limpley Stoke	20	A5
Limpsfield	23	H6
Linbriggs	70	D3
Linby	51	H7
Linchmere	12	B3
Lincoln	52	C5
Lincomb	29	H2
Lincombe	5	H5
Lindal in Furness	55	F2
Lindale	55	H1
Lindean	76	C7
Lindertis	82	E2
Lindfield	13	G4
Lindford	12	B3
Lindifferon	82	E6
Lindley	50	D1
Lindores	82	D6
Lindridge	29	F2
Lindsaig	73	H3
Lindsell	33	K6
Lindsey	34	D4
Linford Hants.	10	C4
Linford Thur.	24	C4
Lingague	54	B6
Lingdale	63	H5
Lingen	28	C2
Lingfield	23	G7
Lingwood	45	H5
Linhead	98	E5
Linhope	69	K3
Linicro	93	J5
Linkenholt	21	G6
Linkhill	14	D5
Linkinhorne	4	D3
Linklater	107	D9
Linksness Ork.	107	B7
Linksness Ork.	107	E6
Linktown	76	A1
Linley	38	C6
Linley Green	29	F3
Linlithgow	75	H3
Linlithgow Bridge	75	H3
Linn of Muick Cottage	90	B6
Linnels	70	E7
Linney	16	B5
Linshiels	70	D3
Linsiadar	100	E4
Linsidemore	96	C2
Linslade	32	C6
Linstead Parva	35	H1
Linstock	61	F1
Linthwaite	50	D1
Lintlaw	77	G5
Lintmill	98	D4
Linton Cambs.	33	J4
Linton Derbys.	40	E4
Linton Here.	29	F6
Linton Kent	14	C3
Linton N.Yorks.	56	E3
Linton W.Yorks.	57	J5
Linton-on-Ouse	57	K3
Lintzford	62	C1
Linwood Hants.	10	C4
Linwood Lincs.	52	E4
Linwood Renf.	74	C4
Lionacleit	92	C7
Lional	101	H1
Liphook	12	B3
Liscombe	7	G2
Liskeard	4	C4
Liss	11	J2
Liss Forest	11	J2
Lissett	59	H4
Lissington	52	E4
Liston	34	C4

Lisvane	18	E3
Liswerry	19	G3
Litcham	44	C4
Litchborough	31	H3
Litchfield	21	H6
Litherland	48	C3
Litlington Cambs.	33	G4
Litlington E.Suss.	13	J6
Little Abington	33	J4
Little Addington	32	C1
Little Alne	30	C2
Little Amwell	33	G7
Little Assynt	102	D6
Little Aston	40	C6
Little Atherfield	11	F7
Little Ayton	63	G5
Little Baddow	24	D1
Little Badminton	20	A3
Little Ballinluig	82	A2
Little Bampton	60	D1
Little Bardfield	33	K5
Little Barford	32	E3
Little Barningham	45	F2
Little Barrington	30	D7
Little Barugh	58	D2
Little Bealings	35	G4
Little Bedwyn	21	F5
Little Bentley	35	F6
Little Berkhamsted	23	F1
Little Billing	32	B2
Little Birch	28	E5
Little Bispham	55	G5
Little Blakenham	35	F4
Little Bollington	49	G4
Little Bookham	22	E6
Little Bowden	42	A7
Little Bradley	33	K3
Little Brampton	38	C7
Little Braxted	34	C7
Little Brechin	83	G1
Little Brickhill	32	C5
Little Bridgeford	40	A3
Little Brington	31	H2
Little Bromley	34	E6
Little Broughton	60	B3
Little Budworth	48	E6
Little Burstead	24	C2
Little Burton	59	H5
Little Bytham	42	D4
Little Carlton Lincs.	53	H4
Little Carlton Notts.	51	K7
Little Casterton	42	D5
Little Catwick	59	H5
Little Cawthorpe	53	G4
Little Chalfont	22	C2
Little Chart	14	E3
Little Chesterford	33	J4
Little Cheverell	20	C6
Little Chishill	33	H5
Little Clacton	35	F7
Little Clifton	60	B4
Little Comberton	29	J4
Little Common	14	C7
Little Compton	30	D5
Little Corby	61	F1
Little Cowarne	29	F3
Little Coxwell	21	F2
Little Crakehall	62	D7
Little Creich	96	D3
Little Cressingham	44	C6
Little Crosby	48	C2
Little Cubley	40	D2
Little Dalby	42	A4
Little Dens	99	J6
Little Dewchurch	28	E5
Little Downham	43	J7
Little Driffield	59	G4
Little Dunham	44	C4
Little Dunkeld	82	B3
Little Dunmow	33	K6
Little Easton	33	K6
Little Eaton	41	F1
Little Ellingham	44	E6
Little End	23	J1
Little Eversden	33	G3
Little Fakenham	34	D1
Little Faringdon	21	F1
Little Fencote	62	D7
Little Fenton	58	B6
Little Finborough	34	E3
Little Fransham	44	C4
Little Gaddesden	32	C7
Little Garway	28	D6
Little Gidding	42	E7
Little Glemham	35	H3
Little Glenshee	82	A4
Little Gorsley	29	F6
Little Gransden	33	F3
Little Green	34	E1
Little Grimsby	53	G3
Little Gruinard	95	F3
Little Habton	58	D2
Little Hadham	33	H6
Little Hale	42	E1
Little Hallingbury	33	H7
Little Hampden	22	B1
Little Harrowden	32	B1
Little Haseley	21	K1
Little Hautbois	45	G3
Little Haven	16	B3
Little Hay	40	D5
Little Hayfield	50	C4
Little Haywood	40	C3
Little Heath	41	F7
Little Hereford	28	E2
Little Holtby	62	D7
Little Horkesley	34	D5
Little Hormead	33	H6
Little Horsted	13	H5
Little Horwood	31	J5
Little Houghton	32	B3
Little Hucklow	50	D5
Little Hulton	49	G2
Little Hungerford	21	J4
Little Idoch	99	F6
Little Kimble	22	B1
Little Kineton	30	E3
Little Kingshill	22	B2
Little Langford	10	B1
Little Laver	23	J1
Little Lawford	31	F1
Little Leigh	49	F5
Little Leighs	34	B7
Little Lever	49	G2
Little Ley	90	E3
Little Linford	32	B4
Little London E.Suss.	13	J5
Little London Hants.	21	G6
Little London Hants.	21	K6
Little London I.o.M.	54	C5
Little London Lincs.	43	H3
Little London Lincs.	43	F3

Little London	53	G5
Lincs.		
Little London Norf.	43	J3
Little London Norf.	44	B6
Little Longstone	50	D5
Little Malvern	29	G4
Little Maplestead	34	C5
Little Marcle	29	F5
Little Marlow	22	B3
Little Massingham	44	B3
Little Melton	45	F5
Little Mill	19	G1
Little Milton	21	K1
Little Missenden	22	C2
Little Musgrave	61	J5
Little Ness	38	D4
Little Neston	48	B5
Little Newcastle	16	C2
Little Newsham	62	C5
Little Oakley Essex	35	G6
Little Oakley Northants.	42	B7
Little Orton	60	E1
Little Ouseburn	57	K3
Little Parndon	23	H1
Little Paxton	32	E2
Little Petherick	3	G1
Little Plumstead	45	H4
Little Ponton	42	C2
Little Raveley	33	F1
Little Ribston	57	J4
Little Rissington	30	C6
Little Rogart	96	E1
Little Ryburgh	44	D3
Little Ryle	71	F2
Little Salkeld	61	G3
Little Sampford	33	K5
Little Saxham	34	B2
Little Scatwell	95	K6
Little Shelford	33	H3
Little Smeaton	51	H1
Little Snoring	44	D2
Little Sodbury	20	A3
Little Somborne	10	E1
Little Somerford	20	C3
Little Stainton	62	E4
Little Stanney	48	D5
Little Staughton	32	E2
Little Steeping	53	H6
Little Stonham	35	F3
Little Stretton Leics.	41	J6
Little Stretton Shrop.	38	D6
Little Strickland	61	G4
Little Stukeley	33	F1
Little Sutton	48	C5
Little Swinburne	70	E6
Little Tey	34	C6
Little Thetford	33	J1
Little Thirkleby	57	K2
Little Thorpe	63	F2
Little Thurlow	33	K3
Little Thurrock	24	C4
Little Torboll	96	E2
Little Torrington	6	C4
Little Totham	34	C7
Little Town	60	D5
Little Urswick	55	F2
Little Wakering	25	F3
Little Walden	33	J4
Little Waldingfield	34	D4
Little Walsingham	44	D2
Little Waltham	34	B7
Little Warley	24	C2
Little Weighton	59	F6
Little Welland	29	H5
Little Welnetham	34	C3
Little Wenham	34	E5
Little Wenlock	39	F5
Little Whittington	35	G1
Green		
Little Whittington	70	E7
Little Wilbraham	33	J3
Little Witcombe	29	J7
Little Witley	29	G2
Little Wittenham	21	J2
Little Wolford	30	D5
Little Wratting	33	K4
Little Wymondley	33	F6
Little Wyrley	40	C5
Little Yeldham	34	B5
Littlebeck	63	K6
Littleborough Gt.Man.	49	J1
Littleborough Notts.	52	B4
Littlebourne	15	G2
Littlebredy	8	E6
Littlebury	33	J5
Littlebury Green	33	H5
Littledean	29	F7
Littleferry	97	F2
Littleham Devon	6	C3
Littleham Devon	7	J7
Littlehampton	12	D6
Littlehempston	5	J4
Littlehoughton	71	H2
Littlemill E.Ayr.	67	J2
Littlemill High.	97	G6
Littlemore	21	J1
Littleover	41	F2
Littleport	43	J7
Littlestone-on-Sea	15	F5
Littlethorpe	57	J3
Littleton Ches.	48	D6
Littleton Hants.	11	F1
Littleton P. & K.	82	D4
Littleton Som.	8	D1
Littleton Surr.	22	D5
Littleton Drew	20	B3
Littleton-on-Severn	19	J3
Littleton Panell	20	C6
Littletown	62	E2
Littlewick Green	22	B4
Littleworth Oxon.	21	G2
Littleworth Staffs.	40	C4
Littleworth Worcs.	29	H3
Litley Green	33	K7
Litton Derbys.	50	D5
Litton N.Yorks.	56	E2
Litton Som.	19	J6
Litton Cheney	8	E5
Liurbost	101	F5
Liverpool	48	C3
Liverpool Airport	48	D4
Liversedge	57	G7
Liverton Devon	5	J3
Liverton R. & C.	63	J5
Liverton Street	14	D3
Livingston	75	J4
Livingston Village	75	J4
Lixwm	47	K5
Lizard	2	D7
Llaingoch	46	A4
Llaithddu	37	K7
Llan	37	H5

Llan-dafal	18	E1
Llan-faes	46	E5
Llan-y-pwll	48	C7
Llanaber	37	F4
Llanaelhaearn	36	C1
Llanaeron	26	D2
Llanafan	27	F1
Llanafan-fawr	27	J3
Llanafan-fechan	27	J3
Llanallgo	46	C4
Llanarmon	36	D2
Llanarmon Dyffryn	38	A2
Ceiriog		
Llanarmon-yn-Ial	47	K7
Llanarth Cere.	26	D3
Llanarth Mon.	28	C7
Llanarthney	17	J2
Llanasa	47	K4
Llanbabo	46	B4
Llanbadarn Fawr	36	E7
Llanbadarn	27	K1
Fynydd		
Llanbadarn-y-	28	A4
garreg		
Llanbadoc	19	G1
Llanbadrig	46	B3
Llanbeder	19	H2
Llanbedr Gwyn.	36	E3
Llanbedr Powys	28	B6
Llanbedr Powys	28	A4
Llanbedr-Dyffryn-	47	K7
Clwyd		
Llanbedr-y-cennin	47	F6
Llanbedrgoch	46	D4
Llanbedrog	36	C2
Llanberis	46	D6
Llanbethery	18	D5
Llanbister	28	A1
Llanblethian	18	C4
Llanboidy	17	G2
Llanbradach	18	E2
Llanbrynmair	37	H5
Llancarfan	18	D4
Llancayo	19	G1
Llancynfelyn	37	F6
Llandaff	18	E4
Llandaff North	18	E4
Llandanwg	36	E3
Llandawke	17	F3
Llanddaniel Fab	46	C5
Llanddarog	17	J3
Llanddeiniol	26	E1
Llanddeiniolen	46	D6
Llandderfel	37	J2
Llanddeusant	27	G6
Carmar.		
Llanddeusant	46	B4
I.o.A.		
Llanddew	27	K5
Llanddewi	17	H6
Llanddewi-Brefi	27	F3
Llanddewi	28	C7
Rhydderch		
Llanddewi Velfrey	16	E3
Llanddewi	28	A2
Ystradenni		
Llanddewi'r Cwm	27	K4
Llanddoged	47	G6
Llanddona	46	D5
Llanddowror	17	F3
Llanddulas	47	H5
Llanddwywe	36	E3
Llanddyfnan	46	D5
Llandefaelog	17	H3
Llandefaelog Fach	27	K5
Llandefaelog-tre'r-	28	A6
graig		
Llandefalle	28	A5
Llandegfan	46	D5
Llandegla	47	K7
Llandegley	28	A2
Llandegveth	19	G2
Llandegwning	36	B2
Llandeilo	17	K2
Llandeilo	17	G3
Abercywyn		
Llandeilo Graban	27	K4
Llandeilo'r-Fan	27	H5
Llandeloy	16	B2
Llandenny	19	H1
Llandevenny	19	H3
Llandinabo	28	E6
Llandinam	37	K6
Llandissilio	16	E2
Llandogo	19	J1
Llandough	18	E4
V. of Glam.		
Llandough	18	C4
V. of Glam.		
Llandovery	27	G5
Llandow	18	C4
Llandre Carmar.	27	F4
Llandre Carmar.	16	E2
Llandre Cere.	37	F7
Llandrillo	37	K2
Llandrillo-yn-Rhôs	47	G4
Llandrindod Wells	27	K2
Llandrinio	38	B4
Llandudno	47	F4
Llandudno	47	F5
Junction		
Llandwrog	46	C7
Llandybie	17	K3
Llandyfriog	26	C4
Llandyfrydog	46	C4
Llandygai	46	D5
Llandygwydd	26	B4
Llandyrnog	47	K6
Llandysilio	38	B4
Llandyssil	38	A6
Llandysul	26	D4
Llanegryn	37	F5
Llanegwad	17	H2
Llaneilian	46	C3
Llanelian-yn-Rhôs	47	K7
Llanelidan	47	K7
Llanelieu	28	A6
Llanellen	28	C7
Llanelli	17	J5
Llanelltyd	37	G4
Llanelly	28	B7
Llanelly Hill Mon.	28	B7
Llanelwedd	27	K3
Llanelwy	47	J5
(St. Asaph)		
Llanenddwyn	36	E3
Llanengan	36	B3
Llanerch-y-medd	46	C4
Llanerfyl	37	K5
Llanfachreth	37	G3
Llanfaelog	46	B5
Llanfaelrhys	36	B3
Llanfaenor	28	D7
Llanfaes Powys	27	K6
Llanfaethlu	46	B4
Llanfaglan	46	C6
Llanfair	36	E3

Llanfair Caereinion	38	A5
Llanfair Clydogau	27	F3
Llanfair Dyffryn	47	K7
Clwyd		
Llanfair-Nant-Gwyn	16	E1
Llanfair-Orllwyn	26	C4
Llanfair Talhaiarn	47	H5
Llanfair Waterdine	28	B1
Llanfair-yn-neubwll	46	B5
Llanfairfechan	46	E5
Llanfairpwll-	46	D5
gwyngyll		
Llanfairynghornwy	46	B3
Llanfallteg	16	E3
Llanfallteg West	16	E3
Llanfaredd	27	K3
Llanfarian	26	E1
Llanfechain	38	A3
Llanfechell	46	B3
Llanfendigaid	36	E5
Llanferres	47	K6
Llanfflewyn	46	B4
Llanfigael	46	B4
Llanfihangel ar-arth	17	H1
Llanfihangel	28	C7
Crucorney		
Llanfihangel Glyn	37	J1
Myfyr		
Llanfihangel Nant	27	J5
Bran		
Llanfihangel-nant-	28	A3
Melan		
Llanfihangel	28	A2
Rhydithon		
Llanfihangel Rogiet	19	H3
Llanfihangel-Tal-y-	28	A6
llyn		
Llanfihangel uwch-	17	H2
gwili		
Llanfihangel-y-	27	F1
Creuddyn		
Llanfihangel-y-	36	E1
pennant Gwyn.		
Llanfihangel-y-	37	F5
pennant Gwyn.		
Llanfihangel-yng-	37	K4
Ngwynfa		
Llanfilo	28	A5
Llanfoist	28	B7
Llanfor	37	J2
Llanfrechfa	19	G2
Llanfrothen	37	F1
Llanfrynach	27	K6
Llanfwrog Denb.	47	K7
Llanfwrog I.o.A.	46	B4
Llanfyllin	38	A4
Llanfynydd	17	J2
Llanfynydd Flints.	48	B7
Llanfyrnach	17	F1
Llangadfan	37	K4
Llangadog	27	G6
Llangadwaladr	46	B6
I.o.A.		
Llangadwaladr	38	A2
Powys		
Llangaffo	46	C6
Llangain	17	G3
Llangammarch	27	J4
Wells		
Llangan	18	C4
Llangarron	28	E6
Llangasty-Talyllyn	28	A6
Llangathen	17	J2
Llangattock	28	B7
Llangattock	28	D7
Lingoed		
Llangattock-Vibon-	28	D7
Avel		
Llangedwyn	38	A3
Llangefni	46	C5
Llangeinor	18	C3
Llangeitho	27	F3
Llangeler	17	G1
Llangelynin	36	E5
Llangendeirne	17	H3
Llangennech	17	J4
Llangennith	17	H5
Llangenny	28	B7
Llangernyw	47	G6
Llangian	36	B3
Llangiwg	18	A1
Llanglydwen	16	E2
Llangoed	46	E5
Llangoedmor	26	A4
Llangollen	38	B1
Llangolman	16	E2
Llangorse	28	A6
Llangorwen	37	F7
Llangovan	19	H1
Llangower	37	J2
Llangranog	26	C3
Llangristiolus	46	C5
Llangrove	28	E7
Llangua	28	C6
Llangunllo	28	B1
Llangunnor	17	J2
Llangurig	27	J1
Llangwm Conwy	37	J1
Llangwm Pembs.	16	C4
Llangwm-isaf	19	H1
Llangwnnadl	36	B2
Llangwyfan	47	K6
Llangwyllog	46	C5
Llangwyryfon	26	E1
Llangybi Cere.	27	F3
Llangybi Gwyn.	36	D1
Llangybi Mon.	19	G2
Llangyfelach	17	K5
Llangynhafal	47	K6
Llangynidr	28	A7
Llangyniew	38	A5
Llangynin	17	G3
Llangynog Carmar.	17	G3
Llangynog Powys	37	K3
Llangynwyd	18	B3
Llanhamlach	27	K6
Llanharan	18	D3
Llanharry	18	D3
Llanhennock	19	G2
Llanhilleth	19	F1
Llanidloes	37	J7
Llaniestyn	36	B2
Llanigon	28	B5
Llanilar	27	F1
Llanilid	18	C3
Llanishen Cardiff	18	E3
Llanishen Mon.	19	H1
Llanllawddog	17	H2
Llanllechid	46	E6
Llanllowell	19	G1
Llanllugan	37	K5
Llanllwch	17	G3
Llanllwchaiarn	38	A6
Llanllwni	26	D4
Llanllyfni	46	C7
Llanllywel	19	G2
Llanmadoc	17	H5
Llanmaes	18	C5

Llanmartin	19	G3
Llanmerewig	38	A6
Llanmihangel	18	C4
Llanmiloe	17	F4
Llanmorlais	17	J5
Llannefydd	47	H5
Llannerch	47	J5
Llannerch-y-Môr	47	K5
Llannon	17	J4
Llannor	36	C2
Llanon	26	E2
Llanover	19	G1
Llanpumsaint	17	H2
Llanreithan	16	B2
Llanrhaeadr	47	J6
Llanrhaeadr-ym-	38	A3
Mochnant		
Llanrhian	16	B1
Llanrhidian	17	J5
Llanrhos	47	F4
Llanrhyddlad	46	B4
Llanrhystud	26	E2
Llanrothal	28	D7
Llanrug	46	D6
Llanrumney	19	F3
Llanrwst	47	F6
Llansadurnen	17	F3
Llansadwrn	17	K1
Carmar.		
Llansadwrn I.o.A.	46	D5
Llansaint	17	G4
Llansamlet	17	K5
Llansanffraid Glan	47	G5
Conwy		
Llansannan	47	H6
Llansannor	18	C4
Llansantffraed	28	A6
Llansantffraed-	27	J2
Cwmdeuddwr		
Llansantffraed-in-	27	K3
Elvel		
Llansantffraid	26	E2
Llansantffraid-ym-	38	B3
Mechain		
Llansawel Carmar.	17	K1
Llansawel (Briton	18	A2
Ferry) N.P.T.		
Llansilin	38	B3
Llansoy	19	H1
Llanspyddid	27	K6
Llanstadwell	16	C4
Llansteffan	17	G3
Carmar.		
Llanstephan	28	A4
Powys		
Llantarnam	19	G2
Llanteg	16	E3
Llanthony	28	B6
Llantilio Crossenny	28	C7
Llantilio Pertholey	28	C7
Llantood	26	A4
Llantrisant Mon.	19	G2
Llantrisant R.C.T.	18	D3
Llantrithyd	18	D3
Llantwit Fardre	18	D3
Llantwit Major	18	C5
Llantysilio	38	A1
Llanuwchllyn	37	H2
Llanvaches	19	H2
Llanvair-Discoed	19	H2
Llanvapley	28	C7
Llanvetherine	28	C7
Llanveynoe	28	C5
Llanvihangel	19	G1
Gobion		
Llanvihangel-	28	D7
Ystern-Llewern		
Llanwarne	28	E6
Llanwddyn	37	K4
Llanwenog	26	D4
Llanwern	19	G3
Llanwinio	17	F2
Llanwnda Gwyn.	46	C7
Llanwnda Pembs.	16	C1
Llanwnen	26	E4
Llanwnog	37	K6
Llanwonno	18	D2
Llanwrda	27	G5
Llanwrin	37	G5
Llanwrthwl	27	J2
Llanwrtyd	27	H4
Llanwrtyd Wells	27	H4
Llanwyddelan	37	K5
Llanyblodwel	38	B3
Llanybri	17	G3
Llanybydder	26	E4
Llanycefn	16	E2
Llanychaer Bridge	16	C1
Llanycil	37	J2
Llanycrwys	27	F4
Llanymawddwy	37	J4
Llanymynech	38	B3
Llanynghenedl	46	B4
Llanynys	47	K6
Llanyre	27	K2
Llanystumdwy	36	D2
Llanywern	28	A6
Llawhaden	16	D3
Llawnt	38	B2
Llawr-y-dref	36	B3
Llawryglyn	37	J6
Llay	48	C7
Llechcynfarwy	46	B4
Llechfaen	27	K6
Llechryd Caerp.	18	E1
Llechryd Cere.	26	B4
Llechrydau	38	B2
Lledrod Cere.	27	F1
Lledrod Powys	38	B3
Llethr	16	B2
Llidiadnenog	17	H1
Llidiardau	37	H2
Llithfaen	36	C1
Lloc	47	K5
Llong	48	B6
Llowes	28	A4
Lloyney	28	B1
Llundain-fach	26	E3
Llwydcoed	18	C1
Llwydiarth	38	A4
Llwyn	38	B7
Llwyn-Madoc	27	J3
Llwyn-onn	26	D3
Llwyn-y-brain	17	F3
Carmar.		
Llwyn-y-brain	27	G5
Carmar.		
Llwyncelyn	26	D3
Llwyndafydd	26	C3
Llwynderw	38	B5
Llwyndyrys	36	C1
Llwyngwril	36	E5
Llwynhendy	17	J5
Llwynmawr	38	B2
Llwynpia	18	C2
Llynclys	38	B3
Llynfaes	46	C5
Llys-y-fran	16	D2
Llysfaen	47	G5
Llyswen	28	A5

Llysworney	18	C4
Llywel	27	H5
Loandhu	97	F4
Loanhead Aber.	91	H1
Loanhead	76	A4
Midloth.		
Loans	74	B7
Loch Baghasdail	84	C3
(Lochboisdale)		
Loch Coire Lodge	103	J5
Loch Eil Outward	87	G7
Bound		
Loch Head D. & G.	64	D6
Loch Head D. & G.	67	K3
Loch na Madadh	92	E5
(Lochmaddy)		
Loch Sgioport	84	D1
Lochailort	86	D6
Lochaline	79	H3
Lochans	64	A5
Locharbriggs	68	E5
Lochawe	80	C5
Lochboisdale	84	C3
(Loch Baghasdail)		
Lochbuie	79	H5
Lochcarron	86	E1
Lochdhu Hotel	105	F4
Lochdon	79	J4
Lochdrum	95	J4
Lochearnhead	81	G5
Lochee	82	E4
Lochend High.	105	H2
Lochend High.	88	C1
Lochfoot	65	K3
Lochgair	73	H1
Lochgarthside	88	C3
Lochgelly	75	K1
Lochgilphead	73	G2
Lochgoilhead	80	D7
Lochgoin	74	D6
Lochhill E.Ayr.	68	B2
Lochhill Moray	97	K5
Lochinch Castle	64	B4
Lochinver	102	C6
Lochlair	83	G3
Lochlane	81	K5
Lochlea	67	J1
Lochluichart	95	K5
Lochmaben	69	F5
Lochmaddy (Loch	92	E5
na Madadh)		
Lochore	75	K1
Lochportain	92	E4
Lochranza	73	H6
Lochside Aber.	83	J1
Lochside High.	103	G3
Lochside High.	104	D5
Lochside High.	105	H3
Lochslin	97	F3
Lochton	67	G5
Lochty	83	G7
Lochuige	79	J2
Lochurr	68	C5
Lochussie	96	B6
Lochwinnoch	74	B5
Lockengate	4	
Lockerbie	69	G5
Lockeridge	20	E5
Lockerley	10	D2
Locking	19	G6
Lockington	59	G5
E.Riding		
Lockington Leics.	41	G3
Lockleywood	39	F3
Locks Heath	11	G4
Locksbottom	23	H5
Lockton	63	K7
Loddington Leics.	42	A5
Loddington	32	B1
Northants.		
Loddiswell	5	H6
Loddon	45	H6
Lode	33	J2
Loders	8	D5
Lodsworth	12	C4
Lofthouse N.Yorks.	57	F2
Lofthouse	57	J7
W.Yorks.		
Loftus	63	J5
Logan D. & G.	64	A6
Logan E.Ayr.	67	K1
Loganlea	75	H4
Loggerheads	39	G2
Loggie	95	H2
Logie Angus	83	H1
Logie Angus	83	F5
Logie Fife	83	F5
Logie Moray	97	H6
Logie Coldstone	90	C4
Logie Hill	96	E4
Logie Newton	90	E1
Logie Pert	83	H1
Logierait	82	A2
Login	16	E2
Lolworth	33	G2
Lonbain	94	C6
Londesborough	58	E5
London	23	G3
London Beach	14	D4
London City	23	H3
Airport		
London Colney	22	E1
London Heathrow	22	D4
Airport		
London Luton	32	E6
Airport		
Londonderry	57	H1
Londonthorpe	42	C2
Londubh	94	E3
Lonemore	96	E3
Long Ashton	19	J4
Long Bennington	42	B1
Long Bredy	8	E5
Long Buckby	31	H2
Long Clawson	42	A3
Long Common	11	G3
Long Compton	40	A3
Staffs.		
Long Compton	30	D5
Warks.		
Long Crendon	21	K1
Long Crichel	9	J3
Long Ditton	22	E5
Long Downs	2	E5
Long Drax	58	C7
Long Duckmanton	51	G5
Long Eaton	41	G2
Long Gill	56	C4
Long Hanborough	31	F7
Long Itchington	31	F2
Long Lawford	31	F1
Long Load	8	D2
Long Marston	32	B3
Herts.		
Long Marston	58	B4
N.Yorks.		

Long Marston Warks. 30 C4
Long Marton 61 H4
Long Melford 34 G4
Long Newnton 20 C2
Long Preston 56 D4
Long Riston 59 H5
Long Stratton 45 F6
Long Street 31 J4
Long Sutton Hants. 22 A7
Long Sutton Lincs. 43 H3
Long Sutton Som. 8 D2
Long Thurlow 34 E2
Long Waste 39 F4
Long Whatton 41 G3
Long Wittenham 21 J2
Longbenton 71 H7
Longborough 30 C6
Longbridge W.Mid. 30 B1
Longbridge Warks. 30 D2
Longbridge Deverill 20 B7
Longburgh 60 E1
Longburton 9 F3
Longcliffe 50 E7
Longcot 21 F2
Longcroft 75 F3
Longcross Devon 4 E3
Longcross Surr. 22 C5
Longden 38 D5
Longdon Staffs. 40 C4
Longdon Worcs. 29 H5
Longdon upon Tern 39 F4
Longdown 7 G6
Longdrum 91 H3
Longfield 24 C5
Longfield Hill 24 C5
Longford Derbys. 40 E2
Longford Glos. 29 H6
Longford Gt.Lon. 22 D4
Longford Shrop. 39 F2
Longford Tel. & W. 39 G4
Longford W.Mid. 41 F7
Longforgan 82 E5
Longformacus 76 E5
Longframlington 71 G3
Longham Dorset 10 B5
Longham Norf. 44 D4
Longhill 99 H5
Longhirst 71 H5
Longhope Glos. 29 F7
Longhorsley 71 G4
Longhoughton 71 H2
Longlands Aber. 90 C2
Longlands Cumb. 60 D3
Longlane Derbys. 40 E2
Longlane W.Berks. 21 J4
Longley Green 29 G3
Longmanhill 99 F4
Longmoor Camp 11 J1
Longmorn 97 K6
Longnewton Sc.Bord. 70 A1
Longnewton Stock. 62 E5
Longney 29 G7
Longniddry 76 C3
Longnor Shrop. 38 D5
Longnor Staffs. 50 C6
Longparish 21 H7
Longridge Lancs. 56 B6
Longridge W.Loth. 75 H4
Longridge Towers 77 H5
Longriggend 75 G3
Longrock 2 B5
Longsdon 49 J7
Longside 99 J6
Longslow 39 F2
Longstanton 33 G2
Longstock 10 E1
Longstowe 33 G3
Longstreet 20 E6
Longthorpe 42 E6
Longton Lancs. 55 H7
Longton Stoke 40 B1
Longtown Cumb. 69 J7
Longtown Here. 28 C6
Longville in the Dale 38 E6
Longwell Green 19 K4
Longwick 22 A1
Longwitton 71 F5
Longworth 21 G2
Longyester 76 D4
Lonmore 93 H7
Looe 4 C5
Loose 14 C2
Loosegate 43 G3
Loosley Row 22 B1
Lopcombe Corner 10 D1
Lopen 8 D3
Loppington 38 D3
Lorbottle 71 F3
Lorbottle Hall 71 F3
Lorgill 93 G7
Lorn 74 B2
Lornty 82 C3
Loscoe 41 G1
Losgaintir 93 F2
Lossiemouth 97 K4
Lossit 72 A2
Lostock Gralam 49 F5
Lostock Green 49 F5
Lostock Junction 49 F2
Lostwithiel 4 B5
Loth 106 F4
Lothbeg 104 E7
Lothersdale 56 E5
Lothmore 104 E7
Loudwater 22 C2
Loughborough 41 H4
Loughor 17 J5
Loughton Essex 23 H2
Loughton M.K. 32 B5
Loughton Shrop. 39 F7
Lound Lincs. 42 D4
Lound Notts. 51 J4
Lound Suff. 45 K6
Lount 41 F4
Lour 83 F3
Louth 53 G4
Love Clough 56 D7
Lovedean 11 H3
Lover 10 D2
Loversall 51 H3
Loves Green 24 C1
Lovington 8 E1
Low 55 H1
Low Ballevain 66 A1
Low Barlay 65 F5
Low Bentham 56 B3
Low Bolton 62 B7

Low Bradfield 50 E3
Low Bradley 57 F5
Low Braithwaite 61 F2
Low Brunton 70 E6
Low Burnham 51 K2
Low Burton 57 H1
Low Catton 58 D4
Low Coniscliffe 62 D5
Low Craighead 67 G3
Low Crosby 61 F1
Low Dinsdale 62 E5
Low Eggborough 58 B7
Low Entercommon 62 D6
Low Etherley 62 C4
Low Gate 70 E7
Low Habberley 29 H1
Low Ham 8 D2
Low Hawsker 63 J2
Low Haygarth 61 H1
Low Hesket 61 F2
Low Hesleyhurst 71 F4
Low Hutton 58 D3
Low Laithe 57 G3
Low Leighton 50 C4
Low Marishes 58 E2
Low Mill 63 H7
Low Moor 56 C5
Low Newton-by-the-Sea 71 H1
Low Risby 52 C1
Low Row Cumb. 70 A7
Low Row N.Yorks. 62 A7
Low Santon 52 C1
Low Stillaig 73 H4
Low Street 45 H3
Low Torry 75 J2
Low Toynton 53 F5
Low Waters 75 F5
Low Wood 55 G1
Low Worsall 62 E5
Lowdham 41 J1
Lower Achachenna 80 B5
Lower Aisholt 7 K2
Lower Apperley 29 H6
Lower Ashton 7 G7
Lower Assendon 22 A3
Lower Auchalick 73 H3
Lower Barewood 28 C3
Lower Beeding 13 F4
Lower Benefield 42 C7
Lower Berry Hill 28 E7
Lower Bockhampton 9 G5
Lower Boddington 31 F3
Lower Boscaswell 2 A5
Lower Bourne 22 B7
Lower Brailes 30 E5
Lower Breakish 86 C2
Lower Broadheath 29 H3
Lower Broughton 49 H3
Lower Brynamman 27 G7
Lower Bullingham 28 E5
Lower Burgate 10 C3
Lower Caldecote 32 E4
Lower Cam 20 A1
Lower Camster 105 H4
Lower Chapel 27 K5
Lower Chute 21 G6
Lower Crossings 50 C4
Lower Darwen 56 B7
Lower Dean 32 D2
Lower Diabaig 94 D5
Lower Dicker 13 J5
Lower Dinchope 38 D7
Lower Down 38 C7
Lower Drift 2 B6
Lower Dunsforth 57 K3
Lower Earley 22 A4
Lower Egleton 29 F4
Lower End 32 B2
Lower Everleigh 20 E6
Lower Failand 19 J4
Lower Farringdon 11 J1
Lower Freystrop 16 C3
Lower Froyle 22 A7
Lower Gabwell 5 K4
Lower Gledfield 96 C2
Lower Godney 19 H7
Lower Green Kent 23 K7
Lower Green Norf. 44 D2
Lower Green Staffs. 40 B5
Lower Green Bank 55 J4
Lower Halstow 24 E5
Lower Hardres 15 G2
Lower Hawthwaite 54 E1
Lower Hayton 38 E7
Lower Hergest 28 B3
Lower Heyford 31 F6
Lower Higham 24 D4
Lower Holbrook 35 F5
Lower Hordley 38 C3
Lower Horsebridge 13 J5
Lower Kilchattan 72 B1
Lower Killeyan 72 A6
Lower Kingcombe 8 E5
Lower Kinnerton 48 C6
Lower Langford 19 H5
Lower Largo 83 F7
Lower Lemington 30 D5
Lower Lovacott 6 D3
Lower Lydbrook 28 E7
Lower Lye 28 D2
Lower Machen 19 F3
Lower Maes-coed 28 C5
Lower Moor 29 J4
Lower Nazeing 23 G1
Lower Oakfield 75 K1
Lower Oddington 30 D6
Lower Ollach 86 B1
Lower Penarth 18 E4
Lower Penn 40 A6
Lower Pennington 10 E5
Lower Peover 49 G5
Lower Quinton 30 C4
Lower Seagry 20 C3
Lower Shelton 32 C4
Lower Shiplake 22 A4
Lower Shuckburgh 31 F2
Lower Slaughter 30 C6
Lower Stanton St. Quintin 20 C3
Lower Stoke 24 E4
Lower Stondon 32 E5
Lower Street 45 H2
Lower Sundon 32 D6
Lower Swanwick 11 F4
Lower Swell 30 C6
Lower Tean 40 C2
Lower Thurlton 45 J6
Lower Thurnham 55 H4
Lower Town I.o.S. 2 C1
Lower Town Pembs. 16 C1
Lower Tysoe 30 E4
Lower Upham 11 G3
Lower Vexford 7 K2
Lower Wallop 38 C5
Lower Walton 49 F4
Lower Weare 19 H6

Lower Welson 28 B3
Lower Whitley 49 F5
Lower Wield 21 K7
Lower (Nether) Winchendon 31 J7
Lower Withington 49 H6
Lower Woodend 22 B3
Lower Woodford 10 C1
Lower Wraxall 8 E4
Lower Wyche 29 G4
Lowesby 42 A5
Lowestoft 45 K6
Lowestoft End 45 K6
Loweswater 60 C4
Lowfield Heath 23 F7
Lowgill Cumb. 61 H7
Lowgill Lancs. 56 B3
Lowick Cumb. 55 F1
Lowick Northants. 42 C7
Lowick Northumb. 77 J7
Lownie Moor 83 F3
Lowsonford 30 C2
Lowther 61 G4
Lowther Castle 61 G4
Lowthorpe 59 G4
Lowton 49 F3
Lowton Common 49 F3
Loxbeare 7 H4
Loxhill 12 D3
Loxhore 6 E2
Loxley 30 D3
Loxton 19 G6
Loxwood 12 D3
Lubachoinnich 96 B2
Lubcroy 95 K1
Lubenham 42 A7
Lubfearn 95 K4
Lubmore 95 F3
Lubreoch 81 F3
Luccombe 7 H1
Luccombe Village 11 G7
Lucker 77 K7
Luckett 4 D3
Luckington 20 B3
Lucklawhill 83 F5
Luckwell Bridge 7 H2
Lucton 28 D2
Ludag 84 C3
Ludborough 53 F3
Ludchurch 16 E3
Luddenden 57 F7
Luddenham Court 25 F5
Luddesdown 24 C5
Luddington N.Lincs. 52 B1
Luddington Warks. 30 C3
Luddington in the Brook 42 E7
Ludford Lincs. 53 F4
Ludford Magna 53 F4
Ludford Parva 52 E4
Ludgvan 2 B5
Ludham 45 H4
Ludlow 28 E1
Ludney 53 G3
Ludstock 29 F5
Ludwell 9 J2
Ludworth 62 E2
Luffincott 6 B6
Luffness 76 C2
Lugar 67 K1
Luggiebank 75 F3
Lugton 74 C5
Lugwardine 28 E4
Luib 86 B2
Luibeilt 80 D1
Lulham 28 D4
Lullington Derbys. 40 E4
Lullington Som. 20 A6
Lulsgate Bottom 19 J5
Lulsley 29 G3
Lulworth Camp 9 H6
Lumb 57 F7
Lumbutts 56 E7
Lumby 57 K6
Lumphanan 90 D4
Lumphinnans 75 K1
Lumsdaine 77 G4
Lumsden 90 C2
Lunan 83 H2
Lunanhead 83 F2
Luncarty 82 B5
Lund E.Riding 59 F5
Lund N.Yorks. 58 C6
Lundavra 80 B1
Lunderton 99 K6
Lundie Angus 82 D4
Lundie High. 87 H3
Lundin Links 83 F7
Lunga 79 J7
Lunna 109 D6
Lunning 109 E6
Lunnon 17 J7
Lunsford's Cross 14 C6
Lunt 48 C2
Luntley 28 C3
Luppitt 7 K5
Lupton 55 J1
Lurgashall 12 C4
Lurignich 80 A2
Lusby 53 G6
Luss 74 B1
Lussagiven 72 E2
Lusta 93 H6
Lustleigh 7 F7
Luston 28 D2
Luthermuir 83 H1
Luthrie 82 E6
Luton Devon 7 J5
Luton Devon 5 K3
Luton Luton 32 D6
Luton Med. 24 D5
Lutterworth 41 H7
Lutton Devon 5 F5
Lutton Lincs. 43 H3
Lutton Northants. 42 E7
Luxborough 7 H2
Luxulyan 4 A5
Lybster High. 105 F2
Lybster High. 105 H5
Lydacott 6 C5
Lydbury North 38 C7
Lydcott 6 E2
Lydd 15 F5
Lydd Airport 15 F5
Lydd-on-Sea 15 F5
Lydden 15 H3
Lyddington 42 B6
Lydeard St. Lawrence 7 K2
Lydford 6 D7
Lydford-on-Fosse 8 E1
Lydgate 56 E7
Lydham 38 C6
Lydiard Millicent 20 D3
Lydiate 48 C2
Lydlinch 9 G3

Lydney 19 K1
Lydstep 16 D5
Lye 40 B7
Lye Green 22 C1
Lyford 21 G2
Lymbridge Green 15 G3
Lyme Regis 8 C5
Lymekilns 74 E5
Lyminge 15 G3
Lymington 10 E5
Lyminster 12 D6
Lymm 49 F4
Lymore 10 E5
Lympne 15 G4
Lympsham 19 G6
Lympstone 7 H7
Lynaberack 88 E5
Lynchat 88 E4
Lyndhurst 10 E4
Lyndon 42 C5
Lyne Aber. 91 H4
Lyne Sc.Bord. 76 A6
Lyne Surr. 22 D5
Lyne of Gorthleck 88 C2
Lyne of Skene 91 F3
Lyne Station 76 A7
Lyneal 38 D2
Lynedale House 93 J6
Lynegar 105 H3
Lyneham Oxon. 30 D6
Lyneham Wilts. 20 D4
Lyneholmeford 70 A6
Lynemore High. 89 H2
Lynemore Moray 89 J1
Lynemouth 71 H4
Lyness 107 C8
Lynford 44 C6
Lyng Norf. 44 E4
Lyng Som. 8 C2
Lynmouth 7 F1
Lynsted 25 F5
Lynton 7 F1
Lyon's Gate 9 F4
Lyonshall 28 C3
Lyrabus 72 A4
Lytchett Matravers 9 J5
Lytchett Minster 9 J5
Lyth 105 H2
Lytham 55 G7
Lytham St. Anne's 55 G7
Lythe 63 K5
Lythe Hill 12 C3
Lythes 107 D9
Lythmore 105 F2

M

Mabe Burnthouse 2 E5
Mabie 65 K3
Mablethorpe 53 J4
Macclesfield 49 J5
Macclesfield Forest 49 J5
Macduff 99 F4
Machan 75 F5
Machany 82 A6
Macharioch 66 B3
Machen 19 F3
Machrie Arg. & B. 72 A4
Machrie Arg. & B. 72 B6
Machrie N.Ayr. 73 H7
Machrihanish 66 A2
Machrins 72 B1
Machynlleth 37 G5
Mackworth 41 F2
Macmerry 76 C3
Macterry 99 F6
Madderty 82 A5
Maddiston 75 H3
Madehurst 12 C5
Madeley Staffs. 39 G1
Madeley Tel. & W. 39 G1
Madeley Heath 39 G1
Madford 7 K4
Madingley 33 G3
Madjeston 9 H2
Madley 28 D5
Madresfield 29 H4
Madron 2 B5
Maen Porth 2 E6
Maenaddwyn 46 C4
Maenclochog 16 D2
Maendy 18 D4
Maentwrog 37 F1
Maer 39 G2
Maerdy Carmar. 17 K2
Maerdy Carmar. 17 K2
Maerdy Conwy 37 K1
Maerdy Mon. 19 G1
Maerdy R.C.T. 18 C2
Maes-Glas 47 K5
Maes-glas (Greenfield) 19 F3
Maes-glas 18 B2
Maes-Treylow 28 B2
Maesbrook 38 B3
Maesbury 38 C3
Maesbury Marsh 38 C3
Maesgwynne 17 F2
Maeshafn 48 B6
Maesllyn 26 C4
Maesmynis 27 K4
Maesteg 18 B2
Maesybont 17 J3
Maescrugiau 26 D4
Maesycwmmer 18 E2
Magdalen Laver 23 J1
Maggieknockater 98 B6
Magham Down 13 K5
Maghull 48 C2
Magor 19 H3
Maiden Bradley 9 G1
Maiden Law 62 C2
Maiden Newton 8 E5
Maiden Wells 16 C5
Maidencombe 5 K4
Maidenhead 22 B3
Maidens 67 G3
Maiden's Green 22 C4
Maidensgrove 22 A3
Maidenwell Cornw. 4 B3
Maidenwell Lincs. 53 G5
Maidford 31 H3
Maids' Moreton 31 J5
Maidstone 14 C2
Maidwell 42 A7
Mail 109 D10
Mains of Ardestie 83 G4
Mains of Balgavies 83 G2
Mains of Ballhall 83 G2
Mains of Ballindarg 83 F2
Mains of Burgie 97 H6
Mains of Culsh 99 G6
Mains of Dillavaird 91 F6
Mains of Drum 91 G4
Mains of Dudwick 91 H1
Mains of Faillie 88 E1
Mains of Fedderate 99 G6
Mains of Glack 91 F2
Mains of Glassaugh 98 D4

Mains of Glenbuchat 90 B3
Mains of Linton 91 F4
Mains of Melgund 83 G2
Mains of Pitfour 99 H6
Mains of Pittrichie 91 G2
Mains of Sluie 97 H6
Mains of Tannachy 98 B4
Mains of Thornton 91 F6
Mains of Tig 67 F5
Mains of Watten 105 H3
Mainsriddle 65 K5
Mainstone 38 B7
Maisemore 29 H6
Makendon 70 D3
Makerstoun 76 E7
Malacleit 92 C4
Malborough 5 H7
Malden Rushett 22 E5
Maldon 24 E1
Malham 56 E3
Maligar 93 K5
Mallaig 86 C5
Mallaigmore 86 D5
Mallaigvaig 86 C5
Malleny Mills 75 K4
Mallsheugh 74 D5
Malling 81 G7
Malltraeth 46 C6
Mallwyd 37 H4
Malmesbury 20 C3
Malmsmead 7 F1
Malpas Ches. 38 D1
Malpas Cornw. 3 F4
Malpas Newport 19 G2
Maltby S.Yorks. 51 H3
Maltby Stock. 63 F5
Maltby le Marsh 53 H4
Maltman's Hill 14 E3
Malton 58 D2
Malvern Link 29 G4
Malvern Wells 29 G4
Mambeg 74 A2
Mamble 29 F1
Mamhead 7 H7
Mamhilad 19 G1
Manaccan 2 E6
Manafon 38 A5
Manais 93 G3
Manaton 7 F7
Manby 53 G4
Mancetter 41 F6
Manchester 49 H3
Manchester Airport 49 H4
Mancot Royal 48 C6
Mandally 87 J4
Manea 43 H7
Maneight 67 K3
Manfield 62 D5
Mangaster 108 C5
Mangotsfield 19 K4
Mangurstadh 100 C4
Mankinholes 56 E7
Manley 48 E5
Manmoel 18 E1
Mannal 78 A3
Manningford Abbots 20 E6
Manningford Bohune 20 E6
Manningford Bruce 20 E6
Mannings Heath 13 F4
Mannington 10 B4
Manningtree 35 F5
Mannofield 91 H4
Manorbier 16 D5
Manordeifi 26 B4
Manordeilo 17 K2
Manorowen 16 C1
Mansell Gamage 28 C4
Mansell Lacy 28 D4
Mansergh 56 B1
Mansfield 51 H6
Mansfield Woodhouse 51 H6
Mansriggs 55 F1
Manston Dorset 9 H3
Manston Kent 25 K5
Manswood 9 J4
Manthorpe Lincs. 42 C2
Manthorpe Lincs. 42 D4
Manton N.Lincs. 52 C2
Manton Rut. 42 B5
Manton Wilts. 20 E5
Manuden 33 H6
Maolachy 79 K6
Maperton 9 F2
Maple Cross 22 D2
Maplebeck 51 K6
Mapledurham 21 K4
Mapledurwell 21 K6
Maplehurst 12 E4
Mapleton 40 D1
Mapperley 41 G1
Mapperton 8 E5
Mappleborough Green 30 B2
Mappleton 59 J5
Mapplewell 51 F2
Mappowder 9 G4
Mar Lodge 89 H5
Marazion 2 C5
Marbury 38 E1
March 43 H6
Marcham 21 H2
Marchamley 38 E3
Marchington 40 D3
Marchington Woodlands 40 D3
Marchwiel 38 C1
Marchwood 10 E3
Marcross 18 C5
Marcus 83 G2
Marden Here. 28 E4
Marden Kent 14 C3
Marden T. & W. 71 J6
Marden Wilts. 20 D6
Marden Beech 14 C3
Marden Thorn 14 C3
Mardy 28 C7
Mare Green 8 C2
Marefield 42 A5
Mareham le Fen 53 F6
Mareham on the Hill 53 F6
Maresfield 13 H4
Marfleet 59 H7
Marford 48 C7
Margam 18 A3
Margaret Marsh 9 H3
Margaret Roding 23 J1
Margaretting 24 C1
Margate 25 K4
Margnaheglish 73 J7
Margreig 65 J3
Margrove Park 63 H5
Marham 44 B5
Marhamchurch 6 A5
Marholm 42 E5

Marian Cwm 47 J5
Marian-Glas 46 D4
Mariansleigh 7 F3
Marishader 93 K5
Maristow House 4 E4
Mark 19 G7
Mark Causeway 19 G7
Mark Cross 13 J3
Markbeech 23 H7
Markby 53 H5
Markdhu 64 B3
Market Bosworth 41 G5
Market Deeping 42 E4
Market Drayton 39 F2
Market Harborough 42 A7
Market Lavington 20 D6
Market Overton 42 B4
Market Rasen 52 E4
Market Stainton 53 F5
Market Street 45 G3
Market Warsop 51 H6
Market Weighton 58 E5
Market Weston 34 D1
Markethill 82 D4
Markfield 41 G4
Markham 18 E1
Markham Moor 51 K5
Markinch 82 D7
Markington 57 H3
Marks Gate 23 H2
Marks Tey 34 D6
Marksbury 19 K5
Markwell 4 D5
Markyate 32 D7
Marland 49 H1
Marlborough 20 E5
Marldon 5 J4
Marlesford 35 H3
Marley Green 38 E1
Marley Hill 62 D1
Marlingford 45 F5
Marloes 16 A4
Marlow 22 B3
Marlpit Hill 23 H7
Marnhull 9 G3
Marnoch 98 D5
Marple 49 J4
Marr 51 H2
Marrel 105 F7
Marrick 62 B7
Marrister 109 E6
Marros 17 F4
Marsden T. & W. 71 K7
Marsden W.Yorks. 50 C1
Marsett 56 E1
Marsh 8 B3
Marsh Baldon 21 J2
Marsh Benham 21 H5
Marsh Chapel 53 G3
Marsh Gibbon 31 H6
Marsh Green Devon 7 J6
Marsh Green Kent 23 H7
Marsh Green Tel. & W. 39 F4
Marsh Lane 51 G5
Marsh Street 7 H1
Marshall's Heath 32 E7
Marshalsea 8 C4
Marsham 45 F3
Marshaw 55 J4
Marshborough 15 H2
Marshbrook 38 D7
Marshchapel 53 G3
Marshfield Newport 19 F3
Marshfield S.Glos. 20 A4
Marshgate 4 B1
Marshside 48 C1
Marshwood 8 C5
Marske 62 B7
Marske-by-the-Sea 63 H4
Marston Ches. 49 F5
Marston Here. 28 C3
Marston Lincs. 42 B1
Marston Oxon. 21 J1
Marston Staffs. 40 B3
Marston Staffs. 40 A4
Marston Warks. 40 E6
Marston Wilts. 20 C6
Marston Magna 8 E2
Marston Meysey 20 E2
Marston Montgomery 40 D2
Marston Moretaine 32 C4
Marston on Dove 40 E3
Marston St. Lawrence 31 G4
Marston Stannett 28 E3
Marston Trussell 41 J7
Marstow 28 E7
Marsworth 32 C7
Marten 21 F5
Marthall 49 H5
Martham 45 J4
Marthwaite 61 H7
Martin Hants. 10 B3
Martin Lincs. 52 E6
Martin Drove End 10 B2
Martin Hussingtree 29 H2
Martinhoe 6 E1
Martinscroft 49 F4
Martinstown 9 F6
Martlesham 35 G4
Martlesham Heath 35 G4
Martletwy 16 D3
Martley 29 G2
Martock 8 D3
Marton Ches. 49 H6
Marton Cumb. 55 F2
Marton E.Riding 59 H6
Marton Lincs. 52 B4
Marton Middbro. 63 G5
Marton N.Yorks. 57 K3
Marton N.Yorks. 58 D1
Marton Shrop. 38 B5
Marton Warks. 31 F2
Marton Abbey 58 B3
Marton-le-Moor 57 J2
Martyr Worthy 11 G1
Martyr's Green 22 D6
Maruig 100 E7
Marwick 106 B5
Marwood 6 D2
Mary Tavy 5 F3
Marybank 96 B6
Maryburgh 96 C6
Maryfield 109 D8
Marygold 77 G5
Maryhill Aber. 99 G6
Maryhill Glas. 74 D4
Marykirk 83 H1
Marylebone Gt.Lon. 23 F3
Marylebone Gt.Man. 48 E2
Marypark 89 J1
Maryport Cumb. 60 B3
Maryport D. & G. 64 B7

Marystow 6 C7
Maryton 83 H2
Marywell Aber. 91 H5
Marywell Aber. 90 D5
Marywell Angus 83 H3
Masham 57 H1
Mashbury 33 K7
Mastrick 91 G4
Matching 33 J7
Matching Green 33 J7
Matching Tye 33 J7
Matfen 71 F6
Matfield 23 K7
Mathern 19 J2
Mathon 29 G4
Mathry 16 B1
Matlaske 45 F2
Matlock 51 F6
Matlock Bank 50 E6
Matlock Bath 50 E7
Matson 29 H7
Matterdale End 60 E4
Mattersey 51 J4
Mattingley 22 A6
Mattishall 44 E4
Mattishall Burgh 44 E4
Mauchline 67 K1
Maud 99 H6
Maufant 3 K7
Maugersbury 30 C6
Maughold 54 D4
Mauld 87 K1
Maulden 32 D5
Maulds Meaburn 61 H5
Maunby 57 J1
Maund Bryan 28 E3
Maundown 7 J3
Mautby 45 J4
Mavesyn Ridware 40 C4
Maw Green 40 C6
Mawbray 60 B2
Mawdesley 48 D1
Mawdlam 18 B3
Mawgan 2 E6
Mawla 2 D4
Mawnan 2 E6
Mawnan Smith 2 E6
Maxey 42 E5
Maxstoke 40 E7
Maxton Kent 15 H3
Maxton Sc.Bord. 70 B1
Maxwellheugh 77 F7
Maxwelltown 65 K3
Maxworthy 4 C1
Maybole 67 H3
Mayen 98 D6
Mayfield E.Suss. 13 J4
Mayfield Midloth. 76 B4
Mayfield Staffs. 40 D1
Mayford 22 C6
Mayland 25 F1
Maylandsea 25 F1
Maynard's Green 13 J5
Maypole I.o.S. 2 C1
Maypole Kent 25 H5
Maypole Green 45 J6
Maywick 109 C10
Meabhag 93 G2
Mead End 10 B2
Meadle 22 B1
Meadowhall 51 F3
Meadowmill 76 C3
Meadowtown 38 C5
Meal Bank 61 G7
Mealabost 101 G2
Mealasta 100 B5
Meals 53 H3
Mealsgate 60 D2
Meanley 56 C5
Mearbeck 56 D3
Meare 19 H7
Mearns 74 D5
Mears Ashby 32 B2
Measham 41 F4
Meathop 55 H1
Meavy 5 F4
Medbourne 42 B6
Meddon 6 A4
Meden Vale 51 H6
Medmenham 22 B3
Medomsley 62 C1
Medstead 11 H1
Meer End 30 D1
Meerbrook 49 J6
Meesden 33 H5
Meeth 6 D5
Meggethead 69 G1
Meidrim 17 F2
Meifod Denb. 47 J7
Meifod Powys 38 A4
Meigle 82 D3
Meikle Earnock 75 F5
Meikle Grenach 73 J4
Meikle Kilmory 73 J4
Meikle Rahane 74 A2
Meikle Strath 90 E7
Meikle Tarty 91 H2
Meikle Wartle 91 F1
Meikleour 82 C4
Meinciau 17 H3
Meir 40 B1
Meirheath 40 B1
Melbost 101 G4
Melbourn 33 G4
Melbourne Derbys. 41 F3
Melbourne E.Riding 58 D5
Melbury 6 B4
Melbury Abbas 9 H3
Melbury Bubb 8 E4
Melbury Osmond 8 E4
Melbury Sampford 8 E4
Melby 109 A7
Melchbourne 32 D2
Melchet Court 10 D2
Melcombe Bingham 9 G4
Melcombe Regis 9 F6
Meldon Devon 6 D6
Meldon Northumb. 71 G5
Meldreth 33 G4
Melfort 79 K6
Melgarve 88 B5
Melgum 90 C4
Meliden (Gallt Melyd) 47 J4
Melin-y-coed 47 G6
Melin-y-ddol 37 K5
Melin-y-grug 37 K5
Melin-y-Wig 37 K1
Melincourt 18 B1
Melincryddan 18 A2
Melinthorpe 61 G4
Melkinthorpe 61 G4
Melkridge 70 C7
Melksham 20 C5
Melksham Forest 20 C5

Melldalloch 73 H3
Melling Lancs. 55 J2
Melling Mersey. 48 C2
Melling Mount 48 D2
Mellis 34 E1
Mellon Charles 94 E2
Mellon Udrigle 94 E2
Mellor Gt.Man. 49 J4
Mellor Lancs. 56 B6
Mellor Brook 56 B6
Mells 20 A7
Melmerby Cumb. 61 H3
Melmerby N.Yorks. 57 F1
Melmerby N.Yorks. 57 J2
Melplash 8 D5
Melrose Aber. 99 F4
Melrose Sc.Bord. 76 D7
Melsetter 107 B9
Melsonby 62 C6
Meltham 50 C1
Melton 35 G3
Melton Constable 44 E2
Melton Mowbray 42 A4
Melton Ross 52 D1
Meltonby 58 D4
Melvaig 94 D3
Melverley 38 C4
Melverley Green 38 C4
Melvich 104 D2
Membury 8 B4
Memsie 99 H4
Memus 83 F2
Menabilly 4 A5
Menai Bridge (Porthaethwy) 46 D5
Mendham 45 G7
Mendlesham 35 F2
Mendlesham Green 34 E2
Menethorpe 58 D3
Menheniot 4 C4
Menie House 91 H2
Mennock 68 D3
Menston 57 G5
Menstrie 75 G1
Mentmore 32 C7
Meoble 86 D6
Meole Brace 38 D4
Meon 11 G4
Meonstoke 11 H3
Meopham 24 C5
Meopham Green 24 C5
Mepal 43 H7
Meppershall 32 E5
Merbach 28 C4
Mercaston 40 E1
Mere Ches. 49 G4
Mere Wilts. 9 H1
Mere Brow 48 D1
Mere Green 40 D6
Mereworth 23 K6
Mergie 91 F6
Meriden 40 E7
Merkland 65 H3
Merley 10 B5
Merlin's Bridge 16 C3
Merridge 8 B1
Merrifield 5 J6
Merrington 38 D3
Merrion 16 C5
Merriott 8 D3
Merrivale 5 F3
Merrow 22 D6
Merry Hill Herts. 22 E2
Merry Hill W.Mid. 40 B7
Merrymeet 4 C4
Mersham 15 F4
Merstham 23 F6
Merston 12 B6
Merstone 11 G6
Merther 3 F4
Merthyr 17 G2
Merthyr Cynog 27 J5
Merthyr Dyfan 18 E5
Merthyr Mawr 18 B4
Merthyr Tydfil 18 D1
Merthyr Vale 18 D2
Merton Devon 6 D4
Merton Gt.Lon. 23 F5
Merton Norf. 44 C6
Merton Oxon. 31 G7
Mertyn 47 K5
Mervinslaw 70 B2
Meshaw 7 F4
Messing 34 C7
Messingham 52 B2
Metfield 45 G7
Metheringham 52 D6
Methil 76 B1
Methlem 36 A2
Methley 57 J7
Methlick 91 G1
Methven 82 B5
Methwold 44 B6
Methwold Hythe 44 B6
Metrocentre 71 H7
Mettingham 45 H6
Metton 45 F2
Mevagissey 4 A6
Mexborough 51 G3
Mey 105 H1
Meysey Hampton 20 E1
Miabhag 100 C7
Miabhig 100 C4
Mial 94 D4
Michaelchurch 28 E6
Michaelchurch Escley 28 C5
Michaelchurch-on-Arrow 28 B3
Michaelston-le-Pit 18 E4
Michaelston-y-Fedw 19 F3
Michaelstow 4 A3
Micheldever 11 G1
Michelmersh 10 E2
Mickfield 35 F2
Mickle Trafford 48 D6
Mickleby 63 K5
Mickleham 22 E6
Micklehurst 49 J2
Mickleover 41 F2
Micklethwaite 60 D1
Mickleton Dur. 62 A4
Mickleton Glos. 30 C4
Mickletown 57 J7
Mickley 57 H2
Mickley Square 71 F7
Mid Ardlaw 99 H4
Mid Beltie 90 E4
Mid Cairncross 90 D7
Mid Calder 75 J4
Mid Clyth 105 H5
Mid Lavant 12 B6
Mid Letter 80 B7
Mid Lix 81 G5
Mid Mossdale 61 K7
Mid Sannox 73 J6
Mid Yell 108 E3
Midbea 106 D3
Middle Assendon 22 A3
Middle Aston 31 F6
Middle Barton 31 F6
Middle Claydon 31 J6
Middle Drums 83 G2
Middle Handley 51 G5
Middle Harling 44 D7
Middle Kames 73 H2
Middle Littleton 30 B4
Middle Maes-coed 28 C5
Middle Mill 16 B2
Middle Rasen 52 D4
Middle Rigg 82 B7
Middle Salter 56 B3
Middle Town 2 C1
Middle Tysoe 30 E4
Middle Wallop 10 D1
Middle Winterslow 10 D1
Middle Woodford 10 C1
Middlebie 69 H6
Middleham 57 G1
Middlehill Aber. 99 G6
Middlehill Cornw. 4 C4
Middlehope 38 D7
Middlemarsh 9 F4
Middlesbrough 63 F4
Middleshaw 55 J1
Middlesmoor 57 F2
Middlestone Moor 62 D3
Middlestown 50 E1
Middleton Aber. 91 G3
Middleton Angus 83 G3
Middleton Cumb. 56 B1
Middleton Derbys. 50 E7
Middleton Derbys. 50 D6
Middleton Essex 34 C4
Middleton Gt.Man. 49 H2
Middleton Hants. 21 H7
Middleton Lancs. 55 H4
Middleton Midloth. 76 B5
Middleton N.Yorks. 58 D1
Middleton Norf. 44 A4
Middleton Northants. 42 B7
Middleton Northumb. 71 F5
Middleton Northumb. 77 J7
Middleton P. & K. 82 C7
Middleton P. & K. 82 C3
Middleton Shrop. 38 B6
Middleton Shrop. 28 E1
Middleton Shrop. 38 C3
Middleton Suff. 35 J2
Middleton Swan. 17 H6
Middleton W.Yorks. 57 G5
Middleton W.Yorks. 57 H7
Middleton Warks. 40 D6
Middleton Bank Top 71 F5
Middleton Cheney 31 F4
Middleton Green 40 B2
Middleton Hall 70 E1
Middleton-in-Teesdale 62 A4
Middleton of Potterton 91 H3
Middleton-on-Leven 63 F5
Middleton-on-Sea 12 C7
Middleton on the Hill 28 E2
Middleton-on-the-Wolds 59 F5
Middleton One Row 62 E5
Middleton Park 91 H3
Middleton Priors 39 F7
Middleton Quernhow 57 J2
Middleton St. George 62 E5
Middleton Scriven 39 F7
Middleton Stoney 31 G6
Middleton Tyas 62 D6
Middletown Cumb. 60 A6
Middletown Powys 38 C4
Middlewich 49 G6
Middlewood 49 J4
Middlewood Green 34 E2
Middleyard 74 D7
Middlezoy 8 C1
Middridge 62 D4
Midfield 103 H2
Midford 20 A5
Midge Hall 55 J7
Midgeholme 61 H1
Midgham 21 J5
Midgley W.Yorks. 50 E1
Midgley W.Yorks. 57 F7
Midhopestones 50 E3
Midhurst 12 B4
Midlem 70 A1
Midpark 73 J5
Midsomer Norton 19 K6
Midtown High. 103 H2
Midtown High. 94 E3
Midtown of Barras 91 G6
Midville 53 G7
Migdale 96 D2
Migvie 90 C4
Milarrochy 74 C1
Milber 5 J3
Milbethill 98 E5
Milborne Port 9 F3
Milborne St. Andrew 9 H5
Milborne Wick 9 F2
Milbourne 71 G6
Milburn 61 H4
Milbury Heath 19 K2
Milcombe 31 F5
Milden 34 D4
Mildenhall Suff. 34 B1
Mildenhall Wilts. 21 F4
Mile Elm 20 C5
Mile End Essex 34 D6
Mile End Glos. 28 E7
Milebrook 28 C1
Milebush 14 C3
Mileham 44 D4
Milesmark 75 J2
Milfield 77 H7
Milford Derbys. 41 F1
Milford Devon 6 A3
Milford Shrop. 38 D3
Milford Staffs. 40 B3
Milford Surr. 22 C7
Milford Haven (Aberdaugleddau) 16 C4
Milford on Sea 10 D5
Milkwall 19 J1
Mill Bank 57 F7
Mill End Bucks. 22 A3
Mill End Herts. 33 G5
Mill End Green 33 K6
Mill Green Essex 24 C1
Mill Green Shrop. 39 F3
Mill Hill 23 F2
Mill Houses 56 B3
Mill Lane 22 A6
Mill of Camsail 74 A2
Mill of Colp 99 F6
Mill of Elrick 99 H6
Mill of Fortune 81 J5
Mill of Kingoodie 91 G2
Mill of Monquich 91 G5
Mill of Uras 91 G7
Mill Street 44 E4
Milland 12 B4
Millbank 99 J6
Millbeck 60 D4
Millbounds 106 E4
Millbreck 99 J6
Millbridge 22 B7
Millbrook Beds. 32 D5
Millbrook Cornw. 4 E5
Millbrook S'ham. 10 E3
Millburn Aber. 90 D2
Millburn Aber. 90 E1
Millcombe 5 J6
Millcorner 14 D5
Millden 91 H3
Milldens 83 G2
Millearne 82 A6
Millenheath 38 E2
Millerhill 76 B4
Miller's Dale 50 D5
Millholme 61 G7
Millhouse Arg. & B. 73 H3
Millhouse Cumb. 60 E3
Millhousebridge 69 G5
Millikenpark 74 C4
Millington 58 E4
Millmeece 40 A2
Millness 87 K1
Millom 54 E1
Millport 73 K5
Millthrop 61 H7
Milltimber 91 G4
Milltown Aber. 90 C3
Milltown D. & G. 69 J6
Milltown Derbys. 51 F6
Milltown Devon 6 D2
Milltown High. 97 G7
Milltown High. 95 K6
Milltown of Aberdalgie 82 B5
Milltown of Auchindoun 98 B6
Milltown of Craigston 99 F5
Milltown of Edinvillie 97 K7
Milltown of Rothiemay 98 D6
Milltown of Towie 90 C3
Milnathort 82 C7
Milngavie 74 D3
Milnrow 49 J1
Milnsbridge 50 D1
Milnthorpe 55 H1
Milovaig 93 G6
Milrig 74 D7
Milson 29 F1
Milstead 14 E2
Milston 20 E7
Milton Angus 82 E3
Milton Cambs. 33 H2
Milton Cumb. 70 A7
Milton D. & G. 68 D5
Milton D. & G. 65 J3
Milton Derbys. 41 F3
Milton High. 96 E4
Milton High. 97 G6
Milton High. 94 D7
Milton High. 96 C7
Milton High. 105 J3
Milton High. 88 B1
Milton Moray 98 D4
Milton N.Som. 19 G5
Milton Newport 19 G3
Milton Notts. 51 K5
Milton Oxon. 31 F5
Milton Oxon. 21 H2
Milton P. & K. 82 A4
Milton Pembs. 16 D4
Milton Stir. 81 G7
Milton Stir. 74 C1
Milton Stoke 49 J7
Milton W.Dun. 74 C3
Milton Abbas 9 H4
Milton Abbot 4 E3
Milton Bridge 76 A4
Milton Bryan 32 C5
Milton Clevedon 9 F1
Milton Combe 4 E4
Milton Damerel 6 B4
Milton Ernest 32 D3
Milton Green 48 D7
Milton Hill 21 H2
Milton Keynes 32 B5
Milton Keynes Village 32 B5
Milton Lilbourne 20 E5
Milton Lockhart 75 G6
Milton Malsor 31 J3
Milton Morenish 81 H4
Milton of Auchinhove 90 D4
Milton of Balgonie 82 E7
Milton of Cairnborrow 98 C6
Milton of Callander 81 G7
Milton of Campfield 90 E4
Milton of Campsie 74 E3
Milton of Coldwells 91 H1
Milton of Cullerlie 91 F4
Milton of Cushnie 90 D3
Milton of Dalcapon 82 A2
Milton of Inveramsay 91 F2
Milton of Noth 90 D2
Milton of Tullich 90 B5
Milton on Stour 9 G2
Milton Regis 24 E5
Milton-under-Wychwood 30 D7
Miltonduff 97 J5
Miltonhill 97 H5
Miltonise 64 B3
Milverton 7 K3
Milwich 40 B2
Minard 73 H1
Minard Castle 73 H1
Minchington 9 J3
Minchinhampton 20 B1
Mindrum 77 G7
Minehead 7 H1
Minera 48 B7
Minety 20 D2
Minffordd Gwyn. 37 G4
Minffordd Gwyn. 36 E2
Mingearraidh 84 C2
Miningsby 53 G6
Minions 4 C3
Minishant 67 H2
Minley Manor 22 B6
Minllyn 37 H4
Minnes 91 H2
Minnigaff 64 E4
Minnonie 99 F4
Minskip 57 J3
Minstead 10 D3
Minster Kent 25 F4
Minster Kent 25 K5
Minster Lovell 30 E7
Minsterley 38 C5
Minsterworth 29 G7
Minterne Magna 9 F4
Minting 52 E5
Mintlaw 99 J6
Minto 70 A1
Minton 38 D6
Minwear 16 D3
Minworth 40 D6
Miodar 78 B3
Mirbister 106 C5
Mireland 105 J2
Mirfield 57 G7
Miserden 20 C1
Miskin R.C.T. 18 D3
Miskin R.C.T. 18 D2
Misson 51 J3
Misterton Leics. 41 H7
Misterton Notts. 51 K3
Misterton Som. 8 D4
Mitcham 23 F5
Mitchel Troy 28 D7
Mitcheldean 29 F7
Mitchell 3 F3
Mitchelland 61 F7
Mitcheltroy Common 19 H1
Mitford 71 G5
Mithian 2 E3
Mitton 40 A4
Mixbury 31 H5
Moar 81 G3
Moat 69 K6
Mobberley 49 G5
Moccas 28 C4
Mochdre Conwy 47 G5
Mochdre Powys 37 K7
Mochrum 64 D6
Mockbeggar 14 C3
Mockerkin 60 B4
Modbury 5 G5
Moddershall 40 B2
Modsarie 103 J2
Moelfre I.o.A. 46 D4
Moelfre Powys 38 A3
Moffat 69 F3
Mogerhanger 32 E4
Moin'a'choire 72 B4
Moine House 103 H2
Moira 41 F4
Mol-chlach 85 K3
Molash 15 F2
Mold (Yr Wyddgrug) 48 B6
Molehill Green 33 J6
Molescroft 59 G5
Molesworth 32 D1
Mollance 65 H4
Molland 7 G3
Mollington Ches. 48 C5
Mollington Oxon. 31 F4
Mollinsburn 75 F3
Monachty 26 E2
Monachyle 81 F6
Moncreiffe 82 C6
Monevechadan 80 C7
Monewden 35 G3
Moneydie 82 B5
Moniaive 68 C4
Monifieth 83 F4
Monikie 83 F4
Monimail 82 D6
Monington 26 A4
Monk Fryston 58 B7
Monk Sherborne 21 K6
Monk Soham 35 G2
Monk Street 33 K6
Monken Hadley 23 F2
Monkhill 60 E1
Monkhopton 39 F6
Monkland 28 D3
Monkleigh 6 C3
Monknash 18 C4
Monkokehampton 6 D5
Monks Eleigh 34 D4
Monk's Gate 13 F4
Monks' Heath 49 H5
Monks Kirby 41 G7
Monks Risborough 22 B1
Monkseaton 71 J6
Monkshill 99 F6
Monksilver 7 J2
Monkstadt 93 J5
Monkswood 19 G1
Monkton Devon 7 K5
Monkton Kent 25 J5
Monkton S.Ayr. 67 H1
Monkton T. & W. 71 J7
Monkton Combe 20 A5
Monkton Deverill 9 H1
Monkton Farleigh 20 A5
Monkton Heathfield 8 B2
Monkton Up Wimborne 10 B3
Monkwearmouth 62 E1
Monkwood 11 H1
Monmore Green 40 B6
Monmouth (Trefynwy) 28 E7
Monnington on Wye 28 C4
Monreith 64 D6
Montacute 8 D3
Monteach 99 G6
Montford 38 D4
Montford Bridge 38 D4
Montgarrie 90 D3
Montgomery (Trefaldwyn) 38 B6
Montgreenan 74 B6
Montrave 82 E7
Montrose 83 J2
Monxton 21 G7
Monyash 50 D6
Monymusk 90 E3
Monzie 81 K5
Moodiesburn 74 E3
Moonzie 82 E6
Moor Allerton 57 J6
Moor Cock 56 B3
Moor Crichel 9 J4
Moor End Cumb. 55 J2
Moor End E.Riding 58 E6
Moor Monkton 58 B4
Moor Nook 56 B6
Moor Row 60 B5
Moor Side 53 F7
Moorby 53 F6
Moorcot 28 C3
Moordown 10 B5
Moore 48 E4
Moorends 51 J1
Moorgreen 41 G1
Moorhall 51 F5
Moorhampton 28 C4
Moorhouse Cumb. 60 E1
Moorhouse Notts. 51 K6
Moorland or Northmoor Green 8 C1
Moorlinch 8 C1
Moorsholm 63 H5
Moorside 49 J2
Moortown I.o.W. 11 F6
Moortown Lincs. 52 D3
Morangie 96 E3
Morar 86 C5
Morborne 42 E6
Morchard Bishop 7 F5
Morcombelake 8 C5
Morcott 42 C5
Morda 38 B3
Morden Dorset 9 J5
Morden Gt.Lon. 23 F5
Mordiford 28 E5
Mordington Holdings 77 H5
Mordon 62 E4
More 38 C6
Morebath 7 H3
Morebattle 70 C1
Morecambe 55 H3
Morefield 95 H2
Moreleigh 5 H5
Morenish 81 H4
Moresby 60 A4
Morestead 11 G2
Moreton Dorset 9 H6
Moreton Essex 23 J1
Moreton Here. 28 E2
Moreton Mersey. 48 B4
Moreton Oxon. 21 K1
Moreton Corbet 38 E3
Moreton-in-Marsh 30 D5
Moreton Jeffries 29 F4
Moreton Morrell 30 E3
Moreton on Lugg 28 E4
Moreton Pinkney 31 G4
Moreton Say 39 F2
Moreton Valence 20 A1
Moretonhampstead 7 F7
Morfa Bychan 36 E2
Morfa Glas 18 B1
Morfa Nefyn 36 B1
Morgan's Vale 10 C2
Mork 19 J1
Morland 61 G4
Morley Derbys. 41 F1
Morley Dur. 62 C4
Morley W.Yorks. 57 H7
Morley Green 49 H4
Morley St. Botolph 44 E5
Morningside Edin. 76 A3
Morningside N.Lan. 75 G5
Morningthorpe 45 G6
Morpeth 71 G5
Morphie 83 J1
Morrey 40 D4
Morriston S.Ayr. 67 G3
Morriston Swan. 17 K5
Morroch 86 C6
Morston 44 E1
Mortehoe 6 C1
Mortimer 21 K5
Mortimer West End 21 K5
Mortimer's Cross 28 D2
Mortlake 23 F4
Morton Derbys. 51 G6
Morton Lincs. 42 E3
Morton Lincs. 52 B3
Morton Notts. 51 K7
Morton S.Glos. 19 K2
Morton Shrop. 38 B3
Morton Bagot 30 C2
Morton-on-Swale 62 E7
Morton on the Hill 45 F4
Morvah 2 A5
Morval 4 C5
Morvich High. 87 F2
Morvich High. 96 E1
Morvil 16 D1
Morville 39 F6
Morwellham 4 E4
Morwenstow 6 A4
Morwick Hall 71 H3
Mosborough 51 G4
Moscow 74 C6
Mosedale 60 E3
Moselden Height 50 C1
Moseley W.Mid. 40 C7
Moseley Worcs. 29 H3
Moss Arg. & B. 78 A3
Moss S.Yorks. 51 H1
Moss Wrex. 48 C7
Moss Bank 48 E3
Moss Nook 49 H4
Moss of Barmuckity 97 K5
Moss Side 55 G6
Moss-side High. 97 F6
Moss-side Moray 98 D5
Mossat 90 C3
Mossbank 108 D5
Mossblown 67 J1
Mossburnford 70 B2
Mossdale 65 G3
Mossend 75 F4
Mossgiel 67 J1
Mosshead 90 D1
Mosside of Ballinshoe 83 F2
Mossley 49 J2
Mossley Hill 48 C4
Mosspaul Hotel 69 K4
Mosstodloch 98 B4
Mosston 83 G3
Mosterton 8 D4
Mostyn 47 K4
Motcombe 9 H2
Motherby 61 F4
Motherwell 75 F5
Mottingham 23 H4
Mottisfont 10 E2
Mottistone 11 F6
Mottram in Longdendale 49 J3
Mottram St. Andrew 49 H5
Mouldsworth 48 E5
Moulin 82 A2
Moulsecoomb 13 G6
Moulsford 21 J3
Moulsham 24 D1
Moulsoe 32 C4
Moulton Ches. 49 F6
Moulton Lincs. 43 G3
Moulton N.Yorks. 62 D6
Moulton Northants. 31 J2
Moulton Suff. 33 K2
Moulton Chapel 43 F4
Moulton St. Mary 45 H5
Moulton Seas End 43 G3
Mounie Castle 91 F2
Mount Cornw. 2 E3
Mount Cornw. 4 B4
Mount High. 97 G7
Mount Bures 34 D5
Mount Hawke 2 E4
Mount Manisty 48 C5
Mount Oliphant 67 H2
Mount Pleasant Derbys. 41 F1
Mount Pleasant Suff. 35 J1
Mount Tabor 57 F7
Mountain Ash 18 D2
Mountain Cross 75 K6
Mountain Water 16 C2
Mountbenger 69 J1
Mountblairy 98 E5
Mountfield 14 C5
Mountgerald 96 C5
Mountjoy 3 F2
Mountnessing 24 C2
Mounton 19 J2
Mountsorrel 41 H4
Mountstuart 73 K5
Mousehole 2 B6
Mouswald 69 F6
Mow Cop 49 H7
Mowden 62 D5
Mowhaugh 70 D1
Mowsley 41 J7
Mowtie 91 G6
Moxley 40 B6
Moy High. 87 H6
Moy High. 88 B6
Moy High. 88 E1
Moy House 97 H5
Moyles Court 10 C4
Moylgrove 26 A4
Muasdale 72 E6
Much Birch 28 E5
Much Cowarne 29 F4
Much Dewchurch 28 D5
Much Hadham 33 H7
Much Hoole 55 H7
Much Marcle 29 F5
Much Wenlock 39 F5
Muchalls 91 G5
Muchelney 8 D2
Muchlarnick 4 C5
Muchra 69 H2
Muchrachd 87 J1
Mucking 24 C3
Mucklestone 39 G2
Muckleton 38 E3
Muckletown 90 D2
Muckton 53 G4
Mudale 103 H5
Muddiford 6 D2
Muddles Green 13 J5
Muddleswood 13 F5
Mudeford 10 C5
Mudford 8 E3
Mudgley 19 H7
Mugeary 85 K1
Mugginton 40 E1
Muggleswick 62 B1
Muie 96 D1
Muir 89 H6
Muir of Fowlis 90 D3
Muir of Lochs 98 B4
Muir of Ord 96 C6
Muirden 99 F5
Muirdrum 83 G4
Muirhead Aber. 90 D3
Muirhead Angus 82 E4
Muirhead Fife 82 D7
Muirhead Moray 97 H5
Muirhead N.Lan. 74 E4
Muirhouses 75 J2
Muirkirk 68 B1
Muirmill 75 F2
Muirtack Aber. 91 H1
Muirtack Aber. 99 G6
Muirton 96 E5
Muirton of Ardblair 82 C3
Muirton of Ballochy 83 H1
Muirtown 82 A6
Muiryfold 99 F5
Muker 62 A7
Mulbarton 45 F5
Mulben 98 B5
Mulhagery 101 F7
Mullach Charlabhaigh 100 E3
Mullacott Cross 6 D1
Mullion 2 D7
Mumby 53 J5
Munderfield Row 29 F3
Munderfield Stocks 29 F3
Mundesley 45 H2
Mundford 44 B6
Mundham 45 H6
Mundon 24 E1
Mundurno 91 H3
Munerigie 87 J4
Mungasdale 95 F2
Mungoswells 76 C3
Mungrisdale 60 E3
Munlochy 96 D6
Munnoch 74 A6
Munsley 29 F4
Munslow 38 E7
Murchington 6 E7
Murcott 31 G7
Murdostoun 75 G5
Murkle 105 G2
Murlaganmore 81 G4
Murlaggan High. 87 G5
Murlaggan High. 87 K6
Murra 107 B7
Murroes 83 F4
Murrow 43 G5
Mursley 32 B6
Murston 25 F5
Murthill 83 F2
Murthly 82 B4
Murton Cumb. 61 J4
Murton Dur. 62 E2
Murton Northumb. 77 H6
Murton York 58 C4
Musbury 8 B5
Muscoates 58 C1
Musdale 80 A5
Musselburgh 76 B3
Muston Leics. 42 B2
Muston N.Yorks. 59 H2
Mustow Green 29 H1
Mutford 45 J7
Muthill 81 K6
Mutterton 7 J5
Mybster 105 G3
Myddfai 27 G5
Myddle 38 D3
Myddlewood 38 D3
Mydroilyn 26 D3
Mylor 3 F5
Mylor Bridge 3 F5
Mynachlog-ddu 16 E1
Myndtown 38 C7
Mynydd-bach 19 H2
Mynydd Llandygai 46 E6
Mynytho 36 C2
Myrebird 91 F5
Mytchett 22 B6
Mytholm 56 E7
Mytholmroyd 57 F7
Myton-on-Swale 57 K3

N

Naast 94 E3
Naburn 58 B5
Nackington 15 G2
Nacton 35 G4
Nafferton 59 G4
Nailbridge 29 F7
Nailsea 19 H4
Nailstone 41 G5
Nailsworth 20 B2
Nairn 97 F6
Nancegollan 2 D5
Nancledra 2 B5
Nanhoron 36 B2
Nannau 37 G3
Nannerch 47 K6
Nanpantan 41 H4
Nanpean 3 G3
Nanstallon 4 A4
Nant-ddu 27 K7
Nant-glas 27 J2
Nant Peris 46 E7
Nant-y-derry 19 G1
Nant-y-dugoed 37 J4
Nant-y-groes 27 K2
Nant-y-moel 18 C2
Nant-y-Pandy 46 E5
Nanternis 26 C3
Nantgaredig 17 H2
Nantgarw 18 E3
Nantglyn 47 J6
Nantlle 46 D7
Nantmawr 38 B3
Nantmel 27 K2
Nantmor 37 F1
Nantwich 49 F7
Nantycaws 17 H3
Nantyffyllon 18 B2
Nantyglo 18 E1
Naphill 22 B2
Nappa 56 D4
Napton on the Hill 31 F2
Narberth (Arberth) 16 E3
Narborough Leics. 41 H6
Narborough Norf. 44 B4
Narrachan 80 A6
Nasareth 46 C7
Naseby 31 H1
Nash Bucks. 31 J5
Nash Here. 28 C2
Nash Newport 19 G3
Nash Shrop. 28 E1
Nash V. of Glam. 18 C4
Nash Lee 22 B1
Nassington 42 D6
Nasty 33 G6
Nateby Cumb. 61 J6
Nateby Lancs. 55 H5
Nately Scures 22 A6
Natland 55 J1
Naughton 34 E4
Naunton Glos. 30 C6
Naunton Worcs. 29 H5
Naunton Beauchamp 29 J3
Navenby 52 C7
Navestock 23 J2
Navestock Side 23 J2
Navidale 105 F7
Navity 96 E5
Nawton 58 C1
Nayland 34 D5
Nazeing 23 H1
Neacroft 10 C5
Neal's Green 41 F7
Neap 109 E7
Near Cotton 40 C1
Near Sawrey 60 E7
Neasham 62 E5
Neath (Castell-Nedd) 18 A2
Neatham 22 A7
Neatishead 45 H3
Nebo Cere. 26 E2
Nebo Conwy 47 G7
Nebo Gwyn. 46 C7
Nebo I.o.A. 46 C3
Necton 44 C5
Nedd 102 D5
Nedderton 71 H5
Nedging Tye 34 E4
Needham 45 G7
Needham Market 34 E3
Needingworth 33 G1
Neen Savage 29 F1
Neen Sollars 29 F1
Neenton 39 F7
Nefyn 36 C1
Neilston 74 C5
Nelson Caerp. 18 E2
Nelson Lancs. 56 D6
Nelson Village 71 H6
Nemphlar 75 G6
Nempnett Thrubwell 19 J5
Nenthall 61 J2
Nenthead 61 J2
Nenthorn 76 E7
Nerabus 72 A5
Nercwys 48 B6
Neriby 72 B4
Nerston 74 E5
Nesbit 77 H7
Ness 48 C5
Ness of Tenston 107 B6
Nesscliffe 38 C4

Neston Ches. 48 B5
Neston Wilts. 20 B5
Nether Alderley 49 H5
Nether Auchendrane 67 H2
Nether Barr 64 E4
Nether Blainslie 76 D6
Nether Broughton 41 J3
Nether Burrow 56 B2
Nether Cerne 9 F5
Nether Compton 8 E3
Nether Crimond 91 G2
Nether Dalgliesh 69 H3
Nether Dallachy 98 B4
Nether End 50 E5
Nether Exe 7 H6
Nether Glasslaw 99 G5
Nether Handwick 82 E3
Nether Haugh 51 G3
Nether Headon 51 K5
Nether Heselden 56 D2
Nether Heyford 31 H3
Nether Kellet 55 J3
Nether Kinmundy 99 J6
Nether Langwith 51 H5
Nether Lenshie 98 E6
Nether Moor 51 F6
Nether Padley 50 E5
Nether Pitforthie 91 G7
Nether Poppleton 58 B4
Nether Silton 63 F7
Nether Stowey 7 K2
Nether Urquhart 82 C7
Nether Wallop 10 E1
Nether Wasdale 60 C6
Nether Wellwood 68 B1
Nether Whitacre 40 E6
Nether (Lower) Winchendon 31 J7
Nether Worton 31 F5
Netheravon 20 E7
Netherbrae 99 F5
Netherbrough 107 C6
Netherburn 75 G6
Netherbury 8 D5
Netherby Cumb. 69 J6
Netherby N.Yorks. 57 J5
Nethercott 31 F6
Netherend 19 J2
Netherfield E.Suss. 14 C6
Netherfield Notts. 41 J1
Netherfield S.Lan. 75 F6
Netherhall 74 A4
Netherhampton 10 C1
Netherley 91 G5
Nethermill 69 F5
Nethermuir 99 H6
Netherseal 40 E4
Nethershield 67 K1
Netherstreet 20 C5
Netherthird D. & G. 65 H5
Netherthird E.Ayr. 67 K2
Netherthong 50 D1
Netherthorpe 51 H4
Netherton Angus 83 G2
Netherton Ches. 48 E5
Netherton Devon 5 J3
Netherton Mersey. 48 C2
Netherton Northumb. 70 E3
Netherton Oxon. 21 H2
Netherton P. & K. 82 C2
Netherton S.Lan. 75 H5
Netherton W.Mid. 40 B7
Netherton W.Yorks. 50 E1
Netherton W.Yorks. 50 D1
Netherton Worcs. 29 J4
Nethertown Cumb. 60 A6
Nethertown Ork. 105 J1
Netherwitton 71 G5
Netherwood D. & G. 65 K3
Netherwood E.Ayr. 68 B1
Nethy Bridge 89 H2
Netley Abbey 11 F4
Netley Marsh 10 E3
Nettlebed 22 A3
Nettlebridge 19 K7
Nettlecombe Dorset 8 E5
Nettlecombe Som. 7 J2
Nettleden 32 D7
Nettleham 52 D5
Nettlestead Kent 23 K6
Nettlestead Suff. 34 E4
Nettlestead Green 23 K6
Nettlestone 11 H5
Nettleton Lincs. 52 E2
Nettleton Wilts. 20 B4
Netton Devon 5 F6
Netton Wilts. 10 C1
Neuadd Cere. 26 D3
Neuadd I.o.A. 46 B3
Neuadd Powys 27 J4
Nevendon 24 D2
Nevern 16 D1
Nevill Holt 42 B6
New Abbey 65 K4
New Aberdour 99 G4
New Addington 23 G5
New Alresford 11 G1
New Alyth 82 D3
New Arley 40 E6
New Ash Green 24 C5
New Barn 24 C5
New Barnet 23 F2
New Belses 70 A1
New Bewick 71 F1
New Bolingbroke 53 G7
New Bradwell 32 B4
New Bridge 65 K3
New Brighton Hants. 11 J4
New Brighton Mersey. 48 C3
New Brinsley 51 G7
New Broughton 48 C7
New Buckenham 44 E6
New Byth 99 G5
New Cheriton 11 G2
New Costessey 45 F5
New Cross 27 F1
New Cumnock 68 B2
New Deer 99 G6
New Duston 31 J2
New Earswick 58 C4
New Edlington 51 H3
New Elgin 97 K5
New Ellerby 59 H6

New Eltham 23 H4
New End 30 B2
New England 42 E5
New Farnley 57 H6
New Ferry 48 C4
New Fryston 57 K7
New Galloway 65 G3
New Gilston 83 F7
New Grimsby 2 B1
New Hartley 71 J6
New Haw 22 D5
New Hedges 16 E4
New Holland 59 G7
New Houghton Derbys. 51 H6
New Houghton Norf. 44 B3
New Houses 56 D2
New Hutton 61 G7
New Hythe 14 C2
New Inn Carmar. 17 H1
New Inn Fife 82 D7
New Inn Mon. 19 H1
New Inn Torfaen 19 F2
New Invention Shrop. 28 B1
New Invention W.Mid. 40 B5
New Lanark 75 G6
New Lane 48 D1
New Leake 53 H7
New Leeds 99 H5
New Leslie 90 D2
New Longton 55 J7
New Luce 64 B4
New Mains Cornw. 2 B5
New Mains of Ury 91 G6
New Malden 23 F5
New Marske 63 H4
New Marton 38 C2
New Mill Cornw. 2 B5
New Mill Herts. 32 C7
New Mill W.Yorks. 50 D2
New Mill End 32 E7
New Mills Cornw. 3 F3
New Mills Derbys. 49 J4
New Mills Mon. 19 J1
New Mills Powys 37 K5
New Milton 10 D5
New Mistley 35 F5
New Moat 16 D2
New Orleans 66 B2
New Park 4 B2
New Pitsligo 99 G5
New Polzeath 3 G1
New Quay (Ceinewydd) 26 C3
New Rackheath 45 G4
New Radnor 28 B2
New Rent 61 F3
New Romney 15 F5
New Rossington 51 J3
New Row 56 B6
New Sawley 41 G2
New Scone 82 C5
New Silksworth 62 D1
New Town E.Loth. 76 C3
New Town L.Isl. 13 H4
New Town Glos. 30 B5
New Tredegar 18 E1
New Ulva 73 F2
New Walsoken 43 H5
New Waltham 53 F2
New Winton 76 C3
New Yatt 30 E7
New York Lincs. 53 F7
New York T. & W. 71 J6
Newark Ork. 106 G3
Newark Peter. 43 F5
Newark-on-Trent 52 B7
Newarthill 75 F5
Newbarn 71 G3
Newbarns 55 F2
Newbiggin Cumb. 61 H4
Newbiggin Cumb. 61 G2
Newbiggin Cumb. 55 F3
Newbiggin Dur. 62 A4
Newbiggin N.Yorks. 57 F1
Newbiggin N.Yorks. 62 A7
Newbiggin Northumb. 70 E7
Newbiggin-by-the-Sea 71 J5
Newbigging-on-Lune 61 J6
Newbigging Aber. 91 G5
Newbigging Aber. 89 J6
Newbigging Angus 83 F4
Newbigging Angus 83 F4
Newbigging Angus 82 D3
Newbigging S.Lan. 75 J6
Newbold Derbys. 51 F5
Newbold Leics. 41 G4
Newbold on Avon 31 F1
Newbold on Stour 30 D4
Newbold Pacey 30 D3
Newbold Verdon 41 G5
Newborough I.o.A. 46 C6
Newborough Peter. 43 F5
Newborough Staffs. 40 D3
Newbottle 35 G5
Newbourne 35 G4
Newbridge (Cefn Bychan) Caerp. 19 F2
Newbridge Cornw. 2 B5
Newbridge Cornw. 4 D4
Newbridge Edin. 75 K3
Newbridge Hants. 10 E3
Newbridge I.o.W. 11 F6
Newbridge Oxon. 21 H1
Newbridge Pembs. 16 C1
Newbridge Wrex. 38 B1
Newbridge-on-Usk 19 G2
Newbridge on Wye 27 K3
Newbrough 70 D7
Newburgh Aber. 99 H5
Newburgh Aber. 91 H2
Newburgh Fife 82 D6
Newburgh Lancs. 48 D1
Newburgh Sc.Bord. 69 J2
Newburn 71 G7
Newbury Cumb. 21 H5
Newby Lancs. 56 D5
Newby N.Yorks. 56 C2
Newby N.Yorks. 62 C2
Newby Bridge 55 G1
Newby East 61 F1
Newby West 60 E1

Newby Wiske 57 J1
Newcastle Bridgend 18 C4
Newcastle Mon. 28 D7
Newcastle Shrop. 38 B7
Newcastle Emlyn (Castell Newydd Emlyn) 26 C4
Newcastle International Airport 71 G6
Newcastle-under-Lyme 40 A1
Newcastle upon Tyne 71 H7
Newcastleton 69 K5
Newchapel Pembs. 17 F1
Newchapel Stoke 49 H7
Newchapel Surr. 23 G7
Newchurch Carmar. 17 G2
Newchurch I.o.W. 11 G6
Newchurch Kent 15 F4
Newchurch Lancs. 56 D7
Newchurch Lancs. 56 D6
Newchurch Mon. 19 H2
Newchurch Powys 28 B3
Newcott 8 B4
Newcraighall 76 B3
Newdigate 22 E7
Newell Green 22 B4
Newenden 14 D5
Newent 29 G6
Newerne 19 K1
Newfield Dur. 62 D3
Newfield Dur. 62 D1
Newfield High. 96 E4
Newgale 16 B2
Newgate 44 E1
Newgate Street 23 G1
Newgord 108 E2
Newhall Ches. 39 F1
Newhall Derbys. 40 E3
Newham Gt.Lon. 23 G3
Newham Northumb. 71 G1
Newham Hall 71 G1
Newhaven 13 H6
Newhey 49 J1
Newholm 63 K5
Newhouse 75 F4
Newick 13 H4
Newington Kent 15 G4
Newington Kent 24 E5
Newington Oxon. 21 K2
Newington Bagpath 20 B2
Newland Glos. 19 J1
Newland N.Yorks. 58 C7
Newland Worcs. 29 G4
Newlandrig 76 B4
Newlands Northumb. 62 B1
Newlands Sc.Bord. 70 A4
Newland's Corner 22 D7
Newlands of Geise 105 F2
Newlyn 2 B6
Newlyn East 3 F3
Newmachar 91 G3
Newmains 75 G5
Newmarket Suff. 33 K2
Newmarket W.Isles 101 G4
Newmill Aber. 91 F6
Newmill Aber. 99 G6
Newmill Aber. 91 G2
Newmill Moray 98 C5
Newmill Sc.Bord. 69 K2
Newmill of Inshewan 83 F1
Newmills 96 D5
Newmiln P. & K. 82 C4
Newmiln P. & K. 82 B5
Newmilns 74 D7
Newnham Glos. 29 F7
Newnham Hants. 22 A6
Newnham Herts. 33 F5
Newnham Kent 14 E2
Newnham Northants. 31 G3
Newnham Worcs. 29 F2
Newnham Paddox 41 G7
Newnoth 90 D1
Newport Cornw. 6 B7
Newport Devon 6 D2
Newport E.Riding 58 E6
Newport Essex 33 J5
Newport Glos. 19 K2
Newport High. 105 G6
Newport I.o.W. 11 G6
Newport (Casnewydd) Newport 19 G3
Newport Norf. 45 K4
Newport Pembs. 16 D1
Newport Tel. & W. 39 G4
Newport-on-Tay 83 F5
Newport Pagnell 32 B4
Newpound Common 12 D4
Newquay 3 F2
Newquay (Cornwall) Airport 3 F2
Newseat 91 F1
Newsham Lancs. 55 J6
Newsham N.Yorks. 62 C5
Newsham N.Yorks. 57 J1
Newsham Northumb. 71 H6
Newsholme E.Riding 58 D7
Newsholme Lancs. 56 D4
Newstead 71 G1
Newstead Notts. 51 H7
Newstead Sc.Bord. 76 D7
Newthorpe 57 K6
Newton Aber. 98 C6
Newton Aber. 91 G6
Newton Arg. & B. 73 J1
Newton Bridgend 18 B4
Newton Cambs. 43 H4
Newton Cambs. 33 H4
Newton Ches. 48 D7
Newton Ches. 48 E5
Newton Cumb. 55 F2
Newton D. & G. 69 G4
Newton Gt.Man. 49 J3
Newton Here. 28 C5
Newton Here. 28 D3
Newton High. 105 J4
Newton High. 96 E7

Newton High. 105 H3
Newton High. 102 E5
Newton High. 96 C6
Newton High. 96 E5
Newton Lancs. 56 B4
Newton Lancs. 55 J2
Newton Lincs. 42 D2
Newton Moray 98 B4
Newton N.Ayr. 73 H5
Newton Norf. 44 C4
Newton Northants. 42 B7
Newton Northumb. 71 F7
Newton Notts. 41 J1
Newton P. & K. 81 K4
Newton Pembs. 16 C2
Newton Pembs. 16 C4
Newton Sc.Bord. 70 B1
Newton Staffs. 40 C3
Newton Suff. 34 D4
Newton Swan. 17 K6
Newton W.Loth. 75 J3
Newton W.Yorks. 57 K7
Newton Warks. 31 G1
Newton Wilts. 10 D2
Newton Abbot 5 J3
Newton Arlosh 60 C1
Newton Aycliffe 62 D4
Newton Bewley 63 F4
Newton Blossomville 32 C3
Newton Bromswold 32 D2
Newton Burgoland 41 F5
Newton by Toft 52 D4
Newton Ferrers 5 F6
Newton Flotman 45 G6
Newton Harcourt 41 J6
Newton Kyme 57 K5
Newton-le-Willows Mersey. 48 E3
Newton-le-Willows N.Yorks. 57 H1
Newton Longville 32 B5
Newton Mearns 74 D5
Newton Morrell 62 D6
Newton Mountain 16 C4
Newton Mulgrave 63 J5
Newton of Affleck 83 F4
Newton of Ardtoe 86 C7
Newton of Balcanquhal 82 C6
Newton of Dalvey 97 H6
Newton of Falkland 82 D7
Newton of Leys 96 D7
Newton-on-Ouse 58 B3
Newton-on-Rawcliffe 63 K7
Newton-on-the-Moor 71 G3
Newton on Trent 52 B5
Newton Popplefor 7 J7
Newton Purcell 31 H5
Newton Regis 40 E5
Newton Reigny 61 F3
Newton St. Cyres 7 G6
Newton St. Faith 45 G4
Newton St. Loe 20 A5
Newton St. Petrock 6 C4
Newton Solney 40 E3
Newton Stacey 21 H7
Newton Stewart 64 E4
Newton Tony 21 F7
Newton Tracey 6 D3
Newton under Roseberry 63 G5
Newton upon Derwent 58 D5
Newton Valence 11 J1
Newtonairds 68 D5
Newtongrange 76 B4
Newtonhill 91 H5
Newtonmill 83 H1
Newtonmore 88 E5
Newtown B.Gwent 28 A7
Newtown Bucks. 22 C1
Newtown Ches. 48 D7
Newtown Cumb. 70 A7
Newtown Derbys. 49 J4
Newtown Hants. 11 H3
Newtown Hants. 21 H5
Newtown Hants. 10 D3
Newtown Hants. 11 G2
Newtown Hants. 11 G3
Newtown Here. 29 G5
Newtown Here. 29 F4
Newtown High. 87 K4
Newtown I.o.M. 54 C6
Newtown I.o.W. 11 F5
Newtown Northumb. 71 F3
Newtown Northumb. 71 F1
Newtown Poole 10 B5
Newtown (Y Drenewydd) Powys 38 A6
Newtown Shrop. 38 D2
Newtown Staffs. 49 J6
Newtown Staffs. 50 C6
Newtown Wilts. 9 J2
Newtown in St. Martin 2 E6
Newtown Linford 41 H4
Newtown St. Boswells 76 D7
Newtown Unthank 41 G5
Newtyle 82 D3
Neyland 16 C4
Nibley Glos. 19 K1
Nibley S.Glos. 19 K3
Nicholashayne 7 K4
Nicholaston 17 J6
Nidd 57 J3
Niddrie 76 A3
Nigg Aberdeen 91 H4
Nigg High. 97 F4
Nightcott 7 G3
Nilig 47 J7
Nimlet 20 A4
Nine Ashes 23 J1
Nine Elms 20 E3
Nine Mile Burn 75 K5
Ninebanks 61 J2
Ninemile Bar or Crocketford 65 J3
Ninfield 14 C6
Ningwood 11 F6
Nisbet 70 B1
Niton 11 G7
Nitshill 74 D4
Nizels 23 J6
No Man's Heath Ches. 38 E1

No Man's Heath Warks. 40 E5
Noak Hill 23 J2
Noblehill 65 K3
Nobottle 31 H2
Nocton 52 D6
Noddsdale 74 A4
Noke 31 G7
Nolton 16 B3
Nomansland Devon 7 G4
Nomansland Wilts. 10 D3
Noneley 38 D3
Nonington 15 H2
Nook Cumb. 69 K6
Nook Cumb. 55 J1
Noonsbrough 109 B7
Noranside 83 F1
Norbiton 22 E5
Norbreck 55 G5
Norbury Ches. 38 E1
Norbury Derbys. 40 D1
Norbury Gt.Lon. 23 G5
Norbury Shrop. 38 C6
Norbury Staffs. 39 G3
Norchard 29 H2
Nordelph 43 J5
Norden 9 J6
Nordley 39 F6
Norham 77 H6
Norland Town 57 F7
Norley 48 E5
Norleywood 10 E5
Norman Cross 42 E6
Normanby N.Lincs. 52 B1
Normanby N.Yorks. 58 D1
Normanby R. & C. 63 G5
Normanby-by-Spital 52 D4
Normanby by Stow 52 B4
Normanby le Wold 52 E3
Normandy 22 C6
Normann's Ruh 79 F3
Norman's Bay 13 K6
Norman's Green 7 J5
Normanton Derby 41 F2
Normanton Leics. 42 B1
Normanton Lincs. 42 C1
Normanton Notts. 51 K7
Normanton Rut. 42 C5
Normanton W.Yorks. 57 J7
Normanton le Heath 41 F4
Normanton on Soar 41 H3
Normanton-on-the-Wolds 41 J2
Normanton on Trent 51 K6
Normoss 55 G6
Norrington Common 20 B5
Norris Hill 41 F4
North Anston 51 H4
North Ascot 22 C5
North Aston 31 F6
North Baddesley 10 E2
North Ballachulish 80 B1
North Balloch 67 H4
North Barrow 9 F2
North Barsham 44 D2
North Benfleet 24 D3
North Bersted 12 C6
North Berwick 76 D2
North Boarhunt 11 H3
North Bogbain 98 B5
North Bovey 7 F7
North Bradley 20 B6
North Brentor 6 C7
North Brewham 9 G1
North Buckland 6 C1
North Burlingham 45 H4
North Cadbury 9 F2
North Cairn 66 D6
North Camp 22 B6
North Carlton Lincs. 52 C5
North Carlton Notts. 51 H4
North Cave 58 E6
North Cerney 20 D1
North Chailey 13 G4
North Charford 10 C2
North Charlton 71 G1
North Cheriton 9 F2
North Cliffe 58 E6
North Clifton 52 B5
North Cockerington 53 G3
North Coker 8 E3
North Connel 80 A4
North Cornelly 18 B3
North Cotes 53 G2
North Cove 45 J7
North Cowton 62 D6
North Crawley 32 C4
North Cray 23 H4
North Creake 44 C2
North Curry 8 C2
North Dallens 80 A3
North Dalton 59 F4
North Dawn 107 D7
North Deighton 57 J4
North Duffield 58 C6
North Elkington 53 F3
North Elmham 44 D3
North Elmsall 51 G1
North End Bucks. 32 B6
North End Essex 33 K7
North End Hants. 21 H5
North End N.Som. 19 H5
North End Norf. 44 E6
North End Northumb. 71 G3
North End Ports. 11 H4
North End W.Suss. 12 E5
North Erradale 94 D3
North Essie 99 J5
North Ferriby 59 F7
North Frodingham 59 H4
North Gorley 10 C3
North Green 45 G7
North Grimston 58 E3
North Hayling 11 J4
North Hazelrigg 77 J7
North Heasley 7 F2
North Heath 12 D5
North Hill 4 C3
North Hinksey 21 H1
North Holmwood 22 E7
North Huish 5 H5
North Hykeham 52 C6
North Johnston 16 C3
North Kelsey 52 D2
North Kessock 96 D7
North Killingholme 52 E1

North Kilvington 57 K1
North Kilworth 41 J7
North Kyme 52 E7
North Lancing 12 E6
North Lee 22 B1
North Leigh 30 E7
North Leverton with Habblesthorpe 51 K4
North Littleton 30 B4
North Lopham 44 E7
North Luffenham 42 C5
North Marden 12 B5
North Marston 31 J6
North Middleton 76 B5
North Millbrex 99 G6
North Molton 7 F3
North Moreton 21 J3
North Mundham 12 B6
North Muskham 51 K7
North Newbald 59 F6
North Newington 31 F5
North Newnton 20 E6
North Newton 8 B1
North Nibley 20 A2
North Oakley 21 J6
North Ockendon 23 J3
North Ormesby 63 G4
North Ormsby 53 F3
North Otterington 62 E7
North Owersby 52 D3
North Perrott 8 D4
North Petherton 8 B1
North Petherwin 4 C2
North Pickenham 44 C5
North Piddle 29 J3
North Poorton 8 E5
North Queensferry 75 K2
North Radworthy 7 F2
North Rauceby 42 D1
North Reston 53 G4
North Rigton 57 H5
North Rode 49 H6
North Roe 108 C4
North Runcton 44 A4
North Sandwick 108 E3
North Scale 54 E3
North Scarle 52 B6
North Seaton 71 H5
North Shian 80 A3
North Shields 71 J7
North Shoebury 25 F3
North Side 43 F6
North Skelton 63 H5
North Somercotes 53 H3
North Stainley 57 H2
North Stainmore 61 K5
North Stifford 24 C3
North Stoke B. & N.E.Som. 19 K5
North Stoke Oxon. 21 K3
North Stoke W.Suss. 12 D5
North Stoneham 11 F3
North Street Hants. 11 H1
North Street Kent 15 F2
North Street W.Berks. 21 K4
North Sunderland 77 K4
North Tamerton 6 B6
North Tarbothill 91 H3
North Tawton 6 E5
North Third 75 F2
North Thoresby 53 F3
North Tidworth 21 F7
North Togston 71 H3
North Town Devon 6 D5
North Town Hants. 22 B6
North Tuddenham 44 E4
North Walsham 45 G2
North Waltham 21 J7
North Warnborough 22 A6
North Watten 105 H3
North Weald Bassett 23 H1
North Wheatley 51 K4
North Whilborough 5 J4
North Wick 19 J5
North Widcombe 19 J6
North Willingham 52 E4
North Wingfield 51 G6
North Witham 42 C3
North Wootton Dorset 9 F3
North Wootton Norf. 44 A3
North Wootton Som. 19 J7
North Wraxall 20 B4
North Wroughton 20 E3
North Yardhope 70 E3
Northacre 44 D6
Northall Green 44 E4
Northallerton 62 E7
Northam Devon 6 C3
Northam S'ham. 11 F3
Northampton 31 J2
Northaw 23 F1
Northay 8 B3
Northborough 42 E5
Northbourne 15 J2
Northbrook 31 F6
Northburnhill 99 G6
Northchapel 12 C4
Northchurch 22 C1
Northcote Manor 6 E4
Northcott 6 B6
Northdyke 106 B5
Northend B. & N.E.Som. 20 A5
Northend Bucks. 22 A2
Northend Warks. 30 E3
Northfield Aber. 99 G4
Northfield Aberdeen 91 G4
Northfield High. 105 J4
Northfield Sc.Bord. 77 H4
Northfield W.Mid. 30 B1
Northfleet 24 C4
Northhouse 69 K3
Northiam 14 D5
Northill 32 E4
Northington 21 J7
Northlands 53 G7
Northleach 30 C7
Northleigh Devon 7 K6
Northleigh Devon 6 D6
Northlew 6 D6
Northmoor 21 H1
Northmoor Green or Moorland 8 C1
Northmuir 82 E2
Northney 11 J4
Northolt 22 E3
Northop 48 B6

Northop Hall 48 B6
Northorpe Lincs. 43 F2
Northorpe Lincs. 52 B3
Northorpe Lincs. 42 D4
Northover 8 E2
Northowram 57 G7
Northpunds 109 D10
Northrepps 45 G2
Northton (Taobh Tuath) 92 E3
Northtown 107 D8
Northway 29 J5
Northwich 49 F5
Northwick 19 J3
Northwold 44 B6
Northwood Gt.Lon. 22 D2
Northwood I.o.W. 11 F5
Northwood Shrop. 38 C2
Northwood Green 29 G7
Norton Glos. 29 H6
Norton Halton 48 E4
Norton Herts. 33 F5
Norton I.o.W. 10 E6
Norton N.Yorks. 58 D2
Norton Northants. 31 H2
Norton Notts. 51 H5
Norton Powys 28 C2
Norton S.Yorks. 51 H1
Norton S.Yorks. 51 G2
Norton Shrop. 38 E5
Norton Shrop. 39 G5
Norton Shrop. 38 D7
Norton Stock. 63 F4
Norton Suff. 34 D2
Norton W.Mid. 40 A7
Norton W.Suss. 12 C6
Norton Wilts. 20 B3
Norton Worcs. 29 H3
Norton Worcs. 30 B4
Norton Bavant 20 C7
Norton Bridge 40 A3
Norton Canes 40 C5
Norton Canon 28 C4
Norton Disney 52 B7
Norton Ferris 9 G1
Norton Fitzwarren 7 K3
Norton Green 10 E6
Norton Hawkfield 19 J5
Norton Heath 24 C1
Norton in Hales 39 G2
Norton in the Moors 49 H7
Norton-Juxta-Twycross 41 F5
Norton-le-Clay 57 J2
Norton Lindsey 30 D2
Norton Malreward 19 J5
Norton Mandeville 23 J1
Norton St. Philip 20 A6
Norton sub Hamdon 8 D3
Norton Subcourse 45 J6
Norton Wood 28 C4
Norwell 51 K6
Norwell Woodhouse 51 K6
Norwich 45 G5
Norwich Airport 45 G4
Norwick 108 F1
Norwood Green 22 E4
Norwood Hill 23 F7
Noseley 42 A6
Noss Mayo 5 F6
Nosterfield 57 H1
Nostie 86 E2
Notgrove 30 C6
Nottage 18 B4
Nottingham High. 105 H6
Nottingham Nott. 41 H1
Notton W.Yorks. 51 F1
Notton Wilts. 20 C5
Nounsley 34 B1
Noutard's Green 29 G2
Nowton 34 C2
Nox 38 D4
Noyadd Trefawr 26 B4
Nuffield 21 K3
Nun Monkton 58 B4
Nunburnholme 58 E5
Nuneaton 41 F6
Nuneham Courtenay 21 J2
Nunney 20 A7
Nunnington 58 C2
Nunnington Park 7 J3
Nunthorpe 63 G5
Nunton 10 C2
Nunwick N.Yorks. 57 J2
Nunwick Northumb. 70 D6
Nup End Bucks. 32 B7
Nup End Glos. 29 H6
Nursling 10 E3
Nursted 11 J2
Nurton 40 A6
Nutbourne W.Suss. 12 D5
Nutbourne W.Suss. 11 J4
Nutfield 23 G6
Nuthall 41 H1
Nuthampstead 33 H5
Nuthurst W.Suss. 12 E4
Nuthurst Warks. 30 C1
Nutley E.Suss. 13 H3
Nutley Hants. 21 K7
Nutwell 51 J2
Nyadd 75 F1
Nybster 105 J2
Nyetimber 12 B7
Nyewood 11 J2
Nymet Rowland 7 F5
Nymet Tracey 7 F5
Nympsfield 20 B1
Nynehead 7 K3
Nythe 8 D1
Nyton 12 C6

O

Oad Street 24 E5
Oadby 41 J5
Oak Cross 6 D6
Oakamoor 40 C1
Oakbank Arg. & B. 79 J4
Oakbank W.Loth. 75 J4
Oakdale 18 E2
Oake 7 K3
Oaken 40 A5
Oakenclough 55 J5
Oakengates 39 G4
Oakenhead 97 K5
Oakenshaw Dur. 62 C3
Oakenshaw W.Yorks. 57 G7
Oakford Cere. 26 D3
Oakford Devon 7 H3

Oakfordbridge 7 H3
Oakgrove 49 J6
Oakham 42 B5
Oakhanger 11 J1
Oakhill 19 K7
Oakington 33 H2
Oaklands *Conwy* 47 G7
Oaklands *Herts.* 33 F7
Oakle Street 29 G3
Oakley *Beds.* 32 D3
Oakley *Bucks.* 31 H1
Oakley *Fife* 75 J2
Oakley *Hants.* 21 J6
Oakley *Suff.* 35 F1
Oakley Green 22 C4
Oakley Park 37 J7
Oakridge Lynch 20 C1
Oaks 38 D5
Oaksey 20 C2
Oakshaw Ford 70 A6
Oakthorpe 41 F4
Oaktree Hill 62 E7
Oakwoodhill 12 E3
Oakworth 57 F6
Oalinlongart 73 K2
Oare *Kent* 25 G5
Oare *Som.* 7 G1
Oare *Wilts.* 20 E5
Oasby 42 D2
Oatfield 66 A2
Oathlaw 83 F2
Oban 79 K5
Obley 28 C1
Oborne 9 F3
Occlestone Green 49 F6
Occold 35 F1
Occumster 105 H5
Ochiltree 67 K1
Ochr-y-Mynydd 18 D1
Ochtermuthill 81 K6
Ochtertyre *P. & K.* 81 K5
Ochtertyre *Stir.* 75 F1
Ockbrook 41 G2
Ockham 22 D6
Ockle 86 B7
Ockley 12 E3
Ocle Pychard 28 E4
Octon 59 G3
Odcombe 8 E3
Odd Down 20 A5
Oddingley 29 J3
Oddington 31 G7
Oddsta 108 E3
Odell 32 C3
Odie 106 F5
Odiham 22 A6
Odstock 10 C2
Odstone 41 F5
Offchurch 30 E2
Offenham 30 B4
Offerton 49 J4
Offham *E.Suss.* 13 H5
Offham *Kent* 23 K6
Offord Cluny 33 F2
Offord D'Arcy 33 F2
Offton 7 K6
Offwell 7 K6
Ogbourne Maizey 20 E4
Ogbourne St. 20 E4
  Andrew
Ogbourne St. 20 E4
  George
Ogden 57 F6
Ogil 83 F1
Ogle 71 G6
Ogmore 18 B4
Ogmore-by-Sea 18 B4
Ogmore Vale 18 C2
Oil Terminal 107 C8
Okeford Fitzpaine 9 H3
Okehampton 6 D6
Okehampton Camp 6 D6
Okraquoy 109 D9
Old 31 J1
Old Aberdeen 91 H4
Old Alresford 11 G1
Old Arley 40 E6
Old Basford 41 H1
Old Basing 21 K6
Old Belses 70 A1
Old Bewick 71 F1
Old Bolingbroke 53 G6
Old Brampton 51 F5
Old Bridge of Urr 65 H4
Old Buckenham 44 E6
Old Burghclere 21 H6
Old Byland 58 B1
Old Cleeve 7 J1
Old Clipstone 51 J6
Old Colwyn 47 G5
Old Craig 91 H2
Old Craighall 76 B3
Old Crombie 98 D5
Old Dailly 67 G4
Old Dalby 41 J3
Old Deer 99 H6
Old Ellerby 59 H6
Old Felixstowe 35 H5
Old Fletton 42 E6
Old Glossop 50 C3
Old Goginan 37 F7
Old Goole 58 D7
Old Gore 29 F6
Old Grimsby 2 B1
Old Hall 53 F1
Old Heath 34 E6
Old Hill 40 B7
Old Hutton 55 J1
Old Kea 3 F4
Old Kilpatrick 74 C3
Old Kinnernie 91 F4
Old Knebworth 33 F6
Old Leake 53 H7
Old Leslie 90 D2
Old Malton 58 D2
Old Micklefield 57 K6
Old Milverton 30 D2
Old Montsale 25 G2
Old Netley 11 F3
Old Newton 34 E2
Old Philpstoun 75 J3
Old Poltalloch 79 K7
Old Radnor 28 B3
Old Rattray 99 J5
Old Rayne 90 E2
Old Romney 15 F5
Old Scone 82 C5
Old Shields 75 G3
Old Sodbury 20 A3
Old Somerby 42 C2
Old Stratford 31 J4
Old 59 G4
  Sunderlandwick
Old Swarland 71 G3
Old Swinford 40 B7
Old Town *Cumb.* 55 J1
Old Town *I.o.S.* 2 C1
Old Town 70 C1
  Northumb.

Old Tupton 51 F6
Old Warden 32 E4
Old Weston 32 E1
Old Windsor 22 C4
Old Wives Lees 15 F2
Old Woking 22 D6
Old Wolverton 32 K4
Old Woods 38 D3
Oldberrow 30 C2
Oldborough 7 F5
Oldbury *Kent* 23 J6
Oldbury *Shrop.* 39 G6
Oldbury *W.Mid.* 40 B6
Oldbury *Warks.* 41 F6
Oldbury Naite 19 K2
Oldbury on the Hill 20 B3
Oldbury-on-Severn 19 K2
Oldcastle 28 C6
Oldcastle Heath 38 D1
Oldcotes 51 H4
Oldfield *H.Yorks.* 57 F6
Oldfield *Worcs.* 29 H2
Oldford 20 A6
Oldhall *Aber.* 90 C5
Oldhall *High.* 105 H3
Oldhamstocks 77 F3
Oldhurst 33 F1
Oldland 19 K4
Oldmeldrum 91 G2
Oldmill 90 D4
Oldpark 39 F5
Oldridge 7 G6
Oldshore Beg 102 D3
Oldshore More 102 E3
Oldstead 58 B1
Oldtown of Aigas 96 B7
Oldtown of Ord 98 E5
Oldwalls 17 H5
Oldways End 7 G3
Oldwhat 99 G5
Olgrinmore 105 F3
Oliver 69 G1
Oliver's Battery 11 F2
Ollaberry 108 C4
Ollerton *Ches.* 49 G5
Ollerton *Notts.* 51 J6
Ollerton *Shrop.* 39 F3
Olmstead Green 33 K4
Olney 32 B3
Olrig House 105 G2
Olton 40 D7
Olveston 19 J3
Ombersley 29 H2
Ompton 51 J6
Onchan 54 C6
Onecote 50 C7
Onen 28 D1
Ongar Hill 43 J3
Ongar Street 28 C2
Onibury 28 D1
Onich 80 B1
Onllwyn 27 H7
Onneley 39 G1
Onslow Village 22 C7
Opinan *High.* 94 E2
Opinan *High.* 94 D4
Orange Lane 77 F6
Orbliston 98 B5
Orbost 93 H7
Orby 53 H6
Orcadia 73 K4
Orchard 73 K2
Orchard Portman 8 B2
Orchard Wyndham 7 J2
Orcheston 20 D7
Orcop 28 D6
Orcop Hill 28 D6
Ord 86 C3
Ordhead 90 E3
Ordie 90 C4
Ordiequish 98 B5
Ordsall 51 K5
Ore 14 D6
Oreham Common 13 F5
Oreston 5 F5
Oreton 39 F7
Orford *Suff.* 35 J4
Orford *Warr.* 49 F3
Orgreave 40 D4
Orleton *Here.* 28 D2
Orleton *Worcs.* 29 F2
Orleton Common 28 D2
Orlingbury 32 B1
Ormacleit 84 C1
Ormesby 63 G5
Ormesby St. 45 J4
  Margaret
Ormesby St. 45 J4
  Michael
Ormiscaig 94 E2
Ormiston 76 C4
Ormsaigmore 79 F1
Ormsary 73 F2
Ormskirk 48 D2
Ormwe 105 G2
Orphir 107 C7
Orpington 23 H5
Orrell 48 E2
Orrisdale 54 C4
Orrok House 91 H3
Orroland 65 H6
Orsett 24 C3
Orslow 40 A4
Orston 42 A1
Orton *Cumb.* 61 H6
Orton *Northants.* 32 B1
Orton Longueville 42 E6
Orton-on-the-Hill 41 F5
Orton Waterville 42 E6
Orwell 33 G4
Osbaldeston 56 B6
Osbaldwick 58 C4
Osbaston *Leics.* 41 G5
Osbaston *Tel.&W.* 38 E4
Osbournby 42 D2
Oscroft 48 E6
Ose 93 J7
Osgathorpe 41 G4
Osgodby *Lincs.* 52 D3
Osgodby *N.Yorks.* 58 C6
Osgodby *N.Yorks.* 59 G1
Oskaig 86 B1
Osmaston *Derby* 41 F2
Osmaston *Derbys.* 40 D1
Osmington 9 G6
Osmington Mills 9 G6
Osmotherley 63 F7
Osnaburgh or 83 F6
  Dairsie
Osney 21 J1
Ospringe 15 F2
Ossett 57 H7
Ossington 51 K6
Ostend 25 F2
Osterley 22 E4
Oswaldkirk 58 C2
Oswaldtwistle 56 C7
Oswestry 38 B3

Otford 23 J6
Otham 14 C2
Othery 8 C1
Otley *Suff.* 35 G3
Otley *W.Yorks.* 57 H5
Otter 73 H3
Otter Ferry 73 H2
Otterbourne 11 F2
Otterburn 56 D4
  N.Yorks.
Otterburn 70 D4
  Northumb.
Otterburn Camp 70 D4
Otterden Place 14 E2
Otterham 4 B1
Otterhampton 19 F7
Ottershaw 22 D5
Otterswick 108 E4
Otterton 7 J7
Ottery St. Mary 7 J6
Ottinge 15 G3
Ottringham 59 J7
Oughterby 60 D1
Oughtershaw 56 D1
Oughtibridge 51 F3
Oulston 58 B2
Oulton *Cumb.* 60 D1
Oulton *Norf.* 45 F3
Oulton *Staffs.* 40 B2
Oulton *Suff.* 45 K6
Oulton *W.Yorks.* 57 J7
Oulton Broad 45 K6
Oulton Street 45 F3
Oundle 42 D7
Ousby 61 H3
Ousdale 105 F6
Ousden 34 B3
Ousefleet 58 E7
Ouston *Dur.* 62 D1
Ouston 71 F6
  Northumb.
Out Newton 59 K7
Out Rawcliffe 55 H5
Outgate 60 E7
Outhgill 61 J6
Outlands 39 G3
Outlane 50 C1
Outwell 43 J5
Outwood *Surr.* 23 G7
Outwood 57 J7
  W.Yorks.
Ovenden 57 F7
Over *Cambs.* 33 G2
Over *Ches.* 49 F6
Over *S.Glos.* 19 J3
Over Compton 8 E3
Over End 50 E5
Over Haddon 50 E6
Over Kellet 55 J2
Over Kiddington 31 F6
Over Norton 30 E6
Over Peover 49 G5
Over Rankeilour 82 E6
Over Silton 63 F7
Over Stowey 7 K2
Over Stratton 8 D3
Over Tabley 49 G4
Over Wallop 10 D1
Over Whitacre 40 E6
Over (Upper) 31 J7
  Winchendon
Over Worton 31 F6
Overbister 106 F3
Overbrae 99 G5
Overbury 29 J5
Overcombe 9 F6
Overleigh 8 D1
Overpool 48 C5
Overscaig Hotel 103 G6
Overseal 40 E4
Oversland 15 F2
Oversley Green 30 B3
Overstone 32 B2
Overstrand 45 G1
Overton *Aber.* 91 F3
Overton *Aberdeen* 91 G3
Overton *Hants.* 21 J7
Overton *Lancs.* 55 H4
Overton *N.Yorks.* 58 B4
Overton *Shrop.* 28 E1
Overton *Swan.* 17 H6
Overton *Wrex.* 38 C1
Overtown 75 G5
Overy Staithe 44 C1
Oving *Bucks.* 31 J6
Oving *W.Suss.* 12 C6
Ovingdean 13 G6
Ovingham 71 F7
Ovington *Dur.* 62 C5
Ovington *Essex* 34 B4
Ovington *Hants.* 11 G1
Ovington *Norf.* 44 D5
Ovington 71 F7
  Northumb.
Ower 10 E3
Owermoigne 9 G6
Owlswick 22 A1
Owmby 52 D2
Owmby-by-Spital 52 D4
Owlsebury 11 G2
Owston 42 A5
Owston Ferry 52 B2
Owstwick 59 J6
Owthorpe 41 J2
Oxborough 44 B5
Oxcliffe Hill 55 H3
Oxcombe 53 G5
Oxen End 33 K6
Oxen Park 55 G1
Oxenhall 29 G6
Oxenholme 61 G7
Oxenhope 57 F6
Oxenton 29 J5
Oxenwood 21 G6
Oxford 21 J1
Oxhill 30 E4
Oxley 40 B5
Oxley Green 34 D7
Oxley's Green 13 K4
Oxnam 70 B2
Oxnead 45 G3
Oxnop Ghyll 62 A7
Oxshott 22 E5
Oxspring 50 E2
Oxted 23 G6
Oxton *Mersey.* 48 C4
Oxton *Notts.* 51 J7
Oxton *Sc.Bord.* 76 C5
Oxwich 17 H6
Oxwich Green 17 J6
Oxwick 44 D3
Oykel Bridge 95 K1
Oyne 90 E2
Ozleworth 20 A2

P
Pabail Iarach 101 H4
Pabail Uarach 101 H4

Packington 41 F4
Padanaram 83 F2
Padbury 31 J5
Paddington 23 F3
Paddlesworth 15 G3
Paddock Wood 23 K7
Paddockhaugh 97 K6
Paddockhole 69 H5
Paddolgreen 38 E2
Padiham 56 C6
Padside 57 G4
Padstow 3 G1
Padworth 21 K5
Pagham 12 B7
Paglesham 25 F2
  Churchend
Paglesham 25 F2
  Eastend
Paibeil 92 C5
Paible 93 F2
Paignton 5 J4
Pailton 41 G7
Painscastle 28 A4
Painshawfield 71 F7
Painswick 20 B1
Paisley 74 C4
Pakefield 45 K6
Pakenham 34 D2
Pale 37 J2
Palestine 21 F7
Paley Street 22 B4
Palgowan 67 H5
Palgrave 35 F1
Pallinsburn House 77 G7
Palmerscross 97 K5
Palmerstown 18 E5
Palnackie 65 J5
Palnure 64 E4
Palterton 51 G6
Pamber End 21 K6
Pamber Green 21 K6
Pamber Heath 21 K5
Pamington 29 J5
Pamphill 9 J4
Pampisford 33 H4
Pan 107 C8
Panborough 19 H7
Panbride 83 G4
Pancrasweek 6 A5
Pandy *Gwyn.* 37 F5
Pandy *Mon.* 28 C6
Pandy *Powys* 37 J5
Pandy *Wrex.* 38 A2
Pandy Tudur 47 G6
Panfield 34 B6
Pangbourne 21 K4
Pannal 57 J4
Panpunton 28 B1
Pant *Shrop.* 38 B3
Pant *Wrex.* 38 B1
Pant Glas 36 D1
Pant *Gwyn.* 37 H3
Pant-lasau 17 K4
Pant Mawr 37 H7
Pant-pastynog 47 J6
Pant-y-dwr 27 J1
Pant-y-ffridd 38 A5
Pantasaph 47 K5
Panteg 19 G2
Pantglas 38 G6
Pantgwyn 26 B4
Panton 52 E5
Pantperthog 37 G5
Pantyffordd 48 B7
Pantyffynnon 17 K3
Panxworth 45 H4
Papcastle 60 C3
Papple 76 D3
Papplewick 51 H7
Papworth Everard 33 F2
Papworth St. 33 F2
  Agnes
Par 4 A5
Parbold 48 D1
Parbrook 8 E1
Parc 37 H2
Parc-Seymour 19 H2
Parcllyn 26 B3
Parcrhydderch 27 F3
Pardshaw 60 B4
Parham 35 H2
Parish Holm 68 C1
Park 98 D5
Park Corner 21 K3
Park End 70 D6
Park Gate 11 G4
Park Lane 38 D2
Park Street 22 E1
Parkend *Cumb.* 60 D3
Parkend *Glos.* 19 K1
Parkeston 35 G5
Parkford 83 F2
Parkgate *Ches.* 48 B5
Parkgate *D.&G.* 69 F5
Parkgate *S.Yorks.* 51 G3
Parkgate *Surr.* 23 F7
Parkham 6 B3
Parkham Ash 6 B3
Parkhill *Angus* 83 H3
Parkhill *P.&K.* 82 C4
Parkhouse 19 J1
Parkhurst 11 F5
Parkmill 17 J6
Parkmore 98 B6
Parkneuk 91 F7
Parkstone 10 B5
Parley Cross 10 B5
Parracombe 6 E1
Parrog 16 D1
Parson Drove 43 G5
Parsonby 60 C3
Partick 74 D4
Partington 49 G3
Partney 53 H6
Parton *Cumb.* 60 A4
Parton *D.&G.* 65 G3
Partridge Green 12 E5
Parwich 50 D7
Passenham 31 J5
Passfield 12 B3
Passingford Bridge 23 H2
Paston 45 H2
Patchacott 6 C6
Patcham 13 G6
Patchole 6 E1
Patchway 19 J3
Pateley Bridge 57 G3
Path of Condie 82 B6
Pathe 8 C1
Pathfinder Village 7 G6
Pathhead *Aber.* 83 J1
Pathhead *E.Ayr.* 68 B2
Pathhead *Fife* 76 A1
Pathhead *Midloth.* 76 B4
Patmore Heath 33 H6
Patna 67 J2
Patney 20 D6
Patrick 54 B5
Patrick Brompton 62 D7

Patrington 59 K7
Patrishow 28 B6
Patrixbourne 15 G2
Patterdale 60 E5
Pattingham 40 A6
Pattishall 31 H3
Pattiswick 34 C6
Paul 2 B6
Paulerspury 31 J4
Paull 59 H7
Paulton 19 K6
Pauperhaugh 71 G4
Pavenham 32 C3
Pawlett 19 F7
Pawston 77 G7
Paxford 30 C5
Paxhill Park 13 G4
Paxton 77 H5
Payhembury 7 J5
Paynes Hall 33 G7
Paythorne 56 D4
Peacehaven 13 H6
Peacemarsh 9 H2
Peachley 29 H3
Peak Dale 50 C5
Peak Forest 50 D5
Peakirk 42 E5
Pean Hill 25 H5
Pearsie 82 E2
Pease Pottage 13 F3
Peasedown St. 20 A6
  John
Peasemore 21 H4
Peasenhall 35 H2
Peaslake 22 D7
Peasmarsh 14 D5
Peaston 76 C4
Peastonbank 76 C4
Peat Inn 83 F7
Peathill 99 H4
Peatling Magna 41 H6
Peatling Parva 41 H7
Peaton 38 E7
Pebble Coombe 23 F6
Pebmarsh 34 C5
Pebworth 30 C4
Pecket Well 56 E7
Peckforton 48 E7
Peckleton 41 G5
Pedmore 40 B7
Pedwell 8 D1
Peebles 76 A6
Peel 54 B5
Pegswood 71 H5
Peighinn nan 84 C1
  Aoireann
Peinchorran 86 B1
Peinlich 93 K7
Pelaw 71 H7
Pelcomb Bridge 16 C3
Pelcomb Cross 16 C3
Peldon 34 D7
Pelsall 40 C5
Pelton 62 D1
Pelutho 60 C2
Pelynt 4 C5
Pemberton 48 E2
Pembrey 17 H4
Pembridge 28 C3
Pembroke (Penfro) 16 C4
Pembroke Dock 16 C4
  (Doc Penfro)
Pembury 23 K7
Pen-bont 37 F7
  Rhydybeddau
Pen-clawdd 17 J5
Pen-ffordd 16 D2
Pen-groes-oped 19 G1
Pen-llyn 46 B4
Pen-sarn *Gwyn.* 36 E3
Pen-sarn *Gwyn.* 36 D1
Pen-twyn 19 J1
Pen-y-banc 17 K2
Pen-y-bont 27 G5
  Carmar.
Pen-y-bont *Powys* 37 K4
Pen-y-bont *Powys* 38 B3
Pen-y-Bont ar 18 C4
  Ogwr (Bridgend)
Pen-y-bryn 37 F4
Pen-y-cae 27 H7
Pen-y-cae-mawr 19 H2
Pen-y-cefn 47 K5
Pen-y-clawdd 19 H1
Pen-y-coedcae 18 D3
Pen-y-fai 18 B3
Pen-y-garn 17 J1
Pen-y-garreg 27 F4
Pen-y-Gwryd Hotel 46 E7
Pen-y-Park 28 B4
Pen-y-sarn 46 C3
Pen-y-stryt 47 K7
Pen-yr-heol 28 E7
Penallt 28 E7
Penally 16 E5
Penalt 28 E6
Penare 3 G4
Penarth 18 E4
Penboyr 17 G1
Penbryn 26 B3
Pencader 17 H1
Pencaenewydd 36 D1
Pencaitland 76 C4
Pencarreg 26 E4
Pencelli 27 K6
Pencoed 18 C3
Pencombe 28 E3
Pencoyd 28 E6
Pencraig *Here.* 28 E6
Pencraig *Powys* 37 K3
Pendeen 2 A5
Penderyn 18 C1
Pendine 17 F4
Pendlebury 49 G2
Pendleton 56 C6
Pendock 29 G5
Pendomer 8 E3
Pendoylan 18 D4
Penegoes 37 G5
Penffordd 16 D2
  Carmar.
Pengam 18 E2
Penge 23 G4
Pengenffordd 28 A5
Pengorffwysfa 46 C3
Pengover Green 4 C4
Penhale 2 D7
Penhallow 2 E3
Penhalvean 2 E5
Penhow 19 H2
Penhurst 13 K5
Peniarth 37 F5
Penicuik 76 A4
Peniel 17 H2
Penifiler 93 K7
Peninver 66 B1
Penisa'r Waun 46 D6
Penisarcwn 37 K4
Penistone 50 E2

Penjerrick 2 E5
Penketh 48 E4
Penkill 67 G4
Penkridge 40 B4
Penley 38 D2
Penllech 36 B2
Penllergaer 17 K5
Penllyn 18 C4
Penmachno 47 F7
Penmaen 17 J6
Penmaenmawr 47 F5
Penmaenpool 37 F4
Penmark 18 D5
Penmon 46 E4
Penmorfa 36 E1
Penmynydd 46 D5
Penn *Bucks.* 22 C2
Penn *W.Mid.* 40 A6
Penn Street 22 C2
Pennal 37 F5
Pennan 99 G4
Pennance 2 E4
Pennant *Cere.* 26 E2
Pennant *Powys* 37 H6
Pennant Melangell 37 K3
Pennard 17 J6
Pennerley 38 C6
Penninghame 64 D4
Pennington 55 F2
Pennsylvania 20 A4
Penny Bridge 55 G1
Pennyfuir 79 K4
Pennyghael 79 G5
Pennyglen 67 G2
Pennygown 79 H3
Pennymoor 7 G4
Penparc *Cere.* 26 B4
Penparc *Pembs.* 16 B7
Penparcau 36 E7
Penperlleni 19 G1
Penpillick 4 A5
Penpol 2 E5
Penpoll 4 B5
Penpont *D.&G.* 68 D4
Penpont *Powys* 27 J6
Penprysg 18 C3
Penrherber 17 F1
Penrhiw-llan 26 C4
Penrhiw-pal 26 C4
Penrhiwceiber 18 D2
Penrhiwgoch 17 J3
Penrhos *Gwyn.* 36 C2
Penrhos *I.o.A.* 46 A4
Penrhos *Mon.* 28 D7
Penrhos *Powys* 27 H7
Penrhos-garnedd 46 D5
Penrhyn Bay 47 G4
  (Bae Penrhyn)
Penrhyn-coch 37 F7
Penrhyn-side 47 G4
Penrhyndeudraeth 37 F2
Penrhys 18 D2
Penrice 17 H6
Penrith 61 G3
Penrose 3 F1
Penruddock 61 F4
Penryn 2 E5
Pensarn *Carmar.* 17 H3
Pensarn *Conwy* 47 H5
Pensax 29 G2
Pensby 48 B4
Penselwood 9 G1
Pensford 19 K5
Pensham 29 J4
Penshaw 62 E1
Penshurst 23 J7
Pensilva 4 C4
Pensnett 40 B7
Pentewan 4 A6
Pentir 46 D6
Pentire 2 E2
Pentireglaze 3 G1
Pentlepoir 16 E4
Pentlow 34 C4
Pentney 44 B4
Penton Mewsey 21 G7
Pentraeth 46 D5
Pentre *Powys* 37 K3
Pentre *Powys* 28 B2
Pentre *Powys* 38 B6
Pentre *R.C.T.* 18 C2
Pentre *Shrop.* 38 C4
Pentre *Wrex.* 38 C1
Pentre-bach 27 J5
Pentre Berw 46 C5
Pentre-bont 37 F7
Pentre-bwlch 38 A1
Pentre-celyn 47 K7
  Denb.
Pentre-celyn 37 H5
  Powys
Pentre-chwyth 17 K5
Pentre-cwrt 17 G1
Pentre-Dolau- 27 J4
  Honddu
Pentre-dwr 17 K5
Pentre Galar 16 E1
Pentre Gwenlais 17 K3
Pentre Gwynfryn 36 E3
Pentre Halkyn 48 B5
Pentre Isaf 47 G6
Pentre Llanrhaeadr 47 J6
Pentre-Llwyn- 27 J3
  llwyd
Pentre-llyn- 47 H7
  cymmer
Pentre Maelor 38 C1
Pentre-piod 37 H2
Pentre-Poeth 19 F3
Pentre Saron 47 J6
Pentre-tafarn-y- 47 G6
  fedw
Pentre-ty-gwyn 27 H5
Pentrebach *M.Tyd.* 18 D1
Pentrebach *Swan.* 17 K4
Pentrecagal 26 C4
Pentreclwydau 18 B1
Pentredwr 38 A1
Pentrefelin 17 J2
  Carmar.
Pentrefelin *Cere.* 27 F4
Pentrefelin 47 G5
  Conwy
Pentrefelin *Gwyn.* 36 E2
Pentrefelin *Powys* 38 A3
Pentrefoelas 47 G7
Pentregat 26 C3
Pentreheyling 38 B6
Pentre'r beirdd 38 A4
Pentre'r-felin 27 J5
Pentrich 51 F7
Pentridge 10 B3
Pentwyn 19 F2
Pentyrch 18 E3
Penuwch 26 E2
Penwithick 4 A5
Penwortham 55 J7
Penwyllt 27 H7

Penybont 28 A2
Penybontfawr 37 K3
Penybryn 18 E2
Penycae 38 B1
Penycwm 16 B2
Penyffordd 48 C6
Penygarnedd 38 A3
Penygraig 18 C2
Penygroes 17 J3
  Carmar.
Penygroes *Gwyn.* 46 C7
Penywaun 18 C1
Penzance 2 B5
Penzance Heliport 2 B5
Peopleton 29 J3
Peover Heath 49 G5
Peper Harow 22 C7
Peplow 39 F3
Perceton 74 B6
Percie 90 D5
Perham Down 21 F7
Perivale 22 E3
Perkhill 90 D4
Perkins Beach 38 C5
Perlethorpe 51 J5
Perranarworthal 2 E5
Perranporth 2 E3
Perranuthnoe 2 C6
Perranzabuloe 2 E3
Perry Barr 40 C6
Perry Green 33 H7
Perry Street 24 C4
Pershall 40 A3
Pershore 29 J4
Persie House 82 C2
Pert 83 H1
Pertenhall 32 D2
Perth 82 C5
Perthy 38 C2
Perton 40 A6
Peter Tavy 5 F3
Peterborough 42 E6
Peterburn 94 D3
Peterchurch 28 C5
Peterculter 91 G4
Peterhead 99 K6
Peterlee 63 F2
Peter's Green 32 E7
Peters Marland 6 C4
Petersfield 11 J2
Peterstone 19 F3
  Wentlooge
Peterstow 28 E6
Petham 15 G2
Petrockstow 6 D5
Pett 14 D6
Pettaugh 35 F3
Pettinain 75 H6
Pettistree 35 G3
Petton *Devon* 7 J3
Petton *Shrop.* 38 D3
Petty 91 F1
Pettycur 76 A2
Pettymuick 91 H2
Petworth 12 C4
Pevensey 13 K6
Pevensey Bay 13 K6
Pewsey 20 E5
Phesdo 90 E7
Philham 6 A3
Philiphaugh 69 K1
Phillack 2 C5
Philleigh 3 F5
Philpstoun 75 J3
Phocle Green 29 F6
Phoenix Green 22 A6
Phones 88 E5
Phorp 97 H6
Pibsbury 8 D2
Pica 60 B4
Piccadilly Corner 45 G7
Piccotts End 22 D1
Pickerells 23 J1
Pickering 58 E1
Picket Piece 21 G7
Picket Post 10 C4
Pickford Green 40 E7
Pickhill 57 J1
Picklescott 38 D6
Pickletillem 83 F5
Pickmere 49 F5
Pickston 82 A5
Pickwell *Devon* 6 C1
Pickwell *Leics.* 42 A4
Pickworth *Lincs.* 42 D2
Pickworth *Rut.* 42 C4
Picton *Ches.* 48 D5
Picton *N.Yorks.* 63 F6
Piddinghoe 13 H6
Piddington 32 B3
  Northants.
Piddington *Oxon.* 31 H7
Piddletrenthide 9 G5
Pidley 33 G1
Piercebridge 62 D5
Pierowall 106 D3
Pigdon 71 G5
Pikehall 50 D7
Pilgrims Hatch 23 J2
Pilham 52 B3
Pill 19 J4
Pillaton 4 D4
Pillerton Hersey 30 D4
Pillerton Priors 30 D4
Pilleth 28 B2
Pilley *Glos.* 29 J7
Pilley *Hants.* 10 E5
Pilley *S.Yorks.* 51 F2
Pilling 55 H5
Pilling Lane 55 G5
Pillowell 19 K1
Pilning 19 J3
Pilsbury 50 D6
Pilsdon 8 D5
Pilsgate 42 D5
Pilsley *Derbys.* 51 G6
Pilsley *Derbys.* 50 E5
Piltdown 13 H4
Pilton *Devon* 6 D2
Pilton *Northants.* 42 D7
Pilton *Rut.* 42 C5
Pilton *Som.* 19 J7
Pimperne 9 J4
Pinchbeck 43 F3
Pinchbeck Bars 43 F3
Pinchbeck West 43 F3
Pinchinthorpe 63 G5
Pinfold 48 C1
Pinhay 8 C5
Pinhoe 7 H6
Pinkneys Green 22 B3
Pinley Green 30 D2
Pinminnoch 67 F4
Pinmore 67 G4

Place	Page	Grid
Pinn	7	K7
Pinner	22	E3
Pinner Green	22	E2
Pinvin	29	J4
Pinwherry	67	F5
Pinxton	51	K7
Pipe and Lyde	28	E4
Pipe Gate	39	G1
Pipe Ridware	40	C4
Piperhill	73	J5
Piperhill	97	F6
Pipers Pool	4	C2
Pipewell	42	B7
Pippacott	6	D2
Pipton	28	A5
Pirbright	22	C6
Pirnmill	73	G6
Pirton *Herts.*	32	E5
Pirton *Worcs.*	29	H4
Pisgah	81	J7
Pishill	22	A3
Pistyll	36	C1
Pitagowan	81	K1
Pitblae	99	H4
Pitcairngreen	82	B5
Pitcairns	82	B6
Pitcaple	91	F2
Pitch Green	22	A1
Pitch Place	22	C6
Pitchcombe	20	B1
Pitchcott	31	J7
Pitchford	38	E5
Pitcombe	9	F1
Pitcot	18	B4
Pitcox	76	E3
Pitcur	82	D4
Pitfichie	90	E3
Pitgrudy	96	E2
Pitinnan	91	F1
Pitkennedy	83	G2
Pitkevy	82	D7
Pitlessie	82	E7
Pitlochry	82	A2
Pitmedden	91	G2
Pitminster	8	B3
Pitmuies	83	G3
Pitmunie	90	E3
Pitnacree	82	A2
Pitney	8	D2
Pitroddie	82	D5
Pitscottie	83	F6
Pitsea	24	D3
Pitsford	31	J2
Pitsford Hill	7	J2
Pitstone	32	C7
Pitstone Green	32	C7
Pitt *Devon*	7	J4
Pitt *Hants.*	11	F2
Pittendreich	97	J5
Pittentrail	96	E1
Pittenweem	83	G7
Pittington	62	E2
Pittodrie House	90	E2
Pitton	10	D1
Pity Me	62	D2
Pixey Green	35	G1
Place Newton	58	E2
Plaidy	99	F5
Plains	75	F4
Plaish	38	E6
Plaistow	12	D3
Plaitford	10	D3
Plas	17	H2
Plas Gogerddan	37	F7
Plas Gwynant	46	E7
Plas Isaf	37	K1
Plas Llwyd	47	H5
Plas Llwyngwern	37	G5
Plas Llysyn	37	J6
Plas Nantyr	38	A2
Plas-rhiw-Saeson	37	J5
Plas-yn-Cefn	47	J5
Plasisaf	47	H6
Plastow Green	21	J5
Platt	23	K6
Platt Bridge	49	F2
Platt Lane	38	E2
Plawsworth	62	D2
Plaxtol	23	K6
Play Hatch	22	A4
Playden	14	E5
Playford	35	G4
Playing Place	3	F4
Plealey	38	D5
Plean	75	G2
Pleasance	82	D6
Pleasington	56	B7
Pleasley	51	H6
Plenmeller	70	C7
Pleshey	33	K7
Plockton	86	E5
Ploughfield	28	C4
Plowden	38	C7
Ploxgreen	38	C5
Pluckley	14	E3
Pluckley Thorne	14	E3
Plumbland	60	C3
Plumley	49	G5
Plumpton *Cumb.*	61	F3
Plumpton *E.Suss.*	13	G5
Plumpton End	31	J4
Plumpton Green	13	G5
Plumpton Head	61	G3
Plumstead *Gt.Lon.*	23	H4
Plumstead *Norf.*	45	F2
Plumtree	41	J2
Plungar	42	A2
Plush	9	G4
Plwmp	26	C3
Plym Bridge	5	F5
Plymouth	4	E5
Plymouth City Airport	5	F4
Plympton	5	F5
Plymstock	5	F5
Plymtree	7	J5
Pockley	58	C1
Pocklington	58	E5
Pocombe Bridge	7	G6
Pode Hole	43	F3
Podimore	8	E2
Podington	32	C2
Podmore	39	G2
Pointon	42	E2
Pokesdown	10	C5
Polanach	80	A2
Polapit Tamar	6	B7
Polbae	67	F5
Polbain	102	B7
Polbathic	4	D5
Polbeth	75	J4
Polchar	89	F4
Poldean	69	G4
Pole Moor	50	C1
Polebrook	42	D7
Polegate	13	J6
Poles	96	E2
Polesworth	40	E5
Polglass	95	G1
Polgooth	3	G3
Polgown	68	C3
Poling	12	D6
Poling Corner	12	D6
Polkerris	4	A5
Poll a' Charra	84	C3
Polla	103	F3
Polldubh	80	C1
Pollie	104	C7
Pollington	51	J1
Polloch	79	J1
Pollokshaws	74	D4
Polmassick	3	G4
Polmont	75	H3
Polnoon	74	D5
Polperro	4	C5
Polruan	4	B5
Polsham	19	J7
Polstead	34	D5
Poltalloch	73	G1
Poltimore	7	H6
Polton	76	A4
Polwarth	77	F5
Polyphant	4	C2
Polzeath	3	G1
Pond Street	33	H5
Ponders End	23	G2
Pondersbridge	43	F6
Ponsanooth	2	E5
Ponsonby	60	B6
Ponsworthy	5	H3
Pont Aber	27	G6
Pont Ceri	26	B4
Pont Crugnant	37	H6
Pont Cyfyng	47	F7
Pont Dolgarrog	47	F6
Pont-faen	27	J5
Pont-Henri	17	H4
Pont Nedd Fechan	18	C1
Pont Pen-y-benglog	46	E6
Pont Rhyd-sarn	37	H3
Pont Rhyd-y-cyff	18	B3
Pont-rhyd-y-groes	27	G1
Pont-rug	46	D6
Pont Walby	18	B1
Pont-y-pant	47	F7
Pont yr Alwen	47	H7
Pontamman	17	K3
Pontantwn	17	H3
Pontardawe	18	A1
Pontarddulais	17	J4
Pontarfynach (Devil's Bridge)	27	G1
Pontargothi	17	J2
Pontarsais	17	H2
Pontblyddyn	48	B6
Pontbren Llwyd	18	B6
Pontefract	57	K7
Ponteland	71	G6
Ponterwyd	37	G7
Pontesbury	38	D5
Pontesford	38	D5
Pontfadog	38	B2
Pontfaen	16	D1
Ponthir	19	G2
Ponthirwaun	26	B4
Pontllanfraith	18	E2
Pontlliw	17	K4
Pontllyfni	46	C7
Pontlottyn	18	E1
Pontnewydd	19	F1
Pontnewynydd	19	F1
Pontrhydfendigaid	27	G2
Pontrhydyfen	18	A2
Pontrhydyrun	19	F2
Pontrilas	28	C6
Pontrobert	38	A4
Ponts Green	13	K5
Pontshaen	26	D4
Pontshill	29	F6
Pontsticill	27	K7
Pontwelly	17	H1
Pontyates	17	H4
Pontyberem	17	J3
Pontybodkin	48	B7
Pontyclun	18	D3
Pontycymer	18	C2
Pontygwaith	18	D2
Pontymister	19	F3
Pontypool	19	F1
Pontypridd	18	D3
Pontywaun	19	F2
Pooksgreen	10	E3
Pool *Cornw.*	2	D4
Pool *W.Yorks.*	57	H5
Pool Bank	55	H1
Pool of Muckhart	82	B7
Pool Quay	38	B4
Pool Street	34	B5
Poole	10	B5
Poole Keynes	20	C2
Poolewe	94	E3
Pooley Bridge	61	F4
Poolhill	29	G6
Pope Hill	16	C4
Popeswood	22	B5
Popham	21	J7
Poplar	23	G3
Porchfield	11	F5
Porin	95	K6
Poringland	45	G5
Porkellis	2	D5
Porlock	7	G1
Porlock Weir	7	G1
Port Allen	82	D5
Port Appin	80	A3
Port Askaig	72	C4
Port Bannatyne	73	J4
Port Carlisle	69	H7
Port Charlotte	72	A5
Port Clarence	63	G4
Port Driseach	73	H3
Port e Vullen	54	D4
Port Ellen	72	B6
Port Elphinstone	91	F3
Port Erin	54	B7
Port Erroll	91	J1
Port Eynon	17	H6
Port Gaverne	4	A2
Port Glasgow	74	B3
Port Henderson	94	D4
Port Isaac	3	G1
Port Logan	64	A6
Port Mòr	85	K7
Port Mulgrave	63	H5
Port-na-Con	103	G2
Port na Craig	82	A2
Port nan Giúran (Portnaguran)	101	H4
Port nan Long	92	D4
Port Nis	101	H1
Port o' Warren	65	J5
Port of Menteith	81	G7
Port Penrhyn	46	D5
Port Quin	3	G1
Port Ramsay	79	K3
Port St. Mary	54	B7
Port Solent	11	H4
Port Sunlight	48	C4
Port Talbot	18	A3
Port Wemyss	72	A2
Port William	64	D6
Portachoillan	73	F5
Portavadie	73	H4
Portbury	19	H4
Portchester	11	H4
Portencross	73	K6
Portesham	9	F6
Portessie	98	C4
Portfield	79	J5
Portfield Gate	16	C3
Portgate	6	C7
Portgordon	98	B4
Portgower	105	F7
Porth *Cornw.*	3	F2
Porth *R.C.T.*	18	D2
Porth Colmon	36	A2
Porth Mellin	2	D7
Porth Navas	2	E6
Porth-y-waen	38	B3
Porthaethwy (Menai Bridge)	46	D5
Porthallow *Cornw.*	2	E6
Porthallow *Cornw.*	4	C5
Porthcawl	18	B4
Porthcothan	3	F1
Porthcurno	2	A6
Porthgain	16	B1
Porthkerry	18	D5
Porthleven	2	D6
Porthmadog	36	E2
Porthmeor	2	B5
Portholland	3	G4
Porthoustock	3	F6
Porthpean	4	A5
Porthtowan	2	D4
Porthyrhyd *Carmar.*	27	G5
Porthyrhyd *Carmar.*	17	J3
Portincaple	74	A1
Portington	58	D6
Portinnisherrich	80	A6
Portinscale	60	D4
Portishead	19	H4
Portknockie	98	C4
Portlethen	91	H5
Portlethen Village	91	H5
Portloe	3	G5
Portmahomack	97	G3
Portmeirion	36	E2
Portmore	10	E5
Portnacroish	80	A3
Portnahaven	72	A2
Portnalong	85	J1
Portnaluchaig	86	C6
Portobello	76	B3
Porton	10	C1
Portpatrick	64	A5
Portreath	2	D4
Portree	93	K7
Portscatho	3	F5
Portsea	11	H4
Portskerra	104	D2
Portskewett	19	J3
Portslade	13	F6
Portslade-by-Sea	13	F6
Portslogan	64	A5
Portsmouth	11	H5
Portsonachan	80	B5
Portsoy	98	D4
Portswood	11	F3
Portuairk	79	F1
Portway *Here.*	28	C4
Portway *Worcs.*	30	B1
Portwrinkle	4	D5
Portyerrock	64	E7
Poslingford	34	B4
Postbridge	5	G3
Postcombe	22	A2
Postling	15	G4
Postwick	45	G5
Potarch	90	E5
Potsgrove	32	C6
Pott Row	44	B3
Pott Shrigley	49	J5
Potten End	22	D1
Potter Heigham	45	J3
Potter Street	23	H1
Potterhanworth	52	D6
Potterhanworth Booths	52	D6
Potterne	20	C6
Potterne Wick	20	C6
Potters Bar	23	F1
Potter's Cross	40	A7
Potters Crouch	22	E1
Potterspury	31	J4
Potterton	91	H3
Potto	63	F6
Potton	33	F4
Poughill *Cornw.*	6	A5
Poughill *Devon*	7	G5
Poulner	10	C4
Poulshot	20	C6
Poulton	20	E1
Poulton-le-Fylde	55	G6
Pound Bank	29	G1
Pound Green	13	J4
Pound Hill	13	F3
Poundffald	17	J5
Poundgate	13	H4
Poundland	67	F4
Poundon	31	H6
Poundsbridge	23	J7
Poundsgate	5	H3
Poundstock	4	C1
Povey Cross	23	F7
Pow Green	29	G4
Powburn	71	F2
Powderham	7	H7
Powerstock	8	E5
Powfoot	69	G7
Powick	29	H3
Powler's Piece	6	B4
Powmill	75	J1
Poxwell	9	G6
Poyle	22	D4
Poynings	13	F5
Poyntington	9	F2
Poynton *Ches.*	49	J4
Poynton *Tel. & W.*	38	E4
Poynton Green	38	E4
Poyntzfield	96	E5
Poys Street	35	H1
Poyston Cross	16	C3
Poystreet Green	34	D3
Praa Sands	2	C6
Pratis	82	E7
Pratt's Bottom	23	H5
Praze-an-Beeble	2	D5
Predannack Wollas	2	D7
Prees	38	E2
Prees Green	38	E2
Prees Higher Heath	38	E2
Preesall	55	G5
Preesgweene	38	B2
Pren-gwyn	26	D4
Prenbrigog	48	B6
Prendergast	16	C3
Prendwick	71	F2
Prenteg	36	E1
Prenton	48	C4
Prescot	48	D3
Prescott	38	D3
Presley	97	H6
Pressen	77	G7
Prestatyn	47	J4
Prestbury *Ches.*	49	H5
Prestbury *Glos.*	29	J6
Presteigne	28	C2
Presthope	38	E6
Prestleigh	19	K7
Prestolee	49	G2
Preston *B. & H.*	13	G6
Preston *Devon*	5	J3
Preston *Dorset*	9	G6
Preston *E.Loth.*	76	D3
Preston *E.Riding*	59	H6
Preston *Glos.*	29	F5
Preston *Glos.*	20	D1
Preston *Herts.*	32	E6
Preston *Kent*	25	G5
Preston *Kent*	25	J5
Preston *Lancs.*	55	J7
Preston *Northumb.*	71	G1
Preston *Rut.*	42	B5
Preston *Sc.Bord.*	77	F5
Preston *Suff.*	34	D3
Preston *T. & W.*	71	J7
Preston *Wilts.*	20	D4
Preston Bagot	30	C2
Preston Bissett	31	H6
Preston Brockhurst	38	E3
Preston Brook	48	E4
Preston Candover	21	K7
Preston Capes	31	J3
Preston Deanery	31	J3
Preston Gubbals	38	D4
Preston on Stour	30	D4
Preston on the Hill	48	E4
Preston on Wye	28	C4
Preston Plucknett	8	E3
Preston-under-Scar	62	B7
Preston upon the Weald Moors	39	F4
Preston Wynne	28	E4
Prestonpans	76	B3
Prestwich	49	H2
Prestwick *Northumb.*	71	G6
Prestwick *S.Ayr.*	67	H1
Prestwick International Airport	67	H1
Prestwold	41	H3
Prestwood	22	B1
Price Town	18	C2
Prickwillow	43	J7
Priddy	19	J6
Priest Hill	56	B6
Priest Hutton	55	J2
Priestland	74	D7
Priestweston	38	B6
Primethorpe	41	H6
Primrose Green	44	E4
Princes End	40	B6
Princes Gate	16	E3
Princes Risborough	22	B1
Princethorpe	31	F1
Princetown *Caerp.*	28	A7
Princetown *Devon*	5	G3
Prior Muir	83	G6
Prior's Frome	28	E5
Priors Hardwick	31	F3
Priors Marston	31	F3
Priory Wood	28	B4
Priston	19	K5
Prittlewell	24	E3
Privett	11	H2
Prixford	6	D2
Proaig	72	C5
Probus	3	F4
Protstonhill	99	G4
Prudhoe	71	G7
Pubil	81	F3
Publow	19	K5
Puckeridge	33	G6
Puckington	8	C3
Pucklechurch	19	K4
Puddinglake	49	G6
Puddington *Ches.*	48	C5
Puddington *Devon*	7	G4
Puddlebrook	29	F7
Puddledock	44	E6
Puddletown	9	G5
Pudsey	57	H6
Pulborough	12	D5
Puldagon	105	J4
Puleston	39	G3
Pulford	48	C7
Pulham	9	G4
Pulham Market	45	F7
Pulham St. Mary	45	G7
Pulloxhill	32	D5
Pulrossie	96	E3
Pulverbatch	38	D5
Pumpherston	75	J4
Pumsaint	27	F4
Puncheston	16	D2
Puncknowle	8	E6
Punnett's Town	13	K4
Purbrook	11	H4
Purfleet	23	J4
Puriton	19	G7
Purleigh	24	E1
Purley	23	G5
Purley on Thames	21	K4
Purlogue	28	B1
Purls Bridge	43	H7
Purse Caundle	9	F3
Purslow	38	C7
Purston Jaglin	51	G1
Purton *Glos.*	19	K1
Purton *Wilts.*	20	D3
Purton Stoke	20	D2
Purves Hall	77	F6
Pury End	31	J4
Pusey	21	G2
Putley	29	F5
Putloe	20	A1
Putney	23	F4
Putsborough	6	C1
Puttenham *Herts.*	32	B7
Puttenham *Surr.*	22	C7
Puttock End	34	C4
Putts Corner	7	K6
Puxton	19	H5
Pwll	17	H4
Pwll Trap	17	F3
Pwll-y-glaw	18	A2
Pwllcrochan	16	C4
Pwlldefaid	36	A3
Pwllgloyw	27	K5
Pwllheli	36	C2
Pwllmeyric	19	G3
Pye Corner *Herts.*	33	H7
Pye Corner *Newport*	19	G3
Pye Green	40	B4
Pyecombe	13	F5
Pyle *Bridgend*	18	B3
Pyle *I.o.W.*	11	F7
Pylle	9	F1
Pymore	43	H7
Pyrford	22	D6
Pyrton	21	K2
Pytchley	32	B1
Pyworthy	6	B5

Q

Place	Page	Grid
Quabbs	38	B7
Quadring	43	F2
Quadring Eaudike	43	F2
Quainton	31	J7
Quarley	21	F7
Quarmby	50	D1
Quarndon	41	F1
Quarr Hill	11	G5
Quarrier's Village	74	B4
Quarrington	42	D1
Quarrington Hill	62	E3
Quarry Bank	40	B7
Quarrybank	48	E6
Quarrywood	97	J5
Quarter	75	F5
Quatford	39	G6
Quatt	39	G7
Quebec	62	C2
Quedgeley	29	H7
Queen Adelaide	43	J7
Queen Camel	8	E2
Queen Charlton	19	K5
Queen Street	23	K7
Queenborough	25	F4
Queensbury	57	G6
Queensferry	48	C6
Queenzieburn	74	E3
Quemerford	20	D4
Quendale	109	F9
Quendon	33	J5
Queniborough	41	J4
Quenington	20	E1
Quernmore	55	J3
Queslett	40	C6
Quethiock	4	D4
Quholm	107	B6
Quidenham	44	E7
Quidhampton *Hants.*	21	J6
Quidhampton *Wilts.*	10	C1
Quilquox	91	H1
Quina Brook	38	E2
Quindry	107	D8
Quine's Hill	54	C6
Quinhill	73	F5
Quinton *Northants.*	31	J3
Quinton *W.Mid.*	40	B7
Quintrell Downs	3	F2
Quoditch	6	C6
Quoig	81	K5
Quoigs House	81	K7
Quoisley	38	E1
Quorn	41	H4
Quothquan	75	H7
Quoyloo	106	B5
Quoys	108	F1
Quoys of Reiss	105	J3

R

Place	Page	Grid
Raby	48	C5
Rachan	75	K7
Rachub	46	E6
Rackenford	7	G4
Rackham	12	D5
Rackheath	45	G4
Racks	69	F6
Rackwick *Ork.*	107	B8
Rackwick *Ork.*	106	D2
Radbourne	40	E2
Radcliffe *Gt.Man.*	49	G2
Radcliffe *Northumb.*	71	H3
Radcliffe on Trent	41	J2
Radclive	31	H5
Radcot	21	F2
Radford *Oxon.*	31	F6
Radford *W.Mid.*	41	F7
Radford Semele	30	E2
Radipole	9	F6
Radlett	22	E2
Radley	21	J2
Radmore Green	48	E7
Radstock	19	K6
Radstone	31	H4
Radway	30	E4
Radway Green	49	G7
Radwell *Beds.*	32	D3
Radwell *Herts.*	33	F5
Radwinter	33	K5
Radyr	18	E3
Raechester	70	E5
Raemoir House	90	E5
Raffin	102	C5
Rafford	97	H6
Ragdale	41	J4
Raglan	19	H1
Ragnall	52	B5
Rahoy	79	H2
Rainford	48	D2
Rainham *Gt.Lon.*	23	J3
Rainham *Med.*	24	E5
Rainhill	48	D3
Rainhill Stoops	48	E3
Rainow	49	J5
Rainton	57	J2
Rainworth	51	H7
Raisbeck	61	H6
Raise	61	H2
Rait	82	D5
Raithby *Lincs.*	53	G5
Raithby *Lincs.*	53	G4
Rake	12	B4
Raleigh's Cross	7	J2
Ram	17	J1
Ram Lane	14	E3
Ramasaig	93	G7
Rame *Cornw.*	2	E5
Rame *Cornw.*	4	E6
Rampisham	8	E4
Rampside	55	F3
Rampton *Cambs.*	33	H2
Rampton *Notts.*	52	B5
Ramsbottom	49	G1
Ramsbury	21	F4
Ramscraigs	105	G6
Ramsdean	11	J2
Ramsdell	21	J6
Ramsden	30	E7
Ramsden Bellhouse	24	D2
Ramsden Heath	24	D2
Ramsey *Cambs.*	43	F7
Ramsey *Essex*	35	G6
Ramsey *I.o.M.*	54	D4
Ramsey Forty Foot	43	G7
Ramsey Heights	43	F7
Ramsey Island	25	F1
Ramsey Mereside	43	F7
Ramsey St. Mary's	43	F7
Ramsgate	25	K5
Ramsgate Street	44	E2
Ramsgill	57	G2
Ramsholt	35	H4
Ramshorn	40	C1
Ramsnest Common	12	C3
Ranachan	79	J1
Ranby *Lincs.*	53	F5
Ranby *Notts.*	51	J4
Rand	52	E5
Randwick	20	B1
Rangemore	40	D3
Rangeworthy	19	K3
Rankinston	67	J2
Rank's Green	34	B7
Rannoch School	81	G2
Ranochan	86	E6
Ranskill	51	J4
Ranton	40	A3
Ranworth	45	H4
Rapness	106	E3
Rascarrel	65	J6
Raskelf	57	K2
Rassau	28	A7
Rastrick	57	G7
Ratagan	86	E3
Ratby	41	H5
Ratcliffe Culey	41	F6
Ratcliffe on Soar	41	G3
Ratcliffe on the Wreake	41	J4
Ratford Bridge	16	C3
Rathen	99	J4
Rathillet	82	E5
Rathliesbeag	87	J6
Rathmell	56	D3
Ratho	75	K3
Ratho Station	75	K3
Rathven	98	C4
Ratley	30	E4
Ratlinghope	38	D6
Rattar	105	H1
Ratten Row	55	H5
Rattery	5	H4
Rattlesden	34	D3
Rattray	82	C3
Raughton Head	60	E2
Raunds	32	D1
Ravenfield	51	G3
Ravenglass	60	B7
Raveningham	45	H6
Ravenscar	63	J2
Ravensdale	54	C4
Ravensden	32	D3
Ravenshaw	56	E5
Ravenshayes	7	H5
Ravenshead	51	H7
Ravensmoor	49	F7
Ravensthorpe *Northants.*	31	H1
Ravensthorpe *W.Yorks.*	50	E1
Ravenstone *Leics.*	41	G4
Ravenstone *M.K.*	32	B4
Ravenstonedale	61	J6
Ravenstruther	75	H6
Raw	63	J2
Rawcliffe *E.Riding*	58	B4
Rawcliffe *York*	58	B4
Rawcliffe Bridge	58	C7
Rawdon	57	H6
Rawmarsh	51	G3
Rawreth	24	D2
Rawridge	7	K5
Rawtenstall	56	D7
Rawyards	75	F4
Raxton	91	G1
Raydon	34	E5
Raylees	70	E4
Rayleigh	24	E2
Raymond's Hill	8	C5
Rayne	34	B6
Reach	33	J2
Read	56	C6
Reading	22	A4
Reading Street	14	E4
Reagill	61	H5
Rearquhar	96	E2
Rearsby	41	J4
Rease Heath	49	F7
Reaster	105	H2
Reaveley	71	F2
Reawick	109	C8
Reay	104	E2
Reculver	25	J5
Red Dial	60	D2
Red Hill *Hants.*	11	J3
Red Hill *Warks.*	30	C3
Red Lodge	33	K1
Red Oaks Hill	33	J5
Red Post *Cornw.*	6	A5
Red Post *Devon*	5	J4
Red Rock	48	E2
Red Roses	17	F3
Red Row	71	H4
Red Street	49	H7
Red Wharf Bay	46	D4
Redberth	16	D4
Redbourn	32	E7
Redbourne	52	C2
Redbridge	23	H3
Redbrook	19	J1
Redbrook Street	14	E4
Redburn *High.*	96	C5
Redburn *High.*	97	G7
Redcar	63	H4
Redcastle *Angus*	83	H2
Redcastle *High.*	96	C7
Redcliff Bay	19	H4
Redcloak	91	G6
Reddish	49	H3
Redditch	30	B2
Rede	34	C3
Redenhall	45	G7
Redesmouth	70	D5
Redford *Aber.*	83	J1
Redford *Angus*	83	G3
Redford *Dur.*	62	B3
Redford *W.Suss.*	12	B4
Redgrave	34	E1
Redheugh	83	F1
Redhill *Aber.*	90	E1
Redhill *Aber.*	91	F4
Redhill *Moray*	98	D6
Redhill *N.Som.*	19	H5
Redhill *Notts.*	41	H1
Redhill *Surr.*	23	F6
Redhill *Tel. & W.*	39	G4
Redhill Aerodrome	23	F7
Redhouse *Aber.*	90	D2
Redhouse *Arg. & B.*	73	G4
Redhouses	72	B4
Redisham	45	J7
Redland *Bristol*	19	J4
Redland *Ork.*	106	C5
Redlingfield	35	F1
Redlynch *Som.*	9	F1
Redlynch *Wilts.*	10	D2
Redmarley D'Abitot	29	G5
Redmarshall	62	E4
Redmile	42	B2
Redmire	62	B7
Redmoor	4	A4
Rednal *Shrop.*	38	C3
Rednal *W.Mid.*	29	J1
Redpath	76	D7
Redpoint	94	D5
Redruth	2	D4
Redscarhead	76	A6
Redshaw	68	D1
Redstone Bank	16	E3
Redwick *Newport*	19	H3
Redwick *S.Glos.*	19	J3
Redworth	62	D4
Reed	33	G5
Reedham	45	J5
Reedness	58	D7
Reepham *Lincs.*	52	D5
Reepham *Norf.*	45	F3
Reeth	62	B7
Regaby	54	D4
Regil	19	J5
Regoul	97	F6
Reiff	102	B7
Reigate	23	F6
Reighton	59	H2
Reinigeadal	100	E7
Reisgill	105	H5
Reiss	105	J3
Rejerrah	2	E3
Relubbus	2	C5
Relugas	97	G7
Remenham	22	A3
Remenham Hill	22	A3
Remony	81	J3
Rempstone	41	H3
Rendcomb	30	B7
Rendham	35	H2
Rendlesham	35	H3
Renfrew	74	D4
Renhold	32	D3
Renishaw	51	G5
Rennington	71	H2
Renton	74	B3
Renwick	61	G2
Repps	45	J4
Repton	41	F3
Rescobie	83	G2
Resipole	79	J1
Resolis	96	D5
Resolven	18	B1
Resourie	86	E7
Reston	77	G4
Reswallie	83	G2
Retew	3	G3
Retford	51	K4
Rettendon	24	D2
Rettendon Place	24	D2
Retyn	3	F3
Revesby	53	F6
Rew	5	H3
Rewe	7	H6
Reydon	35	J1
Reymerston	44	E5
Reynalton	16	D4
Reynoldston	17	H6
Rezare	4	D3
Rhandirmwyn	27	G4
Rhaoine	96	D1
Rhayader	27	J2
Rhedyn	36	B2
Rhegreanoch	102	C7
Rheindown	96	C7
Rhelonie	96	C2
Rhemore	79	G2
Rhes-y-cae	47	K6
Rhewl *Denb.*	38	A1
Rhewl *Denb.*	47	K6
Rhewl *Shrop.*	38	C2
Rhian	103	H7
Rhicarn	102	C6
Rhiconich	102	E3
Rhidorroch	95	H2
Rhifail	104	C3
Rhigos	18	C1
Rhilochan	96	E1
Rhiroy	95	H3
Rhiw	36	B3
Rhiwargor	37	J3
Rhiwbryfdir	37	F1
Rhiwderin	19	F3
Rhiwlas *Gwyn.*	46	D6
Rhiwlas *Gwyn.*	37	J2
Rhiwlas *Powys*	38	B2
Rhodes Minnis	15	G3
Rhodesia	51	H5
Rhodiad-y-Brenin	16	A2
Rhodmad	27	F2
Rhonadale	73	F7
Rhonehouse or Kelton Hill	65	H5
Rhoose	18	D5
Rhos *Carmar.*	17	G1
Rhos *N.P.T.*	18	A1
Rhos-berse	48	B7
Rhos-ddu	36	C2
Rhos-fawr	36	C2
Rhos-goch *Angl.*	46	C4
Rhôs-on-Sea	47	G4
Rhos-y-bol	46	C4
Rhos-y-brwyner	48	B6
Rhos-y-garth	27	F1
Rhos-y-gwaliau	37	J2
Rhos-y-llan	36	B2
Rhos-y-mawn	47	G6
Rhos-y-Meirch	28	B2
Rhoscolyn	46	A5
Rhoscrowther	16	C4
Rhosesmor	48	B6

Rhosgadfan 46 D7
Rhosgoch 28 A4
Rhoshirwaun 36 A3
Rhoslan 36 D1
Rhoslefain 36 E5
Rhosllanerchrugog 38 B1
Rhosmaen 17 K2
Rhosmeirch 46 C5
Rhosneigr 46 B5
Rhosnesni 48 C7
Rhossili 17 H6
Rhosson 16 A2
Rhostryfan 46 C7
Rhostyllen 38 C1
Rhu 74 A2
Rhuallt 47 J5
Rhubodach 73 J3
Rhuddlan 47 J5
Rhue 95 G2
Rhulen 28 A4
Rhumach 86 C6
Rhunahaorine 73 F6
Rhuthun (Ruthin) 47 K7
Rhyd *Gwyn.* 37 F1
Rhyd *Powys* 37 J5
Rhyd-Ddu 46 D7
Rhyd-rosser 26 E2
Rhyd-uchaf 37 J2
Rhyd-wen 37 J3
Rhyd-wyn 46 B4
Rhyd-y-clafdy 36 C2
Rhyd-y-foel 47 H5
Rhyd-y-fro 18 A1
Rhyd-y-meirch 19 G1
Rhyd-yr-onnen 37 F5
Rhydaman (Ammanford) 17 K3
Rhydargaeau 17 H2
Rhydcymerau 17 J1
Rhydd 29 H4
Rhydding 18 A2
Rhydlanfair 47 G7
Rhydlewis 26 C4
Rhydlios 36 A2
Rhydlydan *Conwy* 47 G7
Rhydlydan *Powys* 37 K6
Rhydolion 36 B3
Rhydowen 26 D4
Rhydspence 28 B4
Rhydtalog 48 B7
Rhydycroesau 38 B2
Rhydyfelin *Cere.* 26 E1
Rhydyfelin *R.C.T.* 18 D3
Rhydymain 37 G3
Rhydymwyn 48 B6
Rhydywrach 16 E3
Rhyl 47 J4
Rhymney 18 E1
Rhyn 38 C2
Rhynd 82 C5
Rhynie *Aber.* 90 C2
Rhynie *High.* 97 F4
Ribbesford 29 G1
Ribbleton 55 J6
Ribchester 56 B6
Ribigill 103 H3
Riby 52 E2
Riccall 58 C6
Riccarton 74 C7
Richard's Castle 28 D2
Richings Park 22 D4
Richmond 62 C6
Richmond upon Thames 22 E4
Rickarton 91 G6
Rickford 19 H6
Rickinghall 34 E1
Rickling 33 H5
Rickling Green 33 J6
Rickmansworth 22 D2
Riddell 70 A1
Riddings 51 G7
Riddlecombe 6 E4
Riddlesden 57 F5
Ridge *Dorset* 9 J6
Ridge *Herts.* 23 F1
Ridge *Wilts.* 9 J1
Ridge Green 23 G7
Ridge Lane 40 E6
Ridgebourne 27 K2
Ridgeway 51 G4
Ridgeway Cross 29 G4
Ridgewell 34 B4
Ridgewood 13 H4
Ridgmont 32 C5
Riding Mill 71 F7
Ridley 24 C5
Ridleywood 48 C7
Ridlington *Norf.* 45 H2
Ridlington *Rut.* 42 B5
Ridsdale 70 E5
Riechip 82 B3
Rievaulx 58 B1
Rigg *D. & G.* 69 H7
Rigg *High.* 94 B6
Riggend 75 F4
Rigmaden Park 56 B1
Rigsby 53 H5
Rigside 75 G7
Rileyhill 40 D4
Rilla Mill 4 C3
Rillington 58 E2
Rimington 56 D5
Rimpton 9 F2
Rimswell 59 K7
Rinaston 16 C2
Ringford 65 G5
Ringland 45 F4
Ringles Cross 13 H4
Ringmer 13 H5
Ringmore 5 G6
Ringorm 97 K7
Ring's End 43 G5
Ringsfield 45 J7
Ringsfield Corner 45 J7
Ringshall *Herts.* 32 C7
Ringshall *Suff.* 34 E3
Ringshall Stocks 34 E3
Ringstead *Norf.* 44 B1
Ringstead *Northants.* 32 C1
Ringwood 10 C4
Ringwould 15 J3
Rinloan 89 K4
Rinmore 90 C3
Rinnigill 107 C8
Rinsey 2 C6
Ripe 13 J6
Ripley *Derbys.* 51 G7
Ripley *Hants.* 10 C5
Ripley *N.Yorks.* 57 H3
Ripley *Surr.* 22 D6
Riplingham 59 F6
Ripon 57 J2
Rippingale 42 E3
Ripple *Kent* 15 J2
Ripple *Worcs.* 29 H5
Ripponden 50 C1
Risabus 72 B6
Risbury 28 E3
Risby 34 B2
Risca 19 F2
Rise 59 H5
Risegate 43 F2
Riseley *Beds.* 32 D2
Riseley *W'ham* 22 A5
Rishangles 35 F2
Rishton 56 C6
Rishworth 50 C1
Risley *Derbys.* 41 G2
Risley *Warr.* 49 F3
Risplith 57 H3
Rispond 103 G2
Rivar 21 G5
Rivenhall 34 C7
Rivenhall End 34 C7
River 12 C4
River Bank 33 J2
River Bridge 19 G7
Riverford Bridge 5 H4
Riverhead 23 J6
Rivington 49 F1
Roa Island 55 F3
Roade 31 J3
Roadhead 70 A6
Roadside *High.* 105 G2
Roadside *Ork.* 106 F3
Roadside of Kinneff 91 G7
Roadwater 7 J2
Roag 93 H7
Roath 19 F4
Roberton *S.Lan.* 68 E1
Roberton *Sc.Bord.* 69 K2
Robertsbridge 14 C5
Robertstown 97 K7
Roberttown 57 G7
Robeston Cross 16 B4
Robeston Wathen 16 D3
Robin Hood *Derbys.* 50 E5
Robin Hood *W.Yorks.* 57 J7
Robin Hood's Bay 63 J2
Robins 12 B4
Roborough *Devon* 6 D4
Roborough *Plym.* 5 F4
Roby 48 D3
Roby Mill 48 E2
Rocester 40 D2
Roch 16 B2
Rochallie 82 C2
Rochdale 49 H1
Roche 3 G2
Rochester *Med.* 24 D5
Rochester *Northumb.* 70 D4
Rochford *Essex* 24 E2
Rochford *Worcs.* 29 F2
Rock *Caerp.* 18 E2
Rock *Cornw.* 3 G1
Rock *Northumb.* 71 H1
Rock *Worcs.* 29 G1
Rock Ferry 48 C4
Rockbeare 7 J6
Rockbourne 10 C3
Rockcliffe *Cumb.* 69 J7
Rockcliffe *D. & G.* 65 J5
Rockfield *Arg. & B.* 73 G5
Rockfield *High.* 97 G3
Rockfield *Mon.* 28 D7
Rockhampton 19 K2
Rockhead 4 A2
Rockingham 42 B6
Rockland All Saints 44 D6
Rockland St. Mary 45 H5
Rockland St. Peter 44 D6
Rockley 20 E4
Rockside 72 A4
Rockwell End 22 A3
Rockwell Green 7 K4
Rodborough 20 B1
Rodbourne 20 C3
Rodbridge Corner 34 C4
Rodd 28 C2
Roddam 71 F1
Rodden 9 F6
Rode 20 B6
Rode Heath 49 H7
Rodeheath 49 H6
Rodel (Roghadal) 93 F3
Roden 38 E4
Rodhuish 7 J2
Rodington 38 E4
Rodley 29 G7
Rodmarton 20 C2
Rodmell 13 H6
Rodmersham 25 F5
Rodney Stoke 19 H6
Rodsley 40 E1
Rodway 19 F7
Roe Green 33 G5
Roecliffe 57 J3
Roehampton 23 F4
Roesound 109 C6
Roffey 12 E3
Rogart 96 E1
Rogate 12 B4
Rogerstone 19 F3
Roghadal (Rodel) 93 F3
Rogiet 19 H3
Roker 63 F1
Rollesby 45 J4
Rolleston *Leics.* 42 A5
Rolleston *Notts.* 51 K7
Rolleston *Staffs.* 40 E3
Rollestone 20 D7
Rolston 59 J5
Rolvenden 14 D4
Rolvenden Layne 14 D4
Romaldkirk 62 A4
Romanby 62 E7
Romannobridge 75 K6
Romansleigh 7 F3
Romford *Dorset* 10 B4
Romford *Gt.Lon.* 23 J3
Romiley 49 J3
Romney Street 23 J5
Romsey 10 E2
Romsley *Shrop.* 39 G7
Romsley *Worcs.* 40 B7
Ronachan 73 F5
Ronague 54 B6
Ronnachmore 72 B5
Rookhope 62 A2
Rookley 11 G6
Rooks Bridge 19 G6
Rookwith 57 H1
Roos 59 J6
Roosecote 55 F3
Rootpark 75 H5
Ropley 11 H1
Ropley Dean 11 H1
Ropley Soke 11 H1
Ropsley 42 C2
Rora 99 J5
Rorandle 90 E3
Rorrington 38 B5
Rosarie 98 B5
Rose 2 E3
Rose Ash 7 F3
Rose Green 34 C6
Roseacre 55 H6
Rosebank 75 G6
Rosebrough 71 G1
Rosebush 16 D2
Rosedale Abbey 63 J7
Roseden 71 F1
Rosehall 96 B1
Rosehearty 99 H4
Rosehill *Aber.* 90 D5
Rosehill *Shrop.* 39 F2
Roseisle 97 J5
Rosemarket 16 C4
Rosemarkie 96 E6
Rosemary Lane 7 K4
Rosemount *P. & K.* 82 C3
Rosemount *S.Ayr.* 67 H1
Rosepool 16 B3
Rosewarne 2 D5
Rosewell 76 A4
Roseworthy 2 D5
Rosgill 61 G5
Roshven 86 D7
Roskhill 93 H7
Rosley 60 E2
Roslin 76 A4
Rosliston 40 E4
Rosneath 74 A2
Ross *D. & G.* 65 G6
Ross *Northumb.* 77 K7
Ross *P. & K.* 81 J5
Ross-on-Wye 29 F6
Ross Priory 74 C2
Rossdhu House 74 B2
Rossett 48 C7
Rossie Farm School 83 H2
Rossie Ochill 82 B6
Rossie Priory 82 D4
Rossington 51 J3
Rosskeen 96 D5
Roster 105 H5
Rostherne 49 G4
Rosthwaite *Cumb.* 60 D5
Rosthwaite *Cumb.* 55 F1
Roston 40 D1
Rosyth 75 K2
Rothbury 71 F3
Rotherby 41 J4
Rotherfield 13 J4
Rotherfield Greys 22 A3
Rotherfield Peppard 22 A3
Rotherham 51 G3
Rothersthorpe 31 J3
Rotherwick 22 A6
Rothes 97 K7
Rothesay 73 J4
Rothiebrisbane 91 F1
Rothienorman 91 F1
Rothiesholm 106 F5
Rothley *Leics.* 41 H4
Rothley *Northumb.* 71 F5
Rothwell *Lincs.* 52 E3
Rothwell *Northants.* 42 B7
Rothwell *W.Yorks.* 57 J7
Rotsea 59 G4
Rottal 82 E1
Rottingdean 13 G6
Rottington 60 A5
Roud 11 G6
Roudham 44 D7
Rough Close 40 B2
Rough Common 15 G2
Rougham *Norf.* 44 C3
Rougham *Suff.* 34 D2
Rougham Green 34 D2
Roughburn 87 K6
Roughlee 56 D5
Roughley 40 D6
Roughton *Lincs.* 53 F6
Roughton *Norf.* 45 G2
Roughton *Shrop.* 39 G6
Roundhay 57 J6
Roundstreet Common 12 D4
Roundway 20 D5
Rous Lench 30 B3
Rousdon 8 B5
Rousham 31 F6
Rousham Gap 31 F6
Routenburn 74 A4
Routh 59 G5
Row *Cornw.* 4 A3
Row *Cumb.* 55 H1
Row *Cumb.* 61 H3
Row Heath 35 F7
Row Town 22 D5
Rowanburn 69 K6
Rowardennan Lodge 74 B1
Rowberrow 19 H6
Rowchoish 80 E7
Rowde 20 C5
Rowen 47 F5
Rowfoot 70 B7
Rowhedge 34 E6
Rowhook 12 E3
Rowington 30 D2
Rowington Green 30 D1
Rowland 50 E5
Rowland's Castle 11 J3
Rowlands Gill 62 C1
Rowledge 22 B7
Rowley *Devon* 7 F4
Rowley *Dur.* 62 B2
Rowley *E.Riding* 59 F6
Rowley *Shrop.* 38 C5
Rowley Regis 40 B7
Rowlstone 28 C6
Rowly 22 D7
Rowner 11 G4
Rowney Green 30 B1
Rownhams 10 E3
Rowrah 60 B5
Rowsham 32 B7
Rowsley 50 E6
Rowstock 21 H3
Rowston 52 D7
Rowthorne 51 G6
Rowton *Ches.* 48 D6
Rowton *Shrop.* 38 C4
Rowton *Tel. & W.* 39 F4
Roxburgh 76 E7
Roxby *N.Lincs.* 52 C1
Roxby *N.Yorks.* 63 J5
Roxton 32 E3
Roxwell 24 C1
Royal British Legion Village 14 C2
Royal Leamington Spa 30 E2
Royal Tunbridge Wells 13 J3
Roybridge 87 J6
Roydon *Essex* 33 H7
Roydon *Norf.* 44 E7
Roydon *Norf.* 44 B3
Roydon Hamlet 23 H1
Royston *Herts.* 33 G4
Royston *S.Yorks.* 51 F1
Royton 49 J2
Ruabon 38 C1
Ruaig 78 B3
Ruan Lanihorne 3 F4
Ruan Major 2 D7
Ruan Minor 2 E7
Ruanaich 78 D5
Ruardean 29 F7
Ruardean Woodside 29 F7
Rubery 29 J1
Ruckcroft 61 G2
Ruckinge 15 F4
Ruckland 53 G5
Ruckley 38 E5
Rudbaxton 16 C2
Rudby 63 F6
Rudchester 71 G7
Ruddington 41 H2
Ruddlemoor 4 A5
Rudford 29 G6
Rudge 20 B6
Rudgeway 19 K3
Rudgwick 12 D3
Rudhall 29 F6
Rudheath 49 F5
Rudley Green 24 E1
Rudry 18 E3
Rudston 59 G3
Rudyard 49 J7
Rufford 48 D1
Rufforth 58 B4
Ruffside 62 A1
Rugby 31 G1
Rugeley 40 C4
Ruilick 96 C7
Ruishton 8 B2
Ruisigearraidh 92 E3
Ruislip 22 D3
Rumbling Bridge 75 J1
Rumburgh 45 H7
Rumford 3 F1
Rumney 19 F4
Rumwell 7 K3
Runacraig 81 G6
Runcorn 48 E4
Runcton 12 B6
Runcton Holme 44 A5
Rundlestone 5 F3
Runfold 22 B7
Runhall 44 E5
Runham 45 J4
Runnington 7 K3
Runsell Green 24 D1
Runswick 63 K5
Runtaleave 82 D1
Runwell 24 D2
Ruscombe 22 A4
Rush Green 23 J3
Rushall *Here.* 29 F5
Rushall *Norf.* 45 F7
Rushall *W.Mid.* 40 C5
Rushall *Wilts.* 20 E6
Rushbrooke 34 C2
Rushbury 38 E6
Rushden *Herts.* 33 G5
Rushden *Northants.* 32 C2
Rushford 44 D7
Rushlake Green 13 K5
Rushmere 45 J7
Rushmere St. Andrew 35 F4
Rushmoor *Surr.* 22 B7
Rushmoor *Tel. & W.* 39 F4
Rushock 29 H1
Rusholme 49 H3
Rushton *Ches.* 48 E6
Rushton *Northants.* 42 B7
Rushton *Shrop.* 39 F5
Rushton Spencer 49 J6
Rushwick 29 H3
Rushyford 62 D4
Ruskie 81 H7
Ruskington 52 D7
Rusko 65 F5
Rusland 55 G1
Rusper 13 F3
Ruspidge 29 F7
Russel 94 E7
Russell's Water 22 A3
Rusthall 23 J7
Rustington 12 D6
Ruston 59 F1
Ruston Parva 59 G3
Ruswarp 63 K6
Rutherend 74 E5
Rutherford 70 B1
Rutherglen 74 E4
Ruthernbridge 4 A4
Ruthin (Rhuthun) 47 K7
Ruthrieston 91 H4
Ruthven *Aber.* 98 D6
Ruthven *Angus* 82 D3
Ruthven *High.* 89 F1
Ruthven *High.* 88 E5
Ruthvoes 3 G2
Ruthwaite 60 D3
Ruthwell 69 G7
Ruyton-XI-Towns 38 C3
Ryal 71 F6
Ryal Fold 56 B7
Ryall 8 D5
Ryarsh 23 K6
Rydal 60 E6
Ryde 11 G5
Rydon 6 B5
Rye 14 E5
Rye Foreign 14 D5
Rye Harbour 14 E6
Rye Park 23 G1
Ryhall 42 D4
Ryhill 51 F1
Ryhope 63 F1
Ryland 52 D4
Rylstone 56 E4
Ryme Intrinseca 8 E3
Ryther 58 B6
Ryton *Glos.* 29 G5
Ryton *N.Yorks.* 58 D2
Ryton *Shrop.* 39 G5
Ryton *T. & W.* 71 G7
Ryton-on-Dunsmore 30 E1

S

Sabden 56 C6
Sackers Green 34 D5
Sacombe 33 G7
Sacriston 62 D2
Sadberge 62 E5
Saddell 73 F7
Saddington 41 J6
Saddle Bow 44 A4
Sadgill 61 F6
Saffron Walden 33 J5
Sageston 16 D4
Saham Toney 44 C5
Saighdinis 92 D5
Saighton 48 D6
St. Abbs 77 H4
St. Agnes 2 E3
St. Albans 22 E1
St. Allen 3 F3
St. Andrews 83 G6
St. Andrews Major 18 E4
St. Anne 3 K4
St. Anne's 55 G7
St. Ann's 69 F4
St. Ann's Chapel *Cornw.* 4 E3
St. Ann's Chapel *Devon* 5 G6
St. Anthony *Cornw.* 2 E6
St. Anthony *Cornw.* 3 F5
St. Arvans 19 J2
St. Asaph (Llanelwy) 47 J5
St. Athan 18 D5
St. Aubin 3 J7
St. Audries 7 K1
St. Austell 4 A5
St. Bees 60 A5
St. Blazey 4 A5
St. Blazey Gate 4 A5
St. Boswells 76 D7
St. Brelade 3 J7
St. Breock 3 G1
St. Breward 4 A3
St. Briavels 19 J1
St. Brides 16 B3
St. Brides Major 18 B4
St. Brides Netherwent 19 H3
St. Bride's-super-Ely 18 D4
St. Brides Wentlooge 19 F3
St. Budeaux 4 E5
St. Buryan 2 B6
St. Catherine 20 A4
St. Catherines 80 C7
St. Clears 17 F3
St. Cleer 4 C4
St. Clement 3 F4
St. Clether 4 C2
St. Columb Major 3 G2
St. Columb Minor 3 F2
St. Columb Road 3 G3
St. Combs 99 J4
St. Cross South Elmham 45 G7
St. Cyrus 83 J1
St. Davids *Fife* 75 K2
St. David's *P. & K.* 82 A5
St. David's (Tyddewi) *Pembs.* 16 A2
St. Day 2 E4
St. Decumans 7 J1
St. Dennis 3 G3
St. Dogmaels 26 A4
St. Dogwells 16 C2
St. Dominick 4 E4
St. Donats 18 C5
St. Edith's Marsh 20 C5
St. Endellion 3 G1
St. Enoder 3 F3
St. Erme 3 F4
St. Erth 2 C5
St. Erth Praze 2 C5
St. Ervan 3 F1
St. Eval 3 F2
St. Ewe 3 G4
St. Fagans 18 E4
St. Fergus 99 K5
St. Fillans 81 H5
St. Florence 16 D4
St. Gennys 4 B1
St. George 47 H5
St. Georges *N.Som.* 19 G5
St. George's *V. of Glam.* 18 D4
St. Germans 4 D5
St. Giles in the Wood 6 D4
St. Giles on the Heath 6 B6
St. Harmon 27 J1
St. Helen Auckland 62 C4
St. Helena 45 F4
St. Helen's *E.Suss.* 14 D6
St. Helens *I.o.W.* 11 H6
St. Helens *Mersey.* 48 E3
St. Helier 3 J7
St. Hilary *Cornw.* 2 C5
St. Hilary *V. of Glam.* 18 D4
St. Hill 13 G3
St. Illtyd 19 F1
St. Ippollitts 33 F6
St. Ishmael 17 G4
St. Ishmael's 16 B4
St. Issey 3 G1
St. Ive 4 D4
St. Ives *Cambs.* 33 G1
St. Ives *Cornw.* 2 C4
St. Ives *Dorset* 10 C4
St. James South Elmham 45 H7
St. John *Chan.I.* 3 J6
St. John *Cornw.* 4 E5
St. John's *I.o.M.* 54 B5
St. John's *Surr.* 22 C6
St. John's *Worcs.* 29 H3
St. John's Chapel *Devon* 6 D3
St. John's Chapel *Dur.* 61 K3
St. John's Fen End 43 J4
St. Johns Hall 62 B3
St. John's Highway 43 J4
St. John's Kirk 75 H7
St. John's Town of Dalry 68 B5
St. Judes 54 C4
St. Just 2 A5
St. Just in Roseland 3 F5
St. Katherines 91 F1
St. Keverne 2 E6
St. Kew 4 A3
St. Kew Highway 4 A3
St. Keyne 4 C4
St. Lawrence *Cornw.* 4 A4
St. Lawrence *Essex* 25 F1
St. Lawrence *I.o.W.* 11 G7
St. Leonards *Bucks.* 22 C1
St. Leonards *Dorset* 10 C4
St. Leonards *E.Suss.* 14 D7
St. Leonards Grange 11 F5
St. Leonard's Street 23 K6
St. Levan 2 A6
St. Lythans 18 E4
St. Mabyn 4 A3
St. Margaret South Elmham 45 H7
St. Margarets *Here.* 28 C5
St. Margarets *Herts.* 33 G7
St. Margaret's at Cliffe 15 J3
St. Margaret's Hope 107 D8
St. Mark's 54 C6
St. Martin *Chan.I.* 3 J5
St. Martin *Chan.I.* 3 K7
St. Martin *Cornw.* 4 C5
St. Martin *Cornw.* 2 E6
St. Martins *P. & K.* 82 C4
St. Martin's *Shrop.* 38 C2
St. Mary Bourne 21 H6
St. Mary Church 18 D4
St. Mary Cray 23 H5
St. Mary Hill 18 C4
St. Mary in the Marsh 15 F5
St. Marychurch 5 K4
St. Mary's 107 D7
St. Mary's Airport 2 C1
St. Mary's Bay 15 F5
St. Mary's Croft 64 A4
St. Mary's Grove 19 H5
St. Mary's Hoo 24 D4
St. Mawes 3 F5
St. Mawgan 3 F2
St. Mellion 4 D4
St. Mellons 19 F3
St. Merryn 3 F1
St. Mewan 3 G3
St. Michael Caerhays 3 G4
St. Michael Penkevil 3 F4
St. Michael South Elmham 45 H7
St. Michaels *Kent* 14 D4
St. Michaels *Worcs.* 28 E2
St. Michael's on Wyre 55 H5
St. Minver 3 G1
St. Monans 83 G7
St. Neot 4 B4
St. Neots 32 E3
St. Nicholas *Pembs.* 16 C1
St. Nicholas *V. of Glam.* 18 D4
St. Nicholas at Wade 25 J5
St. Ninians 75 F1
St. Osyth 35 F7
St. Ouen 3 J6
St. Owen's Cross 28 E6
St. Paul's Cray 23 H5
St. Paul's Walden 32 E6
St. Peter 3 J7
St. Peter Port 3 J5
St. Peter's 25 K5
St. Petrox 16 C5
St. Pinnock 4 C4
St. Quivox 67 H1
St. Sampson 3 J5
St. Saviour 3 H5
St. Stephen 3 G3
St. Stephens *Cornw.* 4 E5
St. Stephens *Cornw.* 6 B7
St. Stephens *Herts.* 22 E1
St. Teath 4 A2
St. Tudy 4 A3
St. Twynnells 16 C5
St. Veep 4 B5
St. Vigeans 83 H3
St. Wenn 3 G2
St. Weonards 28 D6
Saintbury 30 C4
Salachail 80 B2
Salcombe 5 H7
Salcombe Regis 7 K7
Salcott 34 D7
Sale 49 G3
Sale Green 29 J3
Saleby 53 H5
Salehurst 14 C5
Salem *Carmar.* 17 K2
Salem *Cere.* 37 F7
Salem *Gwyn.* 46 D7
Salen *Arg. & B.* 79 G3
Salen *High.* 79 H1
Salesbury 56 B6
Salford *Beds.* 32 C5
Salford *Gt.Man.* 49 H3
Salford *Oxon.* 30 D6
Salford Priors 30 B3
Salfords 23 F7
Salhouse 45 H4
Saline 75 J1
Salisbury 10 C1
Salkeld Dykes 61 G3
Sall 45 F3
Sallachan 80 A1
Sallachry 80 B6
Sallachy *High.* 96 C1
Sallachy *High.* 87 F1
Salmonby 53 G5
Salmond's Muir 83 G4
Salperton 30 B6
Salph End 32 D3
Salsburgh 75 G4
Salt 40 B3
Salt Hill 22 C4
Saltash 4 E5
Saltburn 96 E4
Saltburn-by-the-Sea 63 H4
Saltby 42 B3
Saltcoats 74 A6
Saltcotes 55 G7
Saltdean 13 G6
Salterforth 56 D5
Saltergate 63 K7
Salterhill 97 K5
Salterswall 49 F6
Saltfleet 53 H3
Saltfleetby All Saints 53 H3
Saltfleetby St. Clements 53 H3
Saltfleetby St. Peter 53 H4
Saltford 19 K5
Salthaugh Grange 59 J7
Salthouse 44 E1
Saltley 40 C7
Saltmarshe 58 D7
Saltney 48 C6
Salton 58 D1
Saltwick 71 G5
Saltwood 15 G4
Salvington 12 E6
Salwarpe 29 H2
Salwayash 8 D5
Sambourne 30 B2
Sambrook 39 G3
Samhla 92 C5
Samlesbury 55 J6
Samlesbury Bottoms 56 B7
Sampford Arundel 7 K4
Sampford Brett 7 J1
Sampford Courtenay 6 E5
Sampford Peverell 7 J4
Sampford Spiney 5 F3
Samuelston 76 C3
Sanaigmore 72 A4
Sancreed 2 B6
Sancton 59 F6
Sand 109 C8
Sand Hole 58 E6
Sand Hutton 58 C4
Sand Side 55 F1
Sandaig *Arg. & B.* 78 A3
Sandaig *High.* 86 D4
Sandaig *High.* 86 D3
Sandbach 49 G6
Sandbank 73 K2
Sandbanks 10 B6
Sandend 98 D4
Sanderstead 23 G5
Sandford *Cumb.* 61 J5
Sandford *Devon* 7 G5
Sandford *Dorset* 9 J5
Sandford *I.o.W.* 11 G6
Sandford *N.Som.* 19 H6
Sandford *S.Lan.* 75 F6
Sandford-on-Thames 21 J1
Sandford Orcas 9 F2
Sandford St. Martin 31 F6
Sandfordhill 99 K6
Sandgarth 107 E6
Sandgate 15 H4
Sandgreen 65 F5
Sandhaven 99 H4
Sandhead 64 A5
Sandhills *Dorset* 9 F3
Sandhills *Surr.* 12 C3
Sandhoe 70 E7
Sandholme *E.Riding* 58 E6
Sandholme *Lincs.* 43 G2
Sandhurst *Brack.F.* 22 B5
Sandhurst *Glos.* 29 H6
Sandhurst *Kent* 14 C5
Sandhutton 57 J1
Sandiacre 41 G2
Sandilands 53 J4
Sandiway 49 F5
Sandleheath 10 C3
Sandleigh 21 H1
Sandling 14 C2
Sandness 109 A7
Sandon *Essex* 24 D1
Sandon *Herts.* 33 G5
Sandon *Staffs.* 40 B3
Sandown 11 G6
Sandplace 4 C5
Sandquoy 106 G3
Sandridge *Herts.* 32 E7
Sandridge *Wilts.* 20 C5
Sandringham 44 A3
Sandrocks 13 G4
Sandsend 63 K5
Sandside House 104 E2
Sandsound 109 C8
Sandtoft 51 K2
Sanduck 7 F7
Sandway 14 D2
Sandwich 15 J2
Sandwick *Cumb.* 61 F5
Sandwick *Shet.* 109 D10
Sandwick (Sanndabhaig) *W.Isles* 101 G4
Sandwith 60 A5
Sandy 32 E4
Sandy Haven 16 B4
Sandy Lane *W.Yorks.* 57 G6
Sandy Lane *Wilts.* 20 C5
Sandycroft 48 C6
Sandygate *Devon* 5 J3
Sandygate *I.o.M.* 54 C4
Sandylands 55 H3
Sandyway 28 D6
Sangobeg 103 G2
Sanna 79 F1
Sannaig 72 D4
Sanndabhaig (Sandwick) 101 G4
Sanquhar 68 C3
Santon Bridge 60 C6
Santon Downham 44 C7
Sapcote 41 G6
Sapey Common 29 G2
Sapiston 34 D1
Sapperton *Glos.* 20 C1
Sapperton *Lincs.* 42 D2
Saracen's Head 43 G3
Sarclet 105 J4
Sardis 16 C4
Sarisbury 11 G4
Sarn *Bridgend* 18 C3
Sarn *Powys* 38 B6
Sarn Bach 36 C3
Sarn Meyllteyrn 36 B2
Sarnau *Carmar.* 17 G3
Sarnau *Cere.* 26 C3
Sarnau *Gwyn.* 37 J2
Sarnau *Powys* 38 B4
Sarnesfield 28 C3
Saron *Carmar.* 17 K3
Saron *Carmar.* 17 G1
Saron *Gwyn.* 46 D6
Sarratt 22 D2
Sarre 25 J5

Place	Page	Grid
Sarsden	30	D6
Sarsgrum	103	F2
Sartfield	54	C4
Satley	62	C2
Satterleigh	6	E3
Satterthwaite	60	E7
Sauchen	90	E3
Saucher	82	C4
Sauchie	75	G1
Sauchieburn	83	H1
Sauchrie	67	H2
Saughall	48	C6
Saughall Massie	48	B4
Saughtree	70	A4
Saul	20	A1
Saundby	51	K4
Saundersfoot	16	E4
Saunderton	22	A1
Saunton	6	C2
Sausthorpe	53	G6
Savalbeg	96	C1
Savalmore	96	C1
Sawbridgeworth	33	H7
Sawdon	59	F1
Sawley Derbys.	41	G2
Sawley Lancs.	56	C5
Sawley N.Yorks.	57	H3
Sawston	33	H4
Sawtry	42	E7
Saxby Leics.	42	B4
Saxby Lincs.	52	D4
Saxby All Saints	52	C1
Saxelbye	42	A3
Saxilby	52	B5
Saxlingham	44	E2
Saxlingham Green	45	G6
Saxlingham Nethergate	45	G6
Saxlingham Thorpe	45	G6
Saxmundham	35	H2
Saxon Street	33	K3
Saxondale	41	J2
Saxtead Green	35	G2
Saxtead Little Green	35	G2
Saxthorpe	45	F2
Saxton	57	K6
Sayers Common	13	F5
Scackleton	58	C2
Scadabhagh	93	G2
Scaftworth	51	J3
Scagglethorpe	58	E2
Scalasaig	72	B1
Scalby E.Riding	58	E7
Scalby N.Yorks.	59	G1
Scaldwell	31	J1
Scale Houses	61	G2
Scaleby	69	K7
Scalebyhill	69	K7
Scales Cumb.	60	E4
Scales Cumb.	55	F2
Scalford	42	A3
Scaling	63	J5
Scallasaig	86	E3
Scallastle	79	J4
Scalloway	109	C9
Scalpay	92	C4
Scamblesby	53	F5
Scammadale	79	K5
Scamodale	86	E7
Scampston	58	E2
Scampton	52	C5
Scaniport	88	D1
Scapa	107	D7
Scar	106	F3
Scarborough	59	G1
Scarcewater	3	G3
Scarcliffe	51	G6
Scarcroft	57	J5
Scardroy	95	J6
Scarff	108	B4
Scarfskerry	105	H1
Scargill	62	B5
Scarinish	78	B3
Scarisbrick	48	C1
Scarning	44	D4
Scarrington	42	A1
Scarth Hill	48	D2
Scartho	53	F2
Scaur D. & G.	65	J3
Scaur or Kippford D. & G.	65	J5
Scawby	52	C2
Scawton	58	B1
Scayne's Hill	13	G4
Scealascro	100	D5
Scethrog	28	A6
Schaw	67	J1
Scholar Green	49	H7
Scholes W.Yorks.	57	K6
Scholes W.Yorks.	50	D2
Sciberscross	104	C7
Scleddau	16	C1
Sco Ruston	45	G3
Scofton	51	J4
Scole	35	F1
Scolpaig	92	C4
Scones Lethendy	82	C5
Sconser	86	B1
Scoor	79	F6
Scopwick	52	D7
Scorborough	59	G5
Scorrier	2	E4
Scorriton	5	H4
Scorton Lancs.	55	J5
Scorton N.Yorks.	62	D6
Scotby	61	F1
Scotch Corner	62	D6
Scotforth	55	H4
Scothern	52	D5
Scotland Gate	71	H5
Scotlandwell	82	C7
Scotnish	73	F2
Scots' Gap	71	F5
Scotsburn	96	E4
Scotston Aber.	91	F7
Scotston P. & K.	82	A3
Scotstown	79	K1
Scotter	52	B2
Scotterthorpe	52	B2
Scottlethorpe	42	D3
Scotton Lincs.	52	B3
Scotton N.Yorks.	62	C7
Scotton N.Yorks.	57	J4
Scottow	45	G3
Scoulton	44	D5
Scourie	102	D4
Scourie More	102	D4
Scousburgh	109	F9
Scrabster	105	F1
Scrainwood	70	E3
Scrane End	43	G1
Scraptoft	41	J5
Scratby	45	K4

Place	Page	Grid
Scrayingham	58	D3
Scredington	42	D1
Scremby	53	H6
Scremerston	77	J6
Screveton	42	A1
Scriven	57	J4
Scrooby	51	J3
Scropton	40	D2
Scrub Hill	53	F7
Scruton	62	D7
Sculthorpe	44	C2
Scurlage	17	H6
Sea Palling	45	J3
Seabank	80	A3
Seaborough	8	D4
Seacombe	48	B3
Seacroft Lincs.	53	J6
Seacroft W.Yorks.	57	J6
Seafield Arg. & B.	73	F2
Seafield S.Ayr.	67	H1
Seafield W.Loth.	75	J4
Seaford	13	H7
Seaforth	48	C3
Seagrave	41	J4
Seaham	63	F2
Seahouses	77	K4
Seal	23	J6
Sealand	48	C6
Seale	22	B7
Seamer N.Yorks.	63	F5
Seamer N.Yorks.	59	G1
Seamill	74	A6
Searby	52	D2
Seasalter	25	G5
Seascale	60	B6
Seathwaite Cumb.	60	D5
Seathwaite Cumb.	60	D7
Seatoller	60	D5
Seaton Cornw.	4	D5
Seaton Cumb.	60	B3
Seaton Devon	8	B5
Seaton Dur.	63	F2
Seaton E.Riding	59	H5
Seaton Northumb.	71	J6
Seaton Rut.	42	C6
Seaton Burn	71	H6
Seaton Carew	63	G3
Seaton Delaval	71	J6
Seaton Junction	8	B5
Seaton Ross	58	D5
Seaton Sluice	71	J6
Seatown Aber.	99	K5
Seatown Dorset	8	D5
Seatown Moray	98	C4
Seatown Moray	98	D1
Seave Green	63	G6
Seaview	11	H5
Seaville	60	C1
Seavington St. Mary	8	D3
Seavington St. Michael		
Seawick	35	F7
Sebastopol	19	F2
Sebergham	60	E2
Seckington	40	E5
Second Coast	95	F2
Sedbergh	61	H7
Sedbury	19	J2
Sedbusk	61	K7
Sedgeberrow	30	B5
Sedgebrook	42	B2
Sedgefield	62	E4
Sedgeford	44	B2
Sedgehill	9	H2
Sedgley	40	B6
Sedgwick	55	J1
Sedlescombe	14	C6
Sedlescombe Street	14	C6
Seend	20	C5
Seend Cleeve	20	C5
Seer Green	22	C2
Seething	45	H6
Sefton	48	C2
Seghill	71	H6
Seifton	38	D7
Seilebost	93	F2
Seion	46	D6
Seisdon	40	A6
Seisiadar	101	H4
Selattyn	38	B2
Selborne	11	J1
Selby	58	C6
Selham	12	C4
Selkirk	69	K1
Sellack	28	E6
Sellafield	60	B6
Sellafirth	108	E3
Sellindge	15	F4
Selling	15	F2
Sells Green	20	C5
Selly Oak	40	C7
Selmeston	13	J6
Selsdon	23	G5
Selsey	12	B7
Selsfield Common	13	G3
Selside	56	C2
Selstead	15	H3
Selston	51	G7
Selworthy	7	H1
Semblister	109	C7
Semer	34	D4
Semington	20	B5
Semley	9	H2
Send	22	D6
Send Marsh	22	D6
Senghenydd	18	E2
Sennen	2	A6
Sennen Cove	2	A6
Sennybridge	27	J6
Senwick	65	G6
Sequer's Bridge	5	G5
Sessay	57	K2
Setchey	44	A4
Setley	10	E4
Setter Shet.	109	E8
Setter Shet.	109	C7
Settiscarth	107	C6
Settle	56	D3
Settrington	58	E2
Seven Bridges	20	E2
Seven Kings	23	H3
Seven Sisters	18	A1
Seven Springs	29	J7
Sevenhampton Glos.	30	B6
Sevenhampton Swin.	21	F2
Sevenoaks	23	J6
Sevenoaks Weald	23	J6
Severn Beach	19	J3
Severn Stoke	29	H4
Sevington	15	F3
Sewards End	33	J5

Place	Page	Grid
Sewardstone	23	G2
Sewerby	59	J3
Seworgan	2	E5
Sewstern	42	B3
Sexhow	63	F6
Sgarasta Mhòr	93	F2
Sgiogarstaigh	101	H1
Sgodachail	96	B2
Shabbington	21	K1
Shackerley	40	A5
Shackerstone	41	F5
Shackleford	22	C7
Shadfen	71	H5
Shadforth	62	E2
Shadingfield	45	J7
Shadoxhurst	14	E4
Shadwell	44	D7
Shaftesbury	9	H2
Shafton	51	F1
Shalbourne	21	G5
Shalcombe	11	F6
Shalden	21	K7
Shaldon	5	K3
Shalfleet	11	F6
Shalford Essex	34	B6
Shalford Surr.	22	D7
Shalford Green	34	B6
Shallowford	7	F1
Shalmsford Street	15	F2
Shalstone	31	H5
Shalunt	73	J3
Shambellie	65	K4
Shamley Green	22	D7
Shandon	74	A2
Shandwick	97	F4
Shangton	42	A6
Shankend	70	A3
Shankhouse	71	H6
Shanklin	11	G6
Shannochie	66	D1
Shantron	74	B2
Shantullich	96	D6
Shanzie	82	D2
Shap	61	G5
Shapwick Dorset	9	J4
Shapwick Som.	8	D1
Shardlow	41	G2
Shareshill	40	B5
Sharlston	51	F1
Sharnbrook	32	D3
Sharnford	41	G6
Sharoe Green	55	J6
Sharow	57	J2
Sharpenhoe	32	D5
Sharperton	70	E3
Sharpham House	5	J5
Sharpness	19	K1
Sharpthorne	13	G3
Sharrington	44	E2
Shatterford	39	G7
Shaugh Prior	5	F4
Shavington	49	F7
Shaw Gt.Man.	49	J2
Shaw Swin.	20	E3
Shaw W.Berks.	21	H5
Shaw Wilts.	20	B5
Shaw Mills	57	H3
Shawbury	38	E3
Shawclough	49	H1
Shawell	41	H7
Shawford	11	F2
Shawforth	56	D7
Shawhead	65	J3
Shawtonhill	74	E6
Sheanachie	66	B2
Sheandow	89	K1
Shear Cross	20	B7
Shearington	69	F7
Shearsby	41	J6
Shebbear	6	C5
Shebdon	39	G3
Shebster	105	F2
Shedfield	11	G3
Sheen	50	D6
Sheepscombe	29	H7
Sheepstor	5	F4
Sheepwash Devon	6	C5
Sheepwash Northumb.	71	H5
Sheepway	19	H4
Sheepy Magna	41	F5
Sheepy Parva	41	F5
Sheering	33	J7
Sheerness	25	F4
Sheet	11	J2
Sheffield	51	F4
Sheffield Bottom	21	K5
Sheffield City Airport	51	G4
Sheffield Green	13	H4
Shefford	32	E5
Shefford Woodlands	21	G4
Sheigra	102	D2
Sheinton	39	F5
Shelderton	28	D1
Sheldon Derbys.	50	D6
Sheldon Devon	7	K5
Sheldon W.Mid.	40	D7
Sheldwich	15	F2
Shelf	57	G7
Shelfanger	45	F7
Shelfield	40	C5
Shelford	41	J1
Shellachan Arg. & B.	79	K6
Shellachan Arg. & B.	80	B5
Shellbrook Hill	38	C1
Shelley Essex	23	J1
Shelley Suff.	34	E5
Shelley W.Yorks.	50	E1
Shellingford	21	G2
Shellow Bowells	24	C1
Shelsley Beauchamp	29	G2
Shelsley Walsh	29	G2
Shelton Beds.	32	D2
Shelton Norf.	45	G6
Shelton Notts.	42	A1
Shelton Shrop.	38	D4
Shelton Green	45	G6
Shelve	38	C6
Shelwick	28	E4
Shenfield	24	C2
Shenington	30	E4
Shenley	22	E1
Shenley Brook End	32	B5
Shenley Church End	32	B5
Shenleybury	22	E1
Shenmore	28	C5
Shennanton	64	D4
Shenstone Staffs.	40	D5
Shenstone Worcs.	29	H1
Shenstone Woodend	40	D5

Place	Page	Grid
Shenton	41	F5
Shenval	89	K2
Shepeau Stow	43	G4
Shephall	33	F6
Shepherd's Green	22	A3
Shepherdswell (Sibertswold)	15	H3
Shepley	50	D2
Sheppardstown	105	H5
Shepperdine	19	K2
Shepperton	22	D5
Shepreth	33	G4
Shepshed	41	G4
Shepton Beauchamp	8	D3
Shepton Mallet	19	K7
Shepton Montague	9	F1
Shepway	14	C2
Sheraton	63	F3
Sherborne Dorset	9	F3
Sherborne Glos.	30	C7
Sherborne St. John	21	K6
Sherbourne	30	D2
Sherburn Dur.	62	E2
Sherburn N.Yorks.	59	F2
Sherburn in Elmet	57	K6
Shere	22	D7
Shereford	44	C3
Sherfield English	10	D2
Sherfield on Loddon	21	K6
Sherford	5	H6
Sheriff Hutton	58	C3
Sheriffhales	39	G4
Sheringham	45	F1
Sherington	32	B4
Shernborne	44	B2
Sherramore	88	C5
Sherrington	9	J1
Sherston	20	B3
Sherwood Green	6	D3
Shettleston	74	E4
Shevington	48	E2
Shevington Moor	48	E1
Sheviock	4	D5
Shiel Bridge	87	F3
Shieldaig High.	94	E6
Shieldaig High.	94	E4
Shieldhill	75	G3
Shielfoot	86	C7
Shielhill	83	F1
Shiels	90	E4
Shifford	21	G1
Shifnal	39	G5
Shilbottle	71	G3
Shildon	62	D4
Shillingford Devon	7	H3
Shillingford Oxon.	21	J2
Shillingford St. George	7	H7
Shillingstone	9	H3
Shillington	32	E5
Shillmoor	70	D3
Shilstone	6	D5
Shilton Oxon.	21	F1
Shilton Warks.	41	G7
Shimpling Norf.	45	F7
Shimpling Suff.	34	C3
Shimpling Street	34	C3
Shincliffe	62	D2
Shiney Row	62	E1
Shinfield	22	A5
Shingay	33	G4
Shingle Street	35	H4
Shinner's Bridge	5	H4
Shinness Lodge	103	H7
Shipbourne	23	J6
Shipdham	44	D5
Shipham	19	H6
Shiphay	5	J4
Shiplake	22	A4
Shipley Northumb.	71	G2
Shipley Shrop.	40	A6
Shipley W.Suss.	12	E4
Shipley W.Yorks.	57	G6
Shipley Bridge Devon	5	G4
Shipley Bridge Surr.	23	G7
Shipmeadow	45	H6
Shippon	21	H2
Shipston on Stour	30	D4
Shipton Glos.	30	B7
Shipton N.Yorks.	58	B4
Shipton Shrop.	38	E6
Shipton Bellinger	21	F7
Shipton Gorge	8	D5
Shipton Green	12	B7
Shipton Moyne	20	B3
Shipton-on-Cherwell	31	F7
Shipton-under-Wychwood	30	D7
Shiptonthorpe	58	E5
Shira	80	C6
Shirburn	21	K2
Shirdley Hill	48	C1
Shire Oak	40	C5
Shirebrook	51	H6
Shiremoor	71	J6
Shirenewton	19	H2
Shireoaks	51	H4
Shirl Heath	28	D3
Shirland	51	F7
Shirley Derbys.	40	E1
Shirley Gt.Lon.	23	G5
Shirley Hants.	10	C5
Shirley S'ham.	11	F3
Shirley W.Mid.	30	C1
Shirrell Heath	11	G3
Shirwell	6	D2
Shirwell Cross	6	D2
Shiskine	66	D1
Shobdon	28	C2
Shobrooke	7	G5
Shoburyness	25	F3
Sholden	15	J2
Sholing	11	F3
Shoot Hill	38	D4
Shooter's Hill	23	H4
Shop Cornw.	3	F1
Shop Cornw.	6	A4
Shop Corner	35	G5
Shoreditch	23	G3
Shoreham	23	J5
Shoreham-by-Sea	13	F6
Shoremill	96	E5
Shoresdean	77	H6
Shoreswood	77	H6
Shoretown	96	D5
Shorncote	20	D2
Shorne	24	C4
Shorne Ridgeway	24	C4
Short Cross	38	B5

Place	Page	Grid
Short Green	44	E7
Short Heath Derbys.	41	F4
Short Heath W.Mid.	40	C6
Shortacombe	6	D7
Shortgate	13	H5
Shortgrove	33	J5
Shortlanesend	3	F4
Shorwell	11	F6
Shoscombe	20	A6
Shotesham	45	G6
Shotgate	24	D2
Shotley	35	G5
Shotley Bridge	62	B1
Shotley Gate	35	G5
Shotleyfield	62	B1
Shottenden	15	F2
Shottermill	12	B3
Shottery	30	C3
Shotteswell	31	F4
Shottisham	35	H4
Shottle	51	F7
Shottlegate	41	F1
Shotton Dur.	62	E3
Shotton Flints.	48	C6
Shotton Northumb.	77	G7
Shotton Colliery	62	E2
Shotts	75	G4
Shotwick	48	C5
Shoughlaige-e-Caine	54	C5
Shouldham	44	A5
Shouldham Thorpe	44	A5
Shoulton	29	H3
Shover's Green	13	K3
Shrawardine	38	C4
Shrawley	29	H2
Shrewley	30	D2
Shrewsbury	38	D4
Shrewton	20	D7
Shripney	12	C6
Shrivenham	21	F3
Shropham	44	D6
Shroton (Iwerne Courtney)	9	H3
Shrub End	34	D6
Shucknall	28	E4
Shudy Camps	33	K4
Shurdington	29	J7
Shurlock Row	22	B4
Shurrery	105	F3
Shurrery Lodge	105	F3
Shurton	7	K1
Shustoke	40	E6
Shute Heath	40	A3
Shute	8	B5
Shutford	30	E4
Shuthonger	29	H5
Shutlanger	31	J3
Shuttington	40	E5
Shuttlewood	51	G5
Shuttleworth	49	H1
Siabost	100	E3
Siadar Iarach	101	F2
Siadar Uarach	101	F2
Sibbaldbie	69	G5
Sibbertoft	41	J7
Sibdon Carwood	38	D7
Sibertswold (Shepherdswell)	15	H3
Sibford Ferris	30	E5
Sibford Gower	30	E5
Sible Hedingham	34	B5
Sibsey	53	G7
Sibson Cambs.	42	D6
Sibson Leics.	41	F5
Sibster	105	J3
Sibthorpe	42	A1
Sibton	35	H2
Sicklesmere	34	C3
Sicklinghall	57	J5
Sidbury Devon	7	K6
Sidbury Shrop.	39	F7
Sidcot	19	H6
Sidcup	23	H4
Siddington Ches.	49	H5
Siddington Glos.	20	D2
Sidemoor	29	J1
Sidestrand	45	G2
Sidford	7	K6
Sidlesham	12	B7
Sidley	14	C7
Sidlow	23	F7
Sidmouth	7	K7
Sigford	5	H3
Sigglesthorne	59	H5
Sigingstone	18	C4
Silchester	21	K5
Sileby	41	J4
Silecroft	54	E1
Silfield	45	F6
Silian	26	E3
Silk Willoughby	42	D1
Silkstone	50	E2
Silkstone Common	50	E2
Silksworth	62	E1
Silloth	60	C1
Sills	70	D3
Sillyearn	98	D5
Silpho	63	J3
Silsden	57	F5
Silsoe	32	D5
Silton	9	G2
Silver End	34	C6
Silver Hill E.Suss.	14	C5
Silverburn	76	A4
Silvercraigs	73	G2
Silverdale Lancs.	55	H2
Silverdale Staffs.	40	A1
Silverhill	14	D6
Silverley's Green	35	G1
Silvermoss	91	G1
Silverstone	31	H4
Silverton	7	H5
Silvington	29	F1
Silwick	109	B8
Simonburn	70	D6
Simonsbath	7	F2
Simonstone	56	C6
Simprim	77	G6
Simpson	32	B5
Sinclair's Hill	77	G5
Sinclairston	67	J2
Sinderby	57	J1
Sinderhope	61	K1
Sindlesham	22	A5
Singdean	70	A3
Singleton Lancs.	55	G6
Singleton W.Suss.	12	B5
Singlewell or Ifield	24	C4
Sinnahard	90	C3
Sinnington	58	D1
Sinton Green	29	H2
Sipson	22	D4
Sirhowy	28	A7
Sisland	45	H6
Sissinghurst	14	C4

Place	Page	Grid
Siston	19	K4
Sithney	2	D6
Sittingbourne	25	F5
Siulaisiadar	101	H4
Six Ashes	39	G7
Six Mile Bottom	33	J3
Sixhills	52	E4
Sixmile Cottages	15	G3
Sixpenny Handley	9	J3
Sizewell	35	J2
Skail	104	C4
Skaill Ork.	107	B6
Skaill Ork.	107	E7
Skares Aber.	90	E1
Skares E.Ayr.	67	K2
Skarpigarth	109	A7
Skateraw	77	F3
Skaw	109	E6
Skeabost	93	K6
Skeabrae	106	B5
Skeeby	62	C6
Skeffington	42	A5
Skeffling	53	G1
Skegby	51	H6
Skegness	53	J6
Skelberry	109	G9
Skelbo	96	E2
Skeldon	67	H2
Skeldyke	43	G2
Skellingthorpe	52	C5
Skellister	109	D7
Skellow	51	H1
Skelmanthorpe	50	E1
Skelmersdale	48	D2
Skelmonae	91	G1
Skelmorlie	73	K4
Skelmuir	99	H6
Skelpick	104	C3
Skelton Cumb.	61	F3
Skelton E.Riding	58	D7
Skelton N.Yorks.	62	B6
Skelton N.Yorks.	57	H3
Skelton R. & C.	63	H5
Skelton York	58	B4
Skelton Green	63	H5
Skelwick	106	D3
Skelwith Bridge	60	E6
Skendleby	53	H6
Skenfrith	28	D6
Skerne	59	G4
Skeroblingarry	66	B1
Skerray	103	J2
Sketty	17	K5
Skewen	18	A2
Skewsby	58	C2
Skeyton	45	G3
Skidbrooke	53	H3
Skidby	59	G6
Skilgate	7	H3
Skillington	42	C3
Skinburness	60	C1
Skinflats	75	H2
Skinidin	93	H7
Skinnet	105	G2
Skinningrove	63	J4
Skipness	73	H5
Skipsea	59	H4
Skipton	56	E4
Skipton-on-Swale	57	J1
Skipwith	58	C6
Skirbeck	43	G1
Skirlaugh	59	H6
Skirling	75	J7
Skirmett	22	A3
Skirpenbeck	58	D4
Skirwith Cumb.	61	H3
Skirwith N.Yorks.	56	C2
Skirza	105	J2
Skulamus	86	C2
Skullomie	103	J2
Skye of Curr	89	G2
Slack	90	D1
Slackhall	50	C4
Slackhead	98	C4
Slad	20	B1
Slade	6	D1
Slade Green	23	J4
Slaggyford	61	H1
Slaidburn	56	C4
Slains Park	91	G7
Slaithwaite	50	C1
Slaley	62	A1
Slamannan	75	G3
Slapton Bucks.	32	C6
Slapton Devon	5	J6
Slapton Northants.	31	H4
Slate Haugh	98	C4
Slatenber	56	C2
Slattadale	94	E4
Slattocks	49	H2
Slaugham	13	F4
Slaughden	35	J3
Slaughterford	20	B4
Slawston	42	A6
Sleaford Hants.	12	B3
Sleaford Lincs.	42	D1
Sleagill	61	G5
Sleapford	39	F4
Sledge Green	29	H5
Sledmere	59	F3
Sleights	63	K6
Slepe	9	J5
Slickly	105	H2
Sliddery	66	D1
Sliemore	89	H2
Sligachan	85	K2
Slimbridge	20	A1
Slindon Staffs.	40	A2
Slindon W.Suss.	12	C6
Slinfold	12	E3
Slingsby	58	C2
Slioch	90	D1
Slip End Beds.	32	D7
Slip End Herts.	33	F5
Slipton	32	C1
Slochd	89	F2
Slockavullin	73	G1
Slogarie	65	G4
Sloley	45	G3
Sloothby	53	H5
Slough	22	C4
Sluggan	89	F2
Slyne	55	H3
Smailholm	76	E7
Small Dole	13	F5
Small Hythe	14	D4
Smallbridge	49	J1
Smallburgh	45	H3
Smallburn Aber.	99	J6
Smallburn E.Ayr.	68	B1
Smalley	41	G1
Smallfield	23	G7
Smallridge	8	B4
Smallthorne	49	H7
Smallworth	44	E7
Smannell	21	G7
Smardale	61	J6
Smarden	14	D3

Place	Page	Grid
Smaull	72	A4
Smeale Farm	54	D3
Smeatharpe	7	K4
Smeeth	15	F4
Smeeton Westerby	41	J6
Smelthouses	57	G3
Smerral	105	G5
Smethwick	40	C7
Smirisary	86	C7
Smisby	41	F4
Smith End Green	29	G3
Smithfield	69	K7
Smithincott	7	J4
Smith's Green	33	J6
Smithton	96	E7
Smithy Green	49	G5
Smug Oak	22	E1
Smyrton	67	F5
Smythe's Green	34	D7
Snailbeach	38	C5
Snailwell	33	K2
Snainton	59	F1
Snaith	58	C7
Snape N.Yorks.	57	H1
Snape Suff.	35	H3
Snape Green	48	C1
Snarestone	41	F5
Snarford	52	D4
Snargate	14	E5
Snave	15	F4
Sneachill	29	J3
Snead	38	C6
Sneaton	63	K6
Sneatonthorpe	63	K6
Snelland	52	D4
Snellings	60	A6
Snelston	40	D1
Snetterton	44	D6
Snettisham	44	A2
Snibston	41	G4
Snishival	84	C1
Snitter	71	F3
Snitterby	52	C3
Snitterfield	30	D3
Snitton	28	E1
Snodhill	28	C4
Snodland	24	D5
Snowshill	30	B5
Soar Carmar.	17	K2
Soar Devon	5	H7
Soberton	11	H3
Soberton Heath	11	H3
Sockburn	62	E6
Sodylt Bank	38	C2
Soham	33	J1
Solas	92	D4
Soldon Cross	6	B4
Soldridge	11	H1
Sole Street Kent	15	F3
Sole Street Kent	24	C5
Solihull	30	C1
Solihull Lodge	30	B1
Sollers Dilwyn	28	D3
Sollers Hope	29	F5
Sollom	48	D1
Solsgirth	75	H1
Solva	16	A2
Solwaybank	69	J6
Somerby	42	A4
Somercotes	51	G7
Somerford Keynes	20	D2
Somerley	12	B7
Somerleyton	45	J6
Somersal Herbert	40	D2
Somersby	53	G5
Somersham Cambs.	33	G1
Somersham Suff.	34	E4
Somerton Oxon.	31	F6
Somerton Som.	8	D2
Somerton Suff.	34	C3
Sompting	12	E6
Sonning	22	A4
Sonning Common	22	A3
Sonning Eye	22	A4
Sopley	10	C5
Sopworth	20	B3
Sorbie	64	E6
Sordale	105	G2
Sorisdale	78	D1
Sorn	67	K1
Sornhill	74	D7
Soroba	79	K5
Sortat	105	H2
Sotby	53	F5
Sots Hole	52	E6
Sotterly	45	J7
Soudley	39	G3
Soughton	48	B6
Soulbury	32	B6
Soulby	61	J5
Souldern	31	G5
Souldrop	32	C2
Sound Ches.	39	F1
Sound Shet.	109	C7
Sound Shet.	109	D7
Soundwell	19	K4
Sourhope	70	D1
Sourin	106	D3
Sourton	6	D7
Soutergate	55	F1
South Acre	44	C4
South Allington	5	H7
South Alloa	75	G1
South Ambersham	12	C4
South Anston	51	H4
South Ascot	22	C5
South Ballachulish	80	B2
South Balloch	67	H4
South Bank	63	G4
South Barrow	9	F2
South Beddington	23	F5
South Bellsdyke	75	H2
South Benfleet	24	D3
South Bersted	12	C7
South Blackbog	91	F1
South Bowood	8	D5
South Brent	5	G4
South Brentor	6	C7
South Brewham	9	G1
South Broomhill	71	H4
South Burlingham	45	H5
South Cadbury	9	F2
South Cairn	66	D7
South Carlton	52	C5
South Cave	59	F6
South Cerney	20	D2
South Chard	8	C4
South Charlton	71	G1
South Cheriton	9	F2
South Cliffe	58	E5
South Clifton	52	B5
South Cockerington	53	G4
South Common	13	G5
South Cornelly	18	B4
South Corriegills	66	E1
South Cove	45	J7
South Creagan	80	A3

South Creake 44 C2
South Croxton 41 J4
South Dalton 59 F5
South Darenth 23 J5
South Duffield 58 C6
South Elkington 53 F4
South Elmsall 51 G1
South End *Bucks.* 32 B6
South End *Cumb.* 55 F3
South End 52 E1
N.Lincs.
South Erradale 94 D4
South Fambridge 24 E2
South Fawley 21 G3
South Ferriby 59 F7
South Flobbets 91 F1
South Garth 108 E3
South Godstone 23 G7
South Gorley 10 C3
South Green 24 C2
Essex
South Green *Norf.* 44 E4
South Hall 73 J3
South Hanningfield 24 D2
South Harting 11 J3
South Hayling 11 J5
South Hazelrigg 77 J7
South Heath 22 C1
South Heighton 13 H6
South Hetton 62 E2
South Hiendley 51 F1
South Hill 4 D3
South Hinksey 21 J1
South Hole 6 A4
South Holmwood 22 E7
South Hornchurch 23 J3
South Hourat 74 A5
South Huish 5 G6
South Hykeham 52 C6
South Hylton 62 E1
South Kelsey 52 D3
South Kessock 96 D7
South 52 E1
Killingholme
South Kilvington 57 K1
South Kilworth 41 J7
South Kirkby 51 G1
South Kirkton 91 F4
South Kyme 42 E1
South Lancing 12 E6
South Ledaig 80 A4
South Leigh 21 G1
South Leverton 51 K4
South Littleton 30 B4
South Lopham 44 E7
South Luffenham 42 C5
South Malling 13 H5
South Marston 20 E3
South Milford 57 K6
South Milton 5 H6
South Mimms 23 F1
South Molton 7 F3
South Moor 62 C1
South Moreton 21 J3
South Mundham 12 B6
South Muskham 51 K7
South Newbald 59 F6
South Newington 31 F5
South Newton 10 B1
South Normanton 51 G7
South Norwood 23 G5
South Nutfield 23 G7
South Ockendon 23 J3
South Ormsby 53 G5
South Otterington 57 J1
South Oxhey 22 E2
South Park 23 F7
South Perrott 8 D4
South Petherton 8 D3
South Petherwin 6 B7
South Pickenham 44 C5
South Pool 5 H6
South Queensferry 75 K3
South Radworthy 7 F2
South Rauceby 42 D1
South Raynham 44 C3
South Redbriggs 99 F6
South Reston 53 H4
South Runcton 44 A5
South Scarle 52 B6
South Shian 80 A3
South Shields 71 J7
South Somercotes 53 H3
South Stainley 57 J3
South Stoke 21 K3
Oxon.
South Stoke 12 D6
W.Suss.
South Street 13 G5
E.Suss.
South Street *Kent* 24 C5
South Tawton 6 E6
South Thoresby 53 H5
South Tidworth 21 F7
South Town 11 H1
South Upper 99 H6
Barrack
South Walsham 45 H4
South 22 A7
Warnborough
South Weald 23 J2
South Weston 22 A2
South Wheatley 4 C1
Cornw.
South Wheatley 51 K4
Notts.
South Whiteness 109 C8
South Widcombe 19 J6
South Wigston 41 H6
South 15 F3
Willesborough
South Willingham 52 E4
South Wingate 63 F3
South Wingfield 51 F7
South Witham 42 C4
South Wonston 11 F1
South Woodham 24 E2
Ferrers
South Wootton 44 A3
South Wraxall 20 B5
South Yardley 40 D7
South Zeal 6 E6
Southall 22 E4
Southam *Glos.* 29 J6
Southam *Warks.* 31 F2
Southampton 11 F3
Southampton 11 F3
International
Airport
Southbar 74 C4
Southborough 23 J7
Southbourne 10 C5
Bourne.
Southbourne 11 J4
W.Suss.
Southburgh 44 E5
Southburn 59 F4
Southchurch 25 F3
Southcott 6 D6

Southdean 70 B3
Southease 13 H6
Southend *Aber.* 99 F6
Southend 66 A3
Arg. & B.
Southend 21 K4
W.Berks.
Southend-on-Sea 24 E3
Southerndown 18 B4
Southerness 65 K5
Southery 44 A6
Southfleet 24 C4
Southgate *Gt.Lon.* 23 F2
Southgate *Norf.* 45 F3
Southgate *Norf.* 44 A2
Southgate *Swan.* 17 J6
Southill 32 E4
Southington 21 J7
Southleigh 8 B5
Southminster 25 F2
Southmuir 82 E2
Southoe 32 E2
Southolt 35 F2
Southorpe 42 D5
Southowram 57 G2
Southport 48 C1
Southrepps 45 G2
Southrey 52 E6
Southrop 20 E1
Southrope 21 K7
Southsea *Ports.* 11 H5
Southsea *Wrex.* 48 B7
Southstoke 20 A5
Southtown *Norf.* 45 K5
Southtown *Ork.* 107 D8
Southwaite 61 J6
Cumb.
Southwaite 61 F2
Cumb.
Southwark 23 G4
Southwater 12 E4
Southway 19 J7
Southwell *Dorset* 9 F7
Southwell *Notts.* 51 K7
Southwick *Hants.* 11 H4
Southwick 42 D6
Northants.
Southwick *T. & W.* 62 E1
Southwick 13 F6
W.Suss.
Southwick *Wilts.* 20 B5
Southwold 35 K1
Southwood *Norf.* 45 H5
Southwood *Som.* 8 E1
Sowerby *N.Yorks.* 57 K1
Sowerby *W.Yorks.* 57 F7
Sowerby Bridge 57 F7
Sowerby Row 60 E2
Sowton 7 H6
Soyal 96 C2
Spa Common 45 G2
Spadeadam 70 A6
Spalding 43 F3
Spaldington 58 D6
Spaldwick 32 E1
Spalefield 83 G7
Spalford 52 B6
Spanby 42 D2
Sparham 44 E4
Spark Bridge 55 G1
Sparkford 9 F2
Sparkwell 5 F5
Sparrowpit 50 C4
Sparrow's Green 13 K3
Sparsholt *Hants.* 11 F1
Sparsholt *Oxon.* 21 G3
Spartylea 61 K2
Spaunton 63 J7
Spaxton 8 B1
Spean Bridge 87 J6
Speddoch 68 D5
Speen *Bucks.* 22 B1
Speen *W.Berks.* 21 H5
Speeton 59 H2
Speke 48 D4
Speldhurst 23 J7
Spellbrook 33 H7
Spelsbury 30 E6
Spen Green 49 H6
Spencers Wood 22 A5
Spennithorne 57 G1
Spennymoor 62 D3
Spetchley 29 H3
Spetisbury 9 J4
Spexhall 45 H7
Spey Bay 98 B4
Speybridge 89 H2
Speyview 97 K7
Spilsby 53 H6
Spindlestone 77 K7
Spinkhill 51 G5
Spinningdale 96 D2
Spirthill 20 C4
Spital *High.* 105 G3
Spital *W. & M.* 22 C4
Spital in the Street 52 C3
Spitalbrook 23 G1
Spithurst 13 H5
Spittal *D. & G.* 64 E4
Spittal *Dur.* 62 C1
Spittal *E.Loth.* 76 C3
Spittal *Northumb.* 77 J5
Spittal *Pembs.* 16 C2
Spittal of 90 B6
Glenmuick
Spittal of 82 C1
Glenshee
Spittalfield 82 C3
Spixworth 45 G4
Spofforth 57 J4
Spondon 41 G2
Spooner Row 44 E6
Spoonley 39 F2
Sporle 44 C4
Sportsman's Arms 47 H7
Spott 76 E3
Spratton 31 J2
Spreakley 22 B7
Spreyton 6 E6
Spridlington 52 D4
Springburn 74 E4
Springfield 73 J3
Arg. & B.
Springfield 69 J7
D. & G.
Springfield *Fife* 82 E6
Springfield *Moray* 97 H6
Springfield *P. & K.* 82 C4
Springfield 40 C7
W.Mid.
Springholm 65 J4
Springkell 69 H6
Springleys 91 F1
Springside 74 B7
Springthorpe 52 B4
Springwell 62 D1
Sproatley 59 H6
Sproston Green 49 G6

Sproughton 35 F4
Sprouston 77 F7
Sprowston 45 G4
Sproxton *Leics.* 42 B3
Sproxton *N.Yorks.* 58 C1
Spurstow 48 E7
Square Point 65 H3
Squires Gate 55 G6
Sròndoire 73 G3
Sronphadruig 88 E7
Lodge
Stableford 40 A2
Stackhouse 56 D3
Stackpole 16 C5
Stacksteads 56 D7
Staddiscombe 5 F5
Staddlethorpe 58 E7
Stadhampton 21 K2
Stadhlaigearraidh 84 C1
Staffield 61 G2
Staffin 93 K5
Stafford 40 B3
Stagden Cross 33 K7
Stagsden 32 C4
Stagshaw Bank 70 E7
Stain 105 J2
Stainburn 57 H5
Stainby 42 C3
Staincross 51 F2
Staindrop 62 C4
Staines 22 D4
Stainfield *Lincs.* 42 D3
Stainfield *Lincs.* 52 E5
Stainforth 56 D3
N.Yorks.
Stainforth 51 J1
S.Yorks.
Staining 55 G6
Stainland 50 C1
Stainsacre 63 J2
Stainton *Cumb.* 55 J1
Stainton *Cumb.* 61 F4
Stainton *Dur.* 62 B5
Stainton *Middbro.* 63 F5
Stainton *N.Yorks.* 62 B7
Stainton *S.Yorks.* 51 H3
Stainton by 52 D5
Langworth
Stainton le Vale 52 E3
Stainton with 55 F2
Adgarley
Staintondale 63 J3
Stair *Cumb.* 60 D4
Stair *E.Ayr.* 67 J1
Staithes 63 J5
Stake Pool 55 H5
Stakeford 71 H5
Stalbridge 9 G3
Stalbridge Weston 9 G3
Stalham 45 H3
Stalham Green 45 H3
Stalisfield Green 14 E2
Stalling Busk 56 E1
Stallingborough 53 F1
Stalmine 55 G5
Stalybridge 49 J3
Stambourne 34 B5
Stamford *Lincs.* 42 D5
Stamford 71 H2
Northumb.
Stamford Bridge 58 D4
Stamfordham 71 F6
Stanborough 33 F7
Stanbridge *Beds.* 32 C6
Stanbridge *Dorset* 10 B4
Stanbridge Earls 10 E2
Stanbury 57 F6
Stand 75 F4
Standburn 75 H3
Standeford 40 B5
Standen 14 D3
Standford 12 B3
Standish 48 E1
Standlake 21 G1
Standon *Hants.* 11 F2
Standon *Herts.* 33 G6
Standon *Staffs.* 40 A2
Stane 75 G5
Stanfield 44 D3
Stanford *Beds.* 32 E4
Stanford *Kent* 15 G4
Stanford Bishop 29 F3
Stanford Bridge 29 G2
Stanford Dingley 21 J4
Stanford in the 21 G2
Vale
Stanford-le-Hope 24 C3
Stanford on Avon 31 G1
Stanford on Soar 41 H3
Stanford on Teme 29 G2
Stanford Rivers 23 J1
Stanghow 63 H5
Stanground 43 F6
Stanhoe 44 C2
Stanhope *Dur.* 62 A3
Stanhope 69 G1
Sc.Bord.
Stanion 42 C7
Stanley *Derbys.* 41 G1
Stanley *Dur.* 62 C1
Stanley *P. & K.* 82 C4
Stanley *Staffs.* 49 J7
Stanley *W.Yorks.* 57 J7
Stanley *Wilts.* 20 C4
Stanley Common 41 G1
Stanmer 13 G6
Stanmore *Gt.Lon.* 22 E2
Stanmore 21 H4
W.Berks.
Stannersburn 70 C5
Stanningfield 34 C3
Stannington 71 H6
Northumb.
Stannington 51 F4
S.Yorks.
Stansbatch 28 C2
Stansfield 34 B3
Stanstead 34 C4
Stanstead Abbotts 33 G7
Stansted 24 C5
Stansted Airport 33 J6
Stansted 33 J6
Mountfitchet
Stanton *Derbys.* 40 E4
Stanton *Glos.* 30 B5
Stanton 71 G4
Northumb.
Stanton *Staffs.* 40 D1
Stanton *Suff.* 34 D1
Stanton by Bridge 41 F3
Stanton by Dale 41 G1
Stanton Drew 19 J5
Stanton Fitzwarren 20 E2
Stanton Harcourt 21 H1
Stanton Hill 51 G6
Stanton in Peak 50 E6
Stanton Lacy 28 D1
Stanton-on-the- 41 J1
Wolds

Stanton Prior 19 K5
Stanton St. 20 D5
Bernard
Stanton St. John 20 C3
Stanton St. Quintin 20 C4
Stanton Street 34 D2
Stanton under 41 G4
Bardon
Stanton upon Hine 38 E3
Heath
Stanton Wick 19 K5
Stanwardine in the 38 D3
Fields
Stanway *Essex* 34 D6
Stanway *Glos.* 30 B5
Stanwell 22 D4
Stanwell Moor 22 D4
Stanwick 32 C1
Stanwix 61 F1
Stanydale 109 B7
Staoinebrig 84 C1
Stape 63 J7
Stapehill 10 B4
Stapeley 39 F1
Staple 15 H2
Staple Fitzpaine 8 B3
Staplecross 14 C5
Staplefield 13 F4
Stapleford *Cambs.* 33 H3
Stapleford *Herts.* 33 G7
Stapleford *Leics.* 42 B4
Stapleford *Lincs.* 52 B7
Stapleford *Notts.* 41 G2
Stapleford *Wilts.* 10 B1
Stapleford Abbotts 23 H2
Stapleford Tawney 23 J2
Staplegrove 8 B2
Staplehurst 14 C3
Staplers 11 G6
Stapleton *Bristol* 19 J4
Stapleton *Cumb.* 70 A6
Stapleton *Here.* 28 C2
Stapleton *Leics.* 41 G6
Stapleton 62 D5
N.Yorks.
Stapleton *Shrop.* 38 D5
Stapleton *Som.* 8 D2
Stapley 7 K4
Staploe 32 E2
Staplow 29 F4
Star *Fife* 82 E7
Star *Pembs.* 17 F1
Star *Som.* 19 H6
Starbotton 56 E2
Starcross 7 H2
Starkigarth 109 D10
Starling's Green 33 H5
Starr 67 J4
Starston 45 G7
Startforth 62 B5
Startley 20 C3
Statham 49 F4
Stathe 8 C2
Stathern 42 A2
Station Town 63 F3
Staughton Green 32 E2
Staughton 32 E2
Highway
Staunton *Glos.* 28 E7
Staunton *Glos.* 29 G6
Staunton Harold 41 F3
Hall
Staunton on Arrow 28 C2
Staunton on Wye 28 C4
Staveley *Cumb.* 61 F7
Staveley *Derbys.* 51 G5
Staveley *N.Yorks.* 57 J3
Staveley-in- 55 G1
Cartmel
Staverton *Devon* 5 H4
Staverton *Glos.* 29 H6
Staverton 31 G2
Northants.
Staverton *Wilts.* 20 B5
Staverton Bridge 29 H6
Stawell 8 C1
Stawley 7 J3
Staxigoe 105 J3
Staxton 59 G2
Staylittle 37 H6
Staynall 55 G5
Staythorpe 51 K7
Stean 57 F2
Steane 31 G5
Stearsby 58 C2
Steart 19 F7
Stebbing 33 K6
Stebbing Green 33 K6
Stedham 12 B4
Steel Cross 13 J3
Steele Road 70 A4
Steen's Bridge 28 E3
Steep 11 J2
Steep Marsh 11 J2
Steeple *Dorset* 9 J6
Steeple *Essex* 25 F1
Steeple Ashton 20 C6
Steeple Aston 31 F6
Steeple Barton 31 F6
Steeple Bumpstead 33 K4
Steeple Claydon 31 H6
Steeple Gidding 42 E7
Steeple Langford 10 B1
Steeple Morden 33 F4
Steeton 57 F5
Stein 93 H6
Steinmanhill 99 F6
Stella 71 G7
Stelling Minnis 15 G3
Stemster *High.* 105 G2
Stemster *High.* 105 G4
Stemster House 105 G2
Stenalees 4 A5
Stenhousemuir 75 G2
Stenigot 53 F4
Stenness 108 B5
Stenscholl 93 K5
Stenton *E.Loth.* 76 E3
Stenton *P. & K.* 82 B3
Steornabhagh 101 G4
(Stornoway)
Stepaside 16 E4
Stepney 23 G3
Steppingley 32 D5
Stepps 74 E4
Sternfield 35 H2
Sterridge 6 D1
Stert 20 D6
Stetchworth 33 K3
Stevenage 33 F6
Stevenston 74 A6
Steventon *Hants.* 21 J7
Steventon *Oxon.* 21 H2
Stevington 32 C3
Stewartby 32 D4
Stewarton *D. & G.* 64 E6
Stewarton *E.Ayr.* 74 C6
Stewkley 32 B6
Stewton 53 G4

Steyning 12 E5
Steynton 16 C4
Stibb 6 A4
Stibb Cross 6 C4
Stibb Green 21 F5
Stibbard 44 D3
Stibbington 42 D6
Stichill 77 F7
Sticker 3 G3
Stickford 53 G6
Sticklepath 6 E6
Stickney 53 G7
Stiffkey 44 D1
Stifford's Bridge 29 G4
Stillingfleet 58 B5
Stillington 58 B3
N.Yorks.
Stillington *Stock.* 62 E4
Stilton 42 E7
Stinchcombe 20 A2
Stinsford 9 G5
Stirchley 39 G5
Tel. & W.
Stirchley *W.Mid.* 40 C7
Stirkoke House 105 J3
Stirling *Aber.* 99 K6
Stirling *Stir.* 75 F1
Stirton 56 E4
Stisted 34 B6
Stithians 2 E5
Stittenham 96 D4
Stivichall 30 E1
Stix 81 J3
Stixwould 52 E6
Stoak 48 D5
Stobo 75 K7
Stoborough 9 J6
Stoborough Green 9 J6
Stobwood 75 H5
Stock 24 C2
Stock Green 29 J3
Stock Lane 21 F4
Stock Wood 30 B3
Stockbridge 10 E1
Hants.
Stockbridge *Stir.* 81 J7
Stockbury 24 E5
Stockcross 21 H5
Stockdalewath 60 E2
Stockerston 42 B6
Stocking Pelham 33 H6
Stockingford 41 F6
Stockland 8 B4
Stockland Bristol 19 F7
Stockland English 7 G5
Stockleigh 7 G5
Pomeroy
Stockley 20 C5
Stocklinch 8 C3
Stockport 49 H4
Stocksbridge 50 E3
Stocksfield 71 F7
Stockton *Here.* 28 E2
Stockton *Norf.* 45 H6
Stockton *Shrop.* 39 G6
Stockton *Warks.* 31 F2
Stockton Heath 49 F4
Stockton-on-Tees 63 F4
Stockton on Teme 29 G2
Stockton on the 58 C4
Forest
Stockwood 8 E4
Stodday 55 H4
Stodmarsh 25 J5
Stody 44 E2
Stoer 102 C6
Stoford *Som.* 8 E3
Stoford *Wilts.* 10 B1
Stogumber 7 J2
Stogursey 19 F7
Stoke *Devon* 6 A3
Stoke *Hants.* 21 H6
Stoke *Hants.* 11 H4
Stoke *Med.* 24 E4
Stoke *W.Mid.* 30 E1
Stoke Abbott 8 D4
Stoke Albany 42 B7
Stoke Ash 35 F1
Stoke Bardolph 41 J1
Stoke Bliss 29 F2
Stoke Bruerne 31 J3
Stoke by Clare 34 B4
Stoke-by-Nayland 34 D5
Stoke Canon 7 H6
Stoke Charity 11 F1
Stoke Climsland 4 D3
Stoke D'Abernon 22 E6
Stoke Doyle 42 D7
Stoke Dry 42 B6
Stoke Ferry 44 A6
Stoke Fleming 5 J6
Stoke Gabriel 5 J5
Stoke Gifford 19 K4
Stoke Golding 41 F6
Stoke Goldington 32 B4
Stoke Hammond 32 B6
Stoke Heath 39 F3
Stoke Holy Cross 45 G5
Stoke Lacy 29 F3
Stoke Lyne 31 G6
Stoke Mandeville 32 B1
Stoke Newington 23 G3
Stoke on Tern 39 F3
Stoke-on-Trent 40 A1
Stoke Orchard 29 J6
Stoke Poges 22 C3
Stoke Prior *Here.* 28 E3
Stoke Prior *Worcs.* 29 J2
Stoke Rivers 6 E2
Stoke Rochford 42 C3
Stoke Row 21 K3
Stoke St. Gregory 8 C2
Stoke St. Mary 8 B2
Stoke St. Michael 19 K7
Stoke St. 38 E7
Milborough
Stoke sub Hamdon 8 D3
Stoke Talmage 21 K2
Stoke Trister 9 G2
Stoke Wake 9 G4
Stokeford 9 H6
Stokeham 51 K5
Stokeinteignhead 5 K3
Stokenchurch 22 A2
Stokenham 5 J6
Stokesay 38 D7
Stokesby 45 J4
Stokesley 63 G5
Stolford 19 F7
Ston Easton 19 K6
Stonar Cut 25 K5
Stondon Massey 23 J1
Stone *Bucks.* 31 J7
Stone *Glos.* 19 K2
Stone *Kent* 23 J4
Stone *Kent* 14 C5
Stone *Staffs.* 40 A2
Stone *Worcs.* 29 H1

Stone Allerton 19 G6
Stone Cross 13 K6
E.Suss.
Stone Cross *Kent* 15 F4
Stone Cross *Kent* 13 J3
Stone House 56 C1
Stone Street *Kent* 23 J6
Stone Street *Suff.* 45 H7
Stonebridge 40 E7
Warks.
Stonebroom 51 G7
Stoneferry 59 H6
Stonefield 73 G3
Arg. & B.
Stonefield *S.Lan.* 74 E5
Stonegate 13 K4
Stonegrave 58 C2
Stonehaugh 70 C6
Stonehaven 91 G6
Stonehouse 65 J4
D. & G.
Stonehouse *Glos.* 20 B1
Stonehouse 61 H1
Northumb.
Stonehouse *Plym.* 4 E5
Stonehouse 75 F6
S.Lan.
Stoneleigh 30 E1
Stonely 32 E2
Stoner Hill 11 J2
Stones Green 35 F6
Stonesby 42 B3
Stonesfield 30 E7
Stonestreet Green 15 F4
Stonethwaite 60 D5
Stoney Cross 10 D3
Stoney Middleton 50 E5
Stoney Stanton 41 G6
Stoney Stoke 9 G1
Stoney Stratton 9 F1
Stoney Stretton 38 C5
Stoneyburn 75 H4
Stoneygate 41 J5
Stoneyhills 25 F2
Stoneykirk 64 A5
Stoneywood 91 G3
Stonganess 108 E2
Stonham Aspal 35 F3
Stonnall 40 C5
Stonor 22 A3
Stonton Wyville 42 A6
Stony Houghton 51 G6
Stony Stratford 31 J4
Stonybreck 108 A1
Stoodleigh 7 H4
Stopham 12 D5
Stopsley 32 E6
Stoptide 3 G1
Storeton 48 C4
Stornoway 101 G4
(Steornabhagh)
Stornoway 101 G4
Airport
Storridge 29 G4
Storrington 12 D5
Storth 55 H1
Storwood 58 D5
Stotfield 97 K4
Stotfold 33 F5
Stottesdon 39 F7
Stoughton *Leics.* 41 J5
Stoughton *Surr.* 22 C6
Stoughton 12 B5
W.Suss.
Stoul 86 D5
Stoulton 29 J3
Stour Provost 9 G2
Stour Row 9 H2
Stourbridge 40 A7
Stourpaine 9 H4
Stourport-on- 29 H1
Severn
Stourton *Staffs.* 40 A7
Stourton *Warks.* 30 D5
Stourton *Wilts.* 9 G1
Stourton Caundle 9 G3
Stove 106 F4
Stoven 45 J7
Stow *Lincs.* 52 B4
Stow *Sc.Bord.* 76 C6
Stow Bardolph 44 A5
Stow Bedon 44 D6
Stow cum Quy 33 J2
Stow Longa 32 E1
Stow Maries 24 E2
Stow-on-the-Wold 30 C6
Stowbridge 44 A5
Stowe *Glos.* 19 J1
Stowe *Shrop.* 28 C1
Stowe *Staffs.* 40 C3
Stowell *Glos.* 30 B7
Stowell *Som.* 9 F2
Stowey 19 J6
Stowford 6 C7
Stowlangtoft 34 D2
Stowmarket 34 E3
Stowting 15 G3
Stowupland 34 E3
Stracathro 83 H1
Strachan 90 E5
Strachur 80 B7
Stradbroke 35 G1
Stradishall 34 B3
Stradsett 44 A5
Stragglethorpe 52 C7
Straiton *Edin.* 76 A4
Straiton *S.Ayr.* 67 H3
Straloch *Aber.* 91 G2
Straloch *P. & K.* 82 B1
Stramshall 40 C2
Strang 54 C6
Strannda 93 F3
Stranraer 64 A4
Strata Florida 27 G2
Stratfield Mortimer 21 K5
Stratfield Saye 21 K5
Stratfield Turgis 21 K6
Stratford 23 G3
Stratford St. 35 H3
Andrew
Stratford St. Mary 34 E5
Stratford sub 10 C1
Castle
Stratford Tony 10 B2
Stratford-upon- 30 C3
Avon
Strath 105 H3
Strathan *High.* 102 C4
Strathan *High.* 87 F5
Strathaven 74 E6
Strathblane 74 D3
Strathcarron 95 F7
Strathdon 90 B3
Strathgirnock 90 B5
Strathkanaird 95 H1
Strathkinness 83 F6
Strathmiglo 82 D7
Strathpeffer 96 B6

Strathrannoch 95 K4
Strathtay 82 A2
Strathwhillan 73 J7
Strathy 104 D2
Strathyre 81 G6
Stratton *Cornw.* 6 A5
Stratton *Dorset* 9 F5
Stratton *Glos.* 20 D1
Stratton Audley 31 H6
Stratton-on-the- 19 K6
Fosse
Stratton St. 20 E3
Margaret
Stratton St. 45 G6
Michael
Stratton Strawless 45 G3
Stravanan 73 J5
Stravithie 83 G6
Streat 13 G5
Streatham 23 F4
Streatley *Beds.* 32 D6
Streatley *W.Berks.* 21 J3
Street *Lancs.* 55 J4
Street *N.Yorks.* 63 J6
Street *Som.* 8 D1
Street Dinas 38 C2
Street End *Kent* 15 G2
Street End 12 B7
W.Suss.
Street on the Fosse 9 F1
Streethay 40 D4
Streetlam 62 E7
Streetly 40 C6
Strefford 38 D7
Strelley 41 H1
Strensall 58 C3
Strensham 29 J4
Stretcholt 19 F7
Strete 5 J6
Stretford 49 G3
Stretford Court 28 D3
Strethall 33 H5
Stretham 33 J1
Strettington 12 B6
Stretton *Ches.* 48 E7
Stretton *Derbys.* 51 F6
Stretton *Rut.* 42 C4
Stretton *Staffs.* 40 A4
Stretton *Staffs.* 40 E3
Stretton *Warr.* 49 F4
Stretton en le Field 41 F4
Stretton Grandison 29 F4
Stretton Heath 38 C4
Stretton-on- 31 F1
Dunsmore
Stretton-on-Fosse 30 D5
Stretton Sugwas 28 D4
Stretton under 41 G7
Fosse
Stretton Westwood 38 E6
Stribers 55 G1
Strichen 99 H5
Stringston 7 K1
Strixton 32 C2
Stroat 19 J2
Stromeferry 86 E1
Stromemore 86 E1
Stromness 107 B7
Stronachlachar 81 F7
Strone *Arg. & B.* 73 K2
Strone *High.* 88 C2
Strone *High.* 87 H6
Strone *Stir.* 81 F6
Stronechrubie 102 E7
Stronenaba 87 J6
Stronlonag 73 K2
Stronmilchan 80 C5
Strontian 79 K1
Strontoiller 80 A5
Stronvar 81 G6
Strood 24 D5
Strood Green 12 D4
Stroquhan 68 D5
Stroud *Glos.* 20 B1
Stroud *Hants.* 11 J2
Stroud Common 22 D7
Stroud Green 20 B1
Stroul 74 A2
Stroxton 42 C2
Struan *High.* 85 J1
Struan *P. & K.* 81 K1
Strubby 53 H4
Strumpshaw 45 H5
Struthers 82 E7
Struy 96 B7
Stryt-issa 38 B1
Stryt-yr-hwch 38 C1
Stuartfield 99 H6
Stub Place 60 B7
Stubbington 11 G4
Stubbins 49 G1
Stubhampton 9 J3
Stubley 51 F5
Stubton 42 B1
Stuck *Arg. & B.* 73 J4
Stuck *Arg. & B.* 73 K1
Stuckbeg 74 A1
Stuckgowan 80 E6
Stuckindroin 80 E6
Stuckreoch 73 J1
Stuckton 10 C3
Stud Green 22 B4
Studdon 61 K1
Studfold 56 D2
Studham 32 D7
Studholme 60 D1
Studland 10 B6
Studley *Warks.* 30 B2
Studley *Wilts.* 20 C4
Studley Common 30 B2
Studley Roger 57 H2
Stuggadhoo 54 C6
Stump Cross 33 J4
Stuntney 33 J1
Stunts Green 13 K5
Sturbridge 40 A2
Sturmer 34 B4
Sturminster 9 G3
Common
Sturminster 9 J4
Marshall
Sturminster 9 G3
Newton
Sturry 25 H5
Sturton by Stow 52 B4
Sturton le Steeple 51 K4
Stuston 35 F1
Stutton *N.Yorks.* 57 K5
Stutton *Suff.* 35 F5
Styal 49 H4
Styrrup 51 J3
Suainebost 101 H1
Suardail 101 G4
Succoth *Aber.* 90 C1
Succoth *Arg. & B.* 80 D7
Succothmore 80 C7
Suckley 29 G3

Sudborough 42 C7
Sudbourne 35 J3
Sudbrook Lincs. 42 C1
Sudbrook Mon. 19 J3
Sudbrooke 52 D5
Sudbury Derbys. 40 D2
Sudbury Gt.Lon. 22 E3
Sudbury Suff. 34 C4
Sudgrove 20 C1
Suffield N.Yorks. 63 J3
Suffield Norf. 45 G2
Sugarloaf 14 E4
Sugnall 39 G2
Suie Lodge Hotel 81 F5
Sulby 54 C4
Sulgrave 31 G4
Sulham 21 K4
Sulhamstead 21 K5
Sullington 12 D5
Sullom 108 C5
Sullom Voe Oil Terminal 108 C5
Sully 18 E5
Sumburgh 109 G10
Sumburgh Airport 109 G10
Summer Bridge 57 H3
Summercourt 3 F3
Summerfield 44 B2
Summerhill 48 C7
Summerhouse 62 D5
Summerleaze 19 H3
Summerseat 49 G1
Summertown 21 J1
Summit 49 J1
Sunadale 73 G6
Sunbury 22 E5
Sundaywell 68 D5
Sunderland Cumb. 60 C3
Sunderland T. & W. 62 E1
Sunderland Bridge 62 D3
Sundhope 69 J1
Sundon Park 32 D6
Sundridge 23 H6
Sundrum Mains 67 J1
Sunhill 20 E1
Sunipol 78 E2
Sunk Island 53 F1
Sunningdale 22 C5
Sunninghill 22 C5
Sunningwell 21 H2
Sunniside Dur. 62 C3
Sunniside T. & W. 62 D1
Sunny Bank 60 D7
Sunnylaw 75 F1
Sunnymead 21 J1
Sunnyside Aber. 91 G5
Sunnyside Northumb. 70 E7
Sunnyside W.Suss. 13 G3
Sunwick 77 G5
Surbiton 22 E5
Surfleet 43 F3
Surfleet Seas End 43 F3
Surlingham 45 H5
Sustead 45 F2
Susworth 52 B2
Sutcombe 6 B4
Suton 44 E6
Sutors of Cromarty 97 F5
Sutterton 43 F2
Sutton Beds. 33 F4
Sutton Cambs. 33 H1
Sutton Gt.Lon. 23 F5
Sutton Kent 15 J3
Sutton Lincs. 52 B7
Sutton Norf. 45 H3
Sutton Notts. 42 A2
Sutton Notts. 51 J4
Sutton Oxon. 21 H1
Sutton Pembs. 16 C3
Sutton Peter. 42 E6
Sutton S.Yorks. 51 H1
Sutton Shrop. 39 G7
Sutton Shrop. 39 F2
Sutton Shrop. 38 E4
Sutton Staffs. 39 G3
Sutton Suff. 35 H4
Sutton W.Suss. 12 C5
Sutton Abinger 22 E7
Sutton at Hone 23 J4
Sutton Bassett 42 A7
Sutton Benger 20 C4
Sutton Bonington 41 H3
Sutton Bridge 43 H3
Sutton Cheney 41 G5
Sutton Coldfield 40 D6
Sutton Courtenay 21 H2
Sutton Crosses 43 H3
Sutton Grange 57 H2
Sutton Green 22 D6
Sutton Holms 10 B3
Sutton Howgrave 57 J2
Sutton in Ashfield 51 G7
Sutton-in-Craven 57 F5
Sutton in the Elms 41 H6
Sutton Lane Ends 49 J5
Sutton le Marsh 53 J4
Sutton Leach 48 E3
Sutton Maddock 39 G5
Sutton Mallet 8 C1
Sutton Mandeville 9 J2
Sutton Montis 9 F2
Sutton-on-Hull 59 H6
Sutton on Sea 53 J4
Sutton-on-the-Forest 58 B3
Sutton on the Hill 40 E2
Sutton on Trent 51 K6
Sutton Poyntz 9 G6
Sutton St. Edmund 43 G4
Sutton St. James 43 H4
Sutton St. Nicholas 28 E4
Sutton Scarsdale 51 G6
Sutton Scotney 11 F1
Sutton-under-Brailes 30 D5
Sutton-under-Whitestonecliffe 57 K1
Sutton upon Derwent 58 D5
Sutton Valence 14 D3
Sutton Veny 20 B7
Sutton Waldron 9 H3
Sutton Weaver 48 E5
Sutton Wick 21 H2
Swaby 53 G5
Swadlincote 41 F4
Swaffham 44 C5
Swaffham Bulbeck 33 J2
Swaffham Prior 33 J2
Swafield 45 G2

Swainby 63 F6
Swainshill 28 D4
Swainsthorpe 45 G5
Swainswick 20 A5
Swalcliffe 30 E5
Swalecliffe 25 H5
Swallow 52 E2
Swallow Beck 52 C6
Swallowcliffe 9 J2
Swallowfield 22 A5
Swallownest 71 H1
Swalwell 71 H7
Swampton 21 H6
Swan Street 34 C6
Swanage 10 B7
Swanbach 39 F1
Swanbourne 32 B6
Swanbridge 18 E5
Swancote 39 G6
Swanland 59 F7
Swanlaws 70 C2
Swanley 23 J5
Swanmore 11 G3
Swannington Leics. 41 G4
Swannington Norf. 45 F4
Swanscombe 24 C4
Swansea (Abertawe) 17 K5
Swanton Abbot 45 G3
Swanton Morley 44 E4
Swanton Novers 44 E2
Swanwick Derbys. 51 G7
Swanwick Hants. 11 G4
Swarby 42 D1
Swardeston 45 F5
Swarkestone 41 F3
Swarland 71 G3
Swaton 42 E2
Swavesey 33 G2
Sway 10 D5
Swayfield 42 C3
Swaythling 11 F3
Swaythorpe 59 G3
Sweethouse 4 A4
Sweffling 35 H2
Swell 8 C2
Swepstone 41 F4
Swerford 30 E5
Swettenham 49 H6
Swffryd 19 F2
Swiftsden 14 C5
Swilland 35 F3
Swillbrook 55 H6
Swillington 57 J6
Swimbridge 6 E3
Swimbridge Newland 6 E2
Swinbrook 30 D7
Swincliffe 57 H4
Swinderby 52 B6
Swindon Staffs. 40 A6
Swindon Swin. 20 E3
Swindon Village 29 J6
Swine 59 H6
Swinefleet 58 D7
Swineshead Beds. 32 D2
Swineshead Lincs. 43 F1
Swineshead Bridge 43 F1
Swiney 105 H5
Swinford Leics. 31 G1
Swinford Oxon. 21 H1
Swingfield Minnis 15 H3
Swinhoe 71 H1
Swinhope 53 F3
Swining 109 D6
Swinithwaite 57 F1
Swinscoe 40 D1
Swinside Hall 70 C1
Swinstead 42 D3
Swinton Gt.Man. 49 G2
Swinton N.Yorks. 58 D2
Swinton N.Yorks. 57 K1
Swinton S.Yorks. 51 G3
Swinton Sc.Bord. 77 G6
Swintonmill 77 G6
Swithland 41 H4
Swordale 96 C5
Swordland 86 D5
Swordle 79 G1
Swordly 104 C2
Sworton Heath 49 F4
Swydd-ffynnon 27 F2
Swyncombe 21 K2
Swynnerton 40 A2
Swyre 8 E6
Syde 29 J7
Sydenham Gt.Lon. 23 G4
Sydenham Oxon. 22 A1
Sydenham Damerel 4 E3
Syderstone 44 C2
Sydling St. Nicholas 9 F5
Sydmonton 21 H6
Syerston 42 A1
Syke 49 H1
Sykehouse 51 J1
Sykes 56 B4
Sylen 17 J4
Symbister 109 E6
Symington S.Ayr. 74 B7
Symington S.Lan. 75 H7
Symonds Yat 28 E7
Symondsbury 8 D5
Synod Inn 26 D3
Syre 103 J4
Syreford 30 B6
Syresham 31 H4
Syston Leics. 41 J4
Syston Lincs. 42 C1
Sytchampton 29 H2
Sywell 32 B2

T

Taagan 95 G5
Tabost W.Isles 101 H1
Tabost W.Isles 101 H1
Tacher 105 G4
Tackley 31 F7
Tacleit 100 D4
Tacolneston 45 F6
Tadcaster 57 K5
Taddington 50 D5
Taddiport 6 C4
Tadley 21 K5
Tadlow 33 F4
Tadmarton 30 E5
Tadworth 23 F6
Tafarn-y-bwlch 16 D1
Tafarn-y-Gelyn 47 K6
Tafarnaubach 28 A7
Taff's Well (Ffynnon Taf) 18 E3
Tafolwern 37 H5
Tai-bach 38 A3
Tai'n Lôn 46 C7
Taibach 18 A3
Taicynnhaeaf 37 F4
Tain High. 105 H2
Tain High. 96 E3
Tai'r Bull 27 J6
Tairgwaith 27 G7
Tairlaw 67 J3
Takeley 33 J6
Takeley Street 33 J6
Tal-sarn 26 E3
Tal-y-bont Conwy 47 F6
Tal-y-bont Gwyn. 36 E3
Tal-y-bont Gwyn. 46 E5
Tal-y-Cae 46 E6
Tal-y-cafn 47 F5
Tal-y-llyn 37 G5
Tal-y-wern 37 H5
Talachddu 27 K5
Taladale 37 H3
Talaton 7 J6
Talbenny 16 B3
Talbot Green 18 D3
Talerddig 37 J5
Talgarreg 26 D3
Talgarth 28 A5
Taliesin 37 F6
Talisker 85 J1
Talke 49 H7
Talkin 61 G1
Talla Linnfoots 69 G1
Talladale 95 F4
Talladh-a-Bheithe 81 G2
Tallarn Green 38 D1
Tallentire 60 C3
Talley 17 K1
Tallington 42 D5
Talmine 103 H2
Talog 17 G2
Talsarnau 37 F2
Talskiddy 3 G2
Talwrn I.o.A. 46 C5
Talwrn Wrex. 38 B1
Talybont-on-Usk 28 A6
Talyllyn 28 A6
Talysarn 46 C7
Tamavoid 74 D1
Tamerton Foliot 4 E4
Tamworth 40 E5
Tan-lan 37 F1
Tan-y-fron 47 H6
Tan-y-graig 36 C2
Tan-y-groes 26 B4
Tan-y-pistyll 37 K3
Tandridge 23 G6
Tanerdy 17 H2
Tanfield 62 C1
Tangiers 16 C3
Tanglandford 91 G1
Tangley 21 G6
Tangmere 12 C6
Tangwick 108 B5
Tangy 66 A1
Tankerness 107 E7
Tankersley 51 F2
Tannach 105 J4
Tannachie 91 F6
Tannachy 96 E1
Tannadice 83 F2
Tannington 35 G2
Tannochside 75 G4
Tansley 51 F7
Tansor 42 D6
Tantobie 62 C1
Tanton 63 G5
Tanworth in Arden 30 C1
Tanygrisiau 37 F1
Taobh a' Deas Loch Baghasdail 84 C3
Taobh Siar 100 D7
Taobh Tuath (Northton) 92 E3
Tapeley 6 C3
Taplow 22 C3
Taraphocain 80 B3
Tarbat House 96 E4
Tarbert Arg. & B. 73 G4
Tarbert Arg. & B. 72 E5
Tarbert Arg. & B. 72 E2
Tarbert High. 79 H1
Tarbert (An Tairbeart) W.Isles 100 D7
Tarbet Arg. & B. 80 E7
Tarbet High. 86 D5
Tarbet High. 102 D4
Tarbolton 67 J1
Tarbrax 75 J5
Tardebigge 29 J2
Tardy Gate 55 J7
Tarfside 90 C4
Tarland 90 C4
Tarleton 55 H7
Tarlscough 48 D1
Tarlton 20 C2
Tarnbrook 55 J4
Tarnock 19 G6
Tarporley 48 E6
Tarr 7 K2
Tarrant Crawford 9 J4
Tarrant Gunville 9 J3
Tarrant Hinton 9 J3
Tarrant Keynston 9 J4
Tarrant Launceston 9 J4
Tarrant Monkton 9 J4
Tarrant Rawston 9 J4
Tarrant Rushton 9 J4
Tarrel 97 F3
Tarring Neville 13 H6
Tarrington 29 F4
Tarrnacraig 73 H7
Tarsappie 82 C5
Tarskavaig 86 B4
Tarves 91 G1
Tarvie High. 96 B6
Tarvie P. & K. 82 B1
Tarvin 48 D6
Tarvin Sands 48 D6
Tasburgh 45 G6
Tasley 39 F6
Taston 30 E6
Tatenhill 40 E3
Tatham 56 B3
Tathwell 53 G4
Tatsfield 23 H6
Tattenhall 48 D7
Tatterford 44 C3
Tattersett 44 C3
Tattershall 53 F7
Tattershall Bridge 52 E7
Tattershall Thorpe 53 F7
Tattingstone 35 F5
Tatworth 8 C4
Tauchers 98 B5
Taunton 8 B2
Tavelty 91 F3
Taverham 45 F4

Tavernspite 16 E3
Tavistock 4 E3
Taw Bridge 6 E5
Taw Green 6 E6
Tawstock 6 D3
Taxal 50 C5
Tayburn 74 D6
Taychreggan 80 B5
Tayinloan 72 E6
Taylors Cross 6 A4
Taynafead 80 B6
Taynish 73 F2
Taynton Glos. 29 G6
Taynton Oxon. 30 D7
Taynuilt 80 B4
Tayock 83 H2
Tayovullin 72 A3
Tayport 83 F5
Tayvallich 73 F2
Tealby 52 E3
Team Valley 71 H7
Teanamachar 92 C5
Teangue 86 C4
Teasses 83 F7
Tebay 61 H6
Tebworth 32 C6
Tedburn St. Mary 7 G6
Teddington Glos. 29 J5
Teddington Gt.Lon. 22 E4
Tedstone Delamere 29 F3
Tedstone Wafre 29 F3
Teesside International Airport 62 E5
Teeton 31 H1
Teffont Evias 9 J1
Teffont Magna 9 J1
Tegryn 17 F1
Teigh 42 B4
Teigngrace 5 J3
Teignmouth 5 K3
Telford 39 F5
Telham 14 C6
Tellisford 20 A6
Telscombe 13 H6
Telscombe Cliffs 13 H6
Tempar 81 H2
Templand 69 F5
Temple Cornw. 4 B3
Temple Midloth. 76 B5
Temple Bar 26 E3
Temple Cloud 19 K6
Temple Ewell 15 H3
Temple Grafton 30 C3
Temple Guiting 30 B6
Temple Hirst 58 C7
Temple Normanton 51 G6
Temple Sowerby 61 H4
Templecombe 9 G2
Templeton Devon 7 G4
Templeton Pembs. 16 E3
Templeton Bridge 7 G4
Templewood 83 H1
Tempsford 32 E3
Ten Mile Bank 43 J6
Tenbury Wells 28 E2
Tenby (Dinbych-y-Pysgod) 16 E4
Tendring 35 F6
Tenga 79 G3
Tenterden 14 D4
Tepersie Castle 90 D2
Terally 64 B6
Terling 34 B7
Ternhill 39 F2
Terregles 65 K3
Terrington 58 C2
Terrington St. Clement 43 J3
Terrington St. John 43 J4
Tervieside 89 K1
Teston 14 C2
Testwood 10 E3
Tetbury 20 B2
Tetbury Upton 20 B2
Tetchill 38 C2
Tetcott 6 B6
Tetford 53 G5
Tetney 53 G2
Tetney Lock 53 G2
Tetsworth 21 K1
Tettenhall 40 A5
Tettenhall Wood 40 A6
Tetworth 33 F3
Teuchan 91 J1
Teversal 51 G6
Teversham 33 H3
Teviothead 69 K3
Tewel 91 G6
Tewin 33 F7
Tewkesbury 29 H5
Teynham 25 F5
Thainston 90 E7
Thainstone House 91 F3
Thakeham 12 E5
Thame 22 A1
Thames Ditton 22 E5
Thames Haven 24 D3
Thamesmead 23 H3
Thanington 15 G2
Thankerton 75 H7
Tharston 45 F6
Thatcham 21 J5
Thatto Heath 48 E3
Thaxted 33 K5
The Apes Hall 43 J7
The Bage 28 B4
The Balloch 81 K6
The Banking 91 F1
The Bar 12 E4
The Belfry 40 D6
The Birks 91 F4
The Bog 38 C6
The Bourne 22 B7
The Bratch 40 A6
The Bryn 19 G1
The Burf 29 H2
The Burn 90 D7
The Camp 20 C1
The Chequer 38 D1
The City 22 A2
The Common 10 D1
The Craigs 96 B2
The Cronk 54 C4
The Den 74 B5
The Dicker 13 J6
The Drums 82 E1
The Eaves 19 K1
The Flatt 70 A6
The Folly 32 E7
The Grange Shrop.
The Grange Surr. 23 G7
The Green Arg. & B.
The Green Wilts. 9 H1
The Haven 12 D3
The Headland 63 G3

The Hermitage 23 F6
The Howe 54 B7
The Isle 38 D4
The Knowle 23 K7
The Laurels 45 H6
The Leacon 14 E4
The Lee 22 C1
The Lhen 54 C3
The Lodge 73 K1
The Marsh 38 C6
The Moor E.Suss. 14 C5
The Moor Kent 14 C5
The Mumbles 17 K6
The Mythe 29 H5
The Neuk 91 F5
The Node 33 F7
The Oval 20 A5
The Rhos 16 D3
The Rowe 40 A2
The Sands 22 B7
The Shoe 20 B4
The Smithies 39 F6
The Stocks 14 E5
The Vauld 28 E4
The Wrythe 23 F5
The Wyke 39 G5
Theakston 57 H1
Thealby 52 B1
Theale Som. 19 H7
Theale W.Berks. 21 K4
Thearne 59 G6
Theberton 35 J2
Thedden Grange 11 H1
Theddingworth 41 J7
Theddlethorpe All Saints 53 H4
Theddlethorpe St. Helen 53 H4
Thelbridge Barton 7 F4
Thelnetham 34 E1
Thelveton 45 F7
Thelwall 49 F4
Themelthorpe 44 E3
Thenford 31 G4
Therfield 33 G5
Thetford 44 C7
Theydon Bois 23 H2
Thickwood 20 B4
Thimbleby Lincs. 53 F5
Thimbleby N.Yorks. 63 F7
Thirkleby 57 K2
Thirlby 57 K1
Thirlestane 76 D6
Thirn 57 H1
Thirsk 57 K1
Thistleton Lancs. 55 H6
Thistleton Rut. 42 C4
Thistley Green 33 K1
Thixendale 58 E3
Thockrington 70 E6
Tholomas Drove 43 G5
Tholthorpe 57 K3
Thomas Chapel 16 E4
Thomastown 90 D1
Thompson 44 D6
Thomshill 97 K6
Thong 24 C4
Thoralby 57 F1
Thoresby 51 J5
Thoresway 52 E3
Thorganby Lincs. 53 F3
Thorganby N.Yorks. 58 C5
Thorgill 63 J7
Thorington 35 J1
Thorington Street 34 E5
Thorlby 56 E4
Thorley 33 H7
Thorley Street Herts. 33 H7
Thorley Street I.o.W. 10 E6
Thormanby 57 K2
Thorn Falcon 8 B2
Thornaby-on-Tees 63 F5
Thornage 44 E2
Thornborough Bucks. 31 J5
Thornborough N.Yorks. 57 H1
Thornbury Devon 6 C5
Thornbury Here. 29 F3
Thornbury S.Glos. 19 K3
Thornby 31 H1
Thorncliff 50 C7
Thorncombe 8 C4
Thorncombe Street 22 D7
Thorncote Green 32 E4
Thorndon 35 F2
Thorndon Cross 6 D6
Thorne 51 J1
Thorne St. Margaret 7 J3
Thorner 57 J5
Thornes 40 C5
Thorney Bucks. 22 D4
Thorney Notts. 52 B5
Thorney Peter. 43 F5
Thorney Som. 8 D2
Thorney Hill 10 D4
Thornford 9 F3
Thorngrove 8 C1
Thorngumbald 59 J7
Thornham 44 B1
Thornham Magna 35 F1
Thornham Parva 35 F1
Thornhaugh 42 D5
Thornhill Cardiff 18 E3
Thornhill D. & G. 68 D4
Thornhill Derbys. 50 D4
Thornhill S'ham. 11 F3
Thornhill Stir. 81 H7
Thornhill W.Yorks. 50 E1
Thornholme 59 H3
Thornicombe 9 H4
Thornley Dur. 62 E3
Thornley Dur. 62 D4
Thornliebank 74 D5
Thorns 34 B3
Thornsett 50 C4
Thornthwaite Cumb. 60 D4
Thornthwaite N.Yorks. 57 G4
Thornton Angus 82 E3
Thornton Bucks. 31 J5
Thornton E.Riding 58 D5
Thornton Fife 76 A1
Thornton Lancs. 55 G5
Thornton Leics. 41 G5
Thornton Lincs. 53 F6
Thornton Mersey. 48 C2
Thornton Middbro. 63 F5
Thornton Northumb. 77 H6

Thornton P. & K. 82 B3
Thornton Pembs. 16 C4
Thornton W.Yorks. 57 G6
Thornton Curtis 52 D1
Thornton Hough 48 C4
Thornton-in-Craven 56 E5
Thornton-le-Beans 62 E7
Thornton-le-Clay 58 C3
Thornton le Moor Lincs. 52 D3
Thornton-le-Moor N.Yorks. 57 J1
Thornton-le-Moors 48 D5
Thornton-le-Street 57 K1
Thornton Park 77 H6
Thornton Rust 56 E1
Thornton Steward 57 G1
Thornton Watlass 57 H1
Thorntonhall 74 D5
Thorntonloch 77 F3
Thornwood Common 23 H1
Thornyhill 90 E7
Thornylee 76 C7
Thoroton 42 A1
Thorp Arch 57 K5
Thorpe Derbys. 50 D7
Thorpe E.Riding 59 G5
Thorpe Lincs. 53 H4
Thorpe N.Yorks. 57 F3
Thorpe Norf. 45 J6
Thorpe Notts. 51 K7
Thorpe Surr. 22 D5
Thorpe Abbotts 35 F1
Thorpe Acre 41 H3
Thorpe Arnold 42 A3
Thorpe Audlin 51 G1
Thorpe Bassett 58 E2
Thorpe Bay 25 F3
Thorpe by Water 42 B6
Thorpe Constantine 40 E5
Thorpe Culvert 53 H6
Thorpe End Garden Village 45 G4
Thorpe Green 34 D3
Thorpe Hall 58 B2
Thorpe Hesley 51 F3
Thorpe in Balne 51 H1
Thorpe in the Fallows 52 C4
Thorpe Langton 42 A6
Thorpe Larches 62 E4
Thorpe-le-Soken 35 F6
Thorpe le Street 58 E5
Thorpe Malsor 32 B1
Thorpe Mandeville 31 G4
Thorpe Market 45 G2
Thorpe Morieux 34 D3
Thorpe on the Hill Lincs. 52 C6
Thorpe on the Hill W.Yorks. 57 J7
Thorpe St. Andrew 45 G5
Thorpe St. Peter 53 H6
Thorpe Salvin 51 H4
Thorpe Satchville 42 A4
Thorpe Thewles 62 E4
Thorpe Tilney 52 E7
Thorpe Underwood N.Yorks. 57 K4
Thorpe Waterville 42 D7
Thorpe Willoughby 58 B6
Thorpeness 35 J3
Thorpland 44 A5
Thorrington 34 E7
Thorverton 7 H5
Thrandeston 35 F1
Thrapston 32 D1
Threapland 56 E3
Threapwood 38 D1
Three Bridges 13 F3
Three Burrows 2 E4
Three Chimneys 14 D4
Three Cocks 28 A5
Three Crosses 17 J5
Three Cups Corner 13 K4
Three Holes 43 J5
Three Leg Cross 13 K3
Three Legged Cross 10 B4
Three Mile Cross 22 A5
Threekingham 42 D2
Threemilestone 2 E4
Threlkeld 60 E4
Threshers Bush 23 H1
Threshfield 56 E3
Threxton Hill 44 C5
Thriepley 82 E4
Thrigby 45 J4
Thringarth 62 A4
Thringstone 41 G4
Thrintoft 62 E7
Thriplow 33 H4
Throcking 33 G5
Throckley 71 G7
Throckmorton 29 J3
Throphill 71 G5
Thropton 71 F3
Throwleigh 6 E6
Throwley 14 E2
Throws 33 K6
Thrumpton 41 H2
Thrumster 105 J4
Thrunton 71 F2
Thrupp Glos. 20 B1
Thrupp Oxon. 31 F7
Thrushelton 6 C7
Thrussington 41 J4
Thruxton Hants. 21 F7
Thruxton Here. 28 D5
Thrybergh 51 G3
Thulston 41 G2
Thundergay 73 G6
Thundersley 24 E3
Thundridge 33 G7
Thurcaston 41 H4
Thurcroft 51 H3
Thurdistoft 105 H2
Thurgarton Norf. 45 F2
Thurgarton Notts. 41 J1
Thurgoland 50 E2
Thurlaston Leics. 41 H6
Thurlaston Warks. 31 F1
Thurlbear 8 B2
Thurlby Lincs. 42 E4
Thurlby Lincs. 52 C6
Thurleigh 32 D3
Thurlestone 5 G6
Thurloxton 8 B1
Thurlstone 50 E2
Thurlton 45 J6
Thurlwood 49 H7
Thurmaston 41 J5

Thurnby 41 J5
Thurne 45 J4
Thurnham 14 D2
Thurning Norf. 44 E3
Thurning Northants. 42 D7
Thurnscoe 51 G2
Thurrock Lakeside 23 J4
Thursby 60 E1
Thursford 44 D2
Thursley 12 C3
Thurso 105 G2
Thurstaston 48 B4
Thurston 34 D2
Thurstonfield 60 E1
Thurstonland 50 D1
Thurton 45 H5
Thurvaston 40 E2
Thuster 105 H3
Thuxton 44 E5
Thwaite N.Yorks. 61 K7
Thwaite Suff. 35 F2
Thwaite Head 56 D1
Thwaite St. Mary 45 H6
Thwing 59 G3
Tibbermore 82 B5
Tibberton Glos. 29 G6
Tibberton Tel. & W. 39 F3
Tibberton Worcs. 29 J3
Tibbie Shiels Inn 69 H1
Tibenham 45 F6
Tibertich 79 K7
Tibshelf 51 G6
Tibthorpe 59 F4
Ticehurst 13 K3
Tichborne 11 G1
Tickencote 42 C5
Tickenham 19 H4
Tickhill 51 H3
Ticklerton 38 D6
Ticknall 41 F3
Tickton 59 G5
Tidcombe 21 F6
Tiddington Oxon. 21 K1
Tiddington Warks. 30 D3
Tidebrook 13 K4
Tideford 4 D5
Tidenham 19 J2
Tidenham Chase 19 J2
Tideswell 50 D5
Tidmarsh 21 K4
Tidmington 30 D5
Tidpit 10 B3
Tidworth 21 F7
Tiers Cross 16 C3
Tiffield 31 H3
Tifty 99 F6
Tigerton 83 G1
Tigh a' Gearraidh 92 C4
Tighachnoic 79 H3
Tighnabakr 81 J6
Tighnabruaich 73 H3
Tighnacomaire 80 A1
Tigley 5 H4
Tilbrook 32 D2
Tilbury 24 C4
Tile Cross 40 D7
Tile Hill 30 D1
Tilehurst 21 K4
Tilford 22 B7
Tilgate 13 F3
Tillathrowie 90 C1
Tillers' Green 29 F5
Tillery 91 H2
Tilley 38 E3
Tillicoultry 75 H1
Tillingham 25 F1
Tillington Here. 28 D4
Tillington W.Suss. 12 C4
Tillington Common 28 D4
Tillyarblet 83 G1
Tillybirloch 90 E4
Tillycairn Castle 90 E4
Tillycorthie 91 H2
Tillydrine 90 E5
Tillyfar 99 G6
Tillyfour 90 D3
Tillyfourie 90 E3
Tillygreig 91 G2
Tillypronie 90 C4
Tilmanstone 15 H2
Tilney All Saints 43 J4
Tilney High End 43 J4
Tilney St. Lawrence 43 J4
Tilshead 20 D7
Tilstock 38 E2
Tilston 48 D7
Tilstone Fearnall 48 E6
Tilsworth 32 C6
Tilton on the Hill 42 A5
Tiltups End 20 B2
Timberland 52 E7
Timberland Dales 52 E6
Timbersbrook 49 H6
Timberscombe 7 H1
Timble 57 G4
Timperley 49 G4
Timsbury B. & N.E.Som. 19 K6
Timsbury Hants. 10 E2
Timsgearraidh 100 C4
Timworth Green 34 C2
Tincleton 9 G5
Tindale 61 H1
Tingewick 31 H5
Tingley 57 H7
Tingrith 32 D5
Tinhay 6 C7
Tinney 4 C1
Tinshill 57 H6
Tinsley 51 G3
Tinsley Green 13 F3
Tintagel 4 A2
Tintern Parva 19 J1
Tintinhull 8 D3
Tintwistle 50 C3
Tinwald 69 F5
Tinwell 42 D5
Tippacott 7 F1
Tipperty Aber. 91 F6
Tipperty Aber. 91 H2
Tiptoe 10 D5
Tipton 40 B6
Tipton St. John 7 J6
Tiptree 34 C7
Tiptree Heath 34 C7
Tir-y-dail 17 K3
Tirabad 27 H4
Tirdeunaw 17 K5
Tiree Airport 78 B3
Tirindrish 87 J6
Tirley 29 H6
Tirphil 18 E1
Tirril 61 G4
Tisbury 9 J2
Tissington 50 D7
Tister 105 G2

Titchberry 6 A3
Titchfield 11 G4
Titchmarsh 32 D1
Titchwell 44 B1
Tithby 41 J2
Titley 28 C2
Titsey 23 H6
Titson 6 A5
Tittensor 40 A2
Tittleshall 44 C3
Tiverton *Ches.* 48 E6
Tiverton *Devon* 7 H4
Tivetshall St. Margaret 45 F7
Tivetshall St. Mary 45 F7
Tixall 40 B3
Tixover 42 C5
Toab *Ork.* 107 E7
Toab *Shet.* 109 G10
Tobermory 79 G2
Toberonochy 79 J7
Tobha Mòr 84 C1
Tobson 100 D4
Tocher 90 E1
Tockenham 20 D4
Tockenham Wick 20 D3
Tockholes 56 B7
Tockington 19 K3
Tockwith 57 K4
Todber 9 G2
Toddington *Beds.* 32 D6
Toddington *Glos.* 30 B5
Toddington *W.Suss.* 12 D6
Todenham 30 D5
Todhills *Angus* 83 F4
Todhills *Cumb.* 69 J7
Todlachie 90 E3
Todmorden 56 E7
Todwick 51 G4
Toft *Cambs.* 33 G3
Toft *Lincs.* 42 D4
Toft *Shet.* 108 D5
Toft Hill 62 C4
Toft Monks 45 J6
Toft next Newton 52 D4
Toftcarl 105 J4
Toftrees 44 C3
Tofts 105 J2
Toftwood 44 D4
Togston 71 H3
Tokavaig 86 C3
Tokers Green 22 A4
Tolastadh 101 H3
Tolastadh a' Chaolais 100 D4
Tolastadh Ùr 101 H3
Toll of Birness 91 J1
Tolland 7 K2
Tollard Royal 9 J3
Tollcross 74 E4
Toller Down Gate 8 E4
Toller Fratrum 8 E5
Toller Porcorum 8 E5
Toller Whelme 8 E4
Tollerton *N.Yorks.* 58 B3
Tollerton *Notts.* 41 J2
Tollesbury 25 F1
Tollesby 63 G5
Tolleshunt D'Arcy 34 D7
Tolleshunt Knights 34 D7
Tolleshunt Major 34 C7
Tolpuddle 9 G5
Tolvah 89 F5
Tolworth 22 E5
Tom an Fhuadain 101 F6
Tomatin 89 F2
Tombreck 88 D1
Tomchrasky 87 J3
Tomdoun 87 H4
Tomdow 97 H7
Tomich *High.* 87 K2
Tomich *High.* 96 D4
Tomich *High.* 96 D1
Tomintoul 89 J3
Tomnacross 96 C7
Tomnamoon 97 H6
Tomnaven 90 C1
Tomnavoulin 89 K2
Tomvaich 89 H1
Ton Pentre 18 C2
Ton-teg 18 D3
Tonbridge 23 J7
Tondu 18 B3
Tonfanau 36 E5
Tong 39 G5
Tong Norton 39 G5
Tong Street 57 G6
Tonge 41 G3
Tongham 22 B7
Tongland 65 H5
Tongue 103 H3
Tongue House 103 H3
Tongwynlais 18 E3
Tonna 18 A2
Tonwell 33 G7
Tonypandy 18 C2
Tonyrefail 18 D3
Toot Baldon 21 J1
Toot Hill 23 J1
Toothill 10 E3
Top End 32 D2
Topcliffe 57 J2
Topcroft 45 G6
Topcroft Street 45 G6
Toppesfield 34 B5
Toppings 49 G1
Topsham 7 H7
Topsham Bridge 5 H5
Torastan 78 D1
Torbain 89 J3
Torbeg *Aber.* 90 B4
Torbeg *N.Ayr.* 66 D1
Torbryan 5 J4
Torcastle 87 H7
Torcross 5 J6
Tordarroch 88 D1
Tore 96 D6
Toreduff 97 J5
Toremore *High.* 89 J1
Toremore *High.* 105 G5
Torgyle 87 K3
Torksey 52 B5
Torlum 92 C6
Torlundy 87 H7
Tormarton 20 A4
Tormisdale 72 A2
Tormore 73 G7
Tormsdale 105 G3
Tornagrain 96 E6
Tornahaish 89 K4
Tornaveen 90 E4
Torness 88 C2
Torpenhow 60 C3
Torphichen 75 H3
Torphins 90 E4
Torpoint 4 E5
Torquay 5 K4
Torquhan 76 C6
Torr 5 F5
Torran *Arg. & B.* 79 K7
Torran *High.* 96 E4
Torran *High.* 94 B7
Torrance *E.Dun.* 74 E3
Torrance *S.Lan.* 74 E5
Torrancroy 90 B3
Torrich 97 F6
Torridon 95 F6
Torrin 86 B2
Torrisdale *Arg. & B.* 73 F7
Torrisdale *High.* 103 J2
Torrish 104 E7
Torrisholme 55 H3
Torroble 96 C1
Torry *Aber.* 98 C6
Torry *Aberdeen* 91 H4
Torryburn 75 J2
Torsonce 76 C6
Torterston 99 J6
Torthorwald 69 F6
Tortington 12 C6
Tortworth 20 A2
Torvaig 93 K7
Torver 60 D7
Torwood 75 G2
Torworth 51 J4
Tosberry 6 A3
Toscaig 86 D1
Toseland 33 F2
Tosside 56 C4
Tostarie 78 E3
Tostock 34 D2
Totaig 93 H6
Totamore 78 C2
Tote 93 K7
Totegan 104 D2
Totford 11 G1
Tothill 53 H4
Totland 10 E6
Totley 51 F4
Totnes 5 J4
Toton 41 H2
Totronald 78 C2
Tottenham 23 G2
Tottenhill 44 A4
Totteridge 23 F2
Totternhoe 32 C6
Tottington *Gt.Man.* 49 G1
Tottington *Norf.* 44 C6
Totton 10 E3
Touchen-End 22 B4
Toulton 7 K2
Toux 99 H5
Tovil 14 C2
Tow Law 62 C3
Toward 73 K4
Towcester 31 H4
Towednack 2 B5
Tower Hamlets 23 G3
Towersey 22 A1
Towie *Aber.* 99 G4
Towie *Aber.* 90 D2
Towie *Aber.* 90 C3
Towiemore 98 B6
Town End *Cambs.* 43 H6
Town End *Cumb.* 55 H1
Town Green 48 D2
Town Row 13 J3
Town Street 44 B7
Town Yetholm 70 D1
Townend 74 C3
Townhead 65 G6
Townhead of Greenlaw 65 H4
Townhill 75 K2
Townshend 2 C5
Towthorpe *E.Riding* 59 F3
Towthorpe *York* 58 C4
Towton 57 K6
Towyn 47 H5
Toynton All Saints 53 G6
Toynton Fen Side 53 G6
Toynton St. Peter 53 H6
Toy's Hill 23 H6
Trabboch 67 J1
Traboe 2 E6
Tradespark *High.* 97 F6
Tradespark *Ork.* 107 D7
Trafford Centre 49 G3
Trafford Park 49 G3
Trallong 27 J6
Trallwn *Swan.* 17 K5
Tranch 19 F1
Tranent 76 C3
Trantlebeg 104 D3
Trantlemore 104 D3
Tranwell 71 G5
Trap 17 K3
Traprain 76 D3
Traquair 76 B7
Trawden 56 E6
Trawsfynydd 37 G2
Tre-ddiog 16 B2
Tre-groes 26 D4
Tre-Rhys 26 A4
Tre-vaughan 17 H2
Trealaw 18 C2
Treales 55 H6
Trearddur 46 A5
Treaslane 93 J6
Trebanog 18 D2
Trebanos 18 A1
Trebarrow 4 C1
Trebartha 4 C3
Trebarwith 4 A2
Trebetherick 3 G1
Treborough 7 J2
Trebudannon 3 F2
Trebullett 4 D3
Treburley 4 D3
Trebyan 4 A4
Trecastle 27 H6
Trecwn 16 C1
Trecynon 18 C1
Tredavoe 2 B6
Tredegar 18 E1
Tredington *Glos.* 29 J6
Tredington *Warks.* 30 D4
Tredinnick *Cornw.* 3 G1
Tredinnick *Cornw.* 4 C5
Tredomen 28 A5
Tredrissi 16 D1
Tredunnock 19 G2
Treen 2 A6
Treeton 51 G4
Trefaldwyn (Montgomery) 38 B6
Trefasser 16 B1
Trefdraeth 46 C5
Trefecca 28 A5
Trefeglwys 37 J6
Trefenter 27 F2
Treffgarne 16 C2
Treffynnon (Holywell) *Flints.* 47 K5
Treffynnon *Pembs.* 16 B2
Trefgarn Owen 16 B2
Trefil 28 A7
Trefilan 26 E3
Treflach 38 B3
Trefnanney 38 B4
Trefnant 47 J5
Trefonen 38 B3
Trefor *Gwyn.* 36 C1
Trefor *I.o.A.* 46 B4
Treforest 18 D3
Treforest Industrial Estate 18 E3
Trefriw 47 F6
Trefynwy (Monmouth) 28 E7
Tregadillett 6 B7
Tregaian 46 C5
Tregare 28 D7
Tregaron 27 F3
Tregarth 46 E6
Tregavethan 2 E4
Tregear 3 F3
Tregeare 4 C2
Tregeiriog 38 A2
Tregele 46 B3
Tregidden 2 E6
Treglemais 16 B2
Tregolds 3 F1
Tregole 4 B1
Tregonetha 3 G2
Tregony 3 G4
Tregoyd 28 A5
Treguff 18 D4
Tregurrian 3 F2
Tregynon 37 K6
Trehafod 18 D2
Treharris 18 D2
Treherbert 18 C2
Trekenner 4 D3
Treknow 4 A2
Trelash 4 B1
Trelassick 3 F3
Trelawnyd 47 J5
Trelech 17 F1
Trelech a'r Betws 17 G2
Treleddyd-fawr 16 A2
Trelewis 18 E2
Treligga 4 A2
Trelights 3 G1
Trelill 4 A3
Trelissick 3 F5
Trelleck 19 J1
Trelleck Grange 19 H1
Trelogan 47 K4
Trelystan 38 B5
Tremadog 36 E1
Tremail 4 B2
Tremain 26 B4
Tremaine 4 C2
Tremar 4 C4
Trematon 4 D5
Tremeirchion 47 J5
Tremethick Cross 2 B5
Trenance 3 F2
Trenarren 4 A6
Trench *Tel. & W.* 39 F4
Trench *Wrex.* 38 C2
Treneglos 4 C2
Trenewan 4 B5
Trent 8 E3
Trentham 40 A1
Trentishoe 6 E1
Treoes 18 C4
Treorchy 18 C2
Tre'r-ddol 37 F6
Trerulefoot 4 D5
Tresaith 26 B3
Trescott 40 A6
Trescowe 2 C5
Tresham 20 A2
Treshnish 78 E3
Tresillian 3 F4
Tresinney 4 B2
Tresinwen 16 C1
Treskinnick Cross 4 C1
Tresmeer 4 C2
Tresparrett 4 B1
Tresparrett Posts 4 B1
Tressait 81 K1
Tresta *Shet.* 108 F3
Tresta *Shet.* 109 C7
Treswell 51 K5
Trethurgy 4 A5
Tretio 16 A2
Tretire 28 E6
Tretower 28 A6
Treuddyn 48 B7
Trevalga 4 A2
Trevalyn 48 C7
Trevanson 3 G1
Trevarren 3 G2
Trevarrick 3 G4
Trevaughan 17 F3
Trevellas 2 E3
Trevelmond 4 C4
Treverva 2 E5
Trevescan 2 A6
Trevethin 19 F1
Trevigro 4 D4
Trevine *Arg. & B.* 80 B5
Trevine *Pembs.* 16 B1
Treviscoe 3 G3
Trevone 3 F1
Trevor 38 B1
Trewalder 4 A2
Trewarmett 4 A2
Trewarthenick 3 G4
Trewassa 4 B2
Trewellard 2 A5
Trewen 4 C2
Trewern 38 B4
Trewidland 4 C5
Trewilym 26 A4
Trewint 4 B1
Trewithian 3 F5
Trewoon 3 G3
Trewornan 3 G1
Treyarnon 3 F1
Treyford 12 B5
Triangle 57 F7
Trickett's Cross 10 B4
Trimdon 62 E3
Trimdon Colliery 62 E3
Trimdon Grange 62 E3
Trimingham 45 G2
Trimley St. Martin 35 G5
Trimley St. Mary 35 G5
Trimpley 29 G1
Trimsaran 17 H4
Trimstone 6 D1
Trinafour 81 J1
Trinant 19 F2
Tring 32 C7
Trinity 83 H1
Trislaig 87 G7
Trispen 3 F3
Tritlington 71 H4
Trochry 82 A3
Troedyraur 26 C4
Troedyrhiw 18 D1
Trondavoe 108 C5
Troon *Cornw.* 2 D5
Troon *S.Ayr.* 74 B7
Trosaraidh 84 C3
Troston 34 C1
Troswell 4 C1
Trottiscliffe 23 K6
Trotton 12 B4
Troughend 70 D4
Troustan 73 J3
Troutbeck 61 F6
Troutbeck Bridge 61 F6
Trow Green 19 J1
Trowbridge 20 B6
Trowle Common 20 B6
Trowley Bottom 32 D7
Trows 76 E7
Trowse Newton 45 G5
Trudernish 72 C5
Trudoxhill 20 A7
Trull 8 B2
Trumaisge Arraidh 92 D4
Trumpan 93 H5
Trumpet 29 F5
Trumpington 33 H3
Trunch 45 G2
Trunnah 55 G5
Truro 3 F4
Trusham 7 G7
Trusley 40 E2
Trusthorpe 53 J4
Truthan 3 F3
Trysull 40 A6
Tubney 21 H2
Tuckenhay 5 J5
Tuckingmill 2 D4
Tuddenham *Suff.* 35 F4
Tuddenham *Suff.* 34 B1
Tudeley 23 K7
Tudhoe 62 D3
Tudweiliog 36 B2
Tuffley 29 H7
Tufton *Hants.* 21 H7
Tufton *Pembs.* 16 D2
Tugby 42 A5
Tugford 38 E7
Tughall 71 H1
Tuirnaig 94 E3
Tulchan 82 A5
Tullibody 75 G1
Tullich *Arg. & B.* 80 B6
Tullich *Arg. & B.* 79 K6
Tullich *High.* 97 F4
Tullich *High.* 88 D2
Tullich *Moray* 98 B6
Tullich *Stir.* 81 G4
Tullich Muir 96 E4
Tulliemet 82 A2
Tulloch *Aber.* 91 G1
Tulloch *High.* 96 D2
Tulloch *Moray* 97 H6
Tullochgorm 73 H1
Tullochgribban High 89 G2
Tullochvenus 90 D4
Tulloes 83 G3
Tullybannocher 81 J5
Tullybelton 82 B4
Tullyfergus 82 D3
Tullymurdoch 82 C2
Tullynessle 90 D3
Tumble 17 J3
Tumby 53 F7
Tumby Woodside 53 F7
Tummel Bridge 81 J2
Tundergarth Mains 69 G5
Tunga 101 G4
Tunstall *E.Riding* 59 K6
Tunstall *Kent* 24 E5
Tunstall *Lancs.* 56 B2
Tunstall *N.Yorks.* 62 D7
Tunstall *Norf.* 45 J5
Tunstall *Stoke* 49 H7
Tunstall *Suff.* 35 H3
Tunstead 45 H3
Tunworth 21 K7
Tupsley 28 E4
Tupton 51 F6
Tur Langton 42 A6
Turbiskill 73 F2
Turclossie 99 G5
Turgis Green 21 K6
Turin 83 G2
Turkdean 30 C7
Turnastone 28 C5
Turnberry 67 G3
Turnchapel 4 E5
Turnditch 40 E1
Turner's Green 30 C1
Turners Hill 13 G3
Turners Puddle 9 H5
Turnford 23 G1
Turnworth 9 H4
Turret Bridge 87 K5
Turriff 99 F5
Turton Bottoms 49 G1
Turvey 32 C3
Turville 22 A2
Turville Heath 22 A2
Turweston 31 H5
Tutbury 40 E3
Tutnall 29 J1
Tutshill 19 J2
Tuttington 45 G3
Tuxford 51 K5
Twatt *Ork.* 106 B5
Twatt *Shet.* 109 C7
Twechar 74 E3
Tweedmouth 77 H5
Tweedsmuir 69 F1
Twelveheads 2 E4
Twenty 42 E3
Twerton 20 A5
Twickenham 22 E4
Twigworth 29 H6
Twineham 13 F4
Twinhoe 20 A6
Twinstead 34 C5
Twiss Green 49 F3
Twitchen *Devon* 7 F2
Twitchen *Shrop.* 28 C1
Twizell House 71 G1
Two Bridges 5 G3
Two Dales 50 E6
Two Gates 40 E5
Twycross 41 F5
Twyford *Bucks.* 31 H6
Twyford *Derbys.* 41 F3
Twyford *Dorset* 9 H3
Twyford *Hants.* 11 F2
Twyford *Leics.* 42 A5
Twyford *Norf.* 44 E3
Twyford *Oxon.* 31 F5
Twyford *W'ham* 22 A4
Twyford Common 28 E5
Twyn-y-Sheriff 19 H1
Twyn-yr-odyn 18 E4
Twynholm 65 G5
Twyning 29 H5
Twyning Green 29 H5
Twynllanan 27 G6
Twywell 32 C1
Ty-hen 36 A2
Ty Mawr 37 J1
Ty-mawr 38 A1
Ty-nant *Conwy* 37 J1
Ty-nant *Gwyn.* 37 J3
Ty-uchaf 37 J3
Tyberton 28 C5
Tyburn 40 D6
Tycroes 17 K3
Tycrwyn 38 A4
Tydd Gote 43 H4
Tydd St. Giles 43 H4
Tydd St. Mary 43 H4
Tyddewi (St. David's) 16 A2
Tye Common 24 C2
Tye Green 34 B6
Tyldesley 49 F2
Tyle-garw 18 D3
Tyler Hill 25 H5
Tylers Green *Bucks.* 22 C2
Tyler's Green *Essex* 23 J1
Tylorstown 18 D2
Tylwch 27 J1
Tyn-y-cefn 37 K1
Tyn-y-Cwm 37 H7
Tyn-y-ffridd 38 A2
Tyn-y-graig 27 K4
Ty'n-y-groes 47 F5
Tyndrum 80 E4
Tyneham 9 H6
Tynehead 76 B5
Tynemouth 71 J7
Tynewydd 18 C2
Tyninghame 76 E3
Tynribbie 80 A3
Tynron 68 D4
Tynygraig 27 F2
Tyringham 32 B4
Tythegston 18 B4
Tytherington *Ches.* 49 J5
Tytherington *S.Glos.* 19 K3
Tytherington *Som.* 20 A7
Tytherington *Wilts.* 20 C7
Tytherleigh 8 C4
Tytherton Lucas 20 C4
Tywardreath 4 A5
Tywardreath Highway 4 A5
Tywyn 36 E5

U

Uachdar 92 D6
Uags 86 D1
Ubbeston Green 35 H1
Ubley 19 J6
Uckerby 62 D6
Uckfield 13 H4
Uckinghall 29 H5
Uckington 29 J6
Uddingston 74 E4
Uddington 75 G7
Udimore 14 D6
Udny Green 91 G2
Udny Station 91 H2
Udstonhead 75 F6
Uffcott 20 E4
Uffculme 7 J4
Uffington *Lincs.* 42 D5
Uffington *Oxon.* 21 G3
Uffington *Shrop.* 38 E4
Ufford *Peter.* 42 D5
Ufford *Suff.* 35 G3
Ufton 30 E2
Ufton Nervet 21 K5
Ugborough 5 G5
Uggeshall 35 J1
Ugglebarnby 63 K6
Ugley 33 J6
Ugley Green 33 J6
Ugthorpe 63 J5
Uig *Arg. & B.* 78 C2
Uig *Arg. & B.* 73 K2
Uig *High.* 93 J5
Uig *High.* 93 G6
Uigen 100 C4
Uiginish 93 H7
Uigshader 93 K7
Uisgebhagh 92 D7
Uisken 78 E6
Ulbster 105 J4
Ulcat Row 61 F4
Ulceby *Lincs.* 53 H5
Ulceby *N.Lincs.* 52 E1
Ulceby Cross 53 H5
Ulcombe 14 D3
Uldale 60 D3
Uldale House 61 J7
Uley 20 A2
Ulgham 71 H4
Ullapool 95 H2
Ullenhall 30 C2
Ullenwood 29 J7
Ulleskelf 58 B5
Ullesthorpe 41 H7
Ulley 51 G4
Ullingswick 28 E4
Ullinish 85 J1
Ullock 60 B4
Ulpha 60 C7
Ulrome 59 H4
Ulsta 108 D4
Ulting 24 E1
Uluvalt 79 G5
Ulverston 55 F2
Ulwell 10 B6
Ulzieside 68 C3
Umberleigh 6 E3
Unapool 102 E5
Underbarrow 61 F7
Underhoull 108 E2
Underriver 23 J6
Underwood *Newport* 19 G3
Underwood *Notts.* 51 G7
Undy 19 H3
Unifirth 109 B7
Union Croft 91 G5
Union Mills 54 C6
Unstone 51 F5
Unthank 61 F3
Up Cerne 9 F4
Up Exe 7 H5
Up Hatherley 29 J6
Up Holland 48 E2
Up Marden 11 J3
Up Nately 22 A6
Up Somborne 10 E1
Up Sydling 9 F4
Upavon 20 E6
Upchurch 24 E5
Upcott *Devon* 6 C6
Upcott *Here.* 28 C3
Upend 33 K3
Uphall *Dorset* 8 E4
Uphall *W.Loth.* 75 J3
Uphall Station 75 J3
Upham *Devon* 7 G5
Upham *Hants.* 11 G2
Uphampton 29 H2
Uphill 19 G6
Uplawmoor 74 C5
Upleadon 29 G6
Upleatham 63 H4
Uplees 25 G5
Uploders 8 E5
Uplowman 7 J4
Uplyme 8 C5
Upminster 23 J3
Upottery 7 K5
Upper Affcot 38 D7
Upper Ardroscadale 73 J4
Upper Arley 39 G7
Upper Arncott 31 H7
Upper Aston 40 A6
Upper Astrop 31 G5
Upper Basildon 21 K4
Upper Beeding 12 E5
Upper Benefield 42 C7
Upper Bighouse 104 D3
Upper Boat 18 E3
Upper Boddington 31 F3
Upper Borth 37 F7
Upper Boyndlie 99 H4
Upper Brailes 30 E4
Upper Breakish 86 C2
Upper Breinton 28 D4
Upper Broughton 41 J3
Upper Bucklebury 21 J5
Upper Burgate 10 C3
Upper Burnhaugh 91 G5
Upper Caldecote 32 E4
Upper Camster 105 H4
Upper Catshill 29 J1
Upper Chapel 27 K4
Upper Chute 21 F6
Upper Clatford 21 G7
Upper Coberley 29 J7
Upper Cound 38 E5
Upper Cwmbran 19 F2
Upper Dallachy 98 B4
Upper Dean 32 D2
Upper Denby 50 E2
Upper Derraid 89 H1
Upper Diabaig 94 E5
Upper Dicker 13 J5
Upper Dovercourt 35 G6
Upper Dunsforth 57 K3
Upper Eastern Green 40 E7
Upper Eathie 96 E5
Upper Elkstone 50 C7
Upper End 50 C5
Upper Farringdon 11 J1
Upper Framilode 29 G7
Upper Froyle 22 A7
Upper Gills 105 J1
Upper Glendessarry 87 F5
Upper Godney 19 H7
Upper Gornal 40 B6
Upper Gravenhurst 32 E5
Upper Green *Essex* 33 H5
Upper Green *Mon.* 28 C7
Upper Green *W.Berks.* 21 G5
Upper Gylen 79 K5
Upper Hackney 50 E6
Upper Halliford 22 D5
Upper Halling 24 C5
Upper Hambleton 42 C5
Upper Hardres Court 15 G2
Upper Hartfield 13 H3
Upper Hawkhillock 91 J1
Upper Hayton 38 E7
Upper Heath 38 E7
Upper Helmsley 58 C4
Upper Hergest 28 B3
Upper Heyford 31 F6
Upper Hill 28 D3
Upper Hopton 50 D1
Upper Horsebridge 13 J5
Upper Hulme 50 C6
Upper Inglesham 21 F2
Upper Kilchattan 72 B1
Upper Killay 17 J5
Upper Knockando 97 J7
Upper Lambourn 21 G3
Upper Langwith 51 H6
Upper Largo 83 F7
Upper Lochton 90 E5
Upper Longdon 40 C4
Upper Longwood 39 F5
Upper Ludstone 40 A6
Upper Lybster 105 H5
Upper Lydbrook 29 F7
Upper Maes-coed 28 C5
Upper Midhope 50 E3
Upper Minety 20 D2
Upper Mitton 29 H1
Upper Muirskie 91 G5
Upper North Dean 22 B2
Upper Norwood 23 G4
Upper Obney 82 B4
Upper Oddington 30 D6
Upper Ollach 86 B1
Upper Poppleton 58 B4
Upper Quinton 30 C4
Upper Ridinghill 99 J5
Upper Rissington 30 D6
Upper Rochford 29 F2
Upper Sanday 107 E7
Upper Sapey 29 F2
Upper Scolton 16 C2
Upper Seagry 20 C3
Upper Shelton 32 C4
Upper Sheringham 45 F1
Upper Skelmorlie 74 A4
Upper Slaughter 30 C6
Upper Sonachan 80 B5
Upper Soudley 29 F7
Upper Stoke 41 F7
Upper Stondon 32 E5
Upper Stowe 31 H3
Upper Street *Hants.* 10 C3
Upper Street *Norf.* 45 H4
Upper Street *Suff.* 35 F5
Upper Sundon 32 D6
Upper Swell 30 C6
Upper Tean 40 C2
Upper Thurnham 55 H4
Upper Tillyrie 82 C7
Upper Tooting 23 F4
Upper Town 19 J5
Upper Tysoe 30 E4
Upper Upham 21 F4
Upper Upnor 24 D4
Upper Victoria 83 G4
Upper Wardington 31 F4
Upper Weald 32 B5
Upper Weedon 31 H3
Upper Welson 28 B3
Upper Wield 11 H1
Upper (Over) Winchendon 31 J7
Upper Woodford 10 C1
Upper Wootton 21 J6
Upper Wraxall 20 A4
Upper Wyche 29 G4
Uppermill 49 J2
Upperthong 50 D2
Upperton 12 C4
Uppertown 105 J1
Uppingham 42 B6
Uppington *Dorset* 10 B4
Uppington *Shrop.* 38 E5
Upsall 57 K1
Upsettlington 77 G6
Upshire 23 H1
Upstreet 25 J5
Upton *Bucks.* 31 J7
Upton *Cambs.* 32 E1
Upton *Ches.* 48 D6
Upton *Cornw.* 4 C3
Upton *Devon* 7 J5
Upton *Devon* 5 H6
Upton *Dorset* 9 J5
Upton *Hants.* 21 G6
Upton *Hants.* 10 E3
Upton *Lincs.* 52 B4
Upton *Mersey.* 48 B4
Upton *Norf.* 45 H4
Upton *Northants.* 31 J2
Upton *Notts.* 51 K5
Upton *Notts.* 51 K7
Upton *Oxon.* 21 J3
Upton *Peter.* 42 E5
Upton *Slo.* 22 C4
Upton *Som.* 7 H3
Upton *W.Yorks.* 51 G1
Upton Bishop 29 F6
Upton Cheyney 19 K5
Upton Cressett 39 F6
Upton Cross 4 C3
Upton End 32 E5
Upton Green 45 H4
Upton Grey 21 K7
Upton Hellions 7 G5
Upton Lovell 20 C7
Upton Magna 38 E4
Upton Noble 9 G1
Upton Pyne 7 H6
Upton St. Leonards 29 H7
Upton Scudamore 20 B7
Upton Snodsbury 29 J3
Upton upon Severn 29 H4
Upton Warren 29 J2
Upwaltham 12 C5
Upware 33 J2
Upwell 43 J5
Upwey 9 F6
Upwood 43 F7
Uradale 109 D9
Urafirth 108 C5
Urchany 97 F7
Urchfont 20 D6
Urdimarsh 28 E4
Ure 108 B5
Urgha 93 G2
Urlay Nook 62 E5
Urmston 49 G3
Urquhart *High.* 96 C6
Urquhart *Moray* 97 K5
Urra 63 G6
Urray 96 C6
Ushaw Moor 62 D2
Usk 19 G1
Usselby 52 D3
Utley 57 F5
Uton 7 G6
Utterby 53 G3
Uttoxeter 40 C2
Uwchmynydd 36 A3
Uxbridge 22 D3
Uyeasound 108 E2
Uzmaston 16 C3

V

Valley (Dyffryn) 46 A5
Valley Truckle 4 B2
Valleyfield *D. & G.* 65 G5
Valleyfield *Fife* 75 J2
Valsgarth 108 F1
Vange 24 D3
Vardre 17 K4
Varteg 19 F1
Vatersay (Bhatarsaigh) 84 B5
Vatten 93 H7
Vaul 78 B3
Vaynor 27 K7
Vaynor Park 38 A5
Veaullt 28 A3
Veensgarth 109 D8
Velindre *Pembs.* 16 E1
Velindre *Powys* 28 A5
Vellow 7 J2
Veness 106 E5
Venn 5 H6
Venn Ottery 7 J6
Vennington 38 C5
Ventnor 11 G7
Vernham Dean 21 G6
Vernham Street 21 G6
Vernolds Common 38 D7
Verwood 10 B4
Veryan 3 G5
Vicarage 8 B6
Vickerstown 54 E3
Victoria 3 G2
Vidlin 109 D6
Viewfield 105 F2
Viewpark 75 F4
Vigo 40 C5
Vigo Village 24 C5
Villavin 6 D4
Vinehall Street 14 C5
Vine's Cross 13 J5
Viney Hill 19 K1
Virginia Water 22 C5
Virginstow 6 B6
Virley 34 D7
Vobster 20 A7
Voe *Shet.* 109 D6
Voe *Shet.* 108 C4

Vowchurch 28 C5
Voy 107 B6

W

Wackerfield 62 C4
Wacton 45 F6
Wadborough 29 J4
Waddesdon 31 J7
Waddingham 52 C3
Waddington 56 C5
  Lancs.
Waddington 52 C6
  Lincs.
Waddingworth 52 E5
Wadebridge 3 G1
Wadeford 8 C3
Wadenhoe 42 D7
Wadesmill 33 G7
Wadhurst 13 K3
Wadshelf 51 F5
Wadsley Bridge 51 F3
Wadworth 51 H3
Wadworth Hill 59 J7
Waen 47 K6
Waen-fach 38 B4
Waen-wen 46 D6
Wag 105 F6
Wainfleet All 53 H7
  Saints
Wainfleet Bank 53 H7
Wainhouse Corner 4 B1
Wainscott 24 D4
Wainstalls 57 F7
Waitby 61 J6
Wakefield 57 J7
Wakerley 42 C6
Wakes Colne 34 C6
Walberswick 35 J1
Walberton 12 C6
Walcot Lincs. 42 D2
Walcot Lincs. 52 E7
Walcot N.Lincs. 58 E7
Walcot Shrop. 38 C7
Walcot Tel. & W. 38 E4
Walcot Green 45 F7
Walcote Leics. 41 H7
Walcote Warks. 30 C3
Walcott 45 H2
Walcott Dales 52 E7
Walden 57 F1
Walden Head 56 E1
Walden Stubbs 51 H1
Walderton 11 J3
Walditch 8 D5
Waldley 40 D2
Waldridge 62 D1
Waldringfield 35 G4
Waldron 13 J5
Wales 51 G4
Walesby Lincs. 52 E3
Walesby Notts. 51 J5
Walford Here. 28 C1
Walford Here. 28 E6
Walford Shrop. 38 D3
Walgherton 39 F1
Walgrave 32 B1
Walhampton 10 E5
Walk Mill 56 D6
Walkden 49 G2
Walker 71 H7
Walker Fold 56 B5
Walkerburn 76 B7
Walkeringham 51 K3
Walkerith 51 K3
Walkern 33 F6
Walker's Green 28 E4
Walkhampton 5 F4
Walkington 59 G6
Walkwood 30 B2
Wall Northumb. 70 E7
Wall Staffs. 40 D5
Wall Bank 38 E6
Wall Heath 40 A7
Wall under 38 E6
  Heywood
Wallacehall 69 H6
Wallacetown 67 G3
Wallasey 48 B3
Wallbottle 71 G7
Wallend 24 E4
Waller's Green 29 F5
Wallingford 21 K3
Wallington 23 F7
  Gt.Lon.
Wallington Hants. 11 G4
Wallington Herts. 33 F5
Wallis 16 D2
Wallisdown 10 B5
Walliswood 12 E3
Walls 109 B8
Wallsend 71 J7
Wallyford 76 B3
Walmer 15 J2
Walmer Bridge 55 H7
Walmersley 49 H1
Walmley 40 D6
Walpole 35 H1
Walpole Cross 43 J4
  Keys
Walpole Highway 43 J4
Walpole St. 43 J4
  Andrew
Walpole St. Peter 43 J4
Walsall 40 C6
Walsall Wood 40 C5
Walsden 56 E7
Walsgrave on 41 F7
  Sowe
Walsham le 34 E1
  Willows
Walsoken 43 H4
Walston 75 J6
Walsworth 32 E5
Walterstone 28 C6
Waltham Kent 15 G3
Waltham 53 F2
  N.E.Lincs.
Waltham Abbey 23 H1
Waltham Chase 11 G3
Waltham Cross 23 G1
Waltham Forest 23 G2
Waltham on the 42 A3
  Wolds
Waltham St. 22 B4
  Lawrence
Walthamstow 23 G3
Walton Bucks. 32 B7
Walton Cumb. 70 A7
Walton Derbys. 51 F6
Walton Leics. 41 H7
Walton M.K. 32 B5
Walton Mersey. 48 C3
Walton Peter. 42 E5
Walton Powys 28 B3

Walton Som. 8 D1
Walton Staffs. 40 A2
Walton Suff. 35 G5
Walton Tel. & W. 38 E4
Walton W.Yorks. 51 F1
Walton W.Yorks. 57 K5
Walton Warks. 30 D3
Walton Cardiff 29 J5
Walton East 16 D2
Walton-in-Gordano 19 H4
Walton-le-Dale 55 J7
Walton-on- 22 E5
  Thames
Walton-on-the-Hill 40 B3
  Staffs.
Walton on the Hill 23 F6
  Surr.
Walton on the 35 G6
  Naze
Walton on the 41 H4
  Wolds
Walton-on-Trent 40 E4
Walton Park 65 H3
Walton West 16 B3
Walwen Flints. 47 K5
Walwen Flints. 48 B5
Walwick 70 E6
Walworth 62 D5
Walwyn's Castle 16 B3
Wambrook 8 B4
Wanborough 22 C7
  Surr.
Wanborough 21 F3
  Swin.
Wandel 68 E1
Wandon 71 F1
Wandsworth 23 F4
Wandylaw 71 G1
Wangford Suff. 35 J1
Wangford Suff. 44 B7
Wanlip 41 J4
Wanlockhead 68 D2
Wannock 13 J6
Wansford 59 G4
  E.Riding
Wansford Peter. 42 D6
Wanstead 23 H3
Wanstrow 20 A7
Wanswell 19 K1
Wantage 21 G3
Wapley 20 A4
Wappenbury 30 E2
Wappenham 31 H4
Warblebank 60 D2
Warbleton 13 K5
Warborough 21 J2
Warboys 33 G1
Warbstow 4 C1
Warburton 49 F4
Warcop 61 J5
Ward End 40 D7
Ward Green 34 E2
Warden Kent 25 G4
Warden 70 E7
  Northumb.
Wardgate 40 E1
Wardhouse 90 D1
Wardington 31 F4
Wardle Ches. 49 F7
Wardle Gt.Man. 49 J1
Wardley 42 B5
Wardlow 50 D5
Wardy Hill 43 H7
Ware Herts. 33 G7
Ware Kent 25 J5
Wareham 9 J6
Warehorne 14 E4
Waren Mill 77 K1
Warenford 71 G1
Warenton 77 K1
Wareside 33 G7
Waresley 33 F3
Warfield 22 B4
Wargrave 22 A4
Warham 44 D1
Wark Northumb. 70 D6
Wark Northumb. 77 G7
Warkleigh 6 E3
Warkton 32 B1
Warkworth 31 F4
  Northants.
Warkworth 71 H3
  Northumb.
Warlaby 62 E7
Warland 56 E7
Warleggan 4 B4
Warley 40 C7
Warley Town 57 F7
Warlingham 23 G6
Warmfield 57 J7
Warmingham 49 G6
Warminghurst 12 E5
Warmington 42 E6
  Northants.
Warmington 31 F4
  Warks.
Warminster 20 B7
Warmlake 14 D2
Warmley 19 K4
Warmsworth 51 H2
Warmwell 9 G6
Warndon 29 H3
Warnford 11 H2
Warnham 12 E3
Warningcamp 12 D6
Warninglid 13 F4
Warren Ches. 49 H5
Warren Pembs. 16 C5
Warren House 6 E7
Warren Row 22 B3
Warren Street 14 E2
Warrenby 63 G4
Warrington M.K. 32 B3
Warrington Warr. 49 F4
Warroch 82 B7
Warsash 11 F4
Warslow 50 C7
Warter 58 E4
Warthill 58 C4
Wartle 90 D4
Wartling 13 K6
Wartnaby 42 A3
Warton Lancs. 55 J2
Warton Lancs. 55 H7
Warton 71 F3
  Northumb.
Warton Warks. 40 E5
Warwick Cumb. 61 F1
Warwick Warks. 30 D2
Warwick Bridge 61 F1
Wasbister 106 C4
Wash Common 21 H5
Washaway 4 A4
Washbourne 5 H5
Washfield 7 H4
Washfold 62 B6
Washford 7 J1
Washford Pyne 7 G4
Washingborough 52 D5

Washington 62 E1
  T. & W.
Washington 12 E5
  W.Suss.
Washmere Green 34 D4
Wasing 21 J5
Waskerley 62 B2
Wasperton 30 D3
Wass 58 B2
Watchet 7 J1
Watchfield Oxon. 21 F2
Watchfield Som. 19 G7
Watchgate 61 G7
Watendlath 60 D5
Water 56 D7
Water Eaton 31 G7
Water End Herts. 23 F1
Water End Herts. 32 D7
Water Newton 42 E6
Water Orton 40 D6
Water Stratford 31 H5
Water Yeat 55 F1
Waterbeach 33 H2
Waterbeck 69 H6
Waterfall 50 C7
Waterfoot E.Renf. 74 D5
Waterfoot Lancs. 56 D7
Waterford 33 G7
Waterhead Cumb. 60 E6
Waterhead 68 C5
  D. & G.
Waterhill of Bruxie 99 H6
Waterhouses Dur. 62 C2
Waterhouses 50 C7
  Staffs.
Wateringbury 23 K6
Waterloo Aber. 91 J1
Waterloo Mersey. 48 C3
Waterloo N.Lan. 75 G5
Waterloo Norf. 45 G4
Waterloo P & K. 82 B4
Waterloo Pembs. 16 C4
Waterloo Poole 10 B5
Waterloo Cross 7 J4
Waterloo Port 46 C6
Waterlooville 11 H3
Watermeetings 68 E2
Watermillock 61 F4
Waterperry 21 K1
Waterrow 7 J3
Waters Upton 39 F4
Watersfield 12 D5
Waterside Aber. 90 B3
Waterside Aber. 91 J2
Waterside Bucks. 22 C1
Waterside E.Ayr. 67 J3
Waterside E.Ayr. 74 C6
Waterside E.Dun. 74 E3
Waterstock 21 K1
Waterston 16 C4
Waterthorpe 51 G4
Watford Herts. 22 E2
Watford 31 H2
  Northants.
Wath N.Yorks. 57 J2
Wath N.Yorks. 57 G3
Wath Brow 60 B5
Wath upon Dearne 51 G2
Watlington Norf. 44 A4
Watlington Oxon. 21 K2
Watnall 41 H1
Watten 105 H3
Wattisfield 34 E1
Wattisham 34 E3
Watton E.Riding 59 G5
Watton Norf. 44 D5
Watton at Stone 33 G7
Watton Green 44 D5
Wattston 75 F4
Wattstown 18 D2
Wattsville 18 E2
Waun Fawr 37 F7
Waun y Clyn 17 H4
Waunarlwydd 17 K5
Waunclunda 17 K1
Waunfawr 46 D7
Wavendon 32 C5
Waverbridge 60 D2
Waverton Ches. 48 D6
Waverton Cumb. 60 D2
Wawne 59 G6
Waxham 45 J3
Waxholme 59 K7
Way Gill 56 E3
Way Village 7 G4
Wayford 8 D4
Waytown 8 D5
Weachyburn 98 E5
Weald 21 G1
Wealdstone 22 E3
Weare 19 H6
Weare Giffard 6 C3
Wearhead 61 K2
Wearne 8 D2
Weasenham All 44 C4
  Saints
Weasenham St. 44 C4
  Peter
Weathercote 56 C2
Weatheroak Hill 30 B1
Weaverham 49 F5
Weaverthorpe 59 F2
Webheath 30 B2
Webton 28 D5
Wedderlairs 91 G1
Weddington 41 F6
Wedhampton 20 D6
Wedmore 19 H7
Wednesbury 40 B6
Wednesfield 40 B5
Weedon 32 B7
Weedon Bec 31 H3
Weedon Lois 31 H4
Weeford 40 D5
Week 7 F4
Week Orchard 6 A5
Week St. Mary 4 C1
Weekley 42 B7
Weeley 35 F6
Weeley Heath 35 F7
Weem 81 K3
Weeping Cross 40 B3
Weethley 30 B3
Weeting 44 B7
Weeton E.Riding 59 K7
Weeton Lancs. 55 G6
Weeton N.Yorks. 57 H5
Weir Essex 24 E3
Weir Lancs. 56 D7
Weirbrook 38 C3
Welbeck Abbey 51 H5
Welborne 44 E5
Welbourn 52 C7
Welburn 58 D3
Welbury 62 E6
Welby 42 C2
Welches Dam 43 H7
Welcombe 6 A4

Weldon 42 C7
Welford 41 J7
  Northants.
Welford W.Berks. 21 H4
Welford-on-Avon 30 C3
Welham Leics. 42 A6
Welham Notts. 51 K4
Welham Green 23 F1
Well Hants. 22 A7
Well Lincs. 53 H5
Well N.Yorks. 57 H1
Well End 22 B3
Well Hill 23 H5
Well Town 7 H5
Welland 29 G4
Wellbank 83 F4
Wellesbourne 30 D3
Wellhill 97 G5
Welling 23 H4
Wellingborough 32 B2
Wellingham 44 C3
Wellingore 52 C7
Wellington Cumb. 60 B6
Wellington Here. 28 D4
Wellington Som. 7 K3
Wellington 39 F4
  Tel. & W.
Wellington Heath 29 G4
Wellington Marsh 28 D4
Wellow 20 A6
  B. & N.E.Som.
Wellow I.o.W. 10 E6
Wellow Notts. 51 J6
Wells 19 J7
Wells-next-the-Sea 44 D1
Wellsborough 41 F5
Wellwood 75 J2
Welney 43 J6
Welsh Bicknor 28 E7
Welsh End 38 E2
Welsh Frankton 38 C2
Welsh Hook 16 C2
Welsh Newton 28 E7
Welsh St. Donats 18 D4
Welshampton 38 D2
Welshpool 38 B5
  (Y Trallwng)
Welton 19 K6
  B. & N.E.Som.
Welton Cumb. 60 E2
Welton E.Riding 59 F7
Welton Lincs. 52 D4
Welton Northants. 31 G2
Welton le Marsh 53 H6
Welton le Wold 53 F4
Welwick 59 K7
Welwyn 33 F7
Welwyn Garden 33 F7
  City
Wem 38 E3
Wembdon 8 B1
Wembley 22 E3
Wembury 5 F6
Wembworthy 6 E5
Wemyss Bay 73 K4
Wenallt 37 J1
Wendens Ambo 33 J5
Wendlebury 31 G7
Wendling 44 D4
Wendover 22 B1
Wendron 2 D5
Wendy 33 G4
Wenhaston 35 J1
Wennington 47 G6
  Cambs.
Wennington 33 F1
  Gt.Lon.
Wennington 56 B2
  Lancs.
Wensley Derbys. 50 E6
Wensley N.Yorks. 62 B7
Wentbridge 51 G1
Wentnor 38 C6
Wentworth 33 H1
  Cambs.
Wentworth 51 F3
  S.Yorks.
Wentworth Castle 51 F2
Wenvoe 18 E4
Weobley 28 C3
Weobley Marsh 28 D3
Wepham 12 D6
Wepre 48 B6
Wereham 44 A5
Wergs 40 A5
Wernrheolydd 28 C7
Werrington Cornw. 6 B7
Werrington Peter. 42 E5
Werrington Staffs. 40 B1
Wervil Brook 26 C3
Wervin 48 D5
Wesham 55 H6
Wessington 51 F7
West Aberthaw 18 D5
West Acre 44 B4
West Allerdean 77 H6
West Alvington 5 H6
West Amesbury 20 E7
West Anstey 7 G3
West Ashby 53 F5
West Ashling 12 B6
West Ashton 20 B6
West Auckland 62 C4
West Ayton 59 F1
West Bagborough 7 K2
West Barkwith 52 E4
West Barnby 63 K5
West Barns 76 E3
West Barsham 44 D2
West Bay 8 D5
West Beckham 45 F2
West Benhar 75 G4
West Bergholt 34 D6
West Bexington 8 E6
West Bilney 44 B4
West Blatchington 13 F6
West Boldon 71 J7
West Bradenham 44 D5
West Bradford 56 C5
West Bradley 8 E1
West Bretton 50 E1
West Bridgford 41 H2
West Bromwich 40 C6
West Buckland 6 E2
  Devon
West Buckland 7 K3
  Som.
West Burrafirth 109 B7
West Burton 57 F1
  N.Yorks.
West Burton 12 C5
  W.Suss.
West Butterwick 52 B2
West Byfleet 22 D5
West Cairncake 99 G6
West Caister 45 K4
West Calder 75 J4
West Camel 8 E2

West Cauldcoats 74 E6
West Challow 21 G3
West Charleton 5 H6
West Chelborough 8 E4
West Chevington 71 H4
West Chiltington 12 D5
West Chiltington 12 D5
  Common
West Chinnock 8 D3
West Chisenbury 20 E6
West Clandon 22 D6
West Cliffe 15 J3
West Clyne 97 F1
West Coker 8 E3
West Compton 8 E5
  Dorset
West Compton 19 J7
  Som.
West Cross 17 K6
West Curry 4 C1
West Curthwaite 60 E2
West Dean 12 B5
  W.Sussex
West Dean Wilts. 10 D2
West Deeping 42 E5
West Derby 48 C3
West Dereham 44 A5
West Ditchburn 71 G1
West Down 6 D1
West Drayton 22 D4
  Gt.Lon.
West Drayton 51 K5
  Notts.
West Dullater 81 G7
West Dunnet 105 H1
West Edington 71 G5
West Ella 59 G7
West End Beds. 32 C3
West End 59 G3
  E.Riding
West End Hants. 11 F3
West End Kent 25 H5
West End Lancs. 55 H3
West End Lincs. 53 G3
West End N.Yorks. 57 G4
West End Norf. 45 J4
West End Oxon. 21 H1
West End S.Lan. 75 H6
West End Suff. 35 J7
West End Surr. 22 E5
West End Green 21 K5
West Farleigh 14 C2
West Farndon 31 G3
West Felton 38 C3
West Firle 13 H6
West Fleetham 71 G1
West Garforth 57 J6
West Ginge 21 H3
West Glen 73 J3
West Grafton 21 F5
West Green 22 A6
West Grimstead 10 D2
West Grinstead 12 E4
West Haddlesey 58 B7
West Haddon 31 H1
West Hagbourne 21 J3
West Hagley 40 B7
West Hall 70 A7
West Hallam 41 G1
West Halton 59 F7
West Ham 23 H3
West Handley 51 F5
West Hanney 21 H2
West Hanningfield 24 D2
West Hardwick 51 G1
West Harptree 19 J6
West Harting 11 J2
West Hatch 8 B2
West Heath 22 B6
  Hants.
West Heath 30 B1
  W.Mid.
West Helmsdale 105 F7
West Hendred 21 H3
West Hesleton 59 F2
West Hill Devon 7 J6
West Hill N.Som. 19 H4
West Hoathly 13 G3
West Holme 9 H6
West Horndon 24 C3
West Horrington 19 J7
West Horsley 22 D6
West Horton 77 J7
West Hougham 15 H3
West Huntspill 19 G7
West Hyde 22 D2
West Hythe 15 G4
West Ilsley 21 H3
West Itchenor 11 J4
West Keal 53 G6
West Kennett 20 E5
West Kilbride 74 A6
West Kingsdown 23 J5
West Kington 20 B4
West Kirby 48 B4
West Knapton 58 E2
West Knighton 9 G6
West Knoyle 9 H1
West Kyloe 77 J6
West Lambrook 8 D3
West Langwell 96 D1
West Lavington 12 B4
  W.Suss.
West Lavington 20 D6
  Wilts.
West Leake 41 H3
West Lexham 44 C4
West Lilling 58 C3
West Lingo 83 F7
West Linton 75 K5
West Littleton 20 A4
West Lockinge 21 H3
West Looe 4 C5
West Lulworth 9 H6
West Lutton 59 F3
West Lydford 8 E1
West Lyng 8 C2
West Lynn 44 A4
West Mains 23 H6
West Malling 23 K6
West Malvern 29 G4
West Marden 11 J3
West Markham 51 K5
West Marsh 53 F3
West Marton 56 D4
West Melton 51 G2
West Meon 11 H2
West Meon Hut 11 H2
West Mersea 34 E7
West Milton 8 E5
West Minster 25 F4
West Molesey 22 E5
West Monkton 8 B2
West Moors 10 B4
West Mostard 61 J7

West Muir 83 G1
West Ness 58 C2
West Newton 59 J6
  E.Riding
West Newton 44 A3
  Norf.
West Norwood 23 G4
West Ogwell 5 J3
West Orchard 9 H3
West Overton 20 E5
West Park Aber. 91 F5
West Park 48 E3
  Mersey.
West Parley 10 B5
West Peckham 23 K6
West Pennard 8 E1
West Pentire 2 E2
West Perry 32 E2
West Porlock 7 G1
West Putford 6 B4
West Quantoxhead 7 K1
West Rainton 62 E2
West Rasen 52 D4
West Raynham 44 C3
West Rounton 63 F6
West Row 33 K1
West Rudham 44 C3
West Runton 45 F1
West Saltoun 76 C4
West Sandwick 108 D4
West Scrafton 57 F1
West Shinness 103 H7
  Lodge
West Somerton 45 J3
West Stafford 9 G6
West Stockwith 51 K3
West Stoke 12 B6
West Stonesdale 61 K6
West Stoughton 19 H7
West Stour 9 G2
West Stourmouth 25 J5
West Stow 34 C1
West Stowell 20 E5
West Stratton 21 J7
West Street 14 E2
West Tanfield 57 H2
West Taphouse 4 B4
West Tarbert 73 G4
West Tarring 12 E6
West Thorney 11 J4
West Thurrock 23 J4
West Tilbury 24 C4
West Tisted 11 H2
West Tofts Norf. 44 C6
West Tofts P & K. 82 C4
West Torrington 52 E4
West Town Hants. 11 J5
West Town 19 H5
  N.Som.
West Tytherley 10 D1
West Walton 43 H4
West Walton 43 H4
  Highway
West Wellow 10 D2
West Wemyss 76 B1
West Wick 19 G5
West Wickham 33 K4
  Cambs.
West Wickham 23 G5
  Gt.Lon.
West Williamston 16 D4
West Winch 44 A4
West Winterslow 10 D1
West Wittering 11 J5
West Witton 57 F1
West Woodburn 70 D5
West Woodhay 21 G5
West Woodlands 20 A7
West Worldham 11 J1
West Worlington 7 F4
West Worthing 12 E6
West Wratting 33 K3
West Wycombe 22 B2
West Yell 108 D4
Westbere 25 H5
Westborough 42 B1
Westbourne 10 B5
  Bourne.
Westbourne 11 J4
  W.Suss.
Westbrook 21 H4
Westbury Bucks. 31 H5
Westbury Shrop. 38 C5
Westbury Wilts. 20 B6
Westbury Leigh 20 B6
Westbury-on- 29 G7
  Severn
Westbury on Trym 19 J4
Westbury-sub- 19 J7
  Mendip
Westby 55 G6
Westcliff-on-Sea 24 E3
Westcombe 9 F1
Westcote 30 D6
Westcott Bucks. 31 J7
Westcott Devon 7 J5
Westcott Surr. 22 E7
Westcott Barton 31 F6
Westdean 13 J7
Westdowns 4 A2
Wester 88 C2
  Aberchalder
Wester Badentyre 99 F5
Wester Culbeuchly 98 E4
Wester Dechmont 75 J3
Wester Fintray 91 G3
Wester Foffarty 83 F3
Wester 99 F4
  Greenskares
Wester Gruinards 96 C2
Wester Lealty 96 D4
Wester Lonvine 96 E4
Wester Newburn 83 F7
Wester Ord 91 G4
Wester Quarff 109 D9
Wester Skeld 109 B8
Westerdale High. 105 G3
Westerdale 63 H6
  N.Yorks.
Westerfield Shet. 109 C7
Westerfield Suff. 35 F4
Westergate 12 C6
Westerham 23 H6
Westerleigh 19 K4
Westerton Aber. 91 F5
Westerton Angus 83 H2
Westerton Dur. 62 D3
Westerton P & K. 81 K6
Westerwick 109 B8
Westfield Cumb. 60 A4
Westfield E.Suss. 14 D6
Westfield High. 105 F2
Westfield W.Loth. 75 H3
Westgate Dur. 62 A3
Westgate N.Lincs. 51 K2
Westgate Norf. 71 D1
Westgate 44 D1
  Northumb.

Westgate Hill 57 H7
Westgate on Sea 25 K4
Westhall Aber. 90 E2
Westhall Suff. 45 J7
Westham Dorset 9 F7
Westham E.Suss. 13 K6
Westham Som. 19 G7
Westhampnett 12 B6
Westhay 19 H7
Westhead 48 D2
Westhide 28 E4
Westhill Aber. 91 G4
Westhill Here. 96 E7
Westhope Here. 28 D3
Westhope Shrop. 38 D7
Westhorpe Lincs. 43 F2
Westhorpe Suff. 34 E2
Westhoughton 49 F2
Westhouse 56 B2
Westhouses 51 G7
Westhumble 22 E6
Westing 108 E2
Westlake 5 G5
Westleigh Devon 6 C3
Westleigh Devon 7 J4
Westleigh Gt.Man. 49 F2
Westleton 35 J2
Westley Shrop. 38 C5
Westley Suff. 34 C2
Westley Heights 24 C3
Westley Waterless 33 K3
Westlington 31 J7
Westlinton 69 J7
Westloch 76 A5
Westmarsh 25 J5
Westmeston 13 G5
Westmill 33 G6
Westmuir 82 E2
Westness 106 C5
Westnewton 60 C2
  Cumb.
Westnewton 77 G7
  Northumb.
Weston 20 A5
  B. & N.E.Som.
Weston Ches. 49 G7
Weston Devon 7 K7
Weston Dorset 9 F7
Weston Halton 48 E4
Weston Hants. 11 J2
Weston Herts. 33 F5
Weston Lincs. 43 F3
Weston Moray 97 G5
Weston N.Yorks. 57 G5
Weston 31 G4
  Northants.
Weston Notts. 51 K6
Weston Shrop. 38 E6
Weston Shrop. 38 E6
Weston Staffs. 40 B3
Weston W.Berks. 21 H4
Weston Beggard 28 E4
Weston by Welland 42 A6
Weston Colville 33 K3
Weston Corbett 21 K7
Weston Coyney 40 B1
Weston Favell 31 J2
Weston Green 33 K3
  Cambs.
Weston Green 45 F4
  Norf.
Weston Green 22 E5
  Surr.
Weston Heath 39 G4
Weston Hills 43 F3
Weston-in-Gordano 19 H4
Weston Jones 39 G3
Weston Longville 45 F4
Weston 38 D3
  Lullingfields
Weston-on-the- 31 G7
  Green
Weston-on-Trent 41 G3
Weston Patrick 21 K7
Weston Point 48 D4
Weston Rhyn 38 B2
Weston Subedge 30 C4
Weston-super- 19 G5
  Mare
Weston Turville 32 B7
Weston-under- 40 A4
  Lizard
Weston under 29 F6
  Penyard
Weston under 30 E2
  Wetherley
Weston 40 E1
  Underwood
  Derbys.
Weston 32 B4
  Underwood M.K.
Westonbirt 20 B3
Westoning 32 D5
Westonzoyland 8 C1
Westow 58 D3
Westport 66 A1
  Arg. & B.
Westport Som. 8 C2
Westrigg 75 H4
Westruther 76 E5
Westry 43 G6
Westside 91 G5
Westward 60 D2
Westward Ho! 6 C3
Westwell Kent 14 E3
Westwell Oxon. 30 D7
Westwell Leacon 14 E3
Westwick Cambs. 33 H2
Westwick Dur. 62 B5
Westwick Norf. 45 G3
Westwood Devon 7 J6
Westwood Wilts. 20 B6
Westwood Heath 30 D1
Westwoodside 51 K3
Wether Cote Farm 58 C1
Wetheral 61 F1
Wetherby 57 K5
Wetherden 34 E2
Wetheringsett 35 F2
Wethersfield 34 B5
Wetherup Street 35 F2
Wetley Rocks 40 B1
Wettenhall 49 F6
Wettenhall Green 49 F6
Wetton 50 D7
Wetwang 59 F4
Wetwood 39 G2
Wexcombe 21 F6
Weybourne 45 F1
Weybread 45 G1
Weybridge 22 D5
Weycroft 8 C4
Weydale 105 G2
Weyhill 21 G7
Weymouth 9 F7
Whaddon Bucks. 32 B5
Whaddon Cambs. 33 G4
Whaddon Glos. 29 H7

Whaddon Wilts. 10 C2
Whaddon Gap 33 G4
Whale 61 G4
Whaley 51 H5
Whaley Bridge 50 C4
Whaligoe 105 J4
Whalley 56 C6
Whalton 71 G5
Wham 56 C3
Whaplode 43 G3
Whaplode Drove 43 G4
Whaplode St. Catherine 43 G4
Wharfe 56 C3
Wharles 55 H6
Wharncliffe Side 51 F3
Wharram le Street 58 E3
Wharram Percy 58 E3
Wharton Ches. 49 F6
Wharton Here. 28 E3
Whashton 62 C6
Whatcote 30 D4
Whatfield 34 E4
Whatley 20 A7
Whatlington 14 C6
Whatstandwell 51 F7
Whatton 42 A2
Whauphill 64 E6
Whaw 62 A6
Wheatacre 45 J6
Wheatenhurst 20 A1
Wheathampstead 32 E7
Wheathill 39 F7
Wheatley Hants. 11 J1
Wheatley Oxon. 21 K1
Wheatley Hill 62 E3
Wheatley Lane 56 D6
Wheaton Aston 40 A4
Wheddon Cross 7 H2
Wheedlemont 90 C2
Wheelerstreet 22 C7
Wheelock 49 G7
Wheelton 56 B7
Wheen 90 B7
Wheldrake 58 C5
Whelford 20 E2
Whelpley Hill 22 D1
Whelpo 60 E3
Whenby 58 C3
Whepstead 34 C3
Wherstead 35 F4
Wherwell 21 G7
Wheston 50 D5
Whetley Cross 8 D4
Whetsted 23 K7
Whetstone 41 H6
Whicham 54 E1
Whichford 30 E5
Whickham 71 H7
Whiddon Down 6 E6
Whifflet 75 F4
Whigstreet 83 F3
Whilton 31 H2
Whim 76 A5
Whimple 7 J6
Whimpwell Green 45 H2
Whin Lane End 55 G5
Whinburgh 44 E5
Whinnyfold 91 J1
Whippingham 11 G5
Whipsnade 32 D7
Whipton 7 H6
Whisby 52 C6
Whissendine 42 B4
Whissonsett 44 D3
Whistley Green 22 A4
Whiston Mersey. 48 D3
Whiston Northants. 32 B2
Whiston S.Yorks. 51 G4
Whiston Staffs. 40 C1
Whiston Staffs. 40 A4
Whitbeck 54 E1
Whitbourne 29 G3
Whitburn T. & W. 71 K7
Whitburn W.Loth. 75 H4
Whitby Ches. 48 C5
Whitby N.Yorks. 63 K5
Whitchurch B. & N.E.Som. 19 K5
Whitchurch Bucks. 32 B6
Whitchurch Cardiff 18 E4
Whitchurch Devon 4 E3
Whitchurch Hants. 21 H7
Whitchurch Here. 28 E7
Whitchurch Pembs. 16 B2
Whitchurch Shrop. 38 E1
Whitchurch Canonicorum 8 C5
Whitchurch Hill 21 K4
Whitchurch-on-Thames 21 K4
Whitcombe 9 G6
Whitcott Keysett 38 B7
White Colne 34 C6
White Coppice 49 F1
White Cross Cornw. 3 F3
White Cross Devon 7 J6
White Cross Here. 28 D4
White End 29 H6
White Lackington 9 G5
White Ladies Aston 29 J3
White Mill 17 H2
White Moor 41 F1
White Notley 34 B7
White Pit 53 G5
White Roding 33 J7
White Waltham 22 B4
Whiteacen 97 K7
Whiteash Green 34 B5
Whitebog 99 H5
Whitebridge High. 105 H1
Whitebridge High. 88 B3
Whitebrook 19 J1
Whiteburn 76 D6
Whitecairn 64 C5
Whitecairns 91 H3
Whitecastle 75 J6
Whitechapel 55 J5
Whitechurch 16 E1
Whitecraig 76 B3
Whitecroft 19 K1
Whitecrook 64 B5
Whitecross 2 C5
Whiteface 96 E3
Whitefield Aber. 91 F2
Whitefield Gt.Man. 49 H2
Whitefield High. 88 C2
Whitefield High. 105 H3
Whitefield P. & K. 82 C4
Whiteford 91 F2
Whitegate 49 F6
Whitehall 106 F5
Whitehaven 60 A5
Whitehill Hants. 11 J1
Whitehill Kent 14 E2
Whitehill N.Ayr. 74 A5
Whitehills 98 E4
Whitehouse Aber. 90 E3
Whitehouse Arg. & B. 73 G4
Whitekirk 76 D2
Whitelackington 8 C3
Whitelaw 77 G5
Whiteleen 105 J4
Whitelees 74 B7
Whiteley 11 G4
Whiteley Bank 11 G6
Whiteley Village 22 D5
Whiteleys 64 A5
Whitemans Green 13 G4
Whitemire 97 G6
Whiteparish 10 D2
Whiterashes 91 G2
Whiterow 105 J4
Whiteshill 20 B1
Whiteside Northumb. 70 C7
Whiteside W.Loth. 75 H4
Whitesmith 13 J5
Whitestaunton 8 B3
Whitestone Aber. 90 E5
Whitestone Arg. & B. 73 F7
Whitestone Devon 7 G6
Whitestripe 99 H5
Whiteway 29 J7
Whitewell Aber. 99 H4
Whitewell Lancs. 56 B5
Whiteworks 5 G3
Whitewreath 97 K6
Whitfield Here. 28 D5
Whitfield Kent 15 H3
Whitfield Northants. 31 H4
Whitfield Northumb. 61 J1
Whitfield S.Glos. 19 K2
Whitford Devon 8 B5
Whitford (Chwitffordd) Flints. 47 K5
Whitgift 58 E7
Whitgreave 40 A3
Whithorn 64 E6
Whiting Bay 66 E1
Whitkirk 57 J6
Whitlam 91 G2
Whitland 17 F3
Whitland Abbey 17 F3
Whitletts 67 H1
Whitley N.Yorks. 58 B7
Whitley Read. 22 A5
Whitley Wilts. 20 B5
Whitley Bay 71 J6
Whitley Chapel 62 A1
Whitley Lower 50 E1
Whitley Row 23 H6
Whitlock's End 30 C1
Whitminster 20 A1
Whitmore Dorset 10 B4
Whitmore Staffs. 40 A1
Whitnage 7 J4
Whitnash 30 E2
Whitney 28 B4
Whitrigg Cumb. 60 D1
Whitrigg Cumb. 60 D3
Whitsbury 10 C3
Whitsome 77 G5
Whitson 19 G3
Whitstable 25 H5
Whitstone 4 C1
Whittingham 71 F2
Whittingslow 38 D7
Whittington Derbys. 51 F5
Whittington Glos. 30 B6
Whittington Lancs. 56 B2
Whittington Norf. 44 B6
Whittington Shrop. 38 C2
Whittington Staffs. 40 D5
Whittington Staffs. 40 A7
Whittington Worcs. 29 H3
Whittle-le-Woods 55 J7
Whittlebury 31 H4
Whittlesey 43 F6
Whittlesford 33 H4
Whitton N.Lincs. 59 F7
Whitton Northumb. 71 F3
Whitton Powys 28 B2
Whitton Shrop. 28 E1
Whitton Stock. 62 E4
Whitton Suff. 35 F4
Whittonditch 21 F4
Whittonstall 62 B1
Whitway 21 H6
Whitwell Derbys. 51 H5
Whitwell Herts. 32 E6
Whitwell I.o.W. 11 G7
Whitwell N.Yorks. 62 D7
Whitwell Norf. 45 F3
Whitwell Rut. 42 C5
Whitwell-on-the-Hill 58 D3
Whitwick 41 G4
Whitwood 57 K7
Whitworth 49 H1
Whixall 38 E2
Whixley 57 K4
Whorlton Dur. 62 C5
Whorlton N.Yorks. 63 F6
Whygate 70 C6
Whyle 28 E2
Whyteleafe 23 G6
Wibdon 19 J2
Wibsey 57 G6
Wibtoft 41 G7
Wichenford 29 G2
Wichling 14 E2
Wick Bourne. 10 C5
Wick High. 105 J3
Wick S.Glos. 20 A4
Wick V. of Glam. 18 C4
Wick W.Suss. 12 D6
Wick Wilts. 10 C2
Wick Worcs. 29 J4
Wick Airport 105 J3
Wick Hill Kent 14 D3
Wick Hill W'ham 22 A5
Wick St. Lawrence 19 G5
Wicken Cambs. 33 J1
Wicken Northants. 31 J5
Wicken Bonhunt 33 H5
Wickenby 52 D4
Wickerslack 61 H5
Wickersley 51 G3
Wickford 24 D2
Wickham Hants. 11 G3
Wickham W.Berks. 21 G4
Wickham Bishops 34 C7
Wickham Heath 21 H5
Wickham Market 35 G3
Wickham St. Paul 34 C5
Wickham Skeith 34 E2
Wickham Street Suff. 34 B3
Wickham Street Suff. 34 E2
Wickhambreaux 15 H2
Wickhambrook 34 B3
Wickhamford 30 B4
Wickhampton 45 J5
Wicklewood 44 E5
Wickmere 45 F2
Wickwar 20 A3
Widdington 33 J5
Widdop 56 E6
Widdrington 71 H4
Wide Open 71 H6
Widecombe in the Moor 5 H3
Widegates 4 C5
Widemouth Bay 6 A5
Widewall 107 D8
Widford Essex 24 C1
Widford Herts. 33 H7
Widmerpool 41 J3
Widnes 48 E4
Widworthy 8 B5
Wigan 48 E2
Wiggaton 7 K6
Wiggenhall St. Germans 44 A4
Wiggenhall St. Mary Magdalen 44 A4
Wiggenhall St. Mary the Virgin 43 J4
Wiggenhall St. Peter 44 A4
Wiggington 58 C4
Wigginton Herts. 32 C7
Wigginton Oxon. 30 E5
Wigginton Staffs. 40 E5
Wigglesworth 56 D4
Wiggonby 60 D1
Wiggonholt 12 D5
Wighill 57 K5
Wighton 44 D2
Wightwizzle 50 E3
Wigmore Here. 28 D2
Wigmore Med. 24 E5
Wigsley 52 B5
Wigsthorpe 42 D7
Wigston 41 J6
Wigston Parva 41 G6
Wigthorpe 51 H4
Wigtoft 43 F2
Wigton 60 D2
Wigtown 64 E5
Wilbarston 42 B7
Wilberfoss 58 D4
Wilburton 33 H1
Wilby Norf. 44 E6
Wilby Northants. 32 B2
Wilby Suff. 35 G1
Wilcot 20 E5
Wilcott 38 C4
Wilcrick 19 H3
Wildboarclough 49 J6
Wilden Beds. 32 D3
Wilden Worcs. 29 H1
Wildhern 21 G6
Wildhill 23 F1
Wildsworth 52 B3
Wilford 41 H2
Wilkesley 39 F1
Wilkhaven 97 G3
Wilkieston 75 K4
Willand 7 J4
Willaston Ches. 48 C5
Willaston Ches. 49 F7
Willen 32 B4
Willenhall W.Mid. 40 B6
Willenhall W.Mid. 30 E1
Willerby E.Riding 59 G7
Willerby N.Yorks. 59 G2
Willersey 30 C4
Willersley 28 C4
Willesborough 15 F3
Willesborough Lees 15 F3
Willesden 23 F3
Willesley 20 B3
Willett 7 K2
Willey Shrop. 39 F6
Willey Warks. 41 G7
Williamscot 31 F4
Williamthorpe 51 G6
Willian 33 F5
Willimontswick 70 C7
Willingale 23 J1
Willingdon 13 J6
Willingham Cambs. 33 H2
Willingham Lincs. 52 B4
Willington Beds. 32 E4
Willington Derbys. 40 E3
Willington Dur. 62 C3
Willington T. & W. 71 J7
Willington Warks. 30 D5
Willington Corner 48 E6
Willisham 34 E3
Willitoft 58 D6
Williton 7 J1
Willoughby Lincs. 53 H5
Willoughby Warks. 31 G2
Willoughby-on-the-Wolds 41 J3
Willoughby Waterleys 41 H6
Willoughton 52 C3
Willows Green 34 B7
Willsworthy 6 D7
Wilmcote 30 C3
Wilmington Devon 8 B4
Wilmington E.Suss. 13 J6
Wilmington Kent 23 J4
Wilmslow 49 H4
Wilnecote 40 E5
Wilpshire 56 B6
Wilsden 57 F6
Wilsford Lincs. 42 D1
Wilsford Wilts. 20 E7
Wilsford Wilts. 20 D6
Wilsill 57 G3
Wilsley Green 14 C4
Wilson 41 G3
Wilstead 32 D4
Wilsthorpe 42 D4
Wilstone 32 C7
Wilton Cumb. 60 B5
Wilton N.Yorks. 58 E1
Wilton R. & C. 63 G4
Wilton Sc.Bord. 69 K2
Wilton Som. 8 B2
Wilton Wilts. 21 F5
Wilton Wilts. 10 B1
Wimbish 33 J5
Wimbish Green 33 K5
Wimblebury 40 C4
Wimbledon 23 F4
Wimblington 43 H6
Wimborne Minster 10 B4
Wimborne St. Giles 10 B3
Wimbotsham 44 A5
Wimpole 33 G4
Wimpstone 30 D4
Wincanton 9 G2
Wincham 49 F5
Winchburgh 75 J3
Winchcombe 30 B6
Winchelsea 14 E6
Winchelsea Beach 14 E6
Winchester 11 F2
Winchet Hill 14 C3
Winchfield 22 A6
Winchmore Hill Bucks. 22 C2
Winchmore Hill Gt.Lon. 23 G2
Wincle 49 J6
Wincobank 51 F3
Windermere 61 F7
Winderton 30 E4
Windhill 96 C7
Windlesham 22 C5
Windley 41 F1
Windley Meadows 41 F1
Windmill Hill E.Suss. 13 K5
Windmill Hill Som. 8 C3
Windrush 30 C7
Windsor 22 C4
Windy Yet 74 C5
Windygates 82 E7
Wineham 13 F4
Winestead 59 K7
Winewall 56 E5
Winfarthing 45 F7
Winford 19 J5
Winforton 28 B4
Winfrith Newburgh 9 H6
Wing Bucks. 32 B6
Wing Rut. 42 B5
Wingate 63 F3
Wingates Gt.Man. 49 F2
Wingates Northumb. 71 F4
Wingerworth 51 F6
Wingfield Beds. 32 D6
Wingfield Suff. 35 G1
Wingfield Wilts. 20 B6
Wingham 15 H2
Wingmore 15 G3
Wingrave 32 B7
Winkburn 51 K7
Winkfield 22 C4
Winkfield Row 22 B4
Winkhill 50 C7
Winkleigh 6 E5
Winksley 57 H2
Winksley Banks 57 H2
Winkton 10 C5
Winlaton 71 G7
Winlaton Mill 71 G7
Winless 105 H3
Winmarleigh 55 H5
Winnards Perch 3 G2
Winnersh 22 A4
Winscombe 19 H6
Winsford Ches. 49 F6
Winsford Som. 7 H2
Winsh-wen Swan. 17 K5
Winsham 8 C4
Winshill 40 E3
Winskill 61 G3
Winslade 21 K7
Winsley 20 A5
Winslow 31 J6
Winson 20 D1
Winsor 10 E3
Winster Cumb. 61 F7
Winster Derbys. 50 E6
Winston Dur. 62 C5
Winston Suff. 35 F2
Winstone 20 C1
Winswell 6 C4
Winterborne Came 9 G6
Winterborne Clenston 9 H4
Winterborne Houghton 9 H4
Winterborne Kingston 9 H5
Winterborne Monkton 9 F6
Winterborne Stickland 9 H4
Winterborne Whitechurch 9 H4
Winterborne Zelston 9 H5
Winterbourne S.Glos. 19 K3
Winterbourne W.Berks. 21 H4
Winterbourne Abbas 9 F5
Winterbourne Bassett 20 D4
Winterbourne Dauntsey 10 C1
Winterbourne Earls 10 C1
Winterbourne Gunner 10 C1
Winterbourne Monkton 20 D4
Winterbourne Steepleton 9 F6
Winterbourne Stoke 20 D7
Winterburn 56 E4
Wintercleugh 68 E2
Winteringham 59 F7
Winterley 49 G7
Wintersett 51 F1
Wintershill 11 G3
Winterslow 10 D1
Winterton 52 C1
Winterton-on-Sea 45 J4
Winthorpe Lincs. 53 J6
Winthorpe Notts. 52 B7
Winton Bourne. 10 B5
Winton Cumb. 61 J5
Wintringham 58 E2
Winwick Cambs. 42 E7
Winwick Northants. 31 H1
Winwick Warr. 49 F3
Wirksworth 50 E7
Wirswall 38 E1
Wisbech 43 H5
Wisbech St. Mary 43 H5
Wisborough Green 12 D4
Wiceton 51 K4
Wishaw N.Lan. 75 F5
Wishaw Warks. 40 D6
Wisley 22 D6
Wispington 53 F5
Wissett 35 H1
Wissington 34 D5
Wistanstow 38 D7
Wistanswick 39 F3
Wistaston 49 F7
Wiston Pembs. 16 D3
Wiston S.Lan. 75 H7
Wistow Cambs. 43 F7
Wistow N.Yorks. 58 B6
Wiswell 56 C6
Witcham 33 H1
Witchampton 9 J4
Witchburn 66 B2
Witchford 33 J1
Witcombe 8 D2
Witham 34 C7
Witham Friary 20 A7
Witham on the Hill 42 D4
Withcote 42 B5
Witherenden Hill 13 K4
Witherhurst 13 K4
Witheridge 7 G4
Witherley 41 F6
Withern 53 H4
Withernsea 59 K7
Withernwick 59 J5
Withersdale Street 45 G7
Withersfield 33 K4
Witherslack 55 H1
Witherslack Hall 55 H1
Withiel 3 G2
Withiel Florey 7 H2
Withington Glos. 30 B7
Withington Gt.Man. 49 H3
Withington Here. 28 E4
Withington Shrop. 38 E4
Withington Staffs. 40 C2
Withington Green 49 H5
Withleigh 7 H4
Withnell 56 B7
Withybrook 41 G7
Withycombe 7 J1
Withycombe Raleigh 7 J7
Withyham 13 H3
Withypool 7 G2
Witley 12 C3
Witnesham 35 F3
Witney 30 E7
Wittering 42 D5
Wittersham 14 D5
Witton 83 G1
Witton Bridge 45 H2
Witton Gilbert 62 D2
Witton-le-Wear 62 C3
Witton Park 62 C3
Wiveliscombe 7 J3
Wivelsfield 13 G4
Wivelsfield Green 13 G5
Wivenhoe 34 E6
Wiveton 44 E1
Wix 35 F6
Wixford 30 B3
Wixoe 34 B4
Woburn 32 C5
Woburn Sands 32 C5
Wokefield Park 21 K5
Woking 22 D6
Wokingham 22 B5
Wolborough 5 J3
Wold Newton E.Riding 59 G2
Wold Newton N.E.Lincs. 53 F3
Woldingham 23 G6
Wolfelee 70 A3
Wolferlow 29 F2
Wolferton 44 A3
Wolfhampcote 31 G2
Wolfhill 82 C4
Wolfpits 28 B3
Wolf's Castle 16 C2
Wolfsdale 16 C2
Woll 69 K1
Wollaston Northants. 32 C2
Wollaston Shrop. 38 C4
Wollaston W.Mid. 40 A7
Wollerton 39 F3
Wolsingham 62 B3
Wolstenholme 49 H1
Wolston 31 F1
Wolvercote 21 H1
Wolverhampton 40 B6
Wolverley Shrop. 38 D2
Wolverley Worcs. 29 H1
Wolverton Hants. 21 J6
Wolverton M.K. 32 B4
Wolverton Warks. 30 D2
Wolvesnewton 19 H2
Wolvey 41 G7
Wolviston 63 F4
Wombleton 58 C1
Wombourne 40 A6
Wombwell 51 G2
Womenswold 15 H2
Womersley 51 H1
Wonastow 28 D7
Wonersh 22 D7
Wonson 6 E7
Wonston 11 F1
Wooburn 22 C3
Wooburn Green 22 C3
Wood Burcote 31 H4
Wood Dalling 44 E3
Wood End Beds. 32 D4
Wood End Herts. 33 G6
Wood End Warks. 40 E6
Wood End Warks. 30 C1
Wood Enderby 53 F6
Wood Green 23 G2
Wood Hayes 40 B5
Wood Norton 44 E3
Wood Street Village 22 C6
Woodale 57 F2
Woodbastwick 45 H4
Woodbeck 51 K5
Woodbine 16 C3
Woodborough Notts. 41 J1
Woodborough Wilts. 20 E5
Woodbridge 35 G4
Woodbury 7 J7
Woodbury Salterton 7 J7
Woodchester 20 B1
Woodchurch Kent 14 E4
Woodchurch Mersey. 48 B4
Woodcote Oxon. 21 K3
Woodcote Tel. & W. 39 G4
Woodcott 21 H6
Woodcroft 19 J2
Woodcutts 9 J3
Woodditton 33 K3
Woodeaton 31 G7
Woodend Aber. 90 E3
Woodend Cumb. 60 C7
Woodend High. 88 E2
Woodend High. 79 J1
Woodend Northants. 31 H4
Woodend P. & K. 81 J3
Woodend W.Suss. 12 B6
Woodfalls 10 D2
Woodford Cornw. 6 A4
Woodford Glos. 19 K2
Woodford Gt.Lon. 23 H2
Woodford Gt.Man. 49 H4
Woodford Northants. 32 C1
Woodford Bridge 23 H2
Woodford Green 23 H2
Woodford Halse 31 G3
Woodgate Norf. 44 E4
Woodgate W.Mid. 40 B7
Woodgate W.Suss. 12 C6
Woodgate Worcs. 29 J2
Woodgreen 10 C3
Woodhall 62 A7
Woodhall Spa 52 E6
Woodham Dur. 62 D4
Woodham Surr. 22 D5
Woodham Ferrers 24 D2
Woodham Mortimer 24 E1
Woodham Walter 24 E1
Woodhaven 83 F5
Woodhead 91 F1
Woodhill 39 G7
Woodhorn 71 H5
Woodhouse Cumb. 55 J1
Woodhouse Leics. 41 H4
Woodhouse S.Yorks. 51 G4
Woodhouse Eaves 41 H4
Woodhouses 40 D4
Woodhuish 5 K5
Woodhurst 33 G1
Woodingdean 13 G6
Woodland Devon 5 H4
Woodland Dur. 62 B4
Woodlands Dorset 10 B4
Woodlands Hants. 10 E3
Woodlands Shrop. 39 G7
Woodlands Park 22 B4
Woodleigh 5 H6
Woodlesford 57 J7
Woodley 22 A4
Woodmancote Glos. 20 D1
Woodmancote Glos. 29 J6
Woodmancote W.Suss. 13 F5
Woodmancote W.Suss. 11 J4
Woodmancott 21 J7
Woodmansey 59 G6
Woodmansterne 23 F6
Woodminton 10 B2
Woodmoor 38 B5
Woodnesborough 15 H2
Woodnewton 42 D6
Woodplumpton 55 J6
Woodrising 44 D5
Woodseaves Shrop. 39 F2
Woodseaves Staffs. 39 G3
Woodsend 21 F4
Woodsetts 51 H4
Woodsford 9 G5
Woodside Aberdeen 91 H4
Woodside Brack.F. 22 C4
Woodside D. & G. 69 F6
Woodside Fife 83 F7
Woodside Fife 82 D7
Woodside Herts. 23 F1
Woodside N.Ayr. 74 B5
Woodside P. & K. 82 C4
Woodside Shrop. 28 C1
Woodside W.Mid. 40 B7
Woodstock 31 F7
Woodstock Slop 16 D2
Woodston 42 E6
Woodthorpe Derbys. 51 G5
Woodthorpe Leics. 41 H4
Woodton 45 G6
Woodtown 6 C3
Woodville 41 F4
Woodwalton 43 F7
Woodyates 10 B3
Woofferton 28 E2
Wookey 19 J7
Wookey Hole 19 J7
Wool 9 H6
Woolacombe 6 C1
Woolaston 19 J2
Woolavington 19 G7
Woolbeding 12 B4
Wooler 70 E1
Woolfardisworthy Devon 7 G5
Woolfardisworthy Devon 6 B3
Woolfords Cottages 75 J5
Woolhampton 21 J5
Woolhope 29 F5
Woollage Green 15 H3
Woolland 9 G4
Woollard 19 K5
Woollaton 6 C4
Woolley B. & N.E.Som. 20 A5
Woolley Cambs. 32 E1
Woolley W.Yorks. 51 F1
Woolmer Green 33 F7
Woolmere Green 29 J2
Woolmersdon 8 B1
Woolpit 34 D2
Woolscott 31 F2
Woolstaston 38 D6
Woolsthorpe Lincs. 42 B2
Woolsthorpe Lincs. 42 C3
Woolston S'ham. 11 F3
Woolston Shrop. 38 C3
Woolston Shrop. 38 D7
Woolston Warr. 49 F4
Woolston Green 5 H4
Woolstone M.K. 32 B5
Woolstone Oxon. 21 F3
Woolton 48 D4
Woolton Hill 21 H5
Woolverstone 35 F5
Woolverton 20 A6
Woolwich 23 H4
Woonton 28 C3
Wooperton 71 F1
Woore 39 G1
Wootton Beds. 32 D4
Wootton Hants. 10 D5
Wootton Kent 15 H3
Wootton N.Lincs. 52 D1
Wootton Northants. 31 J3
Wootton Oxon. 31 F7
Wootton Oxon. 21 H1
Wootton Shrop. 28 D1
Wootton Staffs. 40 A3
Wootton Staffs. 40 D1
Wootton Bassett 20 D3
Wootton Bridge 11 G5
Wootton Common 11 G5
Wootton Courtenay 7 H1
Wootton Fitzpaine 8 C5
Wootton Green 32 D4
Wootton Rivers 20 E5
Wootton St. Lawrence 21 J6
Wootton Wawen 30 C2
Worcester 29 H3
Worcester Park 23 F5
Wordsley 40 A7
Wordwell 34 C1
Worfield 39 G6
Work 107 D6
Workington 60 B4
Worksop 51 H5
Worlaby 52 D1
Worlds End Hants. 11 H3
World's End W.Berks. 21 H4
Worle 19 G5
Worleston 49 F7
Worlingham 45 J6
Worlington 33 K1
Worlingworth 35 G2
Wormbridge 28 D5
Wormegay 44 A4
Wormelow Tump 28 D5
Wormhill 50 D5
Wormiehills 83 H4
Wormingford 34 D5
Worminghall 21 K1
Wormington 30 B5
Worminster 19 J7
Wormiston 83 H7
Wormit 82 E5
Wormleighton 31 F3
Wormley Herts. 23 G1
Wormley Surr. 12 C3
Wormshill 14 D2
Wormsley 28 D4
Worplesdon 22 C6
Worrall 51 F3
Worsbrough 51 F2
Worsley 49 G2
Worstead 45 H3
Worsted Lodge 33 J3
Worsthorne 56 D6
Worston 56 C5
Worswell 5 F6
Worth Kent 15 J2
Worth W.Suss. 13 G3
Worth Matravers 9 J7
Wortham 34 E1
Worthen 38 C5
Worthenbury 38 D1
Worthing Norf. 44 E4
Worthing W.Suss. 12 E6
Worthington 41 G3
Wortley Glos. 20 A2
Wortley S.Yorks. 51 F3
Worton 20 C6
Wortwell 45 G7
Wotherton 38 B5
Wotton 22 E7
Wotton-under-Edge 20 A2
Wotton Underwood 31 H7
Woughton on the Green 32 B5
Wouldham 24 D5
Wrabness 35 F5
Wrae 99 F5
Wrafton 6 C2
Wragby 52 E5
Wragholme 53 G3
Wramplingham 45 F5
Wrangham 90 E1
Wrangle 53 H7
Wrangle Lowgate 53 H7
Wrangway 7 K4
Wrantage 8 C2
Wrawby 52 D2
Wraxall N.Som. 19 H4
Wraxall Som. 9 F1
Wray 56 B3
Wray Castle 60 E6
Wraysbury 22 D4
Wrea Green 55 G6
Wreay Cumb. 61 F4
Wreay Cumb. 61 F2
Wrecclesham 22 B7
Wrecsam (Wrexham) 38 C1
Wrekenton 62 D1
Wrelton 58 D1
Wrenbury 38 E1
Wreningham 45 F6
Wrentham 45 J7
Wrenthorpe 57 J7
Wrentnall 38 D5
Wressle 58 D6
Wrestlingworth 33 F4
Wretham 44 D7
Wretton 44 A6
Wrexham (Wrecsam) 38 C1
Wrexham Industrial Estate 38 C1
Wribbenhall 29 G1
Wrightington Bar 48 E1
Wrightpark 74 E1
Wrinehill 39 G1
Wrington 19 H5
Writhlington 19 K6
Writtle 24 C1
Wrockwardine 39 F4

Wroot 51 K2
Wrotham 23 K6
Wrotham Heath 23 K6
Wrotham Hill 24 C5
Wrotham Park 23 F2
Wroughton 20 E3
Wroxall *I.o.W.* 11 G7
Wroxall *Warks.* 30 D1
Wroxeter 38 E5
Wroxham 45 H4
Wroxton 31 F4
Wstrws 26 C4
Wyaston 40 D1
Wyberton 43 G1
Wyboston 32 E3
Wybunbury 39 F1
Wych Cross 13 H3
Wychbold 29 J2
Wyck 11 J1
Wyck Rissington 30 C6
Wycliffe 62 C5
Wycoller 56 E6
Wycomb 42 A3
Wycombe Marsh 22 B2
Wyddial 33 G5
Wye 15 F3
Wyke *Dorset* 9 G2

Wyke *Shrop.* 39 F5
Wyke *W.Yorks.* 57 G7
Wyke Regis 9 F7
Wykeham *N.Yorks.* 59 F1
Wykeham *N.Yorks.* 58 E2
Wyken 39 G6
Wykey 38 C3
Wylam 71 G2
Wylde Green 40 D6
Wyllie 18 E2
Wylye 10 B1
Wymering 11 H4
Wymeswold 41 J3
Wymington 32 C2
Wymondham *Leics.* 42 B4
Wymondham *Norf.* 45 F5
Wyndham 18 C2
Wynford Eagle 8 E5
Wynnstay Park 38 C1
Wynyard 63 F4
Wyre Piddle 29 J4
Wyresdale Tower 56 B4
Wysall 41 J3
Wyson 28 E2
Wythall 30 B1
Wytham 21 H1

Wythburn 60 E5
Wyton 33 F1
Wyverstone 34 E2
Wyverstone Street 34 E2
Wyville 42 B3
Wyvis Lodge 96 B4

Y
Y Bryn 37 H3
Y Drenewydd (Newtown) 38 A6
Y Fan 37 J7
Y Felinheli 46 D6
Y Fenni (Abergavenny) 28 C7
Y Fflint (Flint) 48 B5
Y Ffôr 36 C2
Y Trallwng (Welshpool) 38 B5
Yaddlethorpe 52 B2
Yafford 11 F6
Yafforth 62 E7
Yalding 23 K7
Yanworth 30 B7
Yapham 58 D4
Yapton 12 C6
Yarburgh 53 G3
Yarcombe 8 B4
Yardley 40 D7

Yardley Gobion 31 J4
Yardley Hastings 32 B3
Yardro 28 B3
Yarkhill 29 F4
Yarlet 40 B3
Yarley 19 J7
Yarlington 9 F2
Yarm 63 F5
Yarmouth 10 E6
Yarnacott 6 E2
Yarnbrook 20 B6
Yarnfield 40 A2
Yarnscombe 6 D3
Yarnton 31 F7
Yarpole 28 D2
Yarrow 69 J1
Yarrow Feus 69 J1
Yarrowford 69 K1
Yarsop 28 D4
Yarwell 42 D6
Yate 20 A3
Yateley 22 B5
Yatesbury 20 D4
Yattendon 21 J4
Yatton *Here.* 28 D2
Yatton *N.Som.* 19 H5
Yatton Keynell 20 B4
Yaverland 11 H6
Yaxham 44 E4
Yaxley *Cambs.* 42 E6

Yaxley *Suff.* 35 F1
Yazor 28 D4
Yeading 22 E3
Yeadon 57 H5
Yealand Conyers 55 J2
Yealand Redmayne 55 J2
Yealmpton 5 F5
Yearby 63 H4
Yearsley 58 B2
Yeaton 38 D4
Yeaveley 40 D1
Yedingham 58 E2
Yelford 21 G1
Yelland *Devon* 6 C2
Yelland *Devon* 6 C2
Yelling 33 F2
Yelvertoft 31 G1
Yelverton *Devon* 5 F4
Yelverton *Norf.* 45 G5
Yenston 9 G2
Yeo Vale 6 C3
Yeoford 7 F6
Yeolmbridge 6 B7
Yeomadon 6 B5
Yeovil 8 E3
Yeovil Marsh 8 E3
Yeovilton 8 E2
Yerbeston 16 D4
Yesnaby 107 B6

Yetlington 71 F2
Yetminster 8 E3
Yettington 7 J7
Yetts o'Muckhart 82 B7
Yielden 32 D2
Yiewsley 22 D4
Ynys 36 E2
Ynysboeth 18 D2
Ynysddu 18 E2
Ynyshir 18 D2
Ynyslas 37 F6
Ynysmeudwy 18 A1
Ynystawe 17 K4
Ynysybwl 18 D2
Yockenthwaite 56 E2
Yockleton 38 C4
Yokefleet 58 E7
Yoker 74 D4
Yonder Bognie 98 D6
York 58 C4
Yorkletts 25 G5
Yorkley 19 K1
Yorton 38 E3
Youldon 6 B5
Youldonmoor Cross 6 B5

Yoxall 40 D4
Yoxford 35 H2
Yr Wyddgrug (Mold) 48 B6
Ysbyty Cynfyn 27 G1
Ysbyty Ifan 37 H1
Ysbyty Ystwyth 27 G1
Ysceifiog 47 K5
Ysgubor-y-coed 37 F6
Ystalyfera 18 A1
Ystrad 18 C2
Ystrad Aeron 26 E3
Ystrad Meurig 27 G2
Ystrad Mynach 18 E2
Ystradfellte 27 J7
Ystradffin 27 G4
Ystradgynlais 27 G7
Ystradowen *N.P.T.* 27 G7
Ystradowen *V. of Glam.* 18 D4
Ythanwells 90 E1
Ythsie 91 G1

Z
Zeal Monachorum 7 F5
Zeals 9 G1
Zelah 3 F3
Zennor 2 B5

INDEX TO PLACE NAMES IN IRELAND

Abbreviations

Ant. Antrim	*Kilk.* Kilkenny	*Tyr.* Tyrone
Dub. Dublin	*Tipp.* Tipperary	*Water.* Waterford
		Wexf. Wexford

A
Aasleagh 112 B6
Abbeyfeale 110 C3
Abbeyleix 111 F2
Achill 112 B5
Adare 110 C2
Annahilt 113 G4
Annalong 113 H5
Antrim 113 G3
Ardara 112 D3
Ardee 113 G5
Ardglass 113 H4
Arklow (An tinbhear Mór) 111 G2
Armagh 113 G4
Armoy 113 G2
Arvagh 113 E5
Ashbourne 113 G6
Athboy 113 F6
Athenry 110 D1
Athleague 112 D6
Athlone (Baile Átha Luain) 113 E6
Athy 111 F1
Augher 113 F4
Aughnacloy 113 F4
Aughrim 111 G2
Avoca 111 G2

B
Balbriggan 113 G6
Balieborough 113 F5
Ballaghaderreen 112 D5
Ballina (Béal an Átha) 112 C5
Ballinafad 112 D5
Ballinalack 113 E6
Ballinamore 113 E5
Ballinasloe (Béal Átha na Sluaighe) 110 D1
Ballindine 112 C6
Ballinrobe 112 C6
Ballon 111 F2
Ballybay 113 F5
Ballybofey 113 E3
Ballybrack 110 A4
Ballybunnion 110 B3
Ballycanew 111 G2
Ballycastle *Ant.* 113 G2
Ballycastle *Mayo* 112 C4
Ballyclare 113 G3
Ballyconnell 113 E5
Ballycroy 112 B5
Ballydesmond 110 C3
Ballygar 112 D6
Ballygawley 113 F4
Ballygorman 113 F2
Ballyhale 111 F3
Ballyhaunis 112 D6
Ballyheigue 112 B3
Ballyjamesduff 113 F5
Ballykelly 113 F3
Ballylynan 111 F2
Ballymacarberry 111 E4
Ballymacmague 111 E4
Ballymacoda 111 E4
Ballymahon 113 E6
Ballymakeery 110 C4
Ballymena 113 G3
Ballymoney 113 G2
Ballymote 112 D5
Ballymurphy 111 F2
Ballynahinch 113 H4
Ballyragget 111 F2
Ballyshannon 112 D4
Ballyvaughan 110 C1
Ballyward 113 G4
Baltinglass 111 G2
Banagher 111 E1
Banbridge 113 G4
Bandon 110 D4
Bangor 113 H4
Bangor Erris 112 B5
Banteer 110 C3
Bantry 110 B5
Belcoo 113 E4
Belderg 112 B4

Belfast 113 H4
Belfast City Airport 113 H4
Belfast International Airport 113 G4
Belmullet 112 B5
Beragh 113 F4
Bessbrook 113 G5
Bettystown 111 E1
Birr 113 G5
Blackrock 113 G5
Blackwater 111 G3
Blarney 110 D4
Blessington 111 G1
Bohola 112 C5
Borris 111 F2
Borrisokane 110 D1
Borrisoleigh 111 E2
Boyle 112 D5
Bray (Bré) 111 G1
Broadford 110 C3
Broughshane 113 G3
Bunbeg 112 D3
Bunclody 111 G2
Buncrana 113 E2
Bundoran 112 D4
Burtonport 112 D3
Bushmills 113 G2
Butlers Bridge 113 F5
Buttevant 110 D3

C
Cahermore 110 B5
Cahir 111 E3
Cahirciveen 110 A4
Callan 111 F3
Cappoquin 111 E3
Carlingford 113 G5
Carlow (Ceatharlach) 111 F2
Carndonagh 113 F2
Carnlough 113 G3
Carraroe 110 B1
Carrick-on-Shannon
Carrick-on-Suir (Carraig na Sivire) 111 F3
Carrickfergus 113 H3
Carrickmacross 113 F5
Carrigallen 113 E5
Carrigtwohill 110 D4
Carrowdore 113 H4
Carrowkeel 113 F2
Cashel 111 E3
Castlebar (Caisleán an Bharraigh) 112 C5
Castlebellingham 113 G5
Castleblayney 113 F5
Castlebridge 111 G3
Castlecomer 111 F2
Castleconnell 110 D2
Castlederg 113 E3
Castledermot 111 F2
Castlegregory 110 B3
Castleisland 110 B3
Castlemaine 110 B3
Castlemartyr 111 E4
Castlepollard 113 F6
Castlerea 112 D6
Castletown 111 E1
Castletown Bere 110 B5
Catherdaniel 110 A4
Cavan 113 F5
Celbridge 111 G1
Charlestown 112 D5
Cheekpoint 111 F3
City of Derry Airport 113 F3
Clady 113 E3
Clane 111 G1
Clara 111 E1
Clarecastle 110 C2
Claregalway 110 C1
Claremorris 112 C6

Clashmore 111 E4
Claudy 113 F3
Clifden 112 B6
Cliffonoy 112 D4
Cloghan 111 E1
Clogheen 111 E3
Clonakilty 110 C5
Clonbern 112 D6
Clones 113 F5
Clonmel (Cluain Meala) 111 E3
Clonroche 111 G3
Clonygowan 111 F1
Cloonbannin 110 C3
Clooneagh 113 E5
Cobh (An Cóbh) 110 D4
Coleraine 113 F2
Collooney 112 D5
Comber 113 H4
Cong 112 C6
Cookstown 113 F4
Cootehill 113 F5
Cork (Corcaigh) 110 D4
Cork Airport 110 C2
Corofin 110 C2
Courtmacsherry 110 D5
Courtown 111 G2
Craanford 111 G2
Craigavon 113 G4
Creeslough 113 E2
Cregganbaun 112 B6
Crookhaven 110 B5
Croom 110 D3
Crossgar 113 H4
Crosshaven 110 D4
Crossmaglen 113 G5
Crossmolina 112 C5
Crumlin 113 G4
Crusheen 110 C2
Cullybackey 113 G3
Cushendall 113 G3
Cushendun 113 G2

D
Delvin 113 F6
Dingle 110 A3
Donaghadee 113 H4
Donaghmore 113 F4
Donegal 112 D4
Donoughmore 110 D4
Dooagh 112 B5
Downpatrick 113 H4
Draperstown 113 F3
Drimoleague 110 C5
Drogheda (Droichead Átha) 113 G6
Dromod 113 E5
Dromore *Down* 113 G4
Dromore *Tyr.* 113 E4
Dromore West 112 C5
Drumfree 113 E2
Drumkeeran 112 D5
Drummin 111 F3
Dublin (Baile Átha Cliath) 111 G1
Dublin Airport 113 G6
Dún Laoghaire 111 G1
Dunboyne 113 G6
Duncannon 111 F3
Duncormick 111 G3
Dundalk (Dún Dealgan) 113 G5
Dundonald 113 H4
Dundrum 113 H4
Dungannon 113 F4
Dungarvan *Kilk.* 111 F2
Dungarvan (Dún Garbhán) *Water.* 111 E4
Dungiven 113 F3
Dungloe 112 D3
Dunlavin 111 G1
Dunleer 113 G5
Dunloy 113 G3
Dunmanway 110 C4
Dunmore 112 D6
Dunmore East 111 F3
Dunmurry 113 G4
Dunquin 110 A3

Durrow 111 F2

E
Edenderry 111 F1
Edgeworthstown 113 E6
Eglinton 113 F3
Ennis (Inis) 110 C2
Enniscorthy (Inis Córthaidh) 111 G3
Enniskean 110 C4
Enniskerry 111 G1
Enniskillen 113 E4
Ennistymon 110 C2

F
Farranfore 110 B3
Fermoy 111 G2
Ferns 111 E3
Fethard 111 E3
Fintona 113 F4
Fintown 112 D3
Fivemiletown 113 F4
Foxford 112 C5
Foynes 110 C2
Frenchpark 112 D5
Freshford 111 F2

G
Galbally 110 D3
Galway (Gaillimh) 110 C1
Galway Airport 110 C1
Garvagh 113 F3
Glenamaddy 112 D6
Glengarriff 110 B4
Glengavlen 113 E5
Glenties 112 D3
Gorey 111 G2
Gort 110 C1
Gortahork 112 D2
Graigue 111 F2
Graiguenamanagh 111 F2
Granard 113 E6
Grange 111 E4
Greenore 113 G5
Gweedore 112 D3

H
Halfway 110 D4
Headford 112 C6
Holycross 111 E2
Horseleap 112 D6
Hospital 110 D3
Howth 113 G6
Hurler's Cross 110 C2

I
Inch *Kerry* 110 B3
Inch *Wexf.* 111 G2

J
Johnstown 111 E2

K
Kanturk 110 C3
Keady 113 F5
Kells *Kilk.* 111 F3
Kells (Ceanannus Mór) *Meath* 113 F6
Kenmare 110 B4
Kerry Airport 110 B3
Kilbeggan 111 E1
Kilberry 113 F6
Kilcolgan 110 C1
Kilcommon 111 G1
Kilcoole 111 G1
Kilcormac 111 E1
Kilcullen 111 F1
Kildare 111 F1
Kilkee 110 B2
Kilkeel 113 G5
Kilkenny (Cill Chainnigh) 111 F2

Killala 112 C5
Killaloe 110 D1
Killarney (Cill Airne) 110 B4
Killenaule 111 E2
Killimor 110 D1
Killinchy 113 H4
Killinick 111 G3
Killorglin 110 B4
Killurin 111 G3
Killybegs 112 D4
Kilmacrenan 113 E3
Kilmaine 112 C6
Kilmallock 110 D3
Kilmona 110 D4
Kilmore Quay 111 G3
Kilrea 113 G3
Kilrush 110 B2
Kilteel 111 G1
Kiltimagh 112 C5
Kiltullagh 110 D1
Kingscourt 113 F5
Kinnegad 113 F6
Kinsale 110 D4
Kinvara 110 C1
Kircubbin 113 H4
Knock 112 C6
Knock International Airport 112 C5
Knockalough 110 C2
Knocktopher 111 F3

L
Lanesborough 113 E6
Larne 113 H3
Lauragh 110 B4
Laytown 113 G6
Leap 110 C5
Leighlinbridge 111 F2
Leixlip 111 G1
Letterkenny 113 E3
Lifford 113 E3
Limavady 113 F3
Limerick (Luimneach) 110 D2
Lisbellaw 113 E4
Lisburn 113 G4
Lisdoonvarna 110 C1
Lismore 111 E3
Lisnarrick 113 E4
Lisnaskea 113 E5
Listowel 110 B3
Londonderry (Derry) 113 F3
Longford 113 E6
Loughrea 110 D1
Louisburgh 112 B6
Lucan 111 G1
Lukeswell 111 F3
Lurgan 113 G4

M
Macroom 110 C4
Maghera 113 G3
Magherafelt 113 G3
Malahide 113 G6
Malin More 112 D3
Mallow (Mala) 110 D3
Manorhamilton 112 D4
Markethill 113 G4
May's Corner 113 G4
Middletown 113 F4
Midleton 110 D4
Milestone 111 E2
Milford 113 E3
Millstreet 110 C3
Milltown Malbay 110 C2
Mitchelstown 110 D3
Moate 111 E1
Mohill 113 E5
Moira 113 G4
Monaghan (Muineachán) 113 F5
Monasterevan 111 F1
Moneygall 111 E2

Moneymore 113 G3
Monivea 110 D1
Mount Bellew 112 D6
Mountmellick 111 F1
Mountrath 111 E1
Mountshannon 110 D2
Moville 113 F2
Moyvalley 113 F6
Muine Bheag 111 F2
Mullany's Cross 112 C5
Mullingar (An Muileann gCearr) 113 F6
Mulrany 112 B5
Murrisk 112 B6
Murroogh 110 C1

N
Naas (An Nás) 111 G1
Navan (An Uaimh) 113 F6
Nenagh (An tAonach) 110 D2
New Ross 111 F3
Newbridge (Droichead Nua) 111 F1
Newcastle *Down* 113 H5
Newcastle *Dub.* 111 G1
Newcastle West 110 C3
Newinn 111 E3
Newmarket 110 C3
Newmarket-on-Fergus 110 C2
Newport *Mayo* 112 B5
Newport *Tipp.* 110 D2
Newry 113 G5
Newtown 110 D3
Newtownabbey 113 H4
Newtownards 113 H4
Newtownbutler 113 E5
Newtownmount-kennedy 111 G1
Newtownstewart 113 F3
Ninemilehouse 111 E3
Nobber 113 F5

O
Oldcastle 113 F6
Omagh 113 F4
Oranmore 110 C1

P
Pallas Green 110 D2
Park 113 F3
Partry 112 C6
Pettigo 113 E4
Pomeroy 113 F4
Pontoon 112 C5
Portadown 113 G4
Portaferry 113 H4
Portarlington 111 F1
Portavogie 113 H4
Portlaoise 111 F1
Portlaw 111 F3
Portmagee 110 A4
Portrane 113 G6
Portrush 113 G2
Portsalon 113 E2
Portstewart 113 F2
Portumna 110 D1
Poulgorm Bridge 110 C4

R
Randalstown 113 G3
Raphoe 113 E3
Rathangan 111 F1
Rathdowney 111 E2
Rathdrum 111 G2
Rathfriland 113 G5
Rathkeale 110 C3
Rathkeevin 111 E3
Rathluirc (Charleville) 110 D3
Rathvilly 111 G2
Recess 112 B6
Ringsend 113 F3

Roscommon 112 D6
Roscrea 111 E2
Ross Carbery 110 C5
Rosslare 111 G3
Rosslare Harbour 111 G3
Rosslea 113 F5
Rush 113 G6

S
Saintfield 113 H4
Schull 110 B5
Shanacrane 110 C4
Shannon Airport 110 C2
Shercock 113 F5
Shillelagh 111 G2
Sion Mills 113 E3
Sixmilebridge 110 D2
Sixmilecross 113 F4
Skerries 113 G6
Skibbereen 110 C5
Slane 113 G6
Sligo (Sligeach) 112 D4
Sneem 110 B4
Strabane 113 E3
Stradbally 111 F1
Strandford 113 H4
Stranorlar 113 E3
Strokestown 112 D6
Swinford 112 C5
Swords 113 G6

T
Taghmon 111 G3
Tallow 111 E4
Tandragee 113 G4
Tarbert 110 C2
Templemore 111 E2
Templetuohy 111 E2
Thomastown 111 F3
Thurles (Durlas) 111 E2
Timolin 111 F1
Tipperary 110 D3
Tower 110 D4
Tralee (Trá Lí) 110 B3
Tramore (Trá Mhór) 111 F3
Trim 113 F6
Tuam 112 C6
Tubbercurry 112 D5
Tulla 110 D2
Tullamore (Tulach Mhór) 111 E1
Tullow 111 F2
Tully 113 E4
Tulsk 112 D6

U
Urlingford 111 E2

V
Virginia 113 F5

W
Warrenpoint 113 G5
Waterford (Port Láirgé) 111 F3
Waterford Airport 111 F3
Watergrasshill 110 D4
Wellington Bridge 111 G3
Westport 112 B6
Wexford (Loch Garman) 111 G3
Whitehall 111 F2
Whitehead 113 H3
Wicklow (Cill Mhantáin) 111 G1

Y
Youghal (Eochaill) 111 E4